COCOA

IN A NUTSHELL

COCOA

IN A NUTSHELL

Michael Beam and James Duncan Davidson

O'REILLY®

Beijing · Cambridge · Farnham · Köln · Paris · Sebastopol · Taipei · Tokyo

Cocoa in a Nutshell

by Michael Beam and James Duncan Davidson

Published by O'Reilly & Associates, Inc., 1005 Gravenstein Highway North, Sebastopol, CA 95472.

O'Reilly & Associates books may be purchased for educational, business, or sales promotional use. Online editions are also available for most titles (*safari.oreilly.com*). For more information, contact our corporate/institutional sales department: 800-998-9938 or *corporate@oreilly.com*.

Editor:	Chuck Toporek
Production Editor:	Colleen Gorman
Cover Designer:	Emma Colby
Interior Designers:	David Futato and Bret Kerr

Printing History:

May 2003:	First Edition.

ISBN: 0-596-00462-1

[M]

Table of Contents

Part II. API Quick Reference

Part III. Appendix

Preface

It's practically impossible to know Cocoa inside and out. There was once a discussion between two programmers about Cocoa's large APIs: one was a veteran Perl programmer, the other a Cocoa programmer. The Perl programmer grumbled about the intimidating and verbose Cocoa APIs, saying there was simply too much to remember. Bemused, the Cocoa programmer retorted: "You don't *remember* Cocoa; you look it up!"

The point the Cocoa programmer was trying to impress upon the Perl programmer was that understanding object-oriented programming (OOP) concepts and the architecture of the frameworks is more important than remembering the wordy and numerous method and class names in the Cocoa frameworks.

This book is a compact reference that will hopefully grow worn beside your keyboard. Split into two parts, *Cocoa in a Nutshell* first provides an overview of the frameworks that focuses on both common programming tasks and how the parts of the framework interact with one another. The second part of the book is an API quick reference that frees you from having to remember method and class names so you can spend more time hacking code. This book covers the Cocoa frameworks—Foundation and Application Kit (AppKit)—as of Mac OS X 10.2 (Jaguar).

What Is Cocoa?

Cocoa is a complete set of classes and application programming interfaces (APIs) for building Mac OS X applications and tools. With over 240 classes, Cocoa is divided into two essential frameworks: the Foundation framework and the Application Kit.

The Foundation framework provides a fundamental set of tools for representing fundamental data types, accessing operating system services, threading, messaging, and more. The Application Kit provides the functionality to build graphical user interfaces (GUI) for Cocoa applications. It provides access to the standard Aqua interface components ranging from menus, buttons, and text fields—the building blocks of larger interfaces—to complete, prepackaged interfaces for print dialogs, file operation dialogs, and alert dialogs. The Application

Kit also provides higher-level functionality to implement multiple document applications, text handling, and graphics.

Classes are not the only constituents of the Cocoa frameworks. Some programming tasks, such as sounding a system beep, are best accomplished with a simple C function. Cocoa includes a number of functions for accomplishing tasks such as manipulating byte orders and drawing simple graphics. Additionally, Cocoa defines a number of custom data types and constants to provide a higher degree of abstraction to many method parameters.

The Cocoa Development Environment

Project Builder and Interface Builder are the two most important applications used in Cocoa development. *Project Builder* is the interactive development environment (IDE) for Mac OS X used to manage and edit source files, libraries, frameworks, and resources. Additionally, it provides an interface to the Objective-C compiler, *gcc*, and the GNU debugger, *gdb*.

Interface Builder is used to create GUIs for Cocoa applications by allowing developers to manipulate UI components (such as windows and buttons) graphically using drag and drop. It provides assistance for laying out components by providing visual cues that conform to Apple's Aqua Human Interface Guidelines. From an inspector panel, the behavior and appearance of these components can be tweaked in almost every way the component supports. Interface Builder provides an intuitive way to connect objects by letting the user drag wires between objects. This way, you set up the initial network of objects in the interface. In addition, you can interface without having to compile a single bit of code.

Interface components are not the only objects that can be manipulated with Interface Builder. You can subclass any Cocoa class and create instances of the subclasses. More importantly, you can give these classes instance variables, known as *outlets*, and methods, called *actions*, and hook them up to user interface components. Interface Builder can then create source files for these subclasses, complete header files, and an implementation file including stubs for the action methods. There is much more to Interface Builder and Project Builder than we can cover in this book, but as you can begin to imagine, the tight integration of these two applications create a compelling application development environment.

Cocoa Design Patterns

Cocoa uses many design patterns. *Design patterns* are descriptions of common object-oriented programming practices. Effective application development requires that you know how and where to use patterns in Cocoa. *Cocoa in a Nutshell* discusses these patterns in the context in which they are used. Here is a brief list of the design patterns you will encounter in the book:

Delegation
> In this pattern, one object, the delegate, acts on behalf of another object. Delegation is used to alter the behavior of an object that takes a delegate. The developer's job is to implement any number of methods that may be invoked in the delegate. Delegation minimizes the need to subclass objects to extend their functionality.

Singleton

This pattern ensures that only one object instance of a class exists in the system. A singleton method is an object constructor that creates an instance of the class and maintains a reference to that object. Subsequent invocations of the singleton constructor return the existing object, rather than create a new one.

Notification

Notifications allow decoupling of message senders from multiple message receivers. Cocoa implements this pattern in the notification system used throughout the frameworks. It is discussed in Chapter 2.

Model-View-Control

The Model-View-Controller (MVC) pattern is used extensively in the Application Kit to separate an application into logically distinct units: a model, which knows how to work with application data, the view, which is responsible for presenting the data to the user, and the controller, which handles interaction between the model and the view. Chapter 3 discusses MVC in more detail.

Target/action

The target/action pattern decouples user-interface components, such as buttons and menu items, with the objects (the targets) that implement their actions. In this pattern, an activated control sends an action message to its target. Chapter 3 discusses this topic further.

Responder chain

The responder chain pattern is used in the event handling system to give multiple objects a chance to respond to an event. This topic is discussed in Chapter 3.

Key-value coding

Key-value coding provides an interface for accessing an object's properties indirectly by name. Chapter 2 covers key-value coding more thoroughly.

Benefits

These days, application developers expect a lot from their tools, and users expect a lot from any application they use. Any application or application toolkit that neglects these needs is destined for failure. Cocoa comes through grandly by providing the features needed in applications now and in the future, including:

Framework-based development

Cocoa development is based on its frameworks: the Foundation framework and the Application Kit. With framework-based programming, the system takes a central role in the life of an application by calling out to code that you provide. This role allows the frameworks to take care of an application's behind-the-scene details and lets you focus on providing the functionality that makes your application unique.

"For free" features

Cocoa provides a lot of standard application functionality "for free" as part of the frameworks. These features not only include the large number of user-interface components, but larger application subsystems such as the text-handling system and the document-based application architecture. Because

Apple has gone to great lengths to provide these features as a part of Cocoa, developers can spend less time doing the repetitive work that is common between all applications, and more time adding unique value to their application.

The development environment
As discussed earlier, Project Builder and Interface Builder provide a development environment that is highly integrated with the Cocoa frameworks. Interface Builder is used to quickly build user interfaces, which means less tedious work for the developer.

Cocoa's most important benefit is that it lets you develop applications dramatically faster than with other application frameworks.

Languages

Cocoa's native language is Objective-C. The Foundation and Application Kit frameworks are implemented in Objective-C, and using Objective-C provides access to all features of the frameworks. Chapter 1 covers Objective-C in depth.

Objective-C is not, however, the only language through which you can access the Cocoa frameworks. Through the Java Bridge, Apple provides a way to access the Cocoa frameworks using the Java language. The Java Bridge does not provide a complete solution since many of Cocoa's advanced features, such as the distributed objects system, are not available with Java. This book will not discuss Cocoa application development with Java.

Another option for working with Cocoa is AppleScript. AppleScript has traditionally been associated with simple scripting tasks, but with Mac OS X, Apple enabled AppleScript access to the Cocoa frameworks via AppleScript Studio. AppleScript Studio provides hooks into the Cocoa API so scripters can take their existing knowledge of AppleScript, write an application in Project Builder, and use Interface Builder to give their applications an Aqua interface—all without having to learn Objective-C. This exposes Cocoa to a completely new base of Macintosh developers, who know enough AppleScript to build simple task-driven applications for solving common problems. For more information about AppleScript Studio, see *http://www.apple.com/applescript/studio*.

How This Book Is Organized

This book is split into two parts: the overview of Cocoa familiarizes developers with Cocoa's structure, and the API quick reference contains method name listings and brief descriptions for all Foundation and Application Kit framework classes.

Part I is divided into the following eight chapters:

Chapter 1, *Objective-C*
This chapter introduces the use of Objective-C language. Many object-oriented concepts you may be familiar with from other languages are discussed in the context of Objective-C, which lets you leverage your previous knowledge.

Chapter 2, *Foundation*

This chapter discusses the Foundation framework classes that all programs require for common programming tasks such as data handling, process control, run loop management, and interapplication communication.

Chapter 3, *The Application Kit*

This chapter introduces the Application Kit and details larger abstractions of the Application Kit, such as how events are handled with responder chains, the document-based application architecture, and other design patterns that are important in Cocoa development.

Chapter 4, *Drawing and Imaging*

This chapter discusses Cocoa's two-dimensional (2D) graphics capabilities available in the Application Kit.

Chapter 5, *Text Handling*

This chapter details the architecture of Cocoa's advanced text-handling system, which provides a rich level of text-handling functionality for all Cocoa developers.

Chapter 6, *Networking*

This chapter summarizes networking technologies, such as Rendezvous and URL services, that are accessible from a Cocoa application.

Chapter 7, *Interapplication Communication*

This chapter discusses interapplication communication techniques, including distributed objects, pipes, and distributed notifications.

Chapter 8, *Other Frameworks*

This chapter provides information about the many Objective-C frameworks that can be used in conjunction with Cocoa. These frameworks include those that are part of Mac OS X, such as AddressBook and DiscRecording, as well as frameworks supplied by third-party developers.

Part II contains Foundation and AppKit framework references and, as such, makes up the bulk of the book. First, there's an explanation of the organization of chapters in Part II and how class information is referenced. The rest of the section is divided into eight chapters and a method index. Each chapter focuses on a different part of the Cocoa API.

Chapter 9, *Foundation Types and Constants*

This chapter lists the data types and constants defined by the Foundation framework.

Chapter 10, *Foundation Functions*

This chapter lists the functions defined by the Foundation framework.

Chapter 11, *Application Kit Types and Constants*

This chapter lists the data types and constants defined by the Application Kit.

Chapter 12, *Application Kit Functions*

This chapter lists the functions defined by the Application Kit.

Chapter 13, *Foundation Classes*

This chapter contains the API quick-reference Foundation framework classes.

Chapter 14, *Foundation Protocols*

This smaller chapter covers the handful of protocols declared as part of the Foundation framework.

Chapter 15, *Application Kit Classes*

This chapter provides the API quick reference for Application Kit classes.

Chapter 16, *Application Kit Protocols*

This chapter provides reference to the protocols defined and used in the AppKit.

Method Index

This index contains an alphabetical listing of every method in the Foundation framework and Application Kit. Each method name in the index has a list of classes that implement that method.

Unlike the rest of the book's sections, there is but one short appendix in Part III. Regardless of your experience level as a Mac developer, this section contains valuable resources for Cocoa programmers, including details on how you can partner with Apple to market your application.

Appendix: Resources for Cocoa Developers

This appendix lists vital resources for Cocoa developers, including Apple developer documentation, web sites, mailing lists, books, and details on how to partner with Apple to gain exposure for your applications.

Conventions Used in This Book

This book uses the following typographical conventions:

Italic

Used to indicate new terms, URLs, filenames, file extensions, directories, commands, options, and program names, and to highlight comments in examples. For example, a filesystem path will appear as */Applications/Utilities*.

Constant width

Used to show the contents of files or output from commands.

Constant-width bold

Used in examples and tables to show commands or other text that the user should type literally.

Constant-width italic

Used in examples and tables to show text that should be replaced with user-supplied values, and also to highlight comments in code.

Menus/navigation

Menus and their options are referred to in the text as File → Open, Edit → Copy, etc. Arrows will also signify a navigation path in window options—for example, System Preferences → Screen Effects → Activation means that you would launch System Preferences, click on the icon for the Screen Effects preferences panel, and select the Activation pane within that panel.

Pathnames

Pathnames show the location of a file or application in the filesystem. Directories (or folders for Mac and Windows users) are separated by a forward slash. For example, if you see something like, "...launch the Terminal application (*/Applications/Utilities*)" in the text, you'll know that the Terminal application can be found in the Utilities subfolder of the Applications folder.

↵

A carriage return (↵) at the end of a line of code denotes an unnatural line break—i.e., you should not enter two lines of code, but one continuous line. You'll sometimes see multiple lines with carriage returns because of printing constraints.

%, #

The percent sign (%) shows the user prompt for the default *tcsh* shell; the hash mark (#) is the prompt for the root user.

Menu symbols

When looking at the menus for any application, you will see symbols associated with keyboard shortcuts for a particular command. For example, to open a document in Microsoft Word, go to the File menu and select Open (File → Open), or issue the keyboard shortcut, ⌘-O.

Figure P-1 shows the symbols used in various menus to denote a shortcut.

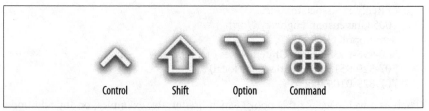

| Control | Shift | Option | Command |

Figure P-1. Keyboard accelerators for issuing commands

You'll rarely see the Control symbol used as a menu command option; it's more often used in association with mouse clicks or for working with the *tcsh* shell.

 Indicates a tip, suggestion, or general note.

 Indicates a warning or caution.

How the Quick Reference Was Generated

You'd have to be a madman to write this book's quick reference by hand. Madmen we are not, so following the example of David Flanagan, author of O'Reilly's *Java in a Nutshell*, Mike wrote a program that would take care of most of the tedious work.

The idea is to attack the problem in two stages. In the first stage, the code enumerates each header file of each Framework that is to be ripped (Foundation and AppKit) and runs each line of each header through a parser. This parser would look for key elements that identify parts of the header, such as @interface,

+ for class methods, – for instance methods, and so forth. Every discovered element was assembled into a cross-linked hierarchy of framework names, class names, or method names. When all headers had been processed, the hierarchy was output into a property list file, which, at the end of the day, weighed in at just over 41,500 lines of text!

Stage two involved reading the contents of this file and running it through several formatting routines that output the XML-formatted text required by the O'Reilly production team.

Each class has a little class hierarchy figure. These figures were autogenerated by drawing into a view (using NSBezierPath) and saving the PDF representation of the view contents to a file. The input data for the program that did all of the drawing was the same property list used to create the API quick reference entries.

Comments and Questions

Please address comments and questions concerning this book to the publisher:

> O'Reilly & Associates, Inc.
> 1005 Gravenstein Highway North
> Sebastopol, CA 95472
> 800-998-9938 (in the United States or Canada)
> 707-829-0515 (international or local)
> 707-829-0104 (fax)

There is a web page for this book, which lists errata, examples, or any additional information. You can access this page at:

> *http://www.oreilly.com/catalog/cocoaian*

To comment or ask technical questions about this book, send email to:

> *bookquestions@oreilly.com*

For more information about books, conferences, Resource Centers, and the O'Reilly Network, see the O'Reilly web site at:

> *http://www.oreilly.com*

Acknowledgments

The authors would like to acknowledge the many people who helped make this book possible.

From Mike

Writing this book has been quite an experience, and it was made possible only by the efforts and support of the people I worked with. My editor, Chuck Toporek, put in a lot of time on this book and kept this first-time author on course and in the right frame of mind with his kind words of encouragement and level-headed advice. He has become a good friend over the past year that we've worked together on this project.

I am grateful to Duncan for his efforts in helping me shape up the book and for contributing the material on Objective-C. Duncan is quite a person to work with, and I look forward to working with him on this book in the future. Any success of this book is due in no small part to both Chuck and Duncan. These two make a great team, and I am fortunate to have the opportunity to work with them.

Thanks to the tech reviewers: Scott Anguish, Sherm Pendley, and the engineers and technical writers at Apple who were kind enough to take time out of their busy lives to review the book. Special thanks go to Malcolm Crawford for going above and beyond the call of duty by providing in-depth comments and suggestions and working closely with us to give the book its final polish. His upbeat attitude and British charm helped us all bring this book to completion.

Derrick Story at the O'Reilly Network took an amazing chance with me by letting me write about Cocoa for *macdevcenter.com*, which gave me the opportunity to get my foot in the door when I was least expecting it. Why he did this baffles me to this day, but I am grateful for it and for his encouragement over the past two years.

Ryan Dionne introduced me to Macs when we were freshman at UT Austin, and he quickly changed my attitude about them (I was a switcher before switching was fashionable). Shortly after that, John Keto of the University of Texas, my teacher and employer, was tricked, by some of the grad students I worked with, into believing that I was some sort of Linux and C guru; let's just say that I quickly became one! I suppose that if either of these things hadn't happened, you wouldn't be reading this acknowledgment. Life's funny sometimes.

All remaining thanks, and all that I am, go to my family and my friends: Mom and Dad, for the love, encouragement, and support during the whole process; my sisters Kristin and Jennifer; and my future parents-in-law, Bill and Lauren, for their love and support; Ryan, Paige, and Tommy for putting up with me and my antisocial behaviors during the past year, and for always having an eye on me and knowing when I needed to get some lunch. As always, my love and appreciation to my fiancée, Heather, (until July 2003!) for being incredibly patient, supportive, and caring during the past year.

From Duncan

I'd like to thank Mike and Chuck for letting me contribute Chapter 1 to the book. They were both very patient and attentive to all of the feedback I contributed to the rest of the book, even when they must have become annoyed by all my suggestions. Chuck, you're a great editor and you've helped me develop as an author, a skill that I never thought I'd have. Mike, I'm honored to have helped you with this book, and I look forward to working with you on it again in the future.

mmalcolm Crawford provided an invaluable service by checking the Objective-C chapter, as well as the rest of the book, in detail, and he really helped shape it into the what you see today. His dinner table discussions, and plenty of red ink stemming from many years of experience, have illuminated several areas of Cocoa and Objective-C for me. This book would not be the book it is without his valuable help.

Finally, thanks to my family and friends who put up with me disappearing during the crunch time leading up to the production of this book. You guys know who you are.

Introducing Cocoa

This part of the book provides a series of chapters that provide a general overview of Cocoa, helping you to quickly come up to speed. The chapters in this part of the book include:

Objective-C

Objective-C is a highly dynamic, message-based *object-oriented* language. Consisting of a small number of additions to ANSI C, Objective-C is characterized by its deferral of many decisions until runtime, supporting its key features of dynamic dispatch, dynamic typing, and dynamic loading. These features support many of the *design patterns* Cocoa uses, including delegation, notification, and Model-View-Controller (MVC). Because it is an extension of C, existing C code and libraries, including those based on C++,* can work with Cocoa-based applications without losing any of the effort that went into their original development.

This chapter is an overview of Objective-C's most frequently used features. If you need more detail about these features or want to see the full language specification, read through Apple's document, *The Objective-C Programming Language*, which is installed as part of the Developer Tools in */Developer/Documentation/ Cocoa/ObjectiveC*.

Objects

The base unit of activity in all object-oriented languages is the *object*—an entity that associates data with operations that can be performed on that data. Objective-C provides a distinct data type, id, defined as a pointer to an object's data that allows you to work with objects. An object may be declared in code as follows:

```
id anObject;
```

For all object-oriented constructs of Objective-C, including method return values, id replaces the default C int as the default return data type.

---

* For more information on using C++ with Objective-C, see the Objective-C++ documentation contained in */Developer/Documentation/ReleaseNotes/Objective-C++.html*.

Dynamic Typing

The id type is completely nonrestrictive. It says very little about an object, indicating only that it is an entity in the system that can respond to messages and be queried for its behavior. This type of behavior, known as *dynamic typing*, allows the system to find the class to which the object belongs and resolve messages into method calls.

Static Typing

Objective-C also supports *static typing*, in which you declare a variable using a pointer to its class type instead of id, for example:

```
NSObject *object;
```

This declaration will turn on some degree of compile time checking to generate warnings when a type mismatch is made, as well as when you use methods not implemented by a class. Static typing can also clarify your intentions to other developers who have access to your source code. However, unlike other languages' use of the term, static typing in Objective-C is used only at compile time. At runtime, all objects are treated as type id to preserve dynamism in the system.

 There are no class-cast exceptions like those present in more strongly typed languages, such as Java. If a variable declared as a Dog turns out to be a Cat, but responds to the messages called on it at runtime, then the runtime won't complain.

Messaging

Objects in Objective-C are largely autonomous, self-contained, opaque entities within the scope of a program. They are not passive containers for state behavior, nor data and a collection of functions that can be applied to that data. The Objective-C language reinforces this concept by allowing any *message*—a request to perform a particular action—to be passed to any object. The object is then expected to respond at runtime with appropriate behavior. In object-oriented terminology, this is called *dynamic binding*.

When an object receives a message at runtime, it can do one of three things:

- Perform the functionality requested, if it knows how.
- Forward the message to some other object that might know how to perform the action.
- Emit a warning (usually stopping program execution), stating that it doesn't know how to respond to the message.

A key feature here is that an object can forward messages that it doesn't know how to deal with to other objects. This feature is one of the significant differences between Objective-C and other object-oriented languages such as Java and C++.

Dynamic binding, as implemented in Objective-C, is different than the *late binding* provided by Java and C++. While the late binding provided by those languages does provide flexibility, it comes with strict compile-time constraints and is enforced at link time. In Objective-C, binding is performed as messages are resolved to methods and is free from constraints until that time.

Structure of a Message

Message expressions in Objective-C are enclosed in square brackets.* The expression consists of the following parts: the object to which the message is sent (the receiver), the message name, and optionally any arguments. For example, the following message can be verbalized as "send a play message to the object identified by the iPod variable":

```
[iPod play];
```

Any arguments in a message expression appear after colons in a message name. For example, to tell the iPod object to set the volume, send it the following message:

```
[iPod setVolume:11];
```

If a message contains multiple arguments, the arguments are typically separated in the message name and follow colons after the corresponding component of the message. For example:

```
[iPod usePlaylist:@"Techno" shuffle:YES];
```

The name of this message is usePlaylist:shuffle:. The colons are part of the method name. If you aren't familiar with this syntax, it may appear a bit odd at first. However, experience shows that structuring messages this way helps code be more self-documenting than in languages such as Java or C++ where parameters are lumped together without appropriate labeling.

Nested messages

Messages can be nested so the return value from one message can become the receiver or parameter for another. For example, to assign the playlist for an iPod to play to the value of an iTunes playlist name without an intermediate variable, use the following:

```
[iPod usePlaylist:[iTunes currentPlaylist]];
```

Messaging nil

Messaging an uninitialized (or *cleared*) object variable (i.e., one with a value of nil) is not an error. If a message doesn't have a return value, nothing will happen. If the message returns an object pointer, it will return nil. If the message returns a scalar value such as an int, it will return 0. Otherwise, the return value is unspecified.

---

* This convention is known as *infix syntax*; it is borrowed from Smalltalk.

How Messages Are Resolved into Methods

When a message is sent to an object, a search determines the implemented method that should be called. The logic of this search is:

1. The runtime inspects the message's target object to determine the object's class.

2. If the class contains an instance method with the same name as the message, the method is executed.

3. If the class does not have a method, the search is moved to the *superclass*. If a method with the same name as the message is found in the superclass, it is executed. This search is continued up the inheritance tree until a match is found.

4. If no match is found, the receiver object is sent the forwardInvocation: message. If the object implements this method, it has the dynamic ability to resolve the problem. This method's default implementation in NSObject simply announces (with an error) that the object doesn't handle the message.

Selectors

While user-friendly names refer to methods in source code, the runtime uses a much more efficient mechanism. At compile time, each method is given a unique value of type SEL called a *selector*. When the runtime performs the message dispatch described in the previous section, it resolves the message to a selector, which is then used to execute the method.

You can use selectors to indicate which method should be called on an object. The following example shows how to use the @selector declaration to get a selector and perform its method on an object:

```
SEL playSelector = @selector(play);
[iPod performSelector:playSelector];
```

A selector identifies a method and is not associated with any particular class. Assuming that a Child class is defined and implements a play method, the following would be valid:

```
[aChild performSelector:playSelector];
```

Using selectors directly can be helpful when you want to execute the same action on a collection of objects. For example, a case of iPod objects, held in an array, could all be told to play by sending the following message to the array:

```
[iPodArray makeObjectsPerformSelector:playSelector];
```

You will also see selectors in the Cocoa framework used in the Target/Action paradigm. For more information about using selectors to call methods on objects, see the NSInvocation class documentation in Chapter 14.

Classes

Objects in Objective-C are defined in terms of a *class*. New classes of objects are specializations of a more general class. Each new class is the accumulation of the class definitions that it inherits from and can expand on that definition by adding new methods and instance variables or redefining existing methods to perform new or expanded functionality. Like Java and Smalltalk, but unlike C++, Objective-C is a *single inheritance language*, meaning that a class can inherit functionality only from a single class.

A class is not just a blueprint for building objects; it is itself an object in the runtime that knows how to build new objects. These new objects are *instances* of the class.

The Root Class

Every class hierarchy begins with a *root class* that has no superclass. While it is possible to define your own root class in Objective-C, the classes you define should inherit, directly or indirectly, from the NSObject class provided by the Foundation framework. The NSObject class defines the behavior required for an object to be used by the Cocoa framework and provides the following functionality:

- Defines the low-level functionality needed to handle object initialization, duplication, and destruction.
- Provides mechanisms to aid Cocoa's memory management model.
- Defines functionality for an object to identify its class membership and provide a reasonable description of the object.

Defining a Class

In Objective-C, classes are defined in two parts, usually separated into two different files:

- An *interface*, which declares a class's methods and instance variables, and names its superclass. The interface is usually specified in a file with the *.h* suffix typical of C header files.
- An *implementation*, which contains the code that defines the class's methods. By convention, files containing the implementation of a class have a *.m* suffix.

The interface

To declare a class and give all the information other classes (and other programs) need to use it, an interface file needs to contain the following information:

- The class that is being inherited from
- The instance variables, if any, that the class adds
- A list of method declarations, if any, indicating what methods the class adds or modifies significantly

Example 1-1 shows simple header file, saved by convention as *Song.h*, containing the interface for the Song class.

Example 1-1. A simple header file for the Song class

```
#import <Cocoa/Cocoa.h>                    // 1

@interface Song : NSObject {               // 2
    id title;                              // 3
}

- (id)title;                               // 4
- (void)setTitle:(id)aTitle;               // 5

@end;                                      // 6
```

Each line is defined as follows:

1. Imports the definitions for the Cocoa frameworks. This line is similar to the #include directive in C, except the compiler ensures that it doesn't include a header file more than once.

2. Declares the name of the class, Song, and specifies NSObject as its superclass.

3. Declares an instance variable named title. The id type indicates that the variable is an object. If we wanted the compiler to enforce type checking for us, we could declare its type as NSString *.

4. Declares an instance method named title that returns an object. The – (minus sign) before the method name indicates that the method is an instance method.

5. Declares an instance method named setTitle that takes an object argument and doesn't return anything.

6. The @end; statement indicates to the compiler the end of the Song class interface.

Scoping instance variables

The object-oriented principle of *encapsulation* means that other programmers shouldn't need to know a class's instance variables. Instead, they need to know only the messages that can be sent to a class. The inclusion of instance variables in the interface file, while required by C, would seem to break encapsulation.

To give a class the ability to enforce encapsulation even though the variables are declared in the header file, the compiler limits the scope of the class's instance variables to the class that declares them and its subclasses. This enforcement can be changed by using the following set of compiler directives:

@private
> These instances are accessible within the class from which they are declared. Subclasses will not be able to access them.

@protected
> These instances are available within the class that declares them and within classes that inherit from them. This is a variable's default scope.

@public
> These instances are available to any class and can be used by code as if they were a field in a C structure. However, the directive should not be used

except when absolutely necessary, because it defeats the purpose of encapsulation.

For example, to ensure that subclasses of the Song class could not directly access the title instance variable, use the @private directive as shown in Example 1-2.

Example 1-2. Constraining a variable's scope

```
#import <Cocoa/Cocoa.h>

@interface Song : NSObject {
@private
    id title;
}

- (id)title;
- (void)setTitle:(id)aTitle;

@end;
```

The implementation

To define how the class works, an implementation file needs to contain implementations of the methods defined in the interface file. Example 1-3 shows the implementation, contained in the source file *Song.m* by convention, of the Song class.

Example 1-3. Implementation of the Song class

```
#import Song.h                    // 1

@implementation Song             // 2

- (id)title {                    // 3
    return title;
}
- (void)setTitle:(id)aTitle {    // 4
    [title autorelease];
    title = [aTitle retain];
}

@end                             // 5
```

Here is a detailed explanation of each part of this code:

1. Imports the header file that contains the interface for the file. Every implementation must import its own interface.

2. Declares that what follows is the implementation of the Song class.

3. Implementation of the title method. This method simply returns the title variable's value. The contents of a method are defined, like C functions, between a pair of braces. Also, the class's instance variables are in the scope of the method and can be referred to directly.

4. Implementation of the setTitle method. This method sets the title variable to the aTitle argument after performing some steps, using the retain and autorelease messages required for proper memory management. For more information about memory management, see the "Memory Management" section, later in this chapter.

5. Indicates to the compiler the end of the Song class implementation.

Notice that the implementation doesn't need to repeat the superclass name or the instance variable declarations.

Special Variables

In addition to a class's instance variables, several other instance variables are defined within the scope of instance methods. These variables are:

isa

    Defined by the NSObject class, the isa variable contains a pointer to the class object. This lets an object introspect itself. It is also what lets the runtime determine what kind of object it is when it resolves messages to methods.

self

    A variable set by the runtime to point at the object the action is performed on—the receiver object of the message. This allows the functionality within a method to send messages to the object on which the method acts.

super

    A variable set by the runtime that behaves similarly to self, except that the resolution of message to method starts with the object's superclass. This allows you to call the functionality of superclasses.

_cmd

    The selector used to call the current method.

Class Methods

Since classes are objects, you can define methods that will act when messages are sent to a class. Class methods are defined in the same way as instance methods, except you use a plus symbol (+) at the beginning of the method declaration instead of a hyphen or minus sign (–). For example, if the Song class keeps track of the number of songs created, a numberOfSongs class method could be provided, as shown in Example 1-4.

Example 1-4. Defining a class method

```
#import <Cocoa/Cocoa.h>

@interface Song : NSObject {
    id title;
}

+ (int)numberOfSongs;
- (id)title;
- (void)setTitle:(id)aTitle;

@end;
```

Similarly, this method's implementation is placed between the @implementation and @end directives in the implementation (*.m*) file. Since a class method operates on the class object, the isa, self, super, and _cmd variables are defined the same way as instance variables.

 There is no *class variable* concept in Objective-C. However, you can achieve much the same effect by declaring a C-style static variable in the same file as the class implementation. This limits the scope of the variable to the *.m* file that contains it.

Overriding Superclass Methods

When a new class is defined, a method can be implemented with the same name as a method in one of the superclasses up the inheritance hierarchy. This new method overrides the original when messages with the method name are sent to the derived class's object. When overriding methods, you can access the superclass's method functionality by sending a message to the special variable super.

For example, if the class of iPod inherits from a more generic MP3Player class that also defines the play method, the subclass's play method may require that the superclass functionality is executed. Example 1-5 shows how this could be achieved by using the super variable.

Example 1-5. Overriding a superclass method

```
- (void)play {
    [self setPlayIndicator:YES];
    [super play];
}
```

When a superclass method is overridden, the method doesn't need to be declared again in the interface (*.h*) file. By convention, an overridden method is listed in the interface file only if you significantly change the way the method works.

 Even though you can override methods of a superclass, you cannot override an inherited variable by declaring a new one with the same name. The compiler will complain if you try.

Creating Object Instances

One of the principal functions of a class object is to serve as a factory for creating new instances. When new objects are created, memory is allocated and its instance variables are initialized. This is accomplished by using the alloc method, defined by the NSObject class, as follows:

```
Song song = [song alloc];
```

The alloc class method dynamically allocates memory, sets the isa variable to a pointer to the class's class object, sets all other variables to 0, and then returns the new object instance. This takes care of the system level tasks that need to be performed when an object is created, but doesn't allow the object to properly initialize itself. To give an opportunity for object-specific initialization, the NSObject class provides the init instance method. To fully create an instance of the Song class, use the following code:

```
Song song = [[song alloc] init];
```

The init method can be overridden in a subclass to assign defaults to instance variables and to take care of other tasks that need to be performed before an object is used.

You can call the alloc and init methods by using separate lines of code. However, since object allocation and initialization are interlinked, calling both methods with one line of code is good practice.

When you override the init method, the superclass's init method (or designated initializer, as covered in the next section) should always be called to ensure that the superclass is initialized properly. Initialization methods should also return self, the object being initialized. Example 1-6 shows an init method for the Song class.

Example 1-6. An initialization method for the Song class

```
- (id)init {                                    // 1
    self = [super init];                        // 2
    // ... Song-specific initialization code
    return self;                                // 3
}
```

The code shown in Example 1-6 performs the following tasks:

1. Declares the init method, which returns an object of type id. The returned object is the newly initialized object.
2. Calls the init method of the superclass (super) to let it properly configure its state. The self variable is set to the return value of the init method because it might return a different instance than the one currently being worked with.
3. Returns the object using the self variable.

Initialization methods return an object of type id so an initialization method can actually return a different object of a different type, if necessary. For example, if a class needs to return a more specialized subtype to better take advantage of a system's runtime configuration, it can release the object originally created, create a new one of the subtype, and return it. This is why programs need to use the object returned by the init method and not the object returned by the alloc method, and why you should make sure that self is set to the init method's return value.

The ability for an initialization method to return a subtype allows for a programming pattern known as *class clusters*. This allows for a large amount of functionality to be exposed behind a small and easy to understand public class definition. For example, there are many different string classes that are represented by the public NSString class.

Designated initializers

A class can provide multiple initialization methods to allow varying levels of customization. When you have multiple initializers, only the *designated initializer* should call the superclass' initializer method. All other initializers must call the designated initializer. This will ensure that your classes always behave properly.

For example, if an initWithTitle: method is defined for the Song class, the more general init method would first need to be called to allow proper initialization of both the Song class and its parent classes before proceeding with specific initialization. Example 1-7 shows an example.

Example 1-7. Calling a designated initializer

```
-(id)initWithTitle:(NSString *)aTitle {
    self = [self init];
    [self setTitle:aTitle];
    return self;
}
```

Memory Management

To properly manage memory, Cocoa provides a *reference counting* mechanism, supported by the NSObject and NSAutoreleasePool classes. As its name suggests, reference counting maintains a count of how many references there are to an object—indicating how many other objects are interested in keeping the object around. Reference counting is not automatic; the compiler has no way to determine an object's lifetime. Therefore, the following NSObject reference counting methods must be called to indicate the level of interest in an object to the memory management system:

retain
> Increments the object's reference count by 1. When you want to register interest in an object that you did not create or copy, indicate interest in it by calling this method.

release
> Decrements the object's reference count by 1. This message is sent to objects created with the alloc method or sent a retain message when you are no longer interested in using them. If this causes the retain count to reach 0, the runtime deallocates the object.

autorelease
> Adds the object to the current *autorelease pool*. This allows you to release your interest in an object without immediately causing the retain count to reach 0. When the autorelease pool is itself released, it sends the release message to every object it contains. This is most useful when you want to pass the object to another object as a return value and won't have the opportunity to release the object later by yourself.

The following set of rules will help you perform accurate reference counting and avoid either leaking memory or prematurely destroying objects:

- Objects created by alloc or copy have a retain count of 1.

- If you want to keep an object received from another mechanism, send it a retain message.

- When you are done with an object created by alloc or copy, or retained by the retain message, send it a release message.

- When you add an object to a collection, such as an array or dictionary (described in Chapter 2), the collection retains it. You are no longer responsible for the object, and you may safely release any interest in it.

- If you need to release interest in an object but need to ensure that it is not immediately destroyed, send an autorelease message so the object is put in the autorelease pool for later release.

 Once you have released interest in an object, you shouldn't send any messages to it. If an object is deallocated because its retain count reached 0, sending a message to the object will cause an error.

Retaining Objects in Accessor Methods

Accessor methods require a bit of caution, especially those where an object's instance variables are set. Because an object passed to a set method may already be held, you must be careful about how memory management is performed. Releasing an object before retaining it can lead to unfortunate side effects and can be the source of much frustration. To ensure that memory management is performed correctly, send the autorelease method to an old object reference before replacing with a new reference. Example 1-8 shows how this rule is applied in the Song class's setTitle: method.

Example 1-8. Memory management in accessor methods

```
- (void)setTitle:(NSString *)aTitle {
    [title autorelease];
    title = [aTitle retain];
}
```

Another way to ensure proper memory management and further increase encapsulation is to make a copy of the parameter, as shown in Example 1-9. This ensures that even if a mutable subtype of NSString were given, any modifications to that parameter would not change the contents of the title variable.

Example 1-9. Copying a parameter to enforce encapsulation

```
- (void)setTitle:(NSString *)aTitle {
    [title autorelease];
    title = [newTitle copy];
}
```

These practices ensure proper memory management in almost all situations you are likely to encounter. However, some fringe cases require care in handling. For more details, see *http://www.stepwise.com/Articles/Technical/2002-06-11.01.html*.

Deallocating Objects

When an object is ready to be destroyed (as determined by the reference counting mechanism), the system will give the object an opportunity to clean up after itself by calling the dealloc method defined by NSObject. If the object has created or retained any other objects' reference by its instance variables, it must implement this method and perform the appropriate tasks to maintain integrity of the reference counting system.

In Example 1-8, the Song class retains the title instance variable in the setTitle: method. To properly implement memory management, you need to balance this retain with a release. Example 1-10 shows the release performed in the Song class's dealloc method.

Example 1-10. Implementing a dealloc method

```
- (void)dealloc {
    [title release];
    [super dealloc];
}
```

This provides proper balance in the reference counting mechanism.

 You should never call the dealloc method yourself. Always let the memory management methods do it.

Categories

Inheritance is not the only way to add functionality to a class. With an Objective-C language construct called a *category*, you can add methods to an existing class, thereby extending its functionality—and the functionality of its subclasses.

A category interface declaration looks like a class interface declaration, with one exception: the category name is listed in parentheses after the class name, and the superclass is not mentioned. For example, if you wanted to add a rot13 method to the NSString class to get the rot13 version of any string, the category interface would be defined as shown in Example 1-11.

Example 1-11. Defining a category interface

```
#import "NSString.h"

@interface NSString (Obfuscation)

- (NSString *)rot13;

@end
```

The category's implementation looks like the implementation of a class itself. Example 1-12 shows an interface implementation.

Example 1-12. Implementation of a category

```
#import "Obfuscation.h"

@implementation NSString (Obfuscation)

- (NSString *)rot13 {
    NSString * rot13string;

    // Perform logic to shift each character by 13
    return rot13string;
}

@end
```

Remember that a category can't declare new instance variables for a class; it can only add methods to an existing class.

 A category is not a substitute for a subclass. You should not redefine methods already in a class or a class's superclass—add only new methods to the class.

Protocols

Class and category interfaces define the methods that belong to a particular class. However, you might want many different classes, otherwise unrelated to one another, to perform the same set of methods. Objective-C does not support multiple inheritance, but because of the language's dynamic nature, its support for *protocols* (declaration of a group of methods under a name) fills the need. A protocol defines the methods that a class is expected to implement in order to function appropriately while leaving the implementation of those methods to the class.

Like classes and categories, protocols are defined in interface header (*.h*) files. To define a set of methods that apply to objects controlled by a media player, define the protocol as shown in Example 1-13.

Example 1-13. Defining a protocol

```
@protocol Playable
- (void)play;
- (void)stop;
@end
```

A class adopts a protocol by listing the protocols in the file's interface declaration. Example 1-14 shows the syntax used in the interface declaration to indicate that the Song class conforms to the Playable protocol.

Example 1-14. Conforming to a protocol in a class interface

```
#import <Cocoa/Cocoa.h>
#import "Playable.h"

@interface Song : NSObject <Playable> {
    id title;
}

- (id)title;
- (void)setTitle:(id)aTitle;

@end;
```

A class or category that adopts a protocol must implement all methods defined by that protocol. The compiler issues a warning if this requirement is not satisfied. Additionally, you can check whether or not objects conform to a particular protocol. If a media player wants to make sure that the Song class conforms to the Playable protocol, the check in Example 1-15 could be used.

Example 1-15. Checking to see if an object conforms to a protocol

```
if([song conformsTo:@protocol(Playable)]) {
    [song play];
} else {
    // Issue a warning or do something else reasonable here
}
```

Naming Conventions

Several naming conventions have become widespread within the Objective-C community. To create code that your peers can maintain more easily, try to use the following conventions:

- Always capitalize class names.
- Begin variable and method names with lowercase letters. If a variable or method name consists of multiple words, capitalize the first letter of the second and any following words. This practice is known as *camelcase*.
- Begin accessor methods that set an instance variable value with the word "set," and make sure the instance variable name follows in camelcase.
- Give accessor methods that return the value of an instance variable the same name as the variable. It is also acceptable—though uncommon—to prefix the variable name with the word "get" and have the instance variable name follow in camelcase.
- Do not begin method names that you create with an underscore. By convention, Apple uses underscores to implement system level private functionality.

We've implemented these conventions throughout the book.

2

Foundation

The Foundation framework provides support for a variety of basic functionalities and data types, including the following:

- Strings, numbers, and collections
- Dates and time
- Binary data
- Means of working with files, including accessing data and working with bundles
- Distributed event notification
- Operating system interaction
- Threading

This chapter discusses these subjects and provides several short examples that demonstrate of the most common methods of the key classes.

Data

The Foundation framework provides many classes and protocols that extend the capabilities of the Objective-C language to represent and work with basic data types, such as strings and numbers, in an object-oriented fashion. Additionally, the Foundation framework provides *application programming interfaces* (APIs) for working with more complex data types, such as dates and collections.

Immutable Versus Mutable Classes

Classes such as NSString and NSArray are *immutable* classes; instances of these classes cannot be altered after they are initialized. Each immutable class, however, has a *mutable* subclass: for example, NSString has the mutable subclass NSMutableString, and NSArray has the subclass NSMutableArray. Mutable subclasses extend their superclass's functionality to allow modification after initialization. Immutable classes are more efficient, but mutable classes are more flexible.

Basic Types

Two of the most basic data types in an application are *strings* and *numbers*. The Foundation framework provides object abstractions in the form of NSString and NSNumber, and an extensive API to manipulate them.

Strings

Foundation's primary class used to represent and manipulate strings is NSString. Instances of NSString can be considered, at their core, an immutable array of Unicode characters, and can represent characters from the alphabets of nearly every written language, past and present. In fact, NSString is a class cluster, which shields the developer from a number of underlying implementation details that make string handling more efficient. This abstraction is generally relevant only when subclassing NSString, so it will not be considered further here.

Objective-C provides a syntax shortcut to create strings in code that is of the form @"...". In code, this looks like:

```
NSString *str = @"Hello";
```

When interpreted by the compiler, this syntax translates into an NSString object that is initialized with the 7-bit ASCII encoded string between the quotes. This string object is created at compile-time and exists for the life of the application. While you may send retain and release messages to an NSString object created from the literal syntax, such an object will never be deallocated. Example 2-1 shows several NSString methods. For more information on using printf-style formatting, see */Developer/Documentation/Cocoa/TasksAndConcepts/Programming Topics/DataFormatting/iFormatStrings.html.*

Example 2-1. Creating instances of, and working with, NSString

```
// The literal syntax for an NSString object
NSString *str = @"Hello";

// Create one string from another string
NSString *str2 = [NSString stringWithString:str];

// You can also create a string using printf style formatting
str = [NSString stringWithFormat:@"%d potatoes", 10];

// The contents of a text file may be used to initialize a string
str = [NSString stringWithContentsOfFile:@"/path/to/file"];

// C character arrays may be used to create a string as well
char *cStr = "Hello again";
str = [NSString stringWithCString:cStr];

// How to get a C string from an NSString
char cStr = [str UTFString];

// Determine the length of a string, which is a count of the
// number of Unicode characters in the string
unsigned int strLength = [str length];
```

Example 2-1. Creating instances of, and working with, NSString (continued)

```
// Append one NSString to another
// str2 = "Hello, World!"
str2 = [str stringByAppendingString:@", World!"];

// Append a format to an NSString
// str3 = "Hello, World! 2003"
NSString *str3 = [str2 stringByAppendingFormat:@" %d", 2003];

// Extract substrings; returns characters 6 to the end
// subStr = @"World! 2003"
NSString *subStr = [str3 substringFromIndex7];

// Returns characters from beginning to character 5
// subStr = @"Hello"
subStr = [str3 substringToIndex:5];

// Returns 6 characters starting at index 7;
// Also see the comment that accompanies NSRange
// subStr = @"World!"
subStr = [str3 substringWithRange:NSMakeRange(7, 6)];

// Case conversion; returns capitalization: "Hello, World"
NSString *firstcaps = [str2 capitalizedString];

// Case conversion; returns lowercase: "hello, world!"
NSString *lower = [str2 lowercaseString];

// Case conversion; returns uppercase: "HELLO, WORLD!"
NSString *upper = [str2 uppercaseString];

// Searching for substrings; returns NSRange {0, 2}
NSRange loc = [str2 rangeOfString:@"He"];

// Searching for substrings; returns NSRange {NSNotFound, 0}
loc = [str2 rangeOfString:@"and"];

// Checking whether a string is a prefix or suffix of another
BOOL r = [str2 hasPrefix:@"Hello, W"];    // Returns YES
BOOL r = [str2 hasSuffix:@"What?"];       // Returns NO
```

NSRange is a Foundation data type used to specify a portion of a series. NSRange is defined as:

```
typedef struct _NSRange {
    unsigned int location;
    unsigned int length;
} NSRange;
```

The location is the starting index of the portion, and the length is the number of elements of the series in the range. Methods that return NSRanges set the location of the range to NSNotFound to indicate an invalid range in the context of the operation.

To initialize an NSString from Unicode characters, first assemble a C array of the Unicode character codes, which are of the type unichar. Example 2-2 shows how to use hexadecimal character codes to specify the Unicode characters for the string "αβγδε":

Example 2-2. Working with Unicode strings and NSString objects

```
// Create the unichar string "αβγδε"
unichar uc[5] = {0x03b1, 0x03b2, 0x03b3, 0x03b4, 0x03b5};

// Initialize an NSString with a Unicode string
NSString *uStr = [NSString stringWithCharacters:&uc length:5];

// Copy the Unicode characters into a buffer
unichar uc2[5] = [uStr characterAtIndex:0];
```

The entire Unicode character set catalog is available at *http://www.unicode.org*. This site offers a way for you to find the hexadecimal code for any character. In addition, Mac OS X also provides the Character Palette utility, found in the Input Menu, which can be used to look up character codes of any Unicode character.

In Example 2-2, the Unicode characters were specified by their hexadecimal code because the default text encoding of source files (*Mac OS Roman* or another 8-bit encoding) doesn't allow direct representation of Unicode characters. However, Project Builder lets you specify *Unicode (UTF-16 and UTF-8)* as the text encoding for a source file, which would let you enter the Unicode characters directly into source strings with the Character Palette. The file encoding is specified globally in the Project Builder preferences, or on a per-file basis in the file's Project Builder info panel.

NSString includes a method used to break a string apart into components, based on a given separator character or string. This might be useful if you need to parse a record line from a text file whose fields are delimited by a character or string. Example 2-3 shows how this works for a string with colon-separated fields.

Example 2-3. Breaking a string up into its components

```
// A sample record from some record set
NSString *rec = @"John:Doe:Austin:TX:etc";

// Break the string into components separated by colons
// Returns the array {John, Doe, Austin, TX, etc}
NSArray *fields = [str componentsSeperatedByString:@":"];

// NSArray can be used to rejoin the components into one string
// Returns "John*Doe*Austin*TX*etc"
NSString *rec2 = [fields componentsJoinedByString:@"*"];
```

NSMutableString extends NSString's functionality to support in-place modification. This additional flexibility is provided at the expense of decreased efficiency. Example 2-4 illustrates several commonly used methods in NSMutableString.

Example 2-4. Using NSMutableString

```
// Create a mutable string from an immutable string
NSString *str = @"Hello, World";
NSMutableString *ms = [NSMutableString stringWithString:str];

// Append one string to another, ms is now "Hello, World!"
[ms appendString:@"!"];

// Insert strings within a string
// ms is now "He_garbage_llo, World!"
[ms insertString:@"_garbage_" atIndex:2];

// Delete part of a string, ms is now "Hello, World!"
[ms deleteCharactersInRange:NSMakeRange(2,9)];

// Replace part of a string with another string
// ms is now "Hello, World."
[ms replaceCharactersInRange:NSMakeRange(12,1) withString:@"."];

// Replace the contents of a string with another string
[ms setString:@"That's all for now."];
```

Comparing strings

NSString provides several methods for comparing strings and testing equality. NSObject declares the method isEqual: to test general object equality. This method works with NSString objects, but the NSString method isEqualToString: more efficiently tests the equality of two objects known to be strings. Using it returns YES if the ids of the two strings are equal (which implies that the variables point to the same object) or if the result of a lexical comparison between the strings is NSOrderedSame.

A comparison that determines the lexical ordering of two strings is carried out with any of several methods, each of which provides varying degrees of control over the scope of the comparison. The method that provides the greatest amount of control is compare:options:range:. The options: argument takes one or both of the following two constants (both can be used with the C bitwise OR operator, |):

NSCaseInsensitiveSearch
Makes the comparison case insensitive.

NSLiteralSearch
Compares the two strings on a byte-by-byte, rather than character-by-character, basis. This comparison can improve speed for some operations, but differing literal sequences may not match when they otherwise would. For example, accented characters may be represented by a composite character (e.g., é), or a combined sequence of two Unicode characters (e.g., e and ´).

The range: argument restricts the comparison to a substring of the receiver. If you want to compare only the first two string characters, specify an NSRange of (0,2) in the range: argument.

Two other related methods are compare:options: and compare:. The first method passes options: to compare:options:range: and makes the range equal to the entire length of the receiver. The second, compare:, passes no options, and again uses the full extent of the receiver as the range. Example 2-5 shows different ways to compare strings.

Example 2-5. Comparing strings

```
NSString *a = @"Right";

// Test for equality; returns YES
BOOL v = [a isEqualToString:@"Right"];

// Determine lexical order of two strings; returns NSOrderedSame
NSComparisonResult r = [a compare:@"Right"];

// Returns NSOrderedDescending; light comes before Right
r = [a compare:@"light"];

// Returns NSOrderedAscending; sight comes after Right
r = [a compare:@"sight"];

// Literal, case-insensitive comparison by setting options
r = [a compare:@"right"
      options:NSCaseInsensitiveSearch | NSLiteralSearch];

// Easier case-insensitive comparison; returns NSOrderedSame
r = [@"next" caseInsensitiveCompare:@"NeXT"];
```

Attributed strings

NSAttributedString provides an API for text strings that contain information about graphical attributes of the text, such as its font, color, size, and kerning. Attributes can be applied to individual characters, ranges of characters, or to the entire length of the string. Like NSString, NSAttributedString is an immutable class with a mutable subclass, NSMutableAttributeString.

The functionality of NSAttributedString as it exists in the Foundation framework is fairly basic. Foundation's functionality is limited to keeping track of the string contents, as well as the various sets of attributes that apply to different ranges of the string. The Application Kit provides most functionality of NSAttributedString related to drawing and displaying text, and is covered more in Chapters 3 and 4.

Working with strings: character sets and scanners

In addition to a rich abstraction for strings, Foundation includes two classes that support string processing: NSScanner and NSCharacterSet.

NSCharacterSet

An NSCharacterSet represents a collection of Unicode characters. A number of sets are predefined and accessible through class methods, including:

- alphanumericCharacterSet
- capitalizedLetterCharacterSet
- controlCharacterSet
- decimalDigitCharacterSet
- letterCharacterSet
- punctuationCharacterSet
- whitespaceAndNewlineCharacterSet
- whitespaceCharacterSet

You can also create a new character set from a string, using characterSetWithCharactersInString:, load in a set from a file with characterSetWithContentsOfFile:, or invert an existing set with invertedSet:.

NSCharacterSet's mutable subclass, NSMutableCharacterSet, allows you to, amongst other modifications, add or remove string characters to or from a set and form a union or intersection with another set. Mutable character sets are, however, less efficient than immutable character sets. If you do not need to change a character set after establishing it, create an immutable copy with copy, and use that.

You would typically use NSCharacterSets to group characters, to let you find part of a particular set when searching an NSString object. You might use NString's rangeOfCharacterFromSet:options:range: method (or a variant thereof) to find the range in the receiver of the first (or in the case of a backwards search, last) character found from the set argument. NSCharacterSets are also used extensively with NSScanner.

NSScanner

An NSScanner object lets you search an NSString object for string and number values, with options for scanning up to or past characters from a given set or string. You would usually initialize a scanner with the string to scan, using scannerWithString: or initWithString. You can configure it to be case-sensitive, or not, with setCaseSensitive; establish a starting point with setScanLocation:; or set its locale with setLocale:. A scanner's locale affects the way it interprets values from the string. In particular, a scanner uses the locale's decimal separator to distinguish the integer and fractional parts of floating-point representations.

After it is configured, a scanner can read numeric values from its string into a variable, using methods such as scanInt:, scanFloat:, and scanDecimal: (the first two methods read scalars; scanDecimal: creates an NSDecimalNumber object). You can search for particular strings or characters by using any of the following methods:

- scanString:intoString:
- scanUpToString:intoString:

- `scanCharactersFromSet:intoString:`
- `scanUpToCharactersFromSet:intoString:`

All of these methods return a Boolean value to indicate the operation's success. Pass a pointer to the variable as the argument to these methods, or pass `nil` to skip a value. Finally, check whether you have reached the end of the input string with the `isAtEnd` method. For example, assume a file, *~/scannerTest.txt*, of the form:

```
EmpId: 7830480 FirstName: Jo LastName: Wong
EmpId: 67567456 FirstName: Toni LastName: Jones
EmpId: 546776 FirstName: Dylan LastName: Blimp
```

Example 2-6 shows how the file may be parsed with `NSScanner`.

Example 2-6. Using NSScanner and NSCharacterSet

```
NSCharacterSet * letterSet , *whiteSet;
letterSet = [NSCharacterSet letterCharacterSet];
whiteSet = [NSCharacterSet whitespaceAndNewlineCharacterSet];

NSString *filePath, *fileString;
NSScanner *scanner;

filePath = [@"~/scannerTest.txt" stringByExpandingTildeInPath];

fileString = [NSString stringWithContentsOfFile:filePath];

scanner = [NSScanner scannerWithString:fileString];

while ( ![scanner isAtEnd] ) {
  NSString *fName, *lName;
  int empId;

  if ( [scanner scanString:@"EmpId: " intoString:nil] ) {

    [scanner scanInt:&empId];

    [scanner scanString:@"FirstName: " intoString:nil];
    [scanner scanCharactersFromSet:letterSet intoString:&fName];

    [scanner scanString:@"LastName: " intoString:nil];
    [scanner scanCharactersFromSet:letterSet intoString:&lName];

    NSLog(@"%@ %@, EmpID: %d", fName, lName, empId);

    [scanner scanCharactersFromSet:whiteSet intoString:nil];
  }
}
```

The code in Example 2-6 produces the following output:

```
Jo Wong, EmpID: 7830480
Toni Jones, EmpID: 67567456
Dylan Blimp, EmpID: 546776
```

Numbers

For many numerical operations dealing with calculations, using C's primitive numerical data types is the easiest and most efficient way to represent numerical data. However, you might need to treat a number as an object to store it in a collection or to store a number in the user defaults database. For such situations, the Foundation framework provides the class NSNumber, which is an Objective-C wrapper class for the standard numeric data types in C. You can initialize instances of NSNumber with a scalar and retrieve a scalar value from a number object. Example 2-7 shows many of the methods used to work with NSNumbers.

Example 2-7. Working with NSNumber

```
// NSNumbers can contain any primitive C type
NSNumber *iN = [NSNumber numberWithInt:1];
NSNumber *fN = [NSNumber numberWithFloat:50.5f];
NSNumber *dN = [NSNumber numberWithDouble:100.45];
NSNumber *cN = [NSNumber numberWithChar:100];
NSNumber *lN = [NSNumber numberWithLong:100];
NSNumber *usN = [NSNumber numberWithUnsignedShort:30];

// Access the value of an NSNumber object
int i = [iN intValue];                          // Returns 1
float f = [fN floatValue];                      // Returns 50.5
double d = [dN doubleValue];                    // Returns 100.45
char c = [cN charValue];                        // Returns 100
long l = [lN longValue];                        // Returns 100
unsigned short us = [usN unsignedShortValue];   // Returns 30

// Test for equality of two numbers; returns YES
BOOL b = [nc isEqualToNumber:nl];

// Determine how one number compares to another in order
NSComparisonResult r = [nc compare:nus];        // NSOrderedDescending
r = [nus compare:ns];                           // NSOrderedAscending
```

NSDecimalNumber extends the capabilities of NSNumber with APIs to perform base-10 arithmetic, and it provides methods to initialize an instance in terms of the number's basic components. Example 2-8 shows how to work with NSDecimalNumber.

Example 2-8. Working with NSDecimalNumber

```
// Planck's Constant (1.04e-34)
NSDecimalNumber *h = [NSDecimalNumber
                        decimalNumberWithManitssa:104
                        exponent:-36
                        isNegative:NO];

// NSDecimalNumber has methods for returning commonly used numbers
NSDecimalNumber *one = [NSDecimalNumber one];    // 1.0
NSDecimalNumber *zero = [NSDecimalNumber zero];  // 0.0
```

Example 2-8. Working with NSDecimalNumber (continued)

```
// NSNumbers that represent system limits
NSDecimalNumber *max = [NSDecimalNumber maximumDecimalNumber];
NSDecimalNumber *min = [NSDecimalNumber minimumDecimalNumber];

// Methods to operate on the numbers
NSDecimalNumber *n;
n = [one decimalNumberByAdding:zero];          // n = 1.0
n = [one decimalNumberBySubtracting:zero];     // n = 1.0
n = [h decimalNumberByMultiplyingBy:c];        // n = 3.16e-26
n = [h decimalNumberByDividingBy:one];         // n = 1.05e-34
n = [c decimalNumberByRaisingToThePower:2];    // n = 9.0e16
```

Each method has corresponding methods that let you determine how to handle rounding and errors (typically by using instances of NSDecimalNumberHandler), which is known as the number's *behavior*. Numbers round to the nearest integer by default; an exception is raised if there is division by zero, or if the result of a calculation exceeds the maximum or minimum numbers that can be represented.

Collections

The Foundation framework offers several important classes for creating and manipulating collections of objects. The primary collection classes are NSArray, NSDictionary, and NSSet:

NSArray
> Stores an ordered, immutable collection of objects, where each member is referenced by its index number. Any given object may appear in an array more than once.

NSSet
> Stores an immutable, unordered collection of unique objects, which support the mathematical idea of a set. NSSet objects are useful when your collection requires you to test an object for membership; NSSet provides a more efficient implementation for testing object membership over that of other collection classes.

NSDictionary
> Stores a collection of objects as key-value pairs; each member has an associated key that identifies that member object.

Each class has subclasses that extend their interfaces to provide mutability.

Arrays

Instances of NSArray represent an ordered collection objects. An index number identifies each member object in the array; indexing begins at zero, just as in C arrays. Example 2-9 gives an overview of NSArray's capabilities.

Example 2-9. Creating and working with NSArray objects

```
// Create an array from several objects
// Objects are separated by commas, and the list must end with nil
NSArray *a = [NSArray arrayWithObjects:@"Hello",@"how",@"are", @"you",nil];
```

Example 2-9. Creating and working with NSArray objects (continued)

```
// If you need an array with one object
NSArray *b = [NSArray arrayWithObject:@"One object"];

// Create an array from the contents of an XML property list
b = [NSArray arrayWithContentsOfFile:@"/path/to/plist"];

// Test arrays for equality
BOOL r = [a isEqualToArray:b];                  // Returns NO

// Determine the number of memebers in a collection
int n = [a count];                              // Returns 4

// Access elements of the array
NSString *one = [a objectAtIndex:0];            // Returns @"Hello"
NSString *end = [a lastObject];                 // Returns @"you"

// Discover the index of an object
unsigned idx = [a indexOfObject:@"how"];        // Returns 1

// Find out if an array contains some object
BOOL result = [a containsObject:@"today"];      // Returns NO

// Obtain a new array by adding an object
NSArray *newA = [a arrayByAddingObject:@"today"];

// Extract subarrays
NSArray *subA = [a subarrayWithRange:NSMakeRange(1,2)];
```

NSMutableArray extends NSArray by adding support for arrays whose contents can be changed after their initialization. Example 2-10 shows how a small set of the mutability methods works.

Example 2-10. A sampling of NSMutableArray methods

```
// Create a mutable array from an immutable array
NSMutableArray *ma = [NSMutableArray arrayWithArray:a];

// Create an empty mutable array
NSMutableArray *ma = [NSMutableArray array];

// Exercise mutability
[ma addObject:@"World"];                    // ma is {World}
[ma insertObject:@"Hello" atIndex:0];       // ma is {Hello, World}
[ma removeObjectAtIndex:0];                 // ma is {World}
[ma removeLastObject];                      // ma is {}
```

Sets

NSSet declares an interface to unordered collections of unique objects. The Foundation framework implements two subclasses of NSSet: NSMutableSet and NSSCountedSet, which is a child class of NSMutableSet. Like arrays and dictionaries, the contents of a set can be any Objective-C object. Example 2-11 shows how to use NSSet.

Example 2-11. Using NSSet

```
// Create a set from the contents of an array
NSSet *set1 = [NSSet setWithArray:anArray];

// Create a set from arbitrary objects
set1 = [NSSet setWithObjects:@"a", @"b", @"c",@"d", nil];

// Create a set from a single object
NSSet *set2 = [NSSet setWithObject:@"a"];

// Determine the size of the set
unsigned int n = [set1 count];              // Returns 4

// Access set members; creates an NSArray from the set contents
NSArray *setObjs = [set1 allObjects];

// You can have a set randomly (essentially) return a member
id object = [set1 anyObject];

// Test for membership, the strength of NSSet; returns YES
BOOL b = [set1 containsObject:@"a"];
b = [set1 containsObject:@"z"];             // Returns NO
id mem = [set1 member:@"a"];                // Returns @"a"
id mem = [set1 member:@"z"];                // Returns nil

// Compare two sets
NSSet *set3 = [NSSet setWithObjects:@"c", @"d", @"e", @"f", nil];
BOOL b = [set2 isSubsetOf:set1];            // Returns YES
b = [set2 intersectsSet:set1];              // Returns YES
b = [set3 intersectsSet:set1];              // Returns NO
b = [set1 isEqualToSet:set2];               // Returns NO
```

Example 2-12 shows what NSMutableSet adds to NSSet.

Example 2-12. Methods provided by NSMutableSet

```
// Add and remove member objects
[set1 addObject:@"e"];                      // set1 now [a, b, c, d, e]
[set1 removeObject:@"a"];                    // set1 now [b, c, d, e]
[set2 removeAllObjects];                     // set1 now []

// Combine sets
[set1 unionSet:set3];                        // set1 now [b, c, d, e, f]
[set1 minusSet:set3];                        // set1 now [b]
[set1 intersectSet:set3];                    // set1 now []
[set1 setSet:set3];                          // set1 now [c, d, e, f]
```

NSCountedSet is based on a slightly different idea of a set than its superclasses. In a standard set, each member object must be unique. Counted sets remove the constraint on uniqueness, making it possible to add an object to a counted set more than once. However, a counted set does not keep multiple references to an object; rather, it keeps a count of the number of times an object was added to the set. Whenever an object is added to the set of which it is already a member, the count for that object is incremented. When an object is removed from a counted set, its count is decremented until it reaches zero, at which point the object is no longer a member of the set. The code in Example 2-13 demonstrates the functionality added by NSCountedSet.

Example 2-13. Methods provided by NSCountedSet

```
// Add and remove objects; inherits methods from NSMutableSet
[set3 addObject:@"b"];              // set3 now [b, c, d, e, f]
[set3 addObject:@"b"];              // Increments count for b to 2
[set3 addObject:@"b"];              // Count for b now 3
[set3 countForObject:@"b"];         // Returns 3
[set3 removeObject:@"b"];
[set3 countForObject:@"b"];         // Returns 2
```

Dictionaries

Cocoa dictionaries provide a collection class that implements the idea of key-value pairs. In a dictionary, member objects are associated with a unique identifier key, used to identify and access the object. Although keys are typically NSString objects, both keys and values may be of any class. Example 2-14 summarizes several commonly used methods of NSDictionary.

Example 2-14. Working with NSDictionary

```
// Create an empty dictionary, useful for
// creating empty mutable dictionaries
NSDictionary *d = [NSDictionary dictionary];

// Initialize a dictionary with contents of an XML property list
d = [NSDictionary dictionaryWithContentsOfFile:@"pList"];

// Create a dictionary from one object with a key
d = [NSDictionary dictionaryWithObject:@"a" forKey:@"A"];

// Create a dictionary with many objects and keys
d = [NSDictionary dictionaryWithObjects:@"a", @"b", nil
                               forKeys:@"A", @"B", nil];

// Count the number of objects in the dictionary;
int n = [d count];                          // Returns 2

// Access objects and keys;
id obj = [d objectForKey:@"A"];             // Returns "a"

// Returns nil since "a" is not a valid key
obj = [d objectForKey:@"a"];

// Returns an array whose members are the keys of the receiver
NSArray *k = [d allKeys];
```

Example 2-14. Working with NSDictionary (continued)

```
// Returns an array with the dictionary's objects
NSArray *v = [d allValues];

// Returns an enumerator for the receiver's keys
NSEnumerator *e = [d keyEnumerator];

// Returns enumerator for objects in dictionary
e = [d objectEnumerator];

// Write contents of dictionary to a file formatted
// as an XML property list
[d writeToFile:@"/path/to/file" atomically:YES];
```

Example 2-15 shows how to work with mutable dictionaries.

Example 2-15. Working with NSMutableDictionary

```
// Create a mutable dictionary from an immutable dictionary
NSMutableDictionary *md;
md = [NSMutableDictionary dictionaryFromDictionary:d];

// Add a key-value pair
[md setObject:@"c" forKey:@"C"];

// Remove an object from the dictionary
[md removeObjectForKey:@"A"];

// You can also remove all objects in one fell swoop
[md removeAllObjects];

// Finally, replace the current contents with the
// contents of another dictionary
[md setDictionary:d];
```

Enumerators

Traditionally, a for-loop is used to enumerate the contents of a collection, which provides access to each member by its index. Since the for-loop technique depends on indexed collection contents, it won't work for non-indexed collections, such as sets and dictionaries. NSEnumerator provides an object-oriented way of iterating over the contents of any collection. Each Foundation collection type implements the method objectEnumerator, which returns an enumerator for the receiver.

To illustrate how NSEnumerator is used in place of the for-loop, consider Examples 2-16 and 2-17. Example 2-16 shows how an array is traditionally enumerated using a for-loop.

Example 2-16. Using a for-loop to enumerate an array's contents

```
// Assume NSArray *array exists
int i;
id object;
```

Example 2-16. Using a for-loop to enumerate an array's contents (continued)

```
for ( i = 0; i < [array count]; i++ ) {
    object = [array objectAtIndex:i];

    // Do something with the object
}
```

Example 2-17 shows how the NSEnumerator class accomplishes the same task.

Example 2-17. Using NSEnumerator to enumerate an array's contents

```
// Assume NSArray *array exists
NSEnumerator *e = [array objectEnumerator];
id object;

while ( object = [e nextObject] ) {

    // Do something with the object
}
```

Some collection classes have variations on the standard objectEnumerator method. For example, the reverseObjectEnumerator method of NSArray lets you access the array's contents from the last item to the first. Another variation is NSDictionary's keyEnumerator method, which lets you enumerate the dictionary's keys instead of its values.

Since the members of an array are indexed, expect an enumerator to return the contents of an array in a predictable order. NSDictionary and NSSet, on the other hand, don't store their contents in a meaningful order, so the order in which the enumerators return the members is unpredictable.

Memory management in collections

Whenever an object is added to a collection, the collection object sends that object a retain message, asserting some ownership over the object that is now a member of the collection. This is true whether the object is added as part of the collection initialization, or at a later point with the addObject:–based methods in mutable collection classes. Objects that are removed from collections receive a release message, as the collection no longer has any interest in maintaining ownership over the object. When a collection is deallocated, all member objects are sent a release message. Example 2-18 shows how this works in practice.

Example 2-18. Collection memory management

```
// anObject has reference count of 1
id anObject = [[ObjectClass alloc] init];

// Assume anArray is an existing mutable array; reference
// count of anObject is now 2.
[anArray addObject:anObject];
```

Example 2-18. Collection memory management (continued)

```
// anObject reference count now 1, still valid because of
// retain sent by the array in addObject:
[anObject release];

// Either of these actions will cause anObject to be released
[anArray removeObject:anObject];
[anArray release];
```

Dates and Time

Cocoa provides three classes to represent date and time information: NSDate, NSCalendarDate, and NSTimeZone. NSDate represents an instant in time, to millisecond precision, as the number of seconds since the absolute reference time, midnight (GMT), January 1, 2001. Many NSDate methods work with time intervals. A time interval is represented by the Foundation data type NSTimeInterval (which is a redefinition of the primitive type double). NSTimeIntervals specify a length of time in units of seconds. Example 2-19 shows how to use NSDate.

Example 2-19. Fundamental methods of NSDate

```
// Create an NSDate set to the current date
NSDate *today = [NSDate date];

// Obtain a date that is many centuries in the future
NSDate *future = [NSDate distantFuture];

// Similarly, obtain a date that is many centuries in the past
NSDate *past = [NSDate distantPast];

// A date that is some number of seconds past the system reference
// date (or before if you supply a negative value)
NSDate *intvl = [NSDate dateWithTimeIntervalSinceReferenceDate:60];

// Check for equality of two dates; returns NO
BOOL b = [today isEqualToDate:intvl];

// These methods return either the earlier or
// the later of the two dates involved.
NSDate *d = [today earlierDate:past];        // Returns past
NSDate *d = [today laterDate:future];        // Returns future

// Obtain Time Intervals
NSTimeInterval d = [intvl timeIntervalSinceReferenceDate];

// Number of seconds between receiver date and current date
d = [today timeIntervalSinceNow];

// Number of seconds between the two dates
d = [today timeIntervalSinceDate:[NSDate date]];

// Number of seconds since 1970, another reference date
d = [today timeIntervalSince1970];
```

NSDate is a lightweight class that represents dates as points in time. NSCalendarDate, a subclass of NSDate, can additionally perform date arithmetic based on the Western Gregorian calendar. NSCalendarDate expands the functionality of NSDate to provide methods that work with dates in terms of days, weeks, months, and years. Example 2-20 summarizes what you can do with NSCalendarDate.

Example 2-20. Working with NSCalendarDate

```
// Create an NSCalendarDate
NSCalendarDate *cd = [NSCalendarDate calendarDate];

// Create an arbitrary calendar date
cd = [NSCalendarDate dateWithYear:2002 month:4 day:10 hour:20
                          minute:3 second:0
                          timeZone:[NSTimeZone systemTimeZone]];

// Retrieve elements of a calendar date
int dce = [cd dayOfCommonEra];     // Returns 730950
int dm = [cd dayOfMonth];          // Returns 10
int dw = [cd dayOfWeek];           // Returns 3
int d = [cd dayOfYear];            // Returns 100
int h = [cd hourOfDay];            // Returns 20
int m = [cd minuteOfHour];         // Returns 3
int s = [cd secondOfMinute];       // Returns 0
int y = [cd yearOfCommonEra];      // Returns 2002
```

Associated with every NSCalendarDate object is an NSTimeZone object. Instances of NSTimeZone capture information about geographic time zones across the planet, such as their name, abbreviation, and "distance" from the reference time zone, GMT, in seconds. Additionally, NSTimeZone is aware of daylight savings time, and capable of translating dates between time zones. NSCalendarDate still stores a date in its lowest form as a time interval from the reference date, which is behavior it inherits from NSDate. NSTimeZone translates that time interval from GMT to a specific time zone. The systemTimeZone method used in Example 2-20 is just one method of NSTimeZone that returns the time zone set on your system. In addition to this method, NSTimeZone declares several other methods, some of which are shown in Example 2-21.

Example 2-21. Working with NSTimeZone

```
// Create time zone objects
NSTimeZone *tz = [NSTimeZone timeZoneWithAbbreviation:@"CST"];

// Obtain the geo-political name of the time zone
// Returns "America/Chicago"
NSString *name = [tz name];

// Get the time zone's abbreviation; Returns CST
NSString *abv = [tz abbreviation];

// Returns whether or not it is daylight saving time; returns NO
BOOL b = [tz isDaylightSavingTime];
```

Example 2-21. Working with NSTimeZone (continued)

```
// The time difference relative to GMT in seconds; Returns -18000
int s = [tz secondsFromGMT];
```

Binary Data

NSData encapsulates a buffer of bytes. Many Foundation framework classes have methods that let you initialize an object from an instance of NSData or convert the object's contents into an NSData object. NSData is a generic object that lets you store and transport data of any kind, any way you like. Example 2-22 gives an example.

Example 2-22. Working with NSData

```
// NSData objects can be created to hold the contents of any data
// buffer, such as a static C character string
char *cData = "This is data, a string of bytes";
NSData *data = [NSData dataWithBytes:cData length:strlen(cData)];

// Create NSData objects from files
data = [NSData dataWithContentsOfFile:@"/path/to/file"];

// Create data objects from resources located by NSURL objects
data = [NSData dataWithContentsOfURL:URLObject];

// Get a C pointer to the data object contents
void *p = [data bytes];

// Copy the contents of data object into a buffer
char buffer[50];
[data getBytes:(void *)buffer];

// Copy a specified number of bytes into the buffer
[data getBytes:buffer length:4];

// Copy a range of bytes from the data object into the buffer
[data getBytes:buffer range:NSMakeRange(5,2)];

// Determine the number of bytes in the data
unsigned l = [data length];
```

Note in the second line that despite initializing an NSData object with a C string, the NSData object is not a string. The data object has no idea what its contents represent, only that it is a collection of bytes. The client that interacts with the data object is responsible for knowing how to interpret the contents.

Like many other Foundation classes, NSData is an immutable class that has a mutable child class, NSMutableData. NSMutableData adds methods to change the length of the stored data (how many bytes are in there) and append data to the stored data, as illustrated in Example 2-23.

Example 2-23. Working with NSMutableData

```
// Create an empty NSData object
NSMutableData *mData = [NSMutableData data];

// Set the size of the internal NSData buffer to 29 bytes
[mData setLength:29];

// Take the data from a buffer and place it
// into the NSData object
[mData appendBytes:cData length:29];
```

Key-Value Coding

Key-value coding lets you access the properties of an object (such as the instance variables) indirectly by using strings referred to as *keys*. Although key-value coding can access instance variables directly, it first tries to use accessor methods to access a property. However, accessor methods are not necessarily mapped to instance variables, which means that an accessor may provide a property value that is computed (perhaps from instance variables).

Key-value coding is a powerful feature of Cocoa that forms the basis of many important technologies. For example, Cocoa's scripting capability is heavily based on the functionality of key-value coding.

The methods that provide an interface to key-value coding are declared in the Foundation framework's NSKeyValueCoding protocol. The principal methods are valueForKey: and takeValue:forKey:, which get and set the instance variable associated with the specified key. NSObject provides default implementations of the methods of NSKeyValueCoding. These default implementations associate keys with instance variables based on a simple set of rules. The methods that return a value, valueForKey: for instance, attempt to access the property specified by the string @"key" using the following means:

1. A public accessor of either the form key or getKey.
2. A private accessor method of either the form _key or _getKey.
3. An instance variable named either key or _key.
4. Finally, if none of these first three attempts results in anything, the method invokes handleQueryWithUnboundKey:. The default implementation raises an exception; classes may choose to provide another implementation suitable to their needs.

Methods that set the values of properties, such as takeValue:forKey:, attempt to access those properties in a similar fashion, assuming again that the key is the string @"key":

1. A public accessor of the form setKey:.
2. A private accessor of the form _setKey:.
3. An instance variable named either key or _key.
4. Finally, if none of these first three rules results in anything, the methods invoke handleTakeValue:forKey:. The default implementation raises an

exception; classes may choose to provide another implementation suitable to their needs.

Example 2-24 shows the interface for a class with three instance variables, a public accessor to one of the instance variables, and a private accessor to another.

Example 2-24. Using key-value coding in a class called KVExample

```
@interface KVExample : NSObject {
    id property1;
    id property2;
    id property3;
}
- (id)property1;     // Public accessor; could be getProperty1
- (id)_property2;    // The private accessor; could be _getProperty2
@end

@implementation KVExample
- (id)init
{
    self = [super init];

    if ( self ) {
        property1 = @"Property 1";
        property2 = @"Property 2";
        property3 = @"Property 3";
    }
    return self;
}

// These two methods return instance variable values
- (id)property1
{
    return property1;
}

- (id)_property2
{
    return property2;
}

// This method returns a property value that is computed,
// rather than stored in an instance variable
-(NSArray *)allProperties
{
    return [NSArray arrayWithObjects:property1, property2, property3, nil];
}
@end
```

Example 2-25 shows how to access each accessor using the key-value coding interface.

Example 2-25. Accessing properties of a class using key-value coding

```
id kv = [[KVExample alloc] init];

NSLog( [kv valueForKey:@"property1"];    // Prints "Property 1"
NSLog( [kv valueForKey:@"property2"];    // Prints "Property 2"
NSLog( [kv valueForKey:@"property3"];    // Prints "Property 3"

// Prints "{Property1, Property2, Property 3}"
NSLog( [kv valueForKey:@"allProperties"]);
```

Working with Files

The Foundation framework provides access to data stored in files in several ways. All of the basic data classes have methods for initializing objects from the contents of files, and for writing the data represented by the object to a file. In addition to these convenience facilities, Foundation provides two classes that provide a much higher level of interaction with files and the filesystem: NSFileManager and NSFileHandle.

The File Manager

The NSFileManager class is an interface that applications use to access and manipulate files and directories in the filesystem; instances of NSFileManager provide a doorway to the filesystem for application developers. Several of NSFileManager's methods call for a handler: argument. The handler is an object that should implement fileManager:willProcessPath: and fileManager:shouldProceedAfterError: methods. These callback methods allow for error handling and confidence testing with respect to the operation being performed. In Example 2-26, nil is passed to handler: for the sake of clarity.

Additionally, methods that deal with movement around in the filesystem and perform operations on files and directories typically return a BOOL value, to indicate an operation's success or failure. Finally, methods that create new files or directories usually take a dictionary with file attributes as an argument. The attributes dictionary may take values to set the file's owner, group owner, modification date, POSIX permissions; determine whether the extension is hidden; and finally, set the HFS type and creator codes. Any unspecified attribute will take on the default value. Example 2-26 shows how to work with file managers and the filesystem.

Example 2-26. Working with NSFileManager

```
// Return the default manager for the filesystem
NSFileManager *fm = [NSFileManager defaultManager];

// Change the current directory; returns YES if successful
BOOL b = [fm changeCurrentDirectoryPath:@"/usr"];

// Return the path to the current directory; returns "/usr"
NSString *p = [fm currentDirectoryPath];
```

Example 2-26. Working with NSFileManager (continued)

```
// Create a new directory at the path with default attributes
b = [fm createDirectoryAtPath:@"/usr/newDir" attributes:nil];

// Working with file attributes using a mutable dictionary
NSMutableDictionary *attr = [NSMutableDictionary dictionary];
[attr setObject:@"mike" forKey:NSFileOwnerAccountName];
[attr setObject:@"admin" forKey:NSFileGroupOwnerAccountName];
[attr setObject:660 forKey:NSFilePosixPermissions];

// Create a new file with these attributes
b = [fm createFileAtPath:@"/usr/newDir/newFile"
                        contents:data attributes:attr];

// Carry out practical filesystem tasks
NSString *p1 = @"/Users/mike/file"
NSString *p2 = @"/Users/mike/Documents/file"
b = [fm movePath:p1 toPath:p2 handler:nil];
b = [fm copyPath:p2 toPath:p1 handler:nil];
b = [fm removeFileAtPath:p2 handler:nil];

// Determine whether a file exists
b = [fm fileExistsAtPath:p1];

// Determine whether a file exists and if it is a directory
// Returns YES; sets dir = NO
BOOL dir;
b = [fm fileExistsAtPath:p1 isDirectory:&dir];

// Check whether the current user can read file at path
b = [fm isReadableAtPath:p1];

// Check whether the current user can write to file at path
b = [fm isWritableAtPath:p1];

// Check whether the current user can execute file at path
b = [fm isExecutableAtPath:p1];

// Check whether the current user can delete file at path
b = [fm isDeletableAtPath:p1];

// Discover the contents of directory at path
NSArray *contents = [fm directoryContentsAtPath:@"/"];

// Determine the directories contained within a directory
NSArray *subpaths = [fm subpathsAtPath:@"/"];

// An enumerator that enumerates the contents at a given path
NSEnumerator *de = [fm enumeratorAtPath:@"/"];
```

Filesystem paths are represented as NSString objects. Any path that you pass to an NSFileManager method must be an absolute path. This means that files in a user's home directory must be referenced as */Users/username/file*, rather than *~/file*. To aid in path manipulation and standardization, NSString provides a number of methods specific to these tasks, many of which are demonstrated in Example 2-27.

Example 2-27. Path manipulation with NSString

```
// The starting path
NSString *p1 = @"~/Documents/class.m";

// Expand the tilde; returns "/Users/mike/Documents/class.m"
p1 = [p1 stringByExpandingTildeInPath];

// Get the last path component; returns "class.m"
p1 = [p1 lastPathComponent];

// This is how you determine the path extension; returns "m"
p1 = [p1 pathExtension];

// Delete the extension; returns "class"
p1 = [p1 stringByDeletingPathExtension];

// Add a path component to a path; returns "/Users/mike/class"
p1 = [@"/Users/mike" stringByAppendingPathComponent:p1];

// Place the tilde back in; returns "~/class"
p1 = [p1 stringByAbbreviatingWithTildeInPath];

// Add an extension; returns "~/class.h"
p1 = [p1 stringByAppendingPathExtension:@"h"];
```

The Foundation framework also provides several functions that return paths to common locations in the filesystem. NSHomeDirectory returns the path to the home directory of the currently logged-in user. NSHomeDirectoryForUser takes a username as an argument and returns the home directory for that user. The function NSTemporaryDirectory returns a string that is the path to the current temporary directory, typically */tmp*.

File Handles

NSFileHandle lets developers access and manipulate file data with a fine degree of control by providing methods for moving a pointer within a file, as well as inserting, deleting, and extracting data from the file. Moreover, in the true spirit of Unix, NSFileHandle can represent a gateway to communication channels such as pipes, sockets, and devices (such as */dev/null, /dev/stderr, /dev/console*). NSFileHandle is covered further in Chapter 6, where methods for asynchronous reading and writing are discussed. Example 2-28 explores some uses of NSFileHandle.

Example 2-28. Working with NSFileHandle

```
// Create a file handle for reading an arbitrary file
NSFileHandle *fh = [NSFileHandle fileHandleForReadingAtPath:p1];
fh = [NSFileHandle fileHandleForReadingAtPath:@"/dev/srandom"];
```

Example 2-28. Working with NSFileHandle (continued)

```
// Create a file handle for writing to a file
fh = [NSFileHandle fileHandleForWritingAtPath:p2];
fh = [NSFileHandle fileHandleForWritingAtPath:@"/dev/null"];

// Create commonly used file handles
fh = [NSFileHandle fileHandleWithStandardError];
fh = [NSFileHandle fileHandleWithStandardInput];
fh = [NSFileHanfle fileHandleWithStandardOutput];
fh = [NSFileHandle fileHandleWithNullDevice];

// Write data to a file handle
NSString *str = @"Other Unix boxes";
NSData *data = [str dataUsingEncoding:NSASCIIStringEncoding];
[fh writeData:data];

// Read data from a file handle;
// this could be used for something like % echo "Hello" | ThisApp
fh = [NSFileHandle fileHandleWithStandardInput];

// Read all available data and converting it to a string
NSData *data = [fh availableData];
NSString *str = [NSString stringWithData:data];

// You can also read a specified number of bytes
data = [fh readDataOfLength:400];

// Or you can read up to an end-of-file
data = [fh readDataToEndOfFile];

// And close it when finished
[fh closeFile];
```

Bundles and Resource Management

A bundle is an abstraction that represents a collection of resources, such as image files, nib files, or loadable code, stored within a folder. Bundles are used pervasively in Mac OS X—applications are themselves bundles, as are preference pane and screensaver modules and application plug-ins. Although bundles are directories, the Finder often presents them to the user as a single file. For a more in-depth discussion of bundles and their usage in Mac OS X, see *Inside Mac OS X: System Overview* (*/Developer/Documentation/Essentials/SystemOverview/SystemOverview.pdf*).

NSBundle provides an interface to bundles in the filesystem. Every Cocoa application has at least one bundle—the main bundle, accessed using the mainBundle method—that represents the application. To load other bundles, use the methods initWithPath: or bundleWithPath:. To access a bundle containing a given class, use bundleForClass:.

Loading Resources

Using NSBundle, you can obtain the paths to resources without knowledge of a bundle's internal directory structure or what localization is used. Methods that find a resource come in two flavors: those that retrieve individual resources, whose names are on the base method name pathForResource:ofType:, and those that return all resources of a type, which are based on the method name pathsForResourceOfType:. The paths returned by these methods are absolute paths in the filesystem. For example, consider the method pathForResource:ofType:. Given the name of the resource (resource file name sans extension) and, optionally, the type (the extension may pass nil or @"" here), this method will return the full path to the specified resource in the main resources directory, which is at *BundleName/Contents/Resources*. If the resource is not found there, then any *.lproj* folders are searched in order according to the user's Language setting in Preferences.

If you want to specify a directory to search in for the resource (as it may not be contained in the *Resources* directory), use the method pathForResource:ofType:inDirectory:. If the resource is not present in the specified directory, the method returns nil. If nil is passed for the parameter inDirectory:, a search is performed through a prioritized list of directories. See the NSBundle documentation for the search order.

In addition to containing resources, bundles may contain other bundles in the form of plug-ins, frameworks, and other applications. Plug-ins and frameworks are generally located in the */BundleName/Contents/PlugIns* and */BundleName/Contents/Frameworks* directories, respectively. You can discover these paths by using the builtInPlugInsPath, privateFrameworksPath and sharedFrameworksPath methods.

Example 2-29 shows how to use these methods to access resources contained within a bundle.

Example 2-29. Accessing bundle resources

```
NSString *imagePath;
NSImage *anImage;
NSBundle *bundle = [NSBundle mainBundle];

// Locate and load a resource
if ( imagePath = [bundle pathForResource:@"mug_shot"
        ofType:@"tiff"] ) {
    anImage = [[NSImage alloc] initWithContentsOfFile:imagePath];
    // Do something with anImage
}

// The path to the frameworks directory
NSString *fPath = [bundle sharedFrameworksPath];
fPath = [bundle privateFrameworksPath];

// Path of the bundle itself
NSString *bPath = [bundle bundlePath];
```

Example 2-29. Accessing bundle resources (continued)

```
// Path to bundle executable
NSString *ePath = [bundle executablePath];

// Obtain the Info.plist dictionary for the bundle
NSDictioanry *iDict = [bundle infoDictionary];
```

Loading Code

Bundles also load new classes into the runtime system. Several methods that do this are provided: load, principalClass, and classNamed:. The load method loads a bundle's executable code into the runtime, if it has not been loaded previously. The method will return YES if loading is successful or if the executable has been loaded already, and NO otherwise.

The principalClass and classNamed: methods not only load a bundle's executable code, but they return a class object for the specified class. In classNamed:, the returned class object is specified by name in an NSString. If no class by the specified name can be located in the bundle, Nil will be returned (Nil is the equivalent of nil for class objects).

The principalClass method returns a class object that is determined by the bundle itself. The bundle's principal class is the class that is generally responsible for the other classes within a bundle. For example, the principal class of most standard Cocoa applications is NSApplication. A bundle's *Info.plist* file contains an entry that identifies the principal class with the key NSPrincipalClass. Bundle developers can specify a class name here for the principal class. If this entry is not present, principalClass returns the class object for the first class loaded in the bundle. Developers can specify the load order of classes by arranging class files in a project in the desired order. Like classNamed:, this method returns Nil if there is an error loading the code or if no executable is found within the bundle.

Example 2-30 shows how to load executable code with NSBundle.

Example 2-30. Loading code using NSBundle

```
Class exampleClass;
id newObject;

// The main bundle
NSBundle *bundle = [NSBundle mainBundle];

// Obtain and instantiate the principal class
if ( exampleClass = [bundle principalClass] ) {
    newObject = [[exampleClass alloc] init];
    // Do something with newObject
}

// Obtain and instantiate a class by name
if ( exampleClass = [bundle classNamed:@"MyClass"] ) {
    newObject = [[exampleClass alloc] init];
    // Do something with newObject
}
```

Archiving Objects

Archiving an object (or a collection of interconnected objects, known as a graph) into a NSData representation is often useful or necessary. Objects that are archived into an NSData object can be transported over network connections or interprocess communication channels and saved to the filesystem. Later, the original graph of objects can be reconstituted from the archive data.

Foundation provides five classes to support the creation and extraction of archives, all subclasses of NSCoder:

- NSArchiver
- NSUnarchiver
- NSKeyedArchiver
- NSKeyedUnarchiver
- NSPortCoder

NSCoder declares the common interface for encoding and decoding objects and other Objective-C data types. For example, the encodeObject method encodes an object into an archive, and methods such as encodeInt: and encodeRect: support encoding C data types such as integers and common Cocoa data structures.

NSCoder does not implement these methods; it is an abstract class. Rather, subclasses implement the appropriate methods for their particular purpose. NSArchiver and NSUnarchiver provide a straightforward way of encoding and decoding objects and scalars, but they have limitations. The biggest limitation is that objects in an archive can be decoded only in the same order in which they were encoded. Because of this constraint, changing an encoding system is difficult once it has been established publicly.

Keyed Archiving

The NSKeyedArchiver and NSKeyedUnarchiver classes solve this problem by associating keys with each object and scalar encoded in an archive. Decoders can use these keys to access an archive's contents in a convenient order that isn't constrained by a design decision made in a previous version of the application.

 Keyed archiving is not available in versions prior to Mac OS X 10.2. If your application supports Mac OS X 10.1, then check whether the coder passed in initWithCoder: or encodeWithCoder: supports keyed archiving. To do this, use the NSCoder method allowsKeyedCoding, which returns YES if keyed coding is supported, and NO otherwise.

The last NSCoder subclass, NSPortCoder, encodes and decodes object proxies in the distributed objects system. NSConnection uses this class, and as such, you should never have to interact with it. Chapter 6 discusses the distributed objects system in more detail.

Consider Examples 2-31 and 2-32. Example 2-31 shows the interface for a hypothetical Employee class. Note in this example that the interface declaration indicates that Employee conforms to the NSCoding protocol.

Example 2-31. Employee class with support for the NSCoding protocol

```
@interface Employee : NSObject < NSCoding > {
    NSString *firstName;
    NSString *lastName;
    int employeeNumber;
}
// Methods left out
@end
```

Example 2-32 shows a way to implement the NSCoding protocol for the Employee class.

Example 2-32. Implementing NSCoding in the Employee class

```
@implementation Employee

- (void)setFirstName:(NSString *)newName
{
    [newName retain];
    [firstName autorelease];
    firstName = newName;
}

- (void)setLastName:(NSString *)newName
{
    [newName retain];
    [lastName autorelease];
    lastName = newName;
}

- (void)encodeWithCoder:(NSCoder *)encoder
{
    if ( [encoder allowsKeyedCoding] ) {
        [encoder encodeObject:firstName forKey:@"First"];
        [encoder encodeObject:lastName forKey:@"Last"];
        [encoder encodeInt: employeeNumber forKey:@"Number"];
    } else {
        [encoder encodeObject:firstName];
        [encoder encodeObject:lastName];
        [encoder encodeValueOfObjCType:@encode(int)
                                    at:&employeeNumber];
    }
}

- (id)initWithCoder:(NSCoder *)decoder
{
    if ( [decoder allowsKeyedCoding] ) {
        // These may be decoded in any order you like
        employeeNumber = [decoder decodeIntForKey:@"Number"];

        // Returned  values are autoreleased
        [self setFirstName: [decoder decodeObjectForKey:@"First"]];
        [self setLastName: [decoder decodeObjectForKey:@"Last"]];
```

Example 2-32. Implementing NSCoding in the Employee class (continued)

```
    } else {
        // These must be decoded in the same order that they
        // were encoded
        [self setFirstName: [decoder decodeObject]];
        [self setLastName: [decoder decodeObject]];
        [decoder decodeValueOfObjCType:@encode(int)
                                     at:&employeeNumber];
    }
    return self;
}

@end
```

User Defoults

User defaults is another term for user application preferences. Mac OS X has a well-designed user defaults system that is accessed in Cocoa through the Foundation class NSUserDefaults. Working with NSUserDefaults is similar to working with an NSDictionary. Default values are stored in the database by keys that the application developer defines in the application. The defaults database is actually a collection of property list files; every application has its own property list file where defaults are stored. You can view these files in *~/Library/Preferences*.

Defaults are organized into *domains*, which are groupings of default values that have varying degrees of visibility to applications. A domain is either *persistent* or *volatile*. Defaults in a persistent domain are stored in the defaults database, while defaults in a volatile domain are applicable only during the lifetime of the NSUserDefaults object that contains those values. NSUserDefaults has five standard domains:

NSArgumentDomain
> Set values for defaults in the argument domain by passing key-value pairs to the application as arguments on the command line, (e.g., % *MyApp -KeyName Value*). The argument domain is volatile, so arguments affect the application only during the application session for which they were specified.

Application
> Application-specific defaults are stored here and kept persistently in the user's defaults database.

NSGlobalDomain
> Defaults stored in the global domain are applicable to all applications run by the user. This persistent domain is stored in the defaults database.

Languages
> The languages domain stores defaults that pertain to language choice and localization.

NSRegistrationDomain
> The registration domain is the lowest-level domain containing application-provided defaults (or "factory settings") used when a default value is otherwise unspecified in a higher domain.

When a default is requested, the domains are searched for the value in order, starting with NSArgumentDomain and ending with NSRegistrationDomain. The search ends at the first discovery of a default value. Thus, if many domains have values for the same default, NSUserDefaults returns the default that occurred in the higher-level domain. You can exploit the search order as a debugging aid by overriding any default by specifying a value in the NSArgumentDomain.

User defaults are capable of storing only what property lists can store, namely NSData, NSNumber, NSString, NSDate, NSArray, and NSDictionary (although convenience methods are also provided to get and set scalar values). Using these data types, you can store information, such as dates, numbers, and text, as well as any object that is archiveable. Example 2-33 shows how to interact with the user defaults system.

Example 2-33. Interacting with the user defaults system using NSUserDefaults

```
// Create an instance of NSUserDefaults
NSUserDefaults *prefs = [NSUserDefaults standardUserDefaults];

// Store and retrieve a string
[prefs setObject:@"Mike Beam" forKey:@"Author"];
NSString *author = [prefs stringForKey:@"Author"];

// Store and retrieve a number
[prefs setFloat:1373.50 forKey:@"NASDAQ"];
[prefs setInt:2002 forKey:@"Year"];
float level = [prefs floatForKey:@"NASDAQ"];
int year = [prefs intForKey:@"Year"];

// Store and retrieve dates
[prefs setObject:[NSDate date] forKey:@"Last Opened"];
NSDate *lastOpenDate = [prefs objectForKey:@"Last Opened"];

// Store collections
[prefs setObject:dictionary forKey:@"A Dictionary"];
[prefs setObject:array forKey:@"An Array"];

// Retrieve collections
NSArray *array = [prefs arrayForKey:@"An Array"];
NSDictionary *dict = [prefs dictionaryForKey:@"A Dictionary"];

// Use the following if you want mutable objects...
NSMutableArray *mArray = [NSMutableArray
    arrayWithArray: [prefs arrayForKey:@"An Array"]];
NSMutableDictionary *mDict = [NSMutableDictionary
    dictionaryWithDictionary: [prefs dictionaryForKey:@"A Dictionary"]];
```

All applications should establish factory default settings in the registration domain. This is done with the registerDefaults method. Establishing defaults in the registration domain often takes place in an overridden initialize class method of one of the first classes loaded in your application. This method works well because it is used to initialize classes when they are first loaded by the runtime system, and it is thus one of the earliest entry points in code execution. This example shows how it might be done for a small number of defaults:

```
+ (void)initialize
{
    NSUserDefaults *prefs;
    NSMutableDictionary *defs;

    prefs = [NSUserDefaults standardUserDefaults];
    [defs setObject:@"May" ForKey:@"Month"];
    [defs setInteger:2002 ForKey:"Year"];
    [prefs registerDefaults:defs];
}
```

If you need to register a large number of defaults, hardcoding them this way might prove cumbersome. For these situations, it may be more convenient to store factory settings in a property list included with the application, which is then read into a dictionary and registered with user defaults:

```
+ (void)initialize
{
    NSString *prefsFile;
    NSUserDefaults *prefs;
    NSDictionary *defs;

    // The factory defaults file is a resource in the application
    // bundle. The path is retrieved using NSBundle.
    prefsFile = [[NSBundle mainBundle]
            pathForResource:@"FactoryDefaults"
            ofType:@"plist"];

    defs = [NSDictionary dictionaryithContentsOfFile:prefsFile];
    prefs = [NSUserDefaults standardUserDefaults];
    [prefs registerDefaults:defs];
}
```

One commonly stored preference is an NSColor. There are, however, no provisions for storing a color directly in the defaults database. One way to store information about colors in the defaults database is to store the color space name and a dictionary of the color component values.. All of these data types are supported by NSUserDefaults. A better solution is to archive the NSColor object into an NSData instance and store it in the preferences, as shown in Example 2-34.

Example 2-34. Storing an NSColor to user defaults

```
// Assume NSColor object color exists
// Store the color
NSUserDefaults *prefs = [NSUserDefaults standardUserDefaults];
NSData *colorData;
colorData = [NSArchiver archivedDataWithRootObject:color];
[prefs setObject:colorData forKey:@"Text Color"];

// Retrieve the color
colorData = [prefs dataForKey:@"Text Color"];
id color = [NSUnarchiver unarchiveObjectWithData:colorData];
```

This technique is not limited to only NSColor. It can work with any class of object that conforms to the NSCoding protocol, the prerequisite for compatibility with Foundation's archiving system.

Notifications

Notifications provide a mechanism for distributing information about events within an application. Notifications provide an alternative to messaging as a means for communicating between objects. Messaging requires that the sender of the message know who the receiver is when the message is dispatched. Effectively, the notifications system decouples the message sender from the message receiver. With notifications, a broadcast paradigm is implemented in which objects post notifications to a *notification center*, which then sends messages to objects (known as observers) which have registered their interest in the type of event, or the originating object.

The notification center is an instance of the NSNotificationCenter class; notifications are instances of the NSNotification class. Every notification object has a name identifying the notification type, an object associated with the notification that provides context for the notification, and an optional userInfo dictionary with which posters may pass additional information. When an observer registers with the notification center, it specifies a method to be invoked in response to the posting of a notification. Upon receiving a notification, the notification center identifies the observers of the specific named notification and invokes a predetermined method in each observer.

To obtain an instance of NSNotificationCenter, use the class method defaultCenter. This returns an application's default notification center. To register an object with the notification center, invoke the NSNotificationCenter method addObserver:selector:name:object:. The first argument in this method is the object that is added as an observer; this object is usually self. The selector: argument provides a method selector for the method that needs to be invoked in response to the notification. The parameter name: is the name of the notification, while the final argument lets you specify the object whose notifications you want to be notified of.

Observers can be flexible when specifying the granularity of which notifications they would like to respond to in the addObserver:selector:name:object: method. For example, if nil is passed to object:, then the observer is notified of all notifications of the specified name, regardless of the originating object. Alternatively, nil can be passed for the notification name and an object can be specified, which causes the observer to be notified of all notifications posted by the indicated object.

Objects that have registered with the notification center are responsible for removing themselves when they no longer wish to receive notifications or when being destroyed. It is particularly important to remove an observer object in the object's dealloc method, since the notification center does not retain observers. If you do not remove objects before they are destroyed, the notification center will attempt to send messages to objects that no longer exist, resulting in a runtime error.

To remove an object from the notification center, use either removeObserver: or removeObserver:name:object:. The first removes the specified object as an observer of all notifications from all objects; this is the method you should use before an object is deallocated. The second method selectively removes the specified object from the notification center.

NSNotificationQueue is a class that lets you change a notification center's delivery behavior. Each thread has its own notification queue, which has two duties. The first is to coalesce notifications so multiple notifications of the same name posted within a short time of one another are posted to the notification center only once. Second, the notification queue allows for asynchronous posting; the standard behavior of NSNotificationCenter handles notifications synchronously.

Cocoa uses notifications extensively. Most objects post notifications of some sort that other objects can use to coordinate actions between objects. For example, Chapter 7 shows how NSFileHandle uses notifications to handle asynchronous communication with a socket. Because of the large number of predefined notifications, we frequently find ourselves registering objects as observers to these notifications.

Operating System Interaction

The Foundation framework provides many services through a small set of classes that allow developers to interact with the underlying operating system in several ways. NSTask is an object-oriented interface to configure and launch a process as a subprocess of the current application. NSProcessInfo lets an application discover information about its current process

Process Info

Example 2-35 shows some of the information you can obtain by using NSProcessInfo.

Example 2-35. Using NSProcessInfo

```
// Get the shared process info object for the current process
NSProcessInfo *proc = [NSProcessInfo processInfo];

// The name and PID of the process
NSString *name = [proc processName];
int pid = [proc processIdentifier];

// The arguments launched with the process
NSArray *args = [proc arguments];

// A dictionary of the environment variables for the process
NSDictionary *env = [proc environment];

// The host name for the host running the process
NSString *host = [proc hostName];

// The operating system version string
```

Example 2-35. Using NSProcessInfo (continued)

```
// Note: this string is NOT appropriate for parsing
NSString *ver = [proc operatingSystemVersionString];
```

Tasks

NSTask is a class that lets a program configure, launch, and communicate with another program as a subprocess. This is something you'll see every time you execute an application you work on from within Project Builder.

An NSTask is launched in a fully configurable execution environment where environment variables, command line options, and other key points of a task may be set. By default, if no environment configuration is provided for a new task, the task inherits the environment of the parent process that launched it.

Setting up and running a task is straightforward. For example, you could run *ls* on the root directory, as shown in Example 2-36.

Example 2-36. The quick and dirty NSTask

```
NSArray *args = [NSArray arrayWithObject:@"/"];
NSTask *task = [NSTask launchedTaskWithLaunchPath:@"/bin/ls
                                        arguments:args];
```

Since no environment was set up for the task, the environment of the parent process is used, which includes sending the standard output of the child process to the standard output of the parent process. The issue of interprocess communication becomes important when working with multiple tasks in an application, since tasks do not share memory space with one another, as do multiple threads of an application. You could improve Example 2-33 so the standard output data can be read from a file handle, rather than being forwarded to the parent processes' standard output. Example 2-37 illustrates the flexibility Cocoa offers for configuring and launching new processes.

Example 2-37. A more complex use of NSTask

```
NSData *data;

// Instantiate and initialize a new task
NSTask *task = [[NSTask alloc] init];

// Create a pipe to communicate with the task
NSPipe *pipe = [NSPipe pipe];

// Get a file handle to read from the pipe
NSFileHandle *fh = [pipe fileHandleForReading];

// Set the path to launch the task at
[task setLaunchPath:@"/bin/ls"];

// Set the arguments; ls takes the directory to list
[task setArguments:[NSArray arrayWithObject:@"/"]];
```

Example 2-37. A more complex use of NSTask (continued)

```
// Connect the pipe to the task's stdout
[task setStandardOutput:pipe];

// Finally, launch it
[task launch];

// Once its launched we can read data from the pipe
data = [fh availableData];
NSLog(@"%s", [data bytes]);
```

If you compile and run this code, you will find the result to be the same as that from Example 2-36. The point of this exercise, however, was to demonstrate how to fine tune a task in every practical manner.

Threaded Programming

Cocoa uses the NSThread class to provide multiple threads of execution in applications. Threads are useful if you want to perform a computationally intensive or time-consuming procedure in the background while allowing the main thread of execution to continue normally. When executing code in the main thread of the application, the flow of execution must stop while that code completes execution. If code takes a long time to execute, the user will notice that the application user interface controls freeze and do not respond to any actions.

To correct this problem, you could isolate the time-consuming code into its own method, and then execute that method in its own thread. This is how NSThread works—using the detachNewThreadSelector:toTarget:withObject: method, as shown in Example 2-38.

Example 2-38. Multithreading an application

```
// This method is invoked in response to some user action
- (void)someActionMethod:(id)sender
{
    [NSThread detachNewThreadSelector:@selector(longCode)
                            toTarget:self withObject:nil];
}

- (void)longCode
{
    NSAutoreleasePool *pool;
    pool = [[NSAutoreleasePool alloc] init];
    BOOL keepGoing = YES;

    while ( keepGoing) {
        // Do something here that will eventually stop by
        // setting keepGoing to NO
    }

    [pool release];
}
```

As illustrated in Example 2-38, threads exit after the natural completion of a method. If the threaded method is to integrate properly with Cocoa objects, then that method is responsible for setting up and destroying its own autorelease pool.

You can also cause a thread to exit before the natural completion of a method's execution by invoking the exit method. In fact, this is the method NSThread uses to cause a thread to exit normally at the end of a method. For example, you could insert a conditional into your threaded processing loop, as shown in Example 2-39.

Example 2-39. Using NSThread's exit method

```
- (void)longCode
{
  NSAutoreleasePool *pool;
  pool = [[NSAutoreleasePool alloc] init];
  BOOL exitEarly = NO;

  while ( YES ) {
    // Your code here, which may set exitEarly = YES

    if ( exitEarly ) {
      [pool release];
      [NSThread exit];
    }

    [pool release];
}
```

NSThread also declares the sleepUntilDate: method, which instructs the thread to take a break until the indicated date is reached. This is demonstrated in Example 2-40.

Example 2-40. Using NSThread's sleepUntilDate: method

```
- (void)longCode
{
    NSAutoreleasePool *pool = [[NSAutoreleasePool alloc] init];
    BOOL keepGoing = YES;

    while ( keepGoing ) {
        // Put the thread to sleep for 10 seconds
        NSDate *d = [NSDate dateWithTimeIntervalFromNow:10.0];
        [NSThread sleepUntilDate:d];

        // Do something here that will eventually stop by
        // setting keepGoing to NO
    }

    [pool release];
}
```

Another useful method of NSThread lets you specify the priority for a thread in the same sense that you can specify a priority for a process using the commands *nice* and *renice*. The method is `setThreadPriority:`, which takes as its argument a float between 0.0 and 1.0. A value of 1.0 gives the thread highest priority, while 0.0 gives the thread lowest priority.

Examples 2-38 through 2-40 indicate that when working with objects in a threaded method, you should always create and destroy an autorelease pool manually for that thread. `NSApplication` defines a thread convenience constructor, which detaches a thread for a specified method, managing the autorelease pool for that thread. This method, declared in `NSApplication`, is `detachDrawingThread:toTarget:withObject:`. The arguments used by this method are the same as `NSThread`'s `detachNewThreadSelector:toTarget:withObject:`, discussed previously in this section.

Locks

One of the difficulties of making applications multithreaded is making certain that data accessible from multiple threads (such as class instance variables) is not accessed simultaneously by multiple threads. Cocoa provides a solution to this problem through the class `NSLock`, which provides a mechanism for coordinating the actions of multiple threads.

Foundation defines the `NSLocking` protocol and three classes that conform to this protocol: `NSLock`, `NSRecursiveLock`, and `NSConditionLock`. For a class to conform to the `NSLocking` protocol, it must implement the `lock` and `unlock` methods. The three classes that do conform to this protocol add methods of their own, as described later in this section.

How Locks Work

Before a thread can execute code that was protected by a lock, a thread must first acquire the lock. A thread acquires a lock by sending a `lock` message to an object that conforms to the `NSLocking` protocol. If a thread has acquired a lock and hasn't yet relinquished it, then any other threads wishing to acquire the lock must stop in their tracks until the current thread releases the lock. By setting a lock in a thread, you prevent other threads from executing a section of code until the lock is removed. Thus, you can prevent threads from simultaneously accessing data by either protecting a common access point to the data with a lock, or by protecting every part of the code that accesses a certain variable with the same lock. This can be done in as shown in Example 2-37. Note that locks are generally created before an application becomes multithreaded, not when the lock is about to be used.

Using locks is one way to make data sharing between threads safe. Using Cocoa's distributed objects system, discussed at the end of this chapter, is another way to transfer data between threads safely.

NSLock

NSLock is the simplest lock in the Foundation framework. Example 2-41 shows how it works.

Example 2-41. Using NSLock to coordinate threads

```
NSLock *aLock = [[NSLock alloc] init];    // Previously created

[aLock lock];                             // Set the lock
[anObject setSomeData:toThisData];
[aLock unlock];                           // Relinquish the lock
```

One shortcoming of the code fragment in Example 2-27 is that if one thread has acquired the lock, aLock, and hasn't yet relinquished it, then other threads attempting to execute this code will be stopped cold while they wait to acquire the lock. This behavior would be undesirable in many situations. Using NSLock's tryLock method is one potential solution. This method attempts to acquire a lock, but doesn't sit around waiting for it. If the lock is immediately available for acquisition, the lock is acquired and tryLock returns YES. If another thread has the lock at the time tryLock is invoked, NO is returned and execution resumes. Thus, you could base the following conditional execution of code on the ability for a thread to acquire a lock:

```
// Use the same aLock from Example 2-41

if ( [aLock tryLock] ) {
    // Run your code here
    [aLock unlock];
}
```

NSRecursiveLock

Sometimes, in sufficiently complex code that has portions protected by locks, a thread attempts to acquire a lock more than once. However, if the thread has already acquired a lock and attempts to do so again, that thread freezes while it waits for the lock to become free. This lock never becomes free, since the thread needs to relinquish it, but the thread is frozen waiting for the lock to become available, ad infinitum.

The solution to this problem is to use a lock that is an instance of the NSRecursiveLock class. This lock lets a thread acquire a single lock multiple times, thus saving itself from the deadlock that would result in the use of NSLock. Example 2-42 shows an example in which a single lock might be acquired more than once by the same thread; this would fail when using an NSLock, so use NSRecursiveLock.

Example 2-42. Using NSRecursiveLock when NSLock would deadlock a thread

```
id rLock = [[NSRecursiveLock alloc] init];
int i;

[rLock lock];
```

Example 2-42. Using NSRecursiveLock when NSLock would deadlock a thread (continued)

```
for ( i = 0; i < 10000; i++ ) {
// Perform some thread-worthy, time-consuming computations

    if ( someCondition == YES ) {
        [rLock lock];
// Do something here
        [rLock unlock];
    }
}
[rLock unlock];
```

NSConditionLock

The third Foundation class that conforms to the NSLocking protocol is the NSConditionLock class. NSConditionLock lets you assign an arbitrary condition when the lock is initialized using initWithCondition:; the condition is just an integer. To acquire the lock, the thread sends the lock either a lockWhenCondition: or a tryLockWhenCondition: message (which are analogous in behavior to lock and tryLock). If the condition passed in these messages is equal to the condition of the receiver lock, then the lock is acquired. Additionally, when relinquishing the lock, you can use the method unlockWithCondition: rather than unlock; this sets the condition of the receiver to the new condition. Example 2-43 shows how to employ NSConditionLock.

Example 2-43. Conditional locking with NSConditionLock

```
id cLock = [[NSConditionLock alloc] initWithCondition:1];

[cLock lock];
// Do something here whose state you want to record
// as a condition in the lock
[cLock unlockWithCondition:0];
```

3

The Application Kit

The bulk of the Application Kit (or AppKit) is comprised of classes for user interface components, from windows and widgets to colors and fonts. From the perspective of an application, the central class is NSApplication, which manages much of the basic application architecture, from loading user interface definitions to setting up the run loop to handle events, which relieves you of much of the nitty-gritty often associated with simply making an application tick. The AppKit also provides many architecture-related classes for document management, printing, and interaction with the workspace.

AppKit Design Patterns

Besides leveraging the design patterns and methodologies used with the Foundation framework, the Application Kit relies heavily on several others. Two that merit special attention are Model-View-Controller and Target/Action.

Model-View-Controller

The Model-View-Controller (MVC) pattern is the driving design pattern in the Application Kit.* The premise of this pattern is that code may be split up into logically distinct units that each perform a specific role:

- The *model* is an object that encapsulates data and provides logic that manipulates that data.
- The *view* is a separate object that only knows how to display data.
- The *controller* is an arbiter between the model and the view. The controller's job is to take data from the model and pass it to the view where it can be

---

* MVC traces its lineage to the first object-oriented programming language, Smalltalk, and has been important ever since.

displayed. If the view is interactive—able to accept user input—then the controller will interpret those actions and instruct the data model to do something in response.

Many views in the MVC pattern may subscribe to the controller, giving the application flexibility to display data in different contexts and formats without heavy modification of the modeling and control logic. This idea is illustrated in Figure 3-1, which shows two views of the same data: a table view of the data and a chart view.

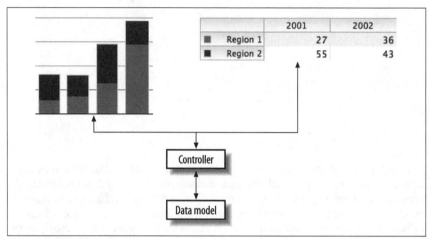

Figure 3-1. MVC used to display two different views of the same data

Target/Action

The Application Kit uses the target/action pattern to decouple UI widgets (controls—typically subclasses of NSControl) from the code that is executed when the user activates the control. In this pattern, a control keeps a reference to a target object that receives an action message. The action message is stored as a selector in an instance variable of the control object. When the user activates the control, the action message is sent to the target. Action messages and targets are generally established in Interface Builder; however, you can change a control's behavior by using the setAction: and setTarget: methods of NSControl. The current target and action of a control may be ascertained programmatically by using the methods target and action.

Nibs

One of the crown jewels of the Cocoa development environment is Interface Builder, a tool for building graphical user interfaces.

Interface Builder creates and stores user interfaces in *nib* files. Perhaps one of the most important aspects of Interface Builder is that it does not generate source code. Nibs are bundles that contain information and archived objects (in this context often referred to as "freeze-dried") that constitute the elements of the user interface (such as windows, widgets and menus, as well as non-UI objects) as they were arranged and configured with Interface Builder. When a nib file is loaded at run time, the elements are reconstituted exactly as they were in Interface Builder.

Every application has a *MainMenu.nib* file that contains the application's main menu structure. For simple applications, this nib might also contain the application's main window. More advanced applications generally have a number of nib files, each of which defines part of the user interface.

From a design perspective, creating a nib for each window (or logical group of windows) facilitates reuse. From a performance perspective, loading nibs into memory takes time, so it is best to keep them small. Thus, when the application launches, it needs to load only the nib containing the first window the user sees, rather than every window in the application, many of which the user may never open (such as the About Box).

Outlets and Actions

Nib files contain definitions for objects that can send messages to other objects in the nib file and be assigned to instance variables of other objects. An object instance variable in Interface Builder is known as an *outlet*. Outlets can be connected to other objects within the nib, and the source code for the class containing the outlet can reference those other nib objects through the outlet instance variable. Objects in nibs also have *actions*, which are methods that other objects may invoke in response to some event, such as a user clicking a button.

When designing a class in Interface Builder, you can create skeleton source files containing instance variables and stubs for action method definitions. In the header file of a class defined in Interface Builder, outlet instance variables have the IBOutlet type modifier and action methods have an IBAction return type, which is synonymous with void. These modifiers help Interface Builder parse class interfaces when importing classes.

When importing class interfaces, Interface Builder recognizes any instance variable of type id as an outlet. You can statically type an instance variable and have Interface Builder import it as an outlet by prepending the type with the IBOutlet modifier. Both of these instance variables are recognized as an outlet:

```
id statusTextField;
IBOutlet NSTextField *statusTextField;
```

However, the following instance variable will not be recognized as an outlet, since it is statically typed and doesn't have the IBOutlet modifier:

```
NSTextField *statusTextField;
```

Interface Builder recognizes methods as actions if they have a void return type and a single parameter named sender. The type of the sender parameter can be id, or a class such as NSButton. Interface Builder looks for the sender parameter name as keyword when parsing methods for actions. If you want more meaningful argument names you can explicitly state that a method is an action using the IBAction return type. Interface Builder would recognize the following lines as action methods:

```
- (void)anAction:(id)sender;
- (void)aButtonAction:(NSButton *)sender;
- (IBAction)aButtonAction:(NSButton *)aButton;
```

However, the following example is not recognized as an action, since the argument is statically typed, not named sender, and the return type is not IBAction:

```
- (void)aButtonAction:(NSButton *)aButton;
```

At any point during the execution of an application, you can load additional nibs. The Application Kit extends the Foundation class NSBundle (discussed in Chapter 2) to provide the ability to load nibs. The most straightforward way to load a nib is with the method loadNibName:owner:. This method searches the application bundle for the best localized nib file variant with the specified name and loads it into memory.

The owner: parameter lets you specify an object that will be the nib's owner. This object can be referenced by other objects in the nib file through the File's Owner proxy object, as illustrated in Figure 3-2. By importing the header for the class of object that will load the nib, you can assign the class for the File's Owner from the Info panel's Custom Class pane. This lets you use the outlets and actions of this class to define connections to objects within the nib.

 File's Owner is only a "promise." It does not guarantee that at runtime, the object will be an instance of the specified class. The developer is responsible for ensuring that the object specified in owner: is an instance of the appropriate class.

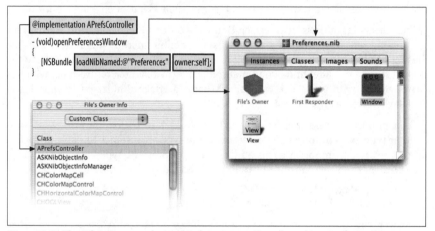

Figure 3-2. The File's Owner relationship between a nib and an object in an application

Application Architecture

The Application Kit's basic architecture is primarily implemented in three classes: NSApplication, NSWindow, and NSView. Figure 3-3 shows the class hierarchy for these classes. Individually, these three classes provide the means for an application to interface with the operating system (and ultimately, the user) via connections to Quartz, the window server, and underlying Unix libraries through Core Foundation. Taken as a whole, these classes form the backbone of the Application Kit's event-handling infrastructure.

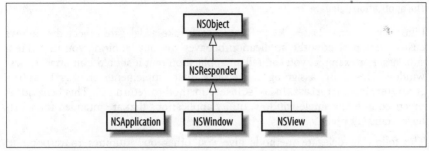

Figure 3-3. The hierarchical relationship between NSApplication, NSWindow, and NSView; these three classes all have a common parent in NSResponder

The Application

Fundamental to every Cocoa application is a singleton instance of NSApplication (accessible by using the class method sharedApplication or the global variable, NSApp). NSApplication provides a link to the window server and other essential operating system services. One of its most important responsibilities is management of the application's *run loop* and event handling. Run loops have the job of managing input from sources such as the mouse and keyboard (through the window server), ports, and timers. As the owner of the application's main run loop, NSApplication is the first stop for event processing in an application. Through a direct connection to the window server, NSApplication accepts events, packages them as Cocoa objects (instances of NSEvent), and dispatches them to the appropriate responder. NSApplication is also responsible for managing autorelease pools.

NSApplication is also concerned with other details, such as managing the main menu of an application, managing an application's Dock menu and icon, opening windows and sheets in modal run loops, hiding and unhiding the application, and application activation and deactivation. NSApplication also enables an application to connect to Mac OS X system services found in its Services menu.

NSApplicationMain

Every application begins with the same function, named main, that every C program starts execution at. Project Builder places this function in the file *main.m* by default, and it has the following very simple implementation:

```
int main(int argc, const char *argv[])
{
    return NSApplicationMain(argc, argv);
}
```

The NSApplicationMain function is responsible for bootstrapping an application and getting it running; it performs three tasks:

1. Instantiates the shared instance of NSApplication.

2. Loads the application's main nib file (specified in the application bundle's *Info.plist* under the key NSMainNibFile).

3. Starts the main run loop by invoking NSApplication's run method.

The application delegate

Like many Cocoa classes, NSApplication can take a delegate object that allows customization of how the application behaves without requiring you to create a subclass. For example, you can tell an application that it should quit after the last window closes by assigning a delegate that implements the application-ShouldTerminateAfterLastWindowIsClosed: method to return YES. This behavior is practiced in many single-window, utility applications that are intended for short-term, transient use.

The following delegate methods give you other opportunities to respond to various changes in the state of the application:

- applicationDidFinishLaunching:
- applicationWillHide:
- applicationDidUnhide:
- applicationWillResignActive:
- applicationDidBecomeActive:
- applicationWillTerminate:

The easiest way to assign a delegate to your application's NSApplication object is from within Interface Builder. *MainMenu.nib*'s File's Owner represents the shared application instance, so you can connect an object directly by using its delegate outlet. It is also possible to assign an application delegate programmatically using NSApplication's setDelegate: method.

The run loop

Run loops monitor the various sources of input for an application—including timers, ports (receiving messages from other applications), Distributed Objects connections, and keyboard and mouse events from the window system—and dispatch them to the various parts of an application for handling. Because of their role in receiving and dispatching events, run loops are often referred to as *event loops*. NSApplication is responsible for creating and managing an application's main run loop.

Run loops work by polling each input source to see if there is input that needs to be processed. Multiple input sources are handled in successive passes through the run loop. If an input source does require processing, then the run loop takes the necessary action to handle that input source. For example, if the run loop determines that a timer needs to be handled, it invokes the method specified by the timer in a target specified by the timer. Once this method invocation has returned, the run loop continues processing input. Figure 3-4 illustrates how this process occurs.

The Foundation class NSRunLoop is used as the interface to run loops. Generally you don't need to create or manage run loops, as this is taken care of by the application. Every thread in an application has a run loop created for it. However, NSApplication starts only the main application thread. If you create a new thread that needs to monitor input sources, you can obtain a reference to the run loop by using NSRunLoop's method currentRunLoop; a run message to this run loop will set it in motion.

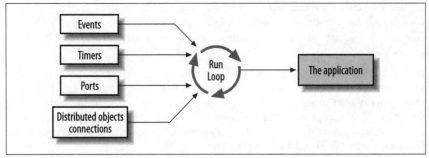

Figure 3-4. How run loops process input sources

The Window

In Cocoa, the window is the foundation of all drawing, and it is a crucial link in the path of an event. Windows are instances of the class NSWindow, or one of its subclasses. The NSWindow class implements many parts of an application's machinery, such as the control of a window's level relative to other windows, window zooming and resizing, miniaturization, hiding and unhiding, activation, and deactivation. A subclass of NSWindow, NSPanel, adds behaviors to windows that make them suitable for utility purposes. The AppKit implements several NSPanel subclasses that give access to standard Mac OS X user interfaces, such Open and Save dialogs in NSOpenPanel and NSSavePanel, the font panel with NSFontPanel, and the Print dialog with NSPrintPanel.

Delegate methods

Like NSApplication, NSWindow defines delegate methods that let you modify the window's default behavior. For example, a controller managing a document might change a window's default closing behavior, as shown in Example 3-1.

Example 3-1. Altering the default closing behavior of a window

```
- (BOOL)windowShouldClose:(NSWindow *)window
{
    // If the document is clean, let the window close
    if ( ![documentData hasUnsavedChanges] ) {
        return YES;
    } else {
        // Run an alert panel to ask the user if they want to
        // save changes; return appropriate value
    }
}
```

The View

NSView, an abstract class that provides support for Cocoa's basic drawing, event-handling, and printing architecture, is the third class in the AppKit trifecta. It is the parent class of every control in Cocoa, from buttons and sliders to tables and color wells. Due to NSView's status as a child class of NSResponder (see Figure 3-2), all NSView subclasses can handle events. Additionally, NSView is the portal to Quartz; all custom drawing and graphics are handled by subclasses of NSView (Chapter 4 discusses NSView's relationship with Quartz and drawing graphics with NSView).

In the Application Kit, an interface's hierarchical composition is manifested as a *view hierarchy* in which every NSView is nested within a parent NSView. Any view may contain zero, one, or several *subviews*, and every subview has exactly one *superview*. The exception is the top-level view at the root of the hierarchy, which is the parent window's *content view* . To access the content view, use the NSWindow methods contentView and setContentView:.

For an example of a view hierarchy, consider the main window of Mail, shown in Figure 3-5. Mail has a fairly simple view hierarchy. The window's top-level content view has two subviews: the NSTextField that displays the number of messages and an NSSplitView. This split view, in turn, has as its subviews an NSTableView and an NSTextView.

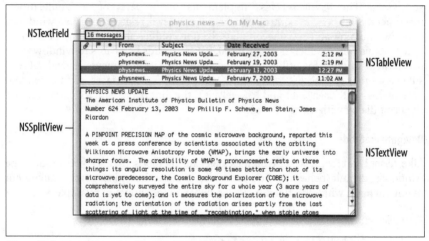

Figure 3-5. View hierarchy of a simple Mail window

There are actually two more view layers in the hierarchy between the split view, the table view, and the text view. Both NSTableView and NSTextView are generally contained within an NSClipView, which is then contained within NSScrollView. The scroll views are the true subviews of the NSSplitView. Thus, for the NSTableView the true hierarchy is NSSplitView → NSScrollView → NSClipView → NSTableView. Furthermore, a clip view is not the only child of a scroll view. The two scrollers are also view objects that are children of the scroll view.

Fortunately, Interface Builder interacts with NSTableView and NSTextView objects that are already part of the scroll view hierarchy, so you don't normally have to interact with the mechanics of scroll and clip views.

Managing the view hierarchy

NSView declares a number of methods that manage the view hierarchy. To add a subview to a view, use the method addSubview:, or addSubview:positioned: relativeTo:. To remove a subview invoke in the subview to remove the method removeFromSuperview. You can easily determine the superview of a view by sending that view a superview message; likewise, the subviews of a viewcan be returned as an NSArray of NSViews by sending that view a subviews message. When building an interface, you don't usually have to interact with the view hierarchy, as Interface Builder takes care of the details.

More important than knowing how to work with the view hierarchy is understanding how a view's geometry is defined both in terms of its coordinate system and the coordinate system of its superview. When a view is added to the hierarchy, it claims a rectangular region of its superview, known as the *frame*, as its own and takes responsibility for drawing in that region and handling events that originate in that region. The view's frame defines the position and size of the view within the coordinate system of its superview. You can modify the view's frame with methods such as setFrame: and setFrameOrigin:.

Another rectangle parameterizes the geometry of a view: the *bounds rectangle*. The bounds rectangle defines the view in terms of its own coordinate system. Another way of looking at it is that the frame gives an external description of the view while the bounds gives an interior description of the view. NSView declares the methods frame and bounds for retrieving these rectangles, which are of type NSRect.

You will often need to convert coordinates in one view's coordinate system to that of another view. NSView provides several methods for converting points, sizes, and rects between coordinate systems. For example, convertPoint:fromView: converts the specified point from the coordinate system of fromView: into the coordinate system of the receiver. The method convertPoint:toView: does the opposite, converting from the receiver's coordinate system to that of toView:. Similar methods convert NSSizes and NSRects.

NSView, being a subclass of NSResponder, is a key component of the event handling system. By subclassing NSView, developers provide event-handling capabilities by simply implementing the relevant event-handling methods (declared in NSResponder), such as mouseMoved:. The event-handling system invokes these methods automatically, when appropriate.

Another feature of NSView is *tracking rectangles*. Tracking rectangles are regions in a view that generate special events as the mouse moves through the rectangle. When the mouse enters a tracking rectangle, a mouse-entered event is generated. When the mouse exits the rectangle, a mouse-exited event is generated. Implement the methods mouseEntered: and mouseExited: to handle these events. Tracking rectangles are defined with the methods addTrackingRect:owner: userData:assumeInside:. This method returns a tag identifying the tracking rectangle. A tracking rectangle may be removed by specifying the tag in the removeTrackingRect: method.

Controls

The most visible aspects of an application are the controls that users interact with. In Cocoa, control objects such as buttons, tables, sliders, and text fields all have a common parent class: NSControl, which is itself a subclass of NSView. Figures 3-6 and 3-7 show the class hierarchies for NSCell and NSControl, and Table 3-1 describes the control classes implemented in the Application Kit.

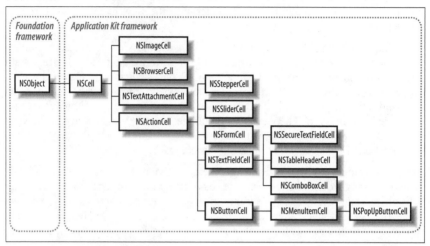

Figure 3-6. NSControl class hierarchy

In general, a Cocoa control must have the ability to do several things:

- Draw itself on the screen.
- Respond to basic events such as a mouseclick or a drag.
- Send action messages to arbitrary objects in response to events.

NSControl gives some amount of control over when and how a control sends the action message to its target. Specifically, you can specify whether the action is to be sent only after the user has finished clicking the control (i.e., when the mouse button is raised), or if the action is to be sent continuously while the mouse button is depressed. You can set this behavior either in Interface Builder or by using the method setContinuous:.

Cells

Most AppKit controls have associated cell classes, and in those cases the cell implements all drawing and event handling, while the control serves as a container within which the cell is drawn. A cursory comparison of NSCell to NSControl makes it appear as though these classes unnecessarily duplicate each other's behavior (see Figure 3-7). For example, both classes declare methods such as intValue, floatValue, doubleValue, stringValue, alignment, and font. The impression is strengthened when considering NSCell's responsibility for drawing many Application Kit controls, and that it takes over other similar roles you would expect from an NSControl. To understand the division of labor between cells and controls, consider the issues of performance and flexibility.

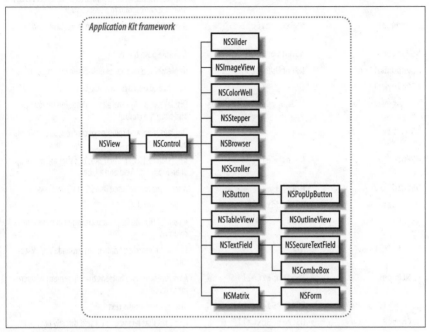

Figure 3-7. NSCellclass hierarchy

Because NSControl is a subclass of NSView, it comes with a lot of baggage (inherited instance variables and data structures) that take memory. As a result, the performance of an application can degrade as the number of NSView instances in an interface increases. NSCell, however, is a much more lightweight object.

Consider now the class NSMatrix. NSMatrix is a subclass of NSControl that manages a rectangular array of NSCells. It is often used in situations when several similar controls are needed, such as for the keypad in the Calculator application, or in a spreadsheet. Consider the case of a 10-column by 10-row spreadsheet. Implementing such a spreadsheet with text views would require 100 instances of NSTextField. However, if you were to build a spreadsheet with an NSMatrix you would have just one instance of an NSView subclass and 100 instances of NSTextFieldCell, a decidedly lighter-weight class than NSTextField. Moreover, when drawing the matrix, there is just a single graphics context switch (as opposed to one context switch per view). You can see the advantage of using cells over views as the size of the spreadsheet increases.

Cells also facilitate the creation of composite controls that are composed of many different parts, such as table or browser views. NSTableView, for example, draws the contents of table columns with NSTextFieldCells. This can be changed to display the contents of a column using NSComboBoxCell or NSButtonCell.

Table 3-1 summarizes the various Application Kit control and cell classes.

Table 3-1. Various Application Kit control and cell classes

Control class	Cell class	Description
NSControl	NSCell	The parent class of all controls; as an abstract class, it does not correspond to a real control
NSBrowser	NSBrowserCell	Displays hierarchical data with levels arranged in columns
NSButton	NSButtonCell	A simple push button
NSPopUpButton	NSPopUpButtonCell	Implements a pop-up or pull-down menu
NSColorWell	N/A	Selects and displays an NSColor
NSImageView	NSImageCell	Displays an image and allows dragging images to and from the control
NSMatrix	N/A	Displays rows and columns of controls, such as radio button controls
NSForm	NSFormCell	An NSMatrix of NSFormCells that are made up of an input text field and a label
NSScroller	N/A	A scrollbar control used in NSScrollViews
NSSlider	NSSliderCell	A slider control
NSTableView	N/A	A control that displays data arranged in rows and columns
NSOutlineView	N/A	Displays hierarchical data in an expandable/collapsible list
NSStepper	NSStepperCell	A control with two buttons that increment or decrement its value
NSTextField	NSTextFieldCell	Displays and inputs text
NSComboBox	NSComboBoxCell	A control that lets you enter text directly or click an attached arrow to reveal a pop-up menu list of items
NSSecureTextField	NSSecureTextFieldCell	A NSTextField subclass that displays all characters as dots

Menus

The NSMenu and NSMenuItem classes implement menus in Cocoa. NSMenu provides an implementation for actual menus, while NSMenuItem represents individual items within menus. An application's menus appear in the main menu bar across the top of the screen. By and large, an application's main menu is assembled in Interface Builder, which provides facilities for editing menu structures and setting menu item targets and actions. Additionally, Interface Builder has several pre-configured menus, such as File and Edit that contain standard menu items familiar to users. An application's main menu is contained in the main nib of an application.

Every application also has a Dock menu, which pops up when you right-click on an application's Dock icon. Dock menus are easily created in Interface Builder by connecting an instance of NSMenu to the File's Owner's dockMenu outlet. Alternatively, the application delegate can supply a Dock menu by implementing the method applicationDockMenu: (this is useful if you want to dynamically reconfigure the menu). A third way of specifying a Dock menu is to assemble the NSMenu object in a nib and specify the nib's file name in the application's *Info.plist* file under the AppleDockMenu key.

NSView objects manage contextual menus. In Interface Builder, every view has a menu outlet, which can be connected to an NSMenu object. The menu that you connect to this outlet will appear as a contextual menu when you right-click over the view. Contextual menus can be assigned to a view by overriding the method menuForEvent: in NSView subclasses. This method has an NSEvent object as the parameter and should be implemented to return an NSMenu. Because an event object is provided in this method, you can use it to return a menu based, for example, on the location of the event within the view. Example 3-5, in the "Event Objects" section, shows how to extract this information from an NSEvent object.

Sheets

Sheets implement window modal (as opposed to *application* modal) dialogs that are attached to the window. Thus, when a dialog pops up asking for attention, it blocks interaction only with that particular window, not the entire application. When a sheet is opened or closed, it appears to slide out of the title bar. Because the sheet is attached to another window, such as a document window, the user never loses track of what dialog belongs with which window. Figure 3-8 shows an example of a sheet.

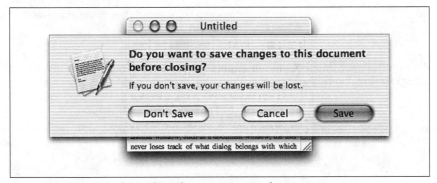

Figure 3-8. A TextEdit sheet asking if you want to save changes

The Application Kit defines a number of convenient functions for displaying standard alert and message sheets, including NSBeginAlertSheet, NSBeginInformationalAlertSheet, and NSBeginCriticalAlertSheet. Each function takes the same parameters; they differ only in the icon displayed on the left of the sheet. The function prototype for NSBeginAlertSheet is the following:

```
void NSBeginAlertSheet(NSString *title,
                       NSString *defaultButton,
                       NSString *alternateButton,
                       NSString *otherButton,
                       NSWindow *docWindow,
                       id modalDelegate,
                       SEL didEndSelector,
                       SEL didDismissSelector,
                       void *contextInfo,
                       NSString *msg, ...)
```

Table 3-2 describes each parameter.

Table 3-2. Parameters for alert sheet functions

Parameter	Description
Title	The title of the sheet, displayed at the top of the sheet in bold-faced font.
defaultButton	The title of the sheet's default button, generally "OK". Passing nil or an empty string will give a localized default button title (i.e., "OK" in English).
alternateButton	The title of the sheet's alternate button, such as "Don't Save," that appears on the left side of the sheet when three buttons are present. Passing nil causes this button to not be created.
otherButton	Title for a third button, such as "Cancel", that appears in the middle. Passing nil causes this button to not be created.
docWindow	The window to which the sheet is attached.
modalDelegate	The object that handles user interaction with the sheet.
didEndSelector	A selector of the method implemented by the modal delegate that will be invoked when the modal session is ended, but before the sheet is dismissed.
didDismissSelector	Selector of the method implemented by the modal delegate is invoked after the sheet is dismissed. This may be NULL if you don't want to end a didDismissSelector.
contextInfo	Pointer to additional data to be passed to didEndSelector or didDismissSelector.
msg	A printf formatted message to be displayed in the sheet. Optional printf-style arguments may follow the message.

An alert similar to the one in Figure 3-8 can be created with a call to NSBeginInformationalAlertSheet, as shown in Example 3-2.

Example 3-2. Creating an alert sheet with NSBeginInformationalAlertSheet

```
NSBeginInformationalAlertSheet(
            @"Do you want to save changes to \
                    this document before closing?"
            @"Save",
            @"Don't Save",
            @"Cancel",
            mainWindow,
            self,
            @selector(sheetDidEnd:returnCode:contextInfo:),
            NULL,
            NULL,
            @"If you don't save, your changes will be lost.");
```

You can display any window as a sheet by using APIs provided by NSApplication. To display a sheet, invoke the following method:

```
beginSheet:modalForWindow:
    modalDelegate:didEndSelector:contextInfo:
```

The first argument, beginSheet:, is the NSWindow we wish to display as a sheet. The modalForWindow: argument specifies the window to which the sheet is attached. Since application execution continues while a sheet is open, the sheet uses a modal delegate to handle user interaction. This delegate is assigned in the modalDelegate: argument. The callback method is indicated in didEndSelector: and has the following signature:

```
- (void)sheetDidEnd:(NSWindow *)sheet
        returnCode:(int)returnCode
        contextInfo:(void *)contextInfo;
```

In this method, contextInfo: is the object passed in the NSApplication method used to open the sheet. It is used to optionally pass arbitrary information between the creator of the sheet and the modal delegate.

To end a document modal session, use NSApplication's methods endSheet: or endSheet:returnCode:. Each method takes the sheet window as a parameter. The second, endSheet:returnCode:, also takes an integer return code that is passed to the didEndSelector: method. Example 3-3 shows how to open and close a sheet in an application.

Example 3-3. Using sheets in an application

```
/*
 * This method is invoked to open a sheet.
 * Assume sheetWindow and mainWindow are Interface Builder
 * outlet instance variables connected to windows in a nib.
 */
- (void)openSheet:(id)sender
{
    SEL selector = @selector(sheetDidEnd:returnCode:contextInfo:);

    [NSApp beginSheet:sheetWindow
        modalForWindow:mainWindow
         modalDelegate:self
        didEndSelector:selector
           contextInfo:NULL];
}


/*
 * This could be the action of the "Cancel" button of the sheet
 * in Figure 3-8.
 */
- (void)cancelSheet:(id)sender
{
    [NSApp endSheet:sheetWindow returnCode:NSCancelButton];
}


/*
 * This could be the action of the "Save" button of the sheet
 * in Figure 3-8.
 */
- (void)acceptSheet:(id)sender
{
    [NSApp endSheet:sheetWindow returnCode:NSOKButton];
}


- (void)sheetDidEnd:(NSWindow *)sheet
        returnCode:(int)returnCode
```

Example 3-3. Using sheets in an application (continued)

```
        contextInfo:(void *)contextInfo
{
    /*
     * Can do something here based on the value of returnCode
     * or do something in the button actions themselves.
     */
    if ( returnCode == NSOKButton ) {
        // If OK was clicked...
    } else if ( returnCode == NSCancelButton ) {
        // If Cancel was clicked....
    }

    [sheet orderOut:nil];
}
```

In this example, NSOKButton and NSCancelButton are global constants often used to identify those buttons in a dialog. The endSheet: methods only end the document modal session; they do not remove the sheet from the screen. To hide the sheet, send an orderOut: message to the sheet window, which Example 3-3 does in the callback method sheetDidEnd:returnCode:contextInfo:.

Finally, there are yet more ways to display sheets: the AppKit classes that implement standard Mac OS X user interfaces, such as NSPrintPanel and NSOpenPanel, all provide ways to display their respective interfaces as document modal sheets.

Drawers

Drawers provide additional window space for an application's interface, and can easily be tucked away from view when not in use. Drawers are ideal for controls that are frequently used, but don't need to be visible at all times. Figure 3-9 shows an example of a drawer in Mail.

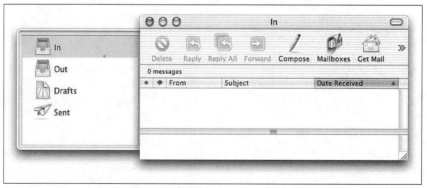

Figure 3-9. The mailboxes drawer from Mail.app

The class NSDrawer defines the behavior of drawers. Interface Builder provides the ability to create drawers and attach them to windows. The window that a drawer is associated with is called the *parent window*. Like windows, drawers contain a view hierarchy. The top-level view of this hierarchy is the drawer's *content view*. NSDrawer objects in Interface Builder have outlets connected to the drawer's parent window and content view. Alternatively, you can set a drawer's parent window of a drawer with the method setParentWindow: and set the content view with setContentView:.

When a drawer opens or closes, it slides from an edge of the parent window. Drawers have a preferred edge of the parent window on which they try to open. Without sufficient room between the preferred edge and the adjacent edge of the screen display, the drawer opens on the opposite side of the window. The preferred edge may be any side of the window: top, bottom, left, or right. You can access this property with setPreferredEdge: and preferredEdge. In these methods, the edge is represented by the data type NSRectEdge, which has the possible constant values NSMinXEdge, NSMaxXEdge, NSMinYEdge, and NSMaxYEdge.

A drawer's state is determined by the state method. The state of a drawer can be specified with NSDrawerClosedState, NSDrawerOpenState, NSDrawerClosingState, or NSDrawerOpeningState. To open a drawer, send an open message. If the drawer is open, nothing happens. To close a drawer, invoke close, which will do nothing if the drawer is already closed. Each method has an counterpart that is appropriate for use as the action of an interface object: open: and close:. Additionally, the toggle: action method closes an open drawer and opens a closed drawer.

Toolbars

Cocoa implements toolbars in the NSToolbar and NSToolbarItem classes. NSToolbar implements the toolbar itself, while NSToolbarItem represents the individual icons and controls within the toolbar.

 Unfortunately, as of the December 2002 release of the Developer Tools, toolbars cannot be created within Interface Builder. Instead, you have to create them manually with code.

To create a toolbar, instantiate an instance of NSToolbar and initialize it with the method initWithIdentifier:. The identifier in this method is a string that identifies the toolbar within an application (it is used, for example, in document-based applications to reflect changes in a toolbar in one document window in all the toolbars of all open document-windows). To attach a toolbar to a window, invoke NSWindow's setToolbar:; the toolbar method of NSWindow returns a window's assigned toolbar.

NSWindow provides a two action methods for interacting with toolbars. The method toggleToolbarShown: hides and shows the toolbar. This is the action for the "Hide Toolbar" menu item (as well as the pill-shaped button on the right side of the window's title bar). Note that toggleToolbarShown: causes the title of this menu item to alternate between "Hide Toolbar" and "Show Toolbar". This method relies on NSToolbar's isVisible and setVisible: methods. isVisible returns YES if the toolbar is present, and NO otherwise; setVisible: takes a BOOL indicating whether the toolbar should be hidden or shown.

NSWindow's `runToolbarCustomizationPalette:` method is the action method for the "Customize Toolbar..." menu item. It uses NSToolbar's `runCustomizationPalette:` and `customizationPaletteIsRunning` methods. The `runCustomizationPalette:` opens a sheet for the customization palette and dismisses the sheet when the user is done.

NSToolbarItem represents the buttons, icons, and controls within a toolbar. The `initWithItemIdentifier:` method initializes instances of NSToolbarItem. The item identifier is a string that uniquely identifies the toolbar item. The Application Kit provides a number of standard toolbar items, such as the "Colors" and "Fonts" items, as well as separator and space items. Passing one of the string constants listed in Table 3-3 creates these standard toolbar items.

Table 3-3. Standard toolbar item identifiers

Item identifier	Description
NSToolbarSeparatorItemIdentifier	The Separator item
NSToolbarSpaceItemIdentifier	The Space item
NSToolbarFlexibleSpaceItemIdentifier	The Flexible Space item
NSToolbarShowColorsItemIdentifier	The Color item, which displays the color panel
NSToolbarShowFontsItemIdentifier	The Fonts item, which displays the font panel
NSToolbarCustomizeToolbarItemIdentifier	The Customize item, which opens the toolbar customization palette
NSToolbarPrintItemIdentifier	The Print item, which sends a `printDocument:` message to `firstResponder`

You can set many attributes in a toolbar item. Minimally, you should assign the toolbar item a label, an image, an action, and a target. The item label is set with the method `setLabel:`. This label appears under the item image in the toolbar. You can also give the toolbar item a more descriptive label that appears in the customization palette by using the method `setPaletteLabel:`. The icon image of the toolbar item is set with `setImage:`, which takes an NSImage as its argument. To set the target/action pair of the toolbar item, use `setTarget:` and `setAction:`. If you do not set the target, the action of the toolbar item is invoked in the first responder that implements it.

A toolbar item can be either a simple icon button, such as the Mailboxes and Junk icons shown in Figure 3-10, or a custom NSView containing any control you wish. The Search field in Figure 3-10 is an example of a toolbar item that uses a custom view rather than an icon button. The simple icon buttons are created by giving the toolbar item an image, as discussed in the last paragraph. To assign a custom view to a toolbar item, use the method `setView:`.

Figure 3-10. The Mail toolbar

NSToolbar relies on a delegate object to supply the toolbar items that populate the toolbar and the customization palette. The delegate should be able to return an NSToolbarItem for every control that might appear in the toolbar. You can set this delegate by sending a setDelegate: message to the toolbar. The delegate is required to implement the following three methods:

toolbar:itemForItemIdentifier:willBeInsertedIntoToolbar:
> This method should return a fully configured instance of NSToolbarItem for the specified toolbar and item identifier. The willBeInsertedIntoToolbar: flag indicates whether the item is about to be inserted into the toolbar. If this parameter is YES, you can expect that the delegate method toolbarWillAddItem: will be called soon.

toolbarAllowedItemIdentifiers:
> This method should return an NSArray of item identifier strings for all items that may go into the toolbar. The order of the item identifiers in the returned array determines the order in which the items appear in the customization palette.

toolbarDefaultItemIdentifiers:
> This method returns an NSArray of item identifiers for the items that make up the default toolbar. The order of the item identifiers in this array determines the order in which items appear in the default toolbar.

Optionally, the toolbar delegate may implement the following two methods:

toolbarWillAddItem:
> Called just before a toolbar item is added to a toolbar. The parameter is a notification posted by the toolbar. The object of this notification is the toolbar to which the item will be added. The toolbar item is available in the userInfo dictionary under the key @"item".

toolbarDidRemoveItem:
> Called just after a toolbar item is removed from a toolbar. The parameter is a notification posted by the toolbar. The object of this notification is the toolbar from which the item will be removed. The toolbar item is available in the userInfo dictionary under the key @"item".

Example 3-4 shows how a toolbar delegate is implemented to create a simple toolbar.

Example 3-4. Implementing a toolbar delegate

```
- (NSArray *)toolbarAllowedItemIdentifiers:(NSToolbar*)toolbar
{
    return [NSArray arrayWithObjects:@"Item1",
                    @"Item2",
                    NSToolbarSeparatorItemIdentifier,
                    NSToolbarSpaceItemIdentifier,
                    NSToolbarFlexibleSpaceItemIdentifier,
                    NSToolbarShowColorsItemIdentifier,
                    NSToolbarCustomizeToolbarItemIdentifier,
                    nil];
}

- (NSArray *)toolbarDefaultItemIdentifiers:(NSToolbar*)toolbar
{
```

Example 3-4. Implementing a toolbar delegate (continued)

```
    return [NSArray arrayWithObjects:@" Item1",
                    NSToolbarFlexibleSpaceItemIdentifier,
                    @"Item2", nil];
}

- (NSToolbarItem *)toolbar:(NSToolbar *)toolbar
        itemForItemIdentifier:(NSString *)itemIdentifier
        willBeInsertedIntoToolbar:(BOOL)flag
{
    NSToolbarItem *item = [[NSToolbarItem alloc]
                    initWithIdentifer:itemIdentifier];

    /*
     * If customize the item based on the identifier;
     * Standard toolbar items fall through and are returned
     */
    if ( [itemIdentifier isEqualToString:@"Item1" ) {
        [item setLabel:@"Do This"];
        [item setAction:@selector(doThis)];
        [item setImage:[NSImage imageNamed:@"DoThis"]];
    } else if ( [itemIdentifier isEqualToString:@"Item12") {
        [item setLabel:@"Do That"];
        [item setAction:@selector(doThat)];
        [item setImage:[NSImage imageNamed:@"DoThat"]];
    }
    return [item autorelease];
}
```

Event Handling

Earlier in this chapter, you learned that NSApplication, NSWindow, and NSView share a common parent class: NSResponder. This class plays a central role in the AppKit event handling system, as it declares the interface to any class that can respond to events.

To handle events, it is often sufficient to understand how to create a suitable subclass of NSResponder (a custom view, for example) and implement the relevant methods (e.g., mouseDown:). The application framework is responsible for ensuring that the appropriate method is invoked on the right object.

The event handling architecture is built on three major ideas: *event messages*, *action messages*, and the *responder chain*. As discussed earlier, events enter an application through the window server and are dispatched by NSApplication, with the method sendEvent:, to forward the event to the appropriate object.

The event model also deals with action messages. Objects, usually interface controls, create actions within the application that can be routed to a target object. The method used to dispatch action messages is NSApplication's sendAction:to:from:. The sendAction: parameter is a selector for the action method to be invoked in the target, the to: parameter is the action's target, and from: is the sender of the action. It is possible that the target is unspecified, in which case the action is sent up the full responder chain, and the first responder object that implements the message responds to it.

As for event handling, a window may be the *key window*, the *main window*, or both. At any point in time, there is only one key and one main window (they may be the same). NSApplication always sends mouse and key events to the key window. NSWindow implements the method sendEvent: to route the event to the proper view within the window. This view is the most tightly nested view within the hierarchy over which the event occurred. If the view does not handle the event, then the event is sent to the view's *next responder*, which is usually its superview.

Action messages, on the other hand, are sent first to the key window's first responder, and follow the responder chain up to the window's content view. If no part of the responder chain handles the action, the window object and window delegate are given a chance to respond to the action. If the main window differs from the key window, the process repeats for the main window. Finally, if the main window and its responder chain do not respond to the action, the NSApplication object and its delegate are given a chance to respond. Thus, mouse and key events are always directed to the key window. If the key window is different from the main window, the main window is not given a chance to handle mouse and key events.

Event Objects

Every event responder method has the event object as its single argument. From this object, you can extract relevant information about the event, such as where the mouse is located in the window, or which key on the keyboard was pressed. Example 3-5 shows how to work with mouse-generated events.

Example 3-5. Working with mouse events

```
- (void)mouseDown:(NSEvent *)theEvent
{
    NSPoint winLoc = [theEvent locationInWindow];
    NSPoint viewLoc = [self convertPoint:winLoc fromView:nil];
}
```

In this example, the locationInWindow method returns an NSPoint object, which gives the location of the event in the window's coordinate system. In the next line, you use the NSView method, convertPoint:fromView:, to convert the point from the coordinate system of one view to the coordinate system of the receiver. By passing nil as the second argument, you convert the point from the base coordinate system of the window to that of the receiver view.

Responding to keyboard events is similar, although the important characteristic is not the location, but the key that is pressed. Example 3-6 shows how to respond to key events. To discover which specific key was pressed, use the characters method.

Example 3-6. Responding to key events

```
- (void)keyDown:(NSEvent *)theEvent
{
    NSString *key = [theEvent characters];

    if ( [key isEqualToString:@"c"] ) {
        // Handle event here for the 'c' key pressed
    }
}
```

The Responder Chain

The final piece of the event model—the glue that holds it all together—is the *responder chain*. The responder chain gives objects that may potentially respond to an event or action a chance to do so. This results in an extremely flexible response model, as the originator of the event or action is decoupled from the ultimate destination.

The responder chain is a series of linked NSResponder objects. When an event or an action occurs, it is dispatched to what is known as the first responder, which is given the first chance to respond to the event or action. If the first responder is incapable of responding, then the next responder object in the chain is given a chance to respond. Events and actions are sent up the responder chain until an object is found that can respond to the message. Typically the Application Kit picks the first responder automatically in response to normal user interaction with the interface. In other words, the object that is clicked or that receives typing is the first responder.

When constructing an interface in Interface Builder, you typically assign a specific object as the target for a control's action. Interface Builder provides a mechanism for actions to be sent to the responder chain, rather than a specific target object. This is done by connecting an object's action to the First Responder proxy object in the nib window.

First Responder represents nil. If a control has a value for its target, it sends its action directly to that target. If the target is nil, this results in a "nil-targeted-action", denoting that the action should be passed to the responder chain (equivalent to passing nil as the message recipient in NSApplication's sendAction:to:from:).

The responder chain pattern is especially convenient when your interface and controller classes are split among several nib files. Using the First Responder in Interface Builder lets you send actions from a control in one nib to an object in another. This is common when working with document-based applications that have the main menu in one nib and the document interface and class in another.

Document-Based Applications

Most applications create, manage, and edit documents. A document can be anything that stores persistent data. Moreover, these applications all duplicate common functionality, such as the ability to create new documents, open existing documents, and manage multiple open documents. Cocoa provides a multiple-document application architecture that implements most of the basic functionality shared by all document-based applications. Cocoa document-based application architecture centers on the NSDocument, NSDocumentController, and NSWindowController classes.

When developing a document-based application, most development effort is likely to be spent implementing subclasses of NSDocument; any document-based application must have at least one NSDocument subclass, but may have more (think of AppleWorks, for example). In MVC terminology, an NSDocument is a controller object; it manages a document's persistent data, and to project that data into a view. This means that minimally an NSDocument subclass must know how to load data into a form useable by the application, as well as how to store this data into a persistent form. A well-implemented document subclass also provides support for printing, undo/redo operations, and edited status tracking.

An NSDocumentController instance is the administrator of a document-based application. It is responsible for servicing user requests to create, open, and save documents. NSDocumentController serves the integral role of the *document factory*. NSDocument knows how to load a file's contents as the document's data, and NSDocumentController knows how to create NSDocument objects under different circumstances. For example, File → New is wired to tell NSDocumentController to create an instance of the application's NSDocument subclass with no initial data. When you choose a file via File → Open, you tell NSDocumentController to create an instance of the document class and load the selected file's contents into that document.

If an application has more than one NSDocument subclass (say, to support different document and data formats), NSDocumentController knows which subclass to instantiate based on the requested document type. Document types are mapped to NSDocument subclasses in the application's *Info.plist*. Each subclass of NSDocumentis tailored to support a different data model (i.e., file format). Instances of the document-based application architecture classes relate to one another in a multi-tier tree. At runtime, a document-based application has a single instance of NSDocumentController (accessed using the sharedDocumentController class method). This instance of NSDocumentController owns and manages zero, one, or more instances of NSDocument. Each NSDocument instance, in turn, owns and manages one or more instances of NSWindowController, which each own an instance of NSWindow. Figure 3-11 shows this arrangement.

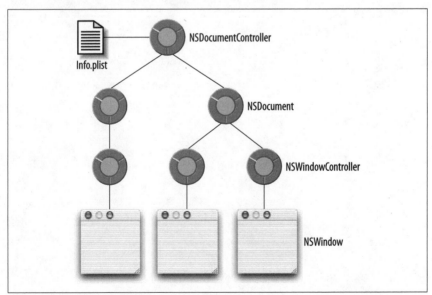

Figure 3-11. The runtime relationship of NSDocumentController, NSDocument, NSWindowController, and NSWindow objects

In simple document-based applications, where every document has just a single window, there may be no need to implement custom NSWindowController classes. The document architecture, however, allows you to create applications where there may be different or replicated views of the same data, e.g., a 3D drawing app where different windows may contain views and controls for wire frame, rendered and points-in-space representations; or a text editor where two windows might show different parts of the same file. In this variation of MVC, two controller classes work with together: NSDocument is the data model controller, and NSWindowController is the view controller. Your NSDocument subclass should manage the data model, and one or more subclasses of NSWindowController manage the windows that present the data.

4

Drawing and Imaging

The Application Kit has a diverse set of graphics classes. These classes range from NSQuickDrawView, which lets developers use legacy graphics code based on the QuickDraw APIs in their Cocoa application, to NSOpenGLView, which provides a way to display OpenGL-based 3D graphics. The focus of this chapter, however, is on the 2D drawing and imaging classes that provide a high-level interface to Mac OS X's graphics system, Quartz. Table 4-1 enumerates the classes discussed in this chapter.

Table 4-1. Application Kit drawing and imaging classes

Class	Description
NSAffineTransform	Defines an interface for creating and applying affine transforms that map points in one coordinate space to another
NSBezierPath	Draws PostScript-style lines and curves that enable the construction of arbitrary paths
NSBitmapImageRep	Interprets bitmapped image data, such as those stored as TIFF, BMP, GIF, JPEG, or PNG file types
NSCachedImageRep	Stores image data as a cached representation
NSColor	Represents a color as an object with support for several color spaces and color calibration
NSCustomImageRep	An image representation that allows the client to determine how the image is rendered
NSEPSImageRep	An image representation subclass that represents PostScript (EPS) formatted image data
NSGraphicsContext	Represents configurations for Quartz's graphics rendering engine and allows the client to determine how characteristics of graphics objects, such as Bezier paths, are rendered
NSImage	Stores and draws an image to screen
NSImageRep	Lets NSImage simultaneously represent an image's data in several formats defined by its six concrete subclasses
NSPDFImageRep	Represents image data stored as a PDF
NSPICTImageRep	Represents image data in Macintosh PICT format

The Role of Quartz

Quartz is the foundation of Cocoa's 2D graphics capabilities. It provides many advanced graphics capabilities, including color management, path-based drawing, transparency, and anti-aliasing. It uses the same fundamental model of drawing as Adobe's Portable Document Format (PDF).

Quartz is actually two individual pieces of software in Mac OS X—*Quartz Compositor* and *Quartz 2D*. The Quartz Compositor is the underlying system service responsible for drawing the graphical user interface to screen from sources such as Quartz 2D, QuickTime, OpenGL, and QuickDraw. Quartz 2D, on the other hand, is an Application Programming Interface (API) for drawing and manipulating 2D graphics. This chapter concentrates on Quartz 2D's drawing functionality.

You can access the Quartz 2D API directly through the *CoreGraphics* framework, but it is far more convenient to use the Cocoa classes that provide an easy-to-use interface to Quartz, including NSBezierPath, NSView, NSImage, and NSGraphicsContext. These classes provide the functionality to render paths, text, and images to screen or to the printed page.

Coordinate Systems

All drawing is performed within an instance of NSView. Each view defines its own *coordinate system*. By default, the origin (0, 0) is in the lower-left corner of the view with positive y-values extending up from, and positive x-values extending to the right of, the origin. Figure 4-1 illustrates this system.

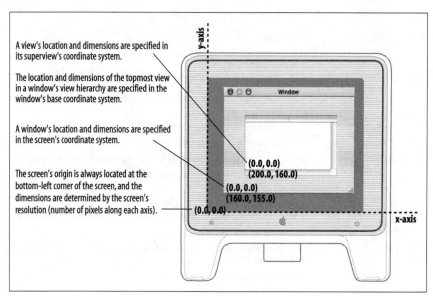

Figure 4-1. View coordinate systems

These coordinates are not tied to any particular output device, but are expressed in terms of points (a unit that is 1/72 of an inch). When Quartz renders graphics, it maps what is drawn in the device-independent coordinate system into the coordinate system of the device. One point is equivalent to one screen pixel.

As covered in Chapter 3, views are arranged in a nested hierarchy, with subviews contained within a superview. Two rectangles characterize a view. The size and position of a view within its superview is determined by its *frame rectangle*. The *bounds rectangle* defines the coordinate system within the view itself. By default, the origin of the bounds rectangle is at (0, 0), and it has the same height and width as the view's frame rectangle. You can access a view's frame using the methods frame and setFrame:, and access the bounds rectangle with bounds and setBounds:. Figure 4-2 shows how the frame and bounds rectangles are related.

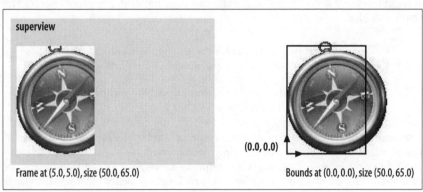

Figure 4-2. The frame and bounds of a view

Resizing the bounds rectangle independently of the frame rectangle lets developers define coordinate systems that are natural for their application, instead of being forced to work in screen coordinates. Additionally, coordinate systems within a view may be translated and rotated independent of other coordinate systems.

Graphics Contexts

A graphics context is a low-level component of the drawing system representing a destination for drawing commands that will be executed and rendered. Instances of the NSGraphicsContext class represent these contexts. The graphics context also provides an interface to manage graphics states and configure a number of rendering options, such as anti-aliasing, image interpolation, and various settings for drawing paths such as line width and join styles.

At any time in the execution of an application, a current context defines the graphics context for all graphics operations. You can obtain this object using the class method currentContext. Multiple graphics contexts are stored on a stack, so that different parts of an application may configure a context specific to their needs. To push a new context onto the stack, use the method saveGraphicsState. Contexts lower in the stack are restored by invoking restoreGraphicsState, which pulls the current context off the stack, making the next lower one current.

You can use a graphics context to determine whether or not the screen is the current drawing destination. This is useful if you have to handle onscreen and off-screen drawing differently (e.g., to a printer). The isDrawingToScreen method returns YES if drawing is done onscreen, and NO otherwise. The convenience class method currentContextDrawingToScreen does the same thing, saving you the step of first invoking currentContext.

Working with Paths

Drawing lines is the most basic function you can perform with Cocoa's drawing classes. The Application Kit encapsulates the low-level, Quartz path-based drawing API in the NSBezierPath class. Minimally, NSBezierPath lets you draw straight lines and Bezier paths, and using this functionality, you can construct any shape you like.

 Bezier curves, or paths, are curved lines based on the mathematics of third-degree polynomials. Because Bezier paths are based on equations, they are resolution-independent and can be scaled to any size without the loss of detail or quality generally experienced with bitmapped graphics.

Drawing with NSBezierPath is in some respects similar to drawing on a sheet of paper with a pencil. Before you can draw a line, you have to place the pencil lead at a point on the page. Drawing a line requires moving the pencil from one point to another. To draw a disjointed line, you pick up the pencil tip from the paper and move it to another location. You might then complete a diagram by drawing a line back to the first point. These actions are reflected in the following NSBezierPath methods, used to construct a path:

- moveToPoint:
- lineToPoint:
- curveToPoint:controlPoint1:controlPoint2:
- closePath

The arguments to the first three methods are all of type NSPoint, a C structure that encapsulates a coordinate pair. Example 4-1 shows the struct declaration for NSPoint.

Example 4-1. The NSPoint struct

```
typedef struct _NSPoint {
  float x;
  float y;
} NSPoint;
```

At any time, there is a current point. The method moveToPoint: moves the current point to the specified point. The methods lineToPoint: and curveToPoint: controlPoint1:controlPoint2: both extend a path from the current point.

Bezier curves (a subset of Bezier paths) are defined by two endpoints and two control points. The line segment connecting an end point to its control point is tangent to the curve at the end point and defines the path's direction. Figure 4-4, later in this chapter, shows the lines connecting each endpoint to their associated control point for the curve that makes up the bottom of the triangle.

Drawing with NSBezierPaths is fundamentally different from drawing with a pencil in that constructing a path is not the same as drawing a path. You can think of a path as an abstract representation that can be rendered into one, or many, views. NSBezierPath provides two methods to render a path: stroke, and fill. stroke draws the outline of the path, while the fill method fills the interior of the path with a color or pattern.

To illustrate this, consider Example 4-2, which draws the image shown in Figure 4-3.

Example 4-2. Code to construct a complex shape using NSBezierPath

```
// The three vertices of a triangle
NSPoint p1 = NSMakePoint(100, 100);
NSPoint p2 = NSMakePoint(200, 300);
NSPoint p3 = NSMakePoint(300, 100);

// Control points
NSPoint c1 = NSMakePoint(200, 200);
NSPoint c2 = NSMakePoint(200, 0);

// Constructing the path for the triangle
NSBezierPath *bp = [NSBezierPath bezierPath];
[bp moveToPoint:p1];
[bp lineToPoint:p2];
[bp lineToPoint:p3];
[bp curveToPoint:p1 controlPoint1:c1 controlPoint2:c2];
[bp closePath];
[bp stroke];
```

For simple drawing, such as constructing rectangles or ellipses, NSBezierPath has two methods: bezierPathWithRect: and bezierPathWithOvalInRect:. Both methods take an NSRect as an argument. In the first method, the NSRect defines the constructed rectangle. In the second method, the specified rectangle determines the boundary of the ellipse. In addition to these two constructors, appendBezierPathWithOvalInRect: and appendBezierPathWithRect: add an ellipse or rectangle to an existing path.

You can also construct arcs with the following three methods:

- appendBezierPathWithArcWithCenter:radius:startAngle:endAngle:clockwise:
- appendBezierPathWithArcWithCenter:radius:startAngle:endAngle:
- appendBezierPathWithArcFromPoint:toPoint:radius:

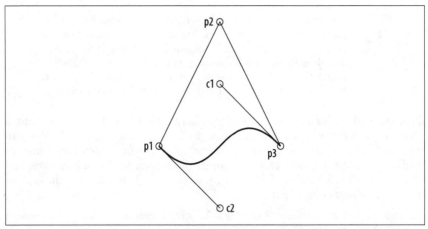

Figure 4-3. The bold line shows the shape resulting from the path in Example 4-2 (the points are labeled with the variable names from Example 4-2)

These methods measure angles in degrees. The first draws an arc centered at the specified center point with a given radius. The arc extends from startAngle: to endAngle:, clockwise or counterclockwise, depending on the value of the clockwise argument. The second method is a wrapper around the first, where clockwise: is NO.

The third method, appendBezierPathWithArcFromPoint:toPoint:radius:, draws an arc from a circle that is inscribed within the angle specified by the current point in a path and the two points specified in the method. The parameter radius: specifies the radius of the circle used to build the arc. This method is more complicated than the other two, so it is illustrated by example. Example 4-3 shows the code used to build the path in Figure 4-4, shown with a bold line.

Example 4-3. Drawing arcs

```
NSPoint p0 = NSMakePoint( 100, 100 );
NSPoint p1 = NSMakePoint( 100, 250 );
NSPoint p2 = NSMakePoint( 200, 250 );

path = [NSBezierPath bezierPath];
[path moveToPoint:p0];
[path appendBezierPathWithArcFromPoint:p1 toPoint:p2 radius:50];
[path stroke];
```

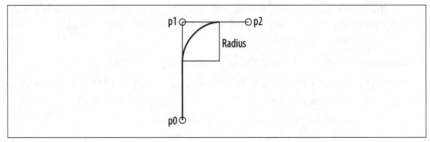

Figure 4-4. The bold line represents the path constructed in Example 4-3

Drawing to Views

To draw in a given view, you must first lock *focus* on the view by sending it a lockFocus message. Quartz interprets all subsequent drawing commands in the context of that view. Once the drawing is done, balance the lockFocus with a matching unlockFocus to the same view.

Custom drawing is implemented in a subclass of NSView. When subclassing NSView, all drawing code is called from an overridden drawRect: method. This method of NSView does nothing by default, but the NSView graphics system is set up to automatically invoke this method at the appropriate times.

While drawRect: does the drawing work, it should never be invoked directly. Instead, to force an immediate redraw of a view, you can send a display message to the view. This causes the receiver to lock its focus, invoke drawRect:, and then unlock its focus before returning control to the caller. To this end, display is functionally similar to the implementation shown in Example 4-4.

Example 4-4. Functional implementation of NSView's display

```
- (void)display
{
  [self lockFocus];
  [self drawRect:[self bounds]];
  [self unlockFocus];
}
```

However, display is still not the interface you usually use to tell a view to redraw its contents. A better method of redrawing tells the view that the contents have changed and lets the view redraw itself the next time through the run loop. You do this by sending the view a setNeedsDisplay: message, with the argument YES to indicate that the view should invoke display in the next run loop pass. If you want to cancel a drawing request, invoke this method passing NO. This allows Quartz to decide the proper time to redraw the contents of a view.

In some circumstances it may be more efficient still to send the view a setNeedsDisplayInRect: message, where the argument is a "dirty" area that needs to be updated. The display system can then determine what rectangle to pass as the argument to a view's drawRect:. In your drawing code, you then ensure that you only update parts of the view that need to be refreshed. Other methods used to cause view updates include:

```
- (void)displayIfNeeded;
- (void)displayIfNeededIgnoringOpacity;
- (void)displayRect:(NSRect)rect;
- (void)displayIfNeededInRect:(NSRect)rect;
- (void)displayRectIgnoringOpacity:(NSRect)rect;
- (void)displayIfNeededInRectIgnoringOpacity:(NSRect)rect;
```

Line Attributes

NSBezierPath lets you change several path-rendering options, such as the line thickness, join style, dash count, miter limit, cap style, and winding rules. You can change a path's attributes with a class method or an instance method. The instance method changes the attributes of only the receiving instance, while the class method changes the default attribute for all instances in the graphics context.

For example, to change the width of a line, use either setLineWidth: or setDefaultLineWidth:. The first changes the line width of the instance to which you send that particular method, while the second class method sets the line width in the graphics context that applies to subsequent renderings of any instance of NSBezierPath.

NSBezierPath provides methods for changing the following attributes:

- Line width
- Path flatness
- Line dashes and phase
- Line cap style
- Line join style
- Miter limit
- Winding rule

You can change any of these attributes for a single instance or for the graphics context, as shown earlier.

Path flatness

Flatness is one attribute that can be set for a curve. A path's *flatness* indicates to the rendering engine how accurately it should reproduce the curve; that is, the flatness is a metric of the curve's granularity or resolution as it is rendered. A higher flatness value corresponds to a rougher curve, which can be rendered more quickly; a lower value corresponds to a smoother curve, which comes at the expense of rendering time. Figure 4-5 shows a curve that is stroked with the default flatness of 0.6, and again with a larger flatness of 100 using a thicker line. Example 4-5 shows the code you need to change the flatness.

Example 4-5. Changing the flatness of a Bezier path

```
- (void)drawRect:(NSRect)aRect
{
    NSBezierPath *path = [NSBezierPath bezierPath];

    [path moveToPoint:NSMakePoint(0, 200)];
    [path curveToPoint:NSMakePoint(500, 200)
        controlPoint1:NSMakePoint(500, 800)
        controlPoint2:NSMakePoint(0, -400)];

    [path setFlatness:100];
    [path stroke];
}
```

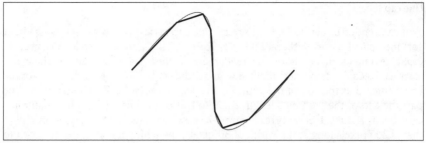

Figure 4-5. The thinner, smooth curve has a default flatness of 0.6; the thicker curve has a flatness of 100

 How jagged a curve appears depends on the flatness and the absolute size of the curve. Endpoints of the curve in Figure 4-5 are 500 pixels apart; if the absolute size of the curve were 10 times as large, a flatness of 100 would create less dramatic jaggedness.

Related to setting the flatness of a rendered curve is the method `bezierPathByFlatteningPath`. This method returns a Bezier path that represents the receiver with all curves approximated as a series of straight lines similar to how changing the flatness renders the curve.

Line dashes and phase

The method `setLineDash:count:phase:` takes three parameters to define a dash pattern for a stroked Bezier path. The first argument is a C array of `float`s that specifies the lengths of alternating stroked and unstroked segments. The second argument indicates the number of elements in the dash pattern array. The final argument indicates where in the dash pattern drawing begins. Consider the three dash patterns in Example 4-6 and the resulting lines in Figure 4-6.

Example 4-6. The code used to generate three dashed lines

```
float pattern1[2] = {50.0, 25.0};
float pattern2[3] = {50.0, 25.0, 75.0};

// The top line in Figure 4-6
[aPath setLineDash:pattern1 count:2 phase:0];

// The middle line in Figure 4-6
[aPath setLineDash:pattern2 count:3 phase:0];

// Bottom line in Figure 4-6
[aPath setLineDash:pattern1 count:2 phase:25];
```

Figure 4-6. Line dash patterns: each line is 400 points long with a line thickness of 10 points

Line cap style

You can render Bezier paths with several line cap styles, which are set using either setLineCapStyle: or setDefaultLineCapStyle:. The line cap style NSButtLine-CapStyle makes the ends of the rendered line flush with the end of the path. NSRoundLineCapStyle renders the line with a radius equal to half the thickness of the line, centered at the end of the path. Finally, NSSquareLineCapStyle extends the line past the end of the path by a length equal to half of the line width. The default line cap style is NSButtLineCapStyle. Figure 4-7 shows various line cap styles on a path that is 200 pixels long and a width of 30 pixels; the white line indicates the path to highlight the position of the endpoints (which is critical when discussing the differences between NSButtLineCapStyle and NSSquareLineCapStyle).

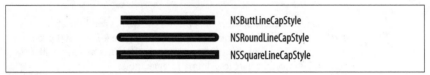

Figure 4-7. Line cap styles

Line join styles

Another property of Bezier paths is the way lines are joined. You can set this property for path objects with setLineJoinStyle:, or set it for the graphics context with setDefaultLineJoinStyle:. The default line join style is NSMiterLine-JoinStyle, in which the outside edges of the lines are extended to a sharp point. You can also create rounded and beveled line join styles using the constants NSRoundLineJoinStyle and NSBevelLineJoinStyle. Figure 4-8 shows examples of the three lines join styles.

Figure 4-8. From left to right: NSMiterLineJoinStyle, NSRoundLineJoinStyle, and NSBevelLineJoinStyle

Miter limit

Miter join styles have a special problem: the join appears as a spike when the angle between the two joined lines is extraordinarily acute (since the join is rendered by extending the outer line edges outward until they meet). To prevent this problem, the graphics context has a *miter limit* that defines a threshold for how small an angle can be before the line join style is changed to a bevel joint. The miter limit is the ratio of the miter length (the diagonal length of the miter extension) to the line width; by default, this is value is 10. To alter this value, use NSBezierPath's class method setDefaultMiterLimit:, or the instance method setMiterLimit:.

Figure 4-9 illustrates a small-angle joint. The joint with the miter join style is drawn with the default miter limit of 10, while the miter limit that produces the bevel joint is reduced to 6. In each example, the line thickness is 20 and the angle between the two lines is about 9.5 degrees.

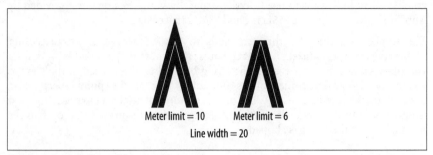

Figure 4-9. The effect of the miter limit

Winding rule

When filling a path, there is another graphics context characteristic to consider: the winding rule. For simple paths such as rectangles and circles, the region that should be filled is unambiguous. However, for complex paths, such as a star with many intersecting line segments, the area that should be filled is less clear. Thus, winding rules are used to determine which regions of a complex intersecting path should be filled.

The two winding rules are *non-zero* (the default) and *even-odd*. The even-odd winding rule works by taking a test point within the region and counting the number of times a ray extending from that point crosses the path. If the number of crossings is odd, then the point is considered "inside" the shape, and its region will be filled. If the number of crossing is even, then the point is considered "outside" the shape, and its enclosing region is not filled.

The non-zero winding rule counts crossings based on the direction of the crossed path. A ray extending from the test point increments its crossing count when it crosses a left-to-right path; it decrements its crossing count when crossing a right-to-left path. If the number of crossings is 1, then the point is "inside;" if the number of crossings is zero, then the point is "outside." Figure 4-10 shows an example of these two winding rules at work.

Figure 4-10. Stars illustrating (from left) the path with no fill, the default non-zero winding rule, and the even-odd winding rule

Drawing Text

For many applications that use text, AppKit's NSTextField or NSTextView classes are sufficient. However, when you need to draw text as part of some custom graphics, you may want to use Cocoa's string drawing functionality, provided by AppKit's extensions to the NSString and NSAttributedString.

The Application Kit adds three methods to the NSString class—drawAtPoint:withAttributes:, drawInRect:withAttributes:, and sizeWithAttributes:—that let you draw strings in views easily. The string being drawn is placed in the view to locate the upper-left corner of its bounding box at the point specified in drawAtPoint:withAttributes:. When using drawInRect:withAttributes:, the text is drawn within the rectangle. If the bounding box of the string is larger than the rectangle, then the string is clipped.

Attributed strings

Attributes are associated with a string by the Foundation class NSAttributedString. Table 4-2 enumerates these attributes.

Table 4-2. Standard Cocoa attributes for NSAttributedString

Attribute identifier	Type	Default value
NSAttachmentAttributeName	NSTextAttachment	No default
NSBackgroundColorAttributeName	NSColor	No default
NSBaselineOffsetAttributeName	NSNumber	0.0
NSFontAttributeName	NSFont	Helvetica 12 points
NSForegroundColorAttributeName	NSColor	Black
NSKernAttributeName	NSNumber	0.0
NSLigatureAttributeName	NSNumber	1
NSLinkAttributeName	id	No default
NSParagraphAttributeName	NSParagraphStyle	[NSParagraphStyle defaultParagraphStyle]
NSSuperscriptAttributeName	NSNumber	0
NSUnderlineStyleAttributeName	NSNumber	0

To create an attributed string, initialize the string with text and assigning to it any of the attributes listed in Table 4-2. Any combination of attributes may be assigned to any subset of characters. For example, the first half of an attributed string might use Lucida Grande with 12-point type, while the second half could use 24-point Tengwar.

Once you have set up the attributes of the string satisfactorily, the string can be drawn in the currently focused view by sending it either a drawAtPoint: or drawInRect: message. These methods are AppKit extensions to NSAttributedString. These methods work in the same way as the NSString extensions discussed previously. You can also determine the size of the bounding box by sending a size message to the attributed string.

Working with Color

Colors in the Application Kit are represented by instances of the NSColor class, which provides an interface for creating colors and setting the color used by the current graphics context. AppKit supports several color spaces that fall into three categories:

Device-dependent
> Color spaces support colors that may appear differently on different devices (such as a color printer or monitor).

Device-independent
> Colors are calibrated so they appear the same on any output device.

Named
> Color spaces represent colors that don't correspond to numerical values, but are referenced in a catalogue of named colors.

The six color spaces supported by the Application Kit are based on these three categories, as detailed in Table 4-3.

Table 4-3. Color spaces supported by the Application Kit

Color space name	Description
NSDeviceCMYKColorSpace	Cyan, magenta, yellow, black, and alpha components
NSDeviceRGBColorSpace	Red, green, blue, and alpha components; or hue, saturation, brightness, and alpha components
NSCalibratedRGBColorSpace	Red, green, blue, and alpha components; or hue, saturation, brightness, and alpha components
NSDeviceWhiteColorSpace	White and alpha components (grayscale)
NSCalibratedWhiteColorSpace	White and alpha components (grayscale)
NSNamedColorSpace	Catalog name and color name components

The color spaces that are NSDevice... are device-dependent color spaces, while those that are NSCalibrated... color spaces are device-independent. Table 4-3 lists constant names defined by AppKit to identify color spaces in code.

To create an instance of NSColor, use any colorWith... class method that takes component values for the color spaces indicated by the method name, such as colorWithCalibratedRed:green:blue:alpha. The parameters passed to these methods as component values are floats ranging between 0 and 1. Values that fall below 0 are interpreted as black, and those above 1 are interpreted as the pure color. Several class methods are also named after colors, such as redColor and blueColor. These methods return an instance of NSColor whose components are set for the specified color and whose color space is NSCalibratedRGBColorSpace.

Example 4-7 shows different ways to create color objects.

Example 4-7. Various ways to create color objects

```
NSColor *c;

// Apple-menu blue in RGB colorspaces
c = [NSColor colorWithCalibratedRed:0.243 green:0.505
             blue:0.863 alpha:1.0];

// Same color in CMYK colorspace
c = [NSColor colorWithDeviceCyan:0.76 magenta:0.50
yellow:0.14 black:0.0 alpha:1.0];
```

NSColor's set method sets the receiver as the current graphics context's color. All subsequent drawing is done in the color that was last set. By default, all drawing is done in black. Example 4-8 demonstrates how this is done in a drawRect: method.

Example 4-8. Setting the color of a graphics context and rendering a path

```
- (void)drawRect:(NSRect)rect
{
  // Construct path

  [[NSColor greyColor] set];
  [bp fill];

  [[NSColor blackColor] set];
  [bp stroke];
}
```

Working with Images

NSImage and NSImageRep are Cocoa's image-handling workhorses. NSImage provides a convenient and easy-to-use frontend to a powerful and flexible backend comprised of NSImageRep's many subclasses. NSImage provides a high level interface for loading, saving, and drawing images onscreen. NSImageRep and its subclasses, on the other hand, provide interfaces for working with specific image formats.

NSImage

NSImage provides the high-level interface for working with images, which includes the ability to load and save images and draw them to screen. With NSImage, you don't need to worry about image formats, which are handled internally by NSImage and the NSImageRep set of classes. To initialize instances of NSImage use these methods:

- initByReferencingFile:
- initByReferencingURL:
- initWithContentsOfFile:
- initWithContentsOfURL:
- initWithData:
- initWithPasteboard:
- initWithSize:

When you initialize anything by reference, as with the first two methods, the data is not loaded until the object actually needs it. This contrasts with initWithContents..., which loads the data and initializes the object immediately. The last method, initWithSize:, initializes an empty image.

imageNamed: is a useful method for creating image objects with images contained in the application bundle. With this method, you don't have to provide a path to the file or include the file extension in the name—NSImage knows where to find it within the bundle.

NSImageView

NSImageView is a subclass of NSControl, and as such, is related to the interface as a control, rather than to graphics, as its name suggests. NSImageView is a small extension to NSControl that lets you display an image. You can set various attributes, such as how the image should scale to fit in the view (i.e., no scaling, proportionally, or stretched) or how it should be aligned in the view (left, right, center, etc.). One of NSImageView's most useful features is its ability to be dragging source and destination; that is, you can drag the image from the view to some other application or document, and when properly implemented, you can drag an image to be displayed in the view.

Compositing

You can also use NSImage to composite images to the screen through Quartz. Earlier in the chapter, we saw that all drawing had to be done within the locked focus of an NSView. Like NSView, NSImage interacts directly with Quartz to accomplish drawing. Compositing combines a source image, your NSImage object, with a destination image, the existing image displayed on the screen, according to a given operation. Table 4-4 lists the various compositing operations.

Table 4-4. Compositing operations and constants

Operation	Effect on destination image
NSCompositeClear	Makes the destination transparent.
NSCompositeCopy	Copies the source image over to the destination image.
NSCompositeDestinationAtop	Draws the destination image wherever both the source and destination images are opaque, and shows the source image wherever the source image is opaque and destination image is transparent. If the overlapping regions of both images are transparent, the composited image is transparent.
NSCompositeDestinationIn	Draws the destination image where overlapping regions of both images are opaque, and is transparent everywhere else.
NSCompositeDestinationOut	Draws the destination image wherever it is opaque but the source image is transparent, and transparent elsewhere.
NSCompositeDestinationOver	Draws the destination image wherever it is opaque, and draws the source image elsewhere.
NSCompositePlusDarker	Draws the sum of the destination and source images, with summed color values approaching 0 (black).

Table 4-4. Compositing operations and constants (continued)

Operation	Effect on destination image
NSCompositePlusLighter	Draws the sum of source and destination images with summed color values approaching 1 (white).
NSCompositeSourceAtop	Draws the source image wherever both images are opaque, draws destination image wherever destination image is opaque but source is transparent, and transparent elsewhere.
NSCompositeSourceIn	Draws the source image wherever both images are opaque, and transparent elsewhere.
NSCompositeSourceOut	Draws the source image wherever it is opaque but the destination is transparent, and draws transparent elsewhere.
NSCompositeSourceOver	Draws the source image wherever it is opaque, and destination elsewhere.
NSCompositeXOR	Draws the exclusive OR of the source and destination image. Works only with black and white images and is thus not recommended for use in color contexts.

The Developer Tools installation includes several sample applications that demonstrate various aspects of the available frameworks. CompositeLab, found in */Developer/Examples/AppKit/CompositeLab*, lets you combine two images with any of the compositing operations listed in Table 4-4; the result is immediate, and you can easily experiment with NSImage compositing. The source code is also available, so you can see how it's implemented. Figure 4-11 shows CompositeLab in action.

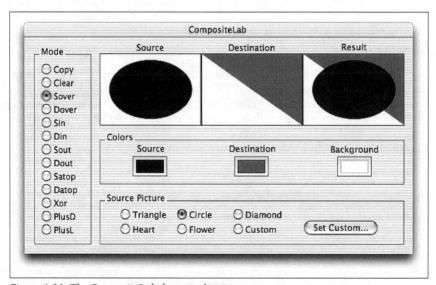

Figure 4-11. The CompositeLab demo application

You can composite an NSImage to screen with any of the following methods:

- compositeToPoint:operation:
- compositeToPoint:fromRect:operation:
- compositeToPoint:fromRect:operation:fraction:
- compositeToPoint:operation:fraction:

In each method, the operation: argument is one of the constants given in Table 4-4. The first argument, compositeToPoint:, is an NSPoint structure indicating where the origin of the image should be placed in the coordinate system of the view whose focus is currently locked; the origin is the lower-left corner of the image. By using a method with a fromRect: parameter, you can specify a cropped portion of the source image to be composited to the point. Finally, the fraction: parameter seen in the last two methods in the list indicates the degree of blending that should occur between the source image and the destination image. This parameter is useful, for example, in an application in which you need to cross-fade between two images, as is often seen in Aqua. The following two methods are also useful for this task:

- (void)dissolveToPoint:fraction:
- (void)dissolveToPoint:fromRect:fraction:

You can also use the following two methods to draw an image:

- drawAtPoint:fromRect:operation:fraction:
- drawInRect:fromRect:operation:fraction:

These methods differ from the compositing methods because they consider the rotation and scaling of the destination coordinate system, drawing the image with the appropriate scaling and rotation applied. The fromRect:, operation:, and fraction: parameters behave as compositing methods.

Example 4-9 demonstrates how to create an NSImage and composite it to a point on screen using the NSCompositeCopy operation.

Example 4-9. Using NSImage

```
// Use a named image
NSImage *image = [NSImage imageNamed:@"buttonImage"];
[image compositeToPoint:NSZeroPoint operation:NSCompositeCopy];
```

Drawing into an image

Compositing an image is considerably faster than rendering a Bezier path or drawing text. Many graphics are static, which means that you don't have to necessarily reconstruct and render a path every time a view is redrawn. Applications can take advantage of the capability to make an instance of NSImage a drawing destination (rather than a view). You can draw a path to an image, and then composite this image to the view. The advantage is that the path need only be rendered once, since redrawing the view involves compositing only the image containing the rendered path. Example 4-10 shows how to accomplish this.

Example 4-10. Drawing to an image

```
NSImage *image = [[NSImage alloc] initWithSize:NSMakeSize( 400, 400 )];

// Lock focus of image, make it a destination for drawing
[image lockFocus];
```

Example 4-10. Drawing to an image (continued)

```
// Set background color to white
[[NSColor whiteColor] set];
NSRectFill( NSMakeRect( 0, 0, 400, 400 )));

// Construct and draw path as you would in drawRect:
[self drawMyPath];
[image unlockFocus];

// Now draw in a view by compositing
[image compositeToPoint:NSZeroPoint operation:NSCompositeCopy];
```

NSImageRep

The relationship between NSImage and NSImageRep in the Application Kit is powerful and has important architectural ramifications. NSImage provides a high-level interface to Cocoa's image manipulation capabilities by defining functionality that is independent of the image's data format. This functionality includes drawing and compositing, which was discussed previously, as well as tasks such as loading and saving image data (which may seem to depend on the data's format, but is implemented in a way that hides the details from clients) and setting/getting attributes of the image such as its display size.

A browse through NSImage's methods reveals that many are used to manage image representations. Image representations are instance of subclasses of NSImageRep; they are bridges between the high-level abstraction of NSImage and the image's data-dependent representation. That is, NSImageRep and its subclasses let NSImage work with multiple formats of data, ranging from EPS and PDF formats to the most prevalent bitmapped image data formats.

AppKit provides six subclasses of NSImageRep; they were described in Table 4-1, and are listed again as follows:

- NSPDFImageRep
- NSEPSImageRep
- NSPictImageRep
- NSCachedImageRep
- NSCustomImageRep
- NSBitmapImageRep

A key feature in the NSImage/NSImageRep relationship is that NSImage usually stores and uses multiple instances of NSImageRep. Some image representations, such as NSEPSImageRep or NSPDFImageRep, are well suited for printing, while others are better suited for onscreen display. For example, it might be best for a bitmap image representation to display an image to a full-color screen, while an EPS image representation would be better suited for output to a PostScript printer due to the ability of EPS to reproduce high resolution graphics.

By keeping multiple image representations handy, a single instance of NSImage can adapt to a variety of display situations, including the ability to adapt to various color depths and output resolutions.

NSImageRep provides a base implementation for image representations that lets you determine many image properties, such as the number of bits in each pixel sample, whether or not the image has an alpha (transparency) channel, the size of the image in pixels, and the name of the color space for the image. Equivalent methods set these image representation properties.

With NSImageRep, you can also draw the image to a view as you can in NSImage by using the draw, drawAtPoint:, and drawInRect: in NSImageRep methods. Most importantly, several class methods let you create an image rep instance from various data sources, such as a file, URL, an NSData object, and even the pasteboard.

Two categories of class methods create new image representations. The methods that begin with imageRep... return an image rep object that most appropriately represents the given data. They are:

- imageRepWithContentsOfFile:
- imageRepWithPasteboard:
- imageRepWithContentsOfURL:

Another set of these convenience constructors include:

- imageRepsWithContentsOfFile:
- imageRepsWithPasteboard:
- imageRepsWithContentsOfURL:

Drawing and Imaging

These methods return an array of NSImageRep objects that are initialized with data from the specified source.

Also of note are the set of class methods that include:

- imageRepClassForData:
- imageRepClassForFileType:
- imageRepClassForPasteboardType:

These methods return the class object for the NSImageRep subclass that best represents the given data.

NSImage provides several methods that manage image representations used by the image object. The methods, addRepresentation: and addRepresentations:, are add image representations to an image. The first takes a single NSImageRep, and the second takes an array of NSImageRep instances. You can find the representations managed by an image by invoking the method representations and remove a representation by using removeRepresentation:.

NSBitmapImageRep

Bitmapped graphics are the types of images you will probably use most. The NSBitmapImageRep class recognizes the following image file formats:

- TIFF
- BMP
- JPEG
- PNG
- Raw image data

Like its parent class, NSBitmapImageRep includes methods that initialize an instance from existing data. To create an empty image data buffer from scratch that creates new images, use the method shown in Example 4-11.

Example 4-11. Creating an empty image data buffer

```
- (id)initWithBitmapDataPlanes:(unsigned char **)planes
      pixelsWide:(int)width
      pixelsHigh:(int)height
      bitsPerSample:(int)bps
      samplesPerPixel:(int)spp
      hasAlpha:(BOOL)alpha
      isPlanar:(BOOL)isPlanar
      colorSpaceName:(NSString *)colorSpaceName
      bytesPerRow:(int)rowBytes
      bitsPerPixel:(int)pixelBits
```

 With over 125 characters in the method name, this is the longest public method name in Cocoa.

You can use the method shown in Example 4-11 to initialize a new blank instance of NSBitmapImageRep with the given properties. Then use either bitmapData or getBitmapDataPlanes: (which one you use depends on whether you passed YES or NO as the isPlanar: argument) to access the data buffers where the actual image data is stored, to give you the means to manipulate bitmap images byte-by-byte. The former returns a pointer of type unsigned char *, and the latter takes an unsigned char ** pointer, which is set to the beginning of the planar (2D) image data. Example 4-12 shows how to manipulate an image's data to invert the image's colors.

Example 4-12. Manipulating an image's data on a byte level

```
// srcImageRep is the NSBitmapImageRep of the source image
int n = [srcImageRep bitsPerPixel] / 8;          // Bytes per pixel
int w = [srcImageRep pixelsWide];
int h = [srcImageRep pixelsHigh];
int rowBytes = [srcImageRep bytesPerRow];
int i;

NSImage *destImage = [[NSImage alloc] initWithSize:NSMakeSize(w, h)];
NSBitmapImageRep *destImageRep = [[[NSBitmapImageRep alloc]
      initWithBitmapDataPlanes:NULL
          pixelsWide:w
          pixelsHigh:h
          bitsPerSample:8
          samplesPerPixel:n
          hasAlpha:[srcImageRep hasAlpha]
          isPlanar:NO
          colorSpaceName:[srcImageRep colorSpaceName]
          bytesPerRow:rowBytes
          bitsPerPixel:NULL] autorelease];
```

Example 4-12. Manipulating an image's data on a byte level (continued)

```
unsigned char *srcData = [srcImageRep bitmapData];
unsigned char *destData = [destImageRep bitmapData];

for ( i = 0; i < rowBytes * h; i++ )
    *(destData + i) = 255 - *(srcData + i);

[destImage addRepresentation:destImageRep];
```

This example works by first creating a new instance of NSBitmapImageRep with the properties you want out of the image. Since the properties will be the same as the source image, use several NSBitmapImageRep methods to determine those properties and use them in the initialization of destImageRep. Next, in the for-statement, use C pointer arithmetic to traverse the buffers obtained immediately before the for-loop, and do the math necessary to invert the image. In this case, subtract the value of each source pixel from 255 and store the result as the value of the destination pixel. Finally, finish things off by adding NSBitmapImageRep's destImageRep to NSImage's destImage. This is a common paradigm for working with bitmap image data in which only the algorithms limit you to operating on the image data.

Transformations

NSAffineTransform provides an interface for defining and applying affine transforms to various parts of the graphics system, such as view coordinate systems, individual Bezier paths or NSPoints. An affine transform is a type of mapping between coordinate systems in which a shape's parallel lines are preserved, but not necessarily the length of line segments or the angles between lines. Out-of-the-box, NSAffineTransform is capable of rotating, translating, and scaling.

To create an affine transform, use the transform convenience constructor. The following example shows how you can create an affine transform object and make a rotation transformation:

```
NSAffineTransform * at = [NSAffineTransform transform];
[at rotateByDegrees:77];
```

To transform a Bezier path using this affine transform object, invoke transformBezierPath:

```
NSBezierPath *newPath = [at transformBezierPath:bp];
```

This method takes the Bezier path to transform as a parameter and returns a new Bezier path that is the transformation of the original. Using a method of NSBezierPath, you can transform a path directly without having a new object returned. The method is transformUsingAffineTransform:, and is used in the following way:

```
[bp transformUsingAffineTransform:rat];
```

Here is how you transform an NSPoint structure:

```
at = [NSAffineTransform transform];
[at translateXBy:100 yBy:50];
NSPoint point = NSMakePoint( 0, 0 );
NSPoint newPoint = [at transformPoint:point];
```

To transform an NSSize, do the following:

```
at = [NSAffineTransform transform];
[at scaleXBy:0.5 yBy:1.5];
NSSize size = NSMakeSize( 100, 100 );
NSSize newSize = [at transforSize:size];
```

The beginning of this chapter discussed graphics contexts and how they control drawing destination properties. One of these properties is a global transformation matrix that is the concatenation of all scaling, translation, and rotation applied by windows and views between and including the screen and the current view.

NSAffineTransform implements two methods that let you alter the graphic context's transformation matrix: set and concat. The first, set, lets you replace the current context's transformation matrix. This is usually not a good idea, since the replacement destroys all information about transformations between windows and views. The other, concat, appends the transformation represented by the receiver to the current context's transformation. All drawing operations subsequent to the invocation of either method have the new transformation applied. Be sure to save the current context before using these methods, and restore that context whenever you complete a drawing operation.

5

Text Handling

Cocoa's text system contains a rich set of features such as text input, layout, display, editing, copying and pasting, and font management. It also includes support for advanced typesetting features such as kerning and ligature, multilingual support with Unicode, and sophisticated layout capabilities.

This chapter discusses the primary classes of Cocoa's text handling system and how they relate to one another. Figure 5-1 shows the hierarchy of classes related to the text system.

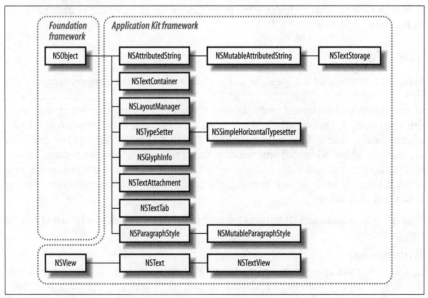

Figure 5-1. Hierarchy of text system class

Text System Architecture

The following four classes make up the core architecture of Cocoa's text handling system:

- NSTextStorage is the backbone data model responsible for storing text.
- NSTextView is responsible for presentation in the view.
- NSLayoutManager and NSTextContainer act as controllers between the model and the view.

The relationship between these core classes is based on the same *Model-View-Controller* (MVC) pattern used throughout the Application Kit (and discussed in Chapter 3). Figure 5-2 shows the division of responsibilities in these four classes using the MVC pattern.

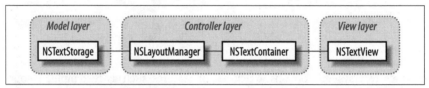

Figure 5-2. How the four core text system classes relate to one another in the MVC pattern

Figure 5-2 shows the relationship between the four classes, but doesn't show the one-to-many relationship that may exist between instances of these classes. Instances of NSTextStorage own and manage one or more NSLayoutManager objects. Similarly, each instance of NSLayoutManager owns one or more NSTextContainer objects, while each text container object is paired with an NSTextView object. The nature of these relationships is what gives Cocoa's text handling system much of its flexibility and power.

NSTextView

NSTextView represents the view, or presentation, layer of the text system; it is the class that facilitates user interaction with the text system. User interaction consists of displaying text onscreen and allowing the user to manipulate what is seen in the text view. NSTextView is a subclass of NSText, which inherits from NSView, which means that text rendering is handled by Quartz. NSTextView provides support for more advanced interactivity features such as drag and drop, rulers, spell checking, cut-and-paste, and speech. It is not only the frontend to the text system, but it is an interface between the text system and almost every relevant Mac OS X technology.

You can create instances of NSTextView within Interface Builder or by using one of two methods:

initWithFrame:
> This method creates the entire network of objects, including the text storage object, layout manager, and text container. When you create a text view within Interface Builder, the entire collection of text system objects is set up in this way.

`initWithFrame:textContainer:`
This method sets the text-view frame and associates the text view with the specified text container. This method is the designated initializer for `NSTextView`.

NSTextStorage

`NSTextStorage` makes up the data storage layer for the text system. `NSTextStorage`'s data is stored as a sequence of Unicode characters, which makes the text system capable of localizing an application in any language. Unicode also contains character sets for mathematics and other technical fields. To see the huge number of characters that Unicode can represent,[*] launch Mac OS X's Character Palette from the Input menu, as shown in Figure 5-3.

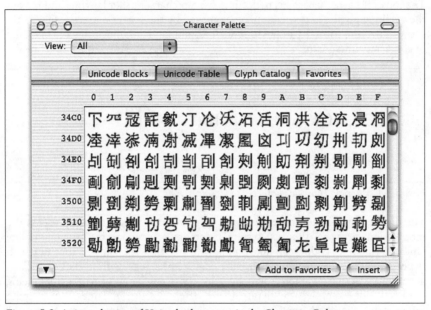

Figure 5-3. A tiny selection of Unicode characters in the Character Palette

`NSTextStorage` is a subclass of `NSMutableAttributedString`. Every character in the text storage, therefore, is associated with a set of attributes that define appearance characteristics such as font and color (a single attributes dictionary will probably be applicable to a range of characters, but it might have a different set of attributes for each character). Cocoa defines a standard set of attributes, which were enumerated in Table 4-2. Additionally, developers may choose to assign their own application specific attributes to text, which could support features such as syntax coloring.

---

[*] You can find out more information about Unicode, including the characters that can be represented, at *http://www.unicode.org*.

Text Handling

As mentioned earlier, NSTextView contains action methods that let controls change the appearance and layout of a selected region of text. These action methods let controls in the user interface (such as a bold-italic-underline button group, or the font and color panels) interact with the contents of the text view. However, using NSTextView's API to effect these attribute changes programmatically is inefficient since those methods are intended for use as user interface actions; it is preferable to use the API provided by NSMutableAttributedString. For example, the method setAttributes:range: takes a dictionary with attribute key-value pairs and a range to which these attributes should be applied. Chapter 2 discusses attributed strings in more detail.

NSLayoutManager

The job of NSLayoutManager is to accurately map characters and glyphs and lay out the resulting glyphs in text containers managed by the layout manager. Figure 5-4 shows a ligature for "Th" in the font Snell Roundhand and illustrates the mapping of characters into glyphs.

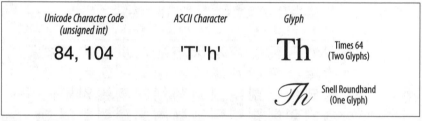

Figure 5-4. Mapping Unicode character codes into glyphs

The distinction between characters and glyphs is important, as it represents the intersection between the text-system's data and view layers. Glyphs, unlike Unicode character codes, can take on many forms, the visual appearance of which depends on the attributes of a particular character such as its font, the other characters around that character, and how ligatures are handled in the font being rendered. For example, the glyph for the letter "T" in the Times font is quite different for the glyph the Zapfino font defines for the same letter. Moreover, multiple characters in a sequence may actually define a single glyph. This is especially true in nonwestern alphabets and in fonts that define ligatures for certain pairs of letters.

 You can find an extreme case of a multi-character glyph in the Zapfino font. Open a TextEdit window, change the active font to Zapfino, and then type the font's name. You'll see multiple glyph substitutions as you type the word, culminating in the use of a single glyph for the entire word—Zapfino's signature.

The flow of information with NSLayoutManager goes in two directions. You just read about the flow from the data model to the view; however, experience shows that information must flow from the view to the data layer whenever you alter the content by typing, making selections, or changing formatting. To facilitate this,

`NSLayoutManager` must be able reconcile the position of selections and the cursor in the glyph stream with character ranges in the storage layer.

The `NSLayoutManager` class has nearly 100 instance methods. Most of these methods are responsible for mapping characters to glyphs, setting attributes of glyphs, and controlling how they are laid out in the view. The API discussed here are the methods that control the text containers that define where text is laid out.

NSTextContainer

`NSTextContainer` defines regions for text display. `NSTextContainer`'s default implementation defines rectangular text regions. However, developers may subclass `NSTextContainer` to provide an implementation that supports irregular layouts. For example, you could subclass `NSTextContainer` to support text layout on circular pages instead of rectangular—strange, but true.

Layout managers store text containers in an indexed array—the order of the text containers in the array is significant, as it determines the order in which the layout manager fills the containers with text. When the first container is filled with text, the layout manager moves to the next, and continues with the remaining containers.

How Text Is Laid Out

When laying out text, `NSLayoutManager` first converts a run of characters into a mapped sequence of glyphs. Once the layout manager knows exactly what needs to be laid out within a text container, it can check with the text container object for guidance in this layout. To do this, `NSLayoutManager` determines the bounding rectangle of the line of glyphs and passes it to the current text container as a proposed layout rectangle. The text container looks at this *proposed rectangle* and compares it to its own *bounding rectangle*. For example, if the proposed rectangle is too long, the text container returns the largest available rectangle for the current line in the text container to the layout manager. Additionally, the text container returns a *remainder rectangle*, which is the difference between the proposed rectangle and the accepted rectangle. `NSLayoutManager` repeats the proposal process with the remainder rectangle, and each successive remainder rectangle until the layout is complete.

When determining how to modify the proposed rectangle, `NSTextContainer` takes into account the direction in which the glyphs are sequenced in a line, and the direction lines are placed relative to their preceding lines. These directions are referred to as the *line sweep direction* and *line movement direction*, respectively. When a text container modifies the proposed rectangle, the text container can shorten the rectangle from the direction of the line sweep, and it is allowed to shift the rectangle in the direction of the line movement. By adhering to these rules, `NSTextContainer` and `NSLayoutManager` can break up a continuous line of glyphs into an arranged set of lines that can be rendered in a view. There is a clear division of responsibility here:

- `NSLayoutManager` is responsible for mapping the characters to glyphs with all the attributes applied.
- `NSTextContainer` is used by the layout manager to break up the glyph line into a series of lines that fit snugly into the region represented by the text container.

The method in NSTextContainer that performs these functions is:

```
lineFragmentRectForProposedRect:sweepDirection:
                movementDirection:remainingRect:
```

The sweepDirection: argument is of type NSLineSweepDirection, and the movementDirection: argument is of type NSLineMovementDirection. NSText-Container returns the remainder rectangle to the sender through the remainingRect: argument, which is a pointer to an NSRect structure. Subclasses override this method to perform custom layout. If the text container object determines that the proposed rectangle cannot fit into the container, then the constant NSZeroRect is returned.

Assembling the Text System

For many applications that work with text, using NSTextView as the frontend interface to the text provides a great deal of functionality. This is by far the easiest way of working with the text system: you only need to drop a text view into your interface using Interface Builder, and you're ready to go.

Using NSTextView's APIs as the sole means of working with the text system does not offer the flexibility that can be achieved by assembling the individual components manually. By starting with an NSTextStorage object and adding layout managers, text containers, and text views, document layouts can have multiple columns and pages, have irregular areas of text, or present the same text in two different layouts.

Before exploring the manually assembly of text components, consider these rules that tell you what you can and cannot do:

- A text storage object may have one or more layout manager objects that it manages.

- Each layout manager instance may manage one or more instances of NSTextContainer.

- Each text container has exactly one text view associated with it.

By varying the structure of the network with respect to the first two rules, you can create the possibilities mentioned earlier.

Several methods in NSTextStorage, NSLayoutManager, and NSTextContainer facilitate assembly and management of the object network.

NSTextStorage
> This class offers the following methods for managing its layout managers:
>
> addLayoutManager:
>> Adds the specified layout manager to the list of layout managers owned by the text storage object
>
> removeLayoutManager:
>> Removes the specified layout manager from the collection of layout managers owned by the text storage object
>
> layoutManagers
>> Returns an NSArray of layout managers currently managed by the text storage object

NSLayoutManager

This class defines the following four methods for managing its collection of NSTextContainers:

addTextContainer:

Adds the specified text container to the end of the list of text containers managed by the layout manager

insertTextContainer:atIndex:

Inserts a text container at the indicated array index into the layout manager's text container array

removeTextContainerAtIndex:

Removes the text container found at the specified index from the layout manager

textContainers

Returns an array of text containers managed by the layout manager

The nature of these methods is differs from those declared by NSTextStorage for managing layout managers. The order of text containers in a layout manager defines the order in which text containers will be filled with text: containers at lower indices will be filled before those at higher indices.

Finally, NSTextContainer associates itself with its partner text view object by using setTextView:. Later, the text view is retrieved with the textView method.

Layout Scenarios

Having control over the layout managers and text containers allows a great deal of flexibility over how a body of text appears onscreen or in print. The possibilities increase when you introduce subclasses of NSTextContainer to the system for defining irregular, or nonrectangular layout regions.

Simple layout

The simplest layout consists of a single view that displays a continuous body of text. This is the layout favored by applications that deal with plain text, such as source code or HTML, as they have little interest in how the text might appear on the printed page. Figure 5-5 shows the object configuration that establishes this "normal" view.

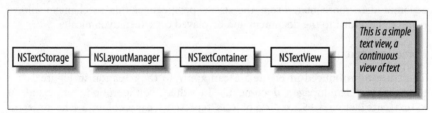

Figure 5-5. Configuration of the core classes for displaying a body of continuous text

Figure 5-5 shows one instance of each of the four core text classes: one text storage object that manages a single layout manager, which in turn manages one text container/text view object pair. The text view exists as a subview of an NSScrollView, which allows the user to scroll through the contents of a larger document that cannot be displayed in one screen. You can build this simply by adding a text view to the application in Interface Builder or by using NSTextView's initWithFrame:.

Paginating text

A more complex text layout, shown in Figure 5-6, is the so-called "page-view," in which the text is displayed onscreen as a series of pages.

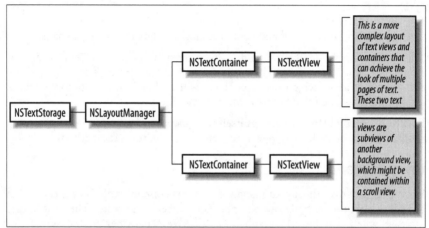

Figure 5-6. A more complex configuration that presents text in a "page-view"

This layout is common in word processors, such as Microsoft Word or TextEdit, where text layout on multiple pages is important. This layout is implemented with a pair of NSTextContainer and NSTextView objects for each page of the document. The layout manager determines the order in which to fill each page according to the order of NSTextContainers in the layout manager's array of text containers. The mechanism NSLayoutManager uses to notify a delegate that the current text container is filled can be a cue to create a new text container/text view pair and accommodate more text. From the user's perspective, this mechanism allows pages to be added to the document and displayed on screen dynamically.

Multicolumn text

The pattern introduced in Figure 5-6 can apply to the situation in Figure 5-7: a multicolumn, multipage document. In this configuration, a pair of NSTextContainer and NSTextView objects represents each column. The order in which columns and pages are filled depends on the order of NSTextContainer objects in the NSLayoutManager instance.

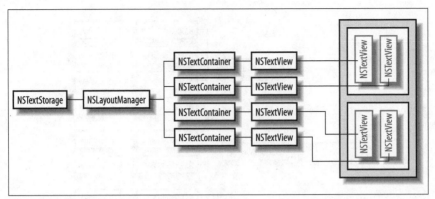

Figure 5-7. Objects involved in creating a multicolumn, multipage document

This gives the illusion of four pages of text, which you might see in a Print Preview window. To create the appearance of a true multicolumn, multipage document (as in Figure 5-7), the column text views are grouped within a regular NSView which represents a page. That page (NSView) may be the same color of the column (the NSTextViews), which means that you only see the text on a solid background. Again, the collection of views that represent a single page is arranged on a gray background view that is a child view of a scroll view.

Multiple simultaneous layouts

As mentioned earlier, NSTextStorage objects are not limited to just one layout manager; they can have many layout managers, if necessary. This scenario lets you lay out the same body of text in multiple styles specified by each layout manager. Figure 5-8 illustrates how multiple layout managers can present text in two layouts simultaneously.

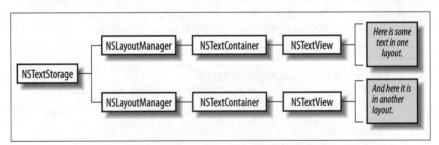

Figure 5-8. Using multiple layout managers to display text data in different layouts

The flexibility achieved through cleverly arranging NSTextViews within NSViews can create many effects, resulting in endless possibilities, as shown in Figure 5-9.

NSLayoutManager Delegation

NSLayoutManager employs a delegate object that may respond to two methods:

*   layoutManager:didCompleteLayoutForTextContainer:atEnd:
*   layoutManagerDidInvalidateLayout:

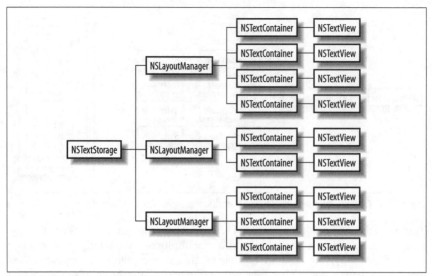

Figure 5-9. You can create complex networks of objects

The first method notifies the delegate when the layout manager finishes formatting the text in the specified text container object. This method can be used to control the appearance of progress indicators in the user interface, or it can enable or disable buttons that control text layout. NSLayoutManager passes nil as the text container argument when it has no more room to lay out its text in the existing text container. This information can be used tohelp you create a new text container/text view pair, which is added to the NSLayoutManager's list of managed text containers.

Example 5-1 demonstrates how to implement layoutManager:didComplete-LayoutForTextContainer:atEnd:. The code in Example 5-1 creates the layout situation shown in Figure 5-6. When a text container fills up with text, the delegate responds by using this method to create additional layout space.

Example 5-1. Creating text containers dynamically

```
- (void)layoutManager:(NSLayoutManager *)lm
        didCompleteLayoutForTextContainer:(NSTextContainer *)tc
        atEnd:(BOOL)flag
{
  if ( !tc ) {
    NSSize tcSize = NSMakeSize( 300, 500 );
    NSTextContainer *cont = [[NSTextContainer alloc]
                               initWithContainerSize: tcSize];
    [[[textStorage layoutManagers]
                       lastObject] addTextContainer: cont];

    NSTextView *tv = [[NSTextView alloc]
                        initWithFrame:[self frameForNewTextView];
                        textContainer:cont];
    [canvas addSubview:tv];
  }
}
```

The delegate method in Example 5-1 is invoked every time the current text container fills up. However, your implementation will work only when the text container passed to you in the argument list is nil, which indicates that the layout manager has filled its current text container. This method deals with a filled text container by creating a new one and adding it to the list of text containers managed by the layout manager. This is accomplished with the NSTextContainer initializer, initWithContainerSize:.

The textStorage variable is an instance variable of the class in which this method is implemented. This instance variable is assigned to the text storage object for the application. To add the new text container, cont, to the list of text containers managed by the layout manager, obtain the layout manager with the layoutManagers method. Since this method returns an NSArray of layout managers, even if there is just one, a lastObject method is sent to get an instance of NSLayoutManager, which receives an addTextContainer: message with cont as the argument.

To create a text view to pair with the text container, use the designate initializer of NSTextView. This initializer requires a frame for the text view, as well as the text container it needs to associate with the text view. Example 5-1 relies on another hypothetical method, frameForNewTextView, to return a frame rect that places the new text view below the previous one. The text view is then added as a subview of canvas. In this example, canvas is best represented by the gray region of Figure 5-7; individual text views are pages displayed in a series on this background view.

6

Networking

Networking is a critical component of many applications today. Networking APIs can take many forms, including TCP/IP communications with the sockets library or interprocess communications using Cocoa's distributed objects system. Mac OS X's Darwin layer includes all standard Unix networking technologies and APIs, which are fully accessible from any Cocoa application. In addition to being able to access the Unix APIs, the Foundation framework implements several classes that give applications a higher-level interface for working with networking technologies. This chapter summarizes Foundation's networking classes, shown in Figure 6-1.

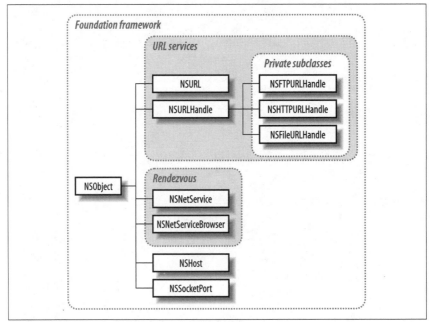

Figure 6-1. Hierarchy of networking-related classes in the Foundation framework

Hosts

NSHost provides services that find host names from addresses and addresses from host names. NSHost relies on the network services available to the operating system, such as LDAP, NetInfo, or the Domain Name Service (DNS). Example 6-1 shows how to use NSHost.

Example 6-1. Using NSHost

```
// Get the NSHost object for the current host
NSHost *host = [NSHost currentHost];

// Get the name of a host
NSString *name = [host name];

// Get the address of a host; returns "xxx.xxx.xxx.xxx" string
NSString *addr = [host address];

// Other ways to create a host object
NSHost *host = [NSHost hostWithAddress:@"www.oreilly.com"];
NSHost *host = [NSHost hostWithName:@"209.204.146.22"];

// If a host has multiple names or address, use the following
NSArray *names = [host names];
NSArray *addrs = [host addresses];
```

URL Resources

Foundation has two classes that facilitate working with URLs: NSURL and NSURLHandle. NSURL represents a Uniform Resource Locator (URL). This class lets applications create, manipulate, and pick apart URLs. NSURLHandle accesses data and resources specified by an instance of NSURL. This class can access resources provided by HTTP, FTP,* and file services.

Working with URLs

NSURL represents a URL—the human-readable host names and paths that various network clients use to locate resources on the local filesystem or over the Internet. NSURL provides a number of methods and initializers that let you create instances in many different ways, as shown in Example 6-2.

 Core Foundation has a type, CFURL, that is "toll-free bridged" to NSURL. As such, the two types can be used interchangeably. CFURL and NSURL are essentially equivalent: NSURL objects can be used in Core Foundation calls that ask for a CFURL, and vice versa. NSURL is just one of several Foundation classes that have a bridged Core Foundation equivalent.

---

* FTP support in NSURLHandle was added in Mac OS X 10.2 and is not available in earlier versions of Mac OS X.

Example 6-2. Creating and initializing instances of NSURL

```
// From a string...
NSURL *url = [NSURL URLWithString:@"http//www.macdevcenter.com"];
url = [[NSURL alloc]
        initWithString: :@"http//www.macdevcenter.com"];

// From a file path...
url = [NSURL fileURLWithPath:@"/Users/mike/Pictures/pic.tiff"];
url = [[NSURL alloc]
    initFileURLWithPath: :@"/Users/mike/Pictures/pic.tiff"];

// Access a URL with scheme, host, and path
url = [[NSURL alloc] initWithScheme:@" FTP" host:@"localhost"
    path:@"/Some/Path"];
```

In Example 6-2, the last initializer, initWithScheme:host:path:, specifies the scheme used by the host the URL points to. In this case, an FTP address was specified; however, the backend to NSURL's data transfer functionality, NSURLHandle, supports HTTP and file URL schemes as well.

NSURL includes an assortment of methods that let you pick apart URLs to extract pieces of information from them, such as the URL path, the host name, the base URL, and the query string. Example 6-3 illustrates several NSURL methods.

Example 6-3. NSURL methods

```
NSURL *url = [NSURL URLWithString:@"http//www.google.com/⏎
search?hl=en&ie=ISO-8859-1&q=NSURL&btnG=Google+Search"];

NSString *s;
s = [url host];             // Returns "www.google.com"
s = [url scheme];           // Returns "HTTP"
s = [url path];             // Returns "/search"

// Returns "//www.google.com/search?hl=en&ie=ISO-8859-1&q=NSURL&btnG=Google+Search"
s = [url resourceSpecifier];

// Returns "hl=en&ie=ISO-8859-1&q=NSURL&btnG=Google+Search"
s = [url query];
```

While NSURLHandle implements data transfer functionality, NSURL provides a handful of convenience methods that can transfer data without having to instantiate NSURLHandle. These methods, whose usage is shown in Example 6-4, include:

- resourceDataUsingCache:
- setResourceData:
- loadResourceDataNotifyingClient:usingCache:

Example 6-4. Using NSURL data access methods

```
// Create an instance of NSURL from an NSString
NSString *urlStr = @"http//host_address/image.jpg";
NSURL *url = [NSURL URLWithString:urlStr];

// Download data from the resource located by a URL
NSData *data = [url resourceDataUsingCache:NO];
NSImage *img = [[NSImage alloc] initWithData:data];

// Write data to a resource located by a URL
NSData *data = [img TIFFRepresentation];
[url setResourceData:data];
```

If YES is passed to the resourceDataUsingCache: method, NSURL attempts to load the resource from the cache if it was loaded previously. If the resource was not loaded, then the host will load it. Passing NO to this method tells NSURL to always fetch the data from the host, even if it has done so already.

> Many Cocoa classes that work with files have methods that let clients interact with files through standard file paths or URLs. For example, you could have replaced the middle two lines of code in Example 6-4 with NSImage's initializer initWithContentsOfURL:, supplying url as the argument.

URL Handles

NSURLHandle provides an interface for uploading and downloading data to and from a resource specified by an instance of NSURL. NSURLHandle actually offloads much of this work to subclasses that implement NSURLHandle's interface to work with various schemes. NSURLHandle's subclasses include NSFileURLHandle, NSFTPURLHandle, and NSHTTPURLHandle. These three subclasses are private—all interaction with them is through NSURLHandle's public interface, which creates the proper subclass based on the provided NSURL object's scheme. For most purposes, the interface provided by NSURL should be sufficient for resource access. NSURLHandle is most useful when you need to create a new subclass to support a URL scheme other than file, FTP, or HTTP.

Managing subclasses

NSURLHandle's subclasses are responsible for implementing the resource acquisition mechanics needed by a URL scheme. When created, that subclass needs to be registered with NSURLHandle using the class method registerURLHandleClass:. The registration process makes NSURLHandle aware of a subclass's availability to handle a new URL scheme.

To determine whether NSURLHandle handles a particular URL scheme, use the class method canInitWithURL:. Additionally, you can retrieve the actual class object used by NSURLHandle for a particular URL scheme by invoking the class method URLHandleClassForURL:.

Rendezvous Network Services

Rendezvous is Apple's implementation of *zero-configuration networking* (Zeroconf). Introduced with the Jaguar release of Mac OS X, Rendezvous brings AppleTalk's ease of use to standard IP networking. This gives the user the ability to browse for printing, file sharing, or any other IP-based services much as was done with the Chooser in earlier versions of the Mac OS.

 For more information on Rendezvous networking, see Apple's Rendezvous developer page at *http://developer.apple.com/macosx/ rendezvous/*, or visit the Zeroconf working group web site at *http:// www.zeroconf.org*.

Foundation provides access to Rendezvous' low-level APIs through the classes NSNetService and NSNetServiceBrowser. An application registers, or *publishes*, a service on the network by using NSNetService. The class NSNetServiceBrowser searches for and discovers services that are registered elsewhere. This section provides an overview of how these classes fit into an application.

NSNetService

NSNetService represents a network service that applications either publish or use as a client. A *network service* can be FTP, Telnet, SSH, HTTP, or something of your own design.

The Picture Sharing application included with the Foundation example code found in the Developer Tools installation (*/Developer/Examples/Foundation/ PictureSharing*) is an example of a custom Rendezvous service. This example has two applications: a server application that publishes a picture sharing service and a client application that browses for picture sharing services.

To set up NSNetService, you must do the following:

1. Configure a listening server socket that clients will connect to.
2. Initialize an NSNetService object with the service domain, type, name and port.
3. Assign a delegate object to this instance.
4. Handle any messages received by the delegate.

Before a service can be published, you must first create a network socket to which clients connect to access the service. While the Net Services API (which collectively refers to NSNetService and NSNetServiceBrowser) has little to do with data transfer between hosts, it has everything to do with advertising a service's existence on a local network. On Mac OS X, several APIs can create a socket: NSSocketPort provides an Objective-C API for sockets, CoreFoundation provides the CFSocket API, and Darwin has the BSD Sockets API. Since this book focuses on how to accomplish tasks with Cocoa, a discussion of the use of NSSocketPort is relevant and will be discussed later, while the Unix and CoreFoundation APIs are beyond the scope of this book.

Initializing NSNetService for publication

NSNetService has two initializers:

- `initWithDomain:type:name:port:`
- `initWithDomain:`

NSNetService's *publication-appropriate* initializer is `initWithDomain:type:name:port:`. The first argument to this method is the domain in which the service is registered. As of Mac OS X 10.2, only the local registration domain, *.local.*, is supported. Since the Zeroconf working group is still hammering out the details of zero-configuration networking, the local domain may not always be *.local.* As such, passing an empty string to `initWithDomain:` is preferable to passing *.local.* as the domain. Doing so tells NSNetService to register the services under the default domain.

The `type:` argument specifies the service type and transport protocol. This string takes the form *_servicetype._tcp.*, where *_servicetype* can be any standard service such as HTTP, FTP, or Telnet, or it may be an arbitrary service type specific to your application, such as *_myservice*.

The *Internet Assigned Numbers Authority* maintains a catalog of service names and a list of ports where applications can find these services. You can find this catalog at *http://www.iana.org/assignments/port-numbers*. The */etc/services* file contains a similar catalog of service names and port numbers.

The third argument, `name:`, is the human-readable name for the service displayed in service browser lists. It can be any UTF8 string you like. Finally, `port:` is the port number to which the service socket is bound. To publish a service, invoke NSNetService's `publish` method. To remove a service from the network, send a `stop` message to the service instance. Example 6-5 shows how an application can create and publish a service.

Example 6-5. Creating and publishing a network service

```
// Socket used for listening for incoming connections bound to port 631
NSSocketPort *s = [[NSSocketPort alloc] initWithTCPPort:631];

NSNetService *serv = [[NSNetService alloc] initWithDomain:@""
                type:@"_ipp._tcp"
                name:@"R&D Printer"
                port:631];

[serv setDelegate:delegateObject];
[serv publish];

// Remove the service from the network
[serv stop];
```

NSNetService tells interested parties that the designated host has a socket listening for connections on the specified port. NSNetService multicasts the address and port information for an open socket to the network. The response message from the Rendezvous host contains additional information that identifies the service name and type. Whether or not a socket is listening on that port is another question; NSNetService puts us on the honor system to make sure everything is configured properly.

The Net Services API uses delegation to drive an application's user interface and for error handling. Setting the delegate of an instance of NSNetService or NSNetServiceBrowser is essential for using these classes effectively.

NSNetService delegate methods

NSNetService declares that the delegates should implement the following methods:

netServiceWillPublish:
> Notifies the delegate that the service is about to be published. The NSNetService that invoked this method is passed in the argument.

netService:didNotPublish:
> Notifies the delegate of an error that occurred while attempting to publish the service. The netService: argument is the NSNetService object that produced the error, and the didNotPublish: argument is an error dictionary containing information about the error. The dictionary contains objects for the keys NSNetServiceErrorCode and NSNetServiceErrorDomain.

netServiceWillResolve:
> Invoked in the delegate when the network is ready to resolve the service. This method is invoked only after sending a resolve message to the service object. The argument is the NSNetService that received the resolve message.

netService:didResolve:
> Notifies the delegate that the service was successfully resolved and is now ready to use. At this point, the address used to connect to the service has been verified and is ready to use.

netService:didNotResolve:
> If an error occurs while attempting to resolve a service, the delegate is notified via this method. The netService: argument is the service instance that produced the error, and the didNotResolve: argument contains the error dictionary. The dictionary keys NSNetServiceErrorCode and NSNetServiceErrorDomain provide information about the error.

netServiceDidStop:
> This method is invoked in the delegate when invoking the stop method in an NSNetService that previously received a publish or resolve message.

Instances of NSNetService either publish or resolve a service, and thus far this chapter has only shown how to publish a service. Services meant for publication can't be used for resolution, and those meant for resolution can't be used for publication.

The delegate methods of NSNetService reflect this division. The three methods netServiceWillResolve:, netService:didResolve:, and netService:didNotResolve: notify the delegate of the status of a service resolution request (in response to a resolve message). The remaining methods, netServiceWillPublish:, netService: didNotPublish:, and netServiceDidStop:, notify the delegate of a publish operation's status. Services meant for publication do not invoke resolution-specific delegate methods, and those services meant for resolution won't ever invoke publication-specific delegate methods.

Implementing these delegate methods is not necessary for a functioning instance of NSNetService. Net services can be published and resolved without having been assigned a delegate; however, without a delegate, there is no way of knowing a particular net service object's status.

Errors

NSNetService declares the delegate methods netService:didNotPublish: and netService:didNotResolve:. These methods notify the delegate of an error that may have occurred in a publish or resolve operation. Each method passes the net service object invoking the methods in the first argument, and a dictionary describing the nature of the error in the second argument.

The error dictionary contains two keys: NSNetServicesErrorDomain and NSNetServicesErrorCode. The first key is for an object that shows where the error occurred: in the lower-level networking layer or in the NSNetService implementation. The NSNetServicesErrorCode key reflects the nature of the error by returning an NSNumber, which corresponds to one of the constants described in Table 6-1.

Table 6-1. Net services error codes

Error code	Description
NSNetServicesUnknownError	An unknown error occurred.
NSNetServicesCollisionError	This error results when a service tries to register a service under a name that is already taken.
NSNetServicesNotFoundError	The service (attempting to be resolved) could not be found on the network.
NSNetServicesActivityInProgress	The net service is busy and cannot process the request.
NSNetServicesBadArgumentError	An invalid argument was used when initializing the NSNetService instance.
NSNetServicesCancelledError	The client cancelled the action.
NSNetServicesInvalidError	The net service was configured improperly.

NSNetServiceBrowser

The NSNetServiceBrowser class is an implementation of Rendezvous' service discovery protocol. This class depends heavily on a delegate, which is the only means of alerting an application to the discovery of a service. NSNetServiceBrowser searches for domains as well as services and uses the same mechanisms in the delegate object to report discovered domains. The methods that a delegate of NSNetServiceBrowser may implement are as follows:

netServiceBrowser:didFindDomain:moreComing:
    Notifies the delegate that a domain was discovered.

netServiceBrowser:didRemoveDomain:moreComing:
    Notifies the delegate when a previously discovered domain becomes unavailable.

`netServiceBrowser:didFindService:moreComing:`
> Notifies the delegate that a service was discovered.

`netServiceBrowser:didRemoveService:moreComing:`
> Notifies the delegate objects that a previously discovered service was removed from the network while searching.

`netServiceBrowser:didNotSearch:`
> If an error occurs, this method notifies the delegate. The first argument is the service browser instance reporting the error, and the second argument is the error dictionary that contains information about the nature of the error.

`netServiceBrowserWillSearch:`
> Notifies the delegate that the network is ready and the search is about to commence. The method is passed the service browser instance that is about to begin searching.

`netServiceBrowserDidStopSearch:`
> Notifies the delegate that a search ended as a result of a stop message to the service browser object. It can perform housekeeping tasks when the search completes.

Several of the delegate methods for `NSNetServiceBrowser` listed here include the `moreComing:` argument. This argument contains a `BOOL` value indicating whether or not more services are to be reported (`NSNetServiceBrowser` may discover services faster than they can be reported). The utility of this flag has to do with how the information is reported through the user interface. The idea is that the user interface should be updated with all available information in one fell swoop. Rather than adding a service name to the browser list every time one is discovered, the delegate method should update the interface only if `moreComing:` reports back with `NO`, saying that there are no further services to report at the time.

Searching for domains

`NSNetServiceBrowser` searches for domains and for services. The previous section discussed the service discovery aspect of `NSNetServiceBrowser`. When searching for domains, you can look for either all domains using the `searchForAllDomains` method or only for those for which you have registration authority with the `searchForRegistrationDomains` method. Example 6-6 shows how to set up a class to search for domains using these methods.

Example 6-6. Searching for domains using NSNetServiceBrowser

```
// Assume the following instance method exists and has been initialized.
NSMutableArray *domains;

- (void)beginDomainSearch
{
  // Assume browser is an instance variable
  browser = [[NSNetServiceBrowser alloc] init];
  [browser searchForAllDomains];

  // Or use [browser searchForRegistrationDomains];
}
```

Example 6-6. Searching for domains using NSNetServiceBrowser (continued)

```
- (void)netServiceBrowser:(NSNetServiceBrowser *)browser
      didFindDomain:(NSString *)domainString
        moreComing:(BOOL)moreComing
{
  [domains addObject:domainString];

  if ( moreComing == NO )
    [self updateUI];
}

- (void)netServiceBrowser:(NSNetServiceBrowser *) browser
     didRemoveDomain:(NSString *)domainString
        moreComing:(BOOL)moreComing
{
  [domains removeObject:domainString];

  if ( moreComing == NO )
    [self updateUI];
}
```

In Example 6-6, note the "Or" comment in the method beginDomainSearch. The comment appears to be relatively innocuous, but it brings up an important point about the capabilities of NSNetServiceBrowser. NSNetServiceBrowser may perform only one search at a time, and this holds true for domain and service searches. If you want to perform multiple searches, either wait for a search to stop and restart your desired search or create multiple instances of NSNetServiceBrowser.

Once the list of domains is obtained, use these strings to specify the domain you would like to search in for services. You also have the option of passing an empty string to indicate that you would like to search in the default domain, as was true when initializing an instance of NSNetService.

Sockets

It is possible to interact with Darwin's BSD sockets API in all of Mac OS X's C-based application environments, including Cocoa. This API is declared primarily in the headers *sys/socket.h* and *netinet/in.h*, and is discussed at length in *Unix Network Programming*, by W. Richard Stevens (Prentice Hall, 1998). Core Foundation also provides an API to sockets with CFSocket. However, discussion of CFSocket is beyond the scope this book. Instead, the next section provides shows how to interact with sockets using the Foundation class NSSocketPort.

In earlier versions of Mac OS X (prior to Mac OS X 10.2), NSSocketPort was used exclusively as part of Cocoa's distributed objects architecture. NSSocketPort created sockets-based distributed objects connections across a network. However, now NSSocketPort provides a convenient alternative to the C sockets API for raw messaging.

NSSocketPort makes it possible to create sockets configured either as local listening sockets (*server sockets*) or sockets connected to a remote host (*client sockets*). The simplest way to initialize a listening socket port object is using the method

Networking

initWithTCPPort:. This method takes a port number as an argument and returns an NSSocketPort object representing a TCP/IP streaming socket. If 0 is passed as the port number, then the operating system selects a port to bind to the socket.

Initialize an NSSocketPort to connect to a remote socket with the method initWithRemoteTCPPort:host:. This method takes as arguments the port number you connect to on the host specified in the second argument. A connection to the remote host is not actually established until data is sent. The *hostname* may be either a domain-name-like hostname, such as www.oreilly.com, or an IPv4-style address, such as 208.201.239.36.

Several of NSSocketPort's methods provide information about the socket, including:

address
> This method returns an NSData object that contains the socket's sockaddr structure, which provides information about the sockets address.

protocol
> This method returns an int specifying the protocol used by the receiver, and protocolFamily returns an int specifying the protocol family used by the receiver.

socketType
> This method returns an int that identifies the receiver's socket type.

The values returned by these methods are the same as the values of the constants used in the BSD sockets API. If you're familiar with socket programming on a Unix system, you should feel right at home with NSSocketPort.

The socket method returns a native OS socket file descriptor, which can then be used with the standard C functions read and write, or to initialize an NSFileHandle. Example 6-7 demonstrates how to use NSSocketPort to create sockets.

Example 6-7. Making sockets with NSSocketPort

```
// Local TCP/IP socket of type SOCK_STREAM listening on port 52279
NSSocketPort *sock= [[NSSocketPort alloc] initWithTCPPort:52279];

// Socket to connect to remote host
sock = [[NSSocketPort alloc]
        initRemoteWithTCPPort:52279 host:@"10.0.1.3"];
```

NSFileHandle

NSFileHandle provides methods that let you read and write data from a file or communication channel asynchronously in the background. Chapter 2 discussed file access with NSFileHandle. This section describes NSFileHandle's asynchronous communications features and how they apply to networking.

You can obtain a socket file descriptor from an instance of NSSocketPort by sending a socket message to the socket port object. With the socket descriptor, you are able to initialize an instance of NSFileHandle with the method initWithFileDescriptor:. The initWithFileDescriptor:closeOnDealloc: method is an extension of this method that specifies whether or not the file descriptor will close when the file handle object is deallocated. By default, the file handle object does not close the file descriptor and ownership of that descriptor remains with the object that created the file handle. To determine an NSFileHandle instance's file descriptor, invoke the method fileDescriptor.

NSFileHandle provides the following three methods for performing asynchronous background communication:

acceptConnectionInBackgroundAndNotify

This method is valid only for NSFileHandle instances initialized with a socket file descriptor (of type SOCK_STREAM), and causes the socket represented by the file handle to listen for new connections. This method returns immediately while a background thread accepts client connections over the socket. Observers are notified of new connections by registering for the notification NSFileHandleAcceptedConnectionNotification. The notification's userInfo dictionary contains a new socket file handle connected to the client that initiated the connection, which frees the listening socket to accept additional connections. You can obtain the socket from the userInfo dictionary through the key NSFileHandleNotificationFileHandleItem.

readInBackgroundAndNotify

This method begins an asynchronous read operation on a socket in the background by invoking the method availableData. This method is generally invoked in the file handle object that represents the socket connected to the client that is obtained from the NSFileHandleAcceptedConnectionNotification userInfo dictionary. When data is read, the connected socket file handle posts an NSFileHandleReadCompletionNotification, whose userInfo dictionary contains the data that was read. You can obtain this NSData object by using the NSFileHandleNotificationDataItem key.

readToEndOfFileInBackgroundAndNotify

This method behaves similarly to readInBackgroundAndNotify, except the NSFileHandle method readToEndOfFile is invoked. When all data has finished being read, the file handle posts an NSFileHandleReadToEndOfFile-CompletionNotification notification. You can obtain the read data from the userInfo dictionary by using the NSFileHandleNotificationDataItem key.

NSFileHandle declares three additional methods that include a ForModes: argument:

- acceptConnectionInBackgroundAndNotifyForModes:
- readInBackgroundAndNotifyForModes:
- readToEndOfFileInBackgroundAndNotifyForModes:

The ForModes: argument specifies which run loop modes each method's notification may be posted in. This specification provides finer control over operation of the notification process.

Example 6-8 shows how to use NSFileHandle to implement a simple server infrastructure.

Example 6-8. Using NSFileHandle for server socket communication

```objc
- (void)startServer
{
  NSSocketPort *sockPort;
  sockPort = [[NSSocketPort alloc] initWithTCPPort:12345];
  int socketFD = [sockPort socket];

  NSFileHandle *listeningSocket;
listeningSocket = [[NSFileHandle alloc]
                 initWithFileDescriptor:socketFD];

  NSNotificationCenter *nc;
  nc = [NSNotificationCenter defaultNotificationCenter];
  [nc addObserver:self
         selector:@selector(spawnChildConnection:)
             name:NSFileHandleConnectionAcceptedNotification
           object:listeningSocket];

  [listeningSocket acceptConnectionInBackgroundAndNotify];
}

  /*
   * This method is invoked in response to
   * NSFileHandleConnectionAcceptedNotification
   */
- (void)spawnChildConnection:(NSNotification *)note
{
NSFileHandle *connectedSocket = [[note userInfo]
     objectForKey:NSFileHandleNotificationFileHandleItem];

  NSNotificationCenter *nc;
  nc = [NSNotificationCenter defaultNotificationCenter];

  [nc addObserver:self
      selector:@selector(processClientData:)
          name:NSFileHandleReadCompletionNotification
        object:connectedSocket];

  // Send a message to the client, acknowledging that the connection was accepted
  [connectedSocket writeData:ackData];

  [connectedSocket readInBackgroundAndNotify];
}

  /*
   * This method is invoked in response to
   * NSFileHandleReadCompletionNotification
   */
- (void)processClientData:(NSNotification *)note
{
  NSData *data = [[note userInfo]
     objectForKey:NSFileHandleNotificationDataItem];
```

```
  // Do something here with your data

  // Tell file handle to continue waiting for data
  [[note object] readInBackgroundAndNotify];
}
```

Example 6-9 shows a client infrastructure using NSFileHandle.

Example 6-9. Using NSFileHandle on the client side

```
- (void)startClient
{
  NSSocketPort *sockPort;
  sockPort = [[NSSocketPort alloc]
      initRemoteWithTCPPort:12345 host:@"10.0.1.3"];
  int sockFD = [sockPort socket];

  NSFileHandle *clientSocket;
  clientSocket = [[NSFileHandle alloc]
      initWithFileDescriptor:sockFD];

  NSNotificationCenter *nc;
  nc = [NSNotificationCenter defaultNotificationCenter];
  [nc addObserver:self
        selector:@selector(processServerData:)
            name: NSFileHandleReadCompletionNotification
          object: clientSocket];

  [clientSocket writeData:dataToWrite];
  [clientSocket readInBackgroundAndNotify];
}

  /*
   * This method is invoked in response to
   * NSFileHandleReadCompletionNotification
   */
- (void) processServerData:(NSNotification *)note
{
  NSData *data = [[note userInfo]
      objectForKey:NSFileHandleNotificationDataItem];

  // Do something here with your data

  // Tell file handle to continue waiting for data
  [[note object] readInBackgroundAndNotify];
}
```

7

Interapplication Communication

Several of Cocoa's classes provide support for interapplication and interthread communication. The Foundation class NSPipe provides an interface to Unix pipes, a long-time staple of Unix interprocess communication (IPC). The Foundation framework also implements a distributed notification system whereby notifications (discussed in Chapter 2) are sent between applications. The NSDistributedNotificationCenter class registers observers with the distributed notification system.

Finally, Cocoa provides a means for high-level IPC, known as distributed objects, that permits object sharing across process boundaries, even on different computers. Figure 7-1 shows the classes involved in interprocess communication.

NSPipe

Instances of NSPipe represent a one-way channel for communication between two tasks. While one task pours data into one end of the pipe, another process reads that data out. You can create a pipe in two ways: with the convenience constructor pipe or with alloc and init. Every pipe has a read and a write end that objects connect to by retrieving NSFileHandle instances using the methods fileHandleForReading and fileHandleForWriting.

NSPipe is also *buffered*, which means that it can store data poured into the write end of the pipe up to a maximum amount that is defined by the underlying operating system. Example 7-1 shows you how to create a pipe by using NSPipe and NSTask.

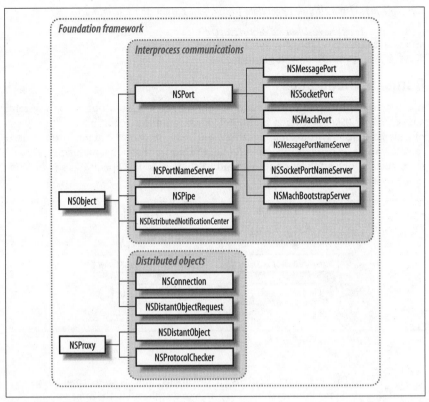

Figure 7-1. IPC classes

Example 7-1. Using NSPipe to get data from an NSTask instance

```
// Instantiate and initialize a new task
NSTask *task = [[NSTask alloc] init];

// Create a pipe to communicate with the task
NSPipe *pipe = [[NSPipe alloc] init];

// Get a file handle to read from the pipe
NSFileHandle *readEnd = [pipe fileHandleForReading];

// Set the path to launch the task at
[task setLaunchPath:@"/bin/ls"];

// Set the arguments; ls takes the directory to list
[task setArguments:[NSArray arrayWithObject:@"/"]];

// Connect the pipe to the task's stdout
[task setStandardOutput:pipe];

// Launch the task
[task launch];
```

Example 7-1. Using NSPipe to get data from an NSTask instance (continued)

```
// Once it's launched we can read data from the pipe
NSData *stdOutData = [readEnd availableData];
NSLog(@"%s", [stdOutData bytes]);
```

Distributed Notifications

As noted in Chapter 2, the Foundation framework's notification system, supported by NSNotification and NSNotificationCenter, coordinates the actions of isolated objects within an application. NSDistributedNotificationCenter is used to receive and dispatch notifications sent between applications, making it possible for objects in one application to respond to changes to the operating environment made by another (see Figure 7-2).

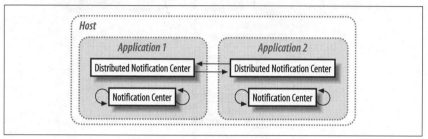

Figure 7-2. Distributed notification centers and notification centers

 Distributed notifications are distributed only as far as applications on the local machine. They are not distributed in the same sense as *distributed objects*, for which communications can occur across a network.

NSDistributedNotificationCenter is a subclass of NSNotificationCenter, and its APIs are almost identical: both require observers to register for notifications, have a default center that is obtained with the defaultCenter class method, and use instances of NSNotification as the vehicle for communication.

Distributed notifications may be posted with standard NSNotificationCenter methods invoked in the distributed notification center:

- postNotificationName:object:
- postNotificationName:object:userInfo:

NSDistributedNotificationCenter provides an additional method: postNotification-Name:object:userInfo:deliverImmediately:

Posting with deliverImmediately set to NO permits normal suspension behavior (described later) of observers. If set to YES, the notification is delivered immediately to all observers, regardless of their suspension behavior or suspension state.

When considering the arguments to these methods, remember the two following points: First, since the "object" is passed to another process, which does not share the same address space, distributed notification filtering is based on an object's string value. Second, the userInfo dictionary is serialized as a property list, so it can be passed to another task (where it is deserialized back into a dictionary). This serialization imposes the restriction that you can only place objects that conform to the NSCoding protocol in the dictionary.

Example 7-2 shows how to set up a distributed notification.

Example 7-2. Using distributed notifications

```
/*
 * In one application we would register with the default
 * distributed notification center...
 */
- (void)registerForNotes
{
    NSDistributedNotificationCenter *dnc;
    dnc = [NSDistributedNotificationCenter defaultCenter];

    [dnc addObserver:self
         selector:@selector(handleDistributedNote:)
         name:@"CocoaNutDistributedNote"
         object:nil];
}

- (void)handleDistributedNote:(NSNotification *)note
{
    NSLog( @"Received Distributed Notification!" );
}

/*
 * ...and another application might post the notification
 */
- (void)postNotes
{
    NSDistributedNotificationCenter *dnc;
    dnc = [NSDistributedNotificationCenter defaultCenter];
    [dnc postNotificationName:@"CocoaNutDistributedNote"
         object:nil];
}
```

Suspending delivery

Distributed notification centers can suspend notification delivery. This is done automatically by NSApplication when an application is not active. To suspend or resume notification delivery manually, use the method setSuspended:, passing YES or NO as appropriate. To inquire into the suspension state of a distributed notification center, use the suspended method.

Suspending a distributed notification center only suspends delivery of notifications by the distributed notification center, not the reception of distributed notifications. In addition to NSNotificationCenter's addObserver:selector: name:object:, the NSDistributedNotificationCenter method addObserver: selector:name:object:suspensionBehavior: can add observers to a distributed notification center. This lets you specify how notifications that would otherwise be sent to the observer should be handled when delivery is suspended.

Interapplication
Communication

`NSDistributedNotificationCenter` has four constants, which are used to specify suspension behaviors:

`NSNotificationSuspensionBehaviorDrop`
> Notifications to observers with this suspension behavior are dropped without further consideration when notification delivery is suspended; it would be as if the notification were never received by the application.

`NSNotificationSuspensionBehaviorCoalesce`
> This suspension behavior causes multiple, identical notifications destined for the observer during suspension to be delivered as a single notification when suspension is lifted.

`NSNotificationSuspensionBehaviorHold`
> Any notification received during delivery suspension is held and delivered to the observer when delivery suspension is removed.

`NSNotificationSuspensionBehaviorDeliverImmediately`
> This behavior causes notifications to the observer to be delivered regardless of the suspension state.

When `YES` is passed to the `postNotificationName:object:userInfo:deliverImmediately:` method, the notification is delivered to all observers regardless of the suspension state of the respective distributed notification centers. Here notification posters have the power to override suspension, whereas observers can override suspension by using the last suspended behavior in the previous list.

Distributed Objects

Cocoa's distributed objects (DO) architecture provides a very high-level interface to interprocess communication. It also lets objects in one application transparently send messages to an object in another application, whether it is on the same or a different computer. Instances of `NSDistantObject` represent objects in a remote application. `NSDistantObject` is a subclass of `NSProxy` (the only other root class in Cocoa besides `NSObject`). `NSDistantObject` relies on the underlying architecture to forward messages and receive return values or exceptions.

DO architecture

Several Foundation classes participate in the distributed objects system. The primary interface for distributed objects, however, is through the class `NSConnection`, which vends objects on the server-side and connects to vended objects on the client-side. Each thread has a shared `NSConnection` object that is obtained through the class method `defaultConnection`.

`NSConnection` relies on several classes to provide support for distributed objects. The lowest-level communication in distributed objects occurs between a pair of `NSPort` objects. `NSPort` is an abstract class that provides an interface for raw messaging. Foundation implements three concrete subclasses of `NSPort`: `NSMachPort`, `NSMessagePort`, and `NSSocketPort`. These subclasses each implement the `NSPort` interface using a different technology. `NSSocketPort`, for example, supports port communications with BSD sockets.

NSConnection objects rely on port name registration services to contact one another and distribute objects. NSPortNameServer provides the interface to port name registration services. Foundation implements a subclass of NSPortNameServer for each of the three types of ports: NSMachBootstrapServer, NSMessagePortNameServer, and NSSocketPortNameServer.

Figure 7-3 shows how distributed object system classes interact.

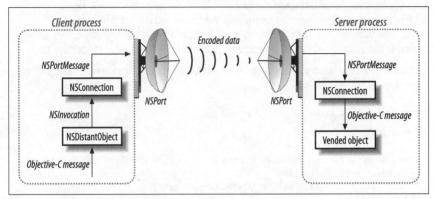

Figure 7-3. The distributed objects system (classes are shown in bold)

Setting up a server

To set up a server with an NSConnection instance, set the root object (the object to be vended) and register the connection. To set the root object, send the NSConnection instance a setRootObject: message. This method makes the specified object available to other processes as a distributed object. To register the connection, send it either registerName: or registerName:withNameServer:. The specified name is the one clients will use to access the vended object; the latter method also lets you specify an NSPortNameServer (see Example 7-3).

When a connection object vends a distributed object, it takes all necessary steps to create the port object and register the port with the port name registration server so other connection objects can locate the vended object.

Example 7-3. How a server vends an object

```
id anObject;  // Assume this object exists

// Get the default connection for the main thread
NSConnection *conn = [NSConnection defaultConnection];

// Set anObject as the root object of the connection
[conn setRootObject:anObject];

// Register the name of the connection so clients can get anObject
if ( [conn registerName:@"Server"] == NO ) {
  // If the name could not be registered, NO is returned
  // and we can handle the error
}
```

Connecting to a remote object

NSConnection instances also provide the route to remote objects from the client side. The class method rootProxyForConnectionWithRegisteredName:host: returns a proxy—an NSDistantObject–for the root object of the NSConnection with the specified name and host, registered with the default NSPortNameServer. You can also specify a port name server with rootProxyForConnectionWith-RegisteredName:host:usingNameServer:. The host name should be an Internet address, such as *myserver.mydomain.com*. Alternatively, by passing "*" as the host, you can specify that the connection should look for an object on all valid hosts. If the host name is nil or empty, then only the local host is searched.

Example 7-4 demonstrates the process by which a client obtains a vended distributed object.

Example 7-4. How a client acquires a vended object

```
id remoteObject;

// Get a proxy to the root object of the connection registered to the name "Server"
remoteObject = [[NSConnection
    rootProxyForConnectionWithRegisteredName:@"Server"
    host:@"*"] retain];
```

DO and threads

Distributed objects can be used to communicate between two threads in the same application the same as it can communicate between two applications on hosts separated by great distances. When using distributed objects to communicate between two threads in the same application, consider the following points: For an NSConnection to run as a server, a run loop must handle incoming messages and requests. If you create the connection in the main thread of an NSApplication-based application, this is taken care of. However, if you vend an object from a different thread, you must tell the thread's run loop to start by sending a run message to the currentRunLoop of the thread.

Making DO more efficient and reliable

Although DO lets you send arbitrary messages to a remote object, doing so creates additional overhead. To encode a message's arguments for transmission over the network, the argument types must be known in advance. If they're not known, the system must send an initial message just to get them, doubling the network traffic for every new message sent. Setting a protocol, by sending the proxy object a setProtocolForProxy: message, removes the need to define methods by the protocol.

```
// Set the protocol of the proxy
[remoteObject setProtocolForProxy:@protocol(rObjectProtocol)];
```

You can still send messages that are not declared in the protocol, but they will incur the additional message overhead. Establishing a protocol for the proxy has the additional benefit of imposing a known API. This reduces the risk that a message will be sent that the remote object does not implement.

You can also make the communication more efficient by employing special Objective-C keywords for distributed messaging. The oneway keyword, for example, is used with methods that return void. The following method might be implemented on a server:

```
-(void oneway)receiveString:(NSString *)string
{
    [self appendString:string];
}
```

When the client sends the proxy a receiveString: message, it does not require a return value. Without the oneway keyword, at least two messages will be sent across the network: the message itself, and a receipt. If the client does not need confirmation, the second message, and attendant overhead, are omitted.

Other keywords are: in, out, and inout, bycopy and byref, the latter two may only be used in protocol definitions. For more information, see */Developer/ Documentation/Cocoa/ObjectiveC/4objc_runtime_overview/Remote_Messaging.html.*

Handling communication failures

Most errors in distributed systems behave the way they would in a standalone application. If you send a message to a remote object that the remote object does not implement, an exception is raised. One additional complication with distributed systems, however, is that the remote application might terminate. In the event of a communication failure—because the remote application has quit, or it has simply ceased to respond—the NSConnection object sends an NSConnectionDidDieNotification to the still-running application's default notification center. Registering for this notification might help you handle connection failures gracefully. You should also implement an applicationWillTerminate method to inform remote objects of your impending disappearance.

8

Other Frameworks

Until this point, this book has focused on Cocoa's core frameworks, Foundation and Application Kit. However, Mac OS X contains *many* frameworks that you can leverage. Just look in */System/Libraray/Frameworks* to see how many there are, or launch the Apple System Profiler (*/Applications/Utilities*) and click on the Frameworks tab.

Not all frameworks, however, are implemented in Objective-C, as are the Foundation framework and Application Kit. Most Mac OS X frameworks are implemented in C since that language provides the most universal API that can be accessed by the widest range of application environments, including Cocoa. Several newer frameworks provide Objective-C interfaces in addition to C.

This chapter looks at some of the Objective-C frameworks provided by Apple. However, Apple isn't the only provider of frameworks. Many free and commercially available Objective-C frameworks are offered by other developers. Several of these third-party frameworks will be mentioned at the end of the chapter. This chapter covers additional Objective-C frameworks, including:

AddressBook
> Provides classes that allow applications to interface with Mac OS X's global Address Book database.

Message
> This small framework provides services to applications for sending email messages.

DiscRecording and DiscRecordingUI
> These two frameworks provide access to the system's disc recording APIs, giving any Cocoa application the ability to burn data to CDs and DVDs.

AddressBook

The AddressBook framework was released with Mac OS X 10.2. This framework provides a consistent, system-wide interface to a user's database of personal contacts. Using the AddressBook framework, applications can access the same information used in Apple's own suite of personal information management applications, including Mail, Address Book, iChat, iCal, and iSync. Figure 8-1 shows the AddressBook framework's class hierarchy.

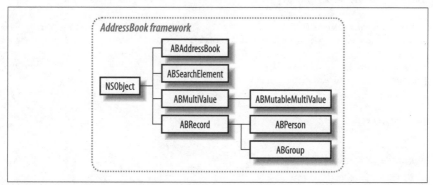

Figure 8-1. The AddressBook framework class hierarchy

ABAddressBook is the main class representing the contacts database. The ABAddressBook class provides access to a collection of records, of two types: people and groups, represented by the classes ABPerson and ABGroup. ABPerson and ABGroup inherit from the class ABRecord, as shown in Figure 8-1. Records are like souped-up dictionaries that store information in property-value pairs (similar to NSDictionary's key-value pairs, but ABRecord properties provide additional functionality).

Both people and group objects store properties, but they are not the same set of properties since a group does not share the characteristics of an individual. To retrieve the value of a property associated with a record, invoke the method valueForProperty: in the ABRecord object in question. To store a value for a record's property, use the method setValue:forProperty:.

ABAddressBook provides methods that access records in the database. The method people returns an NSArray filled with all ABPerson type records, while the method groups returns an NSArray containing all the Address Book's ABGroup type records. Records are added and removed using addRecord: and removeRecord:. Example 8-1 shows how to work with the AddressBook API.

Example 8-1. Working with the AddressBook framework

```
// Instantiate ABAddressBook
ABAddressBook *ab = [ABAddressBook sharedAddressBook];

// Access property values
ABPerson *me = [ab me];
NSString *fName = [me valueForProperty:kABFirstNameProperty];
NSString *lName = [me valueForProperty:kABLastNameProperty];
```

Example 8-1. Working with the AddressBook framework (continued)

```
// Set a property value
[me setValue:@"Michael" forProperty:kABFirstNameProperty];

// Get an array of all people in Address Book
NSArray *everyone = [ab people];

// ...and all groups
NSArray *groups = [ab groups];

// Create a new record
ABPerson *newPerson = [[ABPerson alloc] init];

// Add a record to the Address Book
[ab addRecord: newPerson];

// Remove a record from the Address Book
[ab removeRecord: me];

// Set "me"
[ab setMe:newPerson];

// Save changes to disk
[ab save];
```

Tables 8-1 and 8-2 show the property strings predefined by the AddressBook framework. Table 8-1 contains properties used exclusively by ABPerson objects, while Table 8-2 lists properties common to people and groups. ABGroup has an additional exclusive property, kABGroupNameProperty, which is the name of the group record.

Table 8-1. Property keys used in the AddressBook framework specific to ABPerson records

Property key	Description
kABFirstNameProperty	A person's first name as an NSString
kABLastNameProperty	A person's last name as an NSString
kABFirstNamePhoneticProperty	The phonetic spelling of the person's first name to aid pronunciation
kABLastNamePhoneticProperty	The phonetic spelling of the person's last name to aid pronunciation
kABBirthdayProperty	The person's birthday as an NSDate
kABOrganizationProperty	The person's affiliation as an NSString
kABJobTitleProperty	The job title of the person as an NSString
kABHomePageProperty	The home page of the person as an NSString
kABEmailProperty	The email property for a person as an ABMultiValue of NSStrings (multistring). Values are labeled by kABEmailWorkLabel and kABEmailHomeLabel
kABAddressProperty	The address of a person as an NSDictionary multivalue with the labels kABAddressHomeLabel and kABAddressWorkLabel
kABPhoneProperty	Phone numbers of person as a multistring with the following labels: kABPhoneWorkLabel, kABPhoneHomeLabel, kABPhoneMobileLabel, kABPhoneMainLabel, kABPhoneHomeFAXLabel, kABPhoneWorkFAXLabel, and kABPhonePagerLabel

Table 8-1. Property keys used in the AddressBook framework specific to ABPerson records (continued)

Property key	Description
kABAIMInstantProperty	The AIM screen name of person as a multistring with two labels: kABAIMWorkLabel, and kABAIMHomeLabel
kABJabberInstantProperty	The Jabber screen name of person as a multistring with two labels: kABJabberWorkLabel and kABJabberHomeLabel
kABMSNInstantProperty	The MSN screen name of person as a multistring with two labels: kABMSNWorkLabel and kABMSNHomeLabel
kABYahooInstantProperty	The Yahoo screen name of person as a multistring with two labels: kABYahooWorkLabel and kABYahooHomeLabel
kABICQInstantProperty	The ICQ screen name of person as a multistring with two labels: kABICQWorkLabel and kABICQHomeLabel
kABNoteProperty	The property whose values are an NSString note about the record

Table 8-2. Properties applicable to ABRecord objects (people and groups)

Property key	Description
kABUIDProperty	The UID (unique identifier) property of a record as an NSString
kABCreationDateProperty	The date on which the record was created as an NSDate
kABModificationDateProperty	NSDate specifies the last modification date of the record

In Example 8-1, the save method is invoked in the last line of code, saving changes to the database. Until the save method is invoked, changes only exist in memory, and are not reflected on disk. Once the changes are saved, other applications that use the AddressBook framework are notified that changes have been made to the database (see the *Notifications* section later in this chapter for more information on how this is accomplished).

Working with Multiple-Value Objects

Many property values in the AddressBook are typed as ABMultiValue, which is an object that stores multiple values for a single property. To understand why this might be useful, consider that people tend to have several phone numbers, email addresses, and a work and home address. Rather than create several separate properties for a work and home address, AddressBook defines a generic address property with an ABMultiValue value type.

An ABMultiValue stores the multiple values for a property by index. Each property has a unique identifier, a string label, and a value. Generally, the label is a combination of the property name and "home" or "work" (as shown in Table 8-1). However, it is possible to customize labels for additional values in the multivalue object (such as a summer vacation home address in addition to home and work addresses).

A *primary identifier*, associated with each multivalued property, identifies the subvalue of the multivalue property that a user most strongly associates with a person. For example, if you interact with a person purely on a professional basis, then the primary identifier for that contact's phone property would be for the work value. You can set this identifier in a `ABMutableMultiValue` with the method `setPrimaryIdentifier:`.

You can access values in an `ABMultiValue` object by index with `valueAtIndex:`. It is also possible to access the label and identifier of the object at a particular index with `labelAtIndex:` and `identifierAtIndex:`.

To demonstrate the use of multivalue objects, look closely at `kABAddressProperty`, which is of particular interest since itcontains `NSDictionary` objects as values rather than simple strings. The AddressBook API defines keys used to store values within an address property dictionary. Table 8-3 lists the keys that access values in the dictionaries for `kABAddressProperty`.

Table 8-3. Keys of the address dictionary

Dictionary key	Description
kABAddressStreetKey	The person's street name and number
kABAddressCityKey	The person's city
kABAddressStateKey	The person's state
kABAddressZIPKey	The zip code of the address
kABAddressCountryKey	The country name of the address
kABAddressCountryCodeKey	The two character country code. These standard ISO country codes can be found in the header file *ABGlobals.h*

Example 8-2 shows how to work with the address property and other multi-valued properties in `ABPerson`.

Example 8-2. Working with multivalued properties such as kABAddressProperty

```
ABMultiValue *addr = [p valueForProperty:kABAddressProperty];
int i = [addr indexForIdentifier:[addr primaryIdentifier]];
NSDictionary *prim = [addr valueAtIndex:i];
NSString *street = [prim objectForKey:kABAddressStreetKey];
NSString *state = [prim objectForKey:kABAddressStateKey];

ABMultiValue *aim = [p valueForProperty:kABAIMInstantProperty];

// This statement determines the number of values in the multi-value
int n = [aim count];

NSString *aim1 = [aim valueAtIndex:0];
```

Defining New Properties

It is possible to define your own application-specific keys to store data about a person or group in the contacts database. Because the database contains structured data that can hold values of any property name, the only applications that need know about these additional properties are those that actively look for them. Thus, there is no need to have two separate interfaces for interacting with AddressBook information and information specific to your application.

Add properties to a record by invoking the ABGroup or ABPerson class method addPropertiesAndTypes:. The argument for this method is a dictionary containing the property names as keys and the property types as values. The property type may be one of the following single or multivalue types shown in Table 8-4.

Table 8-4. Single- and multiple-value types

Data type	Single value	Multiple value
NSString	KABStringProperty	kABMultiStringProperty
NSNumber (int)	KABIntegerProperty	kABMultiIntegerProperty
NSNumber (float)	KABRealProperty	kABMultiRealProperty
NSDate	KABDateProperty	kABMultiDateProperty
NSArray	KABArrayProperty	kABMultiArrayProperty
NSDictionary	KABDictionaryProperty	kABMultiDictionaryProperty
NSData	KABDataProperty	kABMultiDataProperty

Example 8-3 shows how to add property-value pairs to a record.

Example 8-3. Defining new properties for a record

```
NSMutableDictionary *newProps = [NSMutableDictionary dictionary];
[newProps setObject:kABStringProperty forKey:@"College"];
[newProps setObject:kABDateProperty forKey:@"Grad Date"];
[ABPerson addPropertiesAndTypes:newProps];

ABAddressBook *ab = [ABAddressBook sharedAddressBook];
ABPerson *me = [ab me];
NSString *c = @"The University of Texas at Austin";
NSDate *d = [NSDate dateWithNaturalLanguageString:@"12/12/02"];
[me setValue:c forProperty:@"College"];
[me setValue:d forProperty:@"Grad Date"];
```

Searching

The AddressBook framework supports searching with the ABSearchElement class. You can create instances of this class with the ABPerson or ABGroup class method searchElementForProperty:label:key:value:comparison:, to which you supply the following search criteria:

searchElementForProperty:
> The record property that will be searched for.

label:
> If the property has multiple values, a label can be specified to restrict the search to one particular element of the multivalue.

key:
> If the property value is a dictionary, the search will be done on the value of the dictionary key specified in this parameter. For example, you could pass kABAddressCityKey here if you want to perform a search against the city of the contact.

value:

The value you are searching for in the property.

comparison:

This parameter specifies how the search process identifies a value as a match. Table 8-5 lists the comparison constants for this parameter.

The searchElementForProperty:label:key:value:comparison: method searches for people or groups, depending on whether it is implemented in the ABPerson or ABGroup class object, respectively.

A search is performed on the AddressBook database by ABAddressBook method recordsMatchingSearchElement:, to which you supply the search element object containing your search criteria. This method returns an array of ABPeople objects or ABGroup objects—depending on which of these two classes you created the search element in—that contains the search results.

Table 8-5. Comparison constants used by ABSearchElement

Comparison constant	Description
kABEqual	Returns records equal to the search value
kABNotEqual	Returns records not equal to the search element value
kABEqualCaseInsensitive	Returns records equal when case is ignored
kABLessThan	Searches for records whose value is less than the search value
kABLessThanOrEqual	Searches for elements less than or equal to the value
kABGreaterThan	Searches for elements greater than the search value
kABGreaterThanOrEqual	Searches for elements greater than or equal to the search value
kABContainsSubStringCaseInsensitive	Searches for records whose value contains the search value as a substring, disregarding case
kABPrefixMatch	Searches for elements that contain the search value as a prefix
kABPrefixMatchCaseInsensitive	Same as kABPrefixMatch, except case-insensitive

ABSearchElement's searchElementForConjunction:children: method can create arbitrarily complex searches by combining search elements into composite search elements using either the kABAndSearch or the kABOrSearch conjunction. The search elements to be combined into the complex search are passed as an array in the children: argument.

Example 8-4 shows how to perform searches in the AddressBook framework.

Example 8-4. Constructing and performing searches

```
ABSearchElement *se1, *se2, *se3;
NSArray *results, *seChildren;

ABAddressBook *ab = [ABAddressBook sharedAddressBook];

// Search against a simple, single-value property
se1 = [ABPerson searchElementForProperty:kABFirstNameProperty
                        label:nil
                        key:nil
```

Example 8-4. Constructing and performing searches (continued)

```
                                    value:@"Michael"
                                    comparison:kABEqual];
results = [ab recordsMatchingSearchElement:se1];

// Search against a key of the kABAddressProperty
se2 = [ABPerson searchElementForProperty:kABAddressProperty
                               label:nil
                               key:kABAddressCityKey
                               value:@"Houston"
                               comparison:kABEqual];
results = [ab recordsMatchingSearchElement:se2];

// Perform a complex search by combining search elements
seChildren = [NSArray arrayWithObjects:se1, se2, nil];
se3 = [ABSearchElement searchElementForConjunction:kABAndSearch
                               children: seChildren];
```

Notifications

The AddressBook framework API defines two notifications that applications may register to observe so they may be notified of changes to the AddressBook database:

kABDatabaseChangedNotification
> Notifies observers of changes the application makes to the database

kABDatabaseChangedExternallyNotification
> Notifies an observer that another application has changed the database

Odds and Ends

You can perform a couple of other operations with records beyond just storing name/value pairs: importing and exporting a vCard representation or associating an image with a person.

Creating a vCard from a record

Creating a vCard is easily accomplished by using the ABRecord method vCardRepresentation. This method returns an NSData object whose data is formatted in the vCard format. This data is written to disk, where it can be read by any number of applications that recognize the vCard format. Going the other way, you can initialize an ABRecord object with vCard data using initWithVCardRepresentation:. This method takes as a parameter an NSData object, which could be initialized with the contents of a vCard file on disk.

Adding an image to a record

To associate an image with a person in the AddressBook, use the methods setTIFFImageData: and TIFFImageData to set and get the person's picture. These methods work with NSData objects whose data is formatted as a TIFF image. These methods interface well with the NSImage methods TIFFRepresentation, which returns an TIFF-formatted `NSData` object, and `initWithData:`, which initializes an `NSImage` object with image data. Example 8-5 shows how to access image data in an Address Book record.

Example 8-5. Accessing image data in a record

```
// Assign an image to a record
NSData *imageData = [[NSData alloc]
                            initWithContentsOfFile:@"image.tiff"];
ABAddressBook *ab = [ABAddressBook sharedAddressBook];
ABRecord *me = [ab me];

[me setTIFFImageData: imageData];
[ab save];

// Retrieve a record's image
NSImage *anImage = [[NSImage alloc] initWithData: [me imageData]];
```

The Message Framework

The message framework, consisting of the single `NSMailDelivery` class, provides the functionality needed to send email messages from within an application. The `NSMailDelivery` class defines three methods:

- `hasDeliveryClassBeenConfigured`
- `deliverMessage:headers:format:protocol:`
- `deliverMessage:subject:to:`

The first method, `hasDeliveryClassBeenConfigured`, returns a `BOOL` value that indicates whether the operating system is configured to send messages. To make sure that any attempt to send a message is not in vain, invoke this method before sending a message, and handle appropriately if `NO` is returned. Message sending is enabled by configuring a default email account in the Internet System Preferences pane.

The second method, `deliverMessage:headers:format:protocol:`, delivers a message whose text is contained in an `NSAttributedString`. The standard message headers, such as "To", "From", and "Subject", are passed in the `headers:` parameter as a dictionary. In this dictionary, the key is the header name. For example, the recipient's email address would be an `NSString` value in the dictionary for the key `@"To"`. Example 8-6 shows how to use this dictionary and the mail delivery methods.

The third parameter specifies the message's format, which can be one of two constants: `NSASCIIMailFormat` or `NSMIMEMailFormat`. If `NSASCIIMailFormat` is specified as the format, then the attributed string is stripped of any rich text formatting information. `NSMIMEMailFormat`, on the other hand, preserves the rich text formatting when sending the message.

The final argument specifies the protocol used to deliver the message. Passing `nil`, which causes the delivery to default to the system default protocol, is preferable. The other choice is to pass the constant `NSSMTPDeliveryProtocol`, specifying that the method should be delivered with the SMTP protocol.

The final method defined in NSMailDelivery is deliverMessage:subject:to:. This convenience method sends the first argument's plain text NSString to the sender specified in the last argument. The subject: argument specifies a subject for the message.

Example 8-6. Using the message framework class NSMailDelivery

```
BOOL status = NO;

// Send an attribute string message
NSAttributedString *msg = [[NSAtrributedString strin alloc]
      initWithString:@"This is a message with no formatting."];

NSMutableDictionary * hdrs = [NSMutableDictionary dictionary];
[hdrs setObject:@"someone@someplace.com" forKey:@"To"];
[hdrs setObject:@"me@myplace.com" forKey:@"From"];
[hdrs setObject:@"Boring email" forKey:@"Subject"];

status = [NSMailDelivery deliverMessage:msg
       headers:hdrs
        format:NSASCIIMailFormat
     protocol:nil];

// Use the convenience method
status = [NSMailDelivery deliverMessage:@"This is another boring email message."
        subject:@"Nothing to important"
              to:@"someone@somplace.com"];
```

In this example, the variable status was set to the return value of the message delivery methods. The return values from these two methods indicate whether or not the message was successfully sent.

Disc Recording Frameworks

The ability to burn data to CDs and DVDs is a centerpiece of the Mac and Apple's Digital Hub strategy. Nearly every Mac sold today can record to CD or DVD media. This creates an opportunity for application developers to provide features in their applications that take advantage of a system's built-in disc burning capabilities.

With Mac OS X 10.2, Apple released two Objective-C frameworks that let applications take advantage of disc capabilities present in most new Macs. These frameworks are *DiscRecording* and *DiscRecordingUI*. Together, they provide an API for assembling content in preparation for recording and performing disc burn and erase operations.

The functionality of the Disc Recoding API is split between two frameworks for a good reason. DiscRecording provides the bulk of the API used for creating content and managing burn operations. DiscRecordingUI, on the other hand, provides no more than several NSPanel subclasses that implement standard user interfaces that applications can use to quickly configure and perform burn and erase operations. By separating the presentation from the mechanics, non-GUI applications can use the DiscRecording APIs. This section begins with a discussion of the DiscRecording framework and finishes with an overview of DiscRecordingUI.

The DiscRecording Framework

The DiscRecording framework provides classes that represent the fundamental parts of a recording process. DiscRecording has APIs that assemble filesystem hierarchies that will be recorded to disc, and APIs that record audio. Figure 8-2 shows this framework's class hierarchy.

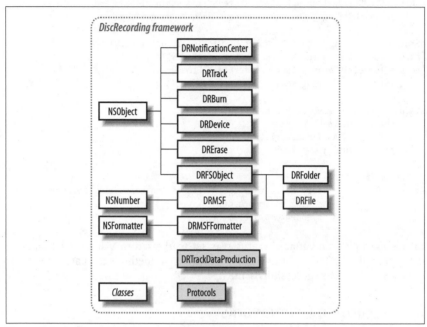

Figure 8-2. DiscRecording framework class hierarchy

The DiscRecording API provides a means to perform two primary tasks that people need their disc recording hardware to accomplish: burning a disc and erasing a disc's contents. These two tasks are represented by the classes DRBurn and DRErase.

DRBurn

DRBurn manages the process of burning a disc. The interface for this class provides several methods used to configure the burn process. Specifically, DRBurn lets you control the behavior of the burn process and specify how media should be handled after it is recorded to (i.e., should the disc be ejected or mounted as a filesystem).

To initialize a DRBurn object, use the method initWithDevice:. This initializer takes a DRDevice object, which represents the physical hardware device used for recording. All DRErase and DRBurn objects have an associated instance of DRDevice that provides information about and controls the hardware. Generally, you won't need to interact with DRDevice objects, except when you need to obtain information about the device, such as its make and model number. Device objects are configured and used mainly by the burning engine.

Use setProperties: to configure burn objects. Table 8-6 enumerates the keys used in this dictionary.

Table 8-6. Keys used in the burn properties dictionary

Key	Description
DRBurnRequestedSpeedKey	NSNumber containing a float that specifies the burn speed in kilobytes per second. The default is DRDeviceBurnSpeedMax.
DRBurnAppendableKey	BOOL specifying whether the disc should be appendable after the initial burn. The default is NO.
DRBurnVerifyDiscKey	BOOL specifying whether the burn should be verified. The default is YES.
DRBurnCompletionActionKey	Specifies the action that should occur after the burn is completed. The options are the default, DRBurnCompletionActionEject, and DRBurnCompletionActionMount.
DRBurnUnderrunProtectionKey	BOOL that turns run protection on and off for devices that support it. The default is YES.
DRBurnTestingKey	BOOL specifying if the burn should be run as a test burn. The default is NO.
DRSynchronousBehaviorKey	BOOL specifying if burn operations will behave synchronously. The default is NO.

DRErase

DRErase represents a disc erasure operation. Like DRBurn objects, DRErase instances are initialized with initWithDevice:. The DiscRecording API supports two types of operations: a quick erase and a complete erase. A quick erase does the minimum amount of work needed to make a disc appear blank, while a complete erase makes sure that every byte of data on the disc is erased. Quick erases, the default type for DRErase, take a couple of minutes to perform, whereas a complete erase can take up to a half an hour.

These two erase types are specified in the API by the constant NSString objects DREraseTypeQuick and DREraseTypeComplete. To specify the type of erase, use the method setEraseType:. The eraseType method returns the current type.

Once an erase object is configured, the erasure operation executes by invoking the start method. This method returns control to the sender immediately. The sender can retrieve information about the progress of an erase operation by polling the status method or listening for notifications.

DRTrack

DRTrack provides the burn with data and describes the track used to burn the data to disc. Instances of DRTrack do not actually store the data that will be recorded; rather, track objects are used as an interface to a data producer that provides the actual data. The DiscRecording framework defines the DRTrackDataProduction protocol to which classes should conform if they want to provide data for a DRTrack object.

Providing data is only part of DRTrack's responsibility. It is also responsible for providing properties of the actual track that will be written to disk. This is done by setting track properties with the setProperties: method. This method takes a dictionary, whose keys come from those listed in Table 8-7. Each key listed in this table must have a value assigned to it, or the burn will fail. The Mt. Fuji (IFF-8090i) specification for CD/DVD devices defines the values these properties may take.

Table 8-7. Required properties for a fully configured DRTrack object

Property key	Description
DRTrackLengthKey	Length of the track
DRBlockSizeKey	Size of each block measured in bytes
DRBlockTypeKey	Type of each block in the track
DRDataFormKey	Data form of each track block
DRSessionFormatKey	Session format of the track
DRTrackModeKey	Mode of the track

DRTrack provides two convenience constructors that prepare a DRTrack to burn audio to a disc or the data contained in a directory structure: trackWithAudioOfLength:producer: for audio and trackForRootFolder: for data.

Preparing audio content

trackWithAudioOfLength:producer: provides audio content to record. In the first parameter, the length's value is specified as an instance of the class DRMSF. This subclass of NSNumber represents lengths and positions on a disc by minutes, seconds, and frames (thus the MSF moniker). A frame is a subdivision of a second, and there are 75 frames in a second. A frame corresponds to one block on a track, and is thus the smallest possible division of space on a disc. The producer: parameter is an object that conforms to the DRTrackDataProduction protocol. The data producer prepares data and provides it to the track during the burn process.

Preparing data content

The second DRTrack convenience constructor is trackForRootFolder:. This method takes a single parameter, which is of type DRFolder. DRFolder is one of two subclasses of the class DRFSObject, which represents a generic filesystem object. The other subclass is DRFile. DRFile and DRFolder both construct a filesystem that will be reproduced on a CD or DVD.

To successfully create a data track, you need to know that files and folders are related to one another in a one-to-many, parent-child relationship, and are arranged in trees. Thus, each folder in the structure may have many children, which are folders or files, and each child has exactly one parent, which must be a folder. Only folders may have children; files may not. This mirrors the organization of any filesystem you're used to working with. Additionally, files and folders may either be *real* or *virtual*. A real file or folder corresponds to a real file or folder that exists on the user's source volume. Because they represent actual objects in the source filesystem, real filesystem objects may not be modified once they are added to the data track preparation.

To create a real `DRFile`, use either the convenience constructor `fileWithPath:` or the initializer `initWithPath:`. Both methods take as an argument the path to an actual file on disk. A `DRFile` object is capable of representing real files, aliases, and symbolically linked files. Similarly, to create a real `DRFolder`, use either the convenience constructor `folderWithPath:` or the initializer `initWithPath:`.

A virtual filesystem object is a placeholder for a file or folder that will be created when the filesystem is written to the disc. The process of assembling virtual files and folders is often referred to as creating a filesystem in the API, referring to the methods in `DRFile` and `DRFolder` used to construct the filesystem. Using virtual folders, a program can construct a filesystem that will be created on the disc by adding children to folder objects. These children may be real or virtual `DRFSObjects`. Virtual `DRFolders` are the only filesystem objects that may contain children. Thus real files and folders, and virtual files, are all leaf nodes in the filesystem.

When a virtual filesystem object is created, a name is assigned to the object that will be the file or folder name in the end product. Virtual files are also assigned an `NSData` object that contains what will become the file contents on the destination media. Alternatively, a virtual file object can be associated with an object that conforms to the `DRDataTrackProduction` protocol as a means of creating a file's contents. You can create a virtual folder by invoking the `DRFolder` class method `folderWithName:` or the initializer `initWithName:`. Virtual files may be created with `virtualFileWith-Name:data:` or `virtualFileWithName:dataProducer:`. In the former method, the parameter is an `NSData` object, while the latter method requires an object that conforms to the `DRTrackDataProduction` protocol. There are also equivalent initializers, `initWithName:data:` and `initWithName:dataProducer:`.

Children are added to a `DRFolder` by invoking the method `addChild:`, and they are removed using the method `removeChild:`. The count method returns the number of children within a folder.. children returns an `NSArray` of a folder's children. While a real folder may not have any children, you can convert a real folder into a virtual folder to add children to the directory structure. When a folder is converted from real to virtual, the converted folder's pre-existing contents remain real. Real folders are made virtual by invoking `makeVirtual`. Once a filesystem structure is created—by choosing a real file or folder or building one from scratch using a combination of real and virtual filesystem objects—the root `DRFolder` of the tree creates a `DRTrack` with the convenience constructor `trackForRootFolder:`.

Example 8-7 shows how to prepare data to be burned to disc.

Example 8-7. Preparing data for burning

```
// Prepare a real folder or file
DRFolder *rFolder = [DRFolder folderWithPath:@"/Users/mike"];
DRFile *rFile = [DRFile fileWithPath:@"/Users/mike/someDoc.txt"];

// Work with virtual filesystem objects
DRFolder *root = [DRFolder folderWithName:@"Root Folder"];
DRFile *vFile = [DRFile fileWithName:@"Fake File" data:someNSData];

[rFolder makeVirtual];
[rFolder addChild:vFile];
[root addChild:rFolder];
[root addChild:rFile];
```

Example 8-7. Preparing data for burning (continued)

```
// Create a DRTrack object to hold the data
DRTrack *track = [DRTrack trackForRootFolder:root];
```

The DiscRecordingUI Framework

DiscRecordingUI implements a standard front-end interface to the DiscRecording framework. From reading the previous section, you know that instances of the classes DRBurn and DRErase represent burn and erase operations. The classes of DiscRecordingUI provide an interface to configure instances of DRBurn and DRErase, as well as monitor the progress of recording and erase operations.

Figure 8-3 shows the classes of the DiscRecordingUI framework. Each one is a subclass of NSPanel. DRSetupPanel is an abstract superclass that provides facilities for device selection and handling needed by burn and erase setup panels.

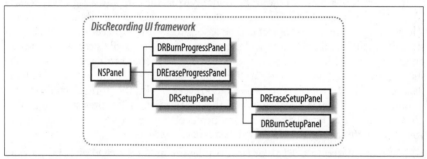

Figure 8-3. DiscRecordingUI framework class hierarchy

DRBurnSetupPanel, shown in Figure 8-4, is an interface that configures and executes a burn operation. DREraseSetupPanel, shown in Figure 8-5, provides an interface for configuring and executing disc erase operations.

How to record

To create a burn or erase setup panel, invoke setupPanel in either DRBurnSetupPanel or DREraseSetupPanel. Once an instance of either class is obtained, invoke the DRSetupPanel method runSetupPanel, which displays the panel on the screen. Setup panels run as *modal windows*, which means you can't interact with any other part of the application while the window is open.

The method runSetupPanel is blocking, so execution in the thread it was invoked in stops until the user clicks the panel's Cancel or Burn/Erase buttons. This method returns with an int, indicating which button the user clicked. The return value is equal to one of the constants NSOKButton or NSCancelButton. This return value determines the next course of action: either continue on with our application or begin a burn/erase operation.

In the case of a burn setup panel, after determining that the Burn button was pressed, we can obtain an instance of DRBurn whose state reflects the configuration made in the setup panel. This object is obtained with the method burnObject.

Figure 8-4. The burn disc panel

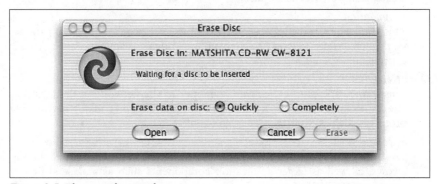

Figure 8-5. The erase disc panel

The next step, after preparing your layout is to instantiate `DRBurnProgressPanel` and start the burn process. To create a burn progress panel, invoke the class method `progressPanel`. You can start burn operations by using `beginProgressPanelForBurn:layout:`, to which you supply our burn object and the object representing your layout. Example 8-8 performs these tasks in code.

Example 8-8. Using setup panels in DiscRecordingUI

```
- (IBAction)showBurnPanel:(id)sender
{
    DRBurnSetupPanel *bp = [DRBurnSetupPanel setupPanel];
    int status = [bp runSetupPanel];

    if ( status == NSOKButton ) {
        DRBurn *burn = [bp burnObject];
        DRBurnProgressPanel *pp = [DRBurnProgressPanel progressPanel];
```

Example 8-8. Using setup panels in DiscRecordingUI (continued)

```
    // Assume aLayout has been prepared previously
    [pp beginProgressPanelForBurn: burn layout:aLayout];
  }
}
```

Third-Party Frameworks

In addition to the frameworks provided by Apple, several third-party objective frameworks are available. One of the most notable is the collection of frameworks from The Omni Group. Omni makes not only the same frameworks developers use in their applications, but also the source code for the frameworks.

Omni provides the following frameworks, whose source code can be downloaded from Omni's developer web site (*http://www.omnigroup.com/developer/sourcecode*):

OmniBase
> This framework provides several low-level classes that provide allocation and initialization debugging aids, classes that aid interaction with the Objective-C runtime, and an exception handling mechanism that is an alternative to the standard one provided in Cocoa.

OmniFoundation
> This framework provides several extensions to Cocoa's Foundation framework, including classes that handle strings, scanning, and regular expressions.

OmniNetworking
> This framework is an Objective-C wrapper to the networking libraries that already exist in Mac OS X. OmniNetworking supports major networking protocols such as Multicast, TCP, and UDP.

OmniAppKit
> This framework provides lots of neat controls, such as a calendar and chasing arrows, as well as larger application components such as a skeletal preferences system and Find panel.

OWF
> The Omni Web Framework is the base architecture for OmniWeb that handles all content retrieval and parsing, and other functions related to Internet application development. Omni says: "If OmniFoundation is the Objective-C programmer's Swiss Army Knife, then OWF is their double barrel, rotary laser cannon."

OmniHTML
> This framework handles HTML parsing and is also used in OmniWeb.

These frameworks provide no documentation. However, with the source code available, learning how to use them should be fun.

Another notable framework is the MiscKit, maintained by the Object Foundation. The framework contains a plethora of miscellany. Undoubtedly, many of you will find the offerings of the MiscKit useful and interesting. Information about MiscKit, as well as resources and the actual framework, is available at *http://www.misckit.com*.

In addition to these larger frameworks, many smaller collections of classes are constantly growing and improving. The Cocoa development community is outputting several free, open source classes. The Softtrak software database, available on Stepwise's site (*http://www.stepwise.com*), maintains information about the third-party frameworks available for Cocoa.

API Quick Reference

This part of the book provides a quick reference to Cocoa's primary frameworks: Foundation and Application Kit. This part starts out with a quick overview of how to use the Cocoa quick reference to better help you understand its organization and structure. The chapters in this part aren't meant to be read from start to finish, but instead are intended to be used as a reference to keep by your side while programming.

Chapters in this part of the book include:

Additionally, Part II begins with an explanation of *How to Use This Quick Reference*, and wraps up with an index that contains an alphabetical listing of every method in the Foundation and Application Kit frameworks, called the *Method Index*.

How to Use This Quick Reference

Part II crams a great deal of information about Cocoa into a relatively small space. In this chapter we take a look at how this information is organized and how to read the quick-reference entries.

Organization of the Quick Reference

Chapters 13 and 15 cover the classes of the Foundation and Application Kit frameworks. Chapters 14 and 16 contain quick-reference entries for the protocols of these two frameworks. Within these four chapters quick-reference entries are arranged alphabetically. Finally, the Method Index contains an alphabetical listing of every method in the Foundation framework and Application Kit. Each method name in the index has a list of classes that implement that method. Here's how to read a quick reference entry.

Description

Following the title of each quick-reference entry is a brief description of the class or protocol. Descriptions may be as short as a couple of lines, or as long as several paragraphs of text.

Hierarchy

Every class in the quick reference has a figure illustrating the hierarchy of the class, and any protocols adopted by the class or its ancestors. In the hierarchy figure classes appear as rectangles containing the name of the class, and formal Objective-C protocols appear as rectangles with rounded corners. The root object of each hierarchy (either NSObject or NSProxy) is at the left of the figure, with subclasses extending horizontally to the right. Subclasses are connected by a solid line, which denotes an inheritance relationship. The protocols adopted by any class in the hierarchy appear vertically beneath the class. Note that the hierarchy only shows the superclasses of a class. Subclasses of the class, if any exist, are listed after the class synopsis in the "Subclasses" cross-reference.

Synopsis

The synopsis is the most important part of the class reference, providing a list of the methods that are part of the class interface. Additionally, the class synopsis provides a list of methods that a delegate object might implement, as well as a list of notifications that the class can post. Each class synopsis begins with the class interface declaration as it would appear in the class header file. The interface declaration displays the class name, superclass name, and any protocols that the class adopts. For example, NSDate has the following interface declaration in its class synopsis:

> @interface NSDate : NSObject <NSCoding, NSCopying>

Following the interface declaration is a list of methods that are a part of the class's interface. This includes all methods that may be declared in a category of a method. The class interface method list is ended with @end. Following the class method list is a list of methods a delegate object may implement, and a list of notifications that instances of the class may post to the notification center.

Protocol synopses take on two forms, depending on whether the protocol is formal or informal. *Formal protocols* enclose the method list as follows:

> @protocol ProtocolName
>
> // Methods
>
> @end

While an *informal protocol* synopsis appears as a category interface declaration:

> @interface NSObject (ProtocolName)
>
> // Methods
>
> @end

Functional grouping of methods

Methods in the class synopsis are broken up into several optional categories, within which the methods are listed alphabetically. A class may have groups of convenience constructors, initializers, and property accessor methods, in addition to class and instance methods. Additionally, the synopsis lists methods a class expects its delegate to respond to, as well as notifications posted by instances of the class. Method groups are separated in the synopsis with C comments, such as // Initializers, // Class Methods, and // Notifications. Protocol synopses group methods either as instance or class methods. Not every class has methods that fall under each of these categorizes. The various categories are as follows (in the same order they would appear in the class synopsis):

Convenience constructors

Lists any convenience constructors of a class. Convenience constructors are class methods that combine object allocation and initialization into one step. By convention, objects returned by convenience constructor have already been sent an autorelease method, and will be released at the end of the event-loop. If you wish to use an object for a longer period of time you must send a retain message to the returned object. Generally speaking, convenience constructors very nearly mirror the initializers of a class. A class may have other factory methods listed in the Class Methods grouping in addition to these convenience constructors.

Initializers

This grouping lists all of the initializers of a class, which is any method that begins with init. When instantiating an class with alloc, you must initialize the new object with one of the class's initializers before it is used. Objects created and initialized in this way have a reference count of 1, unlike objects returned by convenience constructors, which have been autoreleased before they are returned.

Accessor methods

This section lists methods that are used to access the properties of a class. Any instance method that begins with set... is listed here; these are used to set the property indicated in the method name. Conventionally, methods used to access properties are named after the property. For example, NSBezierPath has the method setLineWidth: to set the line width of the path. The associated get-property instance method is lineWidth—the name of the property. Accessor methods are listed alphabetically by the property name, so that the "set" methods appear grouped with their respective property query methods.

Class methods

This section of the synopsis lists all class methods that are not constructors or accessor methods.

Instance methods

This section lists all instance methods that are not initializers or accessor methods.

Implementing methods

This section groups methods that implement the same protocol. For each protocol adopted by the class, there is one subgroup of methods.

Delegate methods

This section lists any methods a delegate of the class may optionally implement. Delegate methods are not part of the class interface; generally, they are declared as a category of the root class, NSObject.

Notifications

This section lists the symbolic names of any notification that the class may post during its lifetime.

9

Foundation Types and Constants

This chapter describes the data types and constants found in the Foundation framework, and is divided into the following sections:

Data types
Enumerations
Global variables
Constants
Exception names

Data Types

This section lists the data types defined by and used in the Foundation framework.

NSCalculationError

```
typedef enum {
  NSCalculationNoError = 0,
  NSCalculationLossOfPrecision,
  NSCalculationUnderflow,
  NSCalculationOverflow,
  NSCalculationDivideByZero
} NSCalculationError;
```

NSComparisonResult

```
typedef enum _NSComparisonResult {
  NSOrderedAscending = -1,
  NSOrderedSame,
  NSOrderedDescending
} NSComparisonResult;
```

NSDecimal

```
typedef struct {
    signed int _exponent:8;
    unsigned int _length:4;
    unsigned int _isNegative:11;
    unsigned int _isCompact:1;
    unsigned int _reserved:18;
    unsigned short _mantissa[NSDecimalMaxSize];
} NSDecimal;
```

NSHashEnumerator

```
typedef struct {
    unsigned _pi;
    unsigned _si void *_bs;
} NSHashEnumerator;
```

NSHashTable

```
typedef struct _NSHashTable
NSHashTable;
```

NSHashTableCallBacks

```
typedef struct {
    unsigned (*hash)(NSHashTable *table, const void *);
    BOOL (*isEqual)(NSHashTable *table, const void *, const void *);
    void (*retain)(NSHashTable *table, const void *);
    void (*release)(NSHashTable *table, void *);
    NSString *(*describe)(NSHashTable *table, const void *);
} NSHashTableCallBacks;
```

NSInsertionPosition

```
typedef enum {
    NSPositionAfter,
    NSPositionBefore,
    NSPositionBeginning,
    NSPositionEnd,
    NSPositionReplace
} NSInsertionPosition;
```

NSMapEnumerator

```
typedef struct {
    unsigned _pi;
    unsigned _si;
    void *_bs;
} NSMapEnumerator;
```

NSMapTable

```
typedef struct _NSMapTable NSMapTable;
```

NSMapTableKeyCallBacks

```
typedef struct {
    unsigned (*hash)(NSMapTable *table, const void *);
    BOOL (*isEqual)(NSMapTable *table, const void *, const void *);
    void (*retain)(NSMapTable *table, const void *);
    void (*release)(NSMapTable *table, void *);
    NSString *(*describe)(NSMapTable *table, const void *);
    const void *notAKeyMarker;
} NSMapTableKeyCallBacks;
```

NSMapTableValueCallBacks

```
typedef struct {
    void (*retain)(NSMapTable *table, const void *);
    void (*release)(NSMapTable *table, void *);
    NSString *(*describe)(NSMapTable *table, const void *);
} NSMapTableValueCallBacks;
```

NSNetServicesError

```
typedef enum {
    NSNetServicesUnknownError = -72000,
    NSNetServicesCollisionError = -72001,
    NSNetServicesNotFoundError = -72002,
    NSNetServicesActivityInProgress = -72003,
    NSNetServicesBadArgumentError = -72004,
    NSNetServicesCancelledError = -72005,
    NSNetServicesInvalidError = -72006
} NSNetServicesError;
```

NSNotificationCoalescing

```
typedef enum {
    NSNotificationNoCoalescing = 0,
    NSNotificationCoalescingOnName = 1,
    NSNotificationCoalescingOnSender = 2
} NSNotificationCoalescing;
```

NSNotificationSuspensionBehavior

```
typedef enum {
    NSNotificationSuspensionBehaviorDrop = 1,
    NSNotificationSuspensionBehaviorCoalesce = 2,
    NSNotificationSuspensionBehaviorHold = 3,
    NSNotificationSuspensionBehaviorDeliverImmediately = 4
} NSNotificationCoalescing;
```

NSObjCValue

```
typedef struct {
  enum _NSObjCValueType type;
  union {
    char charValue;
    short shortValue;
    long longValue;
    long long longlongValue;
    float floatValue;
    double doubleValue;
    bool boolValue;
    SEL selectorValue;
    id objectValue;
    void *pointerValue;
    void *structLocation;
    char *cStringLocation;
  } value;
} NSObjCValue;
```

NSPoint

```
typedef struct _NSPoint {
  float x;
  float y;
} NSPoint;
```

NSPointArray

```
typedef NSPoint *NSPointArray;
```

NSPointPointer

```
typedef NSPoint *NSPointPointer;
```

NSPostingStyle

```
typedef enum {
  NSPostWhenIdle = 1,
  NSPostASAP = 2,
  NSPostNow = 3
} NSPostingStyle;
```

NSPropertyListFormat

```
typedef enum {
  NSPropertyListOpenStepFormat = kCFPropertyListOpenStepFormat,
  NSPropertyListXMLFormat_v1_0 = kCFPropertyListXMLFormat_v1_0,
  NSPropertyListBinaryFormat_v1_0 = kCFPropertyListBinaryFormat_v1_0
} NSPropertyListFormat;
```

NSPropertyListMutabilityOptions

```
typedef enum {
    NSPropertyListImmutable = kCFPropertyListImmutable,
    NSPropertyListMutableContainers = kCFPropertyListMutableContainers,
    NSPropertyListMutableContainersAndLeaves = kCFPropertyListMutableContainersAndLeaves
} NSPropertyListMutabilityOptions;
```

NSRange

```
typedef struct _NSRange {
    unsigned int location;
    unsigned int length;
} NSRange;
```

NSRangePointer

```
typedef NSRange *NSRangePointer;
```

NSRect

```
typedef struct _NSRect {
    NSPoint origin;
    NSSize size;
} NSRect;
```

NSRectArray

```
typedef NSRect *NSRectArray;
```

NSRectEdge

```
typedef enum _NSRectEdge {
    NSMinXEdge = 0,
    NSMinYEdge = 1,
    NSMaxXEdge = 2,
    NSMaxYEdge = 3
} NSRectEdge;
```

NSRectPointer

```
typedef NSRect *NSRectPointer;
```

NSRelativePosition

```
typedef enum {
    NSRelativeAfter = 0,
    NSRelativeBefore
} NSRelativePosition;
```

NSRoundingMode

```
typedef enum {
    NSRoundPlain,
    NSRoundDown,
    NSRoundUp,
    NSRoundBankers
} NSRoundingMode;
```

NSSaveOptions

```
typedef enum {
    NSSaveOptionsYes = 0,
    NSSaveOptionsNo,
    NSSaveOptionsAsk,
} NSSaveOptions;
```

NSSearchPathDirectory

```
typedef enum {
    NSApplicationDirectory = 1,
    NSDemoApplicationDirectory,
    NSDeveloperApplicationDirectory,
    NSAdminApplicationDirectory,
    NSLibraryDirectory,
    NSDeveloperDirectory,
    NSUserDirectory,
    NSDocumentationDirectory,
    NSDocumentDirectory,
    NSAllApplicationsDirectory = 100,
    NSAllLibrariesDirectory = 101
} NSSearchPathDirectory;
```

NSSearchPathDomainMask

```
typedef enum {
    NSUserDomainMask = 1,
    NSLocalDomainMask = 2,
    NSNetworkDomainMask = 4,
    NSSystemDomainMask = 8,
    NSAllDomainsMask = 0x0ffff,
} NSSearchPathDomainMask;
```

NSSize

```
typedef struct _NSSize {
    float width;
    float height;
} NSSize;
```

NSSizeArray

typedef NSSize *NSSizeArray;

NSSizePointer

typedef NSSize *NSSizePointer;

NSStringEncoding

typedef unsigned NSStringEncoding;

NSSwappedDouble

typedef struct {
  unsigned long long v;
} NSSwappedDouble;

NSSwappedFloat

typedef struct {
  unsigned long v;
} NSSwappedFloat;

NSTestComparisonOperation

typedef enum {
  NSEqualToComparison = 0,
  NSLessThanOrEqualToComparison,
  NSLessThanComparison,
  NSGreaterThanOrEqualToComparison,
  NSGreaterThanComparison,
  NSBeginsWithComparison,
  NSEndsWithComparison,
  NSContainsComparison,
} NSTestComparisonOperation;

NSTimeInterval

typedef double NSTimeInterval;

NSUncaughtExceptionHandler

typedef volatile void NSUncaughtExceptionHandler(NSException *exception);

NSURLHandleStatus

typedef enum {
  NSURLHandleNotLoaded = 0,

```
  NSURLHandleLoadSucceeded,
  NSURLHandleLoadInProgress,
  NSURLHandleLoadFailed
} NSURLHandleStatus;
```

NSWhoseSubelementIdentifier

```
typedef enum {
  NSIndexSubelement = 0,
  NSEverySubelement = 1,
  NSMiddleSubelement = 2,
  NSRandomSubelement = 3,
  NSNoSubelement = 4
} NSWhoseSubelementIdentifier;
```

NSZone

```
typedef struct _NSZone NSZone;
```

Enumerations

This section lists the enumeration constants defined by and used in the Foundation framework.

NSNotFound

```
enum {
  NSNotFound = 0x7fffffff
};
```

NSOpenStepUnicodeReservedBase

```
enum {
  NSOpenStepUnicodeReservedBase = 0xF400
};
```

NSProcessInfo (Operating Systems)

```
enum {
  NSWindowsNTOperatingSystem = 1,
  NSWindows95OperatingSystem,
  NSSolarisOperatingSystem,
  NSHPUXOperatingSystem,
  NSMACHOperatingSystem,
  NSSunOSOperatingSystem,
  NSOSF1OperatingSystem
};
```

NSScriptCommand (General Command Execution Errors)

```
enum {
  NSNoScriptError = 0,
  NSReceiverEvaluationScriptError,
  NSKeySpecifierEvaluationScriptError,
  NSArgumentEvaluationScriptError,
  NSReceiversCantHandleCommandScriptError,
  NSRequiredArgumentsMissingScriptError,
  NSArgumentsWrongScriptError,
  NSUnknownKeyScriptError,
  NSInternalScriptError,
  NSOperationNotSupportedForKeyScriptError,
  NSCannotCreateScriptCommandError
};
```

NSScriptObjectSpecifier (Specifier Evaluation Errors)

```
enum {
  NSNoSpecifierError = 0,
  NSNoTopLevelContainersSpecifierError,
  NSContainerSpecifierError,
  NSUnknownKeySpecifierError,
  NSInvalidIndexSpecifierError,
  NSInternalSpecifierError,
  NSOperationNotSupportedForKeySpecifierError
};
```

NSUndoCloseGroupingRunLoopOrdering

```
enum {
  NSUndoCloseGroupingRunLoopOrdering = 350000
};
```

Search Types

```
enum {
  NSCaseInsensitiveSearch = 1,
  NSLiteralSearch = 2,
  NSBackwardsSearch = 4,
  NSAnchoredSearch = 8
};
```

String Encodings

```
enum {
  NSASCIIStringEncoding = 1,
  NSNEXTSTEPStringEncoding = 2,
  NSJapaneseEUCStringEncoding = 3,
  NSUTF8StringEncoding = 4,
  NSISOLatin1StringEncoding = 5,
```

```
    NSSymbolStringEncoding = 6,
    NSNonLossyASCIIStringEncoding = 7,
    NSShiftJISStringEncoding = 8,
    NSISOLatin2StringEncoding = 9,
    NSUnicodeStringEncoding = 10,
    NSWindowsCP1251StringEncoding = 11,
    NSWindowsCP1252StringEncoding = 12,
    NSWindowsCP1253StringEncoding = 13,
    NSWindowsCP1254StringEncoding = 14,
    NSWindowsCP1250StringEncoding = 15,
    NSISO2022JPStringEncoding = 21,
    NSMacOSRomanStringEncoding = 30,
    NSProprietaryStringEncoding = 65536
};
```

Global Variables

This section lists the global variable defined by and used in the Foundation framework.

File Attribute Keys

```
    extern NSString *NSFileType;
    extern NSString *NSFileSize;
    extern NSString *NSFileModificationDate;
    extern NSString *NSFileReferenceCount;
    extern NSString *NSFileDeviceIdentifier;
    extern NSString *NSFileOwnerAccountNumber;
    extern NSString *NSFileGroupOwnerAccountNumber;
    extern NSString *NSFilePosixPermissions;
    extern NSString *NSFileSystemFileNumber;
    extern NSString *NSFileExtensionHidden;
    extern NSString *NSFileHFSCreatorCode;
    extern NSString *NSFileHFSTypeCode;
    extern NSString *NSFileImmutable;
    extern NSString *NSFileAppendOnly;
    extern NSString *NSFileCreationDate;
    extern NSString *NSFileOwnerAccountID;
    extern NSString *NSFileGroupOwnerAccountID;
```

Filesystem Attribute Keys

```
    extern NSString *NSFileSystemSize;
    extern NSString *NSFileSystemFreeSize;
    extern NSString *NSFileSystemNodes;
    extern NSString *NSFileSystemFreeNodes;
    extern NSString *NSFileSystemNumber;
```

File Type Attribute Keys

```
extern NSString *NSFileTypeDirectory;
extern NSString *NSFileTypeRegular;
extern NSString *NSFileTypeSymbolicLink;
extern NSString *NSFileTypeSocket;
extern NSString *NSFileTypeCharacterSpecial;
extern NSString *NSFileTypeBlockSpecial;
extern NSString *NSFileTypeUnknown;
```

Language-Dependent Date/Time Information

```
extern NSString *NSWeekDayNameArray;
extern NSString *NSShortWeekDayNameArray;
extern NSString *NSMonthNameArray;
extern NSString *NSShortMonthNameArray;
extern NSString *NSTimeFormatString;
extern NSString *NSDateFormatString;
extern NSString *NSTimeDateFormatString;
extern NSString *NSShortTimeDateFormatString;
extern NSString *NSAMPMDesignation;
extern NSString *NSHourNameDesignations;
extern NSString *NSYearMonthWeekDesignations;
extern NSString *NSEarlierTimeDesignations;
extern NSString *NSLaterTimeDesignations;
extern NSString *NSThisDayDesignations;
extern NSString *NSNextDayDesignations;
extern NSString *NSNextNextDayDesignations;
extern NSString *NSPriorDayDesignations;
extern NSString *NSDateTimeOrdering;
extern NSString *NSShortDateFormatString;
```

Language-Dependent Numeric Information

```
extern NSString *NSCurrencySymbol;
extern NSString *NSDecimalSeparator;
extern NSString *NSThousandsSeparator;
extern NSString *NSInternationalCurrencyString;
extern NSString *NSPositiveCurrencyFormatString;
extern NSString *NSNegativeCurrencyFormatString;
extern NSString *NSDecimalDigits;
```

NSAppleEvent Timeouts

```
extern const double NSAppleEventTimeOutDefault;
extern const double NSAppleEventTimeOutNone;
```

NSConnectionReplyMode

```
extern NSString *NSConnectionReplyMode;
```

NSDefaultRunLoopMode

```
extern NSString *NSDefaultRunLoopMode;
```

NSJavaSetup Information

```
extern NSString * const NSJavaClasses;
extern NSString * const NSJavaRoot;
extern NSString * const NSJavaPath;
extern NSString * const NSJavaUserPath;
extern NSString * const NSJavaLibraryPath;
extern NSString * const NSJavaOwnVirtualMachine;
extern NSString * const NSJavaPathSeparator;
```

NSHashTable Callbacks

```
extern const NSHashTableCallBacks NSIntHashCallBacks;
extern const NSHashTableCallBacks NSNonOwnedPointerHashCallBacks;
extern const NSHashTableCallBacks NSNonRetainedObjectHashCallBacks;
extern const NSHashTableCallBacks NSObjectHashCallBacks;
extern const NSHashTableCallBacks NSOwnedObjectIdentityHashCallBacks;
extern const NSHashTableCallBacks NSOwnedPointerHashCallBacks;
extern const NSHashTableCallBacks NSPointerToStructHashCallBacks;
```

NSLocalNotificationCenterType

```
extern NSString * const NSLocalNotificationCenterType;
```

NSMapTable Key Call Backs

```
extern const NSMapTableKeyCallBacks NSIntMapKeyCallBacks;
extern const NSMapTableKeyCallBacks NSNonOwnedPointerMapKeyCallBacks;
extern const NSMapTableKeyCallBacks NSNonOwnedPointerOrNullMapKeyCallBacks;
extern const NSMapTableKeyCallBacks NSNonRetainedObjectMapKeyCallBacks;
extern const NSMapTableKeyCallBacks NSObjectMapKeyCallBacks;
extern const NSMapTableKeyCallBacks NSOwnedPointerMapKeyCallBacks;
```

NSMapTable Value Callbacks

```
extern const NSMapTableValueCallBacks NSIntMapValueCallBacks;
extern const NSMapTableValueCallBacks NSNonOwnedPointerMapValueCallBacks;
extern const NSMapTableValueCallBacks NSObjectMapValueCallBacks;
extern const NSMapTableValueCallBacks NSNonRetainedObjectMapValueCallBacks;
extern const NSMapTableValueCallBacks NSOwnedPointerMapValueCallBacks;
```

NSNetServices Errors

```
extern NSString *NSNetServicesErrorCode;
extern NSString *NSNetServicesErrorDomain;
```

NSURL Schemes

```
extern NSString *NSURLFileScheme;
```

NSURLHandle FTP Property Keys

```
extern NSString *NSFTPPropertyUserLoginKey;
extern NSString *NSFTPPropertyUserPasswordKey;
extern NSString *NSFTPPropertyActiveTransferModeKey;
extern NSString *NSFTPPropertyFileOffsetKey;
```

NSURLHandle HTTP Property Keys

```
extern NSString *NSHTTPPropertyStatusCodeKey;
extern NSString *NSHTTPPropertyStatusReasonKey;
extern NSString *NSHTTPPropertyServerHTTPVersionKey;
extern NSString *NSHTTPPropertyRedirectionHeadersKey;
extern NSString *NSHTTPPropertyErrorPageDataKey;
extern NSString *NSHTTPPropertyHTTPProxy;
```

NSUserDefaults Domains

```
extern NSString *NSGlobalDomain;
extern NSString *NSArgumentDomain;
extern NSString *NSRegistrationDomain;
```

Zero Constants

```
extern const NSPoint NSZeroPoint;
extern const NSSize NSZeroSize;
extern const NSRect NSZeroRect;
```

Constants

This section lists the constant macros defined by and used in the Foundation framework.

NSDecimalMaxSize

```
#define NSDecimalMaxSize (8)
```

NSDecimalNoScale

```
#define NSDecimalNoScale SHRT_MAX
```

NSNotAnIntMapKey

#define NSNotAnIntMapKey((const void *)0x80000000)

NSNotAPointerMapKey

#define NSNotAPointerMapKey((const void *)0xffffffff)

Exceptions

This section lists the names of exceptions raised by Foundation classes.

Archiving

extern NSString *NSInconsistentArchiveException;

Connection

extern NSString *NSFailedAuthenticationException;

General Foundation Exception Names

extern NSString *NSGenericException;
extern NSString *NSRangeException;
extern NSString *NSInvalidArgumentException;
extern NSString *NSInternalInconsistencyException;
extern NSString *NSMallocException;
extern NSString *NSObjectInaccessibleException;
extern NSString *NSObjectNotAvailableException;
extern NSString *NSDestinationInvalidException;
extern NSString *NSPortTimeoutException;
extern NSString *NSInvalidSendPortException;
extern NSString *NSInvalidReceivePortException;
extern NSString *NSPortSendException;
extern NSString *NSPortReceiveException;
extern NSString *NSOldStyleException;

Keyed Archiving

extern NSString *NSInvalidArchiveOperationException;
extern NSString *NSInvalidUnarchiveOperationException;

NSDecimalNumber

extern NSString *NSDecimalNumberExactnessException;
extern NSString *NSDecimalNumberOverflowException;

```
extern NSString *NSDecimalNumberUnderflowException;
extern NSString *NSDecimalNumberDivideByZeroException;
```

NSFileHandle

```
extern NSString *NSFileHandleOperationException;
```

NSScriptKeyValueCoding

```
extern NSString *NSOperationNotSupportedForKeyException;
```

NSString Handling

```
extern NSString *NSParseErrorException;
extern NSString *NSCharacterConversionException;
```

10

Foundation Functions

This chapter lists the functions defined by the Foundation framework. The functions are grouped into the following categories:

Assertions
Bundles
Byte ordering
Decimals
Java setup
Hash tables
HFS file types
Map tables
Object allocation
Objective-C runtime
Path utilities
Points
Ranges
Rects
Sizes
Uncaught exceptions
Zones

Assertions

The assertion macros are used within Objective-C methods or C functions to check a condition, and generate an assertion failure if the condition is false. The NSAssert macros are used within Objective-C methods, while the NSCAssert macros are used within C functions. The assertion macros work with a thread's assertion handler, which is an instance of the class NSAssertionHandler. When an assertion is generated the assertion handler will print an error message with the name of the method and class or function in which the assertion failure occurred. The description strings take printf style formatting.

NSAssert
NSAssert(condition, NSString *description)

NSAssert1 through NSAssert5
NSAssert1(condition, NSString *description, arg1)

NSAssert2(condition, NSString *description, arg1, arg2)

NSAssert3(condition, NSString *description, arg1, arg2, arg3)

NSAssert4(condition, NSString *description, arg1, arg2, arg3, arg4)

NSAssert5(condition, NSString *description, arg1, arg2, arg3, arg4, arg5)

NSCAssert
NSCAssert(condition, NSString *description)

NSCAssert1 through NSCAssert5
NSCAssert1(condition, NSString *description, arg1)

NSCAssert2(condition, NSString *description, arg1, arg2)

NSCAssert3(condition, NSString *description, arg1, arg2, arg3)

NSCAssert4(condition, NSString *description, arg1, arg2, arg3, arg4)

NSCAssert5(condition, NSString *description, arg1, arg2, arg3, arg4, arg5)

NSCParameterAssert
NSCParameterAssert(condition)

NSParameterAssert
NSParameterAssert(condition)

Bundles

The bundle functions are used to access localized string resources contained in an application bundle.

NSLocalizedString
NSString *NSLocalizedString(NSString *key, NSString *comment)

NSLocalizedStringFromTable
NSString *NSLocalizedStringFromTable(NSString *key, NSString *tableName, NSString *comment)

NSLocalizedStringFromTableInBundle
NSString *NSLocalizedStringFromTableInBundle(NSString *key, NSString *tableName, NSBundle *bundle, NSString *comment)

NSLocalizedStringWithDefaultValue
NSString NSLocalizedStringWithDefaultValue(NSString *key, NSString *tableName, NSBundle *bundle, NSString *value, NSString *comment)

Byte Ordering

The byte ordering functions are used to convert primitive data type values from big-endian to little-endian, and vice versa.

NSConvertHostDoubleToSwapped
> NSSwappedDouble NSConvertHostDoubleToSwapped(double x)

NSConvertHostFloatToSwapped
> NSSwappedFloat NSConvertHostFloatToSwapped(float x)

NSConvertSwappedDoubleToHost
> double NSConvertSwappedDoubleToHost(NSSwappedDouble x)

NSConvertSwappedFloatToHost
> float NSConvertSwappedFloatToHost(NSSwappedFloat x)

NSHostByteOrder
> unsigned int NSHostByteOrder(void)

NSSwapBigDoubleToHost
> double NSSwapBigDoubleToHost(NSSwappedDouble x)

NSSwapBigFloatToHost
> float NSSwapBigFloatToHost(NSSwappedFloat x)

NSSwapBigIntToHost
> unsigned int NSSwapBigIntToHost(unsigned int x)

NSSwapBigLongLongToHost
> unsigned long long NSSwapBigLongLongToHost(unsigned long long x)

NSSwapBigLongToHost
> unsigned long NSSwapBigLongToHost(unsigned long x)

NSSwapBigShortToHost
> unsigned short NSSwapBigShortToHost(unsigned short x)

NSSwapDouble
> NSSwappedDouble NSSwapDouble(NSSwappedDouble x)

NSSwapFloat
> NSSwappedFloat NSSwapFloat(NSSwappedFloat x)

NSSwapHostDoubleToBig
> NSSwappedDouble NSSwapHostDoubleToBig(double x)

NSSwapHostDoubleToLittle
> NSSwappedDouble NSSwapHostDoubleToLittle(double x)

NSSwapHostFloatToBig
> NSSwappedFloat NSSwapHostFloatToBig(float x)

NSSwapHostFloatToLittle
> NSSwappedFloat NSSwapHostFloatToLittle(float x)

NSSwapHostIntToBig
> unsigned int NSSwapHostIntToBig(unsigned int x)

NSSwapHostIntToLittle
  unsigned int NSSwapHostIntToLittle(unsigned int x)

NSSwapHostLongLongToBig
  unsigned long long NSSwapHostLongLongToBig(unsigned long long x)

NSSwapHostLongLongToLittle
  unsigned long long NSSwapHostLongLongToLittle(unsigned long long x)

NSSwapHostLongToBig
  unsigned long NSSwapHostLongToBig(unsigned long x)

NSSwapHostLongToLittle
  unsigned long NSSwapHostLongToLittle(unsigned long x)

NSSwapHostShortToBig
  unsigned short NSSwapHostShortToBig(unsigned short x)

NSSwapHostShortToLittle
  unsigned short NSSwapHostShortToLittle(unsigned short x)

NSSwapInt
  unsigned int NSSwapInt (unsigned int inv)

NSSwapLittleDoubleToHost
  double NSSwapLittleDoubleToHost(NSSwappedDouble x)

NSSwapLittleFloatToHost
  float NSSwapLittleFloatToHost(NSSwappedFloat x)

NSSwapLittleIntToHost
  unsigned int NSSwapLittleIntToHost(unsigned int x)

NSSwapLittleLongLongToHost
  unsigned long long NSSwapLittleLongLongToHost(unsigned long long x)

NSSwapLittleLongToHost
  unsigned long NSSwapLittleLongToHost(unsigned long x)

NSSwapLittleShortToHost
  unsigned short NSSwapLittleShortToHost(unsigned short x)

NSSwapLong
  unsigned long NSSwapLong(unsigned long inv)

NSSwapLongLong
  unsigned long long NSSwapLongLong(unsigned long long inv)

NSSwapShort
  unsigned short NSSwapShort (unsigned short inv)

Decimals

These functions are used to perform decimal arithmetic with NSDecimal type structs. The Foundation class NSDecimalNumber may also be used for decimal arithmetic.

NSDecimalAdd

    NSCalculationError NSDecimalAdd(NSDecimal *result, const NSDecimal *leftOperand, const NSDecimal *rightOperand, NSRoundingMode roundingMode)

NSDecimalCompact

    void NSDecimalCompact(NSDecimal *number)

NSDecimalCompare

    NSComparisonResult NSDecimalCompare(const NSDecimal *leftOperand, const NSDecimal *rightOperand)

NSDecimalCopy

    void NSDecimalCopy(NSDecimal *destination, const NSDecimal *source)

NSDecimalDivide

    NSCalculationError NSDecimalDivide(NSDecimal *result, const NSDecimal *leftOperand, const NSDecimal *rightOperand, NSRoundingMode roundingMode)

NSDecimalMultiply

    NSCalculationError NSDecimalMultiply(NSDecimal *result, const NSDecimal *leftOperand, const NSDecimal *rightOperand, NSRoundingMode roundingMode)

NSDecimalMultiplyByPowerOf10

    NSCalculationError NSDecimalMultiplyByPowerOf10(NSDecimal *result, const NSDecimal *number, short power, NSRoundingMode roundingMode)

NSDecimalNormalize

    NSCalculationError NSDecimalNormalize(NSDecimal *number1, NSDecimal *number2, NSRoundingMode roundingMode)

NSDecimalPower

    NSCalculationError NSDecimalPower(NSDecimal *result, const NSDecimal *number, unsigned power, NSRoundingMode roundingMode)

NSDecimalRound

    void NSDecimalRound(NSDecimal *result, const NSDecimal *number, int scale, NSRoundingMode roundingMode)

NSDecimalString

    NSString *NSDecimalString(const NSDecimal *dcm, NSDictionary *locale)

NSDecimalSubtract

    NSCalculationError NSDecimalSubtract(NSDecimal *result, const NSDecimal *leftOperand, const NSDecimal *rightOperand, NSRoundingMode roundingMode)

Java Setup

These functions are used to interact with a Java Virtual Machine, Java classes, and the Java-to-Objective-C bridge.

NSJavaBundleCleanup

    void NSJavaBundleCleanup(NSBundle *bundle, NSDictionary *plist)

NSJavaBundleSetup

    id NSJavaBundleSetup(NSBundle *bundle, NSDictionary *plist)

NSJavaClassesForBundle
NSArray *NSJavaClassesForBundle(NSBundle *bundle, BOOL usesyscl, id *vm)

NSJavaClassesFromPath
NSArray *NSJavaClassesFromPath(NSArray *path, NSArray *wanted, BOOL usesyscl, id *vm)

NSJavaNeedsToLoadClasses
BOOL NSJavaNeedsToLoadClasses(NSDictionary *plist)

NSJavaNeedsVirtualMachine
BOOL NSJavaNeedsVirtualMachine(NSDictionary *plist)

NSJavaObjectNamedInPath
id NSJavaObjectNamedInPath(NSString *name, NSArray *path)

NSJavaProvidesClasses
BOOL NSJavaProvidesClasses(NSDictionary *plist)

NSJavaSetup
id NSJavaSetup(NSDictionary *plist)

NSJavaSetupVirtualMachine
id NSJavaSetupVirtualMachine(void)

Hash Tables

These functions are used to create and manipulate hash tables, which are structs of type NSHashTable.

NSAllHashTableObjects
NSArray *NSAllHashTableObjects(NSHashTable *table)

NSCompareHashTables
BOOL NSCompareHashTables(NSHashTable *table1, NSHashTable *table2)

NSCopyHashTableWithZone
NSHashTable *NSCopyHashTableWithZone(NSHashTable *table, NSZone *zone)

NSCountHashTable
unsigned NSCountHashTable(NSHashTable *table)

NSCreateHashTable
NSHashTable *NSCreateHashTable(NSHashTableCallBacks callBacks, unsigned capacity)

NSCreateHashTableWithZone
NSHashTable *NSCreateHashTableWithZone(NSHashTableCallBacks callBacks, unsigned capacity, NSZone *zone)

NSEndHashTableEnumeration
void NSEndHashTableEnumeration(NSHashEnumerator *enumerator)

NSEnumerateHashTable
NSHashEnumerator NSEnumerateHashTable(NSHashTable *table)

NSFreeHashTable
void NSFreeHashTable(NSHashTable *table)

NSHashGet
    void *NSHashGet(NSHashTable *table, const void *pointer)

NSHashInsert
    void NSHashInsert(NSHashTable *table, const void *pointer)

NSHashInsertIfAbsent
    void *NSHashInsertIfAbsent(NSHashTable *table, const void *pointer)

NSHashInsertKnownAbsent
    void NSHashInsertKnownAbsent(NSHashTable *table, const void *pointer)

NSHashRemove
    void NSHashRemove(NSHashTable *table, const void *pointer)

NSNextHashEnumeratorItem
    void *NSNextHashEnumeratorItem(NSHashEnumerator *enumerator)

NSResetHashTable
    void NSResetHashTable(NSHashTable *table)

NSStringFromHashTable
    NSString *NSStringFromHashTable(NSHashTable *table)

HFS File Types

These functions are used to determine the HFS file type of a file, as well as to convert between HFS file types and HFS file codes.

NSFileTypeForHFSTypeCode
    NSString *NSFileTypeForHFSTypeCode(OSType hfsFileTypeCode)

NSHFSTypeCodeFromFileType
    OSType NSHFSTypeCodeFromFileType(NSString *fileTypeString)

NSHFSTypeOfFile
    NSString *NSHFSTypeOfFile(NSString *fullFilePath)

Map Tables

These functions are used to create and manipulate map tables, which are structs of type NSMapTable.

NSAllMapTableKeys
    NSArray *NSAllMapTableKeys(NSMapTable *table)

NSAllMapTableValues
    NSArray *NSAllMapTableValues(NSMapTable *table)

NSCompareMapTables
    BOOL NSCompareMapTables(NSMapTable *table1, NSMapTable *table2)

NSCopyMapTableWithZone
    NSMapTable *NSCopyMapTableWithZone(NSMapTable *table, NSZone *zone)

NSCountMapTable
> unsigned NSCountMapTable(NSMapTable *table)

NSCreateMapTable
> NSMapTable *NSCreateMapTable(NSMapTableKeyCallBacks keyCallBacks, NSMap-TableValueCallBacks valueCallBacks, unsigned capacity)

NSCreateMapTableWithZone
> NSMapTable *NSCreateMapTableWithZone(NSMapTableKeyCallBacks keyCallBacks, NSMapTableValueCallBacks valueCallBacks, unsigned capacity, NSZone *zone)

NSEndMapTableEnumeration
> void NSEndMapTableEnumeration(NSMapEnumerator *enumerator)

NSEnumerateMapTable
> NSMapEnumerator NSEnumerateMapTable(NSMapTable *table)

NSFreeMapTable
> void NSFreeMapTable(NSMapTable *table)

NSMapGet
> void *NSMapGet(NSMapTable *table, const void *key)

NSMapInsert
> void NSMapInsert(NSMapTable *table, const void *key, const void *value)

NSMapInsertIfAbsent
> void *NSMapInsertIfAbsent(NSMapTable *table, const void *key, const void *value)

NSMapInsertKnownAbsent
> void NSMapInsertKnownAbsent(NSMapTable *table, const void *key, const void *value)

NSMapMember
> BOOL NSMapMember(NSMapTable *table, const void *key, void **originalKey, void **value)

NSMapRemove
> void NSMapRemove(NSMapTable *table, const void *key)

NSNextMapEnumeratorPair
> BOOL NSNextMapEnumeratorPair(NSMapEnumerator *enumerator, void **key, void **value)

NSResetMapTable
> void NSResetMapTable(NSMapTable *table)

NSStringFromMapTable
> NSString *NSStringFromMapTable(NSMapTable *table)

Object Allocation

These functions may be used to create and destroy Objective-C objects, as well as to manage the reference counts of objects.

NSAllocateObject
> id NSAllocateObject(Class aClass, unsigned extraBytes, NSZone *zone)

NSCopyObject
> id NSCopyObject(id object, unsigned extraBytes, NSZone *zone)

NSDeallocateObject
    void NSDeallocateObject(id object)

NSDecrementExtraRefCountWasZero
    BOOL NSDecrementExtraRefCountWasZero(id object)

NSExtraRefCount
    unsigned NSExtraRefCount(id object)

NSIncrementExtraRefCount
    void NSIncrementExtraRefCount(id object)

NSShouldRetainWithZone
    BOOL NSShouldRetainWithZone(id anObject, NSZone *requestedZone)

Objective-C Runtime

These functions are used to obtain Objective-C runtime data types such as selectors and class objects. NSLog and NSLogv are used to print information to the standard output of an application.

NSClassFromString
    Class NSClassFromString(NSString *aClassName)

NSGetSizeAndAlignment
    const char *NSGetSizeAndAlignment(const char *typePtr, unsigned int *sizep, unsigned int *alignp)

NSLog
    void NSLog(NSString *format, ...)

NSLogv
    void NSLogv(NSString *format, va_list args)

NSSelectorFromString
    SEL NSSelectorFromString(NSString *aSelectorName)

NSStringFromClass
    NSString *NSStringFromClass(Class aClass)

NSStringFromSelector
    NSString *NSStringFromSelector(SEL aSelector)

Path Utilities

These functions are used to get filesystem paths to common files and directories such as the current user's home directory. NSFullUserName is used to obtain the long username of the current username, while NSUserName returns a user's short username.

NSFullUserName
    NSString *NSFullUserName(void)

NSHomeDirectory
    NSString *NSHomeDirectory(void)

NSHomeDirectoryForUser
    NSString *NSHomeDirectoryForUser(NSString *userName)

NSOpenStepRootDirectory
    NSString *NSOpenStepRootDirectory(void)

NSSearchPathForDirectoriesInDomains
    NSArray *NSSearchPathForDirectoriesInDomains(NSSearchPathDirectory directory,
    NSSearchPathDomainMask domainMask, BOOL expandTilde)

NSTemporaryDirectory
    NSString *NSTemporaryDirectory(void)

NSUserName
    NSString *NSUserName(void)

Points

These functions are used to create and manipulate NSPoint structures.

NSEqualPoints
    BOOL NSEqualPoints(NSPoint aPoint, NSPoint bPoint)

NSMakePoint
    NSPoint NSMakePoint(float x, float y)

NSPointFromString
    NSPoint NSPointFromString(NSString *aString)

NSStringFromPoint
    NSString *NSStringFromPoint(NSPoint aPoint)

Ranges

These functions are used to create and manipulate NSRange structures.

NSEqualRanges
    BOOL NSEqualRanges(NSRange range1, NSRange range2)

NSIntersectionRange
    NSRange NSIntersectionRange(NSRange range1, NSRange range2)

NSLocationInRange
    BOOL NSLocationInRange(unsigned int index, NSRange aRange)

NSMakeRange
    NSRange NSMakeRange(unsigned int location, unsigned int length)

NSMaxRange
    unsigned int NSMaxRange(NSRange range)

NSRangeFromString
    NSRange NSRangeFromString(NSString *aString)

NSStringFromRange
    NSString *NSStringFromRange(NSRange range)

NSUnionRange
    NSRange NSUnionRange(NSRange range1, NSRange range2)

Rects

These functions are used to create and manipulate NSRect structures.

NSContainsRect
    BOOL NSContainsRect(NSRect aRect, NSRect bRect)

NSDivideRect
    void NSDivideRect(NSRect inRect, NSRect *slice, NSRect *rem, float amount, NSRectEdge edge)

NSEqualRects
    BOOL NSEqualRects(NSRect aRect, NSRect bRect)

NSHeight
    float NSHeight(NSRect aRect)

NSInsetRect
    NSRect NSInsetRect(NSRect aRect, float dX, float dY)

NSIntegralRect
    NSRect NSIntegralRect(NSRect aRect)

NSIntersectionRect
    NSRect NSIntersectionRect(NSRect aRect, NSRect bRect)

NSIntersectsRect
    BOOL NSIntersectsRect(NSRect aRect, NSRect bRect)

NSIsEmptyRect
    BOOL NSIsEmptyRect(NSRect aRect)

NSMakeRect
    NSRect NSMakeRect(float x, float y, float w, float h)

NSMaxX
    float NSMaxX(NSRect aRect)

NSMaxY
    float NSMaxY(NSRect aRect)

NSMidX
    float NSMidX(NSRect aRect)

NSMidY
    float NSMidY(NSRect aRect)

NSMinX
    float NSMinX(NSRect aRect)

NSMinY
    float NSMinY(NSRect aRect)

NSMouseInRect
> BOOL NSMouseInRect(NSPoint aPoint, NSRect aRect, BOOL isFlipped)

NSOffsetRect
> NSRect NSOffsetRect(NSRect aRect, float dX, float dY)

NSPointInRect
> BOOL NSPointInRect(NSPoint aPoint, NSRect aRect)

NSRectFromString
> NSRect NSRectFromString(NSString *aString)

NSStringFromRect
> NSString *NSStringFromRect(NSRect aRect)

NSUnionRect
> NSRect NSUnionRect(NSRect aRect, NSRect bRect)

NSWidth
> float NSWidth(NSRect aRect)

Sizes

These functions are used to create and manipulate NSSize structures.

NSEqualSizes
> BOOL NSEqualSizes(NSSize aSize, NSSize bSize)

NSMakeSize
> NSSize NSMakeSize(float width, float height)

NSSizeFromString
> NSSize NSSizeFromString(NSString *aString)

NSStringFromSize
> NSString *NSStringFromSize(NSSize aSize)

Uncaught Exceptions

These two functions are used to get and set the function that an application uses to handle uncaught exceptions.

NSGetUncaughtExceptionHandler
> NSUncaughtExceptionHandler *NSGetUncaughtExceptionHandler(void)

NSSetUncaughtExceptionHandler
> void NSSetUncaughtExceptionHandler(NSUncaughtExceptionHandler *)

Zones

These functions are used to manipulate memory zones, represented by the data type NSZone.

NSAllocateMemoryPages
    void *NSAllocateMemoryPages(unsigned bytes)

NSCopyMemoryPages
    void NSCopyMemoryPages(const void *source, void *dest, unsigned bytes)

NSCreateZone
    NSZone *NSCreateZone(unsigned startSize, unsigned granularity, BOOL canFree)

NSDeallocateMemoryPages
    void NSDeallocateMemoryPages(void *ptr, unsigned bytes)

NSDefaultMallocZone
    NSZone *NSDefaultMallocZone(void)

NSLogPageSize
    unsigned NSLogPageSize(void)

NSPageSize
    unsigned NSPageSize(void)

NSRealMemoryAvailable
    unsigned NSRealMemoryAvailable(void)

NSRecycleZone
    void NSRecycleZone(NSZone *zone)

NSReturnAddress
    void *NSReturnAddress(unsigned frame)

NSRoundDownToMultipleOfPageSize
    unsigned NSRoundDownToMultipleOfPageSize(unsigned bytes)

NSRoundUpToMultipleOfPageSize
    unsigned NSRoundUpToMultipleOfPageSize(unsigned bytes)

NSSetZoneName
    void NSSetZoneName(NSZone *zone, NSString *name)

NSZoneCalloc
    void *NSZoneCalloc(NSZone *zone, unsigned numElems, unsigned byteSize)

NSZoneFree
    void NSZoneFree(NSZone *zone, void *ptr)

NSZoneFromPointer
    NSZone *NSZoneFromPointer(void *ptr)

NSZoneMalloc
    void *NSZoneMalloc(NSZone *zone, unsigned size)

NSZoneName
    NSString *NSZoneName(NSZone *zone)

NSZoneRealloc
    void *NSZoneRealloc(NSZone *zone, void *ptr, unsigned size)

11

Application Kit Types and Constants

This chapter describes the data types and constants found in the Foundation framework, and is divided into the following sections:

Data types
Enumerations
Global variables
Exception names

Data Types

This section lists the data types defined by and used in the Application Kit.

NSAffineTransformStruct

```
typedef struct _NSAffineTransformStruct {
    float m11, m12, m21, m22;
    float tX, tY;
} NSAffineTransformStruct;
```

NSApplicationTerminateReply

```
typedef enum NSApplicationTerminateReply {
    NSTerminateCancel = 0,
    NSTerminateNow = 1,
    NSTerminateLater = 2
} NSApplicationTerminateReply;
```

NSBackingStoreType

```
typedef enum _NSBackingStoreType {
    NSBackingStoreRetained = 0,
    NSBackingStoreNonretained = 1,
    NSBackingStoreBuffered = 2
} NSBackingStoreType;
```

NSBezelStyle

```
typedef enum _NSBezelStyle {
    NSRoundedBezelStyle = 1,
    NSRegularSquareBezelStyle = 2,
    NSThickSquareBezelStyle = 3,
    NSThickerSquareBezelStyle = 4,
    NSShadowlessSquareBezelStyle = 6,
    NSCircularBezelStyle = 7
} NSBezelStyle;
```

NSBezierPathElement

```
typedef enum {
    NSMoveToBezierPathElement,
    NSLineToBezierPathElement,
    NSCurveToBezierPathElement,
    NSClosePathBezierPathElement
} NSBezierPathElement;
```

NSBitmapImageFileType

```
typedef enum _NSBitmapImageFileType {
    NSTIFFFileType,
    NSBMPFileType,
    NSGIFFileType,
    NSJPEGFileType,
    NSPNGFileType
} NSBitmapImageFileType;
```

NSBorderType

```
typedef enum _NSBorderType {
    NSNoBorder = 0,
    NSLineBorder = 1,
    NSBezelBorder = 2,
    NSGrooveBorder = 3
} NSBorderType;
```

NSBoxType

```
typedef enum {
    NSBoxPrimary = 0,
    NSBoxSecondary = 1,
    NSBoxSeparator = 2,
    NSBoxOldStyle = 3
} NSBoxType;
```

NSButtonType

```
typedef enum _NSButtonType {
    NSMomentaryLightButton = 0,
    NSPushOnPushOffButton = 1,
    NSToggleButton = 2,
    NSSwitchButton = 3,
    NSRadioButton = 4,
    NSMomentaryChangeButton = 5,
    NSOnOffButton = 6,
    NSMomentaryPushInButton = 7
} NSButtonType;
```

NSCellAttribute

```
typedef enum _NSCellAttribute {
    NSCellDisabled = 0,
    NSCellState = 1,
    NSPushInCell = 2,
    NSCellEditable = 3,
    NSChangeGrayCell = 4,
    NSCellHighlighted = 5,
    NSCellLightsByContents = 6,
    NSCellLightsByGray = 7,
    NSChangeBackgroundCell = 8,
    NSCellLightsByBackground = 9,
    NSCellIsBordered = 10,
    NSCellHasOverlappingImage = 11,
    NSCellHasImageHorizontal = 12,
    NSCellHasImageOnLeftOrBottom = 13,
    NSCellChangesContents = 14,
    NSCellIsInsetButton = 15,
    NSCellAllowsMixedState = 16
} NSCellAttribute;
```

NSCellImagePosition

```
typedef enum _NSCellImagePosition {
    NSNoImage = 0,
    NSImageOnly = 1,
    NSImageLeft = 2,
    NSImageRight = 3,
    NSImageBelow = 4,
    NSImageAbove = 5,
    NSImageOverlaps = 6
} NSCellImagePosition;
```

NSCellState

```
typedef enum _NSCellState {
    NSMixedState = -1,
    NSOffState = 0,
    NSOnState = 1
} NSCellStateValue;
```

NSCellType

```
typedef enum _NSCellType {
    NSNullCellType = 0,
    NSTextCellType = 1,
    NSImageCellType = 2
} NSCellType;
```

NSCharacterCollection

```
typedef enum {
    NSIdentityMappingCharacterCollection = 0,
    NSAdobeCNS1CharacterCollection = 1,
    NSAdobeGB1CharacterCollection = 2,
    NSAdobeJapan1CharacterCollection = 3,
    NSAdobeJapan2CharacterCollection = 4,
    NSAdobeKorea1CharacterCollection = 5,
} NSCharacterCollection;
```

NSCompositingOperation

```
typedef enum _NSCompositingOperation {
    NSCompositeClear = 0,
    NSCompositeCopy = 1,
    NSCompositeSourceOver = 2,
    NSCompositeSourceIn = 3,
    NSCompositeSourceOut = 4,
    NSCompositeSourceAtop = 5,
    NSCompositeDestinationOver = 6,
    NSCompositeDestinationIn = 7,
    NSCompositeDestinationOut = 8,
    NSCompositeDestinationAtop = 9,
    NSCompositeXOR = 10,
    NSCompositePlusDarker = 11,
    NSCompositeHighlight = 12,
    NSCompositePlusLighter = 13
} NSCompositingOperation;
```

NSControlSize

```
typedef enum _NSControlSize {
    NSRegularControlSize,
    NSSmallControlSize
} NSControlSize;
```

NSControlTint

```
typedef enum _NSControlTint {
    NSDefaultControlTint = 0,
    NSClearControlTint = 7
} NSControlTint;
```

NSDocumentChangeType

```
typedef enum _NSDocumentChangeType {
    NSChangeDone = 0,
    NSChangeUndone = 1,
    NSChangeCleared = 2
} NSDocumentChangeType;
```

NSDragOperation

```
typedef unsigned int NSDragOperation;
```

NSDrawerState

```
typedef enum _NSDrawerState {
    NSDrawerClosedState = 0,
    NSDrawerOpeningState = 1,
    NSDrawerOpenState = 2,
    NSDrawerClosingState = 3
} NSDrawerState;
```

NSEventType

```
typedef enum _NSEventType {
    NSLeftMouseDown = 1,
    NSLeftMouseUp = 2,
    NSRightMouseDown = 3,
    NSRightMouseUp = 4,
    NSMouseMoved = 5,
    NSLeftMouseDragged = 6,
    NSRightMouseDragged = 7,
    NSMouseEntered = 8,
    NSMouseExited = 9,
    NSKeyDown = 10,
    NSKeyUp = 11,
    NSFlagsChanged = 12,
    NSAppKitDefined = 13,
    NSSystemDefined = 14,
    NSApplicationDefined = 15,
    NSPeriodic = 16,
    NSCursorUpdate = 17,
    NSScrollWheel = 22,
    NSOtherMouseDown = 25,
    NSOtherMouseUp = 26,
    NSOtherMouseDragged = 27
} NSEventType;
```

NSFocusRingPlacement

```
typedef enum {
    NSFocusRingOnly = 0,
    NSFocusRingBelow = 1,
```

NSFontAction

```
typedef enum _NSFontAction {
  NSNoFontChangeAction = 0,
  NSViaPanelFontAction = 1,
  NSAddTraitFontAction = 2,
  NSSizeUpFontAction = 3,
  NSSizeDownFontAction = 4,
  NSHeavierFontAction = 5,
  NSLighterFontAction = 6,
  NSRemoveTraitFontAction = 7
} NSFontAction;
```

NSFontTraitMask

```
typedef unsigned int NSFontTraitMask;
```

NSGlyph

```
typedef unsigned int NSGlyph;
```

NSGlyphInscription

```
typedef enum {
  NSGlyphInscribeBase = 0,
  NSGlyphInscribeBelow = 1,
  NSGlyphInscribeAbove = 2,
  NSGlyphInscribeOverstrike = 3,
  NSGlyphInscribeOverBelow = 4
} NSGlyphInscription;
```

NSGlyphLayoutMode

```
typedef enum _NSGlyphLayoutMode {
  NSGlyphLayoutAtAPoint = 0,
  NSGlyphLayoutAgainstAPoint,
  NSGlyphLayoutWithPrevious
} NSGlyphLayoutMode;
```

NSGlyphRelation

```
typedef enum _NSGlyphRelation {
  NSGlyphBelow = 1,
  NSGlyphAbove = 2
} NSGlyphRelation;
```

NSGradientType

```
typedef enum _NSGradientType {
    NSGradientNone = 0,
    NSGradientConcaveWeak = 1,
    NSGradientConcaveStrong = 2,
    NSGradientConvexWeak = 3,
    NSGradientConvexStrong = 4
} NSGradientType;
```

NSImageAlignment

```
typedef enum {
    NSImageAlignCenter = 0,
    NSImageAlignTop,
    NSImageAlignTopLeft,
    NSImageAlignTopRight,
    NSImageAlignLeft,
    NSImageAlignBottom,
    NSImageAlignBottomLeft,
    NSImageAlignBottomRight,
    NSImageAlignRight
} NSImageAlignment;
```

NSImageCacheMode

```
typedef enum {
    NSImageCacheDefault,
    NSImageCacheAlways,
    NSImageCacheBySize,
    NSImageCacheNever
} NSImageCacheMode;
```

NSImageFrameStyle

```
typedef enum {
    NSImageFrameNone = 0,
    NSImageFramePhoto,
    NSImageFrameGrayBezel,
    NSImageFrameGroove,
    NSImageFrameButton
} NSImageFrameStyle;
```

NSImageInterpolation

```
typedef enum {
    NSImageInterpolationDefault,
    NSImageInterpolationNone,
    NSImageInterpolationLow,
    NSImageInterpolationHigh
} NSImageInterpolation;
```

NSImageLoadStatus

```
typedef enum {
    NSImageLoadStatusCompleted,
    NSImageLoadStatusCancelled,
    NSImageLoadStatusInvalidData,
    NSImageLoadStatusUnexpectedEOF,
    NSImageLoadStatusReadError
} NSImageLoadStatus;
```

NSImageRepLoadStatus

```
typedef enum {
    NSImageRepLoadStatusUnknownType = -1,
    NSImageRepLoadStatusReadingHeader = -2,
    NSImageRepLoadStatusWillNeedAllData = -3,
    NSImageRepLoadStatusInvalidData = -4,
    NSImageRepLoadStatusUnexpectedEOF = -5,
    NSImageRepLoadStatusCompleted = -6
} NSImageRepLoadStatus;
```

NSImageScaling

```
typedef enum {
    NSScaleProportionally = 0,
    NSScaleToFit,
    NSScaleNone
} NSImageScaling;
```

NSInterfaceStyle

```
typedef enum {
    NSNoInterfaceStyle = 0,
    NSNextStepInterfaceStyle = 1,
    NSWindows95InterfaceStyle = 2,
    NSMacintoshInterfaceStyle = 3
} NSInterfaceStyle;
```

NSLayoutDirection

```
typedef enum _NSLayoutDirection {
    NSLayoutLeftToRight = 0,
    NSLayoutRightToLeft
} NSLayoutDirection;
```

NSLayoutStatus

```
typedef enum _NSLayoutStatus {
    NSLayoutNotDone = 0,
    NSLayoutDone,
```

```
      NSLayoutCantFit,
      NSLayoutOutOfGlyphs
    } NSLayoutStatus;
```

NSLineBreakMode

```
typedef enum _NSLineBreakMode {
  NSLineBreakByWordWrapping = 0,
  NSLineBreakByCharWrapping,
  NSLineBreakByClipping,
  NSLineBreakByTruncatingHead,
  NSLineBreakByTruncatingTail,
  NSLineBreakByTruncatingMiddle
} NSLineBreakMode;
```

NSLineCapStyle

```
typedef enum {
  NSButtLineCapStyle = 0,
  NSRoundLineCapStyle = 1,
  NSSquareLineCapStyle = 2
} NSLineCapStyle;
```

NSLineJoinStyle

```
typedef enum {
  NSMiterLineJoinStyle = 0,
  NSRoundLineJoinStyle = 1,
  NSBevelLineJoinStyle = 2
} NSLineJoinStyle;
```

NSLineMovementDirection

```
typedef enum {
  NSLineDoesntMove = 0,
  NSLineMovesLeft = 1,
  NSLineMovesRight = 2,
  NSLineMovesDown = 3,
  NSLineMovesUp = 4
} NSLineMovementDirection;
```

NSLineSweepDirection

```
typedef enum {
  NSLineSweepLeft = 0,
  NSLineSweepRight = 1,
  NSLineSweepDown = 2,
  NSLineSweepUp = 3
} NSLineSweepDirection;
```

NSMatrixMode

```
typedef enum _NSMatrixMode {
    NSRadioModeMatrix = 0,
    NSHighlightModeMatrix = 1,
    NSListModeMatrix = 2,
    NSTrackModeMatrix = 3
} NSMatrixMode;
```

NSModalSession

```
typedef struct _NSModalSession *NSModalSession;
```

NSMultibyteGlyphPacking

```
typedef enum _NSMultibyteGlyphPacking {
    NSOneByteGlyphPacking,
    NSJapaneseEUCGlyphPacking,
    NSAsciiWithDoubleByteEUCGlyphPacking,
    NSTwoByteGlyphPacking,
    NSFourByteGlyphPacking,
    NSNativeShortGlyphPacking
} NSMultibyteGlyphPacking;
```

NSOpenGLContextAuxiliary

```
typedef struct _CGLContextObject NSOpenGLContextAuxiliary;
```

NSOpenGLContextParameter

```
typedef enum {
    NSOpenGLCPSwapRectangle = 200,
    NSOpenGLCPSwapRectangleEnable = 201,
    NSOpenGLCPRasterizationEnable = 221,
    NSOpenGLCPSwapInterval = 222,
    NSOpenGLCPSurfaceOrder = 235,
    NSOpenGLCPSurfaceOpacity = 236,
    NSOpenGLCPStateValidation = 301
} NSOpenGLContextParameter;
```

NSOpenGLGlobalOption

```
typedef enum {
    NSOpenGLGOFormatCacheSize = 501,
    NSOpenGLGOClearFormatCache = 502,
    NSOpenGLGORetainRenderers = 503,
    NSOpenGLGOResetLibrary = 504
} NSOpenGLGlobalOption;
```

NSOpenGLPixelFormatAttribute

```
typedef enum {
  NSOpenGLPFAAllRenderers = 1,
  NSOpenGLPFADoubleBuffer = 5,
  NSOpenGLPFAStereo = 6,
  NSOpenGLPFAAuxBuffers = 7,
  NSOpenGLPFAColorSize = 8,
  NSOpenGLPFAAlphaSize = 11,
  NSOpenGLPFADepthSize = 12,
  NSOpenGLPFAStencilSize = 13,
  NSOpenGLPFAAccumSize = 14,
  NSOpenGLPFAMinimumPolicy = 51,
  NSOpenGLPFAMaximumPolicy = 52,
  NSOpenGLPFAOffScreen = 53,
  NSOpenGLPFAFullScreen = 54,
  NSOpenGLPFASampleBuffers = 55,
  NSOpenGLPFASamples = 56,
  NSOpenGLPFAAuxDepthStencil = 57,
  NSOpenGLPFARendererID = 70,
  NSOpenGLPFASingleRenderer = 71,
  NSOpenGLPFANoRecovery = 72,
  NSOpenGLPFAAccelerated = 73,
  NSOpenGLPFAClosestPolicy = 74,
  NSOpenGLPFARobust = 75,
  NSOpenGLPFABackingStore = 76,
  NSOpenGLPFAMPSafe = 78,
  NSOpenGLPFAWindow = 80,
  NSOpenGLPFAMultiScreen = 81,
  NSOpenGLPFACompliant = 83,
  NSOpenGLPFAScreenMask = 84,
  NSOpenGLPFAVirtualScreenCount = 128
} NSOpenGLPixelFormatAttribute;
```

NSOpenGLPixelFormatAuxiliary

```
typedef struct _CGLPixelFormatObject NSOpenGLPixelFormatAuxiliary;
```

NSPopUpArrowPosition

```
typedef enum {
  NSPopUpNoArrow = 0,
  NSPopUpArrowAtCenter = 1,
  NSPopUpArrowAtBottom = 2
} NSPopUpArrowPosition;
```

NSPrinterTableStatus

```
typedef enum _NSPrinterTableStatus {
  NSPrinterTableOK = 0,
  NSPrinterTableNotFound = 1,
  NSPrinterTableError = 2
} NSPrinterTableStatus;
```

NSPrintingOrientation

```
typedef enum {
    NSPortraitOrientation = 0,
    NSLandscapeOrientation = 1
} NSPrintingOrientation;
```

NSPrintingPageOrder

```
typedef enum _NSPrintingPageOrder {
    NSDescendingPageOrder = (-1),
    NSSpecialPageOrder = 0,
    NSAscendingPageOrder = 1,
    NSUnknownPageOrder = 2
} NSPrintingPageOrder;
```

NSPrintingPaginationMode

```
typedef enum {
    NSAutoPagination = 0,
    NSFitPagination = 1,
    NSClipPagination = 2
} NSPrintingPaginationMode;
```

NSProgressIndicatorStyle

```
typedef enum _NSProgressIndicatorStyle {
    NSProgressIndicatorBarStyle = 0,
    NSProgressIndicatorSpinningStyle = 1
} NSProgressIndicatorStyle;
```

NSProgressIndicatorThickness

```
typedef enum _NSProgressIndicatorThickness {
    NSProgressIndicatorPreferredThickness = 14,
    NSProgressIndicatorPreferredSmallThickness = 10,
    NSProgressIndicatorPreferredLargeThickness = 18,
    NSProgressIndicatorPreferredAquaThickness = 12
} NSProgressIndicatorThickness;
```

NSQTMovieLoopMode

```
typedef enum {
    NSQTMovieNormalPlayback,
    NSQTMovieLoopingPlayback,
    NSQTMovieLoopingBackAndForthPlayback
} NSQTMovieLoopMode;
```

NSRequestUserAttentionType

```
typedef enum {
  NSCriticalRequest = 0,
  NSInformationalRequest = 10
} NSRequestUserAttentionType;
```

NSRulerOrientation

```
typedef enum {
  NSHorizontalRuler,
  NSVerticalRuler
} NSRulerOrientation;
```

NSSaveOperationType

```
typedef enum _NSSaveOperationType {
  NSSaveOperation = 0,
  NSSaveAsOperation = 1,
  NSSaveToOperation = 2
} NSSaveOperationType;
```

NSScreenAuxiliaryOpaque

```
typedef struct NSScreenAuxiliary NSScreenAuxiliaryOpaque;
```

NSScrollArrowPosition

```
typedef enum _NSScrollArrowPosition {
  NSScrollerArrowsDefaultSetting = 0,
  NSScrollerArrowsNone = 2
} NSScrollArrowPosition;
```

NSScrollerArrow

```
typedef enum _NSScrollerArrow {
  NSScrollerIncrementArrow = 0,
  NSScrollerDecrementArrow = 1
} NSScrollerArrow;
```

NSScrollerPart

```
typedef enum _NSScrollerPart {
  NSScrollerNoPart = 0,
  NSScrollerDecrementPage = 1,
  NSScrollerKnob = 2,
  NSScrollerIncrementPage = 3,
  NSScrollerDecrementLine = 4,
  NSScrollerIncrementLine = 5,
  NSScrollerKnobSlot = 6
} NSScrollerPart;
```

NSSelectionAffinity

```
typedef enum _NSSelectionAffinity {
    NSSelectionAffinityUpstream = 0,
    NSSelectionAffinityDownstream = 1
} NSSelectionAffinity;
```

NSSelectionDirection

```
typedef enum _NSSelectionDirection {
    NSDirectSelection = 0,
    NSSelectingNext,
    NSSelectingPrevious
} NSSelectionDirection;
```

NSSelectionGranularity

```
typedef enum _NSSelectionGranularity {
    NSSelectByCharacter = 0,
    NSSelectByWord = 1,
    NSSelectByParagraph = 2
} NSSelectionGranularity;
```

NSTableViewDropOperation

```
typedef enum {
    NSTableViewDropOn,
    NSTableViewDropAbove
} NSTableViewDropOperation;
```

NSTabState

```
typedef enum _NSTabState {
    NSSelectedTab = 0,
    NSBackgroundTab = 1,
    NSPressedTab = 2
} NSTabState;
```

NSTabViewItemAuxiliaryOpaque

```
typedef struct NSTabViewItemAuxiliary NSTabViewItemAuxiliaryOpaque;
```

NSTabViewType

```
typedef enum _NSTabViewType {
    NSTopTabsBezelBorder = 0,
    NSLeftTabsBezelBorder = 1,
    NSBottomTabsBezelBorder = 2,
    NSRightTabsBezelBorder = 3,
    NSNoTabsBezelBorder = 4,
```

```
    NSNoTabsLineBorder= 5,
    NSNoTabsNoBorder = 6
} NSTabViewType;
```

NSTextAlignment

```
typedef enum _NSTextAlignment {
    NSLeftTextAlignment = 0,
    NSRightTextAlignment = 1,
    NSCenterTextAlignment = 2,
    NSJustifiedTextAlignment = 3,
    NSNaturalTextAlignment = 4
} NSTextAlignment;
```

NSTextFieldBezelStyle

```
typedef enum {
    NSTextFieldSquareBezel  = 0,
    NSTextFieldRoundedBezel = 1
} NSTextFieldBezelStyle;
```

NSTextTabType

```
typedef enum _NSTextTabType {
    NSLeftTabStopType = 0,
    NSRightTabStopType,
    NSCenterTabStopType,
    NSDecimalTabStopType
} NSTextTabType;
```

NSTickMarkPosition

```
typedef enum _NSTickMarkPosition {
    NSTickMarkBelow = 0,
    NSTickMarkAbove = 1,
    NSTickMarkLeft = NSTickMarkAbove,
    NSTickMarkRight = NSTickMarkBelow
} NSTickMarkPosition;
```

NSTIFFCompression

```
typedef enum _NSTIFFCompression {
    NSTIFFCompressionNone = 1,
    NSTIFFCompressionCCITTFAX3 = 3,
    NSTIFFCompressionCCITTFAX4 = 4,
    NSTIFFCompressionLZW = 5,
    NSTIFFCompressionJPEG = 6,
    NSTIFFCompressionNEXT = 32766,
    NSTIFFCompressionPackBits = 32773,
    NSTIFFCompressionOldJPEG = 32865
} NSTIFFCompression;
```

NSTitlePosition

```
typedef enum _NSTitlePosition {
    NSNoTitle = 0,
    NSAboveTop = 1,
    NSAtTop = 2,
    NSBelowTop = 3,
    NSAboveBottom = 4,
    NSAtBottom = 5,
    NSBelowBottom = 6
} NSTitlePosition;
```

NSToolbarDisplayMode

```
typedef enum {
    NSToolbarDisplayModeDefault,
    NSToolbarDisplayModeIconAndLabel,
    NSToolbarDisplayModeIconOnly,
    NSToolbarDisplayModeLabelOnly
} NSToolbarDisplayMode;
```

NSToolbarSizeMode

```
typedef enum {
    NSToolbarSizeModeDefault,
    NSToolbarSizeModeRegular,
    NSToolbarSizeModeSmall
} NSToolbarSizeMode;
```

NSToolTipTag

```
typedef int NSToolTipTag;
```

NSTrackingRectTag

```
typedef int NSTrackingRectTag;
```

NSTypesetterBehavior

```
typedef enum {
    NSTypesetterLatestBehavior = -1,
    NSTypesetterOriginalBehavior = 0,
    NSTypesetterBehavior_10_2_WithCompatibility = 1,
    NSTypesetterBehavior_10_2 = 2,
} NSTypesetterBehavior;
```

NSTypesetterGlyphInfo

```
typedef struct _NSTypesetterGlyphInfo {
  NSPoint curLocation;
  float extent;
  float belowBaseline;
  float aboveBaseline;
  unsigned glyphCharacterIndex;
  NSFont *font;
  NSSize attachmentSize;
  struct {
    BOOL defaultPositioning:1;
    BOOL dontShow:1;
    BOOL isAttachment:1;
  } _giflags;
} NSTypesetterGlyphInfo;
```

NSUsableScrollerParts

```
typedef enum _NSUsableScrollerParts {
  NSNoScrollerParts = 0,
  NSOnlyScrollerArrows = 1,
  NSAllScrollerParts = 2
} NSUsableScrollerParts;
```

NSWindingRule

```
typedef enum {
  NSNonZeroWindingRule = 0,
  NSEvenOddWindingRule = 1
} NSWindingRule;
```

NSWindowAuxiliaryOpaque

```
typedef struct NSWindowAuxiliary NSWindowAuxiliaryOpaque;
```

NSWindowButton

```
typedef enum {
  NSWindowCloseButton,
  NSWindowMiniaturizeButton,
  NSWindowZoomButton,
  NSWindowToolbarButton,
  NSWindowDocumentIconButton
} NSWindowButton;
```

NSWindowDepth

```
typedef int NSWindowDepth;
```

NSWindowOrderingMode

```
typedef enum _NSWindowOrderingMode {
    NSWindowAbove = 1,
    NSWindowBelow = -1,
    NSWindowOut = 0
} NSWindowOrderingMode;
```

NSWritingDirection

```
typedef enum _NSWritingDirection {
    NSWritingDirectionLeftToRight = 0,
    NSWritingDirectionRightToLeft
} NSWritingDirection;
```

Enumerations

This section lists the enumeration constants defined by and used in the Application Kit.

NSApplication (Modal Session Return Values)

```
enum {
    NSRunStoppedResponse = (-1000),
    NSRunAbortedResponse = (-1001),
    NSRunContinuesResponse = (-1002)
};
```

NSAttributedString (Underlining)

```
enum {
    NSNoUnderlineStyle = 0,
    NSSingleUnderlineStyle
};
```

NSCell (Data Entry Types)

```
enum {
    NSAnyType = 0,
    NSIntType = 1,
    NSPositiveIntType = 2,
    NSFloatType = 3,
    NSPositiveFloatType = 4,
    NSDoubleType = 6,
    NSPositiveDoubleType = 7
};
```

NSCell (State Masks)

```
enum {
  NSNoCellMask = 0,
  NSContentsCellMask = 1,
  NSPushInCellMask = 2,
  NSChangeGrayCellMask = 4,
  NSChangeBackgroundCellMask = 8
};
```

NSColorPanel (Modes)

```
enum {
  NSGrayModeColorPanel = 0,
  NSRGBModeColorPanel = 1,
  NSCMYKModeColorPanel = 2,
  NSHSBModeColorPanel = 3,
  NSCustomPaletteModeColorPanel = 4,
  NSColorListModeColorPanel = 5,
  NSWheelModeColorPanel = 6,
  NSCrayonModeColorPanel = 7
};
```

NSColorPanel (Mode Masks)

```
enum {
  NSColorPanelGrayModeMask = 0x00000001,
  NSColorPanelRGBModeMask = 0x00000002,
  NSColorPanelCMYKModeMask = 0x00000004,
  NSColorPanelHSBModeMask = 0x00000008,
  NSColorPanelCustomPaletteModeMask = 0x00000010,
  NSColorPanelColorListModeMask = 0x00000020,
  NSColorPanelWheelModeMask = 0x00000040,
  NSColorPanelCrayonModeMask = 0x00000080,
  NSColorPanelAllModesMask = 0x0000ffff
};
```

NSDragging (Operations)

```
enum {
  NSDragOperationNone = 0,
  NSDragOperationCopy = 1,
  NSDragOperationLink = 2,
  NSDragOperationGeneric = 4,
  NSDragOperationPrivate = 8,
  NSDragOperationMove = 16,
  NSDragOperationDelete = 32,
  NSDragOperationEvery = UINT_MAX
};
```

NSEvent (Action Flags)

```
enum {
    NSLeftMouseDownMask = 1 << NSLeftMouseDown,
    NSLeftMouseUpMask = 1 << NSLeftMouseUp,
    NSRightMouseDownMask = 1 << NSRightMouseDown,
    NSRightMouseUpMask = 1 << NSRightMouseUp,
    NSMouseMovedMask = 1 << NSMouseMoved,
    NSLeftMouseDraggedMask = 1 << NSLeftMouseDragged,
    NSRightMouseDraggedMask = 1 << NSRightMouseDragged,
    NSMouseEnteredMask = 1 << NSMouseEntered,
    NSMouseExitedMask = 1 << NSMouseExited,
    NSKeyDownMask = 1 << NSKeyDown,
    NSKeyUpMask = 1 << NSKeyUp,
    NSFlagsChangedMask = 1 << NSFlagsChanged,
    NSAppKitDefinedMask = 1 << NSAppKitDefined,
    NSSystemDefinedMask = 1 << NSSystemDefined,
    NSApplicationDefinedMask = 1 << NSApplicationDefined,
    NSPeriodicMask = 1 << NSPeriodic,
    NSCursorUpdateMask = 1 << NSCursorUpdate,
    NSScrollWheelMask = 1 << NSScrollWheel,
    NSOtherMouseDownMask = 1 << NSOtherMouseDown,
    NSOtherMouseUpMask = 1 << NSOtherMouseUp,
    NSOtherMouseDraggedMask = 1 << NSOtherMouseDragged,
    NSAnyEventMask = 0xffffffffU
};
```

NSEvent (Function Key Unicodes)

```
enum {
    NSUpArrowFunctionKey = 0xF700,
    NSDownArrowFunctionKey = 0xF701,
    NSLeftArrowFunctionKey = 0xF702,
    NSRightArrowFunctionKey = 0xF703,
    NSF1FunctionKey = 0xF704,
    NSF2FunctionKey = 0xF705,
    NSF3FunctionKey = 0xF706,
    NSF4FunctionKey = 0xF707,
    NSF5FunctionKey = 0xF708,
    NSF6FunctionKey = 0xF709,
    NSF7FunctionKey = 0xF70A,
    NSF8FunctionKey = 0xF70B,
    NSF9FunctionKey = 0xF70C,
    NSF10FunctionKey = 0xF70D,
    NSF11FunctionKey = 0xF70E,
    NSF12FunctionKey = 0xF70F,
    NSF13FunctionKey = 0xF710,
    NSF14FunctionKey = 0xF711,
    NSF15FunctionKey = 0xF712,
    NSF16FunctionKey = 0xF713,
    NSF17FunctionKey = 0xF714,
    NSF18FunctionKey = 0xF715,
    NSF19FunctionKey = 0xF716,
```

```
    NSF20FunctionKey = 0xF717,
    NSF21FunctionKey = 0xF718,
    NSF22FunctionKey = 0xF719,
    NSF23FunctionKey = 0xF71A,
    NSF24FunctionKey = 0xF71B,
    NSF25FunctionKey = 0xF71C,
    NSF26FunctionKey = 0xF71D,
    NSF27FunctionKey = 0xF71E,
    NSF28FunctionKey = 0xF71F,
    NSF29FunctionKey = 0xF720,
    NSF30FunctionKey = 0xF721,
    NSF31FunctionKey = 0xF722,
    NSF32FunctionKey = 0xF723,
    NSF33FunctionKey = 0xF724,
    NSF34FunctionKey = 0xF725,
    NSF35FunctionKey = 0xF726,
    NSInsertFunctionKey = 0xF727,
    NSDeleteFunctionKey = 0xF728,
    NSHomeFunctionKey = 0xF729,
    NSBeginFunctionKey = 0xF72A,
    NSEndFunctionKey = 0xF72B,
    NSPageUpFunctionKey = 0xF72C,
    NSPageDownFunctionKey = 0xF72D,
    NSPrintScreenFunctionKey = 0xF72E,
    NSScrollLockFunctionKey = 0xF72F,
    NSPauseFunctionKey = 0xF730,
    NSSysReqFunctionKey = 0xF731,
    NSBreakFunctionKey = 0xF732,
    NSResetFunctionKey = 0xF733,
    NSStopFunctionKey = 0xF734,
    NSMenuFunctionKey = 0xF735,
    NSUserFunctionKey = 0xF736,
    NSSystemFunctionKey = 0xF737,
    NSPrintFunctionKey = 0xF738,
    NSClearLineFunctionKey = 0xF739,
    NSClearDisplayFunctionKey = 0xF73A,
    NSInsertLineFunctionKey = 0xF73B,
    NSDeleteLineFunctionKey = 0xF73C,
    NSInsertCharFunctionKey = 0xF73D,
    NSDeleteCharFunctionKey = 0xF73E,
    NSPrevFunctionKey = 0xF73F,
    NSNextFunctionKey = 0xF740,
    NSSelectFunctionKey = 0xF741,
    NSExecuteFunctionKey = 0xF742,
    NSUndoFunctionKey = 0xF743,
    NSRedoFunctionKey = 0xF744,
    NSFindFunctionKey = 0xF745,
    NSHelpFunctionKey = 0xF746,
    NSModeSwitchFunctionKey = 0xF747
};
```

NSEvent (Modifier Flags)

```
enum {
    NSAlphaShiftKeyMask = 1 << 16,
    NSShiftKeyMask = 1 << 17,
    NSControlKeyMask = 1 << 18,
    NSAlternateKeyMask = 1 << 19,
    NSCommandKeyMask = 1 << 20,
    NSNumericPadKeyMask = 1 << 21,
    NSHelpKeyMask = 1 << 22,
    NSFunctionKeyMask = 1 << 23
};
```

NSEvent (Types Defined by the Application Kit)

```
enum {
    NSWindowExposedEventType = 0,
    NSApplicationActivatedEventType = 1,
    NSApplicationDeactivatedEventType = 2,
    NSWindowMovedEventType = 4,
    NSScreenChangedEventType = 8,
    NSAWTEventType = 16
};
```

NSEvent (Types Defined by the System)

```
enum {
    NSPowerOffEventType = 1
};
```

NSFont (Traits)

```
enum {
    NSItalicFontMask = 0x00000001,
    NSBoldFontMask = 0x00000002,
    NSUnboldFontMask = 0x00000004,
    NSNonStandardCharacterSetFontMask = 0x00000008,
    NSNarrowFontMask = 0x00000010,
    NSExpandedFontMask = 0x00000020,
    NSCondensedFontMask = 0x00000040,
    NSSmallCapsFontMask = 0x00000080,
    NSPosterFontMask = 0x00000100,
    NSCompressedFontMask = 0x00000200,
    NSFixedPitchFontMask = 0x00000400,
    NSUnitalicFontMask = 0x01000000
};
```

NSGraphics (Alpha Values)

```
enum {
    NSAlphaEqualToData = 1,
    NSAlphaAlwaysOne = 2
};
```

NSGlyph (Reserved Glyph Codes)

```
enum {
  NSControlGlyph = 0x00FFFFFF,
  NSNullGlyph = 0x0
};
```

NSImageRep (Display Device Matching)

```
enum {
  NSImageRepMatchesDevice
};
```

NSOutlineView (Drop on Index)

```
enum {
  NSOutlineViewDropOnItemIndex = -1
};
```

NSPanel (Alert Panel Return Values)

```
enum {
  NSAlertDefaultReturn = 1,
  NSAlertAlternateReturn = 0,
  NSAlertOtherReturn = -1,
  NSAlertErrorReturn = -2
};
```

NSPanel (Modal Panel Return Values)

```
enum {
  NSOKButton = 1,
  NSCancelButton = 0
};
```

NSPanel (Style Mask)

```
enum {
  NSUtilityWindowMask = 1 << 4,
  NSDocModalWindowMask = 1 << 6,
  NSNonactivatingPanelMask = 1 << 7
};
```

NSRunLoop (Ordering Modes for NSApplication)

```
enum {
  NSUpdateWindowsRunLoopOrdering
};
```

NSRunLoop (Ordering Modes for NSWindow)

```
enum {
    NSDisplayWindowRunLoopOrdering,
    NSResetCursorRectsRunLoopOrdering
};
```

NSSavePanel (Tags for Subviews)

```
enum {
    NSFileHandlingPanelImageButton = 150,
    NSFileHandlingPanelTitleField = 151,
    NSFileHandlingPanelBrowser = 152,
    NSFileHandlingPanelCancelButton = NSCancelButton,
    NSFileHandlingPanelOKButton = NSOKButton,
    NSFileHandlingPanelForm = 155
};
```

NSText (Important Unicodes)

```
enum {
    NSParagraphSeparatorCharacter = 0x2029,
    NSLineSeparatorCharacter = 0x2028,
    NSTabCharacter = 0x0009,
    NSFormFeedCharacter = 0x000c,
    NSNewlineCharacter = 0x000a,
    NSCarriageReturnCharacter = 0x000d,
    NSEnterCharacter = 0x0003,
    NSBackspaceCharacter = 0x0008,
    NSBackTabCharacter = 0x0019,
    NSDeleteCharacter = 0x007f
};
```

NSText (Movement Codes)

```
enum {
    NSIllegalTextMovement = 0,
    NSReturnTextMovement = 0x10,
    NSTabTextMovement = 0x11,
    NSBacktabTextMovement = 0x12,
    NSLeftTextMovement = 0x13,
    NSRightTextMovement = 0x14,
    NSUpTextMovement = 0x15,
    NSDownTextMovement = 0x16
};
```

NSTextAttachment (Attachment Character)

```
enum {
    NSAttachmentCharacter = 0xfffc
};
```

NSTextStorage (Editing)

```
enum {
    NSTextStorageEditedAttributes = 1,
    NSTextStorageEditedCharacters = 2
};
```

NSView (Resizing)

```
enum {
    NSViewNotSizable = 0,
    NSViewMinXMargin = 1,
    NSViewWidthSizable = 2,
    NSViewMaxXMargin = 4,
    NSViewMinYMargin = 8,
    NSViewHeightSizable = 16,
    NSViewMaxYMargin = 32
};
```

NSWindow (Border Masks)

```
enum {
    NSBorderlessWindowMask = 0,
    NSTitledWindowMask = 1 << 0,
    NSClosableWindowMask = 1 << 1,
    NSMiniaturizableWindowMask = 1 << 2,
    NSResizableWindowMask = 1 << 3,
    NSTexturedBackgroundWindowMask= 1 << 8
};
```

Global Variables

This section lists the global variables defined by and used in the Application Kit.

Color Space Names

```
NSString *NSCalibratedWhiteColorSpace;
NSString *NSCalibratedBlackColorSpace;
NSString *NSCalibratedRGBColorSpace;
NSString *NSDeviceWhiteColorSpace;
NSString *NSDeviceBlackColorSpace;
NSString *NSDeviceRGBColorSpace;
NSString *NSDeviceCMYKColorSpace;
NSString *NSNamedColorSpace;
NSString *NSPatternColorSpace;
NSString *NSCustomColorSpace;
```

Display Device (Descriptions)

```
NSString *NSDeviceResolution;
NSString *NSDeviceColorSpaceName;
NSString *NSDeviceBitsPerSample;
NSString *NSDeviceIsScreen;
NSString *NSDeviceIsPrinter;
NSString *NSDeviceSize;
```

NSAccessibility (Actions)

```
NSString *NSAccessibilityPressAction;
NSString *NSAccessibilityIncrementAction;
NSString *NSAccessibilityDecrementAction;
NSString *NSAccessibilityConfirmAction;
NSString *NSAccessibilityPickAction;
```

NSAccessibility (Attributes)

```
NSString *NSAccessibilityRoleAttribute;
NSString *NSAccessibilityRoleDescriptionAttribute;
NSString *NSAccessibilitySubroleAttribute;
NSString *NSAccessibilityHelpAttribute;
NSString *NSAccessibilityTitleAttribute;
NSString *NSAccessibilityValueAttribute;
NSString *NSAccessibilityMinValueAttribute;
NSString *NSAccessibilityMaxValueAttribute;
NSString *NSAccessibilityEnabledAttribute;
NSString *NSAccessibilityFocusedAttribute;
NSString *NSAccessibilityParentAttribute;
NSString *NSAccessibilityChildrenAttribute;
NSString *NSAccessibilityWindowAttribute;
NSString *NSAccessibilitySelectedChildrenAttribute;
NSString *NSAccessibilityVisibleChildrenAttribute;
NSString *NSAccessibilityPositionAttribute;
NSString *NSAccessibilitySizeAttribute;
NSString *NSAccessibilityContentsAttribute;
NSString *NSAccessibilityPreviousContentsAttribute;
NSString *NSAccessibilityNextContentsAttribute;
NSString *NSAccessibilitySelectedTextAttribute;
NSString *NSAccessibilitySelectedTextRangeAttribute;
NSString *NSAccessibilityMainAttribute;
NSString *NSAccessibilityMinimizedAttribute;
NSString *NSAccessibilityCloseButtonAttribute;
NSString *NSAccessibilityZoomButtonAttribute;
NSString *NSAccessibilityMinimizeButtonAttribute;
NSString *NSAccessibilityToolbarButtonAttribute;
NSString *NSAccessibilityProxyAttribute;
NSString *NSAccessibilityGrowAreaAttribute;
NSString *NSAccessibilityMenuBarAttribute;
NSString *NSAccessibilityWindowsAttribute;
NSString *NSAccessibilityFrontmostAttribute;
NSString *NSAccessibilityHiddenAttribute;
NSString *NSAccessibilityMainWindowAttribute;
```

```
NSString *NSAccessibilityFocusedWindowAttribute;
NSString *NSAccessibilityFocusedUIElementAttribute;
NSString *NSAccessibilityHeaderAttribute;
NSString *NSAccessibilityEditedAttribute;
NSString *NSAccessibilityTabsAttribute;
NSString *NSAccessibilityTitleUIElementAttribute;
NSString *NSAccessibilityHorizontalScrollBarAttribute;
NSString *NSAccessibilityVerticalScrollBarAttribute;
NSString *NSAccessibilityOverflowButtonAttribute;
NSString *NSAccessibilityIncrementButtonAttribute;
NSString *NSAccessibilityDecrementButtonAttribute;
NSString *NSAccessibilityFilenameAttribute;
NSString *NSAccessibilityExpandedAttribute;
NSString *NSAccessibilitySelectedAttribute;
NSString *NSAccessibilityColumnTitlesAttribute;
NSString *NSAccessibilitySplittersAttribute;
NSString *NSAccessibilityDocumentAttribute;
NSString *NSAccessibilityOrientationAttribute;
NSString *NSAccessibilityRowsAttribute;
NSString *NSAccessibilityVisibleRowsAttribute;
NSString *NSAccessibilitySelectedRowsAttribute;
NSString *NSAccessibilityColumnsAttribute;
NSString *NSAccessibilityVisibleColumnsAttribute;
NSString *NSAccessibilitySelectedColumnsAttribute;
NSString *NSAccessibilitySortDirectionAttribute;
NSString *NSAccessibilityDisclosingAttribute;
NSString *NSAccessibilityDisclosedRowsAttribute;
NSString *NSAccessibilityDisclosedByRowAttribute;
```

NSAccessibility (Exception Error Code Key)

```
NSString *NSAccessibilityErrorCodeExceptionInfo;
```

NSAccessibility (Notifications)

```
NSString *NSAccessibilityMainWindowChangedNotification;
NSString *NSAccessibilityFocusedUIElementChangedNotification;
NSString *NSAccessibilityApplicationActivatedNotification;
NSString *NSAccessibilityApplicationDeactivatedNotification;
NSString *NSAccessibilityApplicationHiddenNotification;
NSString *NSAccessibilityApplicationShownNotification;
NSString *NSAccessibilityWindowCreatedNotification;
NSString *NSAccessibilityWindowMovedNotification;
NSString *NSAccessibilityWindowResizedNotification;
NSString *NSAccessibilityWindowMiniaturizedNotification;
NSString *NSAccessibilityWindowDeminiaturizedNotification;
NSString *NSAccessibilityValueChangedNotification;
NSString *NSAccessibilityUIElementDestroyedNotification;
```

NSAccessibility (Orientations)

```
NSString *NSAccessibilityHorizontalOrientationValue;
NSString *NSAccessibilityVerticalOrientationValue;
```

NSAccessibility (Roles)

```
NSString *NSAccessibilityUnknownRole;
NSString *NSAccessibilityButtonRole;
NSString *NSAccessibilityRadioButtonRole;
NSString *NSAccessibilityCheckBoxRole;
NSString *NSAccessibilitySliderRole;
NSString *NSAccessibilityTabGroupRole;
NSString *NSAccessibilityTextFieldRole;
NSString *NSAccessibilityStaticTextRole;
NSString *NSAccessibilityTextAreaRole;
NSString *NSAccessibilityScrollAreaRole;
NSString *NSAccessibilityPopUpButtonRole;
NSString *NSAccessibilityMenuButtonRole;
NSString *NSAccessibilityTableRole;
NSString *NSAccessibilityApplicationRole;
NSString *NSAccessibilityGroupRole;
NSString *NSAccessibilityRadioGroupRole;
NSString *NSAccessibilityListRole;
NSString *NSAccessibilityScrollBarRole;
NSString *NSAccessibilityValueIndicatorRole;
NSString *NSAccessibilityImageRole;
NSString *NSAccessibilityMenuBarRole;
NSString *NSAccessibilityMenuRole;
NSString *NSAccessibilityMenuItemRole;
NSString *NSAccessibilityColumnRole;
NSString *NSAccessibilityRowRole;
NSString *NSAccessibilityToolbarRole;
NSString *NSAccessibilityBusyIndicatorRole;
NSString *NSAccessibilityProgressIndicatorRole;
NSString *NSAccessibilityRelevanceIndicatorRole;
NSString *NSAccessibilityWindowRole;
NSString *NSAccessibilityWindowTitleRole;
NSString *NSAccessibilityWindowProxyRole;
NSString *NSAccessibilityDrawerRole;
NSString *NSAccessibilitySystemWideRole;
NSString *NSAccessibilityOutlineRole;
NSString *NSAccessibilityIncrementorRole;
NSString *NSAccessibilityBrowserRole;
NSString *NSAccessibilityComboBoxRole;
NSString *NSAccessibilitySplitGroupRole;
NSString *NSAccessibilitySplitterRole;
NSString *NSAccessibilityColorWellRole;
NSString *NSAccessibilityGrowAreaRole;
NSString *NSAccessibilitySheetRole;
```

NSAccessibility (Subroles)

```
NSString *NSAccessibilityUnknownSubrole;
NSString *NSAccessibilityCloseButtonSubrole;
NSString *NSAccessibilityZoomButtonSubrole;
NSString *NSAccessibilityMinimizeButtonSubrole;
NSString *NSAccessibilityToolbarButtonSubrole;
```

```
NSString *NSAccessibilityTableRowSubrole;
NSString *NSAccessibilityOutlineRowSubrole;
NSString *NSAccessibilitySecureTextFieldSubrole;
```

NSApplication (Shared Application Object)

```
id NSApp;
```

NSAttributedString (Attributes)

```
NSString *NSFontAttributeName;
NSString *NSParagraphStyleAttributeName;
NSString *NSForegroundColorAttributeName;
NSString *NSUnderlineStyleAttributeName;
NSString *NSSuperscriptAttributeName;
NSString *NSBackgroundColorAttributeName;
NSString *NSAttachmentAttributeName;
NSString *NSLigatureAttributeName;
NSString *NSBaselineOffsetAttributeName;
NSString *NSKernAttributeName;
NSString *NSLinkAttributeName;
```

NSAttributedString (Character Shape Attribute)

```
NSString *NSCharacterShapeAttributeName;
```

NSAttributedString (Document Type)

```
NSString *NSPlainTextDocumentType;
NSString *NSRTFTextDocumentType;
NSString *NSRTFDTextDocumentType;
NSString *NSMacSimpleTextDocumentType;
NSString *NSHTMLTextDocumentType;
```

NSAttributedString (Glyph Info Attribute)

```
NSString *NSGlyphInfoAttributeName;
```

NSAttributedString (Underline Masks)

```
unsigned NSUnderlineByWordMask;
unsigned NSUnderlineStrikethroughMask;
```

NSBitmapImageRep (Attributes)

```
NSString *NSImageCompressionMethod;
NSString *NSImageCompressionFactor;
NSString *NSImageDitherTransparency;
NSString *NSImageRGBColorTable;
```

NSString *NSImageInterlaced;
NSString *NSImageColorSyncProfileData;
NSString *NSImageFrameCount;
NSString *NSImageCurrentFrame;
NSString *NSImageCurrentFrameDuration;

NSColor (Grayscale Values)

const float NSWhite;
const float NSLightGray;
const float NSDarkGray;
const float NSBlack;

NSFont (Keys to the AFM Dictionary)

NSString *NSAFMFamilyName;
NSString *NSAFMFontName;
NSString *NSAFMFormatVersion;
NSString *NSAFMFullName;
NSString *NSAFMNotice;
NSString *NSAFMVersion;
NSString *NSAFMWeight;
NSString *NSAFMEncodingScheme;
NSString *NSAFMCharacterSet;
NSString *NSAFMCapHeight;
NSString *NSAFMXHeight;
NSString *NSAFMAscender;
NSString *NSAFMDescender;
NSString *NSAFMUnderlinePosition;
NSString *NSAFMUnderlineThickness;
NSString *NSAFMItalicAngle;
NSString *NSAFMMappingScheme;

NSFont (PostScript Transformation Matrix)

const float *NSFontIdentityMatrix;

NSGraphicsContext (Attributes)

NSString *NSGraphicsContextDestinationAttributeName;
NSString *NSGraphicsContextRepresentationFormatAttributeName;
NSString *NSGraphicsContextPSFormat;
NSString *NSGraphicsContextPDFFormat;

NSInterfaceStyleDefault

NSString *NSInterfaceStyleDefault;

NSPasteboard (Names)

```
NSString *NSGeneralPboard;
NSString *NSFontPboard;
NSString *NSRulerPboard;
NSString *NSFindPboard;
NSString *NSDragPboard;
```

NSPasteboard (Types for Sound Data)

```
NSString *NSSoundPboardType;
```

NSPasteboard (Types for Standard Data)

```
NSString *NSStringPboardType;
NSString *NSFilenamesPboardType;
NSString *NSPostScriptPboardType;
NSString *NSTIFFPboardType;
NSString *NSRTFPboardType;
NSString *NSTabularTextPboardType;
NSString *NSFontPboardType;
NSString *NSRulerPboardType;
NSString *NSFileContentsPboardType;
NSString *NSColorPboardType;
NSString *NSRTFDPboardType;
NSString *HTMLPboardType;
NSString *NSPICTPboardType;
NSString *NSURLPboardType;
NSString *NSPDFPboardType;
NSString *NSVCardPboardType;
NSString *NSFilesPromisePboardType;
```

NSPrintInfo (Dictionary Keys)

```
NSString *NSPrintPaperName;
NSString *NSPrintPaperSize;
NSString *NSPrintMustCollate;
NSString *NSPrintOrientation;
NSString *NSPrintLeftMargin;
NSString *NSPrintRightMargin;
NSString *NSPrintTopMargin;
NSString *NSPrintBottomMargin;
NSString *NSPrintHorizontallyCentered;
NSString *NSPrintVerticallyCentered;
NSString *NSPrintHorizontalPagination;
NSString *NSPrintVerticalPagination;
NSString *NSPrintScalingFactor;
NSString *NSPrintAllPages;
NSString *NSPrintReversePageOrder;
NSString *NSPrintFirstPage;
NSString *NSPrintLastPage;
NSString *NSPrintCopies;
```

```
NSString *NSPrintPrinter;
NSString *NSPrintJobDisposition;
NSString *NSPrintSavePath;
NSString *NSPrintSpoolJob;
NSString *NSPrintPreviewJob;
NSString *NSPrintSaveJob;
NSString *NSPrintCancelJob;
```

NSPrintPanel (Job Style Hints)

```
NSString *NSPrintPhotoJobStyleHint;
```

NSRunLoop (Modes)

```
NSString *NSModalPanelRunLoopMode;
NSString *NSEventTrackingRunLoopMode;
```

NSToolbarItem (Standard Identifiers)

```
NSString *NSToolbarSeparatorItemIdentifier;
NSString *NSToolbarSpaceItemIdentifier;
NSString *NSToolbarFlexibleSpaceItemIdentifier;
NSString *NSToolbarShowColorsItemIdentifier;
NSString *NSToolbarShowFontsItemIdentifier;
NSString *NSToolbarCustomizeToolbarItemIdentifier;
NSString *NSToolbarPrintItemIdentifier;
```

NSWindow (Sizes)

```
NSSize NSIconSize;
NSSize NSTokenSize;
```

NSWindow (Window Levels)

```
NSString *NSNormalWindowLevel
NSString *NSFloatingWindowLevel
NSString *NSSubmenuWindowLevel
NSString *NSTornOffMenuWindowLevel
NSString *NSMainMenuWindowLevel
NSString *NSStatusWindowLevel
NSString *NSModalPanelWindowLevel
NSString *NSPopUpMenuWindowLevel
NSString *NSScreenSaverWindowLevel
```

NSWorkspace (File Operation Constants)

```
NSString *NSWorkspaceMoveOperation;
NSString *NSWorkspaceCopyOperation;
NSString *NSWorkspaceLinkOperation;
NSString *NSWorkspaceCompressOperation;
```

```
NSString *NSWorkspaceDecompressOperation;
NSString *NSWorkspaceEncryptOperation;
NSString *NSWorkspaceDecryptOperation;
NSString *NSWorkspaceDestroyOperation;
NSString *NSWorkspaceRecycleOperation;
NSString *NSWorkspaceDuplicateOperation;
```

NSWorkspace (File Types)

```
NSString *NSPlainFileType;
NSString *NSDirectoryFileType;
NSString *NSApplicationFileType;
NSString *NSFilesystemFileType;
NSString *NSShellCommandFileType;
```

Exceptions

This section lists the names of exceptions raised by Application Kit classes.

```
NSString *NSTextLineTooLongException;
NSString *NSTextNoSelectionException;
NSString *NSWordTablesWriteException;
NSString *NSWordTablesReadException;
NSString *NSTextReadException;
NSString *NSTextWriteException;
NSString *NSPasteboardCommunicationException;
NSString *NSPrintingCommunicationException;
NSString *NSAbortModalException;
NSString *NSAbortPrintingException;
NSString *NSIllegalSelectorException;
NSString *NSAppKitVirtualMemoryException;
NSString *NSBadRTFDirectiveException;
NSString *NSBadRTFFontTableException;
NSString *NSBadRTFStyleSheetException;
NSString *NSTypedStreamVersionException;
NSString *NSTIFFException;
NSString *NSPrintPackageException;
NSString *NSBadRTFColorTableException;
NSString *NSDraggingException;
NSString *NSColorListIOException;
NSString *NSColorListNotEditableException;
NSString *NSBadBitmapParametersException;
NSString *NSWindowServerCommunicationException;
NSString *NSFontUnavailableException;
NSString *NSPPDIncludeNotFoundException;
NSString *NSPPDParseException;
NSString *NSPPDIncludeStackOverflowException;
```

12

Application Kit Functions

This chapter lists the functions defined by the Application Kit. These functions a grouped into the following categories:

Accessibility
Applications
Events
Fonts
Graphics: general
Graphics: window depth
Interface styles
OpenGL
Panels
Pasteboards
System beep

Accessibility

The NSAccessibilityPostNotification function is used to post an accessibility notification, which cannot be posted to the default notification center. The remaining functions are used by the accessibility system in Cocoa to manage what objects are visible to assistive applications.

NSAccessibilityPostNotification
    void NSAccessibilityPostNotification(id element, NSString *notification)

NSAccessibilityUnignoredAncestor
    id NSAccessibilityUnignoredAncestor(id element)

NSAccessibilityUnignoredChildren
    NSArray *NSAccessibilityUnignoredChildren(NSArray *originalChildren)

NSAccessibilityUnignoredChildrenForOnlyChild
    NSArray *NSAccessibilityUnignoredChildrenForOnlyChild(id originalChild)

NSAccessibilityUnignoredDescendant
    id NSAccessibilityUnignoredDescendant(id element)

Applications

These functions are used for various application level tasks, such as loading and running an application, and managing the Services menu for an application.

NSApplicationLoad
    BOOL NSApplicationLoad(void)

NSApplicationMain
    int NSApplicationMain(int argc, const char *argv[ ])

NSPerformService
    BOOL NSPerformService(NSString *itemName, NSPasteboard *pboard)

NSRegisterServicesProvider
    void NSRegisterServicesProvider(id provider, NSString *name)

NSShowsServicesMenuItem
    BOOL NSShowsServicesMenuItem(NSString * itemName)

NSSetShowsServicesMenuItem
    int NSSetShowsServicesMenuItem(NSString * itemName, BOOL enabled)

NSUnRegisterServicesProvider
    void NSUnRegisterServicesProvider(NSString *name)

NSUpdateDynamicServices
    void NSUpdateDynamicServices(void)

Events

This single event-related function is used to obtain an event mask for the specified event type.

NSEventMaskFromType
    unsigned int NSEventMaskFromType(NSEventType type)

Fonts

These two functions are used to manipulate font glyphs.

NSConvertGlyphsToPackedGlyphs
    int NSConvertGlyphsToPackedGlyphs(NSGlyph *glBuf, int count, NSMultibyteGlyphPacking packing, char *packedGlyphs)

NSGlyphInfoAtIndex
    void NSGlyphInfoAtIndex(int IX)

Graphics: General

These functions provide a number of convenient wrappers to common graphics and drawing tasks, such as erasing the contents of a rectangle, drawing various borders, and more.

NSCopyBits
> void NSCopyBits(int srcGState, NSRect srcRect, NSPoint destPoint)

NSCountWindows
> void NSCountWindows(int *count)

NSCountWindowsForContext
> void NSCountWindowsForContext(int context, int *count)

NSDottedFrameRect
> void NSDottedFrameRect(NSRect aRect)

NSDrawBitmap
> void NSDrawBitmap(const NSRect rect, int pixelsWide, int pixelsHigh, int bitsPerSample, int samplesPerPixel, int bitsPerPixel, int bytesPerRow, BOOL isPlanar, BOOL hasAlpha, NSColorSpace colorSpace, const unsigned char *const data[5])

NSDrawButton
> void NSDrawButton(const NSRect aRect, const NSRect clipRect)

NSDrawColorTiledRects
> NSRect NSDrawColorTiledRects(NSRect boundsRect, NSRect clipRect, const NSRectEdge *sides, NSColor **colors, int count)

NSDrawDarkBezel
> void NSDrawDarkBezel(NSRect boundsRect, NSRect clipRect)

NSDrawGrayBezel
> void NSDrawGrayBezel(NSRect boundsRect, NSRect clipRect)

NSDrawGroove
> void NSDrawGroove(NSRect boundsRect, NSRect clipRect)

NSDrawLightBezel
> void NSDrawLightBezel(NSRect boundsRect, NSRect clipRect)

NSDrawTiledRects
> NSRect NSDrawTiledRects(NSRect boundsRect, NSRect clipRect, const NSRectEdge *sides, const float *grays, int count);

NSDrawWhiteBezel
> void NSDrawWhiteBezel(NSRect aRect, NSRect clipRect)

NSDrawWindowBackground
> void NSDrawWindowBackground(NSRect aRect)

NSEraseRect
> void NSEraseRect(const NSRect aRect)

NSFrameRect
    void NSFrameRect(NSRect aRect)

NSFrameRectWithWidth
    void NSFrameRectWithWidth(NSRect aRect, float frameWidth)

NSFrameRectWithWidthUsingOperation
    void NSFrameRectWithWidthUsingOperation(NSRect aRect, float frameWidth, NSCompositingOperation op)

NSGetWindowServerMemory
    int NSGetWindowServerMemory(int context, int *virtualMemory, int *window-BackingMemory, NSString **windowDumpStream)

NSHighlightRect
    void NSHighlightRect(const NSRect aRect)

NSReadPixel
    NSColor *NSReadPixel(NSPoint passedPoint)

NSRectClip
    void NSRectClip(NSRect aRect)

NSRectClipList
    void NSRectClipList(const NSRect *rects, int count)

NSRectFill
    void NSRectFill(const NSRect aRect)

NSRectFillList
    void NSRectFillList(const NSRect *rects, int count)

NSRectFillListWithColors
    void NSRectFillListWithColors(const NSRect *rects, NSColor **colors, int count)

NSRectFillListWithGrays
    void NSRectFillListWithGrays(const NSRect *rects, const float *grays, int count)

NSRectFillUsingOperation
    void NSRectFillUsingOperation(NSRect aRect, NSCompositingOperation op)

NSRectFillListUsingOperation
    void NSRectFillListUsingOperation(const NSRect *rects, int count, NSCompositingOperation op)

NSRectFillListWithColorsUsingOperation
    void NSRectFillListWithColorsUsingOperation(const NSRect *rects, NSColor **colors, int count, NSCompositingOperation op)

NSSetFocusRingStyle
    void NSSetFocusRingStyle(NSFocusRingPlacement placement)

NSWindowList
    void NSWindowList(int size, int list[ ])

NSWindowListForContext
    void NSWindowListForContext(int context, int size, int list[ ])

Graphics: Window Depth

These functions are used to obtain information about the bit-depth of windows.

NSAvailableWindowDepths
    const NSWindowDepth *NSAvailableWindowDepths(void)

NSBestDepth
    NSWindowDepth NSBestDepth(NSString *colorSpace, int bps, int bpp, BOOL planar, BOOL
    *exactMatch)

NSBitsPerPixelFromDepth
    int NSBitsPerPixelFromDepth(NSWindowDepth depth)

NSBitsPerSampleFromDepth
    int NSBitsPerSampleFromDepth(NSWindowDepth depth)

NSColorSpaceFromDepth
    NSString *NSColorSpaceFromDepth(NSWindowDepth depth)

NSNumberOfColorComponents
    int NSNumberOfColorComponents(NSString *colorSpaceName)

NSPlanarFromDepth
    BOOL NSPlanarFromDepth(NSWindowDepth depth)

Interface Styles

Thie function returns the interface style for the specified key and responder objects. Interface styles are described by the **NSInterfaceStyle** enumerator type, which may be one of the following constants:

- NSNoInterfaceStyle
- NSNextStepInterfaceStyle
- NSWindows95InterfaceStyle
- NSMacintoshInterfaceStyle
- NSInterfaceStyleForKey

NSInterfaceStyle
    NSInterfaceStyleForKey(NSString *key, NSResponder *responder)

OpenGL

These functions are used to set and get global OpenGL options, as well as to obtain the version number of the installed OpenGL libraries.

NSOpenGLGetOption
    void NSOpenGLGetOption(NSOpenGLGlobalOption pname, long *param)

NSOpenGLGetVersion
    void NSOpenGLGetVersion(long *major, long *minor)

NSOpenGLSetOption
    void NSOpenGLSetOption(NSOpenGLGlobalOption pname, long param)

Panels

These functions provide a convenient way to display common alert panels and sheets. These functions let us create panels or sheets for informational purposes, to inform the user of an alert, and to inform the user of a critical alert.

NSBeginAlertSheet

    void NSBeginAlertSheet(NSString *title, NSString *defaultButton, NSString *alternateButton, NSString *otherButton, NSWindow *docWindow, id modalDelegate, SEL didEndSelector, SEL didDismissSelector, void *contextInfo, NSString *msg, ...)

NSBeginCriticalAlertSheet

    void NSBeginCriticalAlertSheet(NSString *title, NSString *defaultButton, NSString *alternateButton, NSString *otherButton, NSWindow *docWindow, id modalDelegate, SEL didEndSelector, SEL didDismissSelector, void *contextInfo, NSString *msg, ...)

NSBeginInformationalAlertSheet

    void NSBeginInformationalAlertSheet(NSString *title, NSString *defaultButton, NSString *alternateButton, NSString *otherButton, NSWindow *docWindow, id modalDelegate, SEL didEndSelector, SEL didDismissSelector, void *contextInfo, NSString *msg, ...);

NSGetAlertPanel

    id NSGetAlertPanel(NSString *title, NSString *msg, NSString *default-Button, NSString *alternateButton, NSString *otherButton, ...)

NSGetCriticalAlertPanel

    id NSGetCriticalAlertPanel(NSString *title, NSString *msg, NSString *defaultButton, NSString *alternateButton, NSString *otherButton, ...)

NSGetInformationalAlertPanel

    id NSGetInformationalAlertPanel(NSString *title, NSString *msg, NSString *defaultButton, NSString *alternateButton, NSString *otherButton, ...)

NSReleaseAlertPanel

    void NSReleaseAlertPanel(id alertPanel)

NSRunAlertPanel

    int NSRunAlertPanel(NSString *title, NSString *msg, NSString *default-Button, NSString *alternateButton, NSString *otherButton, ...)

NSRunCriticalAlertPanel

    int NSRunCriticalAlertPanel(NSString *title, NSString *msg, NSString *defaultButton, NSString *alternateButton, NSString *otherButton, ...)

NSRunInformationalAlertPanel

    int NSRunInformationalAlertPanel(NSString *title, NSString *msg, NSString *defaultButton, NSString *alternateButton, NSString *otherButton, ...)

Pasteboards

These functions provide a means to manage pasteboard file types.

NSCreateFileContentsPboardType

    NSString *NSCreateFileContentsPboardType(NSString *fileType)

NSCreateFilenamePboardType

    NSString *NSCreateFilenamePboardType(NSString *fileType)

NSGetFileType
    NSString *NSGetFileType(NSArray *pboardType)

NSGetFileTypes
    NSArray *NSGetFileTypes(NSArray *pboardType)

System Beep

This function is used to sound the system alert sound selected by the user in the Sound system preferences. See the Application Kit class **NSSound** for more information.

NSBeep
    void NSBeep(void)

13

Foundation Classes

This chapter covers the classes of the Foundation framework. The Foundation framework implements a basic set of classes used in data management, application coordination, networking and inter-application communication, as well as for interacting with core operating system services. Chapter 2 discussed in depth many Foundation classes. Chapter 6 discussed several of the Foundation classes related to networking.

NSAppleEventDescriptor   Mac OS X 10.0

This class is primarily used to retrieve information about an Apple Event in a Cocoa application. A handful of methods in the scripting classes of the Foundation framework either take an event descriptor object or return one. For example, in the class NSAppleScript we expect an NSAppleEventDescriptor object to be returned by the script execution methods. This class is only useful for creating event descriptor objects to return to other objects, or to extract information about an Apple Event descriptor. Currently, Cocoa has no mechanism for sending raw Apple Events; for that you must rely on the Carbon Apple Event APIs.

@interface **NSAppleEventDescriptor** : NSObject <NSCopying>
// Initializers
  - (id)**initListDescriptor**;
  - (id)**initRecordDescriptor**;
  - (id)**initWithAEDescNoCopy**:(const AEDesc *)*aeDesc*;
  - (id)**initWithDescriptorType**:(DescType)*descriptorType* **bytes**:(const void *)*bytes* **length**:(unsigned int)*byteCount*;
  - (id)**initWithDescriptorType**:(DescType)*descriptorType* **data**:(NSData *)*data*;

- (id)**initWithEventClass**:(AEEventClass)*eventClass* **eventID**:(AEEventID)*eventID*
  targetDescriptor:(NSAppleEventDescriptor *)*targetDescriptor* **returnID**:(AEReturnID)*returnID*
  transactionID:(AETransactionID)*transactionID*;

// Accessor Methods

- (void)**setDescriptor**:(NSAppleEventDescriptor *)*descriptor* **forKeyword**:(AEKeyword)*keyword*;
- (void)**setAttributeDescriptor**:(NSAppleEventDescriptor *)*descriptor* **forKeyword**:(AEKeyword)*keyword*;
- (void)**setParamDescriptor**:(NSAppleEventDescriptor *)*descriptor* **forKeyword**:(AEKeyword)*keyword*;

// Class Methods

+ (NSAppleEventDescriptor *)**appleEventWithEventClass**:(AEEventClass)*eventClass* **eventID**:(AEEventID)*eventID*
  targetDescriptor:(NSAppleEventDescriptor *)*targetDescriptor* **returnID**:(AEReturnID)*returnID*
  transactionID:(AETransactionID)*transactionID*; **transactionID**:(AETransactionID)*transactionID*;

+ (NSAppleEventDescriptor *)**descriptorWithBoolean**:(Boolean)*boolean*;
+ (NSAppleEventDescriptor *)**descriptorWithDescriptorType**:(DescType)*descriptorType*
  bytes:(const void *)*bytes* **length**:(unsigned int)*byteCount*;
+ (NSAppleEventDescriptor *)**descriptorWithDescriptorType**:(DescType)*descriptorType* **data**:(NSData *)*data*;
+ (NSAppleEventDescriptor *)**descriptorWithEnumCode**:(OSType)*enumerator*;
+ (NSAppleEventDescriptor *)**descriptorWithInt32**:(SInt32)*signedInt*;
+ (NSAppleEventDescriptor *)**descriptorWithString**:(NSString *)*string*;
+ (NSAppleEventDescriptor *)**descriptorWithTypeCode**:(OSType)*typeCode*;
+ (NSAppleEventDescriptor *)**listDescriptor**;
+ (NSAppleEventDescriptor *)**nullDescriptor**;
+ (NSAppleEventDescriptor *)**recordDescriptor**;

// Instance Methods

- (NSAppleEventDescriptor *)**coerceToDescriptorType**:(DescType)*descriptorType*;
- (const AEDesc *)**aeDesc**;
- (NSAppleEventDescriptor *)**attributeDescriptorForKeyword**:(AEKeyword)*keyword*;
- (Boolean)**booleanValue**;
- (NSData *)**data**;
- (NSAppleEventDescriptor *)**descriptorAtIndex**:(long int)*index*;
- (NSAppleEventDescriptor *)**descriptorForKeyword**:(AEKeyword)*keyword*;
- (DescType)**descriptorType**;
- (OSType)**enumCodeValue**;
- (AEEventClass)**eventClass**;
- (AEEventID)**eventID**;
- (void)**insertDescriptor**:(NSAppleEventDescriptor *)*descriptor* **atIndex**:(long int)*index*;
- (SInt32)**int32Value**;
- (AEKeyword)**keywordForDescriptorAtIndex**:(long int)*index*;
- (int)**numberOfItems**;
- (NSAppleEventDescriptor *)**paramDescriptorForKeyword**:(AEKeyword)*keyword*;
- (void)**removeDecriptorAtIndex**:(long int)*index*;
- (void)**removeDescriptorAtIndex**:(long int)*index*;
- (void)**removeDescriptorWithKeyword**:(AEKeyword)*keyword*;
- (void)**removeParamDescriptorWithKeyword**:(AEKeyword)*keyword*;
- (AEReturnID)**returnID**;
- (NSString *)**stringValue**;
- (AETransactionID)**transactionID**;
- (OSType)**typeCodeValue**;

// Methods Implementing NSCopying

- (id)**copyWithZone**:(NSZone *)*zone*;

NSAppleEventManager

This class is used to register objects as handlers of raw Apple Events in a Cocoa application. Instances of this class are not only responsible for registering and unregistering handlers, but are also responsible for dispatching events to the appropriate handler object. An application has a single instance of **NSAppleEventManager** that is shared among its objects; this event manager is obtained using the class method **sharedAppleEventManager**.

@interface **NSAppleEventManager** : NSObject
// *Accessor Methods*
- (void)**setEventHandler:**(id)*handler* **andSelector:**(SEL)*handleEventSelector* **forEventClass:**(AEEventClass)*eventClass*
    andEventID:(AEEventID)*eventID*;
// *Class Methods*
+ (NSAppleEventManager *)**sharedAppleEventManager**;
// *Instance Methods*
- (OSErr)**dispatchRawAppleEvent:**(const AppleEvent *)*theAppleEvent* **withRawReply:**(AppleEvent *)*theReply*
    handlerRefCon:(UInt32)*handlerRefCon*;
- (void)**removeEventHandlerForEventClass:**(AEEventClass)*eventClass* **andEventID:**(AEEventID)*eventID*;

NSAppleScript

This class gives clients the ability to load, compile, and run AppleScripts. This class provides methods to initialize the class with either text source code, or with a precompiled script. With an initialized object, clients can compile or execute scripts. The Application Kit declares an extension to the **NSAppleScript** class that is used to obtain colored source code for a given script.

@interface **NSAppleScript** : NSObject <NSCopying>
// *Initializers*
- (id)**initWithContentsOfURL:**(NSURL *)*url* **error:**(NSDictionary **)*errorInfo*;
- (id)**initWithSource:**(NSString *)*source*;
// *Instance Methods*
- (BOOL)**compileAndReturnError:**(NSDictionary **)*errorInfo*;
- (NSAppleEventDescriptor *)**executeAndReturnError:**(NSDictionary **)*errorInfo*;
- (NSAppleEventDescriptor *)**executeAppleEvent:**(NSAppleEventDescriptor *)*event* **error:**(NSDictionary **)*errorInfo*;
- (BOOL)**isCompiled**;
- (NSAttributedString *)**richTextSource**;
- (NSString *)**source**;
// *Methods Implementing NSCopying*
- (id)**copyWithZone:**(NSZone *)*zone*;

NSArchiver

This class is a concrete subclass of NSCoder used to archive a network of interconnected objects (an object tree) into a data format that can be written to disk. The archive operation returns an NSMutableData object containing this data. To archive an object, the class method archivedDataWithRootObject: is used, which returns an NSData object containing the archived object. Alternatively, we can archive directly to a file using the class method archiveRootObject:toFile:. It is also possible to initialize an instance of NSArchiver with a pointer to an instance of NSMutableData using initForWritingWithMutableData:, thus providing a more persistent archiving engine than if we simply used the class methods.

To retrieve objects from an archive, we use another subclass of NSCoder: NSUnarchiver. NSArchiver and NSUnarchiver support an archival scheme where objects and variables must be unarchived in the same order that they were archived. Mac OS X 10.2 introduced keyed-archiving, whereby every object and variable in an archive has an associated key that frees us from having to be strictly bound to the original archive format. This has great benefits for improving the compatability of data files between versions of an application.

For instances of a class to be archivable, that class must conform to the NSCoding protocol. See the NSCoding protocol description and Chapter 2 for more information about archiving.

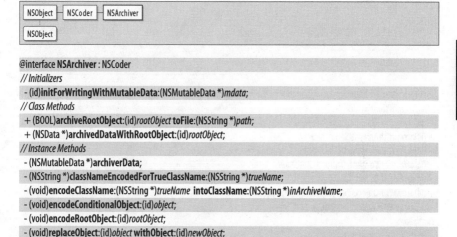

```
@interface NSArchiver : NSCoder
// Initializers
 - (id)initForWritingWithMutableData:(NSMutableData *)mdata;
// Class Methods
 + (BOOL)archiveRootObject:(id)rootObject toFile:(NSString *)path;
 + (NSData *)archivedDataWithRootObject:(id)rootObject;
// Instance Methods
 - (NSMutableData *)archiverData;
 - (NSString *)classNameEncodedForTrueClassName:(NSString *)trueName;
 - (void)encodeClassName:(NSString *)trueName intoClassName:(NSString *)inArchiveName;
 - (void)encodeConditionalObject:(id)object;
 - (void)encodeRootObject:(id)rootObject;
 - (void)replaceObject:(id)object withObject:(id)newObject;
```

NSArray

This class manages an immutable ordered collection of objects. Objects are stored in an array by reference. That is, the pointer to the object is stored rather than the object itself. When the object is added to an array, the array retains it by sending a retain message to the object. When the array is released it sends a release message to each of its members.

There are many methods for querying the contents of the array. The method objectAtIndex: is commonly used to access an object at some position in the array. Conversely, we can determine the index of some object using the method indexOfObject:, which returns the lowest index of the member that is equivalent the specified object. To determine the number of objects contained within the array the count method is invoked.

To enumerate the contents of an array, create an NSEnumerator object for the array using one of two methods: objectEnumerator or reverseObjectEnumerator. A standard object enumerator will return the objects in the order that they exist within the array, while the reverse enumerator will return members starting from the last object and working its way forward. See the NSEnumerator class description for more information on enumerating collections.

Often we want to invoke some method in each member of a collection. NSArray provides a method that saves us from the burden of having to enumerate the contents of the array and send the message manually. This method is makeObjectsPerformSelector:, which will cause the method matching the selector to be invoked in each member of the collection. If you need to invoke a method that takes an argument, then use the method makeObjectsPerformSelector:withObject:.

NSArray is an immutable class. The class NSMutableArray supports ordered collections whose contents can be changed after initialization.

NSArray is toll-free bridged with the Core Foundation type CFArray. As such, NSArray objects can be used interchangeably with the CFArray pointer type, CFArrayRef.

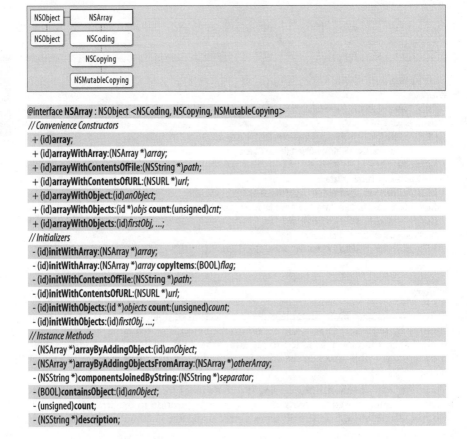

@interface **NSArray** : NSObject <NSCoding, NSCopying, NSMutableCopying>
// Convenience Constructors
+ (id)**array**;
+ (id)**arrayWithArray**:(NSArray *)*array*;
+ (id)**arrayWithContentsOfFile**:(NSString *)*path*;
+ (id)**arrayWithContentsOfURL**:(NSURL *)*url*;
+ (id)**arrayWithObject**:(id)*anObject*;
+ (id)**arrayWithObjects**:(id *)*objs* **count**:(unsigned)*cnt*;
+ (id)**arrayWithObjects**:(id)*firstObj*, ...;
// Initializers
- (id)**initWithArray**:(NSArray *)*array*;
- (id)**initWithArray**:(NSArray *)*array* **copyItems**:(BOOL)*flag*;
- (id)**initWithContentsOfFile**:(NSString *)*path*;
- (id)**initWithContentsOfURL**:(NSURL *)*url*;
- (id)**initWithObjects**:(id *)*objects* **count**:(unsigned)*count*;
- (id)**initWithObjects**:(id)*firstObj*, ...;
// Instance Methods
- (NSArray *)**arrayByAddingObject**:(id)*anObject*;
- (NSArray *)**arrayByAddingObjectsFromArray**:(NSArray *)*otherArray*;
- (NSString *)**componentsJoinedByString**:(NSString *)*separator*;
- (BOOL)**containsObject**:(id)*anObject*;
- (unsigned)**count**;
- (NSString *)**description**;

- (NSString *)**descriptionWithLocale:**(NSDictionary *)*locale;*
- (NSString *)**descriptionWithLocale:**(NSDictionary *)*locale* **indent:**(unsigned)*level;*
- (id)**firstObjectCommonWithArray:**(NSArray *)*otherArray;*
- (void)**getObjects:**(id *)*objects;*
- (void)**getObjects:**(id *)*objects* **range:**(NSRange)*range;*
- (unsigned)**indexOfObject:**(id)*anObject;*
- (unsigned)**indexOfObject:**(id)*anObject* **inRange:**(NSRange)*range;*
- (unsigned)**indexOfObjectIdenticalTo:**(id)*anObject;*
- (unsigned)**indexOfObjectIdenticalTo:**(id)*anObject* **inRange:**(NSRange)*range;*
- (BOOL)**isEqualToArray:**(NSArray *)*otherArray;*
- (id)**lastObject;**
- (void)**makeObjectsPerformSelector:**(SEL)*aSelector;*
- (void)**makeObjectsPerformSelector:**(SEL)*aSelector* **withObject:**(id)*argument;*
- (id)**objectAtIndex:**(unsigned)*index;*
- (NSEnumerator *)**objectEnumerator;**
- (NSArray *)**pathsMatchingExtensions:**(NSArray *)*filterTypes;*
- (NSEnumerator *)**reverseObjectEnumerator;**
- (NSData *)**sortedArrayHint;**
- (NSArray *)**sortedArrayUsingFunction:**(int (*)(id, id, void *))*comparator* **context:**(void *)*context;*
- (NSArray *)**sortedArrayUsingFunction:**(int (*)(id, id, void *))*comparator* **context:**(void *)*context* **hint:**(NSData *)*hint;*
- (NSArray *)**sortedArrayUsingSelector:**(SEL)*comparator;*
- (NSArray *)**subarrayWithRange:**(NSRange)*range;*
- (BOOL)**writeToFile:**(NSString *)*path* **atomically:**(BOOL)*useAuxiliaryFile;*
- (BOOL)**writeToURL:**(NSURL *)*url* **atomically:**(BOOL)*atomically;*

// Methods Implementing NSCoding
- (void)**encodeWithCoder:**(NSCoder *)*aCoder;*
- (id)**initWithCoder:**(NSCoder *)*aDecoder;*

// Methods Implementing NSCopying
- (id)**copyWithZone:**(NSZone *)*zone;*

// Methods Implementing NSMutableCopying
- (id)**mutableCopyWithZone:**(NSZone *)*zone;*

Subclasses

NSMutableArray

NSAssertionHandler Mac OS X 10.0

The NSAssertionHandler class is responsible for assertions that are created using the Foundation framework assertion macros. Every thread has its own assertion handler object that is obtained through the class method currentHandler. NSAssertionHandler provides the methods handleFailureInMethod:object:file:lineNumber:description: and handleFailureInFunction:file:lineNumber:description: to log error messages in response to assertion failures within methods and functions, respectively.

The assertion macros allow the user to check for a given condition—that is, assert that a condition must be true—and if the condition is false, a string is passed to the assertion handler, and the handler is notified of the failed assertion. When the assertion handler receives notification of a failed assertion it will print an error message that includes the user-specified string, as well as the class and method names where the assertion failure occurred. Additionally, an NSInternalInconsistencyException is raised. If this exception is not handled by the application, the application will exit.

The Foundation framework defines six assertion macros that can be used within an Objective-C method (NSAssert, NSAssert1, NSAssert2, etc.) and six macros that may be used within a C function (NSCAssert, NSCAssert1, NSCAssert2, etc.). Each of these macros takes a condition that will be asserted, and a string that will be printed as part of the error message. The numbered macros allow the client to pass additional parameters for printf- style formatted strings.

@interface **NSAssertionHandler** : NSObject
// Class Methods
 + (NSAssertionHandler *)**currentHandler**;
// Instance Methods
 - (void)**handleFailureInFunction**:(NSString *)*functionName* **file**:(NSString *)*fileName* **lineNumber**:(int)*line*
        description:(NSString *)*format*,...;
 - (void)**handleFailureInMethod**:(SEL)*selector* **object**:(id)*object* **file**:(NSString *)*fileName*
        lineNumber:(int)*line* **description**:(NSString *)*format*,...;

NSAttributedString   Mac OS X 10.0

This class represents a string with associated attributes that describe the styled appearance of the string. Attributes are stored in a dictionary. Cocoa defines several keys to identify common attributes such as the font, foreground color, text alignment, line spacing, and more; these keys are listed below in the constants. This class has many methods for querying the attributes of ranges of text within the string. For example, the method **attributesAtIndex:effectiveRange:** returns a dictionary of attributes for the character at index, and by reference the range that the attribute applies to is returned in the second parameter.

The Application Kit implements many extensions to **NSAttributedString** to support more graphical uses of this class. In particular, the AppKit extensions provide support for initializing an attributed string with RTF-formatted data, as well as converting an attributed string to such data. Additionally, these extensions provide for drawing attributed strings into a view, and for managing graphics attributes such as font and ruler characteristics.

NSAttributedString is an immutable class. Mutability is supported in the subclass **NSMutable-AttributedString**.

@interface **NSAttributedString** : NSObject <NSCoding, NSCopying, NSMutableCopying>
// Initializers
 - (id)**initWithAttributedString**:(NSAttributedString *)*attrStr*;
 - (id)**initWithHTML**:(NSData *)*data* **baseURL**:(NSURL *)*base* **documentAttributes**:(NSDictionary **)*dict*;
 - (id)**initWithHTML**:(NSData *)*data* **documentAttributes**:(NSDictionary **)*dict*;

- (id)**initWithPath**:(NSString *)*path* **documentAttributes**:(NSDictionary **)*dict*;
- (id)**initWithRTF**:(NSData *)*data* **documentAttributes**:(NSDictionary **)*dict*;
- (id)**initWithRTFD**:(NSData *)*data* **documentAttributes**:(NSDictionary **)*dict*;
- (id)**initWithRTFDFileWrapper**:(NSFileWrapper *)*wrapper* **documentAttributes**:(NSDictionary **)*dict*;
- (id)**initWithString**:(NSString *)*str*;
- (id)**initWithString**:(NSString *)*str* **attributes**:(NSDictionary *)*attrs*;
- (id)**initWithURL**:(NSURL *)*url* **documentAttributes**:(NSDictionary **)*dict*;

// Class Methods
+ (NSAttributedString *)**attributedStringWithAttachment**:(NSTextAttachment *)*attachment*;
+ (NSArray *)**textFileTypes**;
+ (NSArray *)**textPasteboardTypes**;
+ (NSArray *)**textUnfilteredFileTypes**;
+ (NSArray *)**textUnfilteredPasteboardTypes**;

// Instance Methods
- (NSFileWrapper *)**RTFDFileWrapperFromRange**:(NSRange)*range* **documentAttributes**:(NSDictionary *)*dict*;
- (NSData *)**RTFDFromRange**:(NSRange)*range* **documentAttributes**:(NSDictionary *)*dict*;
- (NSData *)**RTFFromRange**:(NSRange)*range* **documentAttributes**:(NSDictionary *)*dict*;
- (id)**attribute**:(NSString *)*attrName* **atIndex**:(unsigned int)*location* **effectiveRange**:(NSRangePointer)*range*;
- (id)**attribute**:(NSString *)*attrName* **atIndex**:(unsigned int)*location* **longestEffectiveRange**:(NSRangePointer)*range*
      inRange:(NSRange)*rangeLimit*; **inRange**:(NSRange)*rangeLimit*;
- (NSAttributedString *)**attributedSubstringFromRange**:(NSRange)*range*;
- (NSDictionary *)**attributesAtIndex**:(unsigned)*location* **effectiveRange**:(NSRangePointer)*range*;
- (NSDictionary *)**attributesAtIndex**:(unsigned)*location* **longestEffectiveRange**:(NSRangePointer)*range*
      inRange:(NSRange)*rangeLimit*;
- (BOOL)**containsAttachments**;
- (NSRange)**doubleClickAtIndex**:(unsigned)*location*;
- (void)**drawAtPoint**:(NSPoint)*point*;
- (void)**drawInRect**:(NSRect)*rect*;
- (NSDictionary *)**fontAttributesInRange**:(NSRange)*range*;
- (BOOL)**isEqualToAttributedString**:(NSAttributedString *)*other*;
- (unsigned)**length**;
- (unsigned)**lineBreakBeforeIndex**:(unsigned)*location* **withinRange**:(NSRange)*aRange*;
- (unsigned)**nextWordFromIndex**:(unsigned)*location* **forward**:(BOOL)*isForward*;
- (NSDictionary *)**rulerAttributesInRange**:(NSRange)*range*;
- (NSSize)**size**;
- (NSString *)**string**;

// Methods Implementing NSCoding
- (void)**encodeWithCoder**:(NSCoder *)*aCoder*;
- (id)**initWithCoder**:(NSCoder *)*aDecoder*;

// Methods Implementing NSCopying
- (id)**copyWithZone**:(NSZone *)*zone*;

// Methods Implementing NSMutableCopying
- (id)**mutableCopyWithZone**:(NSZone *)*zone*;

Subclasses
NSMutableAttributedString

NSAutoreleasePool

This class is used by Cocoa's memory management system to store objects that have been sent autorelease messages until the end of the current event-loop. At the end of the each pass through the event-loop the autorelease pool is deallocated, thereby releasing any objects referenced by the pool. At the beginning of each pass through the run-loop, a new instance of NSAutoreleasePool is created.

For Cocoa's memory management system to function properly there must be an autorelease pool present. If there is no autorelease pool present then your code will begin to leak memory, as objects will not be released. In this same vein, when you detach a new thread, that thread is responsible for creating its own autorelease pool. Autorelease pools are created just like any other object, using alloc and init. Multiple autorelease pools in a single thread of execution are maintained in a stack whereby objects being autoreleased are sent to the pool at the top of the stack.

The operational method of NSAutoreleasePool is addObject:, which adds the specified object to the pool, causing the object to be released when the pool is itself released. If an object is added multiple times, it will be sent a release message for each time it was added to the pool. You should never have to invoke addObject: yourself; that's the purpose of NSObject's autorelease method.

```
@interface NSAutoreleasePool : NSObject
// Class Methods
  + (void)addObject:(id)anObject;
  + (unsigned int)autoreleasedObjectCount;
  + (void)enableFreedObjectCheck:(BOOL)enable;
  + (void)enableRelease:(BOOL)enable;
  + (unsigned int)poolCountHighWaterMark;
  + (unsigned int)poolCountHighWaterResolution;
  + (void)resetTotalAutoreleasedObjects;
  + (void)setPoolCountHighWaterMark:(unsigned int)count;
  + (void)setPoolCountHighWaterResolution:(unsigned int)res;
  + (void)showPools;
  + (unsigned int)topAutoreleasePoolCount;
  + (unsigned)totalAutoreleasedObjects;
// Instance Methods
  - (void)addObject:(id)anObject;
```

NSBundle

This class represents directories in the filesystem that contain executable binaries, and any resources needed by the executable, such as images, sounds, or nibs. For more information about NSBundle, see Chapter 2.

@interface **NSBundle** : NSObject

// Convenience Constructors

+ (NSBundle *)**bundleForClass**:(Class)*aClass*;

+ (NSBundle *)**bundleWithIdentifier**:(NSString *)*identifier*;

+ (NSBundle *)**bundleWithPath**:(NSString *)*path*;

// Initializers

- (id)**initWithPath**:(NSString *)*path*;

// Class Methods

+ (NSArray *)**allBundles**;

+ (NSArray *)**allFrameworks**;

+ (BOOL)**loadNibFile**:(NSString *)*fileName* **externalNameTable**:(NSDictionary *)*context* **withZone**:(NSZone *)*zone*;

+ (BOOL)**loadNibNamed**:(NSString *)*nibName* **owner**:(id)*owner*;

+ (NSBundle *)**mainBundle**;

+ (NSString *)**pathForResource**:(NSString *)*name* **ofType**:(NSString *)*ext* **inDirectory**:(NSString *)*path*;

+ (NSArray *)**pathsForResourcesOfType**:(NSString *)*ext* **inDirectory**:(NSString *)*subpath*;

+ (NSArray *)**preferredLocalizationsFromArray**:(NSArray *)*localizationsArray*;

+ (NSArray *)**preferredLocalizationsFromArray**:(NSArray *)*localizationsArray*
    forPreferences:(NSArray *)*preferencesArray*;

// Instance Methods

- (NSString *)**builtInPlugInsPath**;

- (NSString *)**bundleIdentifier**;

- (NSString *)**bundlePath**;

- (Class)**classNamed**:(NSString *)*className*;

- (NSAttributedString *)**contextHelpForKey**:(NSString *)*key*;

- (NSString *)**developmentLocalization**;

- (NSString *)**executablePath**;

- (NSDictionary *)**infoDictionary**;

- (BOOL)**isLoaded**;

- (BOOL)**load**;

- (BOOL)**loadNibFile**:(NSString *)*fileName* **externalNameTable**:(NSDictionary *)*context* **withZone**:(NSZone *)*zone*;

- (NSArray *)**localizations**;

- (NSDictionary *)**localizedInfoDictionary**;

- (NSString *)**localizedStringForKey**:(NSString *)*key* **value**:(NSString *)*value* **table**:(NSString *)*tableName*;

- (id)**objectForInfoDictionaryKey**:(NSString *)*key*;

- (NSString *)**pathForAuxiliaryExecutable**:(NSString *)*executableName*;

- (NSString *)**pathForImageResource**:(NSString *)*name*;

- (NSString *)**pathForResource**:(NSString *)*name* **ofType**:(NSString *)*ext*;

- (NSString *)**pathForResource**:(NSString *)*name* **ofType**:(NSString *)*ext* **inDirectory**:(NSString *)*subpath*;

- (NSString *)**pathForResource**:(NSString *)*name* **ofType**:(NSString *)*ext* **inDirectory**:(NSString *)*subpath*
    forLocalization:(NSString *)*localizationName*;

- (NSString *)**pathForSoundResource**:(NSString *)*name*;

- (NSArray *)**pathsForResourcesOfType**:(NSString *)*ext* **inDirectory**:(NSString *)*subpath*;

- (NSArray *)**pathsForResourcesOfType**:(NSString *)*ext* **inDirectory**:(NSString *)*subpath*
    forLocalization:(NSString *)*localizationName*;

- (NSArray *)**preferredLocalizations**;

- (Class)**principalClass**;

- (NSString *)**privateFrameworksPath**;

- (NSString *)**resourcePath**;

- (NSString *)**sharedFrameworksPath**;

- (NSString *)**sharedSupportPath**;

This subclass of NSDate represents dates as users would recognize them on the Western Gregorian calendar. Like NSDate, NSCalendarDate stores a date as the number of seconds since an absolute reference date. However, unlike NSDate, this class is able to return information about the date in terms of minutes, hours, days, weeks, months, and years. For example, using the method dayOfYear we can determine the day of the year a date represents (1 through 366). NSCalendarDate is also capable of providing string representations of dates using the description... methods.

In addition to storing a date value, NSCalendarDate maintains a reference to an NSTimeZone object so that dates may be accurately converted according to the user's time zone. This time zone object is accessed with the methods setTimeZone: and timeZone.

@interface **NSCalendarDate** : NSDate
// Initializers
- (id)**initWithString:**(NSString *)*description;*
- (id)**initWithString:**(NSString *)*description* **calendarFormat:**(NSString *)*format;*
- (id)**initWithString:**(NSString *)*description* **calendarFormat:**(NSString *)*format* **locale:**(NSDictionary *)*dict;*
- (id)**initWithYear:**(int)*year* **month:**(unsigned)*month* **day:**(unsigned)*day* **hour:**(unsigned)*hour*
    minute:(unsigned)*minute* **second:**(unsigned)*second* **timeZone:**(NSTimeZone *)*aTimeZone;*
// Accessor Methods
- (void)**setTimeZone:**(NSTimeZone *)*aTimeZone;*
- (NSTimeZone *)**timeZone;**
- (void)**setCalendarFormat:**(NSString *)*format;*
- (NSString *)**calendarFormat;**
// Class Methods
+ (id)**calendarDate;**
+ (id)**dateWithString:**(NSString *)*description* **calendarFormat:**(NSString *)*format;*
+ (id)**dateWithString:**(NSString *)*description* **calendarFormat:**(NSString *)*format* **locale:**(NSDictionary *)*dict;*
+ (id)**dateWithYear:**(int)*year* **month:**(unsigned)*month* **day:**(unsigned)*day* **hour:**(unsigned)*hour*
    minute:(unsigned)*minute* **second:**(unsigned)*second* **timeZone:**(NSTimeZone *)*aTimeZone;*
// Instance Methods
- (NSCalendarDate *)**dateByAddingYears:**(int)*year* **months:**(int)*month* **days:**(int)*day* **hours:**(int)*hour*
    minutes:(int)*minute* **seconds:**(int)*second;*
- (int)**dayOfCommonEra;**
- (int)**dayOfMonth;**
- (NSString *)**description;**
- (NSString *)**descriptionWithCalendarFormat:**(NSString *)*format;*
- (int)**dayOfWeek;**
- (int)**dayOfYear;**
- (NSString *)**descriptionWithCalendarFormat:**(NSString *)*format* **locale:**(NSDictionary *)*locale;*
- (NSString *)**descriptionWithLocale:**(NSDictionary *)*locale;*
- (int)**hourOfDay;**
- (int)**minuteOfHour;**
- (int)**monthOfYear;**
- (int)**secondOfMinute;**

- (int)**yearOfCommonEra**;
- (void)**years:**(int *)*yp* **months:**(int *)*mop* **days:**(int *)*dp* **hours:**(int *)*hp* **minutes:**(int *)*mip* **seconds:**(int *)*sp*
  sinceDate:(NSCalendarDate *)*date*;

NSCharacterSet

A character set represents a collection of Unicode characters. An instance of NSCharacterSet is a static entity; NSCharacterSet's subclass NSMutableCharacterSet defines an interface to a dynamic set of Unicode characters.

NSCharacterSet is toll-free bridged with the Core Foundation type CFCharacterSet. As such, NSCharacterSet objects can be used interchangeably with the CFCharacterSet pointer type, CFCharacterSetRef.

@interface **NSCharacterSet** : NSObject <NSCoding, NSCopying, NSMutableCopying>
// Class Methods
+ (NSCharacterSet *)**alphanumericCharacterSet**;
+ (NSCharacterSet *)**capitalizedLetterCharacterSet**;
+ (NSCharacterSet *)**characterSetWithBitmapRepresentation:**(NSData *)*data*;
+ (NSCharacterSet *)**characterSetWithCharactersInString:**(NSString *)*aString*;
+ (NSCharacterSet *)**characterSetWithContentsOfFile:**(NSString *)*fName*;
+ (NSCharacterSet *)**characterSetWithRange:**(NSRange)*aRange*;
+ (NSCharacterSet *)**controlCharacterSet**;
+ (NSCharacterSet *)**decimalDigitCharacterSet**;
+ (NSCharacterSet *)**decomposableCharacterSet**;
+ (NSCharacterSet *)**illegalCharacterSet**;
+ (NSCharacterSet *)**letterCharacterSet**;
+ (NSCharacterSet *)**lowercaseLetterCharacterSet**;
+ (NSCharacterSet *)**nonBaseCharacterSet**;
+ (NSCharacterSet *)**punctuationCharacterSet**;
+ (NSCharacterSet *)**uppercaseLetterCharacterSet**;
+ (NSCharacterSet *)**whitespaceAndNewlineCharacterSet**;
+ (NSCharacterSet *)**whitespaceCharacterSet**;
// Instance Methods
- (NSData *)**bitmapRepresentation**;
- (BOOL)**characterIsMember:**(unichar)*aCharacter*;
- (BOOL)**hasMemberInPlane:**(uint8_t)*thePlane*;
- (NSCharacterSet *)**invertedSet**;
- (BOOL)**isSupersetOfSet:**(NSCharacterSet *)*theOtherSet*;
- (BOOL)**longCharacterIsMember:**(UTF32Char)*theLongChar*;
// Methods Implementing NSCoding
- (void)**encodeWithCoder:**(NSCoder *)*aCoder*;
- (id)**initWithCoder:**(NSCoder *)*aDecoder*;
// Methods Implementing NSCopying
- (id)**copyWithZone:**(NSZone *)*zone*;

// Methods Implementing NSMutableCopying
- (id)**mutableCopyWithZone:**(NSZone *)*zone*;

Subclasses
NSMutableCharacterSet

NSClassDescription

This class provides an intelligent interface to Foundation's key-value coding capabilities (see **NSKeyValueCoding** in Chapter 2). The main purpose of this class is to provide an interface for objects to determine the properties and characteristics of a class. **NSClassDescription** is an abstract class, upon which Foundation implements the concrete subclass NSScriptClassDescription.

@interface **NSClassDescription** : NSObject
// Class Methods
+ (NSClassDescription *)**classDescriptionForClass:**(Class)*aClass*;
+ (void)**invalidateClassDescriptionCache**;
+ (void)**registerClassDescription:**(NSClassDescription *)*description* **forClass:**(Class)*aClass*;
// Instance Methods
- (NSArray *)**attributeKeys**;
- (NSArray *)**attributeKeys**;
- (NSClassDescription *)**classDescription**;
- (NSString *)**inverseForRelationshipKey:**(NSString *)*relationshipKey*;
- (NSString *)**inverseForRelationshipKey:**(NSString *)*relationshipKey*;
- (NSArray *)**toManyRelationshipKeys**;
- (NSArray *)**toManyRelationshipKeys**;
- (NSArray *)**toOneRelationshipKeys**;
- (NSArray *)**toOneRelationshipKeys**;
// Notifications
NSClassDescriptionNeededForClassNotification;

Subclasses
NSScriptClassDescription

NSCloneCommand

Instances of this class clone the specified object and then insert the cloned object into the location specified in the script. If no location is specified, the default location is used. This class is used in Cocoa's implementation of built-in AppleScript support, and as such clients should not need to access instances of this class directly.

```
@interface NSCloneCommand : NSScriptCommand
// Accessor Methods
- (void)setReceiversSpecifier:(NSScriptObjectSpecifier *)receiversRef;
// Instance Methods
- (NSScriptObjectSpecifier *)keySpecifier;
```

NSCloseCommand

Mac OS X 10.0

Instances of this class close the specified object, which in Cocoa is generally an instance of NSWindow or NSDocument. This class is used in Cocoa's implementation of built-in AppleScript support, and as such clients should not need to access instances of this class directly.

```
@interface NSCloseCommand : NSScriptCommand
// Instance Methods
- (NSSaveOptions)saveOptions;
```

NSCoder

Mac OS X 10.0

This class defines an abstract interface for subclasses that implement object archival functionality. The Foundation framework implements five concreate subclasses: NSArchiver and NSUnarchiver are used for non-keyed archiving, while NSKeyedArchiver and NSKeyedUnarchiver provide support for keyed-archiving. NSPortCoder is used by the distributed objects system to send object proxies across a connection. For more information, see the class references for these five classes, the protocol reference for the NSCoding protocol, and Chapter 2.

```
@interface NSCoder : NSObject
// Accessor Methods
- (void)setObjectZone:(NSZone *)zone;
- (NSZone *)objectZone;
// Instance Methods
- (BOOL)allowsKeyedCoding;
- (void)decodeArrayOfObjCType:(const char *)itemType count:(unsigned)count at:(void *)array;
- (BOOL)decodeBoolForKey:(NSString *)key;
- (const uint8_t *)decodeBytesForKey:(NSString *)key returnedLength:(unsigned *)lengthp;
- (void *)decodeBytesWithReturnedLength:(unsigned *)lengthp;
- (NSData *)decodeDataObject;
- (double)decodeDoubleForKey:(NSString *)key;
- (float)decodeFloatForKey:(NSString *)key;
- (int32_t)decodeInt32ForKey:(NSString *)key;
- (int64_t)decodeInt64ForKey:(NSString *)key;
```

- (int)**decodeIntForKey**:(NSString *)*key*;
- (NSColor *)**decodeNXColor**;
- (id)**decodeNXObject**;
- (id)**decodeObject**;
- (id)**decodeObjectForKey**:(NSString *)*key*;
- (NSPoint)**decodePoint**;
- (NSPoint)**decodePointForKey**:(NSString *)*key*;
- (id)**decodePropertyList**;
- (NSRect)**decodeRect**;
- (NSRect)**decodeRectForKey**:(NSString *)*key*;
- (NSSize)**decodeSize**;
- (NSSize)**decodeSizeForKey**:(NSString *)*key*;
- (void)**decodeValueOfObjCType**:(const char *)*type* **at**:(void *)*data*;
- (void)**decodeValuesOfObjCTypes**:(const char *)*types, ...*;
- (void)**encodeArrayOfObjCType**:(const char *)*type* **count**:(unsigned)*count* **at**:(const void *)*array*;
- (void)**encodeBool**:(BOOL)*boolv* **forKey**:(NSString *)*key*;
- (void)**encodeBycopyObject**:(id)*anObject*;
- (void)**encodeByrefObject**:(id)*anObject*;
- (void)**encodeBytes**:(const uint8_t *)*bytesp* **length**:(unsigned)*lenv* **forKey**:(NSString *)*key*;
- (void)**encodeBytes**:(const void *)*byteaddr* **length**:(unsigned)*length*;
- (void)**encodeConditionalObject**:(id)*object*;
- (void)**encodeConditionalObject**:(id)*objv* **forKey**:(NSString *)*key*;
- (void)**encodeDataObject**:(NSData *)*data*;
- (void)**encodeDouble**:(double)*realv* **forKey**:(NSString *)*key*;
- (void)**encodeFloat**:(float)*realv* **forKey**:(NSString *)*key*;
- (void)**encodeInt32**:(int32_t)*intv* **forKey**:(NSString *)*key*;
- (void)**encodeInt64**:(int64_t)*intv* **forKey**:(NSString *)*key*;
- (void)**encodeInt**:(int)*intv* **forKey**:(NSString *)*key*;
- (void)**encodeNXObject**:(id)*object*;
- (void)**encodeObject**:(id)*object*;
- (void)**encodeObject**:(id)*objv* **forKey**:(NSString *)*key*;
- (void)**encodePoint**:(NSPoint)*point*;
- (void)**encodePoint**:(NSPoint)*point* **forKey**:(NSString *)*key*;
- (void)**encodePropertyList**:(id)*aPropertyList*;
- (void)**encodeRect**:(NSRect)*rect*;
- (void)**encodeRect**:(NSRect)*rect* **forKey**:(NSString *)*key*;
- (void)**encodeRootObject**:(id)*rootObject*;
- (void)**encodeSize**:(NSSize)*size*;
- (void)**encodeSize**:(NSSize)*size* **forKey**:(NSString *)*key*;
- (void)**encodeValueOfObjCType**:(const char *)*type* **at**:(const void *)*addr*;
- (void)**encodeValuesOfObjCTypes**:(const char *)*types, ...*;
- (BOOL)**containsValueForKey**:(NSString *)*key*;
- (unsigned)**systemVersion**;
- (unsigned)**versionForClassName**:(NSString *)*className*;

Subclasses

NSArchiver, NSKeyedArchiver, NSKeyedUnarchiver, NSPortCoder, NSUnarchiver

NSConditionLock

NSConditionLock is a class that implements the NSLocking protocol and is used to perform thread locks that are associated with specific, user-defined conditions. The idea behind NSConditionLock is that a thread can acquire a lock only if some arbitrary condition has been satisfied. See Chapter 2.

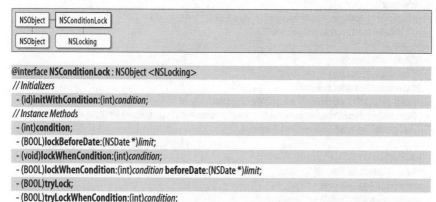

@interface **NSConditionLock** : NSObject <NSLocking>

// Initializers

- (id)**initWithCondition**:(int)*condition*;

// Instance Methods

- (int)**condition**;

- (BOOL)**lockBeforeDate**:(NSDate *)*limit*;

- (void)**lockWhenCondition**:(int)*condition*;

- (BOOL)**lockWhenCondition**:(int)*condition* **beforeDate**:(NSDate *)*limit*;

- (BOOL)**tryLock**;

- (BOOL)**tryLockWhenCondition**:(int)*condition*;

- (void)**unlockWithCondition**:(int)*condition*;

// Methods Implementing NSLocking

- (void)**lock**;

- (void)**unlock**;

NSConnection

This class declares the interface to objects that manage communications between objects that reside in separate processes. The NSConnection class forms the groundwork for Cocoa's distributed objects system, which is described in more detail in Chapter 6. NSConnection supports inter-process communication on the local host, as well as between two hosts over a network. NSConnection is frequently used to facilitate communication between threads in a multithreaded application. Clients use the NSConnection class primarily for vending objects (making them available to other processes), accessing vended objects, and for fine-tuning communication parameters.

@interface **NSConnection** : NSObject

// Convenience Constructors

+ (NSConnection *)**connectionWithReceivePort**:(NSPort *)*receivePort* **sendPort**:(NSPort *)*sendPort*;

+ (NSConnection *)**connectionWithRegisteredName**:(NSString *)*name* **host**:(NSString *)*hostName*;

+ (NSConnection *)**connectionWithRegisteredName**:(NSString *)*name* **host**:(NSString *)*hostName*
   usingNameServer:(NSPortNameServer *)*server*;

// Initializers

- (id)**initWithReceivePort**:(NSPort *)*receivePort* **sendPort**:(NSPort *)*sendPort*;

// Accessor Methods

- (void)**setRequestTimeout**:(NSTimeInterval)*ti*;

- (NSTimeInterval)**requestTimeout**;
- (void)**setReplyTimeout**:(NSTimeInterval)*ti*;
- (NSTimeInterval)**replyTimeout**;
- (void)**setRootObject**:(id)*anObject*;
- (id)**rootObject**;
- (void)**setDelegate**:(id)*anObject*;
- (id)**delegate**;
- (void)**setIndependentConversationQueueing**:(BOOL)*yorn*;
- (BOOL)**independentConversationQueueing**;

// *Class Methods*
+ (NSArray *)**allConnections**;
+ (id)**currentConversation**;
+ (NSConnection *)**defaultConnection**;
+ (NSDistantObject *)**rootProxyForConnectionWithRegisteredName**:(NSString *)*name* **host**:(NSString *)*hostName*;
+ (NSDistantObject *)**rootProxyForConnectionWithRegisteredName**:(NSString *)*name* **host**:(NSString *)*hostName*
    usingNameServer:(NSPortNameServer *)*server*;

// *Instance Methods*
- (void)**invalidate**;
- (void)**addRunLoop**:(NSRunLoop *)*runloop*;
- (void)**enableMultipleThreads**;
- (void)**addRequestMode**:(NSString *)*rmode*;
- (BOOL)**isValid**;
- (NSArray *)**localObjects**;
- (BOOL)**multipleThreadsEnabled**;
- (NSPort *)**receivePort**;
- (BOOL)**registerName**:(NSString *)*name*;
- (BOOL)**registerName**:(NSString *)*name* **withNameServer**:(NSPortNameServer *)*server*;
- (NSArray *)**remoteObjects**;
- (void)**removeRequestMode**:(NSString *)*rmode*;
- (void)**removeRunLoop**:(NSRunLoop *)*runloop*;
- (NSArray *)**requestModes**;
- (NSDistantObject *)**rootProxy**;
- (void)**runInNewThread**;
- (NSPort *)**sendPort**;
- (NSDictionary *)**statistics**;

// *Methods Implemented by the Delegate*
- (BOOL)**authenticateComponents**:(NSArray *)*components* **withData**:(NSData *)*signature*;
- (NSData *)**authenticationDataForComponents**:(NSArray *)*components*;
- (BOOL)**connection**:(NSConnection *)*ancestor* **shouldMakeNewConnection**:(NSConnection *)*conn*;
- (BOOL)**connection**:(NSConnection *)*connection* **handleRequest**:(NSDistantObjectRequest *)*doreq*;
- (id)**createConversationForConnection**:(NSConnection *)*conn*;
- (BOOL)**makeNewConnection**:(NSConnection *)*conn* **sender**:(NSConnection *)*ancestor*;

NSCountCommand

Mac OS X 10.0

Instances of this class serve to count the number of objects contained within the container object specified as part of this command. This class is used in Cocoa's implementation of built-in AppleScript support, and as such clients should not need to access instances of this class directly.

@interface **NSCountCommand** : NSScriptCommand

NSCountedSet

This class extends the functionality of NSMutableSet by associating with each member of the set a count of how many times the object has been added to the set. By keeping a count with each object, NSCountedSet essentially removes the restriction that every member of a set must be unique. NSCountedSet reimplements several of NSMutableSet's methods to support the object counter. The one new method in NSCountedSet is countForObject:, which will return the counter value for the specified object. If the object is not a member of the set, this method returns 0. This count can be viewed as the number of occurences of the object within the set.

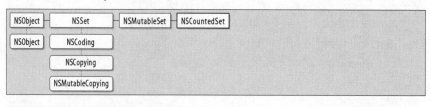

@interface **NSCountedSet** : NSMutableSet
// Initializers
- (id)**initWithArray:**(NSArray *)*array*;
- (id)**initWithCapacity:**(unsigned)*numItems*;
- (id)**initWithSet:**(NSSet *)*set*;
// Instance Methods
- (void)**addObject:**(id)*object*;
- (unsigned)**countForObject:**(id)*object*;
- (NSEnumerator *)**objectEnumerator**;
- (void)**removeObject:**(id)*object*;

NSCreateCommand

This class provides support for the *Make* AppleScript command, which is used to create new instances of the specified object. This class is used in Cocoa's implementation of built-in AppleScript support, and as such clients should not need to access instances of this class directly.

@interface **NSCreateCommand** : NSScriptCommand
// Instance Methods

Foundation
Classes

- (NSScriptClassDescription *)**createClassDescription**;
- (NSDictionary *)**resolvedKeyDictionary**;

NSData

This class is used to store immutable data as a string of bytes. In essence, NSData is an Objective-C wrapper around a C data buffer. To access the buffer directly, use the **bytes** method, which returns a pointer to the buffer. The number of bytes contained in the buffer is found by invoking the **length** method. Additionally, NSData provides a handful of methods for copy bytes from the data object into a buffer. These methods include **getBytes:**, **getBytes:length:**, and **getBytes:range:**. All three of these methods take in the first parameter a generic C pointer to the buffer in which the bytes are copied.

NSData is toll-free bridged with the Core Foundation type **CFData**. As such, NSData objects can be used interchangeably with the **CFData** pointer type, **CFDataRef**.

Note that NSData is an immutable class, which means the contents of the data object cannot be changed after initialization.

@interface **NSData** : NSObject <NSCoding, NSCopying, NSMutableCopying>
// Convenience Constructors
+ (id)**data**;
+ (id)**dataWithBytes:**(const void *)*bytes* **length:**(unsigned)*length*;
+ (id)**dataWithBytesNoCopy:**(void *)*bytes* **length:**(unsigned)*length*;
+ (id)**dataWithBytesNoCopy:**(void *)*bytes* **length:**(unsigned)*length* **freeWhenDone:**(BOOL)*b*;
+ (id)**dataWithContentsOfFile:**(NSString *)*path*;
+ (id)**dataWithContentsOfMappedFile:**(NSString *)*path*;
+ (id)**dataWithContentsOfURL:**(NSURL *)*url*;
+ (id)**dataWithData:**(NSData *)*data*;
// Initializers
- (id)**initWithBytes:**(const void *)*bytes* **length:**(unsigned)*length*;
- (id)**initWithBytesNoCopy:**(void *)*bytes* **length:**(unsigned)*length*;
- (id)**initWithBytesNoCopy:**(void *)*bytes* **length:**(unsigned)*length* **freeWhenDone:**(BOOL)*b*;
- (id)**initWithContentsOfFile:**(NSString *)*path*;
- (id)**initWithContentsOfMappedFile:**(NSString *)*path*;
- (id)**initWithContentsOfURL:**(NSURL *)*url*;
- (id)**initWithData:**(NSData *)*data*;
// Instance Methods
- (const void *)**bytes**;
- (NSString *)**description**;
- (unsigned)**deserializeAlignedBytesLengthAtCursor:**(unsigned *)*cursor*;
- (void)**deserializeBytes:**(void *)*buffer* **length:**(unsigned)*bytes* **atCursor:**(unsigned *)*cursor*;
- (void)**deserializeDataAt:**(void *)*data* **ofObjCType:**(const char *)*type* **atCursor:**(unsigned *)*cursor*
    context:(id <NSObjCTypeSerializationCallBack>)*callback*;
- (int)**deserializeIntAtCursor:**(unsigned *)*cursor*;

- (int)**deserializeIntAtIndex**:(unsigned)*index*;
- (void)**deserializeInts**:(int *)*intBuffer* **count**:(unsigned)*numInts* **atCursor**:(unsigned *)*cursor*;
- (void)**deserializeInts**:(int *)*intBuffer* **count**:(unsigned)*numInts* **atIndex**:(unsigned)*index*;
- (void)**getBytes**:(void *)*buffer*;
- (void)**getBytes**:(void *)*buffer* **length**:(unsigned)*length*;
- (void)**getBytes**:(void *)*buffer* **range**:(NSRange)*range*;
- (BOOL)**isEqualToData**:(NSData *)*other*;
- (unsigned)**length**;
- (NSData *)**subdataWithRange**:(NSRange)*range*;
- (BOOL)**writeToFile**:(NSString *)*path* **atomically**:(BOOL)*useAuxiliaryFile*;
- (BOOL)**writeToURL**:(NSURL *)*url* **atomically**:(BOOL)*atomically*;
// *Methods Implementing NSCoding*
- (void)**encodeWithCoder**:(NSCoder *)*aCoder*;
- (id)**initWithCoder**:(NSCoder *)*aDecoder*;
// *Methods Implementing NSCopying*
- (id)**copyWithZone**:(NSZone *)*zone*;
// *Methods Implementing NSMutableCopying*
- (id)**mutableCopyWithZone**:(NSZone *)*zone*;

Subclasses

NSMutableData

NSDate

This class represents a date and time as the number of seconds since the absolute reference date, which is defined as midnight, January 1, 2001, GMT. This class allows you to compare dates, compute time intervals between dates, and obtain string representations of the NSDate object. The dates represented by NSDate are not suitable for presentation to human users. NSDateFormatter objects are used by NSCell objects to convert raw dates into human readable representations. If your application requires the ability to work with date information in terms of a calendar—that is, days, weeks, months, years, and so on—the Foundation framework provides the NSDate subclass NSCalendarDate.

NSDate is toll-free bridged with the Core Foundation type CFDate. As such, NSDate objects can be used interchangeably with the CFDate pointer type, CFDateRef.

See the NSCalendarDate class description for more information. Additionally, Chapter 2 provides more detailed information on the use of NSDate.

@interface **NSDate** : NSObject <NSCoding, NSCopying>
// *Convenience Constructors*
+ (id)**date**;
+ (id)**dateWithString**:(NSString *)*aString*;
+ (id)**dateWithTimeIntervalSince1970**:(NSTimeInterval)*secs*;
+ (id)**dateWithTimeIntervalSinceNow**:(NSTimeInterval)*secs*;
+ (id)**dateWithTimeIntervalSinceReferenceDate**:(NSTimeInterval)*secs*;

```
// Initializers
- (id)init;
- (id)initWithString:(NSString *)description;
- (id)initWithTimeInterval:(NSTimeInterval)secsToBeAdded sinceDate:(NSDate *)anotherDate;
- (id)initWithTimeIntervalSinceNow:(NSTimeInterval)secsToBeAddedToNow;
- (id)initWithTimeIntervalSinceReferenceDate:(NSTimeInterval)secsToBeAdded;
// Class Methods
+ (id)distantFuture;
+ (id)distantPast;
+ (id) dateWithNaturalLanguageString:(NSString *)string;
+ (id) dateWithNaturalLanguageString:(NSString *)string locale:(NSDictionary *)dict;
+ (NSTimeInterval)timeIntervalSinceReferenceDate;
// Instance Methods
- (id)addTimeInterval:(NSTimeInterval)seconds;
- (NSComparisonResult)compare:(NSDate *)other;
- (NSCalendarDate *)dateWithCalendarFormat:(NSString *)format timeZone:(NSTimeZone *)aTimeZone;
- (NSString *)description;
- (NSString *)descriptionWithCalendarFormat:(NSString *)format timeZone:(NSTimeZone *)aTimeZone
    locale:(NSDictionary *)locale;
- (NSString *)descriptionWithLocale:(NSDictionary *)locale;
- (NSDate *)earlierDate:(NSDate *)anotherDate;
- (BOOL)isEqualToDate:(NSDate *)otherDate;
- (NSDate *)laterDate:(NSDate *)anotherDate;
- (NSTimeInterval)timeIntervalSince1970;
- (NSTimeInterval)timeIntervalSinceDate:(NSDate *)anotherDate;
- (NSTimeInterval)timeIntervalSinceNow;
- (NSTimeInterval)timeIntervalSinceReferenceDate;
// Methods Implementing NSCoding
- (void)encodeWithCoder:(NSCoder *)aCoder;
- (id)initWithCoder:(NSCoder *)aDecoder;
// Methods Implementing NSCopying
- (id)copyWithZone:(NSZone *)zone;
```

Subclasses

NSCalendarDate

NSDateFormatter

Mac OS X 10.0

This class is used to convert NSDate values into a human-readable date and time string, as well as to convert textual date and time representations into NSDate objects. NSDate-Formatter is quite flexible in terms of the variety of supported textual representations, including such standards as 1/1/02, January 1, 2002, and natural language expressions such as "Today" or "Tomorrow". NSDateFormatter is used primarily by NSTextFieldCell instances to present date information to the user in an appropriate format.

@interface **NSDateFormatter** : NSFormatter

// Initializers

- (id)**initWithDateFormat**:(NSString *)*format* **allowNaturalLanguage**:(BOOL)*flag*;

// Instance Methods

- (BOOL)**allowsNaturalLanguage**;

- (NSString *)**dateFormat**;

NSDecimalNumber Mac OS X 10.0

This subclass of NSNumber provides an object-oriented wrapper for performing base-10 arithmetic operations. Instances of NSDecimalNumber are created with a string such as "10.2e4" using decimalNumberWithString:, or by specifying the mantissa, exponent, and whether or not it is negative in the method decimalNumberWith-Mantissa:exponent:isNegative:.

Arithmetic operations are performed on two decimal number objects using methods such as decimalNumberByAdding:, decimalNumberByMultiplying:, and so forth. The value of the decimal number can be accessed as a double by sending a doubleValue message to the object.

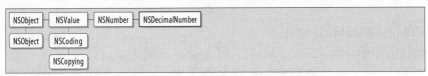

@interface **NSDecimalNumber** : NSNumber

// Initializers

- (id)**initWithDecimal**:(NSDecimal)*dcm*;

- (id)**initWithMantissa**:(unsigned long long)*mantissa* **exponent**:(short)*exponent* **isNegative**:(BOOL)*flag*;

- (id)**initWithString**:(NSString *)*numberValue*;

- (id)**initWithString**:(NSString *)*numberValue* **locale**:(NSDictionary *)*locale*;

// Class Methods

+ (NSDecimalNumber *)**decimalNumberWithDecimal**:(NSDecimal)*dcm*;

+ (NSDecimalNumber *)**decimalNumberWithMantissa**:(unsigned long long)*mantissa*
    exponent:(short)*exponent* **isNegative**:(BOOL)*flag*;

+ (NSDecimalNumber *)**decimalNumberWithString**:(NSString *)*numberValue*;

+ (NSDecimalNumber *)**decimalNumberWithString**:(NSString *)*numberValue* **locale**:(NSDictionary *)*locale*;

+ (id <NSDecimalNumberBehaviors>)**defaultBehavior**;

+ (NSDecimalNumber *)**maximumDecimalNumber**;

+ (NSDecimalNumber *)**minimumDecimalNumber**;

+ (NSDecimalNumber *)**notANumber**;

+ (NSDecimalNumber *)**one**;

+ (void)**setDefaultBehavior**:(id <NSDecimalNumberBehaviors>)*behavior*;

+ (NSDecimalNumber *)**zero**;

// Instance Methods

- (NSComparisonResult)**compare**:(NSNumber *)*decimalNumber*;

- (NSDecimalNumber *)**decimalNumberByAdding**:(NSDecimalNumber *)*decimalNumber*;

- (NSDecimalNumber *)**decimalNumberByAdding**:(NSDecimalNumber *)*decimalNumber*
    withBehavior:(id <NSDecimalNumberBehaviors>)*behavior*;

- (NSDecimalNumber *)**decimalNumberByDividingBy**:(NSDecimalNumber *)*decimalNumber*;

- (NSDecimalNumber *)**decimalNumberByDividingBy**:(NSDecimalNumber *)*decimalNumber*
    withBehavior:(id <NSDecimalNumberBehaviors>)*behavior*;

- (NSDecimalNumber *)**decimalNumberByMultiplyingBy**:(NSDecimalNumber *)*decimalNumber*;

- (NSDecimalNumber *)**decimalNumberByMultiplyingBy**:(NSDecimalNumber *)*decimalNumber*
    withBehavior:(id <NSDecimalNumberBehaviors>)*behavior;*
- (NSDecimalNumber *)**decimalNumberByMultiplyingByPowerOf10**:(short)*power;*
- (NSDecimalNumber *)**decimalNumberByMultiplyingByPowerOf10**:(short)*power*
    withBehavior:(id <NSDecimalNumberBehaviors>)*behavior;*
- (NSDecimalNumber *)**decimalNumberByRaisingToPower**:(unsigned)*power;*
- (NSDecimalNumber *)**decimalNumberByRaisingToPower**:(unsigned)*power*
    withBehavior:(id <NSDecimalNumberBehaviors>)*behavior;*
- (NSDecimalNumber *)**decimalNumberByRoundingAccordingToBehavior**:
    (id <NSDecimalNumberBehaviors>)*behavior;*
- (NSDecimalNumber *)**decimalNumberBySubtracting**:(NSDecimalNumber *)*decimalNumber;*
- (NSDecimalNumber *)**decimalNumberBySubtracting**:(NSDecimalNumber *)*decimalNumber*
    withBehavior:(id <NSDecimalNumberBehaviors>)*behavior;*
- (NSDecimal)**decimalValue;**
- (NSString *)**descriptionWithLocale**:(NSDictionary *)*locale;*
- (double)**doubleValue;**
- (const char *)**objCType;**

NSDecimalNumberHandler Mac OS X 10.0

This class is used to customize the behavior of NSDecimalNumber-based arithmetic without having to subclass. In particular, NSDecimalNumberHandler allows clients to specify how NSDecimalNumber objects should handle rounding and errors.

@interface **NSDecimalNumberHandler** : NSObject <NSCoding, NSDecimalNumberBehaviors>
// Initializers
- (id)**initWithRoundingMode**:(NSRoundingMode)*roundingMode* **scale**:(short)*scale* **raiseOnExactness**:(BOOL)*exact*
    raiseOnOverflow:(BOOL)*overflow* **raiseOnUnderflow**:(BOOL)*underflow* **raiseOnDivideByZero**:(BOOL)*divideByZero;*
// Class Methods
+ (id)**decimalNumberHandlerWithRoundingMode**:(NSRoundingMode)*roundingMode*
    scale:(short)*scale* **raiseOnExactness**:(BOOL)*exact* **raiseOnOverflow**:(BOOL)*overflow*
    raiseOnUnderflow:(BOOL)*underflow* **raiseOnDivideByZero**:(BOOL)*divideByZero;*
+ (id)**defaultDecimalNumberHandler;**
// Methods Implementing NSCoding
- (void)**encodeWithCoder**:(NSCoder *)*aCoder;*
- (id)**initWithCoder**:(NSCoder *)*aDecoder;*
// Methods Implementing NSDecimalNumberBehaviors
- (NSRoundingMode)**roundingMode;**
- (short)**scale;**
- (NSDecimalNumber *)**exceptionDuringOperation**:(SEL)*operation* **error**:(NSCalculationError)*error*
    leftOperand:(NSDecimalNumber *)*leftOperand* **rightOperand**:(NSDecimalNumber *)*rightOperand;*

NSDeleteCommand 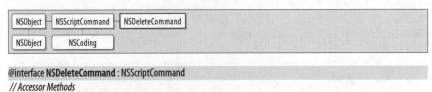 Mac OS X 10.0

Instances of this class delete the indicated object or objects. This class is used in Cocoa's implementation of built-in AppleScript support, and as such clients should not need to access instances of this class directly.

@interface **NSDeleteCommand** : NSScriptCommand
// *Accessor Methods*
 - (void)**setReceiversSpecifier**:(NSScriptObjectSpecifier *)*receiversRef*;
// *Instance Methods*
 - (NSScriptObjectSpecifier *)**keySpecifier**;

NSDeserializer Mac OS X 10.0

This class provides an interface to objects that convert property list–formatted data into a structure of property list objects in memory. Note that this class has been deprecated and clients should instead use the class NSPropertyListSerialization.

@interface **NSDeserializer** : NSObject
// *Class Methods*
 + (id)**deserializePropertyListFromData**:(NSData *)*data* **atCursor**:(unsigned *)*cursor* **mutableContainers**:(BOOL)*mut*;
 + (id)**deserializePropertyListFromData**:(NSData *)*serialization* **mutableContainers**:(BOOL)*mut*;
 + (id)**deserializePropertyListLazilyFromData**:(NSData *)*data* **atCursor**:(unsigned *)*cursor* **length**:(unsigned)*length*
    mutableContainers:(BOOL)*mut*;

NSDictionary Mac OS X 10.0

This class manages a collection of objects as key-value pairs: objects are identified by a unique key within the dictionary. A key-value pair within a dictionary is called an entry. NSDictionary is an immutable class whose contents cannot be altered after they have been initially set. If you need a mutable dictionary, use NSMutableDictionary instead. A dictionary key is typically an NSString, but according to the API the key can be any object that is type id. The fact that a key can be an object of any type opens the way for interesting design possibilities in Cocoa.

NSDictionary has three primitive methods upon which the rest of the API is based. They are count, objectForKey:, and keyEnumerator. The count method returns the number of objects contained in the dictionary. The method objectForKey: is used to access an object in the dictionary. Finally, keyEnumerator will return an NSEnumerator object that will enumerate the keys of the dictionary. In addition to keyEnumerator, NSDictionary responds to objectEnumerator for enumerating the contents of the dictionary. Note that there is no order in a dictionary as there is in an array. When enumerating the contents of a dictionary, there is no guarantee regarding the order that member objects will be returned by the enumerator.

Foundation
Classes

Often we want to send a message to each member of a collection. NSDictionary provides a method that save us from the burden of having to enumerate the contents of the dictionary and send the message manually. This method is makeObjectsPerformSelector:, which will cause the method matching the selector to be invoked in each member of the collection. If you need to invoke a method that takes an argument, then use the method makeObjectsPerformSelector:withObject:.

NSDictionary is toll-free bridged with the Core Foundation type CFDictionary. As such, NSDictionary objects can be used interchangeably with the CFDictionary pointer type, CFDictionaryRef.

@interface **NSDictionary** : NSObject <NSCoding, NSCopying, NSMutableCopying>
// *Convenience Constructors*
+ (id)**dictionary**;
+ (id)**dictionaryWithContentsOfFile**:(NSString *)*path*;
+ (id)**dictionaryWithContentsOfURL**:(NSURL *)*url*;
+ (id)**dictionaryWithDictionary**:(NSDictionary *)*dict*;
+ (id)**dictionaryWithObject**:(id)*object* **forKey**:(id)*key*;
+ (id)**dictionaryWithObjects**:(NSArray *)*objects* **forKeys**:(NSArray *)*keys*;
+ (id)**dictionaryWithObjects**:(id *)*objects* **forKeys**:(id *)*keys* **count**:(unsigned)*count*;
+ (id)**dictionaryWithObjectsAndKeys**:(id)*firstObject*, ...;
// *Initializers*
- (id)**initWithContentsOfFile**:(NSString *)*path*;
- (id)**initWithContentsOfURL**:(NSURL *)*url*;
- (id)**initWithDictionary**:(NSDictionary *)*otherDictionary*;
- (id)**initWithDictionary**:(NSDictionary *)*otherDictionary* **copyItems**:(BOOL)*aBool*;
- (id)**initWithObjects**:(NSArray *)*objects* **forKeys**:(NSArray *)*keys*;
- (id)**initWithObjects**:(id *)*objects* **forKeys**:(id *)*keys* **count**:(unsigned)*count*;
- (id)**initWithObjectsAndKeys**:(id)*firstObject*, ...;
// *Instance Methods*
- (NSArray *)**allKeys**;
- (NSArray *)**allKeysForObject**:(id)*anObject*;
- (NSArray *)**allValues**;
- (unsigned)**count**;
- (NSString *)**description**;
- (NSString *)**descriptionInStringsFileFormat**;
- (NSString *)**descriptionWithLocale**:(NSDictionary *)*locale*;
- (NSString *)**descriptionWithLocale**:(NSDictionary *)*locale* **indent**:(unsigned)*level*;
- (NSDate *)**fileCreationDate**;
- (BOOL)**fileExtensionHidden**;
- (NSNumber *)**fileGroupOwnerAccountID**;
- (NSString *)**fileGroupOwnerAccountName**;
- (OSType)**fileHFSCreatorCode**;
- (OSType)**fileHFSTypeCode**;
- (BOOL)**fileIsAppendOnly**;

- (BOOL)**fileIsImmutable**;
- (NSDate *)**fileModificationDate**;
- (NSNumber *)**fileOwnerAccountID**;
- (NSString *)**fileOwnerAccountName**;
- (unsigned long)**filePosixPermissions**;
- (unsigned long long)**fileSize**;
- (unsigned long)**fileSystemFileNumber**;
- (unsigned long)**fileSystemNumber**;
- (NSString *)**fileType**;
- (BOOL)**isEqualToDictionary**:(NSDictionary *)*otherDictionary*;
- (NSEnumerator *)**keyEnumerator**;
- (NSArray *)**keysSortedByValueUsingSelector**:(SEL)*comparator*;
- (NSEnumerator *)**objectEnumerator**;
- (id)**objectForKey**:(id)*aKey*;
- (NSArray *)**objectsForKeys**:(NSArray *)*keys* **notFoundMarker**:(id)*marker*;
- (BOOL)**writeToFile**:(NSString *)*path* **atomically**:(BOOL)*useAuxiliaryFile*;
- (BOOL)**writeToURL**:(NSURL *)*url* **atomically**:(BOOL)*atomically*;
// *Methods Implementing NSCoding*
- (void)**encodeWithCoder**:(NSCoder *)*aCoder*;
- (id)**initWithCoder**:(NSCoder *)*aDecoder*;
// *Methods Implementing NSCopying*
- (id)**copyWithZone**:(NSZone *)*zone*;
// *Methods Implementing NSMutableCopying*
- (id)**mutableCopyWithZone**:(NSZone *)*zone*;

Subclasses

NSMutableDictionary

NSDirectoryEnumerator

This subclass of NSEnumerator enumerates the contents of a directory at a specified path. The objects returned by the directory enumerator are strings of the pathnames of all files and subdirectories contained within the directory represented by the enumerator. Enumeration is recursive; that is, the contents of a child directory will be enumerated when encountered. Instances of this class are returned by the NSFileManager method **enumeratorAtPath:**.

@interface **NSDirectoryEnumerator** : NSEnumerator
// *Instance Methods*
- (NSDictionary *)**directoryAttributes**;
- (NSDictionary *)**fileAttributes**;
- (void)**skipDescendents**;

NSDistantObject

This subclass of NSProxy is used in distributed objects applications to locally represent objects that have been vended by a remote process. NSDistantObject operates by forwarding any messages it receives to the local NSConnection object, which then passes the invocation to the NSConnection object of the remote process. Return values received by the NSConnection object are passed to the message originator through the same instance of NSDistantObject that forwarded the message.

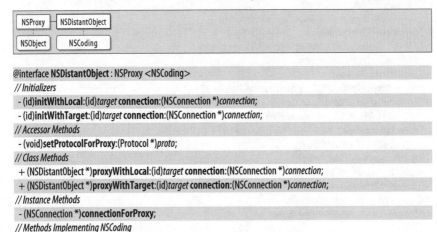

```
@interface NSDistantObject : NSProxy <NSCoding>
// Initializers
  - (id)initWithLocal:(id)target connection:(NSConnection *)connection;
  - (id)initWithTarget:(id)target connection:(NSConnection *)connection;
// Accessor Methods
  - (void)setProtocolForProxy:(Protocol *)proto;
// Class Methods
  + (NSDistantObject *)proxyWithLocal:(id)target connection:(NSConnection *)connection;
  + (NSDistantObject *)proxyWithTarget:(id)target connection:(NSConnection *)connection;
// Instance Methods
  - (NSConnection *)connectionForProxy;
// Methods Implementing NSCoding
  - (void)encodeWithCoder:(NSCoder *)aCoder;
  - (id)initWithCoder:(NSCoder *)aDecoder;
```

NSDistantObjectRequest

This class is used by the distributed objects system to assist handling invocations between objects that reside in different processes. This class is used internally by the distributed objects system, and as such clients should never need to access instances of this class. If a client needs to process events handled by an NSConnection object, they may implement the NSConnection delegate method connection:handleRequest:.

```
@interface NSDistantObjectRequest : NSObject
// Instance Methods
  - (NSConnection *)connection;
  - (id)conversation;
  - (NSInvocation *)invocation;
  - (void)replyWithException:(NSException *)exception;
```

NSDistributedLock

This class provides an interface to an object that can be used by multiple applications to control access to a shared resource (such as a file). This class works by creating an entry in the filesystem at a path known to each application that is interested in acquiring a lock to access the shared resource.

A distributed lock object is initialized with a filesystem entry using the method initWith-Path:. To acquire a lock, thus making it safe to access a resource, we use the method tryLock. This method returns a BOOL indicating whether or not it was successful in attempting to acquire a lock. To relinquish a previously acquired lock, use the method unlock.

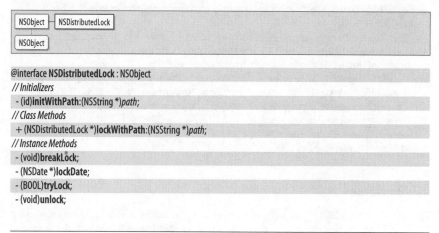

```
@interface NSDistributedLock : NSObject
// Initializers
    - (id)initWithPath:(NSString *)path;
// Class Methods
    + (NSDistributedLock *)lockWithPath:(NSString *)path;
// Instance Methods
    - (void)breakLock;
    - (NSDate *)lockDate;
    - (BOOL)tryLock;
    - (void)unlock;
```

NSDistributedNotificationCenter

This class extends the functionality of its superclass, NSNotificationCenter, by providing a means of sending notifications to objects in other tasks. Every task has a default distributed notification center that objects send notifications to, as well as register themselves as observers. To obtain your application's distributed notification center object, use the factory method defaultCenter.

To register an object as a receiver of a specified notification we use the method addObserver:selector:name:object:. The observer is the object that wishes to be notified of the notification identified by name:. The argument selector: specifies what method should be invoked in response to the notification. The object: parameter allows us to restrict the notifications the observer responds to those posted by the specified object. To remove an observer, invoke the method removeObserver:, which removes the observer for all notifications. To be selective about what notifications from which objects to stop observing, use the method removeObserver:name:object:.

NSNotificationCenter provides three methods for posting notifications: postNotification:, post-NotificationName:object:, and postNotification-Name:object:userInfo:. Each of these methods offers different levels of control over how the notification is posted.

For more information about the notifications system, see Chapter 2.

```
NSObject ─ NSNotificationCenter ─ NSDjstributedNotificationCenter
NSObject
```

@interface **NSDistributedNotificationCenter** : NSNotificationCenter
// Accessor Methods
- (void)**setSuspended**:(BOOL)*suspended*;
- (BOOL)**suspended**;
// Class Methods
+ (id)**defaultCenter**;
+ (NSDistributedNotificationCenter *)**notificationCenterForType**:(NSString *)*notificationCenterType*;
// Instance Methods
- (void)**addObserver**:(id)*observer* **selector**:(SEL)*aSelector* **name**:(NSString *)*aName* **object**:(NSString *)*anObject*;
- (void)**addObserver**:(id)*observer* **selector**:(SEL)*selector* **name**:(NSString *)*name* **object**:(NSString *)*object*
    suspensionBehavior:(NSNotificationSuspensionBehavior)*suspensionBehavior*;
- (void)**postNotificationName**:(NSString *)*aName* **object**:(NSString *)*anObject*;
- (void)**postNotificationName**:(NSString *)*aName* **object**:(NSString *)*anObject* **userInfo**:(NSDictionary *)*aUserInfo*;
- (void)**postNotificationName**:(NSString *)*name* **object**:(NSString *)*object* **userInfo**:(NSDictionary *)*userInfo*
    deliverImmediately:(BOOL)*deliverImmediately*;
- (void)**removeObserver**:(id)*observer* **name**:(NSString *)*aName*
  object:(NSString *)*anObject*;

NSEnumerator

Mac OS X 10.0

This class enumerates the contents of a collection. Instances of this class are created by the collection classes, generally with the method objectEnumerator. NSArray declares the method reverseObjectEnumerator, and NSDictionary declares keyEnumerator as additional methods that create instances of NSEnumerator.

To obtain the next object in an enumerator, we invoke the method nextObject. This will return an object, and advance the enumerator position forward in the collection. When the enumerator has exhausted the collection, nextObject returns nil. Enumerators cannot be reset; once you have enumerated a collection, you must obtain an new enumerator from the collection to start again. The method allObjects is used to return an NSArray of the objects that have not yet been enumerated. See Chapter 2 for more information on collections and enumerators.

```
NSObject ─ NSEnumerator
NSObject
```

@interface **NSEnumerator** : NSObject
// Instance Methods
- (NSArray *)**allObjects**;
- (id)**nextObject**;

Subclasses
NSDirectoryEnumerator

NSException

This class implements the Foundation framework's exception-handling system. Exceptions are used in Cocoa as a mechanism to deal with special conditions in the execution of a program that may require special handling. Clients can use NSException objects to raise exceptions (creating a special condition), as well as to retrieve information about an exception. For details on exception handling, see Chapter 2.

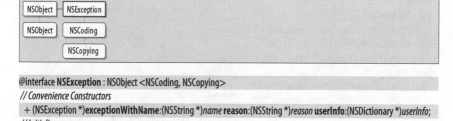

@interface **NSException** : NSObject <NSCoding, NSCopying>
// Convenience Constructors
  + (NSException *)**exceptionWithName**:(NSString *)name **reason**:(NSString *)reason **userInfo**:(NSDictionary *)userInfo;
// Initializers
  - (id)**initWithName**:(NSString *)aName **reason**:(NSString *)aReason **userInfo**:(NSDictionary *)aUserInfo;
// Class Methods
  + (void)**raise**:(NSString *)name **format**:(NSString *)format **arguments**:(va_list)argList;
  + (void)**raise**:(NSString *)name **format**:(NSString *)format, ...;
// Instance Methods
  - (NSString *)**name**;
  - (void)**raise**;
  - (NSString *)**reason**;
  - (NSDictionary *)**userInfo**;
// Methods Implementing NSCoding
  - (void)**encodeWithCoder**:(NSCoder *)aCoder;
  - (id)**initWithCoder**:(NSCoder *)aDecoder;
// Methods Implementing NSCopying
  - (id)**copyWithZone**:(NSZone *)zone;

NSExistsCommand

Instances of this class are used to check whether or not the specified object exists. This class is used in Cocoa's implementation of built-in AppleScript support, and as such clients should not need to access instances of this class directly.

@interface **NSExistsCommand** : NSScriptCommand

NSFileHandle

This class is used to read and write data to and from an open file or open communications channel, such as a networking socket. The class provides methods for working with files, and contains methods and notifications useful for implementing asynchronous background socket communication.

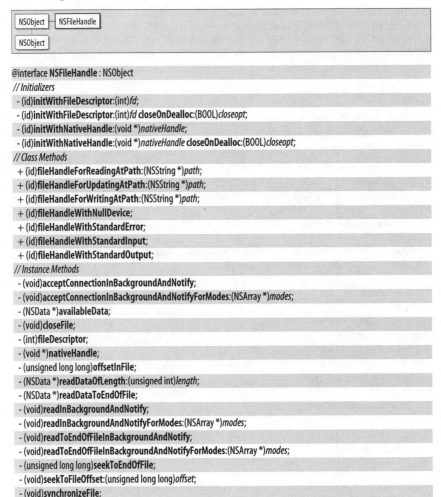

@interface **NSFileHandle** : NSObject
// *Initializers*
- (id)**initWithFileDescriptor**:(int)*fd*;
- (id)**initWithFileDescriptor**:(int)*fd* **closeOnDealloc**:(BOOL)*closeopt*;
- (id)**initWithNativeHandle**:(void *)*nativeHandle*;
- (id)**initWithNativeHandle**:(void *)*nativeHandle* **closeOnDealloc**:(BOOL)*closeopt*;
// *Class Methods*
+ (id)**fileHandleForReadingAtPath**:(NSString *)*path*;
+ (id)**fileHandleForUpdatingAtPath**:(NSString *)*path*;
+ (id)**fileHandleForWritingAtPath**:(NSString *)*path*;
+ (id)**fileHandleWithNullDevice**;
+ (id)**fileHandleWithStandardError**;
+ (id)**fileHandleWithStandardInput**;
+ (id)**fileHandleWithStandardOutput**;
// *Instance Methods*
- (void)**acceptConnectionInBackgroundAndNotify**;
- (void)**acceptConnectionInBackgroundAndNotifyForModes**:(NSArray *)*modes*;
- (NSData *)**availableData**;
- (void)**closeFile**;
- (int)**fileDescriptor**;
- (void *)**nativeHandle**;
- (unsigned long long)**offsetInFile**;
- (NSData *)**readDataOfLength**:(unsigned int)*length*;
- (NSData *)**readDataToEndOfFile**;
- (void)**readInBackgroundAndNotify**;
- (void)**readInBackgroundAndNotifyForModes**:(NSArray *)*modes*;
- (void)**readToEndOfFileInBackgroundAndNotify**;
- (void)**readToEndOfFileInBackgroundAndNotifyForModes**:(NSArray *)*modes*;
- (unsigned long long)**seekToEndOfFile**;
- (void)**seekToFileOffset**:(unsigned long long)*offset*;
- (void)**synchronizeFile**;
- (void)**truncateFileAtOffset**:(unsigned long long)*offset*;
- (void)**waitForDataInBackgroundAndNotify**;
- (void)**waitForDataInBackgroundAndNotifyForModes**:(NSArray *)*modes*;
- (void)**writeData**:(NSData *)*data*;

NSFileManager   Mac OS X 10.0

This class provides an interface that clients can use to interact with the filesystem. This provides all of the standard file and directory manipulation facilities for copying, moving, changing working directories, and more.

```
@interface NSFileManager : NSObject
// Class Methods
+ (NSFileManager *)defaultManager;
// Instance Methods
- (BOOL)changeCurrentDirectoryPath:(NSString *)path;
- (BOOL)changeFileAttributes:(NSDictionary *)attributes atPath:(NSString *)path;
- (NSArray *)componentsToDisplayForPath:(NSString *)path;
- (NSData *)contentsAtPath:(NSString *)path;
- (BOOL)contentsEqualAtPath:(NSString *)path1 andPath:(NSString *)path2;
- (BOOL)copyPath:(NSString *)src toPath:(NSString *)dest handler:(id)handler;
- (BOOL)createDirectoryAtPath:(NSString *)path attributes:(NSDictionary *)attributes;
- (BOOL)createFileAtPath:(NSString *)path contents:(NSData *)data attributes:(NSDictionary *)attr;
- (BOOL)createSymbolicLinkAtPath:(NSString *)path pathContent:(NSString *)otherpath;
- (NSString *)currentDirectoryPath;
- (NSArray *)directoryContentsAtPath:(NSString *)path;
- (NSString *)displayNameAtPath:(NSString *)path;
- (NSDirectoryEnumerator *)enumeratorAtPath:(NSString *)path;
- (NSDictionary *)fileAttributesAtPath:(NSString *)path traverseLink:(BOOL)yorn;
- (BOOL)fileExistsAtPath:(NSString *)path;
- (BOOL)fileExistsAtPath:(NSString *)path isDirectory:(BOOL *)isDirectory;
- (NSDictionary *)fileSystemAttributesAtPath:(NSString *)path;
- (const char *)fileSystemRepresentationWithPath:(NSString *)path;
- (BOOL)isDeletableFileAtPath:(NSString *)path;
- (BOOL)isExecutableFileAtPath:(NSString *)path;
- (BOOL)isReadableFileAtPath:(NSString *)path;
- (BOOL)isWritableFileAtPath:(NSString *)path;
- (BOOL)linkPath:(NSString *)src toPath:(NSString *)dest handler:(id)handler;
- (BOOL)movePath:(NSString *)src toPath:(NSString *)dest handler:(id)handler;
- (NSString *)pathContentOfSymbolicLinkAtPath:(NSString *)path;
- (BOOL)removeFileAtPath:(NSString *)path handler:(id)handler;
- (NSString *)stringWithFileSystemRepresentation:(const char *)str length:(unsigned)len;
- (NSArray *)subpathsAtPath:(NSString *)path;
```

NSFormatter

This class declares an abstract interface for objects that an instance of NSCell can use to create, interpret, and validate a textual representation of the cell's contents that is suited for human readability. The Foundation framework provides two concrete classes that are used to format numeric and time and date values: NSNumberFormatter and NSDateFormatter.

```
@interface NSFormatter : NSObject <NSCoding, NSCopying>
// Instance Methods
- (NSAttributedString *)attributedStringForObjectValue:(id)obj withDefaultAttributes:(NSDictionary *)attrs;
- (NSString *)editingStringForObjectValue:(id)obj;
```

- (BOOL)**getObjectValue:**(id *)*obj* **forString:**(NSString *)*string* **errorDescription:**(NSString **)*error;*
- (BOOL)**isPartialStringValid:**(NSString *)*partialString* **newEditingString:**(NSString **)*newString*
   errorDescription:(NSString **)*error;*
- (BOOL)**isPartialStringValid:**(NSString **)*partialStringPtr*
   proposedSelectedRange:(NSRangePointer)*proposedSelRangePtr* **originalString:**(NSString *)*origString*
   originalSelectedRange:(NSRange)*origSelRange* **errorDescription:**(NSString **)*error;*
- (NSString *)**stringForObjectValue:**(id)*obj;*
// *Methods Implementing NSCoding*
- (void)**encodeWithCoder:**(NSCoder *)*aCoder;*
- (id)**initWithCoder:**(NSCoder *)*aDecoder;*
// *Methods Implementing NSCopying*
- (id)**copyWithZone:**(NSZone *)*zone;*

Subclasses

NSDateFormatter, NSNumberFormatter

NSGetCommand Mac OS X 10.0

Instances of this class are used to retrieve a user-specified value from the specified object. This class is used in Cocoa's implementation of built-in AppleScript support, and as such clients should not need to access instances of this class directly.

@interface **NSGetCommand** : NSScriptCommand

NSHost Mac OS X 10.0

This class is used to perform host name lookup and IP address translation. Translations are provided by any services available to the operating system such as NetInfo, LDAP, or DNS. Instances of **NSHost** are created using one of three class methods: current-Host, hostWithAddress:, and hostWithName:. The first, currentHost, returns an **NSHost** object that contains information about the host running the application process. The methods hostWithName: and hostWithAddress: create **NSHost** objects for the host with the specified name or address. The name used in hostWithName: can be a simple host name, or it can be a fully qualified domain name. When creating a host object with hostWithAddress:, the IP address is specified as a string in dotted decimal format, such as 192.168.254.198. Once an instance of **NSHost** has been created, it can be queried for the IP addresses and names that the host identifies with.

@interface **NSHost** : NSObject
// *Convenience Constructors*
+ (NSHost *)**hostWithAddress:**(NSString *)*address;*
+ (NSHost *)**hostWithName:**(NSString *)*name;*

```
// Class Methods
  + (NSHost *)currentHost;
  + (void)flushHostCache;
  + (BOOL)isHostCacheEnabled;
  + (void)setHostCacheEnabled:(BOOL)flag;
// Instance Methods
  - (NSString *)address;
  - (NSArray *)addresses;
  - (BOOL)isEqualToHost:(NSHost *)aHost;
  - (NSString *)name;
  - (NSArray *)names;
```

NSIndexSpecifier

This class represents the scripting language reference form used to specify an object in a collection according to its indexed position in the collection.

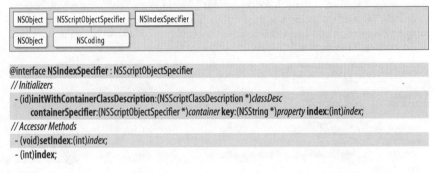

```
@interface NSIndexSpecifier : NSScriptObjectSpecifier
// Initializers
  - (id)initWithContainerClassDescription:(NSScriptClassDescription *)classDesc
    containerSpecifier:(NSScriptObjectSpecifier *)container key:(NSString *)property index:(int)index;
// Accessor Methods
  - (void)setIndex:(int)index;
  - (int)index;
```

NSInvocation

This class encapsulates information about an Objective-C message such as the selector and the target of the message. NSInvocations are useful for statically storing a message and are often used with timers, and for message forwarding.

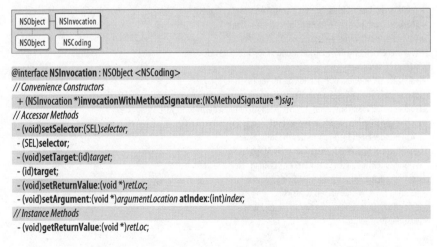

```
@interface NSInvocation : NSObject <NSCoding>
// Convenience Constructors
  + (NSInvocation *)invocationWithMethodSignature:(NSMethodSignature *)sig;
// Accessor Methods
  - (void)setSelector:(SEL)selector;
  - (SEL)selector;
  - (void)setTarget:(id)target;
  - (id)target;
  - (void)setReturnValue:(void *)retLoc;
  - (void)setArgument:(void *)argumentLocation atIndex:(int)index;
// Instance Methods
  - (void)getReturnValue:(void *)retLoc;
```

```
- (void)invoke;
- (void)getArgument:(void *)argumentLocation atIndex:(int)index;
- (BOOL)argumentsRetained;
- (void)invokeWithTarget:(id)target;
- (NSMethodSignature *)methodSignature;
- (void)retainArguments;
// Methods Implementing NSCoding
- (void)encodeWithCoder:(NSCoder *)aCoder;
- (id)initWithCoder:(NSCoder *)aDecoder;
```

NSKeyedArchiver
Mac OS X 10.2

This class is a concrete subclass of NSCoder that encodes objects and scalar values into a
data format that can be stored in a file. NSKeyedArchiver is different from NSArchiver in that
each object and scalar in the archive has an associated name or key. These keys make
it possible to decode the archive piecemeal; that is, in an order that is different from
the original encoding. Clients have the option of picking and choosing which objects
to decode. Non-keyed archives suffer from the limitation that the entirety of an archive
must be decoded at once, and in the order that it was encoded. Archiving is described
in greater detail in Chapter 2.

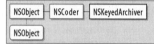

```
@interface NSKeyedArchiver : NSCoder
// Initializers
- (id)initForWritingWithMutableData:(NSMutableData *)data;
// Accessor Methods
- (void)setDelegate:(id)delegate;
- (id)delegate;
- (void)setOutputFormat:(NSPropertyListFormat)format;
- (NSPropertyListFormat)outputFormat;
- (void)setClassName:(NSString *)codedName forClass:(Class)cls;
// Class Methods
+ (BOOL)archiveRootObject:(id)rootObject toFile:(NSString *)path;
+ (NSData *)archivedDataWithRootObject:(id)rootObject;
+ (NSString *)classNameForClass:(Class)cls;
+ (void)setClassName:(NSString *)codedName forClass:(Class)cls;
// Instance Methods
- (void)encodeConditionalObject:(id)objv forKey:(NSString *)key;
- (void)encodeBool:(BOOL)boolv forKey:(NSString *)key;
- (void)encodeBytes:(const uint8_t *)bytesp length:(unsigned)lenv forKey:(NSString *)key;
- (void)encodeDouble:(double)realv forKey:(NSString *)key;
- (void)encodeFloat:(float)realv forKey:(NSString *)key;
- (void)encodeInt32:(int32_t)intv forKey:(NSString *)key;
- (void)encodeInt64:(int64_t)intv forKey:(NSString *)key;
- (void)encodeInt:(int)intv forKey:(NSString *)key;
- (NSString *)classNameForClass:(Class)cls;
- (void)encodeObject:(id)objv forKey:(NSString *)key;
- (void)finishEncoding;
```

// Methods Implemented by the Delegate

  - (void)**archiver:**(NSKeyedArchiver *)*archiver* **didEncodeObject:**(id)*object*;

  - (id)**archiver:**(NSKeyedArchiver *)*archiver* **willEncodeObject:**(id)*object*;

  - (void)**archiver:**(NSKeyedArchiver *)*archiver* **willReplaceObject:**(id)*object* **withObject:**(id)*newObject*;

  - (void)**archiverDidFinish:**(NSKeyedArchiver *)*archiver*;

  - (void)**archiverWillFinish:**(NSKeyedArchiver *)*archiver*;

NSKeyedUnarchiver

Mac OS X 10.2

This concrete subclass of **NSCoder** provides a means to decode objects that have been encoded in a keyed archive. The companion class **NSKeyedArchiver** provides the means to create such keyed archives from a set of objects. Archiving is described in greater detail in Chapter 2.

@interface **NSKeyedUnarchiver** : NSCoder

// Initializers

  - (id)**initForReadingWithData:**(NSData *)*data*;

// Accessor Methods

  - (void)**setDelegate:**(id)*delegate*;

  - (id)**delegate**;

  - (void)**setClass:**(Class)*cls* **forClassName:**(NSString *)*codedName*;

// Class Methods

  + (Class)**classForClassName:**(NSString *)*codedName*;

  + (void)**setClass:**(Class)*cls* **forClassName:**(NSString *)*codedName*;

  + (id)**unarchiveObjectWithData:**(NSData *)*data*;

  + (id)**unarchiveObjectWithFile:**(NSString *)*path*;

// Instance Methods

  - (int32_t)**decodeInt32ForKey:**(NSString *)*key*;

  - (const uint8_t *)**decodeBytesForKey:**(NSString *)*key* **returnedLength:**(unsigned *)*lengthp*;

  - (double)**decodeDoubleForKey:**(NSString *)*key*;

  - (Class)**classForClassName:**(NSString *)*codedName*;

  - (BOOL)**containsValueForKey:**(NSString *)*key*;

  - (BOOL)**decodeBoolForKey:**(NSString *)*key*;

  - (float)**decodeFloatForKey:**(NSString *)*key*;

  - (int64_t)**decodeInt64ForKey:**(NSString *)*key*;

  - (int)**decodeIntForKey:**(NSString *)*key*;

  - (id)**decodeObjectForKey:**(NSString *)*key*;

  - (void)**finishDecoding**;

// Methods Implemented by the Delegate

  - (Class)**unarchiver:**(NSKeyedUnarchiver *)*unarchiver* **cannotDecodeObjectOfClassName:**(NSString *)*name*
     originalClasses:(NSArray *)*classNames*;

  - (id)**unarchiver:**(NSKeyedUnarchiver *)*unarchiver* **didDecodeObject:**(id)*object*;

  - (void)**unarchiver:**(NSKeyedUnarchiver *)*unarchiver* **willReplaceObject:**(id)*object* **withObject:**(id)*newObject*;

  - (void)**unarchiverDidFinish:**(NSKeyedUnarchiver *)*unarchiver*;

  - (void)**unarchiverWillFinish:**(NSKeyedUnarchiver *)*unarchiver*;

Foundation Classes

NSLock

NSLock implements thread locks that can be used to let multiple threads in an application access the same data without clashing. The use of NSLock, and locking in general, is discussed in detail in Chapter 2.

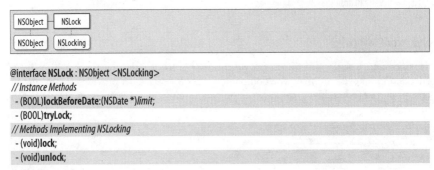

```
@interface NSLock : NSObject <NSLocking>
// Instance Methods
  - (BOOL)lockBeforeDate:(NSDate *)limit;
  - (BOOL)tryLock;
// Methods Implementing NSLocking
  - (void)lock;
  - (void)unlock;
```

NSLogicalTest

Instances of this class represent logical operations—such as AND, OR, and NOT—on a set of Boolean tests. These Boolean tests are represented by instances of the class NSSpecifierTest. Instances of this class are initialized with one of three initializers: initAndTestWithTests:, initOrTestWithTests:, and initNotTestWithTest:. The AND and OR initializers both take an NSArray of test objects, while the NOT initializer requires only one test object. When an NSLogicalTest object is evaluated (by receiving an isTrue message), it sends isTrue messages to each of its component test objects, and then evaluate those results based on the type of logical test being performed.

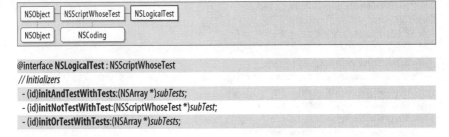

```
@interface NSLogicalTest : NSScriptWhoseTest
// Initializers
  - (id)initAndTestWithTests:(NSArray *)subTests;
  - (id)initNotTestWithTest:(NSScriptWhoseTest *)subTest;
  - (id)initOrTestWithTests:(NSArray *)subTests;
```

NSMachBootstrapServer

This subclass of NSPortNameServer returns and accepts instances of NSMachPort. NSConnection objects use port name servers to register and discover communication ports that can be used for distributed objects connections. Additional subclasses of NSPortNameServer that handle other types of ports are NSSocketPortNameServer and NSMessagePortNameServer.

@interface **NSMachBootstrapServer** : NSPortNameServer
// Class Methods
+ (id)**sharedInstance**;
// Instance Methods
- (NSPort *)**portForName**:(NSString *)name;
- (NSPort *)**portForName**:(NSString *)name **host**:(NSString *)host;
- (BOOL)**registerPort**:(NSPort *)port **name**:(NSString *)name;

NSMachPort

This subclass of NSPort provides an object-oriented wrapper to Mach IPC ports, which can be used either as endpoint for distributed object connections, or for raw messaging. NSMachPort objects only support local messaging; NSSocketPort provides support for remote messaging over a network.

@interface **NSMachPort** : NSPort
// Initializers
- (id)**initWithMachPort**:(int)machPort;
// Class Methods
+ (NSPort *)**portWithMachPort**:(int)machPort;
// Instance Methods
- (int)**machPort**;
- (void)**removeFromRunLoop**:(NSRunLoop *)runLoop **forMode**:(NSString *)mode;
- (void)**scheduleInRunLoop**:(NSRunLoop *)runLoop **forMode**:(NSString *)mode;
// Methods Implemented by the Delegate
- (void)**handleMachMessage**:(void *)msg;

NSMessagePort

This subclass of NSPort provides an interface to objects that serve as endpoints for distributed objects connections between processes on the same machine. NSMachPort provides similar functionality that is implemented using Mach IPC ports, while NSSocketPort supports messaging over a network.

@interface **NSMessagePort** : NSPort

NSMessagePortNameServer

This subclass of NSPortNameServer accepts and returns instances of NSMessagePort. NSConnection objects use port name servers to register and discover communication ports that can be used for distributed objects connections. Additional subclasses of NSPortNameServer that handle other types of ports are NSMachBootstrapServer and NSSocketPortNameServer.

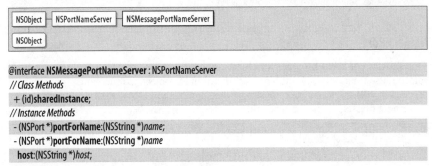

@interface **NSMessagePortNameServer** : NSPortNameServer
// Class Methods
+ (id)**sharedInstance**;
// Instance Methods
- (NSPort *)**portForName**:(NSString *)name;
- (NSPort *)**portForName**:(NSString *)name
host:(NSString *)host;

NSMethodSignature

This class provides an interface used to query information about a method including such characteristics as the number and types of arguments, and the return type. Instances of NSMethodSignature are created using NSObject's methodSignature-ForSelector: method.

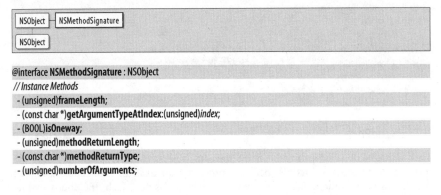

@interface **NSMethodSignature** : NSObject
// Instance Methods
- (unsigned)**frameLength**;
- (const char *)**getArgumentTypeAtIndex**:(unsigned)index;
- (BOOL)**isOneway**;
- (unsigned)**methodReturnLength**;
- (const char *)**methodReturnType**;
- (unsigned)**numberOfArguments**;

NSMiddleSpecifier

This class represents the scripting language reference form used to specify the object that lies in the middle of a collection of objects.

@interface **NSMiddleSpecifier** : NSScriptObjectSpecifier

NSMoveCommand

Instances of this class represent move operations and, when executed, perform such operations on the specified objects.

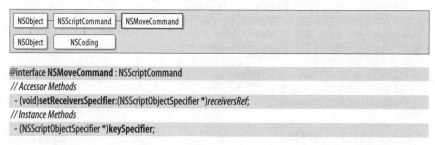

@interface **NSMoveCommand** : NSScriptCommand
// Accessor Methods
- (void)**setReceiversSpecifier**:(NSScriptObjectSpecifier *)*receiversRef*;
// Instance Methods
- (NSScriptObjectSpecifier *)**keySpecifier**;

NSMutableArray

This class extends the API of NSArray to allow for mutable, ordered collections of objects. NSMutableArray provides five primitive methods, which form the basis for the rest of its methods: addObject:, insertObject:atIndex:, removeLastObject, removeObjectAtIndex:, and replaceObjectAtIndex:withObject:. When an object is added to an array, the array asserts some ownership over the object by sending it a retain message. Likewise, when an object is removed from an array, it is sent a release message by the array.

NSMutableArray is toll-free bridged with the Core Foundation type CFArray. As such, NSMutableArray objects can be used interchangeably with the CFArray pointer type, CFArrayRef.

@interface **NSMutableArray** : NSArray
// Initializers
- (id)**initWithCapacity**:(unsigned)*numItems*;
// Accessor Methods
- (void)**setArray**:(NSArray *)*otherArray*;
// Class Methods
+ (id)**arrayWithCapacity**:(unsigned)*numItems*;
// Instance Methods
- (void)**addObject**:(id)*anObject*;
- (void)**addObjectsFromArray**:(NSArray *)*otherArray*;
- (void)**exchangeObjectAtIndex**:(unsigned)*idx1* **withObjectAtIndex**:(unsigned)*idx2*;
- (void)**insertObject**:(id)*anObject* **atIndex**:(unsigned)*index*;
- (void)**removeAllObjects**;
- (void)**removeLastObject**;
- (void)**removeObject**:(id)*anObject*;
- (void)**removeObject**:(id)*anObject* **inRange**:(NSRange)*range*;
- (void)**removeObjectAtIndex**:(unsigned)*index*;

- (void)**removeObjectIdenticalTo**:(id)*anObject*;
- (void)**removeObjectIdenticalTo**:(id)*anObject* **inRange**:(NSRange)*range*;
- (void)**removeObjectsFromIndices**:(unsigned *)*indices* **numIndices**:(unsigned)*count*;
- (void)**removeObjectsInArray**:(NSArray *)*otherArray*;
- (void)**removeObjectsInRange**:(NSRange)*range*;
- (void)**replaceObjectAtIndex**:(unsigned)*index* **withObject**:(id)*anObject*;
- (void)**replaceObjectsInRange**:(NSRange)*range* **withObjectsFromArray**:(NSArray *)*otherArray*;
- (void)**replaceObjectsInRange**:(NSRange)*range* **withObjectsFromArray**:(NSArray *)*otherArray*
    range:(NSRange)*otherRange*;
- (void)**sortUsingFunction**:(int (*)(id, id, void *))*compare*
  context:(void *)*context*;
- (void)**sortUsingSelector**:(SEL)*comparator*;

NSMutableAttributedString

Mac OS X 10.0

NSMutableAttributedString is a subclass of NSAttributedString that allows the contents and attributes of the string to be altered after the object has been initialized, which is normally not possible with its immutable superclass.

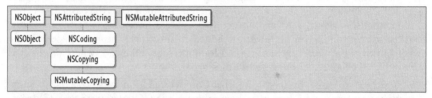

@interface **NSMutableAttributedString** : NSAttributedString
// Accessor Methods
- (void)**setAttributes**:(NSDictionary *)*attrs* **range**:(NSRange)*range*;
- (void)**setAlignment**:(NSTextAlignment)*alignment* **range**:(NSRange)*range*;
- (void)**setAttributedString**:(NSAttributedString *)*attrString*;
// Instance Methods
- (void)**appendAttributedString**:(NSAttributedString *)*attrString*;
- (void)**addAttribute**:(NSString *)*name* **value**:(id)*value* **range**:(NSRange)*range*;
- (void)**addAttributes**:(NSDictionary *)*attrs* **range**:(NSRange)*range*;
- (void)**applyFontTraits**:(NSFontTraitMask)*traitMask* **range**:(NSRange)*range*;
- (void)**beginEditing**;
- (void)**deleteCharactersInRange**:(NSRange)*range*;
- (void)**endEditing**;
- (void)**fixAttachmentAttributeInRange**:(NSRange)*range*;
- (void)**fixAttributesInRange**:(NSRange)*range*;
- (void)**fixFontAttributeInRange**:(NSRange)*range*;
- (void)**fixParagraphStyleAttributeInRange**:(NSRange)*range*;
- (void)**insertAttributedString**:(NSAttributedString *)*attrString* **atIndex**:(unsigned)*loc*;
- (NSMutableString *)**mutableString**;
- (BOOL)**readFromURL**:(NSURL *)*url* **options**:(NSDictionary *)*options* **documentAttributes**:(NSDictionary **)*dict*;
- (void)**removeAttribute**:(NSString *)*name* **range**:(NSRange)*range*;
- (void)**replaceCharactersInRange**:(NSRange)*range* **withAttributedString**:(NSAttributedString *)*attrString*;
- (void)**replaceCharactersInRange**:(NSRange)*range* **withString**:(NSString *)*str*;
- (void)**subscriptRange**:(NSRange)*range*;
- (void)**superscriptRange**:(NSRange)*range*;

- (void)**unscriptRange:**(NSRange)*range;*
- (void)**updateAttachmentsFromPath:**(NSString *)*path;*

Subclasses

NSTextStorage

NSMutableCharacterSet

This class extends the interface of NSCharacterSet to allow clients to modify the contents of the character set after it has been initialized. Clients may add and remove characters specified in a string or numeric range, and new sets may be created from the union or intersection of two existing sets.

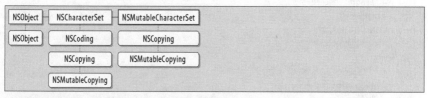

@interface **NSMutableCharacterSet** : NSCharacterSet <NSCopying, NSMutableCopying>
// Instance Methods
- (void)**addCharactersInRange:**(NSRange)*aRange;*
- (void)**addCharactersInString:**(NSString *)*aString;*
- (void)**formIntersectionWithCharacterSet:**(NSCharacterSet *)*otherSet;*
- (void)**formUnionWithCharacterSet:**(NSCharacterSet *)*otherSet;*
- (void)**invert;**
- (void)**removeCharactersInRange:**(NSRange)*aRange;*
- (void)**removeCharactersInString:**(NSString *)*aString;*
// Methods Implementing NSCopying
- (id)**copyWithZone:**(NSZone *)*zone;*
// Methods Implementing NSMutableCopying
- (id)**mutableCopyWithZone:**(NSZone *)*zone;*

NSMutableData

This class adds mutable functionality to NSData, allowing the contents of the data object to be altered after initialization. NSMutableData provides two methods for adjusting the size of the underlying data buffer: increaseLengthBy:,and setLength:. The first of these increases the size of the buffer by the indicated number of bytes, while the latter sets the size of the buffer to the specified number of bytes.

Data is added to a mutable data object using either appendData: or appendBytes:length. appendData: joins the specified NSData object to the end of the receiver, while appendBytes:length: appends to the receiver the number of bytes specified in length from the buffer pointer to in the first parameter.

NSMutableData also provides replaceBytesInRange:withBytes: and replaceBytesInRange:withBytes:length: to directly alter the contents of the underlying data buffer. If you want to zero a portion of data, use the method resetBytesInRange:.

NSMutableData is toll-free bridged with the Core Foundation type CFData. As such, NSMutable-Data objects can be used interchangeably with the CFData pointer type, CFDataRef.

```
NSObject ── NSData ── NSMutableData
NSObject    NSCoding
            NSCopying
            NSMutableCopying
```

@interface **NSMutableData** : NSData

// Initializers

- (id)**initWithCapacity**:(unsigned)*capacity*;

- (id)**initWithLength**:(unsigned)*length*;

// Accessor Methods

- (void)**setData**:(NSData *)*data*;

- (void)**setLength**:(unsigned)*length*;

// Class Methods

+ (id)**dataWithCapacity**:(unsigned)*aNumItems*;

+ (id)**dataWithLength**:(unsigned)*length*;

// Instance Methods

- (void)**appendBytes**:(const void *)*bytes* **length**:(unsigned)*length*;

- (void)**appendData**:(NSData *)*other*;

- (void)**increaseLengthBy**:(unsigned)*extraLength*;

- (void *)**mutableBytes**;

- (void)**replaceBytesInRange**:(NSRange)*range* **withBytes**:(const void *)*bytes*;

- (void)**replaceBytesInRange**:(NSRange)*range* **withBytes**:(const void *)*replacementBytes*
    length:(unsigned)*replacementLength*;

- (void)**resetBytesInRange**:(NSRange)*range*;

- (void)**serializeAlignedBytesLength**:(unsigned)*length*;

- (void)**serializeDataAt**:(const void *)*data* **ofObjCType**:(const char *)*type*
    context:(id <NSObjCTypeSerializationCallBack>)*callback*;

- (void)**serializeInt**:(int)*value*;

- (void)**serializeInt**:(int)*value* **atIndex**:(unsigned)*index*;

- (void)**serializeInts**:(int *)*intBuffer* **count**:(unsigned)*numInts*;

- (void)**serializeInts**:(int *)*intBuffer* **count**:(unsigned)*numInts* **atIndex**:(unsigned)*index*;

NSMutableDictionary   Mac OS X 10.0

NSDictionary, being an immutable class, does not allow clients to add, remove, or replace member objects after initialization. NSMutableDictionary, on the other hand, allows for the kinds of operations that alter the contents of the collection. Objects can be added to a mutable dictionary by invoking setObject:forKey:, and objects may be removed using removeObjectForKey:. When an object is added to a dictionary it is sent a retain message; when the object is removed, the dictionary will offset the retain with a release message.

NSMutableDictionary is toll-free bridged with the Core Foundation type CFDictionary. As such, NSMutableDictionary objects can be used interchangeably with the CFDictionary pointer type, CFDictionaryRef.

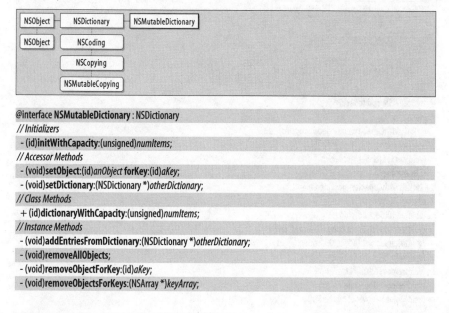

@interface **NSMutableDictionary** : NSDictionary

// Initializers

- (id)**initWithCapacity**:(unsigned)*numItems*;

// Accessor Methods

- (void)**setObject**:(id)*anObject* **forKey**:(id)*aKey*;

- (void)**setDictionary**:(NSDictionary *)*otherDictionary*;

// Class Methods

+ (id)**dictionaryWithCapacity**:(unsigned)*numItems*;

// Instance Methods

- (void)**addEntriesFromDictionary**:(NSDictionary *)*otherDictionary*;

- (void)**removeAllObjects**;

- (void)**removeObjectForKey**:(id)*aKey*;

- (void)**removeObjectsForKeys**:(NSArray *)*keyArray*;

NSMutableSet

Mac OS X 10.0

This class extends the functionality of NSSet by allowing objects to be added to and removed from the set; NSSet does not allow clients to add, remove, or replace objects in a set after initialization. This mutable subclass of NSSet provides an interface for those operations.

To add an object to a mutable set, use the method addObject:. If the object is already present in the set, this method has no effect. When an object is added to a set, it is sent a retain message by that set. The method removeObject: will remove the specified object from the set if it is a member. When an object is removed from a set, it is sent a release message by the set to counteract the retain message it was sent when added to the set.

NSMutableSet also implements a number of methods that are useful for combining sets in various ways. The method unionSet: will add each member of the parameter set into the receiver if the receiver does not already contain that object. The method minusSet: will remove from the receiver each object that is present in both sets, while the method intersectSet: will remove from the receiver each object that isn't a member of the set specified in the argument.

NSMutableSet is toll-free bridged with the Core Foundation type CFSet. As such, NSMutableSet objects can be used interchangeably with the CFSet pointer type, CFSetRef.

@interface **NSMutableSet** : NSSet
// Initializers
- (id)**initWithCapacity**:(unsigned)*numItems*;
// Accessor Methods
- (void)**setSet**:(NSSet *)*otherSet*;
// Class Methods
+ (id)**setWithCapacity**:(unsigned)*numItems*;
// Instance Methods
- (void)**addObject**:(id)*object*;
- (void)**addObjectsFromArray**:(NSArray *)*array*;
- (void)**intersectSet**:(NSSet *)*otherSet*;
- (void)**minusSet**:(NSSet *)*otherSet*;
- (void)**removeAllObjects**;
- (void)**removeObject**:(id)*object*;
- (void)**unionSet**:(NSSet *)*otherSet*;

Subclasses

NSCountedSet

NSMutableString

Mac OS X 10.0

NSString creates immutable strings that cannot be changed after the object has been created. NSMutableString adds methods that allow the contents of NSMutableString objects to be altered after object initialization. This class provides methods for replacing portions of a string with another string, inserting strings within the existing string, appending strings and formats, as well as deleting portions of strings.

NSMutableString is toll-free bridged with the Core Foundation type CFString. As such, NSMutable-String objects can be used interchangeably with the CFString pointer type, CFStringRef.

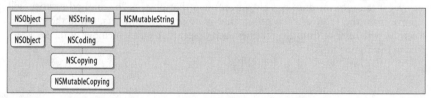

@interface **NSMutableString** : NSString
// Initializers
- (id)**initWithCapacity**:(unsigned)*capacity*;
// Accessor Methods
- (void)**setString**:(NSString *)*aString*;

```
// Class Methods
 + (id)stringWithCapacity:(unsigned)capacity;
// Instance Methods
 - (void)appendFormat:(NSString *)format, ...;
 - (void)appendString:(NSString *)aString;
 - (void)deleteCharactersInRange:(NSRange)range;
 - (void)insertString:(NSString *)aString atIndex:(unsigned)loc;
 - (void)replaceCharactersInRange:(NSRange)range withString:(NSString *)aString;
 - (unsigned int)replaceOccurrencesOfString:(NSString *)target
     withString:(NSString *)replacement options:(unsigned)opts range:(NSRange)searchRange;
```

NSNameSpecifier   Mac OS X 10.2

This class represents the scripting language reference form used to specify an object in a collection according to the object's name.

```
@interface NSNameSpecifier : NSScriptObjectSpecifier
// Initializers
 - (id)initWithContainerClassDescription:(NSScriptClassDescription *)classDesc
     containerSpecifier:(NSScriptObjectSpecifier *)container key:(NSString *)property name:(NSString *)name;
// Accessor Methods
 - (void)setName:(NSString *)name;
 - (NSString *)name;
```

NSNetService   Mac OS X 10.2

NSNetService represents a network service that applications either publish or use as a client. A network service can be anything such as FTP, Telnet, SSH, HTTP, or any of the well-known services. A service can also be something of your own design. NSNet-Service provides application level access to the low-level Multicast DNS responder APIs. For more information about Rendezvous and the Net Services APIs in Foundation, see Chapter 6.

```
@interface NSNetService : NSObject
// Initializers
 - (id)initWithDomain:(NSString *)domain type:(NSString *)type name:(NSString *)name;
 - (id)initWithDomain:(NSString *)domain type:(NSString *)type name:(NSString *)name port:(int)port;
// Accessor Methods
 - (void)setDelegate:(id)delegate;
 - (id)delegate;
 - (void)setProtocolSpecificInformation:(NSString *)specificInformation;
 - (NSString *)protocolSpecificInformation;
```

```
// Instance Methods
- (NSString *)name;
- (NSArray *)addresses;
- (NSString *)domain;
- (void)publish;
- (void)removeFromRunLoop:(NSRunLoop *)aRunLoop forMode:(NSString *)mode;
- (void)resolve;
- (void)scheduleInRunLoop:(NSRunLoop *)aRunLoop forMode:(NSString *)mode;
- (void)stop;
- (NSString *)type;
// Methods Implemented by the Delegate
- (void)netService:(NSNetService *)sender didNotPublish:(NSDictionary *)errorDict;
- (void)netService:(NSNetService *)sender didNotResolve:(NSDictionary *)errorDict;
- (void)netServiceDidResolveAddress:(NSNetService *)sender;
- (void)netServiceDidStop:(NSNetService *)sender;
- (void)netServiceWillPublish:(NSNetService *)sender;
- (void)netServiceWillResolve:(NSNetService *)sender;
```

NSNetServiceBrowser   Mac OS X 10.2

NSNetServiceBrowser is the complement to NSNetService and it serves two purposes: searching for network domains, and searching for network services advertised on a given domain. When searching for domains we can either look for all domains, or only those that we have registration authority in. These searches are performed by invoking the methods searchForAllDomains and searchForRegistrationDomains, respectively. For more information about Rendezvous and the Net Services APIs in Foundation, see Chapter 6.

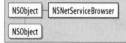

```
@interface NSNetServiceBrowser : NSObject
// Initializers
- (id)init;
// Accessor Methods
- (void)setDelegate:(id)delegate;
- (id)delegate;
// Instance Methods
- (void)removeFromRunLoop:(NSRunLoop *)aRunLoop forMode:(NSString *)mode;
- (void)scheduleInRunLoop:(NSRunLoop *)aRunLoop forMode:(NSString *)mode;
- (void)searchForAllDomains;
- (void)searchForRegistrationDomains;
- (void)searchForServicesOfType:(NSString *)type inDomain:(NSString *)domainString;
- (void)stop;
// Methods Implemented by the Delegate
- (void)netServiceBrowser:(NSNetServiceBrowser *)aNetServiceBrowser didFindDomain:(NSString *)domainString
    moreComing:(BOOL)moreComing;
- (void)netServiceBrowser:(NSNetServiceBrowser *)aNetServiceBrowser didFindService:(NSNetService *)aNetService
    moreComing:(BOOL)moreComing;
- (void)netServiceBrowser:(NSNetServiceBrowser *)aNetServiceBrowser didNotSearch:(NSDictionary *)errorDict;
```

- (void)**netServiceBrowser:**(NSNetServiceBrowser *)*aNetServiceBrowser* **didRemoveDomain:**(NSString *)*domainString*
  moreComing:(BOOL)*moreComing;*

- (void)**netServiceBrowser:**(NSNetServiceBrowser *)*aNetServiceBrowser* **didRemoveService:**(NSNetService *)*aNetService*
  moreComing:(BOOL)*moreComing;*

- (void)**netServiceBrowserDidStopSearch:**(NSNetServiceBrowser *)*aNetServiceBrowser;*

- (void)**netServiceBrowserWillSearch:**(NSNetServiceBrowser *)*aNetServiceBrowser;*

NSNotification Mac OS X 10.0

Notifications provide a mechanism for objects that have no other way to communicate with each other. The model used is a multicast model, in which client objects **register** themselves with a notification center to be notified in response to a certain event, which is encapsulated in an NSNotification object. NSNotification represents both notifications to the notification center, and the notifications that are sent out to the observers of a particular notification.

Clients generally interact with notifications as receivers; that is, they don't create notifications, but extract key bits of information out of received notifications. To obtain information about a notification we use the three methods **name**, **userInfo**, and **object**, which return the notification name, **userInfo** dictionary, and the notification's associated object, respectively.

```
@interface NSNotification : NSObject <NSCoding, NSCopying>
// Convenience Constructors
  + (id)notificationWithName:(NSString *)aName object:(id)anObject;
  + (id)notificationWithName:(NSString *)aName object:(id)anObject userInfo:(NSDictionary *)aUserInfo;
// Instance Methods
  - (NSString *)name;
  - (id)object;
  - (NSDictionary *)userInfo;
// Methods Implementing NSCoding
  - (void)encodeWithCoder:(NSCoder *)aCoder;
  - (id)initWithCoder:(NSCoder *)aDecoder;
// Methods Implementing NSCopying
  - (id)copyWithZone:(NSZone *)zone;
```

NSNotificationCenter Mac OS X 10.0

This class is the core of Cocoa's notification system. Objects **register** with the default notification center to receive notifications posted by other objects. The default notification center, which is also used for system notifications, is obtained using the class method **defaultCenter**.

To **register** an object as a receiver of a specified notification, we use the method **addObserver:selector:name:object:**. The observer is the object that wishes to be notified of the notification identified by **name:**. The **selector:** argument is the selector for the method to be invoked in Observer:. The object: parameter allows us to restrict the notifications to which the observer responds to those posted by the specified object. To remove an observer we invoke the method removeObserver:, which removes the observer for all notifications. If we want to be selective about what notifications from which objects we wish to stop observing, we can use the method removeObserver:name:object:.

NSNotificationCenter provides three methods for posting notifications: postNotification:, postNotificationName:object:, and postNotificationName:object:userInfo:. Each of these methods offers different levels of control over how the notification is posted.

For more information about the notifications system, see Chapter 2.

@interface **NSNotificationCenter** : NSObject
// Class Methods
 + (id)**defaultCenter**;
// Instance Methods
 - (void)**addObserver**:(id)*observer* **selector**:(SEL)*aSelector* **name**:(NSString *)*aName* **object**:(id)*anObject*;
 - (void)**postNotification**:(NSNotification *)*notification*;
 - (void)**postNotificationName**:(NSString *)*aName* **object**:(id)*anObject*;
 - (void)**postNotificationName**:(NSString *)*aName* **object**:(id)*anObject* **userInfo**:(NSDictionary *)*aUserInfo*;
 - (void)**removeObserver**:(id)*observer*;
 - (void)**removeObserver**:(id)*observer* **name**:(NSString *)*aName* **object**:(id)*anObject*;

Subclasses
NSDistributedNotificationCenter

NSNotificationQueue   Mac OS X 10.0

This class acts as a buffer for notification centers. Notification queues can be used to allow greater control over the timing of notifications and how they are posted to the notification center. Each thread has its own notification queue, which is associated with the default notification center. For more information about the notification system, see Chapter 2.

@interface **NSNotificationQueue** : NSObject
// Initializers
 - (id)**initWithNotificationCenter**:(NSNotificationCenter *)*notificationCenter*;
// Class Methods
 + (NSNotificationQueue *)**defaultQueue**;
// Instance Methods
 - (void)**dequeueNotificationsMatching**:(NSNotification *)*notification* **coalesceMask**:(unsigned)*coalesceMask*;
 - (void)**enqueueNotification**:(NSNotification *)*notification* **postingStyle**:(NSPostingStyle)*postingStyle*;
 - (void)**enqueueNotification**:(NSNotification *)*notification* **postingStyle**:(NSPostingStyle)*postingStyle*
    coalesceMask:(unsigned)*coalesceMask* **forModes**:(NSArray *)*modes*;

NSNull

This simple class represents a NULL value as an object. The utility of this is that an instance of NSNull can be added to any of the Foundation collections, which don't provide for the inclusion of nil. To create an instance of NSNull, simply use the class method null.

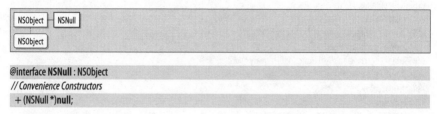

```
@interface NSNull : NSObject
// Convenience Constructors
 + (NSNull *)null;
```

NSNumber

NSNumber is a wrapper class for the C primitive numeric data types. Using this class, clients can store values of primitive data types, such as int and float, in Cocoa collection classes such as NSArray or NSDictionary, which only handle Objective-C objects.

```
@interface NSNumber : NSValue
// Convenience Constructors
 + (NSNumber *)numberWithBool:(BOOL)value;
 + (NSNumber *)numberWithChar:(char)value;
 + (NSNumber *)numberWithDouble:(double)value;
 + (NSNumber *)numberWithFloat:(float)value;
 + (NSNumber *)numberWithInt:(int)value;
 + (NSNumber *)numberWithLong:(long)value;
 + (NSNumber *)numberWithLongLong:(long long)value;
 + (NSNumber *)numberWithShort:(short)value;
 + (NSNumber *)numberWithUnsignedChar:(unsigned char)value;
 + (NSNumber *)numberWithUnsignedInt:(unsigned int)value;
 + (NSNumber *)numberWithUnsignedLong:(unsigned long)value;
 + (NSNumber *)numberWithUnsignedLongLong:(unsigned long long)value;
 + (NSNumber *)numberWithUnsignedShort:(unsigned short)value;
// Initializers
 - (id)initWithBool:(BOOL)value;
 - (id)initWithChar:(char)value;
 - (id)initWithDouble:(double)value;
 - (id)initWithFloat:(float)value;
 - (id)initWithInt:(int)value;
 - (id)initWithLong:(long)value;
 - (id)initWithLongLong:(long long)value;
 - (id)initWithShort:(short)value;
```

Foundation
Classes

- (id)**initWithUnsignedChar:**(unsigned char)*value;*
- (id)**initWithUnsignedInt:**(unsigned int)*value;*
- (id)**initWithUnsignedLong:**(unsigned long)*value;*
- (id)**initWithUnsignedLongLong:**(unsigned long long)*value;*
- (id)**initWithUnsignedShort:**(unsigned short)*value;*
// *Instance Methods*
- (BOOL)**boolValue;**
- (char)**charValue;**
- (NSComparisonResult)**compare:**(NSNumber *)*otherNumber;*
- (NSDecimal)**decimalValue;**
- (NSString *)**descriptionWithLocale:**(NSDictionary *)*locale;*
- (double)**doubleValue;**
- (float)**floatValue;**
- (int)**intValue;**
- (BOOL)**isEqualToNumber:**(NSNumber *)*number;*
- (long long)**longLongValue;**
- (long)**longValue;**
- (short)**shortValue;**
- (NSString *)**stringValue;**
- (unsigned char)**unsignedCharValue;**
- (unsigned int)**unsignedIntValue;**
- (unsigned long long)**unsignedLongLongValue;**
- (unsigned long)**unsignedLongValue;**
- (unsigned short)**unsignedShortValue;**

Subclasses

NSDecimalNumber

NSNumberFormatter   Mac OS X 10.0

This concrete subclass of NSFormatter converts the numeric contents of a cell into a user-specified textual representation; textual representations can also be converted to NSDecimalNumber objects used to store numeric cell values.

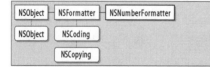

@interface **NSNumberFormatter** : NSFormatter
// *Accessor Methods*
- (void)**setAttributedStringForNil:**(NSAttributedString *)*newAttributedString;*
- (NSAttributedString *)**attributedStringForNil;**
- (void)**setNegativeFormat:**(NSString *)*format;*
- (NSString *)**negativeFormat;**
- (void)**setMaximum:**(NSDecimalNumber *)*aMaximum;*
- (NSDecimalNumber *)**maximum;**
- (void)**setAllowsFloats:**(BOOL)*flag;*
- (BOOL)**allowsFloats;**
- (void)**setPositiveFormat:**(NSString *)*format;*

- (NSString *)**positiveFormat**;
- (void)**setMinimum**:(NSDecimalNumber *)*aMinimum*;
- (NSDecimalNumber *)**minimum**;
- (void)**setAttributedStringForZero**:(NSAttributedString *)*newAttributedString*;
- (NSAttributedString *)**attributedStringForZero**;
- (void)**setRoundingBehavior**:(NSDecimalNumberHandler *)*newRoundingBehavior*;
- (NSDecimalNumberHandler *)**roundingBehavior**;
- (void)**setFormat**:(NSString *)*format*;
- (NSString *)**format**;
- (void)**setHasThousandSeparators**:(BOOL)*flag*;
- (BOOL)**hasThousandSeparators**;
- (void)**setLocalizesFormat**:(BOOL)*flag*;
- (BOOL)**localizesFormat**;
- (void)**setDecimalSeparator**:(NSString *)*newSeparator*;
- (NSString *)**decimalSeparator**;
- (void)**setAttributedStringForNotANumber**:(NSAttributedString *)*newAttributedString*;
- (NSAttributedString *)**attributedStringForNotANumber**;
- (void)**setTextAttributesForNegativeValues**:(NSDictionary *)*newAttributes*;
- (NSDictionary *)**textAttributesForNegativeValues**;
- (void)**setTextAttributesForPositiveValues**:(NSDictionary *)*newAttributes*;
- (NSDictionary *)**textAttributesForPositiveValues**;
- (void)**setThousandSeparator**:(NSString *)*newSeparator*;
- (NSString *)**thousandSeparator**;

NSObject

NSObject is the root class of the Cocoa frameworks. This class defines the base functionality that enables objects to work with the Objective-C runtime.

```
@interface NSObject <NSObject>
// Initializers
- (id)init;
// Class Methods
+ (id)alloc;
+ (id)allocWithZone:(NSZone *)zone;
+ (Class)class;
+ (BOOL)conformsToProtocol:(Protocol *)protocol;
+ (id)copyWithZone:(NSZone *)zone;
+ (NSString *)description;
+ (void)initialize;
+ (IMP)instanceMethodForSelector:(SEL)aSelector;
+ (NSMethodSignature *)instanceMethodSignatureForSelector:(SEL)aSelector;
+ (BOOL)instancesRespondToSelector:(SEL)aSelector;
+ (BOOL)isSubclassOfClass:(Class)aClass;
+ (void)load;
+ (id)mutableCopyWithZone:(NSZone *)zone;
+ (id)new;
```

```
+ (void)poseAsClass:(Class)aClass;
+ (void)setVersion:(int)aVersion;
+ (Class)superclass;
+ (int)version;
// Instance Methods
- (void)URL:(NSURL *)sender resourceDataDidBecomeAvailable:(NSData *)newBytes;
- (void)URL:(NSURL *)sender resourceDidFailLoadingWithReason:(NSString *)reason;
- (void)URLResourceDidCancelLoading:(NSURL *)sender;
- (void)URLResourceDidFinishLoading:(NSURL *)sender;
- (id)awakeAfterUsingCoder:(NSCoder *)aDecoder;
- (unsigned long)classCode;
- (Class)classForArchiver;
- (Class)classForCoder;
- (Class)classForKeyedArchiver;
- (Class)classForPortCoder;
- (NSString *)className;
- (id)copy;
- (void)dealloc;
- (void)doesNotRecognizeSelector:(SEL)aSelector;
- (void)forwardInvocation:(NSInvocation *)anInvocation;
- (IMP)methodForSelector:(SEL)aSelector;
- (NSMethodSignature *)methodSignatureForSelector:(SEL)aSelector;
- (id)mutableCopy;
- (void)performSelector:(SEL)aSelector withObject:(id)anArgument afterDelay:(NSTimeInterval)delay;
- (void)performSelector:(SEL)aSelector withObject:(id)anArgument afterDelay:(NSTimeInterval)delay
    inModes:(NSArray *)modes;
- (void)performSelectorOnMainThread:(SEL)aSelector withObject:(id)arg waitUntilDone:(BOOL)wait;
- (void)performSelectorOnMainThread:(SEL)aSelector withObject:(id)arg waitUntilDone:(BOOL)wait
    modes:(NSArray *)array;
- (id)replacementObjectForArchiver:(NSArchiver *)archiver;
- (id)replacementObjectForCoder:(NSCoder *)aCoder;
- (id)replacementObjectForKeyedArchiver:(NSKeyedArchiver *)archiver;
- (id)replacementObjectForPortCoder:(NSPortCoder *)coder;
// Methods Implementing NSObject
- (BOOL)isEqual:(id)object;
- (unsigned)hash;
- (Class)superclass;
- (Class)class;
- (id)self;
- (NSZone *)zone;
- (id)performSelector:(SEL)aSelector;
- (id)performSelector:(SEL)aSelector withObject:(id)object;
- (id)performSelector:(SEL)aSelector withObject:(id)object1 withObject:(id)object2;
- (BOOL)isProxy;
- (BOOL)isKindOfClass:(Class)aClass;
- (BOOL)isMemberOfClass:(Class)aClass;
- (BOOL)conformsToProtocol:(Protocol *)aProtocol;
- (BOOL)respondsToSelector:(SEL)aSelector;
- (id)retain;
- (oneway void)release;
```

```
- (id)autorelease;
- (unsigned)retainCount;
- (NSString *)description;
```

Subclasses

NSObject is a root class.

NSPipe

This class provides an interface to objects that represent Unix pipes that can be used to transfer data between applications. Pipes are one-way communication channels with a read-end and a write-end. NSFileHandle objects representing these ends of the pipes are obtained by invoking fileHandleForReading and fileHandleForWriting.

```
@interface NSPipe : NSObject
// Convenience Constructors
  + (id)pipe;
// Initializers
  - (id)init;
// Instance Methods
  - (NSFileHandle *)fileHandleForReading;
  - (NSFileHandle *)fileHandleForWriting;
```

NSPort

This class is an abstract class that declares the interface to objects that serve as endpoints for communication between two threads or tasks. Cocoa's distributed objects system implements interprocess communication using subclasses of NSPort. The Foundation framework implements three concrete subclasses of NSPort: NSMessagePort, NSMachPort, and NSSocketPort. NSMessagePort and NSMachPort are used for local communications only, while NSSocketPort can be used for either local or remote communication over a network.

```
@interface NSPort : NSObject <NSCoding, NSCopying>
// Convenience Constructors
  + (NSPort *)port;
// Accessor Methods
  - (void)setDelegate:(id)anId;
  - (id)delegate;
// Class Methods
  + (id)allocWithZone:(NSZone *)zone;
```

// Instance Methods
- (void)**addConnection:**(NSConnection *)*conn* **toRunLoop:**(NSRunLoop *)*runLoop* **forMode:**(NSString *)*mode;*
- (BOOL)**isValid;**
- (void)**invalidate;**
- (void)**removeConnection:**(NSConnection *)*conn* **fromRunLoop:**(NSRunLoop *)*runLoop* **forMode:**(NSString *)*mode;*
- (void)**removeFromRunLoop:**(NSRunLoop *)*runLoop* **forMode:**(NSString *)*mode;*
- (unsigned)**reservedSpaceLength;**
- (void)**scheduleInRunLoop:**(NSRunLoop *)*runLoop* **forMode:**(NSString *)*mode;*
- (BOOL)**sendBeforeDate:**(NSDate *)*limitDate* **components:**(NSMutableArray *)*components* **from:**(NSPort *)*receivePort*
    reserved:(unsigned)*headerSpaceReserved;*
- (BOOL)**sendBeforeDate:**(NSDate *)*limitDate* **msgid:**(unsigned)*msgID* **components:**(NSMutableArray *)*components*
    reserved:(unsigned)*headerSpaceReserved;*
// Methods Implementing NSCoding
- (void)**encodeWithCoder:**(NSCoder *)*aCoder;*
- (id)**initWithCoder:**(NSCoder *)*aDecoder;*
// Methods Implementing NSCopying
- (id)**copyWithZone:**(NSZone *)*zone;*
// Methods Implemented by the Delegate
- (void)**handlePortMessage:**(NSPortMessage *)*message;*

Subclasses

NSMessagePort, NSSocketPort

NSPortCoder   Mac OS X 10.0

This concrete subclass of NSCoder is used by the distributed objects system to encode, transmit, and decode object proxies between two NSConnection objects residing in separate processes (objects, too, can be transmitted using this class).

@interface **NSPortCoder** : NSCoder
// Initializers
- (id)**initWithReceivePort:**(NSPort *)*rcvPort* **sendPort:**(NSPort *)*sndPort* **components:**(NSArray *)*comps;*
// Class Methods
+ (id) **portCoderWithReceivePort:**(NSPort *)*rcvPort* **sendPort:**(NSPort *)*sndPort* **components:**(NSArray *)*comps;*
// Instance Methods
- (NSConnection *)**connection;**
- (NSPort *)**decodePortObject;**
- (void)**dispatch;**
- (void)**encodePortObject:**(NSPort *)*aport;*
- (BOOL)**isBycopy;**
- (BOOL)**isByref;**

NSPortMessage   Mac OS X 10.0

Instances of this class represent low-level interapplication communication meesages. Cocoa's distributed objects system uses this class extensively for communications between applications on the same host machine. Associated with each port messages is a sending NSPort, a receiving NSPort, and an array of message components that may be instances of NSData or NSPort. Instances of this class are initialized using the method init-WithSendPort:receivePort:components:. Messages are sent by invoking the method sendBeforeDate:. Finally, the components method is used to retrieve the components of a port message, while sendPort and receivePort are used to retrieve the port message's send and receive port objects. Applications should make use of the high-level Distributed Objects API for interapplication communication, and resort to raw messaging with port messages for exceptional circumstances.

```
NSObject ── NSPortMessage
NSObject
```

@interface **NSPortMessage** : NSObject

// Initializers

- (id)**initWithSendPort**:(NSPort *)*sendPort* **receivePort**:(NSPort *)*replyPort* **components**:(NSArray *)*components*;

// Accessor Methods

- (void)**setMsgid**:(unsigned)*msgid*;
- (unsigned)**msgid**;

// Instance Methods

- (NSArray *)**components**;
- (NSPort *)**receivePort**;
- (BOOL)**sendBeforeDate**:(NSDate *)*date*;
- (NSPort *)**sendPort**;

NSPortNameServer

Mac OS X 10.0

This class is used by the distributed objects system to provide port registration services for NSConnection objects. Instances of NSPortNameServer are obtained using the class method systemDefaultPortNameServer. Ports are registered using the method registerPort:name:, and unregistered with removePortForName:. To locate a port, invoke portForName: or portForName:host:; the former is used to locate ports on the local host, while the latter is used to locate ports over a network.

```
NSObject ── NSPortNameServer
NSObject
```

@interface **NSPortNameServer** : NSObject

// Class Methods

+ (NSPortNameServer *)**systemDefaultPortNameServer**;

// Instance Methods

- (NSPort *)**portForName**:(NSString *)*name*;
- (NSPort *)**portForName**:(NSString *)*name* **host**:(NSString *)*host*;
- (BOOL)**registerPort**:(NSPort *)*port* **name**:(NSString *)*name*;
- (BOOL)**removePortForName**:(NSString *)*name*;

Subclasses

NSMachBootstrapServer, NSMessagePortNameServer, NSSocketPortNameServer

NSPositionalSpecifier

This class represents the scripting language reference form used to specify an insertion point in a collection of objects in relation to another object in the container.

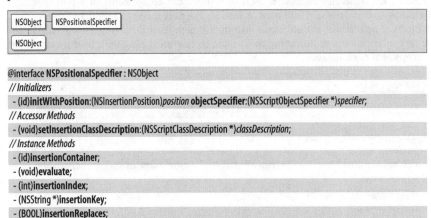

@interface **NSPositionalSpecifier** : NSObject
// Initializers
  - (id)**initWithPosition:**(NSInsertionPosition)*position* **objectSpecifier:**(NSScriptObjectSpecifier *)*specifier*;
// Accessor Methods
  - (void)**setInsertionClassDescription:**(NSScriptClassDescription *)*classDescription*;
// Instance Methods
  - (id)**insertionContainer**;
  - (void)**evaluate**;
  - (int)**insertionIndex**;
  - (NSString *)**insertionKey**;
  - (BOOL)**insertionReplaces**;

NSProcessInfo

This class provides an way for applications to discover information about their current process and host. This information includes such things as the execution arguments, environment variables, process ID, and the process name. Using NSProcessInfo, clients may also discover information about the host, such as the host name, and the operating system name and version. NSProcessInfo returns the operating system version in a human-readable form that is unsuitable for parsing.

@interface **NSProcessInfo** : NSObject
// Accessor Methods
  - (void)**setProcessName:**(NSString *)*newName*;
  - (NSString *)**processName**;
// Class Methods
  + (NSProcessInfo *)**processInfo**;
// Instance Methods
  - (NSDictionary *)**environment**;
  - (NSString *)**globallyUniqueString**;
  - (unsigned int)**operatingSystem**;
  - (NSString *)**operatingSystemName**;
  - (NSString *)**operatingSystemVersionString**;
  - (int)**processIdentifier**;
  - (NSArray *)**arguments**;
  - (NSString *)**hostName**;

NSPropertyListSerialization

This class provides functionality to convert organizations of property list objects (NSArray, NSDictionary, NSData, NSString, and NSNumber) to and from XML or binary data formats.

```
NSObject — NSPropertyListSerialization
NSObject
```

@interface **NSPropertyListSerialization** : NSObject
// *Class Methods*
+ (NSData *)**dataFromPropertyList**:(id)*plist* **format**:(NSPropertyListFormat)*format*
    errorDescription:(NSString **)*errorString*;
+ (BOOL)**propertyList**:(id)*plist* **isValidForFormat**:(NSPropertyListFormat)*format*;
+ (id)**propertyListFromData**:(NSData *)*data* **mutabilityOption**:(NSPropertyListMutabilityOptions)*opt*
    format:(NSPropertyListFormat *)*format* **errorDescription**:(NSString **)*errorString*;

NSPropertySpecifier

This class represents the scripting language reference form used to specify an attribute of an object or a relationship between the target object and one or more additional objects.

```
NSObject — NSScriptObjectSpecifier — NSPropertySpecifier
NSObject          NSCoding
```

@interface **NSPropertySpecifier** : NSScriptObjectSpecifier

NSProtocolChecker

This class is used to provide a proxy for an object (the protocol checker's delegate) that filters messages sent to the object based on a formal protocol. Cocoa's distributed objects system uses this class to improve the performance of a distributed objects connection by limiting the messages sent an object to those agreed upon in a protocol. Instances of NSProtocolChecker are initialized with the method initWithTarget:protocol:. Target: is the object the protocol check will act as a proxy for, while protocol: is the protocol that defines what methods will be forwarded to the target object by the protocol checker. Note that the argument type for protocol: is a protocol object: Protocol *. To obtain a pointer to a protocol, use the @protocol(protocolName) compiler directive.

```
NSProxy — NSProtocolChecker
NSObject
```

@interface **NSProtocolChecker** : NSProxy
// *Initializers*
- (id)**initWithTarget**:(NSObject *)*anObject* **protocol**:(Protocol *)*aProtocol*;
// *Class Methods*
+ (id)**protocolCheckerWithTarget**:(NSObject *)*anObject* **protocol**:(Protocol *)*aProtocol*;

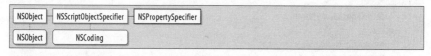

```
// Instance Methods
- (Protocol *)protocol;
- (NSObject *)target;
```

NSProxy

This class is the only other root class in the Cocoa frameworks besides NSObject. NSProxy defines an interface to objects that stand-in for other objects. The concrete subclass, NSDistantObject, is an integral part of the distributed objects system where proxy objects are used to represent in a process objects that have been vended by another process.

Distributed messaging is not, however, the only use of proxy objects. They can also stand-in for objects that have not yet been created. When the proxy object receives a message for the object it is representing, then it can load the object and replace itself with the real object. This is useful for objects that may be too expensive resource-wise to create when their existence may not be needed.

```
@interface NSProxy <NSObject>
// Class Methods
+ (id)alloc;
+ (id)allocWithZone:(NSZone *)zone;
+ (Class)class;
+ (BOOL)respondsToSelector:(SEL)aSelector;
// Instance Methods
- (void)dealloc;
- (NSString *)description;
- (void)forwardInvocation:(NSInvocation *)invocation;
- (NSMethodSignature *)methodSignatureForSelector:(SEL)sel;
// Methods Implementing NSObject
- (BOOL)isEqual:(id)object;
- (unsigned)hash;
- (Class)superclass;
- (Class)class;
- (id)self;
- (NSZone *)zone;
- (id)performSelector:(SEL)aSelector;
- (id)performSelector:(SEL)aSelector
  withObject:(id)object;
- (id)performSelector:(SEL)aSelector withObject:(id)object1 withObject:(id)object2;
- (BOOL)isProxy;
- (BOOL)isKindOfClass:(Class)aClass;
- (BOOL)isMemberOfClass:(Class)aClass;
- (BOOL)conformsToProtocol:(Protocol *)aProtocol;
- (BOOL)respondsToSelector:(SEL)aSelector;
- (id)retain;
- (oneway void)release;
- (id)autorelease;
```

```
- (unsigned)retainCount;
- (NSString *)description;
```

Subclasses

NSProxy is a root class.

NSQuitCommand Mac OS X 10.0

Instances of this class causes its specified application to quit when executed. This class participates in Cocoa's scripting system.

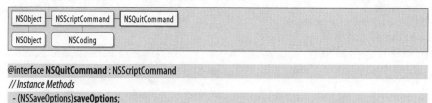

```
@interface NSQuitCommand : NSScriptCommand
// Instance Methods
- (NSSaveOptions)saveOptions;
```

NSRandomSpecifier Mac OS X 10.0

This class represents the scripting language reference form used to specify an arbitrary object in a collection of objects.

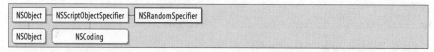

```
@interface NSRandomSpecifier : NSScriptObjectSpecifier
```

NSRangeSpecifier Mac OS X 10.0

This class represents the scripting language reference form used to specify a range of objects within a collection.

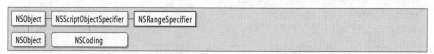

```
@interface NSRangeSpecifier : NSScriptObjectSpecifier
// Initializers
- (id)initWithContainerClassDescription:(NSScriptClassDescription *)classDesc
    containerSpecifier:(NSScriptObjectSpecifier *)container key:(NSString *)property
    startSpecifier:(NSScriptObjectSpecifier *)startSpec endSpecifier:(NSScriptObjectSpecifier *)endSpec;
// Accessor Methods
- (void)setStartSpecifier:(NSScriptObjectSpecifier *)startSpec;
- (NSScriptObjectSpecifier *)startSpecifier;
- (void)setEndSpecifier:(NSScriptObjectSpecifier *)endSpec;
- (NSScriptObjectSpecifier *)endSpecifier;
```

NSRecursiveLock

This class is an implementation of the NSLocking protocol that provides a lock that may be acquired multiply by a single thread without creating a deadlock condition. See Chapter 2 for more information on how locking works.

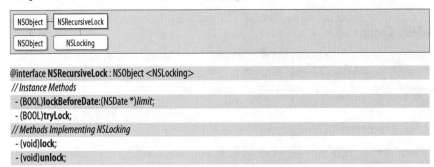

```
@interface NSRecursiveLock : NSObject <NSLocking>
// Instance Methods
 - (BOOL)lockBeforeDate:(NSDate *)limit;
 - (BOOL)tryLock;
// Methods Implementing NSLocking
 - (void)lock;
 - (void)unlock;
```

NSRelativeSpecifier

This class represents the scripting language reference form used to specify the position of one object relative to another.

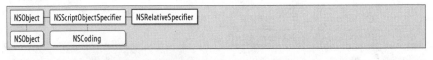

```
@interface NSRelativeSpecifier : NSScriptObjectSpecifier
// Initializers
 - (id)initWithContainerClassDescription:(NSScriptClassDescription *)classDesc
      containerSpecifier:(NSScriptObjectSpecifier *)container key:(NSString *)property
      relativePosition:(NSRelativePosition)relPos baseSpecifier:(NSScriptObjectSpecifier *)baseSpecifier;
// Accessor Methods
 - (void)setRelativePosition:(NSRelativePosition)relPos;
 - (NSRelativePosition)relativePosition;
 - (void)setBaseSpecifier:(NSScriptObjectSpecifier *)baseSpecifier;
 - (NSScriptObjectSpecifier *)baseSpecifier;
```

NSRunLoop

This class manages input sources for a thread. In Cocoa, input sources may include mouse and keyboard events, as well as NSPorts, NSTimers, and NSConnections. NSRunLoop serves as an interface between an application and the rest of the operating system. When events from the mouse, keyboard, or other peripherals are received in the operating system, they are forwarded to the active application through that application's run-loop. The run-loop monitors all of its input sources continuously for events, and dispatches them to the appropriate object in an application. For more information on NSRunLoop and event handling in Cocoa, see Chapter 3.

Every instance of NSApplication creates and manages its own run-loop. This is the main run-loop of the application. Because this run-loop is created for us, we don't need to use any of the NSRunLoop APIs. However, new threads do not have a run-loop object associated with them. For a thread to participate in event handling and notification from other run-loop sources, create a run-loop for any the thread. If you need to have access to a run-loop object, then you can obtain a pointer to the run-loop of the current thread by invoking the class method currentRunLoop. If you need to start your own run-loop in a thread, you must first create the run-loop using alloc and init, and send a run message to the run-loop object.

NSRunLoop objects are based on Core Foundation CFRunLoop objects. The method getCFRunLoop returns an NSRunLoop's underlying Core Foundation run-loop.

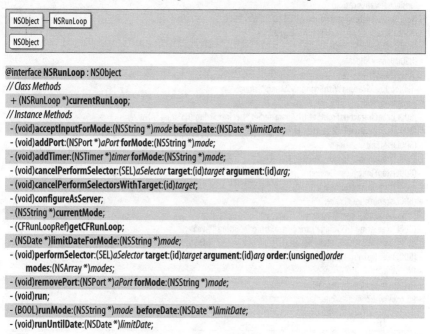

@interface **NSRunLoop** : NSObject

// Class Methods

+ (NSRunLoop *)**currentRunLoop**;

// Instance Methods

- (void)**acceptInputForMode:**(NSString *)*mode* **beforeDate:**(NSDate *)*limitDate*;
- (void)**addPort:**(NSPort *)*aPort* **forMode:**(NSString *)*mode*;
- (void)**addTimer:**(NSTimer *)*timer* **forMode:**(NSString *)*mode*;
- (void)**cancelPerformSelector:**(SEL)*aSelector* **target:**(id)*target* **argument:**(id)*arg*;
- (void)**cancelPerformSelectorsWithTarget:**(id)*target*;
- (void)**configureAsServer**;
- (NSString *)**currentMode**;
- (CFRunLoopRef)**getCFRunLoop**;
- (NSDate *)**limitDateForMode:**(NSString *)*mode*;
- (void)**performSelector:**(SEL)*aSelector* **target:**(id)*target* **argument:**(id)*arg* **order:**(unsigned)*order* **modes:**(NSArray *)*modes*;
- (void)**removePort:**(NSPort *)*aPort* **forMode:**(NSString *)*mode*;
- (void)**run**;
- (BOOL)**runMode:**(NSString *)*mode* **beforeDate:**(NSDate *)*limitDate*;
- (void)**runUntilDate:**(NSDate *)*limitDate*;

NSScanner

Mac OS X 10.0

This class declares an API for objects that can interpret and convert a string into individual number and string values. When you create a scanner object, you assign it the string to scan. Scanner objects are created with the method scannerWithString:, or initialized with initWithString:. A scanner works by interpreting and converting string and number values based on the scan message sent to the scanner object. For example, if the method scanInt: is invoked, the scanner will scan through the string searching from the next available integer. Scanning usually happens within a loop, until the entire string has been scanned. Clients can test whether or not the scanner is at the end of the string using the method isAtEnd.

```
@interface NSScanner : NSObject <NSCopying>
// Convenience Constructors
 + (id)scannerWithString:(NSString *)string;
// Initializers
 - (id)initWithString:(NSString *)string;
// Accessor Methods
 - (void)setCaseSensitive:(BOOL)flag;
 - (BOOL)caseSensitive;
 - (void)setScanLocation:(unsigned)pos;
 - (unsigned)scanLocation;
 - (void)setCharactersToBeSkipped:(NSCharacterSet *)set;
 - (NSCharacterSet *)charactersToBeSkipped;
 - (void)setLocale:(NSDictionary *)dict;
 - (NSDictionary *)locale;
// Class Methods
 + (id)localizedScannerWithString:(NSString *)string;
// Instance Methods
 - (BOOL)scanCharactersFromSet:(NSCharacterSet *)set intoString:(NSString **)value;
 - (BOOL)scanDecimal:(NSDecimal *)dcm;
 - (BOOL)isAtEnd;
 - (BOOL)scanDouble:(double *)value;
 - (BOOL)scanFloat:(float *)value;
 - (BOOL)scanHexInt:(unsigned *)value;
 - (BOOL)scanInt:(int *)value;
 - (BOOL)scanLongLong:(long long *)value;
 - (BOOL)scanString:(NSString *)string intoString:(NSString **)value;
 - (BOOL)scanUpToCharactersFromSet:(NSCharacterSet *)set intoString:(NSString **)value;
 - (BOOL)scanUpToString:(NSString *)string intoString:(NSString **)value;
 - (NSString *)string;
// Methods Implementing NSCopying
 - (id)copyWithZone:(NSZone *)zone;
```

NSScriptClassDescription

This class is used by Cocoa's scripting information to encapsulate information about scriptable classes, and to provide an interface to determine characteristics and properties of scriptable objects.

```
@interface NSScriptClassDescription : NSClassDescription
// Initializers
 - (id)initWithSuiteName:(NSString *)suiteName className:(NSString *)className dictionary:(NSDictionary *)dict;
// Instance Methods
 - (unsigned long)appleEventCode;
 - (unsigned long)appleEventCodeForKey:(NSString *)key;
 - (NSScriptClassDescription *)classDescriptionForKey:(NSString *)key;
 - (NSString *)className;
 - (NSString *)defaultSubcontainerAttributeKey;
```

- (BOOL)**isLocationRequiredToCreateForKey**:(NSString *)*toManyRelationshipKey*;
- (BOOL)**isReadOnlyKey**:(NSString *)*key*;
- (NSString *)**keyWithAppleEventCode**:(unsigned long)*code*;
- (BOOL)**matchesAppleEventCode**:(unsigned long)*code*;
- (SEL)**selectorForCommand**:(NSScriptCommandDescription *)*commandDef*;
- (NSString *)**suiteName**;
- (NSScriptClassDescription *)**superclassDescription**;
- (BOOL)**supportsCommand**:(NSScriptCommandDescription *)*commandDef*;
- (NSString *)**typeForKey**:(NSString *)*key*;

NSScriptCoercionHandler

This class is used by Cocoa's scripting system to translate one scripting data type into another data type, which is a common task in key-value coding operations.

@interface **NSScriptCoercionHandler** : NSObject
// Class Methods
  + (NSScriptCoercionHandler *)**sharedCoercionHandler**;
// Instance Methods
  - (id)**coerceValue**:(id)*value* **toClass**:(Class)*toClass*;
  - (void)**registerCoercer**:(id)*coercer* **selector**:(SEL)*selector* **toConvertFromClass**:(Class)*fromClass* **toClass**:(Class)*toClass*;

NSScriptCommand

This class represents a scripting statement in Cocoa's scripting system. A scripting statement is something like "set bounds of front window to 1104, 360, 1280, 561}". When an application receives the Apple Event corresponding to this script statement, it is translated into an instance NSScriptCommand.

@interface **NSScriptCommand** : NSObject <NSCoding>
// Initializers
  - (id)**initWithCommandDescription**:(NSScriptCommandDescription *)*commandDef*;
// Accessor Methods
  - (void)**setReceiversSpecifier**:(NSScriptObjectSpecifier *)*receiversRef*;
  - (NSScriptObjectSpecifier *)**receiversSpecifier**;
  - (void)**setDirectParameter**:(id)*directParameter*;
  - (id)**directParameter**;
  - (void)**setScriptErrorNumber**:(int)*num*;
  - (int)**scriptErrorNumber**;
  - (void)**setScriptErrorString**:(NSString *)*str*;
  - (NSString *)**scriptErrorString**;
  - (void)**setArguments**:(NSDictionary *)*args*;

- (NSDictionary *)**arguments**;
// Instance Methods
- (NSScriptCommandDescription *)**commandDescription**;
- (NSDictionary *)**evaluatedArguments**;
- (id)**evaluatedReceivers**;
- (id)**executeCommand**;
- (BOOL)**isWellFormed**;
- (id)**performDefaultImplementation**;
// Methods Implementing NSCoding
- (void)**encodeWithCoder**:(NSCoder *)aCoder;
- (id)**initWithCoder**:(NSCoder *)aDecoder;

Subclasses

NSCloneCommand, NSCloseCommand, NSCountCommand, NSCreateCommand, NSDeleteCommand, NSExists-Command, NSGetCommand, NSMoveCommand, NSQuitCommand, NSSetCommand

---

NSScriptCommandDescription   Mac OS X 10.0

This class represents a scripting command within a Cocoa application, framework, or bundle. The job of this class is to provide information about a class and method, including all argument and return types, that is used to represent a scripting command.

@interface **NSScriptCommandDescription** : NSObject <NSCoding>
// Initializers
- (id)**initWithSuiteName**:(NSString *)suiteName **commandName**:(NSString *)commandName
    dictionary:(NSDictionary *)commandDefDict;
// Instance Methods
- (unsigned long)**appleEventClassCode**;
- (unsigned long)**appleEventCode**;
- (unsigned long)**appleEventCodeForArgumentWithName**:(NSString *)argName;
- (unsigned long)**appleEventCodeForReturnType**;
- (NSArray *)**argumentNames**;
- (NSString *)**commandClassName**;
- (NSString *)**commandName**;
- (NSScriptCommand *)**createCommandInstance**;
- (NSScriptCommand *)**createCommandInstanceWithZone**:(NSZone *)zone;
- (BOOL)**isOptionalArgumentWithName**:(NSString *)argName;
- (NSString *)**returnType**;
- (NSString *)**suiteName**;
- (NSString *)**typeForArgumentWithName**:(NSString *)argName;
// Methods Implementing NSCoding
- (void)**encodeWithCoder**:(NSCoder *)aCoder;
- (id)**initWithCoder**:(NSCoder *)aDecoder;

NSScriptExecutionContext

Every scripting command is executed within some context that determines which objects are involved in the command. This class declares the interface to the shared application object that represents the execution context of scripting commands.

```
@interface NSScriptExecutionContext : NSObject
// Accessor Methods
 - (void)setTopLevelObject:(id)obj;
 - (id)topLevelObject;
 - (void)setObjectBeingTested:(id)obj;
 - (id)objectBeingTested;
 - (void)setRangeContainerObject:(id)obj;
 - (id)rangeContainerObject;
// Class Methods
 + (NSScriptExecutionContext *)sharedScriptExecutionContext;
```

NSScriptObjectSpecifier

This is an abstract class for classes of objects known as *object specifiers*. An object specifier is a representation of a scripting language reference form that is used to identify objects in relation to container objects. Object specifiers are used to represent the portions of an AppleScript used to identify the object that is the target of a script command. For example, in the AppleScript get word 3 of paragraph 15 of the front document there are three object specifiers: word 3, paragraph 15, and front document.

Object specifiers are nested, where more general specifiers are evaluated to provide an evaluation context for their nested child specifier. In the example, the specifier front paragraph is evaluated first to provide a container in which the specifier paragraph 15 can be evaluated. The scripting system evaluates object specifiers in this way to determine what object in the application should be the recipient of the command being executed.

The Foundation framework implements several subclasses of NSScriptObjectSpecifier. These subclasses implement object specifiers that represent the various AppleScript language constructs (reference forms) used to identify the targets of script commands.

```
@interface NSScriptObjectSpecifier : NSObject <NSCoding>
// Initializers
 - (id)initWithContainerClassDescription:(NSScriptClassDescription *)classDesc
     containerSpecifier:(NSScriptObjectSpecifier *)container key:(NSString *)property;
 - (id)initWithContainerSpecifier:(NSScriptObjectSpecifier *)container key:(NSString *)property;
// Accessor Methods
 - (void)setEvaluationErrorNumber:(int)error;
 - (int)evaluationErrorNumber;
```

Foundation
Classes

- (void)**setContainerIsObjectBeingTested**:(BOOL)*flag*;
- (BOOL)**containerIsObjectBeingTested**;
- (void)**setChildSpecifier**:(NSScriptObjectSpecifier *)*child*;
- (NSScriptObjectSpecifier *)**childSpecifier**;
- (void)**setKey**:(NSString *)*key*;
- (NSString *)**key**;
- (void)**setContainerIsRangeContainerObject**:(BOOL)*flag*;
- (BOOL)**containerIsRangeContainerObject**;
- (void)**setContainerClassDescription**:(NSScriptClassDescription *)*classDesc*;
- (NSScriptClassDescription *)**containerClassDescription**;
- (void)**setContainerSpecifier**:(NSScriptObjectSpecifier *)*subRef*;
- (NSScriptObjectSpecifier *)**containerSpecifier**;
// *Instance Methods*
- (NSScriptObjectSpecifier *)**evaluationErrorSpecifier**;
- (int *)**indicesOfObjectsByEvaluatingWithContainer**:(id)*container* **count**:(int *)*count*;
- (NSScriptClassDescription *)**keyClassDescription**;
- (id)**objectsByEvaluatingSpecifier**;
- (id)**objectsByEvaluatingWithContainers**:(id)*containers*;
// *Methods Implementing NSCoding*
- (void)**encodeWithCoder**:(NSCoder *)*aCoder*;
- (id)**initWithCoder**:(NSCoder *)*aDecoder*;

Subclasses

NSIndexSpecifier, NSMiddleSpecifier, NSNameSpecifier, NSPropertySpecifier, NSRandomSpecifier, NSRange-
Specifier, NSRelativeSpecifier, NSUniqueIDSpecifier, NSWhoseSpecifier

---

NSScriptSuiteRegistry Mac OS X 10.0

Instances of this class are used to manage an application's scripting information, and
as such it is an integral component in Cocoa's built-in support for scripting. Application scripting information is supplied by *script suites*. A script suite is made up of a
suite definition and script terminologies. Cocoa supports the two standard script suites
out of the box: (Core and Text). Script suites define how an application may be
controlled by scripting, and at a lower level the information provided by script suite
tells the application how to translate Apple Events it receives into script commands
and object specifiers. This class is used primarily internally by Cocoa's scripting
system, and as such you should never have to interact with it directly.

@interface **NSScriptSuiteRegistry** : NSObject
// *Class Methods*
+ (void)**setSharedScriptSuiteRegistry**:(NSScriptSuiteRegistry *)*registry*;
+ (NSScriptSuiteRegistry *)**sharedScriptSuiteRegistry**;
// *Instance Methods*
- (NSData *)**aeteResource**:(NSString *)*languageName*;
- (unsigned long)**appleEventCodeForSuite**:(NSString *)*suiteName*;
- (NSBundle *)**bundleForSuite**:(NSString *)*suiteName*;
- (NSScriptClassDescription *)**classDescriptionWithAppleEventCode**:(unsigned long)*classCode*;

- (NSDictionary *)**classDescriptionsInSuite**:(NSString *)*suiteName*;
- (NSScriptCommandDescription *)**commandDescriptionWithAppleEventClass**:(unsigned long)*eventClass*
  andAppleEventCode:(unsigned long)*commandCode*;
- (NSDictionary *)**commandDescriptionsInSuite**:(NSString *)*suiteName*;
- (void)**loadSuiteWithDictionary**:(NSDictionary *)*dict* **fromBundle**:(NSBundle *)*bundle*;
- (void)**loadSuitesFromBundle**:(NSBundle *)*bundle*;
- (void)**registerClassDescription**:(NSScriptClassDescription *)*classDesc*;
- (void)**registerCommandDescription**:(NSScriptCommandDescription *)*commandDef*;
- (NSString *)**suiteForAppleEventCode**:(unsigned long)*code*;
- (NSArray *)**suiteNames**;

NSScriptWhoseTest

Mac OS X 10.0

This class is used in Cocoa's scripting system to represent the Boolean expression of an NSScriptWhoseSpecifier. NSScriptWhoseTest is an abstract class that defines only the single method isTrue. This method is invoked to evaluate the expression represented by the NSScriptWhoseTest object, and returns a BOOL. Foundation implements two concrete subclasses of this class: NSLogicalTest and NSSpecifierTest.

@interface **NSScriptWhoseTest** : NSObject <NSCoding>
// Instance Methods
- (BOOL)**isTrue**;
// Methods Implementing NSCoding
- (void)**encodeWithCoder**:(NSCoder *)*aCoder*;
- (id)**initWithCoder**:(NSCoder *)*aDecoder*;

Subclasses
NSLogicalTest, NSSpecifierTest

NSSerializer

Mac OS X 10.0

This class converts a collection of property-list objects (NSDictionary, NSArray, NSString, and NSData) in memory into a form that can be saved to a file, for example. This class has been deprecated, and clients should instead use the class NSPropertyListSerialization.

@interface **NSSerializer** : NSObject
// Class Methods
+ (NSData *)**serializePropertyList**:(id)*aPropertyList*;
+ (void)**serializePropertyList**:(id)*aPropertyList* **intoData**:(NSMutableData *)*mdata*;

This class implements a unordered collection of unique objects. NSSet is based on the mathematical idea of a *set*, where each member is unique, and the order of elements is unimportant. What is important in a set is object membership. NSSet objects are often used in situations where an application needs to quickly determine whether or not an object is a member of a collection. As such, NSSet is able to more efficiently make this determination than NSArray.

To test whether or not an object is a member of set, use the method containsObject:, which returns a BOOL. Alternatively, the method member can be used, which returns the specified object if it exists in the set, and nil otherwise.

To enumerate the contents of a set, we create an instance of NSEnumerator by sending an objectEnumerator message to the set. Note that the order that objects are accessed by the enumerator is not guaranteed, and an order should not be assumed.

Often we want to invoke some method in each member of a collection. NSSet provides a method that saves us from the burden of having to enumerate the contents of the set and send the message to each object manually. This method is makeObjectsPerformSelector:, which will cause the method matching the selector to be invoked in each member of the collection. If you need to invoke a method that takes an argument, then use the method makeObjectsPerformSelector:withObject:.

NSSet provides several methods that are useful for comparing two sets. The method isSubsetOfSet: will return YES if the specified set contains every member of the receiver. The method intersectsSet: returns YES if at least one member of the receiver is present in the specified set. Finally, isEqualToSet: will return YES if the contents of the receiver are equal to the contents of the specified set.

NSSet is toll-free bridged with the Core Foundation type CFSet. As such, NSSet objects can be used interchangeably with the CFSet pointer type, CFSetRef.

```
@interface NSSet : NSObject <NSCoding, NSCopying, NSMutableCopying>
// Convenience Constructors
 + (id)set;
 + (id)setWithArray:(NSArray *)array;
 + (id)setWithObject:(id)object;
 + (id)setWithObjects:(id *)objs count:(unsigned)cnt;
 + (id)setWithObjects:(id)firstObj, ...;
 + (id)setWithSet:(NSSet *)set;
// Initializers
 - (id)initWithArray:(NSArray *)array;
 - (id)initWithObjects:(id *)objects count:(unsigned)count;
 - (id)initWithObjects:(id)firstObj, ...;
 - (id)initWithSet:(NSSet *)set;
 - (id)initWithSet:(NSSet *)set copyItems:(BOOL)flag;
```

```
// Instance Methods
 - (NSArray *)allObjects;
 - (id)anyObject;
 - (BOOL)containsObject:(id)anObject;
 - (unsigned)count;
 - (NSString *)description;
 - (NSString *)descriptionWithLocale:(NSDictionary *)locale;
 - (BOOL)intersectsSet:(NSSet *)otherSet;
 - (BOOL)isEqualToSet:(NSSet *)otherSet;
 - (BOOL)isSubsetOfSet:(NSSet *)otherSet;
 - (void)makeObjectsPerformSelector:(SEL)aSelector;
 - (void)makeObjectsPerformSelector:(SEL)aSelector withObject:(id)argument;
 - (id)member:(id)object;
 - (NSEnumerator *)objectEnumerator;
// Methods Implementing NSCoding
 - (void)encodeWithCoder:(NSCoder *)aCoder;
 - (id)initWithCoder:(NSCoder *)aDecoder;
// Methods Implementing NSCopying
 - (id)copyWithZone:(NSZone *)zone;
// Methods Implementing NSMutableCopying
 - (id)mutableCopyWithZone:(NSZone *)zone;
```

Subclasses

NSMutableSet

NSSetCommand · Mac OS X 10.0

Instances of this class are used in Cocoa's scripting system to set the specified properties of the specified object to the specified value.

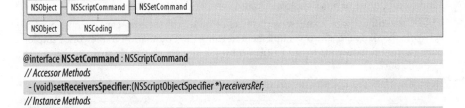

```
@interface NSSetCommand : NSScriptCommand
// Accessor Methods
 - (void)setReceiversSpecifier:(NSScriptObjectSpecifier *)receiversRef;
// Instance Methods
 - (NSScriptObjectSpecifier *)keySpecifier;
```

NSSocketPort Mac OS X 10.0

This subclass of NSPort provides an interface to objects that can serve as endpoints for
distributed objects connections over a network. NSSocketPort is implemented using the
BSD Sockets API, which makes it useful for raw network communications in addition
to serving as a component of the distributed objects system. A socket file descriptor
that is suitable for use with the BSD Sockets API can be obtained by sending a socket
message to an instance of this class.

While local communication is supported in socket ports, it is generally more efficient in terms of resource usage to use NSMachPort or NSMessagePort for local distributed objects connections.

@interface **NSSocketPort** : NSPort

// Initializers

- (id)**init**;
- (id)**initRemoteWithProtocolFamily**:(int)*family* **socketType**:(int)*type* **protocol**:(int)*protocol* **address**:(NSData *)*address*;
- (id)**initRemoteWithTCPPort**:(unsigned short)*port* **host**:(NSString *)*hostName*;
- (id)**initWithProtocolFamily**:(int)*family* **socketType**:(int)*type* **protocol**:(int)*protocol* **address**:(NSData *)*address*;
- (id)**initWithProtocolFamily**:(int)*family* **socketType**:(int)*type* **protocol**:(int)*protocol* **socket**:(NSSocketNativeHandle)*sock*;
- (id)**initWithTCPPort**:(unsigned short)*port*;

// Instance Methods

- (NSData *)**address**;
- (int)**protocol**;
- (int)**protocolFamily**;
- (NSSocketNativeHandle)**socket**;
- (int)**socketType**;

NSSocketPortNameServer

Mac OS X 10.0

This subclass of NSPortNameServer accepts and returns instances of NSSocketPort. NSConnection objects use port name servers to register and discover communication ports that can be used for distributed objects connections. Additional subclasses of NSPortNameServer that handle other types of ports are NSMachBootstrapServer and NSMessagePortNameServer.

Unlike the other port name server classes, NSSocketPortNameServer can operate over a network. NSSocketPortNameServer is implemented using the Foundation framework's implementation of Rendezvous found in NSNetService. Clients are able to discover socket ports by name only.

Note: this class did not function in versions of Mac OS X prior to 10.2.

@interface **NSSocketPortNameServer** : NSPortNameServer

// Accessor Methods

- (void)**setDefaultNameServerPortNumber**:(unsigned short)*portNumber*;
- (unsigned short)**defaultNameServerPortNumber**;

// Class Methods

+ (id)**sharedInstance**;

// Instance Methods

- (NSPort *)**portForName**:(NSString *)*name*;
- (NSPort *)**portForName**:(NSString *)*name* **host**:(NSString *)*host*;

- (NSPort *)**portForName:**(NSString *)*name* **host:**(NSString *)*host*
    nameServerPortNumber:(unsigned short)*portNumber*;
- (BOOL)**registerPort:**(NSPort *)*port* **name:**(NSString *)*name*;
- (BOOL)**registerPort:**(NSPort *)*port* **name:**(NSString *)*name*
    nameServerPortNumber:(unsigned short)*portNumber*;
- (BOOL)**removePortForName:**(NSString *)*name*;

NSSpecifierTest

This class represents a single Boolean expression. NSSpecifierTest is initialized with the method initWithObjectSpecifier:comparisonOperator:testObject:. This method will initialize the specifier test to compare testObject: with the object specifier by the ...ObjectSpecifier: parameter; the comparison is made using the indicated comparisonOperator:, which is a constant of type NSTestComparisonOperation.

@interface **NSSpecifierTest** : NSScriptWhoseTest
// Initializers
- (id)**initWithObjectSpecifier:**(NSScriptObjectSpecifier *)*obj1*
    comparisonOperator:(NSTestComparisonOperation)*compOp* **testObject:**(id)*obj2*;

NSSpellServer

This class is used by applications to register a custom spellchecker with the operating system. Developers can use this class to create spellchecking services for all applications that use Cocoa's spellchecking services (through the class NSSpellChecker).

@interface **NSSpellServer** : NSObject
// Accessor Methods
- (void)**setDelegate:**(id)*anObject*;
- (id)**delegate**;
// Instance Methods
- (BOOL)**isWordInUserDictionaries:**(NSString *)*word* **caseSensitive:**(BOOL)*flag*;
- (BOOL)**registerLanguage:**(NSString *)*language* **byVendor:**(NSString *)*vendor*;
- (void)**run**;
// Methods Implemented by the Delegate
- (void)**spellServer:**(NSSpellServer *)*sender* **didForgetWord:**(NSString *)*word* **inLanguage:**(NSString *)*language*;
- (void)**spellServer:**(NSSpellServer *)*sender* **didLearnWord:**(NSString *)*word* **inLanguage:**(NSString *)*language*;
- (NSRange)**spellServer:**(NSSpellServer *)*sender* **findMisspelledWordInString:**(NSString *)*stringToCheck*
    language:(NSString *)*language* **wordCount:**(int *)*wordCount* **countOnly:**(BOOL)*countOnly*;
- (NSArray *)**spellServer:**(NSSpellServer *)*sender* **suggestGuessesForWord:**(NSString *)*word*
    inLanguage:(NSString *)*language*;

Foundation
Classes

NSString Mac OS X 10.0

This is Foundation's primary class for representing and manipulating strings. At their core, instances of NSString are an immutable array of Unicode characters. With built-in, low-level support of Unicode, Cocoa applications can represent nearly every written language in existence, past and present. NSString is toll-free bridged with the Core Foundation type CFString. As such, NSString objects can be used interchangeably with the CFString pointer type, CFStringRef.

```
@interface NSString : NSObject <NSCoding, NSCopying, NSMutableCopying>
// Convenience Constructors
+ (id)string;
+ (id)stringWithCString:(const char *)bytes;
+ (id)stringWithCString:(const char *)bytes length:(unsigned)length;
+ (id)stringWithCharacters:(const unichar *)characters length:(unsigned)length;
+ (id)stringWithContentsOfFile:(NSString *)path;
+ (id)stringWithContentsOfURL:(NSURL *)url;
+ (id)stringWithFormat:(NSString *)format, ...;
+ (id)stringWithString:(NSString *)string;
+ (id)stringWithUTF8String:(const char *)bytes;
// Initializers
- (id)init;
- (id)initWithCString:(const char *)bytes;
- (id)initWithCString:(const char *)bytes length:(unsigned)length;
- (id)initWithCStringNoCopy:(char *)bytes length:(unsigned)length freeWhenDone:(BOOL)freeBuffer;
- (id)initWithCharacters:(const unichar *)characters length:(unsigned)length;
- (id)initWithCharactersNoCopy:(unichar *)characters length:(unsigned)length freeWhenDone:(BOOL)freeBuffer;
- (id)initWithContentsOfFile:(NSString *)path;
- (id)initWithContentsOfURL:(NSURL *)url;
- (id)initWithData:(NSData *)data encoding:(NSStringEncoding)encoding;
- (id)initWithFormat:(NSString *)format arguments:(va_list)argList;
- (id)initWithFormat:(NSString *)format locale:(NSDictionary *)dict arguments:(va_list)argList;
- (id)initWithFormat:(NSString *)format locale:(NSDictionary *)dict, ...;
- (id)initWithFormat:(NSString *)format, ...;
- (id)initWithString:(NSString *)aString;
- (id)initWithUTF8String:(const char *)bytes;
// Class Methods
+ (const NSStringEncoding *)availableStringEncodings;
+ (NSStringEncoding)defaultCStringEncoding;
+ (NSString *)localizedNameOfStringEncoding:(NSStringEncoding)encoding;
+ (id)localizedStringWithFormat:(NSString *)format, ...;
+ (NSString *)pathWithComponents:(NSArray *)components;
// Instance Methods
- (const char *)UTF8String;
```

- (const char *)**cString**;
- (unsigned)**cStringLength**;
- (BOOL)**canBeConvertedToEncoding**:(NSStringEncoding)*encoding*;
- (NSString *)**capitalizedString**;
- (NSComparisonResult)**caseInsensitiveCompare**:(NSString *)*string*;
- (unichar)**characterAtIndex**:(unsigned)*index*;
- (NSString *)**commonPrefixWithString**:(NSString *)*aString* **options**:(unsigned)*mask*;
- (NSComparisonResult)**compare**:(NSString *)*string*;
- (NSComparisonResult)**compare**:(NSString *)*string* **options**:(unsigned)*mask*;
- (NSComparisonResult)**compare**:(NSString *)*string* **options**:(unsigned)*mask* **range**:(NSRange)*compareRange*;
- (NSComparisonResult)**compare**:(NSString *)*string* **options**:(unsigned)*mask* **range**:(NSRange)*compareRange*
     locale:(NSDictionary *)*dict*;
- (unsigned)**completePathIntoString**:(NSString **)*outputName* **caseSensitive**:(BOOL)*flag*
     matchesIntoArray:(NSArray **)*outputArray* **filterTypes**:(NSArray *)*filterTypes*;
- (NSArray *)**componentsSeparatedByString**:(NSString *)*separator*;
- (NSData *)**dataUsingEncoding**:(NSStringEncoding)*encoding*;
- (NSData *)**dataUsingEncoding**:(NSStringEncoding)*encoding* **allowLossyConversion**:(BOOL)*lossy*;
- (NSString *)**decomposedStringWithCanonicalMapping**;
- (NSString *)**decomposedStringWithCompatibilityMapping**;
- (NSString *)**description**;
- (double)**doubleValue**;
- (NSStringEncoding)**fastestEncoding**;
- (const char *)**fileSystemRepresentation**;
- (float)**floatValue**;
- (void)**getCString**:(char *)*bytes*;
- (void)**getCString**:(char *)*bytes* **maxLength**:(unsigned)*maxLength*;
- (void)**getCString**:(char *)*bytes* **maxLength**:(unsigned)*maxLength* **range**:(NSRange)*aRange*
     remainingRange:(NSRangePointer)*leftoverRange*;
- (void)**getCharacters**:(unichar *)*buffer*;
- (void)**getCharacters**:(unichar *)*buffer* **range**:(NSRange)*aRange*;
- (BOOL)**getFileSystemRepresentation**:(char *)*cname* **maxLength**:(unsigned)*max*;
- (void)**getLineStart**:(unsigned *)*startPtr* **end**:(unsigned *)*lineEndPtr* **contentsEnd**:(unsigned *)*contentsEndPtr*
     forRange:(NSRange)*range*;
- (BOOL)**hasPrefix**:(NSString *)*aString*;
- (BOOL)**hasSuffix**:(NSString *)*aString*;
- (unsigned)**hash**;
- (int)**intValue**;
- (BOOL)**isAbsolutePath**;
- (BOOL)**isEqualToString**:(NSString *)*aString*;
- (NSString *)**lastPathComponent**;
- (unsigned int)**length**;
- (NSRange)**lineRangeForRange**:(NSRange)*range*;
- (NSComparisonResult)**localizedCaseInsensitiveCompare**:(NSString *)*string*;
- (NSComparisonResult)**localizedCompare**:(NSString *)*string*;
- (const char *)**lossyCString**;
- (NSString *)**lowercaseString**;
- (NSArray *)**pathComponents**;
- (NSString *)**pathExtension**;
- (NSString *)**precomposedStringWithCanonicalMapping**;
- (NSString *)**precomposedStringWithCompatibilityMapping**;
- (id)**propertyList**;

- (NSDictionary *)**propertyListFromStringsFileFormat**;
- (NSRange)**rangeOfCharacterFromSet**:(NSCharacterSet *)*aSet*;
- (NSRange)**rangeOfCharacterFromSet**:(NSCharacterSet *)*aSet* **options**:(unsigned int)*mask*;
- (NSRange)**rangeOfCharacterFromSet**:(NSCharacterSet *)*aSet*
    options:(unsigned int)*mask* **range**:(NSRange)*searchRange*;
- (NSRange)**rangeOfComposedCharacterSequenceAtIndex**:(unsigned)*index*;
- (NSRange)**rangeOfString**:(NSString *)*aString*;
- (NSRange)**rangeOfString**:(NSString *)*aString* **options**:(unsigned)*mask*;
- (NSRange)**rangeOfString**:(NSString *)*aString* **options**:(unsigned)*mask* **range**:(NSRange)*searchRange*;
- (NSStringEncoding)**smallestEncoding**;
- (NSString *)**stringByAbbreviatingWithTildeInPath**;
- (NSString *)**stringByAppendingFormat**:(NSString *)*format, ...*;
- (NSString *)**stringByAppendingPathComponent**:(NSString *)*str*;
- (NSString *)**stringByAppendingPathExtension**:(NSString *)*str*;
- (NSString *)**stringByAppendingString**:(NSString *)*aString*;
- (NSString *)**stringByDeletingLastPathComponent**;
- (NSString *)**stringByDeletingPathExtension**;
- (NSString *)**stringByExpandingTildeInPath**;
- (NSString *)**stringByPaddingToLength**:(unsigned)*newLength* **withString**:(NSString *)*padString*
    startingAtIndex:(unsigned)*padIndex*;
- (NSString *)**stringByResolvingSymlinksInPath**;
- (NSString *)**stringByStandardizingPath**;
- (NSString *)**stringByTrimmingCharactersInSet**:(NSCharacterSet *)*set*;
- (NSArray *)**stringsByAppendingPaths**:(NSArray *)*paths*;
- (NSString *)**substringFromIndex**:(unsigned)*from*;
- (NSString *)**substringToIndex**:(unsigned)*to*;
- (NSString *)**substringWithRange**:(NSRange)*range*;
- (NSString *)**uppercaseString**;
- (BOOL)**writeToFile**:(NSString *)*path* **atomically**:(BOOL)*useAuxiliaryFile*;
- (BOOL)**writeToURL**:(NSURL *)*url* **atomically**:(BOOL)*atomically*;
// *Methods Implementing NSCoding*
- (void)**encodeWithCoder**:(NSCoder *)*aCoder*;
- (id)**initWithCoder**:(NSCoder *)*aDecoder*;
// *Methods Implementing NSCopying*
- (id)**copyWithZone**:(NSZone *)*zone*;
// *Methods Implementing NSMutableCopying*
- (id)**mutableCopyWithZone**:(NSZone *)*zone*;

Subclasses

NSMutableString, NSSimpleCString

NSTask

Mac OS X 10.0

This class provides an interface for an application to execute other programs as subprocesses. To create an NSTask, use alloc and init. Before a task can be executed, it must be prepared. By default a task inherits the environment of its parent process, which includes attributes such as the current working directory. To specify what program the task should execute, set the launch path of the program in the task using the method setLaunchPath:. Arguments for the executable are provided in an NSArray through the method setArguments:. If you need to pass data to a task and receive data in return, connect an NSPipe or NSFileHandle object to the executable's standard input, output, or error using setStandardInput:, setStandardOutput:, and setStandardError:, respectively.

To execute a task, invoke the method launch. NSTask also provides methods for controlling the execution of a task through the methods interrupt, suspend, terminate, and resume.

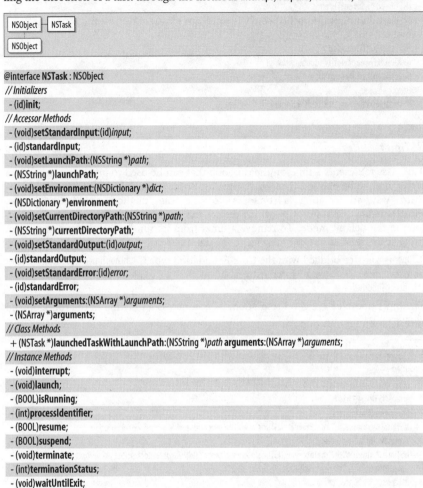

```
@interface NSTask : NSObject
// Initializers
- (id)init;
// Accessor Methods
- (void)setStandardInput:(id)input;
- (id)standardInput;
- (void)setLaunchPath:(NSString *)path;
- (NSString *)launchPath;
- (void)setEnvironment:(NSDictionary *)dict;
- (NSDictionary *)environment;
- (void)setCurrentDirectoryPath:(NSString *)path;
- (NSString *)currentDirectoryPath;
- (void)setStandardOutput:(id)output;
- (id)standardOutput;
- (void)setStandardError:(id)error;
- (id)standardError;
- (void)setArguments:(NSArray *)arguments;
- (NSArray *)arguments;
// Class Methods
+ (NSTask *)launchedTaskWithLaunchPath:(NSString *)path arguments:(NSArray *)arguments;
// Instance Methods
- (void)interrupt;
- (void)launch;
- (BOOL)isRunning;
- (int)processIdentifier;
- (BOOL)resume;
- (BOOL)suspend;
- (void)terminate;
- (int)terminationStatus;
- (void)waitUntilExit;
```

NSThread   Mac OS X 10.0

NSThread provides functionality to run processes as separate threads of execution. NSThread takes a method selector that will be run in its own thread. Threads share the memory space of their parent processes, unlike processes executed by NSTask instances.

```
@interface NSThread : NSObject
// Convenience Constructors
+ (double)threadPriority;
// Class Methods
+ (NSThread *)currentThread;
+ (void)detachNewThreadSelector:(SEL)selector toTarget:(id)target withObject:(id)argument;
+ (void)exit;
+ (BOOL)isMultiThreaded;
+ (BOOL)setThreadPriority:(double)priority;
+ (void)sleepUntilDate:(NSDate *)date;
// Instance Methods
- (NSMutableDictionary *)threadDictionary;
```

NSTimer

This class represents a timer in the run-loop that can be used to invoke a method in a target after some elapsed time, or at regularly spaced intervals. The most straightforward way of creating a time is to use the method scheduledTimerWithTimeInterval:target:selector:userInfo:repeats:, which creates the timer and add it to the current runloop in the default mode. To remove a timer from its run-loop and stopping it from firing again, send an invalidate message to the timer object.

NSTimer is toll-free bridged with the Core Foundation type CFRunLoopTimer. As such, NSTimer objects can be used interchangeably with the CFRunLoopTimer pointer type, CFRunLoopTimerRef.

The timer doesn't have good resolution; its accuracy is a function of the run-loop and what's on it.

```
@interface NSTimer : NSObject
// Convenience Constructors
+ (NSTimer *)timerWithTimeInterval:(NSTimeInterval)ti invocation:(NSInvocation *)invocation
    repeats:(BOOL)yesOrNo;
+ (NSTimer *)timerWithTimeInterval:(NSTimeInterval)ti target:(id)aTarget selector:(SEL)aSelector
    userInfo:(id)userInfo repeats:(BOOL)yesOrNo;
// Initializers
- (id)initWithFireDate:(NSDate *)date interval:(NSTimeInterval)ti target:(id)t selector:(SEL)s
    userInfo:(id)ui repeats:(BOOL)rep;
// Accessor Methods
- (void)setFireDate:(NSDate *)date;
- (NSDate *)fireDate;
// Class Methods
+ (NSTimer *)scheduledTimerWithTimeInterval:(NSTimeInterval)ti invocation:(NSInvocation *)invocation
    repeats:(BOOL)yesOrNo;
+ (NSTimer *)scheduledTimerWithTimeInterval:(NSTimeInterval)ti target:(id)aTarget selector:(SEL)aSelector
    userInfo:(id)userInfo repeats:(BOOL)yesOrNo;
// Instance Methods
- (void)fire;
```

- (NSTimeInterval)**timeInterval**;
- (void)**invalidate**;
- (BOOL)**isValid**;
- (id)**userInfo**;

NSTimeZone

This class represents a time zone—objects that store information about a geographic time zone, such as the name, abbreviation, time from GMT, whether or not daylight savings is in effect, and so on.

NSTimeZone is toll-free bridged with the Core Foundation type CFTimeZone. As such, NSTime-Zone objects can be used interchangeably with the CFTimeZone pointer type, CFTimeZoneRef.

@interface **NSTimeZone** : NSObject <NSCoding, NSCopying>
// Initializers
- (id)**initWithName**:(NSString *)*tzName*;
- (id)**initWithName**:(NSString *)*tzName* **data**:(NSData *)*aData*;
// Class Methods
+ (NSDictionary *)**abbreviationDictionary**;
+ (NSTimeZone *)**defaultTimeZone**;
+ (NSArray *)**knownTimeZoneNames**;
+ (NSTimeZone *)**localTimeZone**;
+ (void)**resetSystemTimeZone**;
+ (void)**setDefaultTimeZone**:(NSTimeZone *)*aTimeZone*;
+ (NSTimeZone *)**systemTimeZone**;
+ (id)**timeZoneForSecondsFromGMT**:(int)*seconds*;
+ (id)**timeZoneWithAbbreviation**:(NSString *)*abbreviation*;
+ (id)**timeZoneWithName**:(NSString *)*tzName*;
+ (id)**timeZoneWithName**:(NSString *)*tzName* **data**:(NSData *)*aData*;
// Instance Methods
- (NSString *)**abbreviation**;
- (NSString *)**abbreviationForDate**:(NSDate *)*aDate*;
- (NSData *)**data**;
- (NSString *)**description**;
- (BOOL)**isDaylightSavingTime**;
- (BOOL)**isDaylightSavingTimeForDate**:(NSDate *)*aDate*;
- (BOOL)**isEqualToTimeZone**:(NSTimeZone *)*aTimeZone*;
- (NSString *)**name**;
- (int)**secondsFromGMT**;
- (int)**secondsFromGMTForDate**:(NSDate *)*aDate*;
// Methods Implementing NSCoding
- (void)**encodeWithCoder**:(NSCoder *)*aCoder*;
- (id)**initWithCoder**:(NSCoder *)*aDecoder*;
// Methods Implementing NSCopying
- (id)**copyWithZone**:(NSZone *)*zone*;

NSUnarchiver

This concrete subclass of NSCoder is used to convert archived data (such as the data produced by NSArchiver) into an object tree, which is restored to the state it was in prior to archiving.

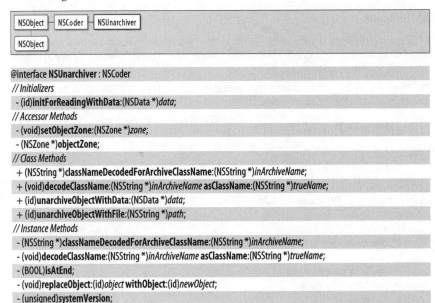

@interface **NSUnarchiver** : NSCoder

// Initializers

- (id)**initForReadingWithData**:(NSData *)*data*;

// Accessor Methods

- (void)**setObjectZone**:(NSZone *)*zone*;

- (NSZone *)**objectZone**;

// Class Methods

+ (NSString *)**classNameDecodedForArchiveClassName**:(NSString *)*inArchiveName*;

+ (void)**decodeClassName**:(NSString *)*inArchiveName* **asClassName**:(NSString *)*trueName*;

+ (id)**unarchiveObjectWithData**:(NSData *)*data*;

+ (id)**unarchiveObjectWithFile**:(NSString *)*path*;

// Instance Methods

- (NSString *)**classNameDecodedForArchiveClassName**:(NSString *)*inArchiveName*;

- (void)**decodeClassName**:(NSString *)*inArchiveName* **asClassName**:(NSString *)*trueName*;

- (BOOL)**isAtEnd**;

- (void)**replaceObject**:(id)*object* **withObject**:(id)*newObject*;

- (unsigned)**systemVersion**;

NSUndoManager

This class provides the basis of Cocoa's undo and redo system. NSUndoManager supports two kinds of undo: simple undo and invocation-based undo. In *simple undo* clients register in the undo manager a target and selector that is used to undo the last operation. In *invocation based* undo the client creates an NSInvocation object that can undo the last operation and record that in the undo manager. In either case, it is the responsibility of the client to specify how the an operation is undone; NSUndoManager simply provides the machinery for keeping track of and executing the supplied selectors or invocations.

@interface **NSUndoManager** : NSObject

// Accessor Methods

- (void)**setActionName**:(NSString *)*actionName*;

- (void)**setGroupsByEvent**:(BOOL)*groupsByEvent*;

- (BOOL)**groupsByEvent**;

- (void)**setRunLoopModes**:(NSArray *)*runLoopModes*;

- (NSArray *)**runLoopModes**;

- (void)**setLevelsOfUndo**:(unsigned)*levels*;

```
- (unsigned)levelsOfUndo;
// Instance Methods
- (void)beginUndoGrouping;
- (BOOL)canRedo;
- (BOOL)canUndo;
- (void)disableUndoRegistration;
- (void)enableUndoRegistration;
- (void)endUndoGrouping;
- (void)forwardInvocation:(NSInvocation *)anInvocation;
- (int)groupingLevel;
- (BOOL)isRedoing;
- (BOOL)isUndoRegistrationEnabled;
- (BOOL)isUndoing;
- (id)prepareWithInvocationTarget:(id)target;
- (void)redo;
- (NSString *)redoActionName;
- (NSString *)redoMenuItemTitle;
- (NSString *)redoMenuTitleForUndoActionName:(NSString *)actionName;
- (void)registerUndoWithTarget:(id)target selector:(SEL)selector object:(id)anObject;
- (void)removeAllActions;
- (void)removeAllActionsWithTarget:(id)target;
- (void)undo;
- (NSString *)undoActionName;
- (NSString *)undoMenuItemTitle;
- (NSString *)undoMenuTitleForUndoActionName:(NSString *)actionName;
- (void)undoNestedGroup;
```

NSUniqueIDSpecifier

Mac OS X 10.2

This class represents the scripting language reference form used to specify an object in a collection based on a unique ID.

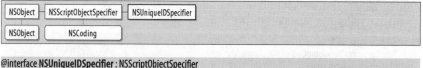

```
@interface NSUniqueIDSpecifier : NSScriptObjectSpecifier
// Initializers
- (id)initWithContainerClassDescription:(NSScriptClassDescription *)classDesc
    containerSpecifier:(NSScriptObjectSpecifier *)container key:(NSString *)property uniqueID:(id)uniqueID;
// Accessor Methods
- (void)setUniqueID:(id)uniqueID;
- (id)uniqueID;
```

NSURL

Mac OS X 10.0

NSURL is a class that represents a URL—the human-readable host names and paths that various networking clients use to locate both remote resources over a network, or resources on the local filesystem. Core Foundation has a type, CFURL, that is toll-free bridged to NSURL, and as such the two types can be used interchangeably.

@interface **NSURL** : NSObject

// Accessor Methods

- (BOOL)**setResourceData**:(NSData *)*data*;

- (BOOL)**setProperty**:(id)*property* **forKey**:(NSString *)*propertyKey*;

// Class Methods

+ (NSURL *)**URLFromPasteboard**:(NSPasteboard *)*pasteBoard*;

+ (id)**URLWithString**:(NSString *)*URLString*;

+ (id)**URLWithString**:(NSString *)*URLString* **relativeToURL**:(NSURL *)*baseURL*;

+ (id)**fileURLWithPath**:(NSString *)*path*;

// Instance Methods

- (NSURLHandle *)**URLHandleUsingCache**:(BOOL)*shouldUseCache*;

- (id) **initWithString**:(NSString *)*URLString*;

- (id) **initWithString**:(NSString *)*URLString* **relativeToURL**:(NSURL *)*baseURL*;

- (NSString *)**absoluteString**;

- (NSURL *)**absoluteURL**;

- (NSURL *)**baseURL**;

- (NSString *)**fragment**;

- (NSString *)**host**;

- (BOOL)**isFileURL**;

- (void)**loadResourceDataNotifyingClient**:(id)*client* **usingCache**:(BOOL)*shouldUseCache*;

- (NSString *)**parameterString**;

- (NSString *)**password**;

- (id) **initFileURLWithPath**:(NSString *)*path*;

- (NSString *)**path**;

- (NSNumber *)**port**;

- (id)**propertyForKey**:(NSString *)*propertyKey*;

- (NSString *)**query**;

- (NSString *)**relativePath**;

- (NSString *)**relativeString**;

- (NSData *)**resourceDataUsingCache**:(BOOL)*shouldUseCache*;

- (NSString *)**resourceSpecifier**;

- (NSString *)**scheme**;

- (id) **initWithScheme**:(NSString *)*scheme* **host**:(NSString *)*host* **path**:(NSString *)*path*;

- (NSURL *)**standardizedURL**;

- (NSString *)**user**;

- (void)**writeToPasteboard**:(NSPasteboard *)*pasteBoard*;

NSURLHandle

Mac OS X 10.0

NSURLHandle provides an interface for uploading and downloading data to and from a resource specified by an NSURL. NSURLHandle actually offloads much of this work to subclasses that implement NSURLHandle's interface to work with various schemes.

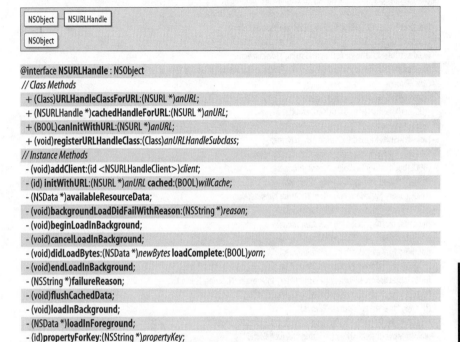

```
@interface NSURLHandle : NSObject
// Class Methods
  + (Class)URLHandleClassForURL:(NSURL *)anURL;
  + (NSURLHandle *)cachedHandleForURL:(NSURL *)anURL;
  + (BOOL)canInitWithURL:(NSURL *)anURL;
  + (void)registerURLHandleClass:(Class)anURLHandleSubclass;
// Instance Methods
  - (void)addClient:(id <NSURLHandleClient>)client;
  - (id) initWithURL:(NSURL *)anURL cached:(BOOL)willCache;
  - (NSData *)availableResourceData;
  - (void)backgroundLoadDidFailWithReason:(NSString *)reason;
  - (void)beginLoadInBackground;
  - (void)cancelLoadInBackground;
  - (void)didLoadBytes:(NSData *)newBytes loadComplete:(BOOL)yorn;
  - (void)endLoadInBackground;
  - (NSString *)failureReason;
  - (void)flushCachedData;
  - (void)loadInBackground;
  - (NSData *)loadInForeground;
  - (id)propertyForKey:(NSString *)propertyKey;
  - (id)propertyForKeyIfAvailable:(NSString *)propertyKey;
  - (void)removeClient:(id <NSURLHandleClient>)client;
  - (NSData *)resourceData;
  - (NSURLHandleStatus)status;
  - (BOOL)writeData:(NSData *)data;
  - (BOOL)writeProperty:(id)propertyValue forKey:(NSString *)propertyKey;
```

NSUserDefaults

Mac OS X 10.0

This class is the entry-point into Mac OS X's user defaults database, which is how user preferences are stored and managed for applications. Instances of this class are created using the class method standardUserDefaults. This class provides methods for storing and accessing arrays, dictionaries, strings, objects, numbers, and data in an application's user defaults database.

```
NSObject — NSUserDefaults
NSObject
```

```
@interface NSUserDefaults : NSObject
// Initializers
  - (id)init;
  - (id)initWithUser:(NSString *)username;
// Accessor Methods
  - (void)setInteger:(int)value forKey:(NSString *)defaultName;
  - (void)setVolatileDomain:(NSDictionary *)domain forName:(NSString *)domainName;
  - (void)setBool:(BOOL)value forKey:(NSString *)defaultName;
  - (void)setFloat:(float)value forKey:(NSString *)defaultName;
  - (void)setObject:(id)value forKey:(NSString *)defaultName;
  - (void)setPersistentDomain:(NSDictionary *)domain forName:(NSString *)domainName;
// Class Methods
  + (void)resetStandardUserDefaults;
  + (NSUserDefaults *)standardUserDefaults;
// Instance Methods
  - (void)addSuiteNamed:(NSString *)suiteName;
  - (NSArray *)arrayForKey:(NSString *)defaultName;
  - (BOOL)boolForKey:(NSString *)defaultName;
  - (NSData *)dataForKey:(NSString *)defaultName;
  - (NSDictionary *)dictionaryForKey:(NSString *)defaultName;
  - (NSDictionary *)dictionaryRepresentation;
  - (float)floatForKey:(NSString *)defaultName;
  - (int)integerForKey:(NSString *)defaultName;
  - (id)objectForKey:(NSString *)defaultName;
  - (BOOL)objectIsForcedForKey:(NSString *)key;
  - (BOOL)objectIsForcedForKey:(NSString *)key inDomain:(NSString *)domain;
  - (NSDictionary *)persistentDomainForName:(NSString *)domainName;
  - (NSArray *)persistentDomainNames;
  - (void)registerDefaults:(NSDictionary *)registrationDictionary;
  - (void)removeObjectForKey:(NSString *)defaultName;
  - (void)removePersistentDomainForName:(NSString *)domainName;
  - (void)removeSuiteNamed:(NSString *)suiteName;
  - (void)removeVolatileDomainForName:(NSString *)domainName;
  - (NSArray *)stringArrayForKey:(NSString *)defaultName;
  - (NSString *)stringForKey:(NSString *)defaultName;
  - (BOOL)synchronize;
  - (NSDictionary *)volatileDomainForName:(NSString *)domainName;
  - (NSArray *)volatileDomainNames;
```

NSValue

Mac OS X 10.0

This class provides an object-oriented interface to C and Objective-C scalar data items, such as numeric primitives, and C structures. Providing an object-oriented wrapper for these non-object types makes it possible for clients to store these types in any of the Foundation collection classes.

```
@interface NSValue : NSObject <NSCoding, NSCopying>
// Convenience Constructors
  + (NSValue *)value:(const void *)value withObjCType:(const char *)type;
  + (NSValue *)valueWithBytes:(const void *)value objCType:(const char *)type;
  + (NSValue *)valueWithNonretainedObject:(id)anObject;
  + (NSValue *)valueWithPoint:(NSPoint)point;
  + (NSValue *)valueWithPointer:(const void *)pointer;
  + (NSValue *)valueWithRange:(NSRange)range;
  + (NSValue *)valueWithRect:(NSRect)rect;
  + (NSValue *)valueWithSize:(NSSize)size;
// Initializers
  - (id)initWithBytes:(const void *)value objCType:(const char *)type;
// Instance Methods
  - (void)getValue:(void *)value;
  - (BOOL)isEqualToValue:(NSValue *)value;
  - (id)nonretainedObjectValue;
  - (const char *)objCType;
  - (NSPoint)pointValue;
  - (void *)pointerValue;
  - (NSRange)rangeValue;
  - (NSRect)rectValue;
  - (NSSize)sizeValue;
// Methods Implementing NSCoding
  - (void)encodeWithCoder:(NSCoder *)aCoder;
  - (id)initWithCoder:(NSCoder *)aDecoder;
// Methods Implementing NSCopying
  - (id)copyWithZone:(NSZone *)zone;
```

Subclasses

NSNumber

NSWhoseSpecifier

This class represents the scripting language reference form used to specify a selection of objects within a collection that matches some provided boolean condition. NSWhoseSpecifier works in conjunction with a test object that represents the matching condition. This test object is an instance of a subclass of NSScriptWhoseTest.

```
┌─────────┐   ┌──────────────────────┐   ┌──────────────────┐
│NSObject ├───┤NSScriptObjectSpecifier├───┤NSWhoseSpecifier  │
└─────────┘   └──────────────────────┘   └──────────────────┘
┌─────────┐   ┌──────────────────────┐
│NSObject │   │      NSCoding        │
└─────────┘   └──────────────────────┘
```

```
@interface NSWhoseSpecifier : NSScriptObjectSpecifier
// Initializers
  - (id)initWithContainerClassDescription:(NSScriptClassDescription *)classDesc
       containerSpecifier:(NSScriptObjectSpecifier *)container key:(NSString *)property test:(NSScriptWhoseTest *)test;
// Accessor Methods
  - (void)setStartSubelementIndex:(int)index;
  - (int)startSubelementIndex;
  - (void)setEndSubelementIndex:(int)index;
  - (int)endSubelementIndex;
```

- (void)**setEndSubelementIdentifier**:(NSWhoseSubelementIdentifier)*subelement*;
- (NSWhoseSubelementIdentifier)**endSubelementIdentifier**;
- (void)**setStartSubelementIdentifier**:(NSWhoseSubelementIdentifier)*subelement*;
- (NSWhoseSubelementIdentifier)**startSubelementIdentifier**;
- (void)**setTest**:(NSScriptWhoseTest *)*test*;
- (NSScglobal variables;iptWhoseTest *)**test**;

14

Foundation Protocols

This chapter covers the protocols of the Foundation framework. The Foundation framework provides a basic set of classes used in data management, application coordination, networking and interapplication communication, as well as interacting with core operating system services. Chapter 2 discussed many Foundation classes in depth; Chapter 6 discussed several of the Foundation classes related to networking.

NSCoding Mac OS X 10.0

This protocol declares an interface is adopted by classes to provide for archiving and unarchiving of instances of the class. The NSCoding protocol defines the two methods initWithCode: and encodeWithCode:. These two methods are the foundation of archiving and distribution in the Foundation framework. Each of these two methods passes an NSCoder object, which is used to perform archiving and unarchiving. The NSCoder class provides the tools to encode and decode objects and C and Objective-C data types. See the NSCoder class description and Chapter 2 for more information.

```
@protocol NSCoding
// Instance Methods
  - (void)encodeWithCoder:(NSCoder *)aCoder;
  - (id)initWithCoder:(NSCoder *)aDecoder;
@end
```

NSComparisonMethods Mac OS X 10.0

This informal protocol declares several methods that are used to perform common comparisons between two objects. In Cocoa's scripting system, comparisons are represented by instances of NSSpecifierTest, which relies on objects implementing either methods from this protocol, or the NSScriptingComparisonMethods protocol.

```
@interface NSObject (NSComparisonMethods)
// Instance Methods
  - (BOOL)isEqualTo:(id)object;
  - (BOOL)isLessThanOrEqualTo:(id)object;
  - (BOOL)isLessThan:(id)object;
  - (BOOL)isGreaterThanOrEqualTo:(id)object;
  - (BOOL)isGreaterThan:(id)object;
  - (BOOL)isNotEqualTo:(id)object;
  - (BOOL)doesContain:(id)object;
  - (BOOL)isLike:(NSString *)object;
  - (BOOL)isCaseInsensitiveLike:(NSString *)object;
@end
```

NSCopying   Mac OS X 10.0

This protocol declares a single method for classes to implement: copyWithZone:. Classes should implement this method to create and return a fully functioning object that is a copy of the receiver. The zone parameter indicates what memory zone the new object should be allocated in; if this parameter is nil, then the instance is allocated in the default zone. Clients generally make copies of objects using NSObject's copy method, which is a convenience method for invoking copyWithZone: with nil as the zone.

```
@protocol NSCopying
// Instance Methods
  - (id)copyWithZone:(NSZone *)zone;
@end
```

NSDecimalNumberBehaviors   Mac OS X 10.0

This protocol defines the interface to objects that control aspects of the behavior of NSDecimalNumber objects. In particular, there are three methods that classes implement to specify rounding behavior, number precision, and a means for handling calculation errors. The Foundation framework implements this protocol in the class NSDecimalNumberHandler.

```
@protocol NSDecimalNumberBehaviors
// Instance Methods
  - (NSRoundingMode)roundingMode;
  - (short)scale;
  - (NSDecimalNumber *)exceptionDuringOperation:(SEL)operation error:(NSCalculationError)error
        leftOperand:(NSDecimalNumber *)leftOperand rightOperand:(NSDecimalNumber *)rightOperand;
@end
```

NSKeyValueCoding   Mac OS X 10.0

This informal protocol provides a way for clients to access a class's instance variables (or other properties) without having to explicitly rely on accessor methods. NSKeyValueCoding provides indirect access to an object's instance variables through the use of strings or keys. The two most commonly used methods in the protocol are takeValue:forKey: and valueForKey:, which are used to set and get the value of an instance variable, respectively.

This protocol, and the associated NSScriptKeyValueCoding protocol, both form the basis of scripting in Cocoa. Chapter 2 goes into more detail about this protocol.

```
@interface NSObject (NSKeyValueCoding)
// Class Methods
+ (BOOL)accessInstanceVariablesDirectly;
+ (BOOL)useStoredAccessor;
// Instance Methods
- (id)valueForKey:(NSString *)key;
- (void)takeValue:(id)value forKey:(NSString *)key;
- (id)storedValueForKey:(NSString *)key;
- (void)takeStoredValue:(id)value forKey:(NSString *)key;
- (id)valueForKeyPath:(NSString *)key;
- (void)takeValue:(id)value forKeyPath:(NSString *)key;
- (NSDictionary *)valuesForKeys:(NSArray *)keys;
- (void)takeValuesFromDictionary:(NSDictionary *)dictionary;
- (id)handleQueryWithUnboundKey:(NSString *)key;
- (void)handleTakeValue:(id)value forUnboundKey:(NSString *)key;
- (void)unableToSetNilForKey:(NSString *)key;
@end
```

NSLocking

This protocol is adopted by a class that implements lock objects. Locks are used in multithreaded applications to coordinate access to shared, thread-sensitive storage, or to control execution of critical portions of code (which usually deal with these same kinds of resources) that two or more threads may attempt to access simultaneously. The protocol declares two methods: lock and unlock. The lock message is used by clients to acquire a lock before executing critical sections of code, and the unlock method is used to relinquish a previously acquired lock.

The Foundation framework defines three classes that adopt the NSLocking protocol: NSLock, NSConditionLock, and NSRecursiveLock. See the class descriptions for these three classes, and Chapter 2 for more information.

```
@protocol NSLocking
// Instance Methods
- (void)lock;
- (void)unlock;
@end
```

NSMutableCopying

This protocol declares the single method mutableCopyWithZone:, which is implemented by classes that wish to allow clients to make mutable copies of themselves. This protocol should be adopted only by classes that have both mutable and immutable variants (for example, NSString and NSMutableString). Clients create mutable copies of objects through NSObject's mutableCopy convenience method, which invokes mutableCopyWithZone: with the default zone.

```
@protocol NSMutableCopying
// Instance Methods
 - (id)mutableCopyWithZone:(NSZone *)zone;
@end
```

NSObjCTypeSerializationCallBack

Mac OS X 10.0

This protocol is adopted by classes that wish to intervene in serialization and deserialization operations. It is obsolete and has been deprecated.

```
@protocol NSObjCTypeSerializationCallBack
// Instance Methods
 - (void)serializeObjectAt:(id *)object ofObjCType:(const char *)type intoData:(NSMutableData *)data;
 - (void)deserializeObjectAt:(id *)object ofObjCType:(const char *)type fromData:(NSData *)data
     atCursor:(unsigned *)cursor;
@end
```

NSObject

Mac OS X 10.0

This protocol defines the interface for so-called *first-class objects*. Objects that conform to the NSObject protocol are able to provide a great deal of information about themselves to other objects, such as their classnames, superclass names, and the protocols that they conform to. Additionally, this protocol declares methods that clients use to determine whether an object can respond to an arbitrary message. Finally, the NSObject protocol declares methods that allow objects to participate in Cocoa's memory management system. In the Foundation framework, the two root classes NSObject and NSProxy conform to this protocol.

```
@protocol NSObject
// Instance Methods
 - (BOOL)isEqual:(id)object;
 - (unsigned)hash;
 - (Class)superclass;
 - (Class)class;
 - (id)self;
 - (NSZone *)zone;
 - (id)performSelector:(SEL)aSelector;
 - (id)performSelector:(SEL)aSelector withObject:(id)object;
 - (id)performSelector:(SEL)aSelector withObject:(id)object1 withObject:(id)object2;
 - (BOOL)isProxy;
 - (BOOL)isKindOfClass:(Class)aClass;
 - (BOOL)isMemberOfClass:(Class)aClass;
 - (BOOL)conformsToProtocol:(Protocol *)aProtocol;
 - (BOOL)respondsToSelector:(SEL)aSelector;
 - (id)retain;
 - (oneway void)release;
 - (id)autorelease;
 - (unsigned)retainCount;
 - (NSString *)description;
@end
```

NSScriptingComparisonMethods Mac OS X 10.0

This informal protocol declares methods that are appropriate for use in comparing scriptable objects. Many Cocoa classes provide default implementations of these methods as part of the built-in support for scripting. This is especially true for the Foundation classes such as NSString, NSNumber, and NSDate that represent basic data types in a scripting environment. When a specifier test object evaluates a Boolean expression, it tries to invoke methods of this protocol in the relevant objects. If neither of the objects implement the necessary methods, then the scripting system will try to invoke methods from the NSComparisonMethods protocol.

```
@interface NSObject (NSScriptingComparisonMethods)
// Instance Methods
 - (BOOL)scriptingIsEqualTo:(id)object;
 - (BOOL)scriptingIsLessThanOrEqualTo:(id)object;
 - (BOOL)scriptingIsLessThan:(id)object;
 - (BOOL)scriptingIsGreaterThanOrEqualTo:(id)object;
 - (BOOL)scriptingIsGreaterThan:(id)object;
 - (BOOL)scriptingBeginsWith:(id)object;
 - (BOOL)scriptingEndsWith:(id)object;
 - (BOOL)scriptingContains:(id)object;
@end
```

NSScriptKeyValueCoding Mac OS X 10.0

This protocol defines additional key-value coding functionality beyond that of NSKeyValueCoding. The additional functionality provides support for scriptability in Cocoa.

```
@interface NSObject (NSScriptKeyValueCoding)
// Instance Methods
 - (id)valueAtIndex:(unsigned)index inPropertyWithKey:(NSString *)key;
 - (id)valueWithName:(NSString *)name inPropertyWithKey:(NSString *)key;
 - (id)valueWithUniqueID:(id)uniqueID inPropertyWithKey:(NSString *)key;
 - (void)replaceValueAtIndex:(unsigned)index inPropertyWithKey:(NSString *)key withValue:(id)value;
 - (void)insertValue:(id)value atIndex:(unsigned)index inPropertyWithKey:(NSString *)key;
 - (void)removeValueAtIndex:(unsigned)index fromPropertyWithKey:(NSString *)key;
 - (void)insertValue:(id)value inPropertyWithKey:(NSString *)key;
 - (id)coerceValue:(id)value forKey:(NSString *)key;
@end
```

Foundation
Protocols

NSScriptObjectSpecifiers Mac OS X 10.0

This informal protocol declares two methods that classes implement to support scriptability. The two methods are objectSpecifier and indicesOfObjectsBy-EvaluatingObjectSpecifier:. The objectSpecifier method, when implemented, should return an instance of NSObjectSpecifier, while the second method listed below is implemented by container objects to return an NSArray of NSNumbers indicating the indices of objects within the container that match the specifier indicated in the argument. See the class description of NSScriptObjectSpecifier in Chapter 13 for more information.

```
@interface NSObject (NSScriptObjectSpecifiers)
// Instance Methods
 - (NSScriptObjectSpecifier *)objectSpecifier;
 - (NSArray *)indicesOfObjectsByEvaluatingObjectSpecifier:(NSScriptObjectSpecifier *)specifier;
@end
```

NSURLHandleClient

This protocol defines methods that clients of NSURLHandle must implement to function as
such. See Chapter 6 for more information.

```
@protocol NSURLHandleClient
// Instance Methods
 - (void)URLHandle:(NSURLHandle *)sender resourceDataDidBecomeAvailable:(NSData *)newBytes;
 - (void)URLHandleResourceDidBeginLoading:(NSURLHandle *)sender;
 - (void)URLHandleResourceDidFinishLoading:(NSURLHandle *)sender;
 - (void)URLHandleResourceDidCancelLoading:(NSURLHandle *)sender;
 - (void)URLHandle:(NSURLHandle *)sender resourceDidFailLoadingWithReason:(NSString *)reason;
@end
```

15

Application Kit Classes

This chapter covers the classes of the Application Kit. The Application Kit implements all of the graphical user interface components of Cocoa, including the complete standard Aqua widget set. Additionally, the Application Kit provides classes for interacting with the Quartz 2D drawing system, and for managing and accessing resources such as colors, fonts, and printers. The Application Kit is discusses in Chapter 3. Chapter 4 and Chapter 5 go into more detail about aspects of the Application Kit.

NSActionCell   Mac OS X 10.0

This subclass of NSCell provides an implementation of the target/action mechanism that is the basis of interface messaging in Cocoa. This mechanism operates by sending a message, often referred to as an *action message* to a *target* object. The majority of controls in the Application Kit rely on the functionality of NSActionCell to notify clients when the control has been activated by the user.

While NSCell implements most of the methods found in NSActionCells, it does so only passively. NSActionCell reimplements many of NSCell's methods to provide an active target/action mechanism and to manage the target and action of a cell. In addition to managing these attributes of a cell, NSActionCell provides the necessary implementation to provide feedback to mouse actions, such as highlighting certain active areas of a control when the mouse hovers above them.

```
NSObject ─── NSCell ─── NSActionCell
NSObject ─── NSCoding
           NSCopying
```

@interface **NSActionCell** : NSCell
// Accessor Methods
- (void)**setFloatingPointFormat**:(BOOL)*autoRange* **left**:(unsigned int)*leftDigits* **right**:(unsigned int)*rightDigits*;

- (void)**setAlignment:**(NSTextAlignment)*mode;*
- (void)**setBordered:**(BOOL)*flag;*
- (void)**setBezeled:**(BOOL)*flag;*
- (void)**setEnabled:**(BOOL)*flag;*
- (void)**setTag:**(int)*anInt;*
- (int)**tag;**
- (void)**setImage:**(NSImage *)*image;*
- (void)**setTarget:**(id)*anObject;*
- (id)**target;**
- (void)**setAction:**(SEL)*aSelector;*
- (SEL)**action;**
- (void)**setObjectValue:**(id)*obj;*
- (void)**setFont:**(NSFont *)*fontObj;*
// Instance Methods
- (double)**doubleValue;**
- (float)**floatValue;**
- (int)**intValue;**
- (NSString *)**stringValue;**
- (NSView *)**controlView;**

Subclasses
NSButtonCell, NSFormCell, NSSliderCell, NSStepperCell, NSTextFieldCell

NSAffineTransform

Mac OS X 10.0

This class is used to perform affine transform operations on **NSBezierPath** objects, as well as on **NSSize**, and **NSPoint** structures. An *affine transform* is an operation in which one coordinate system is mapped to another whereby the parallelism of lines is maintained, but not necessarily their length or angles.

NSAffineTransform has methods for performing several types of operations: rotation, scaling, and translation. These transforms are implemented in the methods **scaleBy:**, **scaleXBy:yBy:**, **rotateByDegrees:**, **rotateByRadians:**, and **translateXBy:yBy:**. Additionally, applications may define their own transformation matrices using the method **setTransformStruct:**. To apply a transform to an object we use **transformBezierPath:**, **transformSize:**, and **transformPoint:**.

@interface **NSAffineTransform** : NSObject <NSCoding, NSCopying>
// Initializers
- (id)**initWithTransform:**(NSAffineTransform *)*transform;*
// Accessor Methods
- (void)**setTransformStruct:**(NSAffineTransformStruct)*transformStruct;*
- (NSAffineTransformStruct)**transformStruct;**
// Class Methods
+ (NSAffineTransform *)**transform;**
// Instance Methods
- (void)**invert;**

```
- (void)concat;
- (void)set;
- (void)appendTransform:(NSAffineTransform *)transform;
- (void)prependTransform:(NSAffineTransform *)transform;
- (void)rotateByDegrees:(float)angle;
- (void)rotateByRadians:(float)angle;
- (void)scaleBy:(float)scale;
- (void)scaleXBy:(float)scaleX yBy:(float)scaleY;
- (NSBezierPath *)transformBezierPath:(NSBezierPath *)aPath;
- (NSPoint)transformPoint:(NSPoint)aPoint;
- (NSSize)transformSize:(NSSize)aSize;
- (void)translateXBy:(float)deltaX yBy:(float)deltaY;
// Methods Implementing NSCoding
- (void)encodeWithCoder:(NSCoder *)aCoder;
- (id)initWithCoder:(NSCoder *)aDecoder;
// Methods Implementing NSCopying
- (id)copyWithZone:(NSZone *)zone;
```

NSApplication

This is one of the three classes that define the overall architecture of the Application Kit, as well as the general behavior of Cocoa applications. The other two classes are NSView and NSResponder. Every AppKit-based application has an instance of NSApplication that is accessible through the global variable NSApp.

```
@interface NSApplication : NSResponder
// Accessor Methods
- (void)setMainMenu:(NSMenu *)aMenu;
- (NSMenu *)mainMenu;
- (void)setDelegate:(id)anObject;
- (id)delegate;
- (void)setWindowsNeedUpdate:(BOOL)needUpdate;
- (void)setAppleMenu:(NSMenu *)menu;
- (void)setApplicationIconImage:(NSImage *)image;
- (NSImage *)applicationIconImage;
- (void)setWindowsMenu:(NSMenu *)aMenu;
- (NSMenu *)windowsMenu;
- (void)setServicesMenu:(NSMenu *)aMenu;
- (NSMenu *)servicesMenu;
- (void)setServicesProvider:(id)provider;
- (id)servicesProvider;
// Class Methods
+ (void)detachDrawingThread:(SEL)selector toTarget:(id)target withObject:(id)argument;
+ (NSApplication *)sharedApplication;
// Instance Methods
- (NSModalSession)beginModalSessionForWindow:(NSWindow *)theWindow;
- (void)activateContextHelpMode:(id)sender;
```

- (void)**abortModal**;
- (void)**activateIgnoringOtherApps**:(BOOL)*flag*;
- (void)**addWindowsItem**:(NSWindow *)*win* **title**:(NSString *)*aString* **filename**:(BOOL)*isFilename*;
- (void)**arrangeInFront**:(id)*sender*;
- (NSModalSession)**beginModalSessionForWindow**:(NSWindow *)*theWindow*
    relativeToWindow:(NSWindow *)*docWindow*;
- (void)**beginSheet**:(NSWindow *)*sheet* **modalForWindow**:(NSWindow *)*docWindow* **modalDelegate**:(id)*modalDelegate*
    didEndSelector:(SEL)*didEndSelector* **contextInfo**:(void *)*contextInfo*;
- (void)**cancelUserAttentionRequest**:(int)*request*;
- (void)**changeColor**:(id)*sender*;
- (void)**changeWindowsItem**:(NSWindow *)*win* **title**:(NSString *)*aString* **filename**:(BOOL)*isFilename*;
- (NSGraphicsContext*)**context**;
- (NSEvent *)**currentEvent**;
- (void)**deactivate**;
- (void)**discardEventsMatchingMask**:(unsigned int)*mask* **beforeEvent**:(NSEvent *)*lastEvent*;
- (void)**endModalSession**:(NSModalSession)*session*;
- (void)**endSheet**:(NSWindow *)*sheet*;
- (void)**endSheet**:(NSWindow *)*sheet* **returnCode**:(int)*returnCode*;
- (void)**finishLaunching**;
- (void)**hide**:(id)*sender*;
- (void)**hideOtherApplications**:(id)*sender*;
- (BOOL)**isActive**;
- (BOOL)**isHidden**;
- (BOOL)**isRunning**;
- (NSWindow *)**keyWindow**;
- (NSWindow *)**mainWindow**;
- (NSWindow *)**makeWindowsPerform**:(SEL)*aSelector* **inOrder**:(BOOL)*flag*;
- (void)**miniaturizeAll**:(id)*sender*;
- (NSWindow *)**modalWindow**;
- (NSEvent *)**nextEventMatchingMask**:(unsigned int)*mask* **untilDate**:(NSDate *)*expiration* **inMode**:(NSString *)*mode*
    dequeue:(BOOL)*deqFlag*;
- (void)**orderFrontColorPanel**:(id)*sender*;
- (void)**orderFrontStandardAboutPanel**:(id)*sender*;
- (void)**orderFrontStandardAboutPanelWithOptions**:(NSDictionary *)*optionsDictionary*;
- (void)**postEvent**:(NSEvent *)*event* **atStart**:(BOOL)*flag*;
- (void)**preventWindowOrdering**;
- (void)**registerServicesMenuSendTypes**:(NSArray *)*sendTypes* **returnTypes**:(NSArray *)*returnTypes*;
- (void)**removeWindowsItem**:(NSWindow *)*win*;
- (void)**replyToApplicationShouldTerminate**:(BOOL)*shouldTerminate*;
- (void)**reportException**:(NSException *)*theException*;
- (int)**requestUserAttention**:(NSRequestUserAttentionType)*requestType*;
- (void)**run**;
- (int)**runModalForWindow**:(NSWindow *)*theWindow*;
- (int)**runModalForWindow**:(NSWindow *)*theWindow* **relativeToWindow**:(NSWindow *)*docWindow*;
- (int)**runModalSession**:(NSModalSession)*session*;
- (void)**runPageLayout**:(id)*sender*;
- (BOOL)**sendAction**:(SEL)*theAction* **to**:(id)*theTarget* **from**:(id)*sender*;
- (void)**sendEvent**:(NSEvent *)*theEvent*;
- (void)**showHelp**:(id)*sender*;
- (void)**stop**:(id)*sender*;
- (void)**stopModal**;

- (void)**stopModalWithCode:**(int)*returnCode;*
- (id)**targetForAction:**(SEL)*theAction;*
- (id)**targetForAction:**(SEL)*theAction* **to:**(id)*theTarget* **from:**(id)*sender;*
- (void)**terminate:**(id)*sender;*
- (BOOL)**tryToPerform:**(SEL)*anAction* **with:**(id)*anObject;*
- (void)**unhide:**(id)*sender;*
- (void)**unhideAllApplications:**(id)*sender;*
- (void)**unhideWithoutActivation;**
- (void)**updateWindows;**
- (void)**updateWindowsItem:**(NSWindow *)*win;*
- (id)**validRequestorForSendType:**(NSString *)*sendType*
  returnType:(NSString *)*returnType;*
- (NSWindow *)**windowWithWindowNumber:**(int)*windowNum;*
- (NSArray *)**windows;**

// Methods Implemented by the Delegate
- (BOOL)**application:**(NSApplication *)*sender* **delegateHandlesKey:**(NSString *)*key;*
- (BOOL)**application:**(NSApplication *)*sender* **openFile:**(NSString *)*filename;*
- (BOOL)**application:**(NSApplication *)*sender* **openTempFile:**(NSString *)*filename;*
- (BOOL)**application:**(NSApplication *)*sender* **printFile:**(NSString *)*filename;*
- (BOOL)**application:**(id)*sender* **openFileWithoutUI:**(NSString *)*filename;*
- (void)**applicationDidBecomeActive:**(NSNotification *)*notification;*
- (void)**applicationDidChangeScreenParameters:**(NSNotification *)*notification;*
- (void)**applicationDidFinishLaunching:**(NSNotification *)*notification;*
- (void)**applicationDidHide:**(NSNotification *)*notification;*
- (void)**applicationDidResignActive:**(NSNotification *)*notification;*
- (void)**applicationDidUnhide:**(NSNotification *)*notification;*
- (void)**applicationDidUpdate:**(NSNotification *)*notification;*
- (NSMenu *)**applicationDockMenu:**(NSApplication *)*sender;*
- (BOOL)**applicationOpenUntitledFile:**(NSApplication *)*sender;*
- (BOOL)**applicationShouldHandleReopen:**(NSApplication *)*sender* **hasVisibleWindows:**(BOOL)*flag;*
- (BOOL)**applicationShouldOpenUntitledFile:**(NSApplication *)*sender;*
- (NSApplicationTerminateReply)**applicationShouldTerminate:**(NSApplication *)*sender;*
- (BOOL)**applicationShouldTerminateAfterLastWindowClosed:**(NSApplication *)*sender;*
- (void)**applicationWillBecomeActive:**(NSNotification *)*notification;*
- (void)**applicationWillFinishLaunching:**(NSNotification *)*notification;*
- (void)**applicationWillHide:**(NSNotification *)*notification;*
- (void)**applicationWillResignActive:**(NSNotification *)*notification;*
- (void)**applicationWillTerminate:**(NSNotification *)*notification;*
- (void)**applicationWillUnhide:**(NSNotification *)*notification;*
- (void)**applicationWillUpdate:**(NSNotification *)*notification;*

// Notifications
NSApplicationDidBecomeActiveNotification;
NSApplicationDidChangeScreenParametersNotification;
NSApplicationDidFinishLaunchingNotification;
NSApplicationDidHideNotification;
NSApplicationDidResignActiveNotification;
NSApplicationDidUnhideNotification;
NSApplicationDidUpdateNotification;
NSApplicationWillBecomeActiveNotification;
NSApplicationWillFinishLaunchingNotification;
NSApplicationWillHideNotification;

NSApplicationWillResignActiveNotification;
NSApplicationWillTerminateNotification;
NSApplicationWillUnhideNotification;
NSApplicationWillUpdateNotification;

NSBezierPath Mac OS X 10.0

This class represents Bezier paths that are vector-based paths based on polynomial formulas. Vector paths are the basis of Quartz 2D. As such, this class provides the most general interface to Quartz 2D from Cocoa.

A Bezier path is constructed from path elements. Complex paths are constructed by appending lines and curves to the path. It is also possible to move to a point, thus creating a broken space in the path. Lines are appended to a path using the method lineToPoint:. Curves are appended using the method curveToPoint:controlPoint1:controlPoint2:. To move to a new location on the canvas, use the method moveToPoint:. In all of these methods, the point referred to is the end point of the element; the starting point is implicitly specified as the endpoint of the last element in the path. Chapter 4 provides a more detailed discussion on the use of NSBezierPath for drawing.

```
@interface NSBezierPath : NSObject <NSCoding, NSCopying>
// Accessor Methods
    - (void)setMiterLimit:(float)miterLimit;
    - (float)miterLimit;
    - (void)setLineDash:(const float *)pattern count:(int)count phase:(float)phase;
    - (void)setCachesBezierPath:(BOOL)flag;
    - (BOOL)cachesBezierPath;
    - (void)setClip;
    - (void)setLineWidth:(float)lineWidth;
    - (float)lineWidth;
    - (void)setWindingRule:(NSWindingRule)windingRule;
    - (NSWindingRule)windingRule;
    - (void)setLineJoinStyle:(NSLineJoinStyle)lineJoinStyle;
    - (NSLineJoinStyle)lineJoinStyle;
    - (void)setAssociatedPoints:(NSPointArray)points atIndex:(int)index;
    - (void)setLineCapStyle:(NSLineCapStyle)lineCapStyle;
    - (NSLineCapStyle)lineCapStyle;
    - (void)setFlatness:(float)flatness;
    - (float)flatness;
// Class Methods
    + (NSBezierPath *)bezierPath;
    + (NSBezierPath *)bezierPathWithOvalInRect:(NSRect)rect;
    + (NSBezierPath *)bezierPathWithRect:(NSRect)rect;
    + (void)clipRect:(NSRect)rect;
    + (float)defaultFlatness;
    + (NSLineCapStyle)defaultLineCapStyle;
```

```
+ (NSLineJoinStyle)defaultLineJoinStyle;
+ (float)defaultLineWidth;
+ (float)defaultMiterLimit;
+ (NSWindingRule)defaultWindingRule;
+ (void)drawPackedGlyphs:(const char *)packedGlyphs atPoint:(NSPoint)point;
+ (void)fillRect:(NSRect)rect;
+ (void)setDefaultFlatness:(float)flatness;
+ (void)setDefaultLineCapStyle:(NSLineCapStyle)lineCapStyle;
+ (void)setDefaultLineJoinStyle:(NSLineJoinStyle)lineJoinStyle;
+ (void)setDefaultLineWidth:(float)lineWidth;
+ (void)setDefaultMiterLimit:(float)limit;
+ (void)setDefaultWindingRule:(NSWindingRule)windingRule;
+ (void)strokeLineFromPoint:(NSPoint)point1 toPoint:(NSPoint)point2;
+ (void)strokeRect:(NSRect)rect;
// Instance Methods
- (void)addClip;
- (void)appendBezierPath:(NSBezierPath *)path;
- (void)appendBezierPathWithArcFromPoint:(NSPoint)point1;
- (void)appendBezierPathWithArcWithCenter:(NSPoint)center radius:(float)radius;
- (void)appendBezierPathWithArcWithCenter:(NSPoint)center radius:(float)radius;
- (void)appendBezierPathWithGlyph:(NSGlyph)glyph inFont:(NSFont *)font;
- (void)appendBezierPathWithGlyphs:(NSGlyph *)glyphs count:(int)count;
- (void)appendBezierPathWithOvalInRect:(NSRect)rect;
- (void)appendBezierPathWithPackedGlyphs:(const char *)packedGlyphs;
- (void)appendBezierPathWithPoints:(NSPointArray)points count:(int)count;
- (void)appendBezierPathWithRect:(NSRect)rect;
- (NSBezierPath *)bezierPathByFlatteningPath;
- (NSBezierPath *)bezierPathByReversingPath;
- (NSRect)bounds;
- (void)closePath;
- (NSPoint)currentPoint;
- (NSBezierPathElement)elementAtIndex:(int)index;
- (NSBezierPathElement)elementAtIndex:(int)index;
- (int)elementCount;
- (void)fill;
- (void)getLineDash:(float *)pattern count:(int *)count phase:(float *)phase;
- (BOOL)isEmpty;
- (void)lineToPoint:(NSPoint)point;
- (void)moveToPoint:(NSPoint)point;
- (void)relativeCurveToPoint:(NSPoint)endPoint;
- (void)relativeLineToPoint:(NSPoint)point;
- (void)relativeMoveToPoint:(NSPoint)point;
- (void)removeAllPoints;
- (void)stroke;
- (void)transformUsingAffineTransform:(NSAffineTransform *)transform;
- (BOOL)containsPoint:(NSPoint)point;
- (NSRect)controlPointBounds;
- (void)curveToPoint:(NSPoint)endPoint;
// Methods Implementing NSCoding
- (void)encodeWithCoder:(NSCoder *)aCoder;
- (id)initWithCoder:(NSCoder *)aDecoder;
```

```
// Methods Implementing NSCopying
- (id)copyWithZone:(NSZone *)zone;
```

NSBitmapImageRep

This subclass of NSImageRep represents bitmapped raster images. NSBitmapImageRep is able to
read and write image data in many of the popular bitmap image data formats: TIFF,
JPEG, Windows Bitmap, PNG, as well as raw data. This class allows applications to
create bitmap image buffers that can be manipulated programmatically, and is thus
useful for image manipulation and filtering applications. To obtain a pointer to the
image data buffer, use the method bitmapData. If the image data is arranged in planes,
rather than interlaced, use the method getBitmapDataPlanes:, which returns a C array of
pointers to the image's data planes. NSBitmapImageRep provides a number of methods for
discovering characteristics of the image data, such as the buffer size, pixel and sample
formats, and more. See Chapter 4 for more information on how Cocoa handles images.

```
@interface NSBitmapImageRep : NSImageRep
// Initializers
- (id)initForIncrementalLoad;
- (id)initWithBitmapDataPlanes:(unsigned char **)planes pixelsWide:(int)width pixelsHigh:(int)height
      bitsPerSample:(int)bps samplesPerPixel:(int)spp hasAlpha:(BOOL)alpha isPlanar:(BOOL)isPlanar
      colorSpaceName:(NSString *)colorSpaceName bytesPerRow:(int)rBytes bitsPerPixel:(int)pBits;
- (id)initWithData:(NSData *)tiffData;
- (id)initWithFocusedViewRect:(NSRect)rect;
// Accessor Methods
- (void)setCompression:(NSTIFFCompression)compression factor:(float)factor;
- (void)setProperty:(NSString *)property withValue:(id)value;
// Class Methods
+ (NSData *)TIFFRepresentationOfImageRepsInArray:(NSArray *)array;
+ (NSData *)TIFFRepresentationOfImageRepsInArray:(NSArray *)array usingCompression:(NSTIFFCompression)comp
+ (void)getTIFFCompressionTypes:(const NSTIFFCompression **)list count:(int *)numTypes;
+ (id)imageRepWithData:(NSData *)tiffData;
+ (NSArray *)imageRepsWithData:(NSData *)tiffData;
+ (NSString *)localizedNameForTIFFCompressionType:(NSTIFFCompression)compression;
+ (NSData *)representationOfImageRepsInArray:(NSArray *)imageReps
      usingType:(NSBitmapImageFileType)storageType properties:(NSDictionary *)properties;
// Instance Methods
- (NSData *)TIFFRepresentation;
- (NSData *)TIFFRepresentationUsingCompression:(NSTIFFCompression)comp factor:(float)factor;
- (unsigned char *)bitmapData;
- (int)bytesPerRow;
- (int)bitsPerPixel;
- (int)bytesPerPlane;
- (BOOL)canBeCompressedUsing:(NSTIFFCompression)compression;
- (void)colorizeByMappingGray:(float)midPoint toColor:(NSColor *)midPointColor
      blackMapping:(NSColor *)shadowColor whiteMapping:(NSColor *)lightColor;
```

```
- (void)getBitmapDataPlanes:(unsigned char **)data;
- (void)getCompression:(NSTIFFCompression *)compression factor:(float *)factor;
- (int)incrementalLoadFromData:(NSData*)data complete:(BOOL)complete;
- (BOOL)isPlanar;
- (int)numberOfPlanes;
- (NSData *)representationUsingType:(NSBitmapImageFileType)storageType
    properties:(NSDictionary *)properties;
- (int)samplesPerPixel;
- (id)valueForProperty:(NSString *)property;
```

NSBox Mac OS X 10.0

This simple subclass of NSView performs two tasks: it can draw a border around itself, as well as title itself. By specifying that the box should have no border or title, NSBox views can be used to transparentlly group other NSView objects by making them subviews of the box view. Interface Builder provides facilities for using NSBox to group views.

```
@interface NSBox : NSView
// Accessor Methods
- (void)setTitle:(NSString *)aString;
- (NSString *)title;
- (void)setBorderType:(NSBorderType)aType;
- (NSBorderType)borderType;
- (void)setBoxType:(NSBoxType)boxType;
- (NSBoxType)boxType;
- (void)setTitlePosition:(NSTitlePosition)aPosition;
- (NSTitlePosition)titlePosition;
- (void)setFrameFromContentFrame:(NSRect)contentFrame;
- (void)setTitleFont:(NSFont *)fontObj;
- (NSFont *)titleFont;
- (void)setContentView:(NSView *)aView;
- (id)contentView;
- (void)setContentViewMargins:(NSSize)offsetSize;
- (NSSize)contentViewMargins;
// Instance Methods
- (NSRect)borderRect;
- (void)sizeToFit;
- (id)titleCell;
- (NSRect)titleRect;
```

NSBrowser Mac OS X 10.0

This NSControl subclass represents an interface widget that displays hierarchical data in a series of columns, much like a Column View in the Finder. If the data is not hierarchical, then NSBrowser displays the data as a list. Data is provided to a browser by its delegate object.

```
@interface NSBrowser : NSControl
// Accessor Methods
 - (void)setTitle:(NSString *)aString ofColumn:(int)column;
 - (void)setDoubleAction:(SEL)aSelector;
 - (SEL)doubleAction;
 - (void)setMatrixClass:(Class)factoryId;
 - (Class)matrixClass;
 - (void)setPathSeparator:(NSString *)newString;
 - (NSString *)pathSeparator;
 - (void)setCellClass:(Class)factoryId;
 - (void)setCellPrototype:(NSCell *)aCell;
 - (id)cellPrototype;
 - (void)setDelegate:(id)anObject;
 - (id)delegate;
 - (void)setReusesColumns:(BOOL)flag;
 - (BOOL)reusesColumns;
 - (void)setHasHorizontalScroller:(BOOL)flag;
 - (BOOL)hasHorizontalScroller;
 - (void)setSeparatesColumns:(BOOL)flag;
 - (BOOL)separatesColumns;
 - (void)setTitled:(BOOL)flag;
 - (void)setMinColumnWidth:(float)columnWidth;
 - (float)minColumnWidth;
 - (void)setMaxVisibleColumns:(int)columnCount;
 - (int)maxVisibleColumns;
 - (void)setSendsActionOnArrowKeys:(BOOL)flag;
 - (BOOL)sendsActionOnArrowKeys;
 - (void)setAllowsMultipleSelection:(BOOL)flag;
 - (BOOL)allowsMultipleSelection;
 - (void)setAllowsBranchSelection:(BOOL)flag;
 - (BOOL)allowsBranchSelection;
 - (void)setAllowsEmptySelection:(BOOL)flag;
 - (BOOL)allowsEmptySelection;
 - (void)setTakesTitleFromPreviousColumn:(BOOL)flag;
 - (BOOL)takesTitleFromPreviousColumn;
 - (void)setAcceptsArrowKeys:(BOOL)flag;
 - (BOOL)acceptsArrowKeys;
 - (BOOL)setPath:(NSString *)path;
 - (NSString *)path;
 - (void)setLastColumn:(int)column;
 - (int)lastColumn;
// Class Methods
 + (Class)cellClass;
```

```
// Instance Methods
- (NSRect)frameOfColumn:(int)column;
- (void)doDoubleClick:(id)sender;
- (void)doClick:(id)sender;
- (void)displayColumn:(int)column;
- (void)addColumn;
- (void)displayAllColumns;
- (int)columnOfMatrix:(NSMatrix *)matrix;
- (void)drawTitleOfColumn:(int)column inRect:(NSRect)aRect;
- (int)firstVisibleColumn;
- (NSRect)frameOfInsideOfColumn:(int)column;
- (BOOL)isLoaded;
- (BOOL)isTitled;
- (int)lastVisibleColumn;
- (void)loadColumnZero;
- (id)loadedCellAtRow:(int)row column:(int)col;
- (NSMatrix *)matrixInColumn:(int)column;
- (int)numberOfVisibleColumns;
- (NSString *)pathToColumn:(int)column;
- (void)reloadColumn:(int)column;
- (void)scrollColumnToVisible:(int)column;
- (void)scrollColumnsLeftBy:(int)shiftAmount;
- (void)scrollColumnsRightBy:(int)shiftAmount;
- (void)scrollViaScroller:(NSScroller *)sender;
- (void)selectAll:(id)sender;
- (void)selectRow:(int)row inColumn:(int)column;
- (id)selectedCell;
- (id)selectedCellInColumn:(int)column;
- (NSArray *)selectedCells;
- (int)selectedColumn;
- (int)selectedRowInColumn:(int)column;
- (BOOL)sendAction;
- (void)tile;
- (NSRect)titleFrameOfColumn:(int)column;
- (float)titleHeight;
- (NSString *)titleOfColumn:(int)column;
- (void)updateScroller;
- (void)validateVisibleColumns;
// Methods Implemented by the Delegate
- (void)browser:(NSBrowser *)sender createRowsForColumn:(int)column inMatrix:(NSMatrix *)matrix;
- (BOOL)browser:(NSBrowser *)sender isColumnValid:(int)column;
- (int)browser:(NSBrowser *)sender numberOfRowsInColumn:(int)column;
- (BOOL)browser:(NSBrowser *)sender selectCellWithString:(NSString *)title inColumn:(int)column;
- (BOOL)browser:(NSBrowser *)sender selectRow:(int)row inColumn:(int)column;
- (NSString *)browser:(NSBrowser *)sender titleOfColumn:(int)column;
- (void)browser:(NSBrowser *)sender willDisplayCell:(id)cell atRow:(int)row column:(int)column;
- (void)browserDidScroll:(NSBrowser *)sender;
- (void)browserWillScroll:(NSBrowser *)sender;
```

NSBrowserCell

Mac OS X 10.0

Instances of this class are responsible for displaying the contents of columns in an NSBrowser, which are NSMatrix views containing a stack of NSBrowserCell objects.

@interface **NSBrowserCell** : NSCell
// Accessor Methods
- (void)**setLeaf**:(BOOL)*flag*;
- (void)**setAlternateImage**:(NSImage *)*newAltImage*;
- (NSImage *)**alternateImage**;
- (void)**setLoaded**:(BOOL)*flag*;
- (void)**setImage**:(NSImage *)*image*;
- (NSImage *)**image**;
// Class Methods
+ (NSImage *)**branchImage**;
+ (NSImage *)**highlightedBranchImage**;
// Instance Methods
- (void)**set**;
- (NSColor *)**highlightColorInView**:(NSView *)*controlView*;
- (BOOL)**isLeaf**;
- (BOOL)**isLoaded**;
- (void)**reset**;

NSButton

Mac OS X 10.0

This NSControl subclass represents a button control in the user interface. A button works by sending out an action message whenever a mouse-down and mouse-up event occurs within the button area. The associated NSCell subclass for NSButton is NSButtonCell, described next.

@interface **NSButton** : NSControl
// Accessor Methods
- (void)**setImagePosition**:(NSCellImagePosition)*aPosition*;
- (NSCellImagePosition)**imagePosition**;
- (void)**setTitle**:(NSString *)*aString*;
- (NSString *)**title**;
- (void)**setAlternateTitle**:(NSString *)*aString*;
- (NSString *)**alternateTitle**;
- (void)**setKeyEquivalentModifierMask**:(unsigned int)*mask*;
- (unsigned int)**keyEquivalentModifierMask**;
- (void)**setImage**:(NSImage *)*image*;

- (NSImage *)**image**;
- (void)**setAlternateImage:**(NSImage *)*image*;
- (NSImage *)**alternateImage**;
- (void)**setKeyEquivalent:**(NSString *)*charCode*;
- (NSString *)**keyEquivalent**;
- (void)**setAttributedTitle:**(NSAttributedString *)*aString*;
- (NSAttributedString *)**attributedTitle**;
- (void)**setAllowsMixedState:**(BOOL)*flag*;
- (BOOL)**allowsMixedState**;
- (void)**setAttributedAlternateTitle:**(NSAttributedString *)*obj*;
- (NSAttributedString *)**attributedAlternateTitle**;
- (void)**setBordered:**(BOOL)*flag*;
- (void)**setSound:**(NSSound *)*aSound*;
- (NSSound *)**sound**;
- (void)**setPeriodicDelay:**(float)*delay* **interval:**(float)*interval*;
- (void)**setTransparent:**(BOOL)*flag*;
- (void)**setButtonType:**(NSButtonType)*aType*;
- (void)**setState:**(int)*value*;
- (int)**state**;
- (void)**setNextState**;

// Instance Methods
- (BOOL)**showsBorderOnlyWhileMouseInside**;
- (NSBezelStyle)**bezelStyle**;
- (void)**getPeriodicDelay:**(float *)*delay* **interval:**(float *)*interval*;
- (void)**highlight:**(BOOL)*flag*;
- (BOOL)**isBordered**;
- (BOOL)**isTransparent**;
- (void)**setBezelStyle:**(NSBezelStyle)*bezelStyle*;
- (void)**setShowsBorderOnlyWhileMouseInside:**(BOOL)*show*;
- (BOOL)**performKeyEquivalent:**(NSEvent *)*key*;

Subclasses

NSPopUpButton

NSButtonCell

Mac OS X 10.0

This subclass of NSActionCell contains the majority of the functionality of a button control. NSButtonCell, like most NSCell subclasses, is responsible for the appearance of the NSButton control; NSButton serves more as a view for NSButtonCell to draw in, and most of NSButton's API is forwarded to NSButtonCell.

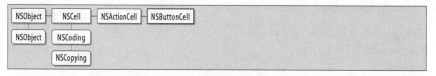

@interface **NSButtonCell** : NSActionCell
// Accessor Methods
- (void)**setPeriodicDelay:**(float)*delay* **interval:**(float)*interval*;
- (void)**setTitle:**(NSString *)*aString*;

- (NSString *)**title**;
- (void)**setAlternateTitle**:(NSString *)*aString*;
- (NSString *)**alternateTitle**;
- (void)**setImagePosition**:(NSCellImagePosition)*aPosition*;
- (NSCellImagePosition)**imagePosition**;
- (void)**setHighlightsBy**:(int)*aType*;
- (int)**highlightsBy**;
- (void)**setAttributedAlternateTitle**:(NSAttributedString *)*obj*;
- (NSAttributedString *)**attributedAlternateTitle**;
- (void)**setAttributedTitle**:(NSAttributedString *)*obj*;
- (NSAttributedString *)**attributedTitle**;
- (void)**setTransparent**:(BOOL)*flag*;
- (void)**setSound**:(NSSound *)*aSound*;
- (NSSound *)**sound**;
- (void)**setKeyEquivalent**:(NSString *)*aKeyEquivalent*;
- (NSString *)**keyEquivalent**;
- (void)**setKeyEquivalentModifierMask**:(unsigned int)*mask*;
- (unsigned int)**keyEquivalentModifierMask**;
- (void)**setKeyEquivalentFont**:(NSFont *)*fontObj*;
- (NSFont *)**keyEquivalentFont**;
- (void)**setKeyEquivalentFont**:(NSString *)*fontName* **size**:(float)*fontSize*;
- (void)**setGradientType**:(NSGradientType)*type*;
- (NSGradientType)**gradientType**;
- (void)**setImageDimsWhenDisabled**:(BOOL)*flag*;
- (BOOL)**imageDimsWhenDisabled**;
- (void)**setAlternateImage**:(NSImage *)*image*;
- (NSImage *)**alternateImage**;
- (void)**setShowsStateBy**:(int)*aType*;
- (int)**showsStateBy**;
- (void)**setButtonType**:(NSButtonType)*aType*;
- (void)**setFont**:(NSFont *)*fontObj*;
// Instance Methods
- (BOOL)**showsBorderOnlyWhileMouseInside**;
- (BOOL)**isOpaque**;
- (BOOL)**isTransparent**;
- (void)**getPeriodicDelay**:(float *)*delay* **interval**:(float *)*interval*;
- (void)**performClick**:(id)*sender*;
- (NSBezelStyle)**bezelStyle**;
- (void)**mouseEntered**:(NSEvent*)*event*;
- (void)**mouseExited**:(NSEvent*)*event*;
- (void)**setBezelStyle**:(NSBezelStyle)*bezelStyle*;
- (void)**setShowsBorderOnlyWhileMouseInside**:(BOOL)*show*;

Subclasses
NSMenuItemCell

NSCachedImageRep
Mac OS X 10.0

This subclass of NSImageRep stores an image's data representation as an image that has been rendered into a window, which is usually an off-screen window. Images represented by NSCachedImageRep can be redrawn very quickly as they have already been rendered to the screen environment.

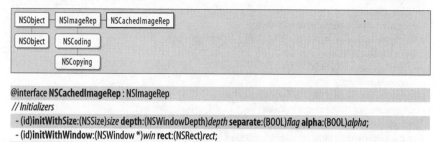

@interface **NSCachedImageRep** : NSImageRep

// Initializers

- (id)**initWithSize**:(NSSize)*size* **depth**:(NSWindowDepth)*depth* **separate**:(BOOL)*flag* **alpha**:(BOOL)*alpha*;
- (id)**initWithWindow**:(NSWindow *)*win* **rect**:(NSRect)*rect*;

// Instance Methods

- (NSRect)**rect**;
- (NSWindow *)**window**;

NSCell

This class is the base superclass for the hierarchy of lightweight objects that know how to draw into a view. Most NSControl classes in the Application Kit defer the implementation of drawing to an associated NSCell. For example, NSButton uses a concrete subclass of NSCell, NSButtonCell, to handle all of the drawing and event handling of a button interface component. Cells provide a leaner alternative to using views in situations when a control appears repeatedly in a view. The interface of NSCell is closely mirrored in NSControl; indeed, many concrete subclasses of NSControl forward most messages to their associated NSCell object.

@interface **NSCell** : NSObject <NSCoding, NSCopying>

// Initializers

- (id)**initImageCell**:(NSImage *)*image*;
- (id)**initTextCell**:(NSString *)*aString*;

// Accessor Methods

- (void)**setBezeled**:(BOOL)*flag*;
- (void)**setType**:(NSCellType)*aType*;
- (NSCellType)**type**;
- (void)**setCellAttribute**:(NSCellAttribute)*aParameter* **to**:(int)*value*;
- (void)**setAllowsMixedState**:(BOOL)*flag*;
- (BOOL)**allowsMixedState**;
- (void)**setTarget**:(id)*anObject*;
- (id)**target**;
- (void)**setAction**:(SEL)*aSelector*;
- (SEL)**action**;
- (void)**setImportsGraphics**:(BOOL)*flag*;
- (BOOL)**importsGraphics**;
- (void)**setTag**:(int)*anInt*;

```
- (int)tag;
- (void)setTitle:(NSString*)aString;
- (NSString*)title;
- (void)setAllowsEditingTextAttributes:(BOOL)flag;
- (BOOL)allowsEditingTextAttributes;
- (void)setEnabled:(BOOL)flag;
- (void)setRepresentedObject:(id)anObject;
- (id)representedObject;
- (void)setAttributedStringValue:(NSAttributedString *)obj;
- (NSAttributedString *)attributedStringValue;
- (void)setSelectable:(BOOL)flag;
- (void)setBordered:(BOOL)flag;
- (void)setDoubleValue:(double)aDouble;
- (double)doubleValue;
- (void)setScrollable:(BOOL)flag;
- (void)setSendsActionOnEndEditing:(BOOL)flag;
- (BOOL)sendsActionOnEndEditing;
- (void)setHighlighted:(BOOL)flag;
- (void)setAlignment:(NSTextAlignment)mode;
- (NSTextAlignment)alignment;
- (void)setWraps:(BOOL)flag;
- (BOOL)wraps;
- (void)setImage:(NSImage *)image;
- (NSImage *)image;
- (void)setEntryType:(int)aType;
- (int)entryType;
- (NSText *)setUpFieldEditorAttributes:(NSText *)textObj;
- (void)setFloatingPointFormat:(BOOL)autoRange left:(unsigned)leftDigits right:(unsigned)rightDigits;
- (void)setFormatter:(NSFormatter *)newFormatter;
- (id)formatter;
- (void)setStringValue:(NSString *)aString;
- (NSString *)stringValue;
- (void)setIntValue:(int)anInt;
- (int)intValue;
- (void)setFloatValue:(float)aFloat;
- (float)floatValue;
- (void)setObjectValue:(id <NSCopying>)obj;
- (id <NSCopying>)objectValue;
- (void)setMenu:(NSMenu *)aMenu;
- (NSMenu *)menu;
- (void)setFont:(NSFont *)fontObj;
- (NSFont *)font;
- (void)setControlSize:(NSControlSize)size;
- (NSControlSize)controlSize;
- (void)setContinuous:(BOOL)flag;
- (void)setState:(int)value;
- (int)state;
- (void)setNextState;
- (int)nextState;
- (void)setEditable:(BOOL)flag;
```

```
// Class Methods
+ (NSMenu *)defaultMenu;
+ (BOOL)prefersTrackingUntilMouseUp;
// Instance Methods
- (NSSize)cellSize;
- (NSColor *)highlightColorWithFrame:(NSRect)cellFrame inView:(NSView *)controlView;
- (NSRect)imageRectForBounds:(NSRect)theRect;
- (BOOL)isEnabled;
- (int)cellAttribute:(NSCellAttribute)aParameter;
- (BOOL)isContinuous;
- (BOOL)isEditable;
- (BOOL)isBordered;
- (BOOL)isBezeled;
- (void)calcDrawInfo:(NSRect)aRect;
- (void)endEditing:(NSText *)textObj;
- (NSSize)cellSizeForBounds:(NSRect)aRect;
- (void)getPeriodicDelay:(float *)delay interval:(float *)interval;
- (BOOL)hasValidObjectValue;
- (void)highlight:(BOOL)flag withFrame:(NSRect)cellFrame inView:(NSView *)controlView;
- (NSComparisonResult)compare:(id)otherCell;
- (void)setControlTint:(NSControlTint)controlTint;
- (BOOL)continueTracking:(NSPoint)lastPoint at:(NSPoint)currentPoint inView:(NSView *)controlView;
- (NSControlTint)controlTint;
- (NSView *)controlView;
- (void)drawInteriorWithFrame:(NSRect)cellFrame inView:(NSView *)controlView;
- (void)drawWithFrame:(NSRect)cellFrame inView:(NSView *)controlView;
- (NSRect)drawingRectForBounds:(NSRect)theRect;
- (void)editWithFrame:(NSRect)aRect inView:(NSView *)controlView editor:(NSText *)textObj
    delegate:(id)anObject event:(NSEvent *)theEvent;
- (BOOL)isEntryAcceptable:(NSString *)aString;
- (BOOL)isHighlighted;
- (BOOL)isOpaque;
- (BOOL)isScrollable;
- (BOOL)isSelectable;
- (NSString *)keyEquivalent;
- (NSMenu *)menuForEvent:(NSEvent *)event inRect:(NSRect)cellFrame ofView:(NSView *)view;
- (int)mouseDownFlags;
- (void)resetCursorRect:(NSRect)cellFrame inView:(NSView *)controlView;
- (void)selectWithFrame:(NSRect)aRect inView:(NSView *)controlView editor:(NSText *)textObj
    delegate:(id)anObject start:(int)selStart length:(int)selLength;
- (int)sendActionOn:(int)mask;
- (BOOL)startTrackingAt:(NSPoint)startPoint inView:(NSView *)controlView;
- (void)stopTracking:(NSPoint)lastPoint at:(NSPoint)stopPoint inView:(NSView *)controlView mouseIsUp:(BOOL)flag;
- (void)takeDoubleValueFrom:(id)sender;
- (void)takeFloatValueFrom:(id)sender;
- (void)takeIntValueFrom:(id)sender;
- (void)takeObjectValueFrom:(id)sender;
- (void)takeStringValueFrom:(id)sender;
- (NSRect)titleRectForBounds:(NSRect)theRect;
- (BOOL)trackMouse:(NSEvent *)theEvent inRect:(NSRect)cellFrame ofView:(NSView *)controlView
    untilMouseUp:(BOOL)flag;
```

```
// Methods Implementing NSCoding
 - (void)encodeWithCoder:(NSCoder *)aCoder;
 - (id)initWithCoder:(NSCoder *)aDecoder;
// Methods Implementing NSCopying
 - (id)copyWithZone:(NSZone *)zone;
```

Subclasses

NSActionCell, NSBrowserCell, NSImageCell, NSTextAttachmentCell

---

NSClipView

This NSView subclass is used in conjunction with NSScrollView to contain the document view of the scroll view (the document view is the view that contains the content of the document, such as text or graphics). The primary responsibility of NSClipView is to implement the scrolling machinery used by NSScrollView. Ordinarily, you should not need to interact with NSClipView unless you are implementing a class that provides functionality similar to NSScrollView.

```
@interface NSClipView : NSView
// Accessor Methods
 - (void)setCopiesOnScroll:(BOOL)flag;
 - (BOOL)copiesOnScroll;
 - (void)setBackgroundColor:(NSColor *)color;
 - (NSColor *)backgroundColor;
 - (void)setDrawsBackground:(BOOL)flag;
 - (BOOL)drawsBackground;
 - (void)setDocumentCursor:(NSCursor *)anObj;
 - (NSCursor *)documentCursor;
 - (void)setDocumentView:(NSView *)aView;
 - (id)documentView;
// Instance Methods
 - (BOOL)autoscroll:(NSEvent *)theEvent;
 - (NSPoint)constrainScrollPoint:(NSPoint)newOrigin;
 - (NSRect)documentRect;
 - (NSRect)documentVisibleRect;
 - (void)scrollToPoint:(NSPoint)newOrigin;
 - (void)viewBoundsChanged:(NSNotification *)notification;
 - (void)viewFrameChanged:(NSNotification *)notification;
```

NSColor

This class represents a color in the Application Kit. Each color has a colorspace associated with it, and the color components that are recognized by that color space. NSColor supports six color spaces identified by the following constants:

- NSDeviceCMYKColorSpace
- NSDeviceWhiteColorSpace

- NSDeviceRGBColor
- NSCalibratedWhiteColorSpace
- NSCalibratedRGBColorSpace
- NSNamedColorSpace

Calibrated colorspaces use Apple's ColorSync technology to ensure that colors look the same on all output devices. Device colorspaces, on the other hand, do not employ ColorSync calibration, and the appearance of colors is thus device-dependent.

The set method is one of the most commonly used methods of NSColor, as it sets the color that all subsequent drawing operations should use. NSColor declares a number of methods for determining the values of various color components, converting colors between colorspaces, creating NSColor objects by changing components of an existing color object, and more. Additionally, there are a number of convenience contructors such as blueColor, redColor, and blackColor that return premade colors without having to specify component values.

@interface **NSColor** : NSObject <NSCoding, NSCopying>
// *Convenience Constructors*
+ (NSColor *)**colorForControlTint**:(NSControlTint)*controlTint*;
+ (NSColor *)**colorFromPasteboard**:(NSPasteboard *)*pasteBoard*;
+ (NSColor *)**colorWithCalibratedHue**:(float)*hue* **saturation**:(float)*saturation* **brightness**:(float)*brightness*
    alpha:(float)*alpha*;
+ (NSColor *)**colorWithCalibratedRed**:(float)*red* **green**:(float)*green* **blue**:(float)*blue* **alpha**:(float)*alpha*;
+ (NSColor *)**colorWithCalibratedWhite**:(float)*white* **alpha**:(float)*alpha*;
+ (NSColor *)**colorWithCatalogName**:(NSString *)*listName* **colorName**:(NSString *)*colorName*;
+ (NSColor *)**colorWithDeviceCyan**:(float)*cyan* **magenta**:(float)*magenta* **yellow**:(float)*yellow*
    black:(float)*black* **alpha**:(float)*alpha*;
+ (NSColor *)**colorWithDeviceHue**:(float)*hue* **saturation**:(float)*saturation* **brightness**:(float)*brightness*
    alpha:(float)*alpha*;
+ (NSColor *)**colorWithDeviceRed**:(float)*red* **green**:(float)*green* **blue**:(float)*blue* **alpha**:(float)*alpha*;
+ (NSColor *)**colorWithDeviceWhite**:(float)*white* **alpha**:(float)*alpha*;
+ (NSColor*)**colorWithPatternImage**:(NSImage*)*image*;
// *Class Methods*
+ (NSColor *)**alternateSelectedControlColor**;
+ (NSColor *)**alternateSelectedControlTextColor**;
+ (NSColor *)**blackColor**;
+ (NSColor *)**blueColor**;
+ (NSColor *)**brownColor**;
+ (NSColor *)**clearColor**;
+ (NSColor *)**controlBackgroundColor**;
+ (NSColor *)**controlColor**;
+ (NSColor *)**controlDarkShadowColor**;
+ (NSColor *)**controlHighlightColor**;
+ (NSColor *)**controlLightHighlightColor**;
+ (NSColor *)**controlShadowColor**;
+ (NSColor *)**controlTextColor**;

```
+ (NSColor *)cyanColor;
+ (NSColor *)darkGrayColor;
+ (NSColor *)disabledControlTextColor;
+ (NSColor *)grayColor;
+ (NSColor *)greenColor;
+ (NSColor *)gridColor;
+ (NSColor *)headerColor;
+ (NSColor *)headerTextColor;
+ (NSColor *)highlightColor;
+ (BOOL)ignoresAlpha;
+ (NSColor *)keyboardFocusIndicatorColor;
+ (NSColor *)knobColor;
+ (NSColor *)lightGrayColor;
+ (NSColor *)magentaColor;
+ (NSColor *)orangeColor;
+ (NSColor *)purpleColor;
+ (NSColor *)redColor;
+ (NSColor *)scrollBarColor;
+ (NSColor *)secondarySelectedControlColor;
+ (NSColor *)selectedControlColor;
+ (NSColor *)selectedControlTextColor;
+ (NSColor *)selectedKnobColor;
+ (NSColor *)selectedMenuItemColor;
+ (NSColor *)selectedMenuItemTextColor;
+ (NSColor *)selectedTextBackgroundColor;
+ (NSColor *)selectedTextColor;
+ (void)setIgnoresAlpha:(BOOL)flag;
+ (NSColor *)shadowColor;
+ (NSColor *)textBackgroundColor;
+ (NSColor *)textColor;
+ (NSColor *)whiteColor;
+ (NSColor *)windowBackgroundColor;
+ (NSColor *)windowFrameColor;
+ (NSColor *)windowFrameTextColor;
+ (NSColor *)yellowColor;
// Instance Methods
- (NSColor *)blendedColorWithFraction:(float)fraction ofColor:(NSColor *)color;
- (float)blueComponent;
- (void)set;
- (float)alphaComponent;
- (float)blackComponent;
- (float)brightnessComponent;
- (NSString *)catalogNameComponent;
- (NSString *)colorNameComponent;
- (NSString *)colorSpaceName;
- (NSColor *)colorUsingColorSpaceName:(NSString *)colorSpace;
- (NSColor *)colorUsingColorSpaceName:(NSString *)colorSpace device:(NSDictionary *)deviceDescription;
- (NSColor *)colorWithAlphaComponent:(float)alpha;
- (float)cyanComponent;
- (void)drawSwatchInRect:(NSRect)rect;
```

- (void)**getCyan:**(float *)*cyan* **magenta:**(float *)*magenta* **yellow:**(float *)*yellow* **black:**(float *)*black*
    alpha:(float *)*alpha;* **brightness:**(float *)*brightness* **alpha:**(float *)*alpha;*
- (void)**getHue:**(float *)*hue* **saturation:**(float *)*saturation*
- (void)**getRed:**(float *)*red* **green:**(float *)*green* **blue:**(float *)*blue* **alpha:**(float *)*alpha;*
- (void)**getWhite:**(float *)*white* **alpha:**(float *)*alpha;*
- (float)**greenComponent;**
- (NSColor *)**highlightWithLevel:**(float)*val;*
- (float)**hueComponent;**
- (NSString *)**localizedCatalogNameComponent;**
- (NSString *)**localizedColorNameComponent;**
- (float)**magentaComponent;**
- (NSImage*)**patternImage;**
- (float)**redComponent;**
- (float)**saturationComponent;**
- (NSColor *)**shadowWithLevel:**(float)*val;*
- (float)**whiteComponent;**
- (void)**writeToPasteboard:**(NSPasteboard *)*pasteBoard;*
- (float)**yellowComponent;**
// Methods Implementing NSCoding
- (void)**encodeWithCoder:**(NSCoder *)*aCoder;*
- (id)**initWithCoder:**(NSCoder *)*aDecoder;*
// Methods Implementing NSCopying
- (id)**copyWithZone:**(NSZone *)*zone;*

NSColorList

This class manages an ordered, named list of NSColors. The operating system itself provides several color lists, which are visible in the Color panel of any application. To obtain an array of available color lists, use the class method **availableColorLists**. To manage the colors contained within a color list we have several methods at our disposal. The method **colorWithKey:** will return the color associated with the indicated key. Colors are added to the list using the method **insertColor:key:atIndex:**. To remove a color, use **removeColorWithKey:**. To change which color is associated with a key, use the method **setColor:forKey:**.

An important feature of color list objects is that they can be written to files that are kept in well-known locations in the filesystem, thus making them easily accessed by other applications. To store a color list to file, use the method **writeToFile:**. Passing **nil** to this method causes the color list to be stored in the users private color lists directory with the filename *listname.clr*. To initialize a color list object from a stored color list, use the initializer **initWithName:fromFile:**.

```
NSObject — NSColorList

NSObject     NSCoding
```

@interface **NSColorList** : NSObject <NSCoding>
// Initializers
- (id)**initWithName:**(NSString *)*name* **fromFile:**(NSString *)*path;*
- (id)**initWithName:**(NSString *)*name;*
// Accessor Methods
- (void)**setColor:**(NSColor *)*color* **forKey:**(NSString *)*key;*

 + (NSArray *)**availableColorLists**;
 + (NSColorList *)**colorListNamed**:(NSString *)*name*;
// Instance Methods
 - (NSString *)**name**;
 - (void)**removeColorWithKey**:(NSString *)*key*;
 - (NSArray *)**allKeys**;
 - (NSColor *)**colorWithKey**:(NSString *)*key*;
 - (void)**insertColor**:(NSColor *)*color* **key**:(NSString *)*key* **atIndex**:(unsigned)*loc*;
 - (BOOL)**isEditable**;
 - (void)**removeFile**;
 - (BOOL)**writeToFile**:(NSString *)*path*;
// Methods Implementing NSCoding
 - (void)**encodeWithCoder**:(NSCoder *)*aCoder*;
 - (id)**initWithCoder**:(NSCoder *)*aDecoder*;
// Notifications
 NSColorListDidChangeNotification;

NSColorPanel

This class implements the system-wide color picker used by all applications. To obtain the shared color panel, use the class method **sharedColorPanel**. NSColorPanel is a subclass of NSPanel, so to display the color panel on screen, invoke NSWindow's orderFront: method. NSColorPanel takes a target and an action that are used to notify the application of the user changing the color selection in the color panel. To obtain the color, use the method **color**.

The color panel optionally displays a slider to change the alpha value of the selected color. This behavior is set with the method **setShowsAlpha:**. To determine if the color panel is set to use alpha, invoke **showsAlpha**. It is also possible for an application to add a color list—which is an instance of NSColorList—to the color panel. Color lists are managed using the methods **attachColorList:** and **detachColorList:**.

The Application Kit provides the class NSColorWell as an interface to Cocoa's color-picking system. It is generally sufficient to use NSColorWell as an interface for users to select colors in an application, as it both displays the color associated with it, and provides a means to open the color panel so the user can choose a new color.

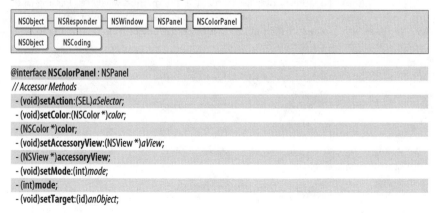

@interface **NSColorPanel** : NSPanel
// Accessor Methods
 - (void)**setAction**:(SEL)*aSelector*;
 - (void)**setColor**:(NSColor *)*color*;
 - (NSColor *)**color**;
 - (void)**setAccessoryView**:(NSView *)*aView*;
 - (NSView *)**accessoryView**;
 - (void)**setMode**:(int)*mode*;
 - (int)**mode**;
 - (void)**setTarget**:(id)*anObject*;

- (void)**setContinuous**:(BOOL)*flag*;
- (void)**setShowsAlpha**:(BOOL)*flag*;
- (BOOL)**showsAlpha**;
// Class Methods
+ (BOOL)**dragColor**:(NSColor *)*color* **withEvent**:(NSEvent *)*theEvent* **fromView**:(NSView *)*sourceView*;
+ (void)**setPickerMask**:(int)*mask*;
+ (void)**setPickerMode**:(int)*mode*;
+ (NSColorPanel *)**sharedColorPanel**;
+ (BOOL)**sharedColorPanelExists**;
// Instance Methods
- (float)**alpha**;
- (void)**attachColorList**:(NSColorList *)*colorList*;
- (void)**detachColorList**:(NSColorList *)*colorList*;
- (BOOL)**isContinuous**;
// Notifications
NSColorPanelColorDidChangeNotification;

NSColorPicker

Mac OS X 10.0

This class implements the NSColorPickingDefault protocol. This class is used to add custom color pickers to the NSColorPanel, which allows applications to add new interfaces that users can use to choose colors.

@interface **NSColorPicker** : NSObject <NSColorPickingDefault>
// Initializers
- (id)**initWithPickerMask**:(int)*mask* **colorPanel**:(NSColorPanel *)*owningColorPanel*;
// Accessor Methods
- (void)**setMode**:(int)*mode*;
// Instance Methods
- (void)**attachColorList**:(NSColorList *)*colorList*;
- (NSColorPanel *)**colorPanel**;
- (void)**detachColorList**:(NSColorList *)*colorList*;
- (void)**insertNewButtonImage**:(NSImage *)*newButtonImage* **in**:(NSButtonCell *)*buttonCell*;
- (NSImage *)**provideNewButtonImage**;
- (void)**viewSizeChanged**:(id)*sender*;
// Methods Implementing NSColorPickingDefault
- (id)**initWithPickerMask**:(int)*mask* **colorPanel**:(NSColorPanel *)*owningColorPanel*;
- (NSImage *)**provideNewButtonImage**;
- (void)**insertNewButtonImage**:(NSImage *)*newButtonImage* **in**:(NSButtonCell *)*buttonCell*;
- (void)**viewSizeChanged**:(id)*sender*;
- (void)**alphaControlAddedOrRemoved**:(id)*sender*;
- (void)**attachColorList**:(NSColorList *)*colorList*;
- (void)**detachColorList**:(NSColorList *)*colorList*;
- (void)**setMode**:(int)*mode*;

NSColorWell

This NSControl subclass provides a user interface element that the user can use to open the color picker and select colors the application can use. This NSControl subclass has no associated NSCell subclass, so NSColorWell controls may not appear in NSMatrix objects, which require NSCell objects as its children. To obtain an NSColor object from the color well, use the method color; to set the color displayed in the well, invoke setColor:.

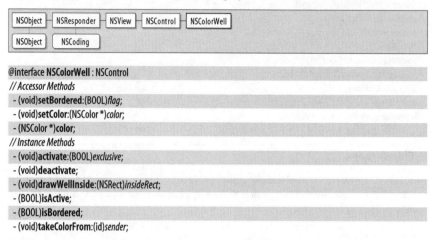

@interface **NSColorWell** : NSControl

// Accessor Methods

- (void)**setBordered**:(BOOL)*flag*;
- (void)**setColor**:(NSColor *)*color*;
- (NSColor *)**color**;

// Instance Methods

- (void)**activate**:(BOOL)*exclusive*;
- (void)**deactivate**;
- (void)**drawWellInside**:(NSRect)*insideRect*;
- (BOOL)**isActive**;
- (BOOL)**isBordered**;
- (void)**takeColorFrom**:(id)*sender*;

NSComboBox

This class provides a combo box interface control to let the user enter a value into the text-field portion of the combo box, or select a value from a pop-up list.

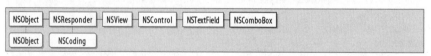

@interface **NSComboBox** : NSTextField

// Initializers

- (id)**initWithCoder**:(NSCoder *)*coder*;

// Accessor Methods

- (void)**setNumberOfVisibleItems**:(int)*visibleItems*;
- (int)**numberOfVisibleItems**;
- (void)**setHasVerticalScroller**:(BOOL)*flag*;
- (BOOL)**hasVerticalScroller**;
- (void)**setCompletes**:(BOOL)*completes*;
- (BOOL)**completes**;
- (void)**setIntercellSpacing**:(NSSize)*aSize*;
- (NSSize)**intercellSpacing**;
- (void)**setItemHeight**:(float)*itemHeight*;
- (float)**itemHeight**;
- (void)**setUsesDataSource**:(BOOL)*flag*;
- (BOOL)**usesDataSource**;

```
- (void)setDataSource:(id)aSource;
- (id)dataSource;
// Instance Methods
- (void)deselectItemAtIndex:(int)index;
- (void)encodeWithCoder:(NSCoder *)coder;
- (int)indexOfItemWithObjectValue:(id)object;
- (void)addItemWithObjectValue:(id)object;
- (void)addItemsWithObjectValues:(NSArray *)objects;
- (int)indexOfSelectedItem;
- (void)insertItemWithObjectValue:(id)object atIndex:(int)index;
- (id)itemObjectValueAtIndex:(int)index;
- (void)noteNumberOfItemsChanged;
- (int)numberOfItems;
- (id)objectValueOfSelectedItem;
- (NSArray *)objectValues;
- (void)reloadData;
- (void)removeAllItems;
- (void)removeItemAtIndex:(int)index;
- (void)removeItemWithObjectValue:(id)object;
- (void)scrollItemAtIndexToTop:(int)index;
- (void)scrollItemAtIndexToVisible:(int)index;
- (void)selectItemAtIndex:(int)index;
- (void)selectItemWithObjectValue:(id)object;
// Methods Implemented by the Delegate
- (void)comboBoxSelectionDidChange:(NSNotification *)notification;
- (void)comboBoxSelectionIsChanging:(NSNotification *)notification;
- (void)comboBoxWillDismiss:(NSNotification *)notification;
- (void)comboBoxWillPopUp:(NSNotification *)notification;
```

NSComboBoxCell
Mac OS X 10.0

This class is the subclass of NSCell that provides the look and feel of the NSComboBox control.

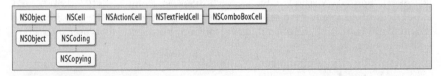

```
@interface NSComboBoxCell : NSTextFieldCell
// Initializers
- (id)initWithCoder:(NSCoder *)coder;
// Accessor Methods
- (void)setNumberOfVisibleItems:(int)visibleItems;
- (int)numberOfVisibleItems;
- (void)setHasVerticalScroller:(BOOL)flag;
- (BOOL)hasVerticalScroller;
- (void)setIntercellSpacing:(NSSize)aSize;
- (NSSize)intercellSpacing;
- (void)setItemHeight:(float)itemHeight;
```

```
- (float)itemHeight;
- (void)setDataSource:(id)aSource;
- (id)dataSource;
- (void)setUsesDataSource:(BOOL)flag;
- (BOOL)usesDataSource;
- (void)setCompletes:(BOOL)completes;
- (BOOL)completes;
// Instance Methods
- (void)addItemsWithObjectValues:(NSArray *)objects;
- (void)addItemWithObjectValue:(id)object;
- (NSString *)completedString:(NSString *)string;
- (void)deselectItemAtIndex:(int)index;
- (void)encodeWithCoder:(NSCoder *)coder;
- (int)indexOfItemWithObjectValue:(id)object;
- (int)indexOfSelectedItem;
- (void)insertItemWithObjectValue:(id)object atIndex:(int)index;
- (id)itemObjectValueAtIndex:(int)index;
- (void)noteNumberOfItemsChanged;
- (int)numberOfItems;
- (id)objectValueOfSelectedItem;
- (NSArray *)objectValues;
- (void)reloadData;
- (void)removeAllItems;
- (void)removeItemAtIndex:(int)index;
- (void)removeItemWithObjectValue:(id)object;
- (void)scrollItemAtIndexToTop:(int)index;
- (void)scrollItemAtIndexToVisible:(int)index;
- (void)selectItemAtIndex:(int)index;
- (void)selectItemWithObjectValue:(id)object;
```

NSControl

Mac OS X 10.0

NSControl is a subclass of NSView that is the base class of all AppKit controls like text fields (NSTextField), buttons (NSButton), table views (NSTableView), color wells (NSColorWell), and more. Controls generally have associated cells that are responsible for presenting the graphical appearance of the control, and responding appropriately to user interaction with the control.

```
@interface NSControl : NSView
// Initializers
- (id)initWithFrame:(NSRect)frameRect;
// Accessor Methods
- (void)setTag:(int)anInt;
- (int)tag;
- (void)setCell:(NSCell *)aCell;
- (id)cell;
- (void)setNeedsDisplay;
```

- (void)**setTarget**:(id)*anObject*;
- (id)**target**;
- (void)**setAction**:(SEL)*aSelector*;
- (SEL)**action**;
- (void)**setFormatter**:(NSFormatter *)*newFormatter*;
- (id)**formatter**;
- (void)**setIgnoresMultiClick**:(BOOL)*flag*;
- (BOOL)**ignoresMultiClick**;
- (void)**setIntValue**:(int)*anInt*;
- (int)**intValue**;
- (void)**setStringValue**:(NSString *)*aString*;
- (NSString *)**stringValue**;
- (void)**setFloatValue**:(float)*aFloat*;
- (float)**floatValue**;
- (void)**setAttributedStringValue**:(NSAttributedString *)*obj*;
- (NSAttributedString *)**attributedStringValue**;
- (void)**setDoubleValue**:(double)*aDouble*;
- (double)**doubleValue**;
- (void)**setEnabled**:(BOOL)*flag*;
- (void)**setFloatingPointFormat**:(BOOL)*autoRange* **left**:(unsigned)*leftDigits* **right**:(unsigned)*rightDigits*;
- (void)**setAlignment**:(NSTextAlignment)*mode*;
- (NSTextAlignment)**alignment**;
- (void)**setObjectValue**:(id)*obj*;
- (id)**objectValue**;
- (void)**setContinuous**:(BOOL)*flag*;
- (void)**setFont**:(NSFont *)*fontObj*;
- (NSFont *)**font**;
// Class Methods
+ (Class)**cellClass**;
+ (void)**setCellClass**:(Class)*factoryId*;
// Instance Methods
- (void)**calcSize**;
- (NSText *)**currentEditor**;
- (BOOL)**abortEditing**;
- (BOOL)**isContinuous**;
- (BOOL)**isEnabled**;
- (void)**mouseDown**:(NSEvent *)*theEvent*;
- (void)**selectCell**:(NSCell *)*aCell*;
- (id)**selectedCell**;
- (int)**selectedTag**;
- (BOOL)**sendAction**:(SEL)*theAction* **to**:(id)*theTarget*;
- (int)**sendActionOn**:(int)*mask*;
- (void)**sizeToFit**;
- (void)**takeDoubleValueFrom**:(id)*sender*;
- (void)**takeFloatValueFrom**:(id)*sender*;
- (void)**takeIntValueFrom**:(id)*sender*;
- (void)**takeObjectValueFrom**:(id)*sender*;
- (void)**takeStringValueFrom**:(id)*sender*;
- (void)**updateCell**:(NSCell *)*aCell*;
- (void)**updateCellInside**:(NSCell *)*aCell*;
- (void)**validateEditing**;

- (void)**drawCell:**(NSCell *)*aCell;*
- (void)**drawCellInside:**(NSCell *)*aCell;*
// Methods Implemented by the Delegate
- (BOOL)**control:**(NSControl *)*control* **didFailToFormatString:**(NSString *)*string* **errorDescription:**(NSString *)*error;*
- (void)**control:**(NSControl *)*control* **didFailToValidatePartialString:**(NSString *)*string*
    errorDescription:(NSString *)*error;*
- (BOOL)**control:**(NSControl *)*control* **isValidObject:**(id)*obj;*
- (BOOL)**control:**(NSControl *)*control* **textShouldBeginEditing:**(NSText *)*fieldEditor;*
- (BOOL)**control:**(NSControl *)*control* **textShouldEndEditing:**(NSText *)*fieldEditor;*
- (BOOL)**control:**(NSControl *)*control* **textView:**(NSTextView *)*textView* **doCommandBySelector:**(SEL)*commandSelector;*
- (void)**controlTextDidBeginEditing:**(NSNotification *)*obj;*
- (void)**controlTextDidChange:**(NSNotification *)*obj;*
- (void)**controlTextDidEndEditing:**(NSNotification *)*obj;*

Subclasses

NSBrowser, NSButton, NSColorWell, NSImageView, NSMatrix, NSScroller, NSSlider, NSStepper, NSTableView, NSTextField

---

NSCursor   Mac OS X 10.0

This class represents a mouse cursor on the screen, and is used to create new cursors that can be used in place of the default arrow cursor. NSView objects often define regions within the view in which the cursor is changed when the mouse is present in those regions. For example, in a text view the cursor changes to an I-beam when the cursor is inside of the text field.

@interface **NSCursor** : NSObject <NSCoding>
// Initializers
- (id)**initWithImage:**(NSImage *)*newImage* **foregroundColorHint:**(NSColor *)*fg*
    backgroundColorHint:(NSColor *)*bg* **hotSpot:**(NSPoint)*hotSpot;*
- (id)**initWithImage:**(NSImage *)*newImage* **hotSpot:**(NSPoint)*aPoint;*
// Accessor Methods
- (void)**setOnMouseEntered:**(BOOL)*flag;*
- (void)**setOnMouseExited:**(BOOL)*flag;*
// Class Methods
+ (NSCursor *)**IBeamCursor;**
+ (NSCursor *)**arrowCursor;**
+ (NSCursor *)**currentCursor;**
+ (void)**hide;**
+ (void)**pop;**
+ (void)**setHiddenUntilMouseMoves:**(BOOL)*flag;*
+ (void)**unhide;**
// Instance Methods
- (void)**set;**
- (NSPoint)**hotSpot;**
- (NSImage *)**image;**
- (BOOL)**isSetOnMouseEntered;**

- (BOOL)**isSetOnMouseExited**;
- (void)**mouseEntered**:(NSEvent *)*theEvent*;
- (void)**mouseExited**:(NSEvent *)*theEvent*;
- (void)**pop**;
- (void)**push**;
// *Methods Implementing NSCoding*
- (void)**encodeWithCoder**:(NSCoder *)*aCoder*;
- (id)**initWithCoder**:(NSCoder *)*aDecoder*;

NSCustomImageRep

This subclass of **NSImageRep** allows you to create images from custom drawing code. For example, one might implement a subclass of **NSCustomImageRep** to draw a complicated Bezier path as the image represented by the particular object. This permits shapes to be drawn in contexts that use images instead of views.

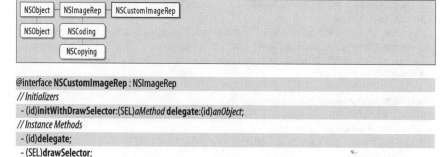

@interface **NSCustomImageRep** : NSImageRep
// *Initializers*
- (id)**initWithDrawSelector**:(SEL)*aMethod* **delegate**:(id)*anObject*;
// *Instance Methods*
- (id)**delegate**;
- (SEL)**drawSelector**;

NSDocument

This class is one of three that comprise Cocoa's document-based application architecture; the other two are **NSDocumentController** and **NSWindowController**. **NSDocument** is an abstract class that defines the fundamental interface for objects that represent documents. This interface includes methods for loading and saving a document's contents, managing a document's windows, handling print jobs, and managing an undo manager. **NSDocument** is never used directly; rather, developers subclass **NSDocument** and implement the key methods to tailor the document to their needs.

@interface **NSDocument** : NSObject
// *Initializers*
- (id)**init**;
- (id)**initWithContentsOfFile**:(NSString *)*fileName* **ofType**:(NSString *)*fileType*;
- (id)**initWithContentsOfURL**:(NSURL *)*url* **ofType**:(NSString *)*fileType*;
// *Accessor Methods*
- (void)**setHasUndoManager**:(BOOL)*flag*;
- (BOOL)**hasUndoManager**;

- (void)**setFileType:**(NSString *)*type*;
- (NSString *)**fileType**;
- (void)**setFileName:**(NSString *)*fileName*;
- (NSString *)**fileName**;
- (void)**setUndoManager:**(NSUndoManager *)*undoManager*;
- (NSUndoManager *)**undoManager**;
- (void)**setPrintInfo:**(NSPrintInfo *)*printInfo*;
- (NSPrintInfo *)**printInfo**;
- (void)**setWindow:**(NSWindow *)*window*;

// *Class Methods*

+ (BOOL)**isNativeType:**(NSString *)*type*;
+ (NSArray *)**readableTypes**;
+ (NSArray *)**writableTypes**;

// *Instance Methods*

- (NSData *)**dataRepresentationOfType:**(NSString *)*type*;
- (NSString *)**displayName**;
- (void)**addWindowController:**(NSWindowController *)*windowController*;
- (BOOL)**canCloseDocument**;
- (NSDictionary *)**fileAttributesToWriteToFile:**(NSString *)*fullDocumentPath* **ofType:**(NSString *)*documentTypeName*
    saveOperation:(NSSaveOperationType)*saveOperationType*;
- (void)**canCloseDocumentWithDelegate:**(id)*delegate* **shouldCloseSelector:**(SEL)*shouldCloseSelector*
    contextInfo:(void *)*contextInfo*;
- (void)**close**;
- (BOOL)**fileNameExtensionWasHiddenInLastRunSavePanel**;
- (NSString *)**fileNameFromRunningSavePanelForSaveOperation:**(NSSaveOperationType)*saveOperation*;
- (NSString *)**fileTypeFromLastRunSavePanel**;
- (NSFileWrapper *)**fileWrapperRepresentationOfType:**(NSString *)*type*;
- (BOOL)**isDocumentEdited**;
- (BOOL)**keepBackupFile**;
- (BOOL)**loadDataRepresentation:**(NSData *)*data* **ofType:**(NSString *)*type*;
- (BOOL)**loadFileWrapperRepresentation:**(NSFileWrapper *)*wrapper* **ofType:**(NSString *)*type*;
- (void)**makeWindowControllers**;
- (BOOL)**preparePageLayout:**(NSPageLayout *)*pageLayout*;
- (BOOL)**prepareSavePanel:**(NSSavePanel *)*savePanel*;
- (IBAction)**printDocument:**(id)*sender*;
- (void)**printShowingPrintPanel:**(BOOL)*flag*;
- (BOOL)**readFromFile:**(NSString *)*fileName* **ofType:**(NSString *)*type*;
- (BOOL)**readFromURL:**(NSURL *)*url* **ofType:**(NSString *)*type*;
- (void)**removeWindowController:**(NSWindowController *)*windowController*;
- (IBAction)**revertDocumentToSaved:**(id)*sender*;
- (BOOL)**revertToSavedFromFile:**(NSString *)*fileName* **ofType:**(NSString *)*type*;
- (BOOL)**revertToSavedFromURL:**(NSURL *)*url* **ofType:**(NSString *)*type*;
- (int)**runModalPageLayoutWithPrintInfo:**(NSPrintInfo *)*printInfo*;
- (void)**runModalPageLayoutWithPrintInfo:**(NSPrintInfo *)*printInfo*
    delegate:(id)*delegate* **didRunSelector:**(SEL)*didRunSelector* **contextInfo:**(void *)*contextInfo*;
- (void)**runModalPrintOperation:**(NSPrintOperation *)*printOperation*
    delegate:(id)*delegate* **didRunSelector:**(SEL)*didRunSelector* **contextInfo:**(void *)*contextInfo*;
- (int)**runModalSavePanel:**(NSSavePanel *)*savePanel* **withAccessoryView:**(NSView *)*accessoryView*;
- (void)**runModalSavePanelForSaveOperation:**(NSSaveOperationType)*saveOperation*
    delegate:(id)*delegate* **didSaveSelector:**(SEL)*didSaveSelector* **contextInfo:**(void *)*contextInfo*;
- (IBAction)**runPageLayout:**(id)*sender*;

- (IBAction)**saveDocument**:(id)*sender*;
- (IBAction)**saveDocumentAs**:(id)*sender*;
- (IBAction)**saveDocumentTo**:(id)*sender*;
- (void)**saveDocumentWithDelegate**:(id)*delegate* **didSaveSelector**:(SEL)*didSaveSelector* **contextInfo**:(void *)*contextInfo*;
- (void)**saveToFile**:(NSString *)*fileName* **saveOperation**:(NSSaveOperationType)*saveOperation*
    delegate:(id)*delegate* **didSaveSelector**:(SEL)*didSaveSelector* **contextInfo**:(void *)*contextInfo*;
- (BOOL)**shouldChangePrintInfo**:(NSPrintInfo *)*newPrintInfo*;
- (BOOL)**shouldCloseWindowController**:(NSWindowController *)*windowController*;
- (void)**shouldCloseWindowController**:(NSWindowController *)*windowController*
    delegate:(id)*delegate* **shouldCloseSelector**:(SEL)*callback* **contextInfo**:(void *)*contextInfo*;
- (BOOL)**shouldRunSavePanelWithAccessoryView**;
- (void)**showWindows**;
- (void)**updateChangeCount**:(NSDocumentChangeType)*change*;
- (BOOL)**validateMenuItem**:(NSMenuItem *)*anItem*;
- (BOOL)**validateUserInterfaceItem**:(id <NSValidatedUserInterfaceItem>)*anItem*;
- (void)**windowControllerDidLoadNib**:(NSWindowController *)*windowController*;
- (void)**windowControllerWillLoadNib**:(NSWindowController *)*windowController*;
- (NSArray *)**windowControllers**;
- (NSString *)**windowNibName**;
- (BOOL)**writeToFile**:(NSString *)*fileName* **ofType**:(NSString *)*type*;
- (BOOL)**writeToFile**:(NSString *)*fullDocumentPath* **ofType**:(NSString *)*documentTypeName*
    originalFile:(NSString *)*fullOriginalDocumentPath* **saveOperation**:(NSSaveOperationType)*saveOperationType*;
- (BOOL)**writeToURL**:(NSURL *)*url* **ofType**:(NSString *)*type*;
- (BOOL)**writeWithBackupToFile**:(NSString *)*fullDocumentPath* **ofType**:(NSString *)*documentTypeName*
    saveOperation:(NSSaveOperationType)*saveOperationType*;

NSDocumentController

Mac OS X 10.0

NSDocumentController is one of three classes that make up the document-based application architecture. The other two classes are NSDocument and NSWindowController. This class is responsible for managing an applications documents, in particular providing an implementation for the File → Open and File → New commands. Additionally, NSDocumentController takes responsibility for ensuring that documents are properly saved and closed before an application terminates.

@interface **NSDocumentController** : NSObject <NSCoding>
// Initializers
- (id)**init**;
// Accessor Methods
- (void)**setShouldCreateUI**:(BOOL)*flag*;
- (BOOL)**shouldCreateUI**;
// Class Methods
+ (id)**sharedDocumentController**;
// Instance Methods
- (BOOL)**closeAllDocuments**;
- (NSArray *)**URLsFromRunningOpenPanel**;
- (void)**addDocument**:(NSDocument *)*document*;

- (IBAction)**clearRecentDocuments**:(id)*sender*;
- (void)**closeAllDocumentsWithDelegate**:(id)*delegate* **didCloseAllSelector**:(SEL)*didAllCloseSelector*
    contextInfo:(void *)*contextInfo*;
- (NSString *)**currentDirectory**;
- (id)**currentDocument**;
- (NSString *)**displayNameForType**:(NSString *)*documentTypeName*;
- (Class)**documentClassForType**:(NSString *)*documentTypeName*;
- (id)**documentForFileName**:(NSString *)*fileName*;
- (id)**documentForWindow**:(NSWindow *)*window*;
- (NSArray *)**documents**;
- (NSArray *)**fileExtensionsFromType**:(NSString *)*documentTypeName*;
- (NSArray *)**fileNamesFromRunningOpenPanel**;
- (BOOL)**hasEditedDocuments**;
- (id)**makeDocumentWithContentsOfFile**:(NSString *)*fileName* **ofType**:(NSString *)*type*;
- (id)**makeDocumentWithContentsOfURL**:(NSURL *)*url* **ofType**:(NSString *)*type*;
- (id)**makeUntitledDocumentOfType**:(NSString *)*type*;
- (IBAction)**newDocument**:(id)*sender*;
- (void)**noteNewRecentDocument**:(NSDocument *)*document*;
- (void)**noteNewRecentDocumentURL**:(NSURL *)*url*;
- (IBAction)**openDocument**:(id)*sender*;
- (id)**openDocumentWithContentsOfFile**:(NSString *)*fileName* **display**:(BOOL)*display*;
- (id)**openDocumentWithContentsOfURL**:(NSURL *)*url* **display**:(BOOL)*display*;
- (id)**openUntitledDocumentOfType**:(NSString*)*type* **display**:(BOOL)*display*;
- (NSArray *)**recentDocumentURLs**;
- (void)**removeDocument**:(NSDocument *)*document*;
- (BOOL)**reviewUnsavedDocumentsWithAlertTitle**:(NSString *)*title* **cancellable**:(BOOL)*cancellable*;
- (void)**reviewUnsavedDocumentsWithAlertTitle**:(NSString *)*title* **cancellable**:(BOOL)*cancellable* **delegate**:(id)*delegate*
    didReviewAllSelector:(SEL)*didReviewAllSelector* **contextInfo**:(void *)*contextInfo*;
- (int)**runModalOpenPanel**:(NSOpenPanel *)*openPanel* **forTypes**:(NSArray *)*openableFileExtensions*;
- (IBAction)**saveAllDocuments**:(id)*sender*;
- (NSString *)**typeFromFileExtension**:(NSString *)*fileNameExtensionOrHFSFileType*;
- (BOOL)**validateMenuItem**:(NSMenuItem *)*anItem*;
- (BOOL)**validateUserInterfaceItem**:(id <NSValidatedUserInterfaceItem>)*anItem*;
// Methods Implementing NSCoding
- (void)**encodeWithCoder**:(NSCoder *)*aCoder*;
- (id)**initWithCoder**:(NSCoder *)*aDecoder*;

NSDrawer
Mac OS X 10.0

This class implements the drawer interface component. Drawers are extensions to windows that contain a content view, and can be opened and closed along one edge of a window to show and hide the contents contained within. One example of an NSDrawer is the Mailboxes drawer in *Mail.app*.

@interface **NSDrawer** : NSResponder
// Initializers
- (id)**initWithContentSize**:(NSSize)*contentSize* **preferredEdge**:(NSRectEdge)*edge*;

```
// Accessor Methods
- (void)setPreferredEdge:(NSRectEdge)edge;
- (NSRectEdge)preferredEdge;
- (void)setParentWindow:(NSWindow *)parent;
- (NSWindow *)parentWindow;
- (void)setTrailingOffset:(float)offset;
- (float)trailingOffset;
- (void)setMinContentSize:(NSSize)size;
- (NSSize)minContentSize;
- (void)setLeadingOffset:(float)offset;
- (float)leadingOffset;
- (void)setMaxContentSize:(NSSize)size;
- (NSSize)maxContentSize;
- (void)setDelegate:(id)anObject;
- (id)delegate;
- (void)setContentSize:(NSSize)size;
- (NSSize)contentSize;
- (void)setContentView:(NSView *)aView;
- (NSView *)contentView;
// Instance Methods
- (void)close;
- (void)close:(id)sender;
- (NSRectEdge)edge;
- (void)open;
- (void)open:(id)sender;
- (void)openOnEdge:(NSRectEdge)edge;
- (int)state;
- (void)toggle:(id)sender;
// Methods Implemented by the Delegate
- (void)drawerDidClose:(NSNotification *)notification;
- (void)drawerDidOpen:(NSNotification *)notification;
- (BOOL)drawerShouldClose:(NSDrawer *)sender;
- (BOOL)drawerShouldOpen:(NSDrawer *)sender;
- (void)drawerWillClose:(NSNotification *)notification;
- (void)drawerWillOpen:(NSNotification *)notification;
- (NSSize)drawerWillResizeContents:(NSDrawer *)sender toSize:(NSSize)contentSize;
// Notifications
NSDrawerDidCloseNotification;
NSDrawerDidOpenNotification;
NSDrawerWillCloseNotification;
NSDrawerWillOpenNotification;
```

NSEPSImageRep

Mac OS X 10.0

This subclass of NSImageRep is capable of rendering an image from Encapsulated Post-Script (EPS) data.

@interface **NSEPSImageRep** : NSImageRep

// Initializers

  - (id)**initWithData:**(NSData *)*epsData*;

// Class Methods

  + (id)**imageRepWithData:**(NSData *)*epsData*;

// Instance Methods

  - (NSData *)**EPSRepresentation**;

  - (NSRect)**boundingBox**;

  - (void)**prepareGState**;

NSEvent Mac OS X 10.0

This class encapsulates the data related to all events in a Cocoa application. **NSEvent** objects are dispatched by **NSApplication** to the appropriate receiver using the method **sendEvent:**. Both key and mouse events are represented by **NSEvent**. All classes that wish to respond to events must inherit from **NSResponder**.

@interface **NSEvent** : NSObject <NSCoding, NSCopying>

// Class Methods

  + (NSEvent *)**enterExitEventWithType:**(NSEventType)*type* **location:**(NSPoint)*location* **modifierFlags:**(unsigned int)*flags*
    timestamp:(NSTimeInterval)*time* **windowNumber:**(int)*wNum*
    context:(NSGraphicsContext*)*context* **eventNumber:**(int)*eNum* **trackingNumber:**(int)*tNum* **userData:**(void *)*data*;

  + (NSEvent *)**keyEventWithType:**(NSEventType)*type* **location:**(NSPoint)*location* **modifierFlags:**(unsigned int)*flags*
    timestamp:(NSTimeInterval)*time* **windowNumber:**(int)*wNum* **context:**(NSGraphicsContext*)*context*
    characters:(NSString *)*keys* **charactersIgnoringModifiers:**(NSString *)*ukeys*

  + (NSEvent *)**mouseEventWithType:**(NSEventType)*type* **location:**(NSPoint)*location* **modifierFlags:**(unsigned int)*flags*
    timestamp:(NSTimeInterval)*time* **windowNumber:**(int)*wNum* **context:**(NSGraphicsContext*)*context*
    eventNumber:(int)*eNum* **clickCount:**(int)*cNum* **pressure:**(float)*pressure*;

  + (NSPoint)**mouseLocation**;

  + (NSEvent *)**otherEventWithType:**(NSEventType)*type* **location:**(NSPoint)*location* **modifierFlags:**(unsigned int)*flags*
    timestamp:(NSTimeInterval)*time* **windowNumber:**(int)*wNum* **context:**(NSGraphicsContext*)*context*
    subtype:(short)*subtype* **data1:**(int)*d1* **data2:**(int)*d2*;

  + (void)**startPeriodicEventsAfterDelay:**(NSTimeInterval)*delay* **withPeriod:**(NSTimeInterval)*period*;

  + (void)**stopPeriodicEvents**;

// Instance Methods

  - (int)**buttonNumber**;

  - (NSString *)**characters**;

  - (NSString *)**charactersIgnoringModifiers**;

  - (int)**clickCount**;

  - (NSGraphicsContext*)**context**;

  - (int)**data1**;

  - (int)**data2**;

  - (float)**deltaX**;

  - (float)**deltaY**;

  - (float)**deltaZ**;

  - (int)**eventNumber**;

- (BOOL)**isARepeat**;
- (unsigned short)**keyCode**;
- (NSPoint)**locationInWindow**;
- (unsigned int)**modifierFlags**;
- (float)**pressure**;
- (short)**subtype**;
- (NSTimeInterval)**timestamp**;
- (int)**trackingNumber**;
- (NSEventType)**type**;
- (void *)**userData**;
- (NSWindow *)**window**;
- (int)**windowNumber**;
// *Methods Implementing NSCoding*
- (void)**encodeWithCoder**:(NSCoder *)*aCoder*;
- (id)**initWithCoder**:(NSCoder *)*aDecoder*;
// *Methods Implementing NSCopying*
- (id)**copyWithZone**:(NSZone *)*zone*;

NSFileWrapper Mac OS X 10.0

This class is used to represent a file, or a set of files contained in a file package, as a single unit of information in a document or application. NSFileWrapper is often used in conjunction with subclasses of NSDocument as a means of conveniently managing a document's data. This class provides functionality that allows clients to edit file attributes and perform file operations. Additionally, clients may assign an icon to represent the file wrapper object in dragging operations.

@interface **NSFileWrapper** : NSObject <NSCoding>
// *Initializers*
- (id)**initDirectoryWithFileWrappers**:(NSDictionary *)*docs*;
- (id)**initRegularFileWithContents**:(NSData *)*data*;
- (id)**initSymbolicLinkWithDestination**:(NSString *)*path*;
- (id)**initWithPath**:(NSString *)*path*;
- (id)**initWithSerializedRepresentation**:(NSData *)*data*;
// *Accessor Methods*
- (void)**setFilename**:(NSString *)*filename*;
- (NSString *)**filename**;
- (void)**setIcon**:(NSImage *)*icon*;
- (NSImage *)**icon**;
- (void)**setFileAttributes**:(NSDictionary *)*attributes*;
- (NSDictionary *)**fileAttributes**;
- (void)**setPreferredFilename**:(NSString *)*filename*;
- (NSString *)**preferredFilename**;
// *Instance Methods*
- (NSString *)**addFileWithPath**:(NSString *)*path*;
- (NSString *)**addFileWrapper**:(NSFileWrapper *)*doc*;
- (NSString *)**addRegularFileWithContents**:(NSData *)*data* **preferredFilename**:(NSString *)*filename*;

AppKit Classes

- (NSString *)**addSymbolicLinkWithDestination:**(NSString *)*path* **preferredFilename:**(NSString *)*filename;*
- (NSDictionary *)**fileWrappers;**
- (BOOL)**isDirectory;**
- (BOOL)**isRegularFile;**
- (BOOL)**isSymbolicLink;**
- (NSString *)**keyForFileWrapper:**(NSFileWrapper *)*doc;*
- (BOOL)**needsToBeUpdatedFromPath:**(NSString *)*path;*
- (NSData *)**regularFileContents;**
- (void)**removeFileWrapper:**(NSFileWrapper *)*doc;*
- (NSData *)**serializedRepresentation;**
- (NSString *)**symbolicLinkDestination;**
- (BOOL)**updateFromPath:**(NSString *)*path;*
- (BOOL)**writeToFile:**(NSString *)*path* **atomically:**(BOOL)*atomicFlag* **updateFilenames:**(BOOL)*updateFilenamesFlag;*
// Methods Implementing NSCoding
- (void)**encodeWithCoder:**(NSCoder *)*aCoder;*
- (id)**initWithCoder:**(NSCoder *)*aDecoder;*

NSFont Mac OS X 10.0

This class represents a single font in an application. NSAttributedString uses NSFont as an attribute that specifies which font a string should be drawn in. NSFont provides access to all of the characteristics of a font, such as the ascender and descender height, italic angle, underline thickness, and more.

@interface **NSFont** : NSObject <NSCoding, NSCopying>
// Convenience Constructors
+ (NSFont *)**fontWithName:**(NSString *)*fontName* **matrix:**(const float *)*fontMatrix;*
+ (NSFont *)**fontWithName:**(NSString *)*fontName* **size:**(float)*fontSize;*
// Class Methods
+ (float)**labelFontSize;**
+ (float)**smallSystemFontSize;**
+ (float)**systemFontSize;**
+ (NSFont *)**boldSystemFontOfSize:**(float)*fontSize;*
+ (NSFont *)**controlContentFontOfSize:**(float)*fontSize;*
+ (NSFont *)**labelFontOfSize:**(float)*fontSize;*
+ (NSFont *)**menuFontOfSize:**(float)*fontSize;*
+ (NSFont *)**messageFontOfSize:**(float)*fontSize;*
+ (NSFont *)**paletteFontOfSize:**(float)*fontSize;*
+ (NSArray *)**preferredFontNames;**
+ (void)**setPreferredFontNames:**(NSArray *)*fontNameArray;*
+ (void)**setUserFixedPitchFont:**(NSFont *)*aFont;*
+ (void)**setUserFont:**(NSFont *)*aFont;*
+ (NSFont *)**systemFontOfSize:**(float)*fontSize;*
+ (NSFont *)**titleBarFontOfSize:**(float)*fontSize;*
+ (NSFont *)**toolTipsFontOfSize:**(float)*fontSize;*

+ (void)**useFont**:(NSString *)*fontName*;

+ (NSFont *)**userFixedPitchFontOfSize**:(float)*fontSize*;

+ (NSFont *)**userFontOfSize**:(float)*fontSize*;

// Instance Methods

- (void)**set**;

- (float)**ascender**;

- (float)**capHeight**;

- (float)**defaultLineHeightForFont**;

- (float)**descender**;

- (NSString *)**encodingScheme**;

- (NSMultibyteGlyphPacking)**glyphPacking**;

- (NSGlyph)**glyphWithName**:(NSString *)*aName*;

- (BOOL)**isFixedPitch**;

- (float)**italicAngle**;

- (NSSize)**maximumAdvancement**;

- (NSStringEncoding)**mostCompatibleStringEncoding**;

- (unsigned)**numberOfGlyphs**;

- (int)**positionsForCompositeSequence**:(NSGlyph *)*someGlyphs* **numberOfGlyphs**:(int)*numGlyphs*
    pointArray:(NSPointArray)*points*;

- (float)**underlinePosition**;

- (float)**underlineThickness**;

- (float)**xHeight**;

- (NSSize)**advancementForGlyph**:(NSGlyph)*ag*;

- (NSDictionary *)**afmDictionary**;

- (NSRect)**boundingRectForFont**;

- (NSRect)**boundingRectForGlyph**:(NSGlyph)*aGlyph*;

- (NSCharacterSet *)**coveredCharacterSet**;

- (NSString *)**displayName**;

- (NSString *)**familyName**;

- (NSString *)**fontName**;

- (BOOL)**glyphIsEncoded**:(NSGlyph)*aGlyph*;

- (BOOL)**isBaseFont**;

- (const float *)**matrix**;

- (float)**pointSize**;

- (NSPoint)**positionOfGlyph**:(NSGlyph)*aGlyph* **forCharacter**:(unichar)*aChar* **struckOverRect**:(NSRect)*aRect*;

- (NSPoint)**positionOfGlyph**:(NSGlyph)*aGlyph* **struckOverRect**:(NSRect)*aRect* **metricsExist**:(BOOL *)*exist*;

- (NSPoint)**positionOfGlyph**:(NSGlyph)*curGlyph* **precededByGlyph**:(NSGlyph)*prevGlyph* **isNominal**:(BOOL *)*nominal*;

- (NSPoint)**positionOfGlyph**:(NSGlyph)*curGlyph* **struckOverGlyph**:(NSGlyph)*prevGlyph* **metricsExist**:(BOOL *)*exist*;

- (NSPoint)**positionOfGlyph**:(NSGlyph)*thisGlyph* **withRelation**:(NSGlyphRelation)*rel* **toBaseGlyph**:(NSGlyph)*baseGlyph*
    totalAdvancement:(NSSizePointer)*adv* **metricsExist**:(BOOL *)*exist*;

- (NSFont *)**printerFont**;

- (NSFont *)**screenFont**;

- (float)**widthOfString**:(NSString *)*string*;

// Methods Implementing NSCoding

- (void)**encodeWithCoder**:(NSCoder *)*aCoder*;

- (id)**initWithCoder**:(NSCoder *)*aDecoder*;

// Methods Implementing NSCopying

- (id)**copyWithZone**:(NSZone *)*zone*;

This class defines the interface to the system Cocoa uses to coordinate the usage of fonts in an application. Part of **NSFontManager**'s duty is to keep track of the currently selected font, and manage the interaction between the Font Panel, Font menu, and text-bearing objects. To obtain an application's Font Manager, use the class method sharedFontManager.

@interface **NSFontManager** : NSObject
// Accessor Methods
- (void)**setEnabled**:(BOOL)*flag*;
- (void)**setSelectedFont**:(NSFont *)*fontObj* **isMultiple**:(BOOL)*flag*;
- (NSFont *)**selectedFont**;
- (void)**setDelegate**:(id)*anObject*;
- (id)**delegate**;
- (void)**setAction**:(SEL)*aSelector*;
- (SEL)**action**;
- (void)**setFontMenu**:(NSMenu *)*newMenu*;
// Class Methods
+ (void)**setFontManagerFactory**:(Class)*factoryId*;
+ (void)**setFontPanelFactory**:(Class)*factoryId*;
+ (NSFontManager *)**sharedFontManager**;
// Instance Methods
- (NSString *)**localizedNameForFamily**:(NSString *)*family* **face**:(NSString *)*faceKey*;
- (void)**addFontTrait**:(id)*sender*;
- (NSArray *)**availableFontFamilies**;
- (NSArray *)**availableFontNamesWithTraits**:(NSFontTraitMask)*someTraits*;
- (NSArray *)**availableFonts**;
- (NSArray *)**availableMembersOfFontFamily**:(NSString *)*fam*;
- (NSFont *)**convertFont**:(NSFont *)*fontObj*;
- (NSFont *)**convertFont**:(NSFont *)*fontObj* **toFace**:(NSString *)*typeface*;
- (NSFont *)**convertFont**:(NSFont *)*fontObj* **toFamily**:(NSString *)*family*;
- (NSFont *)**convertFont**:(NSFont *)*fontObj* **toHaveTrait**:(NSFontTraitMask)*trait*;
- (NSFont *)**convertFont**:(NSFont *)*fontObj* **toNotHaveTrait**:(NSFontTraitMask)*trait*;
- (NSFont *)**convertFont**:(NSFont *)*fontObj* **toSize**:(float)*size*;
- (NSFont *)**convertWeight**:(BOOL)*upFlag* **ofFont**:(NSFont *)*fontObj*;
- (NSMenu *)**fontMenu**:(BOOL)*create*;
- (BOOL)**fontNamed**:(NSString *)*fName* **hasTraits**:(NSFontTraitMask)*someTraits*;
- (NSFontPanel *)**fontPanel**:(BOOL)*create*;
- (NSFont *)**fontWithFamily**:(NSString *)*family* **traits**:(NSFontTraitMask)*traits* **weight**:(int)*weight* **size**:(float)*size*;
- (BOOL)**isEnabled**;
- (BOOL)**isMultiple**;
- (void)**modifyFont**:(id)*sender*;
- (void)**modifyFontViaPanel**:(id)*sender*;
- (void)**orderFrontFontPanel**:(id)*sender*;
- (void)**removeFontTrait**:(id)*sender*;
- (BOOL)**sendAction**;

- (NSFontTraitMask)**traitsOfFont**:(NSFont *)*fontObj*;
- (int)**weightOfFont**:(NSFont *)*fontObj*;

// Methods Implemented by the Delegate
- (void)**changeFont**:(id)*sender*;
- (BOOL)**fontManager**:(id)*sender* **willIncludeFont**:(NSString *)*fontName*;

NSFontPanel

This class provides an implementation for the font-panel that users interact with to select fonts in an application. The panel provides a list of all available fonts from which the user can select a font, style, size, and preview the font as well. NSFontPanel communicates with NSFontManager to obtain the set of available fonts, as well as to effect any changes that may need to be done in the selected text.

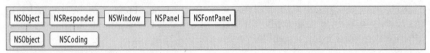

@interface **NSFontPanel** : NSPanel

// Accessor Methods
- (void)**setEnabled**:(BOOL)*flag*;
- (void)**setAccessoryView**:(NSView *)*aView*;
- (NSView *)**accessoryView**;
- (void)**setPanelFont**:(NSFont *)*fontObj* **isMultiple**:(BOOL)*flag*;

// Class Methods
+ (NSFontPanel *)**sharedFontPanel**;
+ (BOOL)**sharedFontPanelExists**;

// Instance Methods
- (void)**reloadDefaultFontFamilies**;
- (BOOL)**isEnabled**;
- (NSFont *)**panelConvertFont**:(NSFont *)*fontObj*;
- (BOOL)**worksWhenModal**;

NSForm

This subclass of NSMatrix implements an interface component that is a stack of NSFormCells, which are a type of cell that represents a titled text entry field.

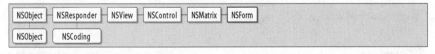

@interface **NSForm** : NSMatrix

// Accessor Methods
- (void)**setTitleAlignment**:(NSTextAlignment)*mode*;
- (void)**setEntryWidth**:(float)*width*;
- (void)**setInterlineSpacing**:(float)*spacing*;
- (void)**setBordered**:(BOOL)*flag*;
- (void)**setBezeled**:(BOOL)*flag*;
- (void)**setTitleFont**:(NSFont *)*fontObj*;

```
- (void)setTextFont:(NSFont *)fontObj;
- (void)setTextAlignment:(int)mode;
```
// Instance Methods
```
- (NSFormCell *)addEntry:(NSString *)title;
- (NSFormCell *)insertEntry:(NSString *)title atIndex:(int)index;
- (id)cellAtIndex:(int)index;
- (int)indexOfCellWithTag:(int)aTag;
- (int)indexOfSelectedItem;
- (void)removeEntryAtIndex:(int)index;
- (void)selectTextAtIndex:(int)index;
- (void)drawCellAtIndex:(int)index;
```

NSFormCell   Mac OS X 10.0

This class is a subclass of NSActionCell that represents a labeled text entry field. The left of
the cell consists of a title, while the right of the cell is an editable text entry field.
NSFormCells are used to implement NSForm controls.

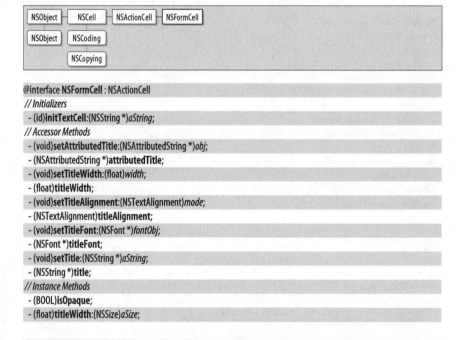

@interface **NSFormCell** : NSActionCell
// Initializers
```
- (id)initTextCell:(NSString *)aString;
```
// Accessor Methods
```
- (void)setAttributedTitle:(NSAttributedString *)obj;
- (NSAttributedString *)attributedTitle;
- (void)setTitleWidth:(float)width;
- (float)titleWidth;
- (void)setTitleAlignment:(NSTextAlignment)mode;
- (NSTextAlignment)titleAlignment;
- (void)setTitleFont:(NSFont *)fontObj;
- (NSFont *)titleFont;
- (void)setTitle:(NSString *)aString;
- (NSString *)title;
```
// Instance Methods
```
- (BOOL)isOpaque;
- (float)titleWidth:(NSSize)aSize;
```

NSGlyphInfo   Mac OS X 10.2

This class is used in attributed strings as a value for the attribute NSGlyphInfoAttributeName.
Glyph info objects are used to specify a mapping between a Unicode character code
and a glyph ID, thus permitting clients to override the default glyph used by a font to
represent some Unicode character.

@interface **NSGlyphInfo** : NSObject <NSCoding>
// Class Methods
+ (NSGlyphInfo *)**glyphInfoWithCharacterIdentifier**:(unsigned int)*cid*
   collection:(NSCharacterCollection)*characterCollection* **baseString**:(NSString *)*theString*;
+ (NSGlyphInfo *)**glyphInfoWithGlyph**:(NSGlyph)*glyph* **forFont**:(NSFont *)*font* **baseString**:(NSString *)*theString*;
+ (NSGlyphInfo *)**glyphInfoWithGlyphName**:(NSString *)*glyphName*
   forFont:(NSFont *)*font* **baseString**:(NSString *)*theString*;
// Instance Methods
- (NSCharacterCollection)**characterCollection**;
- (unsigned int)**characterIdentifier**;
- (NSString *)**glyphName**;
// Methods Implementing NSCoding
- (void)**encodeWithCoder**:(NSCoder *)*aCoder*;
- (id)**initWithCoder**:(NSCoder *)*aDecoder*;

NSGraphicsContext

Mac OS X 10.0

This class is an interface to graphics context objects, which interpret drawing commands based on a number of attributes that make up an environment for rendering. NSGraphicsContext can be used change a number of rendering options, such as whether or not antialiasing should be done, or whether image smoothing and interpolation should be used when drawing images.

@interface **NSGraphicsContext** : NSObject
// Accessor Methods
- (void)**setImageInterpolation**:(NSImageInterpolation)*interpolation*;
- (NSImageInterpolation)**imageInterpolation**;
- (void)**setShouldAntialias**:(BOOL)*antialias*;
- (BOOL)**shouldAntialias**;
- (void)**setFocusStack**:(void *)*stack*;
- (void *)**focusStack**;
- (void)**setPatternPhase**:(NSPoint)*phase*;
- (NSPoint)**patternPhase**;
// Class Methods
+ (NSGraphicsContext *)**currentContext**;
+ (BOOL)**currentContextDrawingToScreen**;
+ (NSGraphicsContext *)**graphicsContextWithAttributes**:(NSDictionary *)*attributes*;
+ (NSGraphicsContext *)**graphicsContextWithWindow**:(NSWindow *)*window*;
+ (void)**restoreGraphicsState**;
+ (void)**saveGraphicsState**;
+ (void)**setCurrentContext**:(NSGraphicsContext *)*context*;
+ (void)**setGraphicsState**:(int)*gState*;
// Instance Methods
- (NSDictionary *)**attributes**;
- (void)**flushGraphics**;
- (void *)**graphicsPort**;

- (BOOL)**isDrawingToScreen**;
- (void)**restoreGraphicsState**;
- (void)**saveGraphicsState**;

NSHelpManager

Mac OS X 10.0

This class provides an interface to an application's help manager object used to provide online help in the application. You won't need to use this class, as Project Builder and Interface Builder provide support for integrating help documents with an application.

@interface **NSHelpManager** : NSObject
// Accessor Methods
- (void)**setContextHelp**:(NSAttributedString *)*attrString* **forObject**:(id)*object*;
// Class Methods
+ (BOOL)**isContextHelpModeActive**;
+ (void)**setContextHelpModeActive**:(BOOL)*active*;
+ (NSHelpManager *)**sharedHelpManager**;
// Instance Methods
- (NSAttributedString *)**contextHelpForObject**:(id)*object*;
- (void)**removeContextHelpForObject**:(id)*object*;
- (BOOL)**showContextHelpForObject**:(id)*object* **locationHint**:(NSPoint)*pt*;

NSImage

Mac OS X 10.0

This class is the general interface to images in the AppKit. Instances of **NSImage** usually have one or more image representations (instances of the class **NSImageRep** or one of its subclasses) associated with them. The purpose of keeping multiple image representations is so the image data can be rendered on a variety of devices, with each image representation providing rendering functionality for a specific device.

@interface **NSImage** : NSObject <NSCoding, NSCopying>
// Convenience Constructors
+ (NSArray *)**imageFileTypes**;
+ (id)**imageNamed**:(NSString *)*name*;
+ (NSArray *)**imagePasteboardTypes**;
+ (NSArray *)**imageUnfilteredFileTypes**;
+ (NSArray *)**imageUnfilteredPasteboardTypes**;
// Initializers
- (id)**initByReferencingFile**:(NSString *)*fileName*;

```
- (id)initByReferencingURL:(NSURL *)url;
- (id)initWithContentsOfFile:(NSString *)fileName;
- (id)initWithContentsOfURL:(NSURL *)url;
- (id)initWithData:(NSData *)data;
- (id)initWithPasteboard:(NSPasteboard *)pasteboard;
- (id)initWithSize:(NSSize)aSize;
// Accessor Methods
- (void)setSize:(NSSize)aSize;
- (NSSize)size;
- (void)setPrefersColorMatch:(BOOL)flag;
- (BOOL)prefersColorMatch;
- (void)setCacheMode:(NSImageCacheMode)mode;
- (NSImageCacheMode)cacheMode;
- (void)setUsesEPSOnResolutionMismatch:(BOOL)flag;
- (BOOL)usesEPSOnResolutionMismatch;
- (void)setFlipped:(BOOL)flag;
- (void)setBackgroundColor:(NSColor *)aColor;
- (NSColor *)backgroundColor;
- (void)setDelegate:(id)anObject;
- (id)delegate;
- (void)setCachedSeparately:(BOOL)flag;
- (void)setCacheDepthMatchesImageDepth:(BOOL)flag;
- (BOOL)cacheDepthMatchesImageDepth;
- (BOOL)setName:(NSString *)string;
- (NSString *)name;
- (void)setScalesWhenResized:(BOOL)flag;
- (BOOL)scalesWhenResized;
- (void)setMatchesOnMultipleResolution:(BOOL)flag;
- (BOOL)matchesOnMultipleResolution;
- (void)setDataRetained:(BOOL)flag;
// Class Methods
+ (BOOL)canInitWithPasteboard:(NSPasteboard *)pasteboard;
// Instance Methods
- (void)addRepresentation:(NSImageRep *)imageRep;
- (NSData *)TIFFRepresentation;
- (NSData *)TIFFRepresentationUsingCompression:(NSTIFFCompression)comp factor:(float)aFloat;
- (void)addRepresentations:(NSArray *)imageReps;
- (void)cancelIncrementalLoad;
- (void)compositeToPoint:(NSPoint)point fromRect:(NSRect)rect operation:(NSCompositingOperation)op;
- (void)compositeToPoint:(NSPoint)point fromRect:(NSRect)rect operation:(NSCompositingOperation)op
    fraction:(float)delta;
- (void)compositeToPoint:(NSPoint)point operation:(NSCompositingOperation)op;
- (void)compositeToPoint:(NSPoint)point operation:(NSCompositingOperation)op fraction:(float)delta;
- (NSImageRep *)bestRepresentationForDevice:(NSDictionary *)deviceDescription;
- (void)dissolveToPoint:(NSPoint)point fraction:(float)aFloat;
- (void)dissolveToPoint:(NSPoint)point fromRect:(NSRect)rect fraction:(float)aFloat;
- (void)drawAtPoint:(NSPoint)point fromRect:(NSRect)fromRect operation:(NSCompositingOperation)op
    fraction:(float)delta;
- (void)drawInRect:(NSRect)rect fromRect:(NSRect)fromRect operation:(NSCompositingOperation)op
    fraction:(float)delta;
```

- (BOOL)**drawRepresentation:**(NSImageRep *)*imageRep* **inRect:**(NSRect)*rect*;
- (BOOL)**isCachedSeparately**;
- (BOOL)**isDataRetained**;
- (BOOL)**isFlipped**;
- (BOOL)**isValid**;
- (void)**lockFocus**;
- (void)**lockFocusOnRepresentation:**(NSImageRep *)*imageRepresentation*;
- (void)**recache**;
- (void)**removeRepresentation:**(NSImageRep *)*imageRep*;
- (NSArray *)**representations**;
- (void)**unlockFocus**;

// Methods Implementing NSCoding
- (void)**encodeWithCoder:**(NSCoder *)*aCoder*;
- (id)**initWithCoder:**(NSCoder *)*aDecoder*;

// Methods Implementing NSCopying
- (id)**copyWithZone:**(NSZone *)*zone*;

// Methods Implemented by the Delegate
- (void)**image:**(NSImage*)*image* **didLoadPartOfRepresentation:**(NSImageRep*)*rep* **withValidRows:**(int)*rows*;
- (void)**image:**(NSImage*)*image* **didLoadRepresentation:**(NSImageRep*)*rep* **withStatus:**(NSImageLoadStatus)*status*;
- (void)**image:**(NSImage*)*image* **didLoadRepresentationHeader:**(NSImageRep*)*rep*;
- (void)**image:**(NSImage*)*image* **willLoadRepresentation:**(NSImageRep*)*rep*;
- (NSImage *)**imageDidNotDraw:**(id)*sender* **inRect:**(NSRect)*aRect*;

NSImageCell   Mac OS X 10.0

This cell class is responsible for drawing an image in a frame. NSImageCell provides
methods that allow clients to specify the frame style, as well as how images that do not
fit in the cell bounds should be scaled.

@interface **NSImageCell** : NSCell <NSCoding, NSCopying>
// Accessor Methods
- (void)**setImageAlignment:**(NSImageAlignment)*newAlign*;
- (NSImageAlignment)**imageAlignment**;
- (void)**setImageScaling:**(NSImageScaling)*newScaling*;
- (NSImageScaling)**imageScaling**;
- (void)**setImageFrameStyle:**(NSImageFrameStyle)*newStyle*;
- (NSImageFrameStyle)**imageFrameStyle**;

// Methods Implementing NSCoding
- (void)**encodeWithCoder:**(NSCoder *)*aCoder*;
- (id)**initWithCoder:**(NSCoder *)*aDecoder*;

// Methods Implementing NSCopying
- (id)**copyWithZone:**(NSZone *)*zone*;

This is an abstract class that defines a general interface to image representations. NSImageRep subclasses allow NSImage to work with various image data formats using the common interface declared in NSImageRep.

```
@interface NSImageRep : NSObject <NSCoding, NSCopying>
// Accessor Methods
 - (void)setSize:(NSSize)aSize;
 - (NSSize)size;
 - (void)setPixelsWide:(int)anInt;
 - (int)pixelsWide;
 - (void)setBitsPerSample:(int)anInt;
 - (int)bitsPerSample;
 - (void)setOpaque:(BOOL)flag;
 - (void)setPixelsHigh:(int)anInt;
 - (int)pixelsHigh;
 - (void)setAlpha:(BOOL)flag;
 - (void)setColorSpaceName:(NSString *)string;
 - (NSString *)colorSpaceName;
// Class Methods
 + (BOOL)canInitWithData:(NSData *)data;
 + (BOOL)canInitWithPasteboard:(NSPasteboard *)pasteboard;
 + (NSArray *)imageFileTypes;
 + (NSArray *)imagePasteboardTypes;
 + (Class)imageRepClassForData:(NSData *)data;
 + (Class)imageRepClassForFileType:(NSString *)type;
 + (Class)imageRepClassForPasteboardType:(NSString *)type;
 + (id)imageRepWithContentsOfFile:(NSString *)filename;
 + (id)imageRepWithContentsOfURL:(NSURL *)url;
 + (id)imageRepWithPasteboard:(NSPasteboard *)pasteboard;
 + (NSArray *)imageRepsWithContentsOfFile:(NSString *)filename;
 + (NSArray *)imageRepsWithContentsOfURL:(NSURL *)url;
 + (NSArray *)imageRepsWithPasteboard:(NSPasteboard *)pasteboard;
 + (NSArray *)imageUnfilteredFileTypes;
 + (NSArray *)imageUnfilteredPasteboardTypes;
 + (void)registerImageRepClass:(Class)imageRepClass;
 + (NSArray *)registeredImageRepClasses;
 + (void)unregisterImageRepClass:(Class)imageRepClass;
// Instance Methods
 - (BOOL)draw;
 - (BOOL)drawAtPoint:(NSPoint)point;
 - (BOOL)drawInRect:(NSRect)rect;
 - (BOOL)hasAlpha;
 - (BOOL)isOpaque;
```

```
// Methods Implementing NSCoding
 - (void)encodeWithCoder:(NSCoder *)aCoder;
 - (id)initWithCoder:(NSCoder *)aDecoder;
// Methods Implementing NSCopying
 - (id)copyWithZone:(NSZone *)zone;
// Notifications
 NSImageRepRegistryDidChangeNotification;
```

Subclasses

NSBitmapImageRep, NSCachedImageRep, NSCustomImageRep, NSEPSImageRep, NSPDFImageRep, NSPICTImageRep

---

NSImageView   Mac OS X 10.0

This subclass of NSView is responsible for drawing an image in a frame, and provides functionality that allows users to set the displayed image by dropping an image over the view. Clients may access the NSImage displayed in the image view using the methods setImage: and image. The associated cell for this class is NSImageCell.

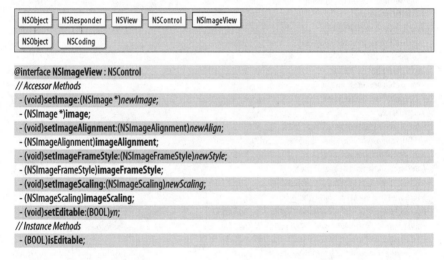

```
@interface NSImageView : NSControl
// Accessor Methods
 - (void)setImage:(NSImage *)newImage;
 - (NSImage *)image;
 - (void)setImageAlignment:(NSImageAlignment)newAlign;
 - (NSImageAlignment)imageAlignment;
 - (void)setImageFrameStyle:(NSImageFrameStyle)newStyle;
 - (NSImageFrameStyle)imageFrameStyle;
 - (void)setImageScaling:(NSImageScaling)newScaling;
 - (NSImageScaling)imageScaling;
 - (void)setEditable:(BOOL)yn;
// Instance Methods
 - (BOOL)isEditable;
```

NSInputManager   Mac OS X 10.0

This class is a key component of Cocoa's text input system, which also consists of the classes NSInputServer and NSTextView. This class sits between NSInputServer and NSTextView. Applications don't need to interact with this class directly, unless they are implementing a custom text input and management system.

```
@interface NSInputManager : NSObject <NSTextInput>
// Class Methods
 + (NSInputManager *)currentInputManager;
```

+ (void)**cycleToNextInputLanguage**:(id)*sender*;
+ (void)**cycleToNextInputServerInLanguage**:(id)*sender*;
// Instance Methods
- (BOOL)**handleMouseEvent**:(NSEvent*)*theMouseEvent*;
- (NSImage *)**image**;
- (NSInputManager *)**initWithName**:(NSString *)*inputServerName* **host**:(NSString *)*hostName*;
- (NSString*)**language**;
- (NSString *)**localizedInputManagerName**;
- (void)**markedTextAbandoned**:(id)*cli*;
- (void)**markedTextSelectionChanged**:(NSRange)*newSel* **client**:(id)*cli*;
- (NSInputServer*)**server**;
- (BOOL)**wantsToDelayTextChangeNotifications**;
- (BOOL)**wantsToHandleMouseEvents**;
- (BOOL)**wantsToInterpretAllKeystrokes**;
// Methods Implementing NSTextInput
- (void)**insertText**:(id)*aString*;
- (void)**doCommandBySelector**:(SEL)*aSelector*;
- (void)**setMarkedText**:(id)*aString* **selectedRange**:(NSRange)*selRange*;
- (void)**unmarkText**;
- (BOOL)**hasMarkedText**;
- (long)**conversationIdentifier**;
- (NSAttributedString *)**attributedSubstringFromRange**:(NSRange)*theRange*;
- (NSRange)**markedRange**;
- (NSRange)**selectedRange**;
- (NSRect)**firstRectForCharacterRange**:(NSRange)*theRange*;
- (unsigned int)**characterIndexForPoint**:(NSPoint)*thePoint*;
- (NSArray*)**validAttributesForMarkedText**;

NSInputServer

Mac OS X 10.0

This class is a key component of the subsystem used to receive and process keystrokes, and direct the associated characters to the active text view to be added to the displayed text. The other two key classes of Cocoa's text input system are NSInputManager and NSTextView. This class implements the interfaces declared in the NSInputServiceProvider and NSInputServerMouseTracker protocols. These two protocols declare the bulk of the functionality of NSInputServer. See the descriptions for these two protocols in Chapter 3 for more information.

@interface **NSInputServer** : NSObject <NSInputServerMouseTracker, NSInputServiceProvider>
// Instance Methods
- (id) **initWithDelegate**:(id)*aDelegate* **name**:(NSString *)*name*;
// Methods Implementing NSInputServerMouseTracker
- (BOOL)**mouseDownOnCharacterIndex**:(unsigned)*theIndex* **atCoordinate**:(NSPoint)*thePoint*
    withModifier:(unsigned int)*theFlags* **client**:(id)*sender*;

- (BOOL)**mouseDraggedOnCharacterIndex**:(unsigned)*theIndex* **atCoordinate**:(NSPoint)*thePoint*
    withModifier:(unsigned int)*theFlags* **client**:(id)*sender*;
- (void)**mouseUpOnCharacterIndex**:(unsigned)*theIndex* **atCoordinate**:(NSPoint)*thePoint*
    withModifier:(unsigned int)*theFlags* **client**:(id)*sender*;
// Methods Implementing NSInputServiceProvider
- (void)**insertText**:(id)*aString* **client**:(id)*sender*;
- (void)**doCommandBySelector**:(SEL)*aSelector* **client**:(id)*sender*;
- (void)**markedTextAbandoned**:(id)*sender*;
- (void)**markedTextSelectionChanged**:(NSRange)*newSel* **client**:(id)*sender*;
- (void)**terminate**:(id)*sender*;
- (BOOL)**canBeDisabled**;
- (BOOL)**wantsToInterpretAllKeystrokes**;
- (BOOL)**wantsToHandleMouseEvents**;
- (BOOL)**wantsToDelayTextChangeNotifications**;
- (void)**inputClientBecomeActive**:(id)*sender*;
- (void)**inputClientResignActive**:(id)*sender*;
- (void)**inputClientEnabled**:(id)*sender*;
- (void)**inputClientDisabled**:(id)*sender*;
- (void)**activeConversationWillChange**:(id)*sender* **fromOldConversation**:(long)*oldConversation*;
- (void)**activeConversationChanged**:(id)*sender* **toNewConversation**:(long)*newConversation*;

NSLayoutManager   Mac OS X 10.0

NSLayoutManager is responsible for managing how text is laid out. NSLayoutManager objects
manage a set of NSTextContainer objects, and supervise how text is laid out in these
containers. Additionally, NSLayoutManager is responsible for mapping Unicode character
codes into glyphs that will be displayed in an NSTextView object. In terms of the Model-
View-Controller design pattern, NSTextStorage is the model, NSTextView the view, and
NSLayoutManager and NSTextContainer are controllers between the data layer and the view
layer.

@interface **NSLayoutManager** : NSObject <NSCoding>
// Initializers
- (id)**init**;
// Accessor Methods
- (void)**setDelegate**:(id)*delegate*;
- (id)**delegate**;
- (void)**setDefaultAttachmentScaling**:(NSImageScaling)*scaling*;
- (NSImageScaling)**defaultAttachmentScaling**;
- (void)**setTemporaryAttributes**:(NSDictionary *)*attrs* **forCharacterRange**:(NSRange)*charRange*;
- (void)**setAttachmentSize**:(NSSize)*attachmentSize* **forGlyphRange**:(NSRange)*glyphRange*;
- (void)**setNotShownAttribute**:(BOOL)*flag* **forGlyphAtIndex**:(unsigned)*glyphIndex*;
- (void)**setTypesetter**:(NSTypesetter *)*typesetter*;
- (NSTypesetter *)**typesetter**;
- (void)**setLocation**:(NSPoint)*location* **forStartOfGlyphRange**:(NSRange)*glyphRange*;
- (void)**setCharacterIndex**:(unsigned)*charIndex* **forGlyphAtIndex**:(unsigned)*glyphIndex*;
- (void)**setBackgroundLayoutEnabled**:(BOOL)*flag*;

- (BOOL)**backgroundLayoutEnabled**;
- (void)**setExtraLineFragmentRect**:(NSRect)*fragmentRect* **usedRect**:(NSRect)*usedRect*
  textContainer:(NSTextContainer *)*container*;
- (NSRect)**extraLineFragmentRect**;
- (void)**setLineFragmentRect**:(NSRect)*fragmentRect* **forGlyphRange**:(NSRange)*glyphRange* **usedRect**:(NSRect)*usedRect*;
- (void)**setHyphenationFactor**:(float)*factor*;
- (float)**hyphenationFactor**;
- (void)**setUsesScreenFonts**:(BOOL)*flag*;
- (BOOL)**usesScreenFonts**;
- (void)**setIntAttribute**:(int)*attributeTag* **value**:(int)*val*
  forGlyphAtIndex:(unsigned)*glyphIndex*;
- (void)**setTypesetterBehavior**:(NSTypesetterBehavior)*theBehavior*;
- (NSTypesetterBehavior)**typesetterBehavior**;
- (void)**setTextStorage**:(NSTextStorage *)*textStorage*;
- (NSTextStorage *)**textStorage**;
- (void)**setShowsControlCharacters**:(BOOL)*flag*;
- (BOOL)**showsControlCharacters**;
- (void)**setDrawsOutsideLineFragment**:(BOOL)*flag* **forGlyphAtIndex**:(unsigned)*glyphIndex*;
- (void)**setShowsInvisibleCharacters**:(BOOL)*flag*;
- (BOOL)**showsInvisibleCharacters**;
- (void)**setTextContainer**:(NSTextContainer *)*container* **forGlyphRange**:(NSRange)*glyphRange*;
// Instance Methods
- (void)**addTemporaryAttributes**:(NSDictionary *)*attrs* **forCharacterRange**:(NSRange)*charRange*;
- (void)**addTextContainer**:(NSTextContainer *)*container*;
- (NSSize)**attachmentSizeForGlyphAtIndex**:(unsigned)*glyphIndex*;
- (NSRect)**boundingRectForGlyphRange**:(NSRange)*glyphRange* **inTextContainer**:(NSTextContainer *)*container*;
- (unsigned)**characterIndexForGlyphAtIndex**:(unsigned)*glyphIndex*;
- (NSRange)**characterRangeForGlyphRange**:(NSRange)*glyphRange*
  actualGlyphRange:(NSRangePointer)*actualGlyphRange*;
- (float)**defaultLineHeightForFont**:(NSFont *)*theFont*;
- (void)**deleteGlyphsInRange**:(NSRange)*glyphRange*;
- (void)**drawBackgroundForGlyphRange**:(NSRange)*glyphsToShow* **atPoint**:(NSPoint)*origin*;
- (void)**drawGlyphsForGlyphRange**:(NSRange)*glyphsToShow* **atPoint**:(NSPoint)*origin*;
- (void)**drawUnderlineForGlyphRange**:(NSRange)*glyphRange* **underlineType**:(int)*underlineVal*
  baselineOffset:(float)*baselineOffset* **lineFragmentRect**:(NSRect)*lineRect*
  lineFragmentGlyphRange:(NSRange)*lineGlyphRange* **containerOrigin**:(NSPoint)*containerOrigin*;
- (BOOL)**drawsOutsideLineFragmentForGlyphAtIndex**:(unsigned)*glyphIndex*;
- (NSTextContainer *)**extraLineFragmentTextContainer**;
- (NSRect)**extraLineFragmentUsedRect**;
- (NSTextView *)**firstTextView**;
- (unsigned)**firstUnlaidCharacterIndex**;
- (unsigned)**firstUnlaidGlyphIndex**;
- (float)**fractionOfDistanceThroughGlyphForPoint**:(NSPoint)*point* **inTextContainer**:(NSTextContainer *)*container*;
- (void)**getFirstUnlaidCharacterIndex**:(unsigned *)*charIndex* **glyphIndex**:(unsigned *)*glyphIndex*;
- (unsigned)**getGlyphs**:(NSGlyph *)*glyphArray* **range**:(NSRange)*glyphRange*;
- (unsigned)**getGlyphsInRange**:(NSRange)*glyphsRange* **glyphs**:(NSGlyph *)*glyphBuffer*
  characterIndexes:(unsigned *)*charIndexBuffer* **glyphInscriptions**:(NSGlyphInscription *)*inscribeBuffer*
  elasticBits:(BOOL *)*elasticBuffer*;
- (unsigned)**getGlyphsInRange**:(NSRange)*glyphsRange* **glyphs**:(NSGlyph *)*glyphBuffer*
  characterIndexes:(unsigned *)*charIndexBuffer* **glyphInscriptions**:(NSGlyphInscription *)*inscribeBuffer*
  elasticBits:(BOOL *)*elasticBuffer* **bidiLevels**:(unsigned char *)*bidiLevelBuffer*;

- (NSGlyph)**glyphAtIndex**:(unsigned)*glyphIndex*;
- (NSGlyph)**glyphAtIndex**:(unsigned)*glyphIndex* **isValidIndex**:(BOOL *)*isValidIndex*;
- (unsigned)**glyphIndexForPoint**:(NSPoint)*point* **inTextContainer**:(NSTextContainer *)*container*;
- (unsigned)**glyphIndexForPoint**:(NSPoint)*point* **inTextContainer**:(NSTextContainer *)*container*
    fractionOfDistanceThroughGlyph:(float *)*partialFraction*;
- (NSRange)**glyphRangeForBoundingRect**:(NSRect)*bounds* **inTextContainer**:(NSTextContainer *)*container*;
- (NSRange)**glyphRangeForBoundingRectWithoutAdditionalLayout**:(NSRect)*bounds*
    inTextContainer:(NSTextContainer *)*container*;
- (NSRange)**glyphRangeForCharacterRange**:(NSRange)*charRange*
    actualCharacterRange:(NSRangePointer)*actualCharRange*;
- (NSRange)**glyphRangeForTextContainer**:(NSTextContainer *)*container*;
- (void)**insertGlyph**:(NSGlyph)*glyph* **atGlyphIndex**:(unsigned)*glyphIndex* **characterIndex**:(unsigned)*charIndex*;
- (void)**insertTextContainer**:(NSTextContainer *)*container* **atIndex**:(unsigned)*index*;
- (int)**intAttribute**:(int)*attributeTag* **forGlyphAtIndex**:(unsigned)*glyphIndex*;
- (void)**invalidateDisplayForCharacterRange**:(NSRange)*charRange*;
- (void)**invalidateDisplayForGlyphRange**:(NSRange)*glyphRange*;
- (void)**invalidateGlyphsForCharacterRange**:(NSRange)*charRange* **changeInLength**:(int)*delta*
    actualCharacterRange:(NSRangePointer)*actualCharRange*;
- (void)**invalidateLayoutForCharacterRange**:(NSRange)*charRange* **isSoft**:(BOOL)*flag*
    actualCharacterRange:(NSRangePointer)*actualCharRange*;
- (BOOL)**isValidGlyphIndex**:(unsigned)*glyphIndex*;
- (BOOL)**layoutManagerOwnsFirstResponderInWindow**:(NSWindow *)*window*;
- (NSRect)**lineFragmentRectForGlyphAtIndex**:(unsigned)*glyphIndex*
    effectiveRange:(NSRangePointer)*effectiveGlyphRange*;
- (NSRect)**lineFragmentUsedRectForGlyphAtIndex**:(unsigned)*glyphIndex*
    effectiveRange:(NSRangePointer)*effectiveGlyphRange*;
- (NSPoint)**locationForGlyphAtIndex**:(unsigned)*glyphIndex*;
- (BOOL)**notShownAttributeForGlyphAtIndex**:(unsigned)*glyphIndex*;
- (unsigned)**numberOfGlyphs**;
- (NSRange)**rangeOfNominallySpacedGlyphsContainingIndex**:(unsigned)*glyphIndex*;
- (NSRectArray)**rectArrayForCharacterRange**:(NSRange)*charRange*
    withinSelectedCharacterRange:(NSRange)*selCharRange* **inTextContainer**:(NSTextContainer *)*container*
    rectCount:(unsigned *)*rectCount*;
- (NSRectArray)**rectArrayForGlyphRange**:(NSRange)*glyphRange* **withinSelectedGlyphRange**:(NSRange)*selGlyphRange*
    inTextContainer:(NSTextContainer *)*container* **rectCount**:(unsigned *)*rectCount*;
- (void)**removeTemporaryAttribute**:(NSString *)*name* **forCharacterRange**:(NSRange)*charRange*;
- (void)**removeTextContainerAtIndex**:(unsigned)*index*;
- (void)**replaceGlyphAtIndex**:(unsigned)*glyphIndex* **withGlyph**:(NSGlyph)*newGlyph*;
- (void)**replaceTextStorage**:(NSTextStorage *)*newTextStorage*;
- (NSView *)**rulerAccessoryViewForTextView**:(NSTextView *)*view* **paragraphStyle**:(NSParagraphStyle *)*style*
    ruler:(NSRulerView *)*ruler* **enabled**:(BOOL)*isEnabled*;
- (NSArray *)**rulerMarkersForTextView**:(NSTextView *)*view* **paragraphStyle**:(NSParagraphStyle *)*style*
    ruler:(NSRulerView *)*ruler*;
- (void)**showAttachmentCell**:(NSCell *)*cell* **inRect**:(NSRect)*rect* **characterIndex**:(unsigned)*attachmentIndex*;
- (void)**showPackedGlyphs**:(char *)*glyphs* **length**:(unsigned)*glyphLen* **glyphRange**:(NSRange)*glyphRange*
    atPoint:(NSPoint)*point* **font**:(NSFont *)*font* **color**:(NSColor *)*color* **printingAdjustment**:(NSSize)*printingAdjustment*;
- (NSFont *)**substituteFontForFont**:(NSFont *)*originalFont*;
- (NSDictionary *)**temporaryAttributesAtCharacterIndex**:(unsigned)*charIndex*
    effectiveRange:(NSRangePointer)*effectiveCharRange*;
- (void)**textContainerChangedGeometry**:(NSTextContainer *)*container*;
- (void)**textContainerChangedTextView**:(NSTextContainer *)*container*;

- (NSTextContainer *)**textContainerForGlyphAtIndex**:(unsigned)*glyphIndex*
    effectiveRange:(NSRangePointer)*effectiveGlyphRange*;
- (NSArray *)**textContainers**;
- (void)**textStorage**:(NSTextStorage *)*str* **edited**:(unsigned)*editedMask* **range**:(NSRange)*newCharRange*
    changeInLength:(int)*delta* **invalidatedRange**:(NSRange)*invalidatedCharRange*;
- (NSTextView *)**textViewForBeginningOfSelection**;
- (void)**underlineGlyphRange**:(NSRange)*glyphRange* **underlineType**:(int)*underlineVal*
    lineFragmentRect:(NSRect)*lineRect* **lineFragmentGlyphRange**:(NSRange)*lineGlyphRange*
    containerOrigin:(NSPoint)*containerOrigin*;
- (NSRect)**usedRectForTextContainer**:(NSTextContainer *)*container*;

// Methods Implementing NSCoding
- (void)**encodeWithCoder**:(NSCoder *)*aCoder*;
- (id)**initWithCoder**:(NSCoder *)*aDecoder*;

// Methods Implemented by the Delegate
- (void)**layoutManager**:(NSLayoutManager *)*layoutManager*
    didCompleteLayoutForTextContainer:(NSTextContainer *)*textContainer* **atEnd**:(BOOL)*layoutFinishedFlag*;
- (void)**layoutManagerDidInvalidateLayout**:(NSLayoutManager *)*sender*;

NSMatrix

Mac OS X 10.0

This NSView subclass specializes in organizing groups of cells in a grid, and endowing them with various collective behaviors such as that exhibited by radio buttons. Radio button groups are an example of an interface component implemented with an NSMatrix and NSButtonCells.

@interface **NSMatrix** : NSControl

// Initializers
- (id)**initWithFrame**:(NSRect)*frameRect*;
- (id)**initWithFrame**:(NSRect)*frameRect* **mode**:(int)*aMode* **cellClass**:(Class)*factoryId* **numberOfRows**:(int)*rowsHigh*
    numberOfColumns:(int)*colsWide*;
- (id)**initWithFrame**:(NSRect)*frameRect* **mode**:(int)*aMode* **prototype**:(NSCell *)*aCell* **numberOfRows**:(int)*rowsHigh*
    numberOfColumns:(int)*colsWide*;

// Accessor Methods
- (void)**setAllowsEmptySelection**:(BOOL)*flag*;
- (BOOL)**allowsEmptySelection**;
- (void)**setToolTip**:(NSString *)*toolTipString* **forCell**:(NSCell *)*cell*;
- (void)**setCellClass**:(Class)*factoryId*;
- (Class)**cellClass**;
- (void)**setDelegate**:(id)*anObject*;
- (id)**delegate**;
- (void)**setAutoscroll**:(BOOL)*flag*;
- (void)**setIntercellSpacing**:(NSSize)*aSize*;
- (NSSize)**intercellSpacing**;
- (void)**setValidateSize**:(BOOL)*flag*;
- (void)**setCellBackgroundColor**:(NSColor *)*color*;
- (NSColor *)**cellBackgroundColor**;
- (void)**setMode**:(NSMatrixMode)*aMode*;

- (NSMatrixMode)**mode**;
- (void)**setSelectionByRect**:(BOOL)*flag*;
- (void)**setSelectionFrom**:(int)*startPos* **to**:(int)*endPos* **anchor**:(int)*anchorPos* **highlight**:(BOOL)*lit*;
- (void)**setAutosizesCells**:(BOOL)*flag*;
- (BOOL)**autosizesCells**;
- (void)**setCellSize**:(NSSize)*aSize*;
- (NSSize)**cellSize**;
- (void)**setScrollable**:(BOOL)*flag*;
- (void)**setBackgroundColor**:(NSColor *)*color*;
- (NSColor *)**backgroundColor**;
- (void)**setDoubleAction**:(SEL)*aSelector*;
- (SEL)**doubleAction**;
- (void)**setPrototype**:(NSCell *)*aCell*;
- (id)**prototype**;
- (void)**setState**:(int)*value* **atRow**:(int)*row* **column**:(int)*col*;
- (void)**setDrawsBackground**:(BOOL)*flag*;
- (BOOL)**drawsBackground**;
- (void)**setDrawsCellBackground**:(BOOL)*flag*;
- (BOOL)**drawsCellBackground**;
// Instance Methods
- (BOOL)**acceptsFirstMouse**:(NSEvent *)*theEvent*;
- (void)**addColumn**;
- (void)**addColumnWithCells**:(NSArray *)*newCells*;
- (void)**addRow**;
- (void)**addRowWithCells**:(NSArray *)*newCells*;
- (id)**cellAtRow**:(int)*row* **column**:(int)*col*;
- (NSRect)**cellFrameAtRow**:(int)*row* **column**:(int)*col*;
- (id)**cellWithTag**:(int)*anInt*;
- (NSArray *)**cells**;
- (void)**deselectAllCells**;
- (void)**deselectSelectedCell**;
- (void)**drawCellAtRow**:(int)*row* **column**:(int)*col*;
- (void)**getNumberOfRows**:(int *)*rowCount* **columns**:(int *)*colCount*;
- (BOOL)**getRow**:(int *)*row* **column**:(int *)*col* **forPoint**:(NSPoint)*aPoint*;
- (BOOL)**getRow**:(int *)*row* **column**:(int *)*col* **ofCell**:(NSCell *)*aCell*;
- (void)**highlightCell**:(BOOL)*flag* **atRow**:(int)*row* **column**:(int)*col*;
- (void)**insertColumn**:(int)*column*;
- (void)**insertColumn**:(int)*column* **withCells**:(NSArray *)*newCells*;
- (void)**insertRow**:(int)*row*;
- (void)**insertRow**:(int)*row* **withCells**:(NSArray *)*newCells*;
- (BOOL)**isAutoscroll**;
- (BOOL)**isSelectionByRect**;
- (NSCell *)**makeCellAtRow**:(int)*row* **column**:(int)*col*;
- (void)**mouseDown**:(NSEvent *)*theEvent*;
- (int)**mouseDownFlags**;
- (int)**numberOfColumns**;
- (int)**numberOfRows**;
- (BOOL)**performKeyEquivalent**:(NSEvent *)*theEvent*;
- (void)**putCell**:(NSCell *)*newCell* **atRow**:(int)*row* **column**:(int)*col*;
- (void)**removeColumn**:(int)*col*;
- (void)**removeRow**:(int)*row*;

- (void)**renewRows**:(int)*newRows* **columns**:(int)*newCols*;
- (void)**resetCursorRects**;
- (void)**scrollCellToVisibleAtRow**:(int)*row* **column**:(int)*col*;
- (void)**selectAll**:(id)*sender*;
- (void)**selectCellAtRow**:(int)*row* **column**:(int)*col*;
- (BOOL)**selectCellWithTag**:(int)*anInt*;
- (void)**selectText**:(id)*sender*;
- (id)**selectTextAtRow**:(int)*row* **column**:(int)*col*;
- (id)**selectedCell**;
- (NSArray *)**selectedCells**;
- (int)**selectedColumn**;
- (int)**selectedRow**;
- (BOOL)**sendAction**;
- (void)**sendAction**:(SEL)*aSelector* **to**:(id)*anObject* **forAllCells**:(BOOL)*flag*;
- (void)**sendDoubleAction**;
- (void)**sizeToCells**;
- (void)**sortUsingFunction**:(int (*)(id, id, void *))*compare* **context**:(void *)*context*;
- (void)**sortUsingSelector**:(SEL)*comparator*;
- (void)**textDidBeginEditing**:(NSNotification *)*notification*;
- (void)**textDidChange**:(NSNotification *)*notification*;
- (void)**textDidEndEditing**:(NSNotification *)*notification*;
- (BOOL)**textShouldBeginEditing**:(NSText *)*textObject*;
- (BOOL)**textShouldEndEditing**:(NSText *)*textObject*;
- (NSString *)**toolTipForCell**:(NSCell *)*cell*;

Subclasses

NSForm

NSMenu

Mac OS X 10.0

This class provides an interface to an application's menus. Generally, you won't have to work directly with menus since Interface Builder provides facilities for creating an application's entire menu structure, including the main menu bar, the Dock menu, contextual menus for views, and menus for pop-up buttons. However, if your application requires some degree of dynamicism in its menus, then you will need to use NSMenu's API.

Menus are initialized with initWithTitle:. The string passed in this method appears as the title of the menu. A menu manages a collection of menu items, which are instances of the class NSMenuItem. To manage a menu's items, we have several methods at our disposal. To add an item to the end of the menu, use addItem:; to insert an item at some position in the menu, use insertItem:atIndex:. Menu items are removed from a menu using the methods removeItem: and removeItemAtIndex:.

Menus can also be queried for their menu items. The method itemArray returns an NSArray containing the menu's items. Items can also be retrieved by their index, title, and tag using itemAtIndex:, itemWithTitle:, and itemWithTag:, respectively.

To add a submenu to a menu, first add a menu item to represent that submenu, and then associate another instance of NSMenu with that menu item using the method setSubmenu:forItem:.

```objc
@interface NSMenu : NSObject <NSCoding, NSCopying>
// Convenience Constructors
+ (BOOL)menuBarVisible;
+ (NSZone *)menuZone;
// Initializers
- (id)initWithTitle:(NSString *)aTitle;
// Accessor Methods
- (void)setTearOffMenuRepresentation:(id)menuRep;
- (id)tearOffMenuRepresentation;
- (void)setTitle:(NSString *)aString;
- (NSString *)title;
- (void)setSupermenu:(NSMenu *)supermenu;
- (NSMenu *)supermenu;
- (void)setAutoenablesItems:(BOOL)flag;
- (BOOL)autoenablesItems;
- (void)setSubmenu:(NSMenu *)aMenu forItem:(id <NSMenuItem>)anItem;
- (void)setMenuRepresentation:(id)menuRep;
- (id)menuRepresentation;
- (void)setContextMenuRepresentation:(id)menuRep;
- (id)contextMenuRepresentation;
- (void)setMenuChangedMessagesEnabled:(BOOL)flag;
- (BOOL)menuChangedMessagesEnabled;
// Class Methods
+ (void)popUpContextMenu:(NSMenu*)menu withEvent:(NSEvent*)event forView:(NSView*)view;
+ (void)setMenuBarVisible:(BOOL)visible;
+ (void)setMenuZone:(NSZone *)aZone;
// Instance Methods
- (NSMenu *)attachedMenu;
- (void)addItem:(id <NSMenuItem>)newItem;
- (id <NSMenuItem>)addItemWithTitle:(NSString *)aString action:(SEL)aSelector keyEquivalent:(NSString *)charCode;
- (void)helpRequested:(NSEvent *)eventPtr;
- (int)indexOfItem:(id <NSMenuItem>)index;
- (int)indexOfItemWithRepresentedObject:(id)object;
- (int)indexOfItemWithSubmenu:(NSMenu *)submenu;
- (int)indexOfItemWithTag:(int)aTag;
- (int)indexOfItemWithTarget:(id)target andAction:(SEL)actionSelector;
- (int)indexOfItemWithTitle:(NSString *)aTitle;
- (void)insertItem:(id <NSMenuItem>)newItem atIndex:(int)index;
- (id <NSMenuItem>)insertItemWithTitle:(NSString *)aString action:(SEL)aSelector
    keyEquivalent:(NSString *)charCode atIndex:(int)index;
- (BOOL)isAttached;
- (BOOL)isTornOff;
```

```
- (NSArray *)itemArray;
- (id <NSMenuItem>)itemAtIndex:(int)index;
- (void)itemChanged:(id <NSMenuItem>)item;
- (id <NSMenuItem>)itemWithTag:(int)tag;
- (id <NSMenuItem>)itemWithTitle:(NSString *)aTitle;
- (NSPoint)locationForSubmenu:(NSMenu *)aSubmenu;
- (int)numberOfItems;
- (void)performActionForItemAtIndex:(int)index;
- (BOOL)performKeyEquivalent:(NSEvent *)theEvent;
- (void)removeItem:(id <NSMenuItem>)item;
- (void)removeItemAtIndex:(int)index;
- (void)sizeToFit;
- (void)submenuAction:(id)sender;
- (void)update;
// Methods Implementing NSCoding
- (void)encodeWithCoder:(NSCoder *)aCoder;
- (id)initWithCoder:(NSCoder *)aDecoder;
// Methods Implementing NSCopying
- (id)copyWithZone:(NSZone *)zone;
// Notifications
NSMenuDidAddItemNotification;
NSMenuDidChangeItemNotification;
NSMenuDidRemoveItemNotification;
NSMenuDidSendActionNotification;
NSMenuWillSendActionNotification;
```

NSMenuItem

Mac OS X 10.0

This class declares the interface to objects that make up commands in an NSMenu. NSMenuItems have an associated target and action, and may optionally have a key equivalent that the user can use to activate the menu item. Menu items are also capable of maintaining a state (on, off, or mixed).

```
@interface NSMenuItem : NSObject <NSMenuItem>
// Initializers
- (id)initWithTitle:(NSString *)aString action:(SEL)aSelector keyEquivalent:(NSString *)charCode;
// Accessor Methods
- (void)setAction:(SEL)aSelector;
- (SEL)action;
- (void)setRepresentedObject:(id)anObject;
- (id)representedObject;
- (void)setSubmenu:(NSMenu *)submenu;
- (NSMenu *)submenu;
- (void)setTag:(int)anInt;
- (int)tag;
- (void)setTitle:(NSString *)aString;
- (NSString *)title;
```

- (void)**setTitleWithMnemonic**:(NSString *)*stringWithAmpersand*;
- (void)**setKeyEquivalent**:(NSString *)*aKeyEquivalent*;
- (NSString *)**keyEquivalent**;
- (void)**setTarget**:(id)*anObject*;
- (id)**target**;
- (void)**setKeyEquivalentModifierMask**:(unsigned int)*mask*;
- (unsigned int)**keyEquivalentModifierMask**;
- (void)**setEnabled**:(BOOL)*flag*;
- (void)**setMixedStateImage**:(NSImage *)*image*;
- (NSImage *)**mixedStateImage**;
- (void)**setMnemonicLocation**:(unsigned)*location*;
- (unsigned)**mnemonicLocation**;
- (void)**setOffStateImage**:(NSImage *)*image*;
- (NSImage *)**offStateImage**;
- (void)**setImage**:(NSImage *)*menuImage*;
- (NSImage *)**image**;
- (void)**setState**:(int)*state*;
- (int)**state**;
- (void)**setMenu**:(NSMenu *)*menu*;
- (NSMenu *)**menu**;
- (void)**setOnStateImage**:(NSImage *)*image*;
- (NSImage *)**onStateImage**;

// Class Methods
+ (id <NSMenuItem>)**separatorItem**;
+ (void)**setUsesUserKeyEquivalents**:(BOOL)*flag*;
+ (BOOL)**usesUserKeyEquivalents**;

// Instance Methods
- (BOOL)**hasSubmenu**;
- (BOOL)**isEnabled**;
- (BOOL)**isSeparatorItem**;
- (NSString *)**mnemonic**;
- (NSString *)**userKeyEquivalent**;

// Methods Implementing NSMenuItem
- (id)**initWithTitle**:(NSString *)*aString* **action**:(SEL)*aSelector* **keyEquivalent**:(NSString *)*charCode*;
- (void)**setMenu**:(NSMenu *)*menu*;
- (NSMenu *)**menu**;
- (BOOL)**hasSubmenu**;
- (void)**setSubmenu**:(NSMenu *)*submenu*;
- (NSMenu *)**submenu**;
- (void)**setTitle**:(NSString *)*aString*;
- (NSString *)**title**;
- (BOOL)**isSeparatorItem**;
- (void)**setKeyEquivalent**:(NSString *)*aKeyEquivalent*;
- (NSString *)**keyEquivalent**;
- (void)**setKeyEquivalentModifierMask**:(unsigned int)*mask*;
- (unsigned int)**keyEquivalentModifierMask**;
- (NSString *)**userKeyEquivalent**;
- (unsigned int)**userKeyEquivalentModifierMask**;
- (void)**setMnemonicLocation**:(unsigned)*location*;
- (unsigned)**mnemonicLocation**;
- (NSString *)**mnemonic**;

- (void)**setTitleWithMnemonic**:(NSString *)*stringWithAmpersand*;
- (void)**setImage**:(NSImage *)*menuImage*;
- (NSImage *)**image**;
- (void)**setState**:(int)*state*;
- (int)**state**;
- (void)**setOnStateImage**:(NSImage *)*image*;
- (NSImage *)**onStateImage**;
- (void)**setOffStateImage**:(NSImage *)*image*;
- (NSImage *)**offStateImage**;
- (void)**setMixedStateImage**:(NSImage *)*image*;
- (NSImage *)**mixedStateImage**;
- (void)**setEnabled**:(BOOL)*flag*;
- (BOOL)**isEnabled**;
- (void)**setTarget**:(id)*anObject*;
- (id)**target**;
- (void)**setAction**:(SEL)*aSelector*;
- (SEL)**action**;
- (void)**setTag**:(int)*anInt*;
- (int)**tag**;
- (void)**setRepresentedObject**:(id)*anObject*;
- (id)**representedObject**;

NSMenuItemCell

Mac OS X 10.0

This class is used to represent and draw menu items in a menu view. This class has been deprecated and should not be used in new code. You should use the APIs provided by NSMenu and NSMenuItem instead.

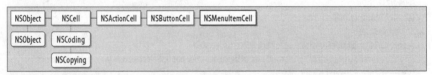

@interface **NSMenuItemCell** : NSButtonCell

// Accessor Methods
- (void)**setNeedsSizing**:(BOOL)*flag*;
- (BOOL)**needsSizing**;
- (void)**setNeedsDisplay**:(BOOL)*flag*;
- (BOOL)**needsDisplay**;
- (void)**setHighlighted**:(BOOL)*flag*;
- (void)**setMenuView**:(NSMenuView *)*menuView*;
- (NSMenuView *)**menuView**;
- (void)**setMenuItem**:(NSMenuItem *)*item*;
- (NSMenuItem *)**menuItem**;
// Instance Methods
- (void)**calcSize**;
- (void)**drawBorderAndBackgroundWithFrame**:(NSRect)*cellFrame* **inView**:(NSView *)*controlView*;
- (void)**drawImageWithFrame**:(NSRect)*cellFrame* **inView**:(NSView *)*controlView*;
- (void)**drawKeyEquivalentWithFrame**:(NSRect)*cellFrame* **inView**:(NSView *)*controlView*;
- (void)**drawSeparatorItemWithFrame**:(NSRect)*cellFrame* **inView**:(NSView *)*controlView*;

- (void)**drawStateImageWithFrame**:(NSRect)*cellFrame* **inView**:(NSView *)*controlView*;
- (void)**drawTitleWithFrame**:(NSRect)*cellFrame* **inView**:(NSView *)*controlView*;
- (NSRect)**imageRectForBounds**:(NSRect)*cellFrame*;
- (float)**imageWidth**;
- (BOOL)**isHighlighted**;
- (NSRect)**keyEquivalentRectForBounds**:(NSRect)*cellFrame*;
- (float)**keyEquivalentWidth**;
- (NSRect)**stateImageRectForBounds**:(NSRect)*cellFrame*;
- (float)**stateImageWidth**;
- (NSRect)**titleRectForBounds**:(NSRect)*cellFrame*;
- (float)**titleWidth**;

Subclasses

NSPopUpButtonCell

NSMenuView   Mac OS X 10.0

This subclass of NSView is used to draw menus. Like NSMenuItemCell, this class has been deprecated, and should not be used in new code. You should use the APIs provided by NSMenu and NSMenuItem instead.

@interface **NSMenuView** : NSView
// *Initializers*
- (id)**initAsTearOff**;
- (id)**initWithFrame**:(NSRect)*frame*;
// *Accessor Methods*
- (void)**setWindowFrameForAttachingToRect**:(NSRect)*screenRect*
    onScreen:(NSScreen *)*screen* **preferredEdge**:(NSRectEdge)*edge* **popUpSelectedItem**:(int)*selectedItemIndex*;
- (void)**setHorizontalEdgePadding**:(float)*pad*;
- (float)**horizontalEdgePadding**;
- (void)**setNeedsDisplayForItemAtIndex**:(int)*index*;
- (void)**setNeedsSizing**:(BOOL)*flag*;
- (BOOL)**needsSizing**;
- (void)**setHighlightedItemIndex**:(int)*index*;
- (int)**highlightedItemIndex**;
- (void)**setHorizontal**:(BOOL)*flag*;
- (void)**setMenu**:(NSMenu *)*menu*;
- (NSMenu *)**menu**;
- (void)**setFont**:(NSFont *)*font*;
- (NSFont *)**font**;
- (void)**setMenuItemCell**:(NSMenuItemCell *)*cell* **forItemAtIndex**:(int)*index*;
// *Class Methods*
+ (float)**menuBarHeight**;
// *Instance Methods*
- (void)**attachSubmenuForItemAtIndex**:(int)*index*;
- (NSMenu *)**attachedMenu**;
- (NSMenuView *)**attachedMenuView**;

- (void)**detachSubmenu**;
- (float)**imageAndTitleOffset**;
- (float)**imageAndTitleWidth**;
- (int)**indexOfItemAtPoint**:(NSPoint)*point*;
- (NSRect)**innerRect**;
- (BOOL)**isAttached**;
- (BOOL)**isHorizontal**;
- (BOOL)**isTornOff**;
- (void)**itemAdded**:(NSNotification *)*notification*;
- (void)**itemChanged**:(NSNotification *)*notification*;
- (void)**itemRemoved**:(NSNotification *)*notification*;
- (float)**keyEquivalentOffset**;
- (float)**keyEquivalentWidth**;
- (NSPoint)**locationForSubmenu**:(NSMenu *)*aSubmenu*;
- (NSMenuItemCell *)**menuItemCellForItemAtIndex**:(int)*index*;
- (void)**performActionWithHighlightingForItemAtIndex**:(int)*index*;
- (NSRect)**rectOfItemAtIndex**:(int)*index*;
- (void)**sizeToFit**;
- (float)**stateImageOffset**;
- (float)**stateImageWidth**;
- (BOOL)**trackWithEvent**:(NSEvent *)*event*;
- (void)**update**;

NSMovie

This class provides an object-oriented wrapper for QuickTime movie data, which allows clients to easily load QuickTime movies into memory. The data represented by an NSMovie object can be any format supported by the QuickTime APIs, including video, sound, and still images. Clients can obtain a pointer to the QuickTime data by sending a QTMovie message to the NSMovie instance; this pointer is suitable for use with any of the QuickTime APIs.

@interface **NSMovie** : NSObject <NSCoding, NSCopying>

// Class Methods
+ (BOOL)**canInitWithPasteboard**:(NSPasteboard*)*pasteboard*;
+ (NSArray*)**movieUnfilteredFileTypes**;
+ (NSArray*)**movieUnfilteredPasteboardTypes**;

// Instance Methods
- (id)**initWithMovie**:(void* /*Movie*/)*movie*;
- (id)**initWithPasteboard**:(NSPasteboard*)*pasteboard*;
- (id)**initWithURL**:(NSURL*)*url* **byReference**:(BOOL)*byRef*;
- (void*/*Movie*/)**QTMovie**;
- (NSURL*)**URL**;

// Methods Implementing NSCoding
- (void)**encodeWithCoder**:(NSCoder *)*aCoder*;
- (id)**initWithCoder**:(NSCoder *)*aDecoder*;

// Methods Implementing NSCopying
- (id)**copyWithZone**:(NSZone *)zone;

NSMovieView

This class provides a means to display an NSMovie in an Cocoa view. NSMovieView has provisions to display in the view controls to control playback and editing of the represented movie. Additionally, action methods declared in the interface allow you to build custom interfaces for controlling movie playback and editing.

@interface **NSMovieView** : NSView
// Accessor Methods
- (void)**setMuted**:(BOOL)mute;
- (void)**setRate**:(float)rate;
- (float)**rate**;
- (void)**setLoopMode**:(NSQTMovieLoopMode)mode;
- (NSQTMovieLoopMode)**loopMode**;
- (void)**setVolume**:(float)volume;
- (float)**volume**;
- (void)**setPlaysEveryFrame**:(BOOL)flag;
- (BOOL)**playsEveryFrame**;
- (void)**setPlaysSelectionOnly**:(BOOL)flag;
- (BOOL)**playsSelectionOnly**;
- (void)**setEditable**:(BOOL)editable;
// Instance Methods
- (void)**cut**:(id)sender;
- (void)**clear**:(id)sender;
- (void)**gotoBeginning**:(id)sender;
- (NSMovie*)**movie**;
- (void* /*MovieController*/)**movieController**;
- (NSRect)**movieRect**;
- (void)**setMovie**:(NSMovie*)movie;
- (void)**copy**:(id)sender;
- (void)**gotoEnd**:(id)sender;
- (void)**gotoPosterFrame**:(id)sender;
- (BOOL)**isControllerVisible**;
- (BOOL)**isEditable**;
- (BOOL)**isMuted**;
- (BOOL)**isPlaying**;
- (void)**paste**:(id)sender;
- (void)**resizeWithMagnification**:(float)magnification;
- (void)**selectAll**:(id)sender;
- (void)**showController**:(BOOL)show **adjustingSize**:(BOOL)adjustSize;
- (NSSize)**sizeForMagnification**:(float)magnification;
- (void)**start**:(id)sender;
- (void)**stepBack**:(id)sender;
- (void)**stepForward**:(id)sender;
- (void)**stop**:(id)sender;

NSMutableParagraphStyle

This class extends the interface of NSParagraphStyle to allow for the characteristics of a paragraph style object to be altered after the object is initialized. See the NSParagraphStyle class description later in this chapter for more information.

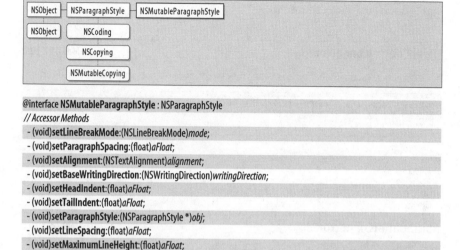

```
@interface NSMutableParagraphStyle : NSParagraphStyle
// Accessor Methods
 - (void)setLineBreakMode:(NSLineBreakMode)mode;
 - (void)setParagraphSpacing:(float)aFloat;
 - (void)setAlignment:(NSTextAlignment)alignment;
 - (void)setBaseWritingDirection:(NSWritingDirection)writingDirection;
 - (void)setHeadIndent:(float)aFloat;
 - (void)setTailIndent:(float)aFloat;
 - (void)setParagraphStyle:(NSParagraphStyle *)obj;
 - (void)setLineSpacing:(float)aFloat;
 - (void)setMaximumLineHeight:(float)aFloat;
 - (void)setTabStops:(NSArray *)array;
 - (void)setMinimumLineHeight:(float)aFloat;
 - (void)setFirstLineHeadIndent:(float)aFloat;
// Instance Methods
 - (void)addTabStop:(NSTextTab *)anObject;
 - (void)removeTabStop:(NSTextTab *)anObject;
```

NSNibConnector

This class represents a connection between two objects in Interface Builder. The Application Kit declares two subclasses that represent the two types of connections supported in Interface Builder: NSNibControlConnection and NSNibOutletConnection.

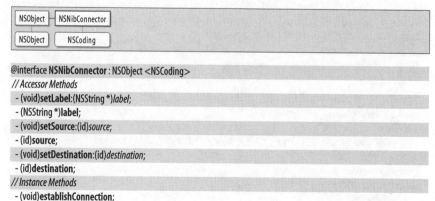

```
@interface NSNibConnector : NSObject <NSCoding>
// Accessor Methods
 - (void)setLabel:(NSString *)label;
 - (NSString *)label;
 - (void)setSource:(id)source;
 - (id)source;
 - (void)setDestination:(id)destination;
 - (id)destination;
// Instance Methods
 - (void)establishConnection;
```

- (void)**replaceObject:**(id)*oldObject* **withObject:**(id)*newObject*;
// *Methods Implementing NSCoding*
- (void)**encodeWithCoder:**(NSCoder *)*aCoder*;
- (id)**initWithCoder:**(NSCoder *)*aDecoder*;

Subclasses
NSNibControlConnector, NSNibOutletConnector

NSNibControlConnector   Mac OS X 10.0

This class represents an *action* connection between two objects in Interface Builder.

@interface **NSNibControlConnector** : NSNibConnector
// *Instance Methods*
- (void)**establishConnection;**

NSNibOutletConnector   Mac OS X 10.0

This class represents an *outlet* connection between two objects in Interface Builder.

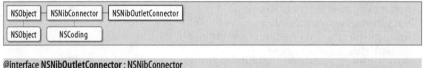

@interface **NSNibOutletConnector** : NSNibConnector
// *Instance Methods*
- (void)**establishConnection;**

NSOpenGLContext   Mac OS X 10.0

This class provides an interface to objects that are responsible for interpreting and rendering calls to the OpenGL API. **NSOpenGLContext** supports rendering on the full screen (as would be done in a game), off-screen, or into an instance of **NSOpenGLView** (which might be useful for data visualization applications).

@interface **NSOpenGLContext** : NSObject
// *Initializers*
- (id)**initWithFormat:**(NSOpenGLPixelFormat *)*format* **shareContext:**(NSOpenGLContext *)*share*;
// *Accessor Methods*
- (void)**setCurrentVirtualScreen:**(int)*screen*;
- (int)**currentVirtualScreen;**
- (void)**setFullScreen;**

- (void)**setOffScreen:**(void *)*baseaddr* **width:**(long)*width* **height:**(long)*height* **rowbytes:**(long)*rowbytes*;
- (void)**setValues:**(const long *)*vals* **forParameter:**(NSOpenGLContextParameter)*param*;
- (void)**setView:**(NSView *)*view*;
- (NSView *)**view**;
// Class Methods
+ (void)**clearCurrentContext**;
+ (NSOpenGLContext *)**currentContext**;
// Instance Methods
- (void)**createTexture:**(unsigned long/*GLenum*/)*target* **fromView:**(NSView*)*view*
    internalFormat:(unsigned long/*GLenum*/)*format*;
- (void)**clearDrawable**;
- (void)**copyAttributesFromContext:**(NSOpenGLContext *)*context* **withMask:**(unsigned long)*mask*;
- (void)**flushBuffer**;
- (void)**getValues:**(long *)*vals* **forParameter:**(NSOpenGLContextParameter)*param*;
- (void)**makeCurrentContext**;
- (void)**update**;

NSOpenGLPixelFormat

Mac OS X 10.0

This class is used by NSOpenGLContext and NSOpenGLView to specify the attributes of an OpenGL pixel format, such as buffer size and type and rendering options.

@interface **NSOpenGLPixelFormat** : NSObject <NSCoding>
// Initializers
- (id)**initWithAttributes:**(NSOpenGLPixelFormatAttribute*)*attribs*;
- (id)**initWithData:**(NSData*)*attribs*;
// Accessor Methods
- (void)**setAttributes:**(NSData*)*attribs*;
- (NSData*)**attributes**;
// Instance Methods
- (void)**getValues:**(long*)*vals* **forAttribute:**(NSOpenGLPixelFormatAttribute)*attrib* **forVirtualScreen:**(int)*screen*;
- (int)**numberOfVirtualScreens**;
// Methods Implementing NSCoding
- (void)**encodeWithCoder:**(NSCoder *)*aCoder*;
- (id)**initWithCoder:**(NSCoder *)*aDecoder*;

NSOpenGLView

Mac OS X 10.0

This subclass of NSView allows applications to render calls to the OpenGL API into a Cocoa view hierarchy. Instances of this class maintain NSOpenGLPixelFormat and NSOpenGLContext objects to control many OpenGL rendering options and parameters.

```
@interface NSOpenGLView : NSView
// Initializers
 - (id)initWithFrame:(NSRect)frameRect pixelFormat:(NSOpenGLPixelFormat*)format;
// Accessor Methods
 - (void)setPixelFormat:(NSOpenGLPixelFormat*)pixelFormat;
 - (NSOpenGLPixelFormat*)pixelFormat;
 - (void)setOpenGLContext:(NSOpenGLContext*)context;
 - (NSOpenGLContext*)openGLContext;
// Class Methods
 + (NSOpenGLPixelFormat*)defaultPixelFormat;
// Instance Methods
 - (void)clearGLContext;
 - (void)reshape;
 - (void)update;
```

NSOpenPanel   Mac OS X 10.0

This subclass of NSSavePanel implements a Mac OS X Open panel with which users are
presented a filesystem browser interface to choose files or directories for the application to open. The Open panel is created by invoking the class method **openPanel**, and is
displayed onscreen using any of the **runModal...** or **beginSheet...** methods. After an Open
panel has been closed by the user, an application can obtain an array of the selected
files or directories as paths or URLs using the method **filenames** or **URLs**.

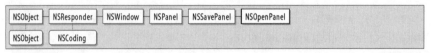

```
@interface NSOpenPanel : NSSavePanel
// Accessor Methods
 - (void)setCanChooseDirectories:(BOOL)flag;
 - (BOOL)canChooseDirectories;
 - (void)setCanChooseFiles:(BOOL)flag;
 - (BOOL)canChooseFiles;
 - (void)setResolvesAliases:(BOOL)flag;
 - (BOOL)resolvesAliases;
 - (void)setAllowsMultipleSelection:(BOOL)flag;
 - (BOOL)allowsMultipleSelection;
// Class Methods
 + (NSOpenPanel *)openPanel;
// Instance Methods
 - (NSArray *)URLs;
 - (void)beginSheetForDirectory:(NSString *)path file:(NSString *)name types:(NSArray *)fileTypes
     modalForWindow:(NSWindow *)docWindow modalDelegate:(id)delegate didEndSelector:(SEL)didEndSelector
     contextInfo:(void *)contextInfo;
 - (NSArray *)filenames;
 - (int)runModalForDirectory:(NSString *)path file:(NSString *)name types:(NSArray *)fileTypes;
 - (int)runModalForDirectory:(NSString *)path file:(NSString *)name types:(NSArray *)fileTypes
     relativeToWindow:(NSWindow*)window;
 - (int)runModalForTypes:(NSArray *)fileTypes;
```

NSOutlineView

This subclass of NSTableView implements a user interface component that can display hierarchical data (such as how a filesystem structure is displayed in the Finder's list view). In an NSOutlineView, users can expand and collapse rows, change the width and order of columns, and edit the contents of the outline. NSOutlineView objects rely on classes that implement the NSOutlineViewDataSource protocol to provide the data to be displayed in the outline.

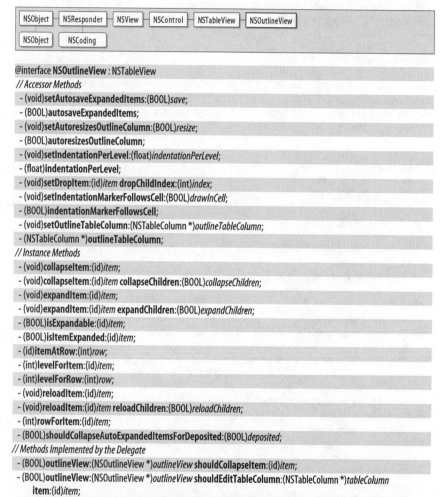

```
@interface NSOutlineView : NSTableView
// Accessor Methods
 - (void)setAutosaveExpandedItems:(BOOL)save;
 - (BOOL)autosaveExpandedItems;
 - (void)setAutoresizesOutlineColumn:(BOOL)resize;
 - (BOOL)autoresizesOutlineColumn;
 - (void)setIndentationPerLevel:(float)indentationPerLevel;
 - (float)indentationPerLevel;
 - (void)setDropItem:(id)item dropChildIndex:(int)index;
 - (void)setIndentationMarkerFollowsCell:(BOOL)drawInCell;
 - (BOOL)indentationMarkerFollowsCell;
 - (void)setOutlineTableColumn:(NSTableColumn *)outlineTableColumn;
 - (NSTableColumn *)outlineTableColumn;
// Instance Methods
 - (void)collapseItem:(id)item;
 - (void)collapseItem:(id)item collapseChildren:(BOOL)collapseChildren;
 - (void)expandItem:(id)item;
 - (void)expandItem:(id)item expandChildren:(BOOL)expandChildren;
 - (BOOL)isExpandable:(id)item;
 - (BOOL)isItemExpanded:(id)item;
 - (id)itemAtRow:(int)row;
 - (int)levelForItem:(id)item;
 - (int)levelForRow:(int)row;
 - (void)reloadItem:(id)item;
 - (void)reloadItem:(id)item reloadChildren:(BOOL)reloadChildren;
 - (int)rowForItem:(id)item;
 - (BOOL)shouldCollapseAutoExpandedItemsForDeposited:(BOOL)deposited;
// Methods Implemented by the Delegate
 - (BOOL)outlineView:(NSOutlineView *)outlineView shouldCollapseItem:(id)item;
 - (BOOL)outlineView:(NSOutlineView *)outlineView shouldEditTableColumn:(NSTableColumn *)tableColumn
        item:(id)item;
 - (BOOL)outlineView:(NSOutlineView *)outlineView shouldExpandItem:(id)item;
 - (BOOL)outlineView:(NSOutlineView *)outlineView shouldSelectItem:(id)item;
 - (BOOL)outlineView:(NSOutlineView *)outlineView shouldSelectTableColumn:(NSTableColumn *)tableColumn;
 - (void)outlineView:(NSOutlineView *)outlineView willDisplayCell:(id)cell
        forTableColumn:(NSTableColumn *)tableColumn item:(id)item;
 - (void)outlineView:(NSOutlineView *)outlineView willDisplayOutlineCell:(id)cell
        forTableColumn:(NSTableColumn *)tableColumn item:(id)item;
```

- (void)**outlineViewColumnDidMove**:(NSNotification *)*notification*;
- (void)**outlineViewColumnDidResize**:(NSNotification *)*notification*;
- (void)**outlineViewItemDidCollapse**:(NSNotification *)*notification*;
- (void)**outlineViewItemDidExpand**:(NSNotification *)*notification*;
- (void)**outlineViewItemWillCollapse**:(NSNotification *)*notification*;
- (void)**outlineViewItemWillExpand**:(NSNotification *)*notification*;
- (void)**outlineViewSelectionDidChange**:(NSNotification *)*notification*;
- (void)**outlineViewSelectionIsChanging**:(NSNotification *)*notification*;
- (BOOL)**selectionShouldChangeInOutlineView**:(NSOutlineView *)*outlineView*;
// *Notifications* **NSOutlineViewSelectionDidChangeNotification**; **NSOutlineViewSelectionIsChangingNotification**;

NSPageLayout   Mac OS X 10.0

This class implements the Mac OS X Page Layout panel, with which users can specify page layout information such as the paper size and orientation. Page layout objects are created with the class layout **pageLayout**. The panel is made visible by invoking either runModal, or runModalWithPrintInfo:. Alternatively, the page layout panel may be displayed as a sheet.

@interface **NSPageLayout** : NSObject
// *Accessor Methods*
- (void)**setAccessoryView**:(NSView *)*aView*;
- (NSView *)**accessoryView**;
- (NSView *)**accessoryView**;
- (void)**setAccessoryView**:(NSView *)*aView*;
// *Class Methods*
+ (NSPageLayout *)**pageLayout**;
+ (NSPageLayout *)**pageLayout**;
// *Instance Methods*
- (void)**beginSheetWithPrintInfo**:(NSPrintInfo *)*printInfo*
    modalForWindow:(NSWindow *)*docWindow* **delegate**:(id)*delegate* **didEndSelector**:(SEL)*didEndSelector*
    contextInfo:(void *)*contextInfo*;
- (void)**convertOldFactor**:(float *)*oldFactor* **newFactor**:(float *)*newFactor*;
- (void)**pickedButton**:(id)*sender*;
- (void)**pickedOrientation**:(id)*sender*;
- (void)**pickedPaperSize**:(id)*sender*;
- (void)**pickedUnits**:(id)*sender*;
- (NSPrintInfo *)**printInfo**;
- (NSPrintInfo *)**printInfo**;
- (void)**readPrintInfo**;
- (void)**readPrintInfo**;
- (int)**runModal**;
- (int)**runModal**;
- (int)**runModalWithPrintInfo**:(NSPrintInfo *)*pInfo*;
- (int)**runModalWithPrintInfo**:(NSPrintInfo *)*pInfo*;
- (void)**writePrintInfo**;
- (void)**writePrintInfo**;

NSPanel

This subclass extends the functionality of NSWindow that is useful for auxiliary and utility windows. In particular, panels are different from windows in several key ways. First, NSPanels adopt the behavior that by default the panel will hide itself when its application becomes inactive. Second, NSPanels are capable of becoming key windows, but they may never have main window status. Additionally, NSPanel object can be made to float above all other windows, making their contents easily accessible when other windows are in front.

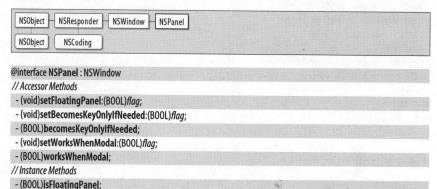

```
@interface NSPanel : NSWindow
// Accessor Methods
  - (void)setFloatingPanel:(BOOL)flag;
  - (void)setBecomesKeyOnlyIfNeeded:(BOOL)flag;
  - (BOOL)becomesKeyOnlyIfNeeded;
  - (void)setWorksWhenModal:(BOOL)flag;
  - (BOOL)worksWhenModal;
// Instance Methods
  - (BOOL)isFloatingPanel;
```

Subclasses

NSColorPanel, NSFontPanel, NSSavePanel

NSParagraphStyle

Instances of this class are used in attributed strings to encapsulate paragraph and ruler characteristics to be applied to a range of text. Paragraph style attributes included such characteristics as paragraph alignment, line height and spacing, paragraph spacing, and more. NSParagraphStyle is an immutable class. If you require mutability, use its subclass, NSMutableParagraphStyle.

```
@interface NSParagraphStyle : NSObject <NSCoding, NSCopying, NSMutableCopying>
// Class Methods
  + (NSParagraphStyle *)defaultParagraphStyle;
  + (NSWritingDirection)defaultWritingDirectionForLanguage:(NSString *)languageName;
// Instance Methods
  - (NSTextAlignment)alignment;
  - (NSWritingDirection)baseWritingDirection;
  - (float)firstLineHeadIndent;
```

```
- (float)headIndent;
- (NSLineBreakMode)lineBreakMode;
- (float)lineSpacing;
- (float)maximumLineHeight;
- (float)minimumLineHeight;
- (float)paragraphSpacing;
- (NSArray *)tabStops;
- (float)tailIndent;
// Methods Implementing NSCoding
- (void)encodeWithCoder:(NSCoder *)aCoder;
- (id)initWithCoder:(NSCoder *)aDecoder;
// Methods Implementing NSCopying
- (id)copyWithZone:(NSZone *)zone;
// Methods Implementing NSMutableCopying
- (id)mutableCopyWithZone:(NSZone *)zone;
```

Subclasses

NSMutableParagraphStyle

NSPasteboard

Mac OS X 10.0

This class provides access to the pasteboard server, which allows applications to share data with one another. A general purpose pasteboard is obtained using the class method generalPasteboard. Alternatively, clients can access one of the standard pasteboards (general, font, ruler, find, and drag), or create a private pasteboard using the class method pasteboardWithName:.

Data is read and written to a pasteboard using the methods dataForType: and setData:forType:, respectively.

```
@interface NSPasteboard : NSObject
// Convenience Constructors
+ (NSPasteboard *)pasteboardByFilteringData:(NSData *)data ofType:(NSString *)type;
+ (NSPasteboard *)pasteboardByFilteringFile:(NSString *)filename;
+ (NSPasteboard *)pasteboardByFilteringTypesInPasteboard:(NSPasteboard *)pboard;
+ (NSPasteboard *)pasteboardWithName:(NSString *)name;
+ (NSPasteboard *)pasteboardWithUniqueName;
// Accessor Methods
- (BOOL)setString:(NSString *)string forType:(NSString *)dataType;
- (BOOL)setData:(NSData *)data forType:(NSString *)dataType;
- (BOOL)setPropertyList:(id)plist forType:(NSString *)dataType;
// Class Methods
+ (NSPasteboard *)generalPasteboard;
+ (NSArray *)typesFilterableTo:(NSString *)type;
// Instance Methods
- (NSString *)availableTypeFromArray:(NSArray *)types;
- (int)addTypes:(NSArray *)newTypes owner:(id)newOwner;
```

- (int)**changeCount**;
- (NSData *)**dataForType**:(NSString *)*dataType*;
- (int)**declareTypes**:(NSArray *)*newTypes* **owner**:(id)*newOwner*;
- (NSString *)**name**;
- (id)**propertyListForType**:(NSString *)*dataType*;
- (NSString *)**readFileContentsType**:(NSString *)*type* **toFile**:(NSString *)*filename*;
- (NSFileWrapper *)**readFileWrapper**;
- (void)**releaseGlobally**;
- (NSString *)**stringForType**:(NSString *)*dataType*;
- (NSArray *)**types**;
- (BOOL)**writeFileContents**:(NSString *)*filename*;
- (BOOL)**writeFileWrapper**:(NSFileWrapper *)*wrapper*;

NSPDFImageRep   Mac OS X 10.0

This is a subclass of NSImageRep that understands how to manipulate, represent, and draw PDF-formatted image data.

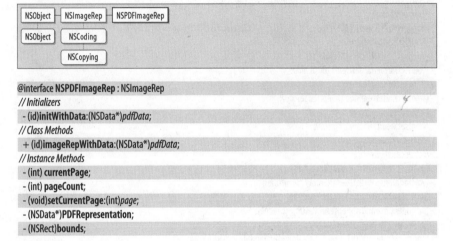

```
@interface NSPDFImageRep : NSImageRep
// Initializers
- (id)initWithData:(NSData*)pdfData;
// Class Methods
+ (id)imageRepWithData:(NSData*)pdfData;
// Instance Methods
- (int) currentPage;
- (int) pageCount;
- (void)setCurrentPage:(int)page;
- (NSData*)PDFRepresentation;
- (NSRect)bounds;
```

NSPICTImageRep   Mac OS X 10.0

This is a subclass of NSImageRep that understands how to manipulate, represent, and draw Macintosh PICT-formatted image data.

```
@interface NSPICTImageRep : NSImageRep
// Initializers
- (id)initWithData:(NSData*)pictData;
// Class Methods
+ (id)imageRepWithData:(NSData*)pictData;
```

```
// Instance Methods
- (NSRect) boundingBox;
- (NSData*)PICTRepresentation;
```

NSPopUpButton

This class implements a pop-up button interface component. A pop-up button is a button that displays a menu when it is activated; the displayed menu can either be a pop-up menu that appears beneath the mouse cursor, or a pull-down menu that is drawn below the button.

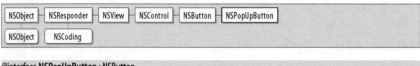

```
@interface NSPopUpButton : NSButton
// Initializers
- (id)initWithFrame:(NSRect)buttonFrame pullsDown:(BOOL)flag;
// Accessor Methods
- (void)setPullsDown:(BOOL)flag;
- (BOOL)pullsDown;
- (void)setTitle:(NSString *)aString;
- (void)setAutoenablesItems:(BOOL)flag;
- (BOOL)autoenablesItems;
- (void)setPreferredEdge:(NSRectEdge)edge;
- (NSRectEdge)preferredEdge;
- (void)setMenu:(NSMenu *)menu;
- (NSMenu *)menu;
// Instance Methods
- (void)addItemWithTitle:(NSString *)title;
- (void)addItemsWithTitles:(NSArray *)itemTitles;
- (int)indexOfItem:(id <NSMenuItem>)item;
- (int)indexOfItemWithRepresentedObject:(id)obj;
- (int)indexOfItemWithTag:(int)tag;
- (int)indexOfItemWithTarget:(id)target andAction:(SEL)actionSelector;
- (int)indexOfItemWithTitle:(NSString *)title;
- (int)indexOfSelectedItem;
- (void)insertItemWithTitle:(NSString *)title atIndex:(int)index;
- (NSArray *)itemArray;
- (id <NSMenuItem>)itemAtIndex:(int)index;
- (NSString *)itemTitleAtIndex:(int)index;
- (NSArray *)itemTitles;
- (id <NSMenuItem>)itemWithTitle:(NSString *)title;
- (id <NSMenuItem>)lastItem;
- (int)numberOfItems;
- (void)removeAllItems;
- (void)removeItemAtIndex:(int)index;
- (void)removeItemWithTitle:(NSString *)title;
- (void)selectItem:(id <NSMenuItem>)item;
- (void)selectItemAtIndex:(int)index;
- (void)selectItemWithTitle:(NSString *)title;
```

```
- (id <NSMenuItem>)selectedItem;
- (void)synchronizeTitleAndSelectedItem;
- (NSString *)titleOfSelectedItem;
```
// Notifications
```
NSPopUpButtonWillPopUpNotification;
```

NSPopUpButtonCell

Mac OS X 10.0

This class is the associated NSCell for an NSPopUpButton object that handles the drawing and mouse-handling for the control.

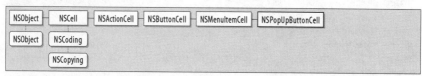

@interface **NSPopUpButtonCell** : NSMenuItemCell
// Initializers
```
- (id)initTextCell:(NSString *)stringValue pullsDown:(BOOL)pullDown;
```
// Accessor Methods
```
- (void)setAltersStateOfSelectedItem:(BOOL)flag;
- (BOOL)altersStateOfSelectedItem;
- (void)setTitle:(NSString *)aString;
- (void)setArrowPosition:(NSPopUpArrowPosition)position;
- (NSPopUpArrowPosition)arrowPosition;
- (void)setPullsDown:(BOOL)flag;
- (BOOL)pullsDown;
- (void)setUsesItemFromMenu:(BOOL)flag;
- (BOOL)usesItemFromMenu;
- (void)setAutoenablesItems:(BOOL)flag;
- (BOOL)autoenablesItems;
- (void)setPreferredEdge:(NSRectEdge)edge;
- (NSRectEdge)preferredEdge;
- (void)setMenu:(NSMenu *)menu;
- (NSMenu *)menu;
```
// Instance Methods
```
- (void)addItemWithTitle:(NSString *)title;
- (void)addItemsWithTitles:(NSArray *)itemTitles;
- (void)attachPopUpWithFrame:(NSRect)cellFrame inView:(NSView *)controlView;
- (void)dismissPopUp;
- (int)indexOfItem:(id <NSMenuItem>)item;
- (int)indexOfItemWithRepresentedObject:(id)obj;
- (int)indexOfItemWithTag:(int)tag;
- (int)indexOfItemWithTarget:(id)target andAction:(SEL)actionSelector;
- (int)indexOfItemWithTitle:(NSString *)title;
- (int)indexOfSelectedItem;
- (void)insertItemWithTitle:(NSString *)title atIndex:(int)index;
- (NSArray *)itemArray;
- (id <NSMenuItem>)itemAtIndex:(int)index;
- (NSString *)itemTitleAtIndex:(int)index;
```

```
- (NSArray *)itemTitles;
- (id <NSMenuItem>)itemWithTitle:(NSString *)title;
- (id <NSMenuItem>)lastItem;
- (int)numberOfItems;
- (void)performClickWithFrame:(NSRect)frame inView:(NSView *)controlView;
- (void)removeAllItems;
- (void)removeItemAtIndex:(int)index;
- (void)removeItemWithTitle:(NSString *)title;
- (void)selectItem:(id <NSMenuItem>)item;
- (void)selectItemAtIndex:(int)index;
- (void)selectItemWithTitle:(NSString *)title;
- (id <NSMenuItem>)selectedItem;
- (void)synchronizeTitleAndSelectedItem;
- (NSString *)titleOfSelectedItem;
// Notifications
NSPopUpButtonCellWillPopUpNotification;
```

NSPrinter   Mac OS X 10.0

This class represents a printer as it is described in its PPD file. Using this class, applications can obtain information about any of the printers found in the Print Center application. To create an instance of NSPrint, use either the method printerWithName: or the method printerWithType:. If the printer indicated by the name or type does not exist in the Print Center printer list, these methods will return nil. In these methods, *Type* refers to the make and model of the printer, while *Name* refers to the name given to the printer in Print Center. Applications can obtain arrays of the names and types of available printers by invoking the class methods printerNames and printerTypes, respectively.

```
@interface NSPrinter : NSObject <NSCoding, NSCopying>
// Convenience Constructors
 + (NSArray *)printerNames;
 + (NSArray *)printerTypes;
 + (NSPrinter *)printerWithName:(NSString *)name;
 + (NSPrinter *)printerWithName:(NSString *)name domain:(NSString *)domain includeUnavailable:(BOOL)flag;
 + (NSPrinter *)printerWithType:(NSString *)type;
// Instance Methods
- (BOOL)acceptsBinary;
- (BOOL)booleanForKey:(NSString *)key inTable:(NSString *)table;
- (NSDictionary *)deviceDescription;
- (NSString *)domain;
- (float)floatForKey:(NSString *)key inTable:(NSString *)table;
- (NSString *)host;
- (NSRect)imageRectForPaper:(NSString *)paperName;
- (int)intForKey:(NSString *)key inTable:(NSString *)table;
- (BOOL)isColor;
```

- (BOOL)**isFontAvailable**:(NSString *)*faceName*;
- (BOOL)**isKey**:(NSString *)*key* **inTable**:(NSString *)*table*;
- (BOOL)**isOutputStackInReverseOrder**;
- (int)**languageLevel**;
- (NSString *)**name**;
- (NSString *)**note**;
- (NSSize)**pageSizeForPaper**:(NSString *)*paperName*;
- (NSRect)**rectForKey**:(NSString *)*key* **inTable**:(NSString *)*table*;
- (NSSize)**sizeForKey**:(NSString *)*key* **inTable**:(NSString *)*table*;
- (NSPrinterTableStatus)**statusForTable**:(NSString *)*tableName*;
- (NSString *)**stringForKey**:(NSString *)*key* **inTable**:(NSString *)*table*;
- (NSArray *)**stringListForKey**:(NSString *)*key* **inTable**:(NSString *)*table*;
- (NSString *)**type**;
// Methods Implementing NSCoding
- (void)**encodeWithCoder**:(NSCoder *)*aCoder*;
- (id)**initWithCoder**:(NSCoder *)*aDecoder*;
// Methods Implementing NSCopying
- (id)**copyWithZone**:(NSZone *)*zone*;

NSPrintInfo

Mac OS X 10.0

This class encapsulates the information related to a print job, such as margin sizes, paper orientation, pagination type, and how the view contents should be positioned on the printed output (centered vertically, horizontally, no centering, etc.). Each application has a shared print info object that is used by default for all print jobs. This object is obtained using the class method **sharedPrintInfo**.

@interface **NSPrintInfo** : NSObject <NSCoding, NSCopying>
// Initializers
- (id)**initWithDictionary**:(NSDictionary *)*attributes*;
// Accessor Methods
- (void)**setUpPrintOperationDefaultValues**;
- (void)**setHorizontallyCentered**:(BOOL)*flag*;
- (void)**setPaperName**:(NSString *)*name*;
- (NSString *)**paperName**;
- (void)**setPaperSize**:(NSSize)*size*;
- (NSSize)**paperSize**;
- (void)**setOrientation**:(NSPrintingOrientation)*orientation*;
- (NSPrintingOrientation)**orientation**;
- (void)**setPrinter**:(NSPrinter *)*printer*;
- (NSPrinter *)**printer**;
- (void)**setJobDisposition**:(NSString *)*disposition*;
- (NSString *)**jobDisposition**;
- (void)**setHorizontalPagination**:(NSPrintingPaginationMode)*mode*;
- (NSPrintingPaginationMode)**horizontalPagination**;

- (void)**setRightMargin**:(float)*margin*;
- (float)**rightMargin**;
- (void)**setTopMargin**:(float)*margin*;
- (float)**topMargin**;
- (void)**setLeftMargin**:(float)*margin*;
- (float)**leftMargin**;
- (void)**setVerticallyCentered**:(BOOL)*flag*;
- (void)**setVerticalPagination**:(NSPrintingPaginationMode)*mode*;
- (NSPrintingPaginationMode)**verticalPagination**;
- (void)**setBottomMargin**:(float)*margin*;
- (float)**bottomMargin**;
// Class Methods
+ (NSPrinter *)**defaultPrinter**;
+ (void)**setDefaultPrinter**:(NSPrinter *)*printer*;
+ (void)**setSharedPrintInfo**:(NSPrintInfo *)*printInfo*;
+ (NSPrintInfo *)**sharedPrintInfo**;
+ (NSSize)**sizeForPaperName**:(NSString *)*name*;
// Instance Methods
- (NSMutableDictionary *)**dictionary**;
- (NSRect)**imageablePageBounds**;
- (BOOL)**isHorizontallyCentered**;
- (BOOL)**isVerticallyCentered**;
// Methods Implementing NSCoding
- (void)**encodeWithCoder**:(NSCoder *)*aCoder*;
- (id)**initWithCoder**:(NSCoder *)*aDecoder*;
// Methods Implementing NSCopying
- (id)**copyWithZone**:(NSZone *)*zone*;

NSPrintOperation

Mac OS X 10.0

Instances of this class work with NSView and NSPrintInfo objects to coordinate the generation of EPS or PDF data suitable for output to a printer device. In Cocoa's printing system, NSPrintInfo objects provide information about output settings such as paper size and margin widths, while NSView objects are responsible for creating the actual output with the same standard drawing APIs used for onscreen drawing.

@interface **NSPrintOperation** : NSObject
// Accessor Methods
- (void)**setPageOrder**:(NSPrintingPageOrder)*order*;
- (NSPrintingPageOrder)**pageOrder**;
- (void)**setCanSpawnSeparateThread**:(BOOL)*canSpawnSeparateThread*;
- (BOOL)**canSpawnSeparateThread**;
- (void)**setJobStyleHint**:(NSString *)*hint*;
- (NSString *)**jobStyleHint**;
- (void)**setPrintInfo**:(NSPrintInfo *)*aPrintInfo*;
- (NSPrintInfo *)**printInfo**;
- (void)**setAccessoryView**:(NSView *)*aView*;

- (NSView *)**accessoryView**;
- (void)**setPrintPanel**:(NSPrintPanel *)*panel*;
- (NSPrintPanel *)**printPanel**;
- (void)**setShowPanels**:(BOOL)*flag*;
- (BOOL)**showPanels**;
// Class Methods
+ (NSPrintOperation *)**EPSOperationWithView**:(NSView *)*aView*
    insideRect:(NSRect)*rect* **toData**:(NSMutableData *)*data*;
+ (NSPrintOperation *)**EPSOperationWithView**:(NSView *)*aView*
    insideRect:(NSRect)*rect* **toData**:(NSMutableData *)*data* **printInfo**:(NSPrintInfo *)*aPrintInfo*;
+ (NSPrintOperation *)**EPSOperationWithView**:(NSView *)*aView* **insideRect**:(NSRect)*rect* **toPath**:(NSString *)*path*
    printInfo:(NSPrintInfo *)*aPrintInfo*;
+ (NSPrintOperation *)**PDFOperationWithView**:(NSView *)*aView*
    insideRect:(NSRect)*rect* **toData**:(NSMutableData *)*data*;
+ (NSPrintOperation *)**PDFOperationWithView**:(NSView *)*aView*
    insideRect:(NSRect)*rect* **toData**:(NSMutableData *)*data* **printInfo**:(NSPrintInfo *)*aPrintInfo*;
+ (NSPrintOperation *)**PDFOperationWithView**:(NSView *)*aView* **insideRect**:(NSRect)*rect* **toPath**:(NSString *)*path*
    printInfo:(NSPrintInfo *)*aPrintInfo*;
+ (NSPrintOperation *)**currentOperation**;
+ (NSPrintOperation *)**printOperationWithView**:(NSView *)*aView*;
+ (NSPrintOperation *)**printOperationWithView**:(NSView *)*aView* **printInfo**:(NSPrintInfo *)*aPrintInfo*;
+ (void)**setCurrentOperation**:(NSPrintOperation *)*operation*;
// Instance Methods
- (void)**cleanUpOperation**;
- (BOOL)**deliverResult**;
- (NSGraphicsContext *)**createContext**;
- (int)**currentPage**;
- (NSGraphicsContext *)**context**;
- (void)**destroyContext**;
- (BOOL)**isCopyingOperation**;
- (BOOL)**runOperation**;
- (void)**runOperationModalForWindow**:(NSWindow *)*docWindow* **delegate**:(id)*delegate*
    didRunSelector:(SEL)*didRunSelector* **contextInfo**:(void *)*contextInfo*;
- (NSView *)**view**;

NSPrintPanel

Mac OS X 10.0

This class provides the Mac OS X Print panel interface for Cocoa applications. To obtain an instance of NSPrintPanel, use the class method **printPanel**. The panel is displayed and run when the **runModal** method is invoked, which will display the print panel as a window. It is also possible to display the print panel as a sheet attached to the document window; this is done with the method **beginSheetWithPrintInfo:modalFor-Window: delegate:didEndSelector:contextInfo:**.

Cocoa allows you to attach an accessory view to the print panel, providing an interface for users to configure options related to how your application handles printing. To set the accessory view, use the method **setAccessoryView:**.

@interface **NSPrintPanel** : NSObject

// *Accessor Methods*

- (void)**setAccessoryView**:(NSView *)*aView*;
- (NSView *)**accessoryView**;
- (void)**setJobStyleHint**:(NSString *)*hint*;
- (NSString *)**jobStyleHint**;

// *Class Methods*

+ (NSPrintPanel *)**printPanel**;

// *Instance Methods*

- (void)**beginSheetWithPrintInfo**:(NSPrintInfo *)*printInfo* **modalForWindow**:(NSWindow *)*docWindow*
    delegate:(id)*delegate* **didEndSelector**:(SEL)*didEndSelector* **contextInfo**:(void *)*contextInfo*;
- (void)**finalWritePrintInfo**;
- (void)**pickedAllPages**:(id)*sender*;
- (void)**pickedButton**:(id)*sender*;
- (void)**pickedLayoutList**:(id)*sender*;
- (int)**runModal**;
- (void)**updateFromPrintInfo**;

NSProgressIndicator

This class implements a progress bar interface component. Cocoa progress indicators may either be determinate or indeterminate. A *determinate* progress indicator shows progress by filling the bar proportionate to the amount of work that has been done. An *indeterminate* progress indicator displays the spinning barber pole to show that an application is busy with a task.

@interface **NSProgressIndicator** : NSView

// *Accessor Methods*

- (void)**setBezeled**:(BOOL)*flag*;
- (void)**setIndeterminate**:(BOOL)*flag*;
- (void)**setMaxValue**:(double)*newMaximum*;
- (double)**maxValue**;
- (void)**setDoubleValue**:(double)*doubleValue*;
- (double)**doubleValue**;
- (void)**setAnimationDelay**:(NSTimeInterval)*delay*;
- (NSTimeInterval)**animationDelay**;
- (void)**setUsesThreadedAnimation**:(BOOL)*threadedAnimation*;
- (BOOL)**usesThreadedAnimation**;
- (void)**setMinValue**:(double)*newMinimum*;
- (double)**minValue**;
- (void)**setControlTint**:(NSControlTint)*tint*;
- (NSControlTint)**controlTint**;
- (void)**setControlSize**:(NSControlSize)*size*;
- (NSControlSize)**controlSize**;

// *Instance Methods*

- (BOOL)**isDisplayedWhenStopped**;
- (void)**setDisplayedWhenStopped**:(BOOL)*isDisplayed*;

- (void)**setStyle:**(NSProgressIndicatorStyle)*style;*
- (void)**sizeToFit;**
- (NSProgressIndicatorStyle)**style;**
- (void)**animate:**(id)*sender;*
- (void)**incrementBy:**(double)*delta;*
- (BOOL)**isBezeled;**
- (BOOL)**isIndeterminate;**
- (void)**startAnimation:**(id)*sender;*
- (void)**stopAnimation:**(id)*sender;*

NSQuickDrawView

This subclass of NSView provides a destination in a Cocoa view for the QuickDraw drawing commands that are part of the Carbon APIs.

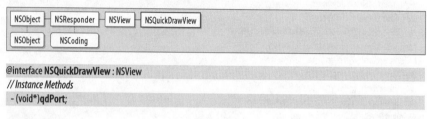

@interface **NSQuickDrawView** : NSView
// Instance Methods
- (void*)**qdPort;**

NSResponder

This abstract class provides the basis of the Application Kit's event handling system. NSResponder is the superclass of the three cornerstone classes of the AppKit: NSApplication, NSView, and NSWindow. The methods in this class are overridden by subclasses to handle mouse and key event handling messages. For more information about AppKit event handling with NSResponder, see Chapter 3.

@interface **NSResponder** : NSObject <NSCoding>
// Accessor Methods
- (void)**setInterfaceStyle:**(NSInterfaceStyle)*interfaceStyle;*
- (NSInterfaceStyle)**interfaceStyle;**
- (void)**setMark:**(id)*sender;*
- (void)**setNextResponder:**(NSResponder *)*aResponder;*
- (NSResponder *)**nextResponder;**
- (void)**setMenu:**(NSMenu *)*menu;*
- (NSMenu *)**menu;**
// Instance Methods
- (BOOL)**acceptsFirstResponder;**
- (BOOL)**becomeFirstResponder;**
- (void)**capitalizeWord:**(id)*sender;*
- (void)**centerSelectionInVisibleArea:**(id)*sender;*
- (void)**changeCaseOfLetter:**(id)*sender;*
- (void)**complete:**(id)*sender;*

```
- (void)deleteBackward:(id)sender;
- (void)deleteForward:(id)sender;
- (void)deleteToBeginningOfLine:(id)sender;
- (void)deleteToBeginningOfParagraph:(id)sender;
- (void)deleteToEndOfLine:(id)sender;
- (void)deleteToEndOfParagraph:(id)sender;
- (void)deleteToMark:(id)sender;
- (void)deleteWordBackward:(id)sender;
- (void)deleteWordForward:(id)sender;
- (void)doCommandBySelector:(SEL)aSelector;
- (void)flagsChanged:(NSEvent *)theEvent;
- (void)flushBufferedKeyEvents;
- (void)helpRequested:(NSEvent *)eventPtr;
- (void)indent:(id)sender;
- (void)insertBacktab:(id)sender;
- (void)insertNewline:(id)sender;
- (void)insertNewlineIgnoringFieldEditor:(id)sender;
- (void)insertParagraphSeparator:(id)sender;
- (void)insertTab:(id)sender;
- (void)insertTabIgnoringFieldEditor:(id)sender;
- (void)insertText:(id)insertString;
- (void)interpretKeyEvents:(NSArray *)eventArray;
- (void)keyDown:(NSEvent *)theEvent;
- (void)keyUp:(NSEvent *)theEvent;
- (void)lowercaseWord:(id)sender;
- (void)mouseDown:(NSEvent *)theEvent;
- (void)mouseDragged:(NSEvent *)theEvent;
- (void)mouseEntered:(NSEvent *)theEvent;
- (void)mouseExited:(NSEvent *)theEvent;
- (void)mouseMoved:(NSEvent *)theEvent;
- (void)mouseUp:(NSEvent *)theEvent;
- (void)moveBackward:(id)sender;
- (void)moveBackwardAndModifySelection:(id)sender;
- (void)moveDown:(id)sender;
- (void)moveDownAndModifySelection:(id)sender;
- (void)moveForward:(id)sender;
- (void)moveForwardAndModifySelection:(id)sender;
- (void)moveLeft:(id)sender;
- (void)moveRight:(id)sender;
- (void)moveToBeginningOfDocument:(id)sender;
- (void)moveToBeginningOfLine:(id)sender;
- (void)moveToBeginningOfParagraph:(id)sender;
- (void)moveToEndOfDocument:(id)sender;
- (void)moveToEndOfLine:(id)sender;
- (void)moveToEndOfParagraph:(id)sender;
- (void)moveUp:(id)sender;
- (void)moveUpAndModifySelection:(id)sender;
- (void)moveWordBackward:(id)sender;
- (void)moveWordBackwardAndModifySelection:(id)sender;
- (void)moveWordForward:(id)sender;
- (void)moveWordForwardAndModifySelection:(id)sender;
```

- (void)**noResponderFor**:(SEL)*eventSelector*;
- (void)**otherMouseDown**:(NSEvent *)*theEvent*;
- (void)**otherMouseDragged**:(NSEvent *)*theEvent*;
- (void)**otherMouseUp**:(NSEvent *)*theEvent*;
- (void)**pageDown**:(id)*sender*;
- (void)**pageUp**:(id)*sender*;
- (BOOL)**performKeyEquivalent**:(NSEvent *)*theEvent*;
- (BOOL)**resignFirstResponder**;
- (void)**rightMouseDown**:(NSEvent *)*theEvent*;
- (void)**rightMouseDragged**:(NSEvent *)*theEvent*;
- (void)**rightMouseUp**:(NSEvent *)*theEvent*;
- (void)**scrollLineDown**:(id)*sender*;
- (void)**scrollLineUp**:(id)*sender*;
- (void)**scrollPageDown**:(id)*sender*;
- (void)**scrollPageUp**:(id)*sender*;
- (void)**scrollWheel**:(NSEvent *)*theEvent*;
- (void)**selectAll**:(id)*sender*;
- (void)**selectLine**:(id)*sender*;
- (void)**selectParagraph**:(id)*sender*;
- (void)**selectToMark**:(id)*sender*;
- (void)**selectWord**:(id)*sender*;
- (BOOL)**shouldBeTreatedAsInkEvent**:(NSEvent *)*theEvent*;
- (void)**showContextHelp**:(id)*sender*;
- (void)**swapWithMark**:(id)*sender*;
- (void)**transpose**:(id)*sender*;
- (void)**transposeWords**:(id)*sender*;
- (BOOL)**tryToPerform**:(SEL)*anAction* **with**:(id)*anObject*;
- (NSUndoManager *)**undoManager**;
- (void)**uppercaseWord**:(id)*sender*;
- (id)**validRequestorForSendType**:(NSString *)*sendType* **returnType**:(NSString *)*returnType*;
- (void)**yank**:(id)*sender*;

// Methods Implementing NSCoding
- (void)**encodeWithCoder**:(NSCoder *)*aCoder*;
- (id)**initWithCoder**:(NSCoder *)*aDecoder*;

Subclasses
NSApplication, NSDrawer, NSView, NSWindow, NSWindowController

NSRulerMarker   Mac OS X 10.0

Instances of this class are used to display symbolic markers in an NSRulerView. An example of ruler view markers are those that text documents use to indicate the position of tab stops or table columns. Markers are initialized with an associated ruler view, a position in that view, an image used to represent the marker in the ruler view, and an NSPoint that specifies what point in the image should be treated as the marker origin.

@interface **NSRulerMarker** : NSObject <NSCoding, NSCopying>

// Initializers
- (id)**initWithRulerView**:(NSRulerView *)*ruler* **markerLocation**:(float)*location* **image**:(NSImage *)*image*
    imageOrigin:(NSPoint)*imageOrigin*;
// Accessor Methods
- (void)**setRepresentedObject**:(id <NSCopying>)*representedObject*;
- (id <NSCopying>)**representedObject**;
- (void)**setImageOrigin**:(NSPoint)*imageOrigin*;
- (NSPoint)**imageOrigin**;
- (void)**setMarkerLocation**:(float)*location*;
- (float)**markerLocation**;
- (void)**setMovable**:(BOOL)*flag*;
- (void)**setImage**:(NSImage *)*image*;
- (NSImage *)**image**;
- (void)**setRemovable**:(BOOL)*flag*;
// Instance Methods
- (void)**drawRect**:(NSRect)*rect*;
- (NSRect)**imageRectInRuler**;
- (BOOL)**isDragging**;
- (BOOL)**isMovable**;
- (BOOL)**isRemovable**;
- (NSRulerView *)**ruler**;
- (float)**thicknessRequiredInRuler**;
- (BOOL)**trackMouse**:(NSEvent *)*mouseDownEvent* **adding**:(BOOL)*isAdding*;
// Methods Implementing NSCoding
- (void)**encodeWithCoder**:(NSCoder *)*aCoder*;
- (id)**initWithCoder**:(NSCoder *)*aDecoder*;
// Methods Implementing NSCopying
- (id)**copyWithZone**:(NSZone *)*zone*;
// Methods Implemented by the Delegate
- (void)**rulerView**:(NSRulerView *)*ruler* **didAddMarker**:(NSRulerMarker *)*marker*;
- (void)**rulerView**:(NSRulerView *)*ruler* **didMoveMarker**:(NSRulerMarker *)*marker*;
- (void)**rulerView**:(NSRulerView *)*ruler* **didRemoveMarker**:(NSRulerMarker *)*marker*;
- (void)**rulerView**:(NSRulerView *)*ruler* **handleMouseDown**:(NSEvent *)*event*;
- (BOOL)**rulerView**:(NSRulerView *)*ruler* **shouldAddMarker**:(NSRulerMarker *)*marker*;
- (BOOL)**rulerView**:(NSRulerView *)*ruler* **shouldMoveMarker**:(NSRulerMarker *)*marker*;
- (BOOL)**rulerView**:(NSRulerView *)*ruler* **shouldRemoveMarker**:(NSRulerMarker *)*marker*;
- (float)**rulerView**:(NSRulerView *)*ruler* **willAddMarker**:(NSRulerMarker *)*marker* **atLocation**:(float)*location*;
- (float)**rulerView**:(NSRulerView *)*ruler* **willMoveMarker**:(NSRulerMarker *)*marker* **toLocation**:(float)*location*;
- (void)**rulerView**:(NSRulerView *)*ruler* **willSetClientView**:(NSView *)*newClient*;

NSRulerView

Mac OS X 10.0

This is a subclass of NSView and is used to draw rulers in an NSScrollView. A ruler view keeps track of the units used to convert measurements between pixels and whatever unit the client specifies should be displayed by the ruler view. A ruler view may contain ruler markers, which are instances of the class NSRulerMarker.

```
@interface NSRulerView : NSView
// Initializers
- (id)initWithScrollView:(NSScrollView *)scrollView orientation:(NSRulerOrientation)orientation;
// Accessor Methods
- (void)setReservedThicknessForAccessoryView:(float)thickness;
- (float)reservedThicknessForAccessoryView;
- (void)setScrollView:(NSScrollView *)scrollView;
- (NSScrollView *)scrollView;
- (void)setOriginOffset:(float)offset;
- (float)originOffset;
- (void)setOrientation:(NSRulerOrientation)orientation;
- (NSRulerOrientation)orientation;
- (void)setClientView:(NSView *)client;
- (NSView *)clientView;
- (void)setReservedThicknessForMarkers:(float)thickness;
- (float)reservedThicknessForMarkers;
- (void)setMarkers:(NSArray *)markers;
- (NSArray *)markers;
- (void)setRuleThickness:(float)thickness;
- (float)ruleThickness;
- (void)setAccessoryView:(NSView *)accessory;
- (NSView *)accessoryView;
- (void)setMeasurementUnits:(NSString *)unitName;
- (NSString *)measurementUnits;
// Class Methods
+ (void)registerUnitWithName:(NSString *)unitName abbreviation:(NSString *)abbreviation
    unitToPointsConversionFactor:(float)conversionFactor tepUpCycle:(NSArray *)stepUpCycle
    stepDownCycle:(NSArray *)stepDownCycle;
// Instance Methods
- (void)addMarker:(NSRulerMarker *)marker;
- (float)baselineLocation;
- (void)drawHashMarksAndLabelsInRect:(NSRect)rect;
- (void)drawMarkersInRect:(NSRect)rect;
- (void)invalidateHashMarks;
- (BOOL)isFlipped;
- (void)moveRulerlineFromLocation:(float)oldLocation toLocation:(float)newLocation;
- (void)removeMarker:(NSRulerMarker *)marker;
- (float)requiredThickness;
- (BOOL)trackMarker:(NSRulerMarker *)marker withMouseEvent:(NSEvent *)event;
```

NSSavePanel

Mac OS X 10.0

This class is an implementation of the complete Mac OS X file Save dialog, which clients can use to present a file browser to users for saving files. It is possible to provide an accessory view to be displayed on the bottom part of the Save panel. Accessory views can be used to provide additional parameters that should be used in the Save operation. A graphics application, for example, may use the accessory view to provide controls for the user to specify compression and format options for the file to be saved.

@interface **NSSavePanel** : NSPanel
// Accessor Methods
- (void)**setTreatsFilePackagesAsDirectories:**(BOOL)*flag*;
- (BOOL)**treatsFilePackagesAsDirectories**;
- (void)**setAccessoryView:**(NSView *)*aView*;
- (NSView *)**accessoryView**;
- (void)**setExtensionHidden:**(BOOL)*flag*;
- (void)**setCanSelectHiddenExtension:**(BOOL)*flag*;
- (void)**setDelegate:**(id)*anObject*;
- (void)**setDirectory:**(NSString *)*path*;
- (NSString *)**directory**;
- (void)**setPrompt:**(NSString *)*prompt*;
- (NSString *)**prompt**;
- (void)**setTitle:**(NSString *)*title*;
- (NSString *)**title**;
- (void)**setRequiredFileType:**(NSString *)*type*;
- (NSString *)**requiredFileType**;
// Class Methods
+ (NSSavePanel *)**savePanel**;
// Instance Methods
- (void)**cancel:**(id)*sender*;
- (void)**beginSheetForDirectory:**(NSString *)*path* **file:**(NSString *)*name* **modalForWindow:**(NSWindow *)*docWindow*
      modalDelegate:(id)*delegate* **didEndSelector:**(SEL)*didEndSelector* **contextInfo:**(void *)*contextInfo*;
- (NSURL *)**URL**;
- (NSString *)**filename**;
- (void)**ok:**(id)*sender*;
- (int)**runModal**;
- (int)**runModalForDirectory:**(NSString *)*path* **file:**(NSString *)*name*;
- (int)**runModalForDirectory:**(NSString *)*path* **file:**(NSString *)*name* **relativeToWindow:**(NSWindow*)*window*;
- (void)**selectText:**(id)*sender*;
- (BOOL)**isExpanded**;
- (BOOL)**isExtensionHidden**;
- (void)**validateVisibleColumns**;
// Methods Implemented by the Delegate
- (NSComparisonResult)**panel:**(id)*sender* **compareFilename:**(NSString *)*file1* **with:**(NSString *)*file2*
      caseSensitive:(BOOL)*caseSensitive*;
- (BOOL)**panel:**(id)*sender* **isValidFilename:**(NSString *)*filename*;
- (BOOL)**panel:**(id)*sender* **shouldShowFilename:**(NSString *)*filename*;
- (NSString *)**panel:**(id)*sender* **userEnteredFilename:**(NSString *)*filename* **confirmed:**(BOOL)*okFlag*;
- (void)**panel:**(id)*sender* **willExpand:**(BOOL)*expanding*;

Subclasses
NSOpenPanel

NSScreen

This class represents a user's monitor, and allows clients to ascertain properties of the display such as width and height in pixels, or color bit-depth. This class works only in the presence of an instance of NSApplication; NSScreen requires that an application have a connection to the window server to obtain information about the screen, which is provided by NSApplication.

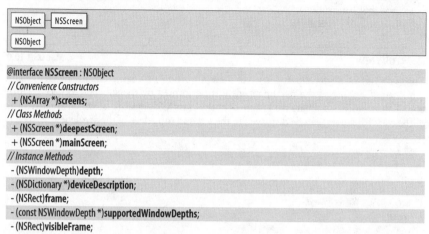

```
@interface NSScreen : NSObject
// Convenience Constructors
 + (NSArray *)screens;
// Class Methods
 + (NSScreen *)deepestScreen;
 + (NSScreen *)mainScreen;
// Instance Methods
 - (NSWindowDepth)depth;
 - (NSDictionary *)deviceDescription;
 - (NSRect)frame;
 - (const NSWindowDepth *)supportedWindowDepths;
 - (NSRect)visibleFrame;
```

NSScroller

This class represents the scrollbar control of a scroll view, and is used to control the scrolling of a document within a scroll view's clip view. There is usually no need to work with NSScroller objects in code, as they are completely configured within a scroll view by Interface Builder.

```
@interface NSScroller : NSControl
// Convenience Constructors
 + (float)scrollerWidth;
 + (float)scrollerWidthForControlSize:(NSControlSize)controlSize;
// Accessor Methods
 - (void)setFloatValue:(float)aFloat knobProportion:(float)percent;
 - (void)setControlTint:(NSControlTint)controlTint;
 - (NSControlTint)controlTint;
 - (void)setArrowsPosition:(NSScrollArrowPosition)where;
 - (NSScrollArrowPosition)arrowsPosition;
 - (void)setControlSize:(NSControlSize)controlSize;
 - (NSControlSize)controlSize;
// Instance Methods
 - (void)checkSpaceForParts;
 - (void)drawArrow:(NSScrollerArrow)whichArrow highlight:(BOOL)flag;
 - (void)drawKnob;
```

```
- (void)drawParts;
- (void)highlight:(BOOL)flag;
- (NSScrollerPart)hitPart;
- (float)knobProportion;
- (NSRect)rectForPart:(NSScrollerPart)partCode;
- (NSScrollerPart)testPart:(NSPoint)thePoint;
- (void)trackKnob:(NSEvent *)theEvent;
- (void)trackScrollButtons:(NSEvent *)theEvent;
- (NSUsableScrollerParts)usableParts;
```

NSScrollView

This subclass of NSView allows a user to view a portion of a large document view using scrollbars. Clipping of the document view is performed by the subclass NSClipView. Horizontal and vertical scrollbars are instances of the class NSScroller. Rulers, which are instances of the class NSRulerView, can be displayed in the left and top edges of the scrollview.

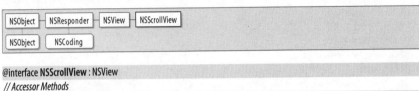

```
@interface NSScrollView : NSView
// Accessor Methods
- (void)setBackgroundColor:(NSColor *)color;
- (NSColor *)backgroundColor;
- (void)setPageScroll:(float)value;
- (float)pageScroll;
- (void)setHorizontalRulerView:(NSRulerView *)ruler;
- (NSRulerView *)horizontalRulerView;
- (void)setHasVerticalRuler:(BOOL)flag;
- (BOOL)hasVerticalRuler;
- (void)setHasHorizontalRuler:(BOOL)flag;
- (BOOL)hasHorizontalRuler;
- (void)setHorizontalPageScroll:(float)value;
- (float)horizontalPageScroll;
- (void)setBorderType:(NSBorderType)aType;
- (NSBorderType)borderType;
- (void)setHorizontalLineScroll:(float)value;
- (float)horizontalLineScroll;
- (void)setRulersVisible:(BOOL)flag;
- (BOOL)rulersVisible;
- (void)setScrollsDynamically:(BOOL)flag;
- (BOOL)scrollsDynamically;
- (void)setHasVerticalScroller:(BOOL)flag;
- (BOOL)hasVerticalScroller;
- (void)setHasHorizontalScroller:(BOOL)flag;
- (BOOL)hasHorizontalScroller;
- (void)setLineScroll:(float)value;
- (float)lineScroll;
- (void)setHorizontalScroller:(NSScroller *)anObject;
- (NSScroller *)horizontalScroller;
- (void)setDocumentCursor:(NSCursor *)anObj;
```

- (NSCursor *)**documentCursor**;
- (void)**setDocumentView**:(NSView *)*aView*;
- (id)**documentView**;
- (void)**setContentView**:(NSClipView *)*contentView*;
- (NSClipView *)**contentView**;
- (void)**setVerticalScroller**:(NSScroller *)*anObject*;
- (NSScroller *)**verticalScroller**;
- (void)**setVerticalRulerView**:(NSRulerView *)*ruler*;
- (NSRulerView *)**verticalRulerView**;
- (void)**setVerticalLineScroll**:(float)*value*;
- (float)**verticalLineScroll**;
- (void)**setVerticalPageScroll**:(float)*value*;
- (float)**verticalPageScroll**;
- (void)**setDrawsBackground**:(BOOL)*flag*;
- (BOOL)**drawsBackground**;

// Class Methods

+ (NSSize)**contentSizeForFrameSize**:(NSSize)*fSize* **hasHorizontalScroller**:(BOOL)*hFlag* **hasVerticalScroller**:(BOOL)*vFlag*
    borderType:(NSBorderType)*aType*;

+ (NSSize)**frameSizeForContentSize**:(NSSize)*cSize* **hasHorizontalScroller**:(BOOL)*hFlag* **hasVerticalScroller**:(BOOL)*vFlag*
    borderType:(NSBorderType)*aType*;

+ (Class)**rulerViewClass**;
+ (void)**setRulerViewClass**:(Class)*rulerViewClass*;

// Instance Methods

- (void)**reflectScrolledClipView**:(NSClipView *)*cView*;
- (void)**scrollWheel**:(NSEvent *)*theEvent*;
- (void)**tile**;
- (NSSize)**contentSize**;
- (NSRect)**documentVisibleRect**;

NSSecureTextField Mac OS X 10.0

NSSecureTextField is a subclass of **NSTextField** that adds the behavior of displaying the contents of the text field as a string of dots so that the value of the string is kept hidden. This is the control a developer would use for password entry fields, or any other text field that displays sensitive values that may need to be hidden.

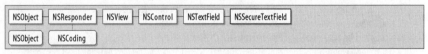

@interface **NSSecureTextField** : NSTextField

NSSecureTextFieldCell Mac OS X 10.0

This class is the cell associated with the **NSSecureTextField** control. NSSecureTextFieldCell is responsible for the appearance of the secure text field control, as well as any mouse event handling that occurs over the cell.

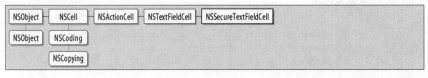

```
@interface NSSecureTextFieldCell : NSTextFieldCell
// Accessor Methods
- (void)setEchosBullets:(BOOL)flag;
- (BOOL)echosBullets;
```

NSSimpleHorizontalTypesetter

Mac OS X 10.0

This concrete subclass of **NSTypesetter** supports left-to-right line layout. This class handles such things as hyphenation, word wrapping, and line-breaking. For more information about Cocoa's text layout engine, see Chapter 5.

```
@interface NSSimpleHorizontalTypesetter : NSTypesetter
// Class Methods
+ (id)sharedInstance;
// Instance Methods
- (void)willSetLineFragmentRect:(NSRect *)aRect forGlyphRange:(NSRange)aRange usedRect:(NSRect *)bRect;
- (NSTypesetterGlyphInfo *)baseOfTypesetterGlyphInfo;
- (void)breakLineAtIndex:(unsigned)location;
- (unsigned)capacityOfTypesetterGlyphInfo;
- (void)clearAttributesCache;
- (void)clearGlyphCache;
- (NSTextContainer *)currentContainer;
- (NSLayoutManager *)currentLayoutManager;
- (NSParagraphStyle *)currentParagraphStyle;
- (NSTextStorage *)currentTextStorage;
- (void)fillAttributesCache;
- (unsigned)firstGlyphIndexOfCurrentLineFragment;
- (void)fullJustifyLineAtGlyphIndex:(unsigned)glyphIndexForLineBreak;
- (unsigned)glyphIndexToBreakLineByHyphenatingWordAtIndex:(unsigned)charIndex;
- (unsigned)glyphIndexToBreakLineByWordWrappingAtIndex:(unsigned)charIndex;
- (unsigned)growGlyphCaches:(unsigned)desiredCapacity fillGlyphInfo:(BOOL)fillGlyphInfo;
- (void)insertGlyph:(NSGlyph)glyph atGlyphIndex:(unsigned)glyphIndex characterIndex:(unsigned)charIndex;
- (NSLayoutStatus)layoutControlGlyphForLineFragment:(NSRect)lineFrag;
- (NSLayoutStatus)layoutControlGlyphForLineFragment:(NSRect)lineFrag;
- (NSLayoutStatus)layoutGlyphsInHorizontalLineFragment:(NSRect *)lineFragmentRect baseline:(float *)baseline;
- (void)layoutGlyphsInLayoutManager:(NSLayoutManager *)layoutManager
    startingAtGlyphIndex:(unsigned)startGlyphIndex maxNumberOfLineFragments:(unsigned)maxNumLines
    nextGlyphIndex:(unsigned *)nextGlyph;
- (void)layoutTab;
- (void)layoutTab;
- (unsigned)sizeOfTypesetterGlyphInfo;
- (void)typesetterLaidOneGlyph:(NSTypesetterGlyphInfo *)gl;
- (void)updateCurGlyphOffset;
```

NSSlider

Mac OS X 10.0

This subclass of NSControl represents a slider control where a user manipulates a knob to select from a range of values: for example, the control in the Volume menu item. The cell for NSSlider is NSSliderCell.

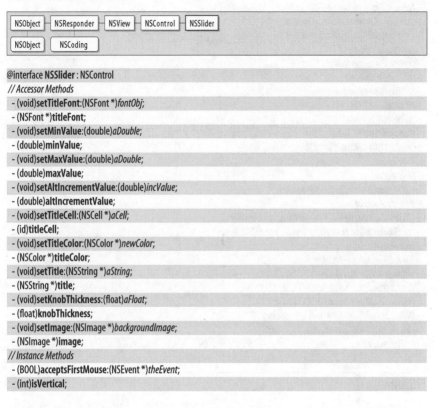

```
@interface NSSlider : NSControl
// Accessor Methods
 - (void)setTitleFont:(NSFont *)fontObj;
 - (NSFont *)titleFont;
 - (void)setMinValue:(double)aDouble;
 - (double)minValue;
 - (void)setMaxValue:(double)aDouble;
 - (double)maxValue;
 - (void)setAltIncrementValue:(double)incValue;
 - (double)altIncrementValue;
 - (void)setTitleCell:(NSCell *)aCell;
 - (id)titleCell;
 - (void)setTitleColor:(NSColor *)newColor;
 - (NSColor *)titleColor;
 - (void)setTitle:(NSString *)aString;
 - (NSString *)title;
 - (void)setKnobThickness:(float)aFloat;
 - (float)knobThickness;
 - (void)setImage:(NSImage *)backgroundImage;
 - (NSImage *)image;
// Instance Methods
 - (BOOL)acceptsFirstMouse:(NSEvent *)theEvent;
 - (int)isVertical;
```

NSSliderCell

Mac OS X 10.0

This is the NSCell subclass for the NSSlider control class, which is an interface element that allows the user to select a value from a range of values by sliding a knob along a track.

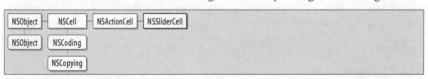

```
@interface NSSliderCell : NSActionCell
// Accessor Methods
 - (void)setTitleColor:(NSColor *)newColor;
 - (NSColor *)titleColor;
 - (void)setMinValue:(double)aDouble;
 - (double)minValue;
 - (void)setMaxValue:(double)aDouble;
```

AppKit
Classes

- (double)**maxValue**;
- (void)**setAltIncrementValue**:(double)*incValue*;
- (double)**altIncrementValue**;
- (void)**setNumberOfTickMarks**:(int)*count*;
- (int)**numberOfTickMarks**;
- (void)**setTickMarkPosition**:(NSTickMarkPosition)*position*;
- (NSTickMarkPosition)**tickMarkPosition**;
- (void)**setKnobThickness**:(float)*aFloat*;
- (float)**knobThickness**;
- (void)**setTitleFont**:(NSFont *)*fontObj*;
- (NSFont *)**titleFont**;
- (void)**setAllowsTickMarkValuesOnly**:(BOOL)*yorn*;
- (BOOL)**allowsTickMarkValuesOnly**;
- (void)**setTitle**:(NSString *)*aString*;
- (NSString *)**title**;
- (void)**setTitleCell**:(NSCell *)*aCell*;
- (id)**titleCell**;
// *Class Methods*
+ (BOOL)**prefersTrackingUntilMouseUp**;
// *Instance Methods*
- (double)**closestTickMarkValueToValue**:(double)*value*;
- (void)**drawBarInside**:(NSRect)*aRect* **flipped**:(BOOL)*flipped*;
- (void)**drawKnob**;
- (void)**drawKnob**:(NSRect)*knobRect*;
- (int)**indexOfTickMarkAtPoint**:(NSPoint)*point*;
- (int)**isVertical**;
- (NSRect)**knobRectFlipped**:(BOOL)*flipped*;
- (NSRect)**rectOfTickMarkAtIndex**:(int)*index*;
- (double)**tickMarkValueAtIndex**:(int)*index*;
- (NSRect)**trackRect**;

NSSound

Mac OS X 10.0

This class is a simple interface for playing AIFF, WAV, and NeXT sound files. An instance of this class is initialized from a file using the method **initWithContentsOfFile:byReference:**. The **byReference:** argument relates to how the sound object should be archived. If this argument is YES, only the name of the sound file will be archived; otherwise, the object data will be archived. There are four methods for controlling playback of the sound: **play**, **pause**, **resume**, and **stop**. Instances of NSSound may take a delegate object, which will be notified when the sound has finished playing.

```
@interface NSSound : NSObject <NSCoding, NSCopying>
// Convenience Constructors
 + (id)soundNamed:(NSString *)name;
 + (NSArray *)soundUnfilteredFileTypes;
```

```
+ (NSArray *)soundUnfilteredPasteboardTypes;
// Initializers
 - (id)initWithContentsOfFile:(NSString *)path byReference:(BOOL)byRef;
 - (id)initWithContentsOfURL:(NSURL *)url byReference:(BOOL)byRef;
 - (id)initWithData:(NSData *)data;
 - (id)initWithPasteboard:(NSPasteboard *)pasteboard;
// Accessor Methods
 - (void)setDelegate:(id)aDelegate;
 - (id)delegate;
 - (BOOL)setName:(NSString *)string;
 - (NSString *)name;
// Class Methods
 + (BOOL)canInitWithPasteboard:(NSPasteboard *)pasteboard;
// Instance Methods
 - (BOOL)isPlaying;
 - (BOOL)pause;
 - (BOOL)play;
 - (BOOL)resume;
 - (BOOL)stop;
 - (void)writeToPasteboard:(NSPasteboard *)pasteboard;
// Methods Implementing NSCoding
 - (void)encodeWithCoder:(NSCoder *)aCoder;
 - (id)initWithCoder:(NSCoder *)aDecoder;
// Methods Implementing NSCopying
 - (id)copyWithZone:(NSZone *)zone;
// Methods Implemented by the Delegate
 - (void)sound:(NSSound *)sound didFinishPlaying:(BOOL)aBool;
```

NSSpellChecker

This class provides an interface to Cocoa's spellchecking service. A shared instance of NSSpellChecker is returned using the class method sharedSpellChecker. To check the spelling of a length of text, invoke the method checkSpellingOfString:startingAt:, which takes the string to check and the offset in the string where the spellcheck should commence. This method will return an NSRange indicating the location of the first misspelled word. Clients then update the contents of the spellchecking panel to notify the user of the discovery of the misspelled word using the method updateSpellingPanelWithMisspelledWord:; passing an empty string here will cause the spellchecking process to terminate. Support for spellchecking services is built into the Cocoa text handling classes. If you wish to implement support for spellchecking into a class of your own, then you must implement the methods declared in the NSChangeSpelling and NSIgnoreMisspelledWords protocols; see the protocol descriptions in Chapter 16 for more information.

```
NSObject ─── NSSpellChecker
NSObject
```

```
@interface NSSpellChecker : NSObject
// Accessor Methods
 - (void)setIgnoredWords:(NSArray *)words inSpellDocumentWithTag:(int)tag;
 - (void)setWordFieldStringValue:(NSString *)aString;
```

- (BOOL)**setLanguage**:(NSString *)*language*;
- (NSString *)**language**;
- (void)**setAccessoryView**:(NSView *)*aView*;
- (NSView *)**accessoryView**;
// Class Methods
+ (NSSpellChecker *)**sharedSpellChecker**;
+ (BOOL)**sharedSpellCheckerExists**;
+ (int)**uniqueSpellDocumentTag**;
// Instance Methods
- (NSRange)**checkSpellingOfString**:(NSString *)*stringToCheck* **startingAt**:(int)*startingOffset*;
- (int)**countWordsInString**:(NSString *)*stringToCount* **language**:(NSString *)*language*;
- (NSRange)**checkSpellingOfString**:(NSString *)*stringToCheck* **startingAt**:(int)*startingOffset*
    language:(NSString *)*language* **wrap**:(BOOL)*wrapFlag* **inSpellDocumentWithTag**:(int)*tag*
    wordCount:(int *)*wordCount*;
- (void)**closeSpellDocumentWithTag**:(int)*tag*;
- (NSArray *)**guessesForWord**:(NSString *)*word*;
- (void)**ignoreWord**:(NSString *)*wordToIgnore* **inSpellDocumentWithTag**:(int)*tag*;
- (NSArray *)**ignoredWordsInSpellDocumentWithTag**:(int)*tag*;
- (NSPanel *)**spellingPanel**;
- (void)**updateSpellingPanelWithMisspelledWord**:(NSString *)*word*;

NSSplitView

Mac OS X 10.0

This NSView subclass displays two subviews either stacked vertically, or side-by-side horizontally, separated by a divider that can be used to resize the subviews within the split view.

@interface **NSSplitView** : NSView
// Accessor Methods
- (void)**setIsPaneSplitter**:(BOOL)*flag*;
- (BOOL)**isPaneSplitter**;
- (void)**setDelegate**:(id)*anObject*;
- (id)**delegate**;
- (void)**setVertical**:(BOOL)*flag*;
// Instance Methods
- (float)**dividerThickness**;
- (BOOL)**isVertical**;
- (void)**adjustSubviews**;
- (void)**drawDividerInRect**:(NSRect)*aRect*;
- (BOOL)**isSubviewCollapsed**:(NSView *)*subview*;
// Methods Implemented by the Delegate
- (BOOL)**splitView**:(NSSplitView *)*sender* **canCollapseSubview**:(NSView *)*subview*;
- (float)**splitView**:(NSSplitView *)*sender* **constrainMaxCoordinate**:(float)*proposedCoord* **ofSubviewAt**:(int)*offset*;
- (float)**splitView**:(NSSplitView *)*sender* **constrainMinCoordinate**:(float)*proposedCoord* **ofSubviewAt**:(int)*offset*;
- (void)**splitView**:(NSSplitView *)*sender* **resizeSubviewsWithOldSize**:(NSSize)*oldSize*;
- (float)**splitView**:(NSSplitView *)*splitView* **constrainSplitPosition**:(float)*proposedPosition* **ofSubviewAt**:(int)*index*;
- (void)**splitViewDidResizeSubviews**:(NSNotification *)*notification*;

- (void)**splitViewWillResizeSubviews:**(NSNotification *)*notification*;
// Notifications
  NSSplitViewDidResizeSubviewsNotification;
  NSSplitViewWillResizeSubviewsNotification;

NSStatusBar

Mac OS X 10.0

This class defines the interface for the system status bar that appears on the right end of the main menu bar. The individual items in the status bar are instances of the class NSStatusItem. Clients obtain the shared system status bar instance using the class method systemStatusBar. Status items are created and added to a status bar by invoking the method statusItemWithLength:, and applications can remove status items that they have created by invoking removeStatusItem:.

@interface **NSStatusBar** : NSObject
// Class Methods
  + (NSStatusBar*)**systemStatusBar;**
// Instance Methods
  - (BOOL) **isVertical;**
  - (float) **thickness;**
  - (void)**removeStatusItem:**(NSStatusItem*)*item*;
  - (NSStatusItem*)**statusItemWithLength:**(float)*length*;

NSStatusItem

Mac OS X 10.0

This class represents the objects that appear in the system status bar at the right end of the main menu bar in every application. This class provides methods to access and manage the characteristics of a status item, such as its title, icon, length, tool tip, target, action, and more. To prevent cluttering of the status bar, status items should be used sparingly and only when no better alternative exists.

@interface **NSStatusItem** : NSObject
// Instance Methods
  - (SEL)**action;**
  - (NSAttributedString*)**attributedTitle;**
  - (BOOL)**highlightMode;**
  - (NSImage*)**image;**
  - (BOOL)**isEnabled;**
  - (float)**length;**
  - (NSMenu*)**menu;**
  - (void)**sendActionOn:**(int)*mask*;
  - (void)**setAction:**(SEL)*action*;

**AppKit
Classes**

- (void)**setAttributedTitle**:(NSAttributedString*)*title*;
- (void)**setEnabled**:(BOOL)*enabled*;
- (void)**setHighlightMode**:(BOOL)*highlightMode*;
- (void)**setImage**:(NSImage*)*image*;
- (void)**setLength**:(float)*length*;
- (void)**setMenu**:(NSMenu*)*menu*;
- (void)**setTarget**:(id)*target*;
- (void)**setTitle**:(NSString*)*title*;
- (void)**setToolTip**:(NSString*)*toolTip*;
- (void)**setView**:(NSView*)*view*;
- (NSStatusBar*)**statusBar**;
- (id)**target**;
- (NSString*)**title**;
- (NSString*)**toolTip**;
- (NSView*)**view**;

NSStepper   Mac OS X 10.0

This is a subclass of NSControl that allows users to change an incremental value by
clicking on portions of the control that either increment or decrement the value of the
control by some predetermined amount.

@interface **NSStepper** : NSControl
// Accessor Methods
- (void)**setMaxValue**:(double)*maxValue*;
- (double)**maxValue**;
- (void)**setMinValue**:(double)*minValue*;
- (double)**minValue**;
- (void)**setAutorepeat**:(BOOL)*autorepeat*;
- (BOOL)**autorepeat**;
- (void)**setIncrement**:(double)*increment*;
- (double)**increment**;
- (void)**setValueWraps**:(BOOL)*valueWraps*;
- (BOOL)**valueWraps**;

NSStepperCell   Mac OS X 10.0

This class is the associated cell for the NSStepper control. As an NSCell subclass, this
NSStepperCell is responsible for the appearence and event handling of an NSStepper control.

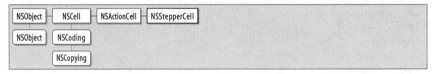

```
@interface NSStepperCell : NSActionCell
// Accessor Methods
 - (void)setMaxValue:(double)maxValue;
 - (double)maxValue;
 - (void)setMinValue:(double)minValue;
 - (double)minValue;
 - (void)setAutorepeat:(BOOL)autorepeat;
 - (BOOL)autorepeat;
 - (void)setIncrement:(double)increment;
 - (double)increment;
 - (void)setValueWraps:(BOOL)valueWraps;
 - (BOOL)valueWraps;
```

NSTableColumn Mac OS X 10.0

This class represents a column in an NSTableView. In particular, NSTableColumn stores display attributes of the table column, such as the display width, whether the table column may be resized, and whether it is editable.

Every column in a table has a unique identifier, which is accessed with the methods setIdentifier: and identifier.

Associated with a table column object are two NSCells: the header cell and the data cell. The header cell is responsible for the appearance of the table column header. To access the table column's header cell, use the methods setHeaderCell: and headerCell.

The data cell of a table column determines how data in the column is displayed. By default the data cell is an instance of NSTextFieldCell, which provides for displayed and editing text data. However, you could change the data cell of a table column to display controls other than a text field. For example, if you wanted to display Boolean information in your table column, you could set the data cell to an instance of NSButtonCell that is configured as a checkbox. If you wanted a column of slider controls, you could set the data cell of the column to an instance of NSSliderCell. To access the data cell use the methods setDataCell: and dataCell.

```
@interface NSTableColumn : NSObject
// Initializers
 - (id)initWithIdentifier:(id)identifier;
// Accessor Methods
 - (void)setTableView:(NSTableView *)tableView;
 - (NSTableView *)tableView;
 - (void)setIdentifier:(id)identifier;
 - (id)identifier;
 - (void)setResizable:(BOOL)flag;
 - (void)setMinWidth:(float)minWidth;
 - (float)minWidth;
 - (void)setHeaderCell:(NSCell *)cell;
 - (id)headerCell;
 - (void)setDataCell:(NSCell *)cell;
```

```
- (id)dataCell;
- (void)setMaxWidth:(float)maxWidth;
- (float)maxWidth;
- (void)setWidth:(float)width;
- (float)width;
- (void)setEditable:(BOOL)flag;
// Instance Methods
- (id)dataCellForRow:(int)row;
- (BOOL)isEditable;
- (BOOL)isResizable;
- (void)sizeToFit;
```

NSTableHeaderCell

Mac OS X 10.0

NSTableHeaderCell is used by NSTableHeaderView to draw the contents of table column headers. This class may be subclassed to customize the appearence of the column headers in a table view.

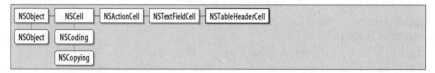

```
@interface NSTableHeaderCell : NSTextFieldCell
```

NSTableHeaderView

Mac OS X 10.0

This class is responsible for managing column headers in a table view. NSTableView objects use NSTableHeaderView to draw the headers, including any labeling and highlighting. NSTableHeaderView relies on NSTableHeaderCell objects to draw the individual header labels.

```
@interface NSTableHeaderView : NSView
// Accessor Methods
- (void)setTableView:(NSTableView *)tableView;
- (NSTableView *)tableView;
// Instance Methods
- (int)columnAtPoint:(NSPoint)point;
- (int)draggedColumn;
- (float)draggedDistance;
- (NSRect)headerRectOfColumn:(int)column;
- (int)resizedColumn;
```

NSTableView

This subclass of NSView organizes information into rows and columns. The information displayed in the table comes from an object that serves as the table view's data source object; data source objects must implement a minimum set of methods declared by the NSTableDataSource informal protocol. Instances of NSTableView are composite objects that manage NSTableColumn objects (one for each column in a table), and NSTableHeaderView objects (to draw the headers over the table columns).

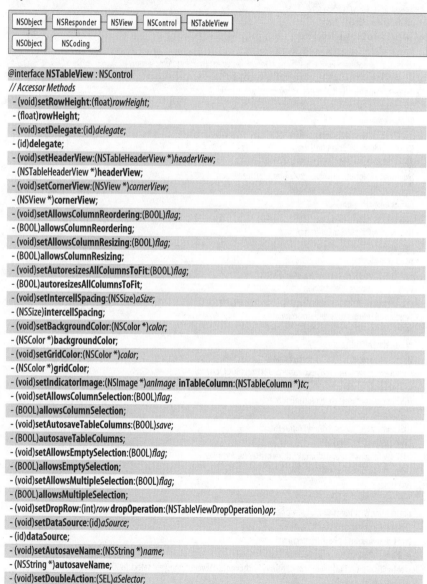

```
@interface NSTableView : NSControl
// Accessor Methods
 - (void)setRowHeight:(float)rowHeight;
 - (float)rowHeight;
 - (void)setDelegate:(id)delegate;
 - (id)delegate;
 - (void)setHeaderView:(NSTableHeaderView *)headerView;
 - (NSTableHeaderView *)headerView;
 - (void)setCornerView:(NSView *)cornerView;
 - (NSView *)cornerView;
 - (void)setAllowsColumnReordering:(BOOL)flag;
 - (BOOL)allowsColumnReordering;
 - (void)setAllowsColumnResizing:(BOOL)flag;
 - (BOOL)allowsColumnResizing;
 - (void)setAutoresizesAllColumnsToFit:(BOOL)flag;
 - (BOOL)autoresizesAllColumnsToFit;
 - (void)setIntercellSpacing:(NSSize)aSize;
 - (NSSize)intercellSpacing;
 - (void)setBackgroundColor:(NSColor *)color;
 - (NSColor *)backgroundColor;
 - (void)setGridColor:(NSColor *)color;
 - (NSColor *)gridColor;
 - (void)setIndicatorImage:(NSImage *)anImage inTableColumn:(NSTableColumn *)tc;
 - (void)setAllowsColumnSelection:(BOOL)flag;
 - (BOOL)allowsColumnSelection;
 - (void)setAutosaveTableColumns:(BOOL)save;
 - (BOOL)autosaveTableColumns;
 - (void)setAllowsEmptySelection:(BOOL)flag;
 - (BOOL)allowsEmptySelection;
 - (void)setAllowsMultipleSelection:(BOOL)flag;
 - (BOOL)allowsMultipleSelection;
 - (void)setDropRow:(int)row dropOperation:(NSTableViewDropOperation)op;
 - (void)setDataSource:(id)aSource;
 - (id)dataSource;
 - (void)setAutosaveName:(NSString *)name;
 - (NSString *)autosaveName;
 - (void)setDoubleAction:(SEL)aSelector;
 - (SEL)doubleAction;
```

- (void)**setHighlightedTableColumn**:(NSTableColumn *)*tc*;
- (NSTableColumn *)**highlightedTableColumn**;
- (void)**setDrawsGrid**:(BOOL)*flag*;
- (BOOL)**drawsGrid**;
- (void)**setVerticalMotionCanBeginDrag**:(BOOL)*flag*;
- (BOOL)**verticalMotionCanBeginDrag**;

// Instance Methods
- (void)**highlightSelectionInClipRect**:(NSRect)*rect*;
- (void)**deselectRow**:(int)*row*;
- (void)**deselectAll**:(id)*sender*;
- (void)**deselectColumn**:(int)*column*;
- (void)**addTableColumn**:(NSTableColumn *)*column*;
- (NSImage*)**dragImageForRows**:(NSArray*)*dragRows* **event**:(NSEvent*)*dragEvent*
        dragImageOffset:(NSPointPointer)*dragImageOffset*;
- (NSRect)**frameOfCellAtColumn**:(int)*column* **row**:(int)*row*;
- (int)**clickedColumn**;
- (int)**clickedRow**;
- (NSImage *)**indicatorImageInTableColumn**:(NSTableColumn *)*tc*;
- (BOOL)**isColumnSelected**:(int)*row*;
- (BOOL)**isRowSelected**:(int)*row*;
- (void)**moveColumn**:(int)*column* **toColumn**:(int)*newIndex*;
- (void)**noteNumberOfRowsChanged**;
- (int)**numberOfColumns**;
- (int)**numberOfRows**;
- (int)**numberOfSelectedColumns**;
- (int)**numberOfSelectedRows**;
- (void)**reloadData**;
- (void)**removeTableColumn**:(NSTableColumn *)*column*;
- (int)**rowAtPoint**:(NSPoint)*point*;
- (NSRange)**rowsInRect**:(NSRect)*rect*;
- (void)**scrollColumnToVisible**:(int)*column*;
- (void)**scrollRowToVisible**:(int)*row*;
- (void)**selectAll**:(id)*sender*;
- (void)**selectColumn**:(int)*column* **byExtendingSelection**:(BOOL)*extend*;
- (void)**selectRow**:(int)*row* **byExtendingSelection**:(BOOL)*extend*;
- (int)**selectedColumn**;
- (NSEnumerator *)**selectedColumnEnumerator**;
- (int)**selectedRow**;
- (NSEnumerator *)**selectedRowEnumerator**;
- (void)**sizeLastColumnToFit**;
- (NSTableColumn *)**tableColumnWithIdentifier**:(id)*identifier*;
- (NSArray *)**tableColumns**;
- (void)**tile**;
- (int)**columnAtPoint**:(NSPoint)*point*;
- (int)**columnWithIdentifier**:(id)*identifier*;
- (NSRange)**columnsInRect**:(NSRect)*rect*;
- (void)**drawGridInClipRect**:(NSRect)*rect*;
- (void)**drawRow**:(int)*row* **clipRect**:(NSRect)*rect*;
- (void)**editColumn**:(int)*column* **row**:(int)*row* **withEvent**:(NSEvent *)*theEvent* **select**:(BOOL)*select*;
- (int)**editedColumn**;
- (int)**editedRow**;

```
- (NSRect)rectOfColumn:(int)column;
- (NSRect)rectOfRow:(int)row;
- (void)textDidBeginEditing:(NSNotification *)notification;
- (void)textDidChange:(NSNotification *)notification;
- (void)textDidEndEditing:(NSNotification *)notification;
- (BOOL)textShouldBeginEditing:(NSText *)textObject;
- (BOOL)textShouldEndEditing:(NSText *)textObject;
// Methods Implemented by the Delegate
- (void)tableView:(NSTableView*)tableView didClickTableColumn:(NSTableColumn *)tableColumn;
- (void)tableView:(NSTableView*)tableView didDragTableColumn:(NSTableColumn *)tableColumn;
- (void)tableView:(NSTableView*)tableView mouseDownInHeaderOfTableColumn:(NSTableColumn *)tableColumn;
- (BOOL)selectionShouldChangeInTableView:(NSTableView *)aTableView;
- (BOOL)tableView:(NSTableView *)tableView shouldEditTableColumn:(NSTableColumn *)tableColumn row:(int)row;
- (BOOL)tableView:(NSTableView *)tableView shouldSelectRow:(int)row;
- (BOOL)tableView:(NSTableView *)tableView shouldSelectTableColumn:(NSTableColumn *)tableColumn;
- (void)tableView:(NSTableView *)tableView willDisplayCell:(id)cell
    forTableColumn:(NSTableColumn *)tableColumn row:(int)row;
- (void)tableViewColumnDidMove:(NSNotification *)notification;
- (void)tableViewColumnDidResize:(NSNotification *)notification;
- (void)tableViewSelectionDidChange:(NSNotification *)notification;
- (void)tableViewSelectionIsChanging:(NSNotification *)notification;
// Notifications
NSTableViewSelectionDidChangeNotification;
NSTableViewSelectionIsChangingNotification;
```

Subclasses

NSOutlineView

NSTabView

This NSView subclass provides a way to display pages of views that can be selected by
tabs identifying each view. The pages of a tab view are actually instances of the class
NSTabViewItem, which is a small class that keeps the tab view, page view, and related
information to presenting it in the tab view.

```
@interface NSTabView : NSView
// Accessor Methods
- (void)setAllowsTruncatedLabels:(BOOL)allowTruncatedLabels;
- (BOOL)allowsTruncatedLabels;
- (void)setDelegate:(id)anObject;
- (id)delegate;
- (void)setTabViewType:(NSTabViewType)tabViewType;
- (NSTabViewType)tabViewType;
- (void)setFont:(NSFont *)font;
- (NSFont *)font;
- (void)setControlSize:(NSControlSize)controlSize;
- (NSControlSize)controlSize;
```

```
- (void)setDrawsBackground:(BOOL)flag;
- (BOOL)drawsBackground;
- (void)setControlTint:(NSControlTint)controlTint;
- (NSControlTint)controlTint;
```
// Instance Methods
```
- (void)addTabViewItem:(NSTabViewItem *)tabViewItem;
- (int)indexOfTabViewItemWithIdentifier:(id)identifier;
- (int)indexOfTabViewItem:(NSTabViewItem *)tabViewItem;
- (void)insertTabViewItem:(NSTabViewItem *)tabViewItem atIndex:(int)index;
- (NSSize)minimumSize;
- (int)numberOfTabViewItems;
- (void)removeTabViewItem:(NSTabViewItem *)tabViewItem;
- (void)selectFirstTabViewItem:(id)sender;
- (void)selectLastTabViewItem:(id)sender;
- (void)selectNextTabViewItem:(id)sender;
- (void)selectPreviousTabViewItem:(id)sender;
- (void)selectTabViewItem:(NSTabViewItem *)tabViewItem;
- (void)selectTabViewItemAtIndex:(int)index;
- (void)selectTabViewItemWithIdentifier:(id)identifier;
- (NSTabViewItem *)selectedTabViewItem;
- (NSTabViewItem *)tabViewItemAtIndex:(int)index;
- (NSTabViewItem *)tabViewItemAtPoint:(NSPoint)point;
- (NSArray *)tabViewItems;
- (void)takeSelectedTabViewItemFromSender:(id)sender;
- (NSRect)contentRect;
```
// Methods Implemented by the Delegate
```
- (void)tabView:(NSTabView *)tabView didSelectTabViewItem:(NSTabViewItem *)tabViewItem;
- (BOOL)tabView:(NSTabView *)tabView shouldSelectTabViewItem:(NSTabViewItem *)tabViewItem;
- (void)tabView:(NSTabView *)tabView willSelectTabViewItem:(NSTabViewItem *)tabViewItem;
- (void)tabViewDidChangeNumberOfTabViewItems:(NSTabView *)TabView;
```

NSTabViewItem   Mac OS X 10.0

This class represents a single tabbed pane within a tab view object. NSTabView objects
maintain an array of NSTabViewItem objects for each of its tabs. Associated with each tab
view item is an identifier, a label that is drawn in the tab itself, and a view that
contains the contents of the tab view item. For most simple uses of tab views, you
won't have to interact with the NSTabView or NSTabViewItem APIs directly, as Interface
Builder is capable of fully configuring a tab view.

```
@interface NSTabViewItem : NSObject <NSCoding>
```
// Initializers
```
- (id)initWithIdentifier:(id)identifier;
- (id)initialFirstResponder;
```
// Accessor Methods
```
- (void)setColor:(NSColor *)color;
- (NSColor *)color;
```

```
- (void)setLabel:(NSString *)label;
- (NSString *)label;
- (void)setIdentifier:(id)identifier;
- (id)identifier;
- (void)setInitialFirstResponder:(NSView *)view;
- (void)setView:(NSView *)view;
- (id)view;
// Instance Methods
- (NSSize)sizeOfLabel:(BOOL)computeMin;
- (NSTabState)tabState;
- (NSTabView *)tabView;
// Methods Implementing NSCoding
- (void)encodeWithCoder:(NSCoder *)aCoder;
- (id)initWithCoder:(NSCoder *)aDecoder;
```

NSText

Mac OS X 10.0

NSText inherits from NSView and is the parent class of NSTextView. It declares the most general interface for objects that manage and display text; however, clients generally interact with NSTextView objects rather than instances of NSText itself.

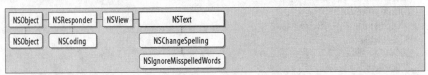

```
@interface NSText : NSView <NSChangeSpelling, NSIgnoreMisspelledWords>
// Accessor Methods
- (void)setHorizontallyResizable:(BOOL)flag;
- (void)setString:(NSString *)string;
- (NSString *)string;
- (void)setDelegate:(id)anObject;
- (id)delegate;
- (void)setSelectedRange:(NSRange)range;
- (NSRange)selectedRange;
- (void)setSelectable:(BOOL)flag;
- (void)setMinSize:(NSSize)newMinSize;
- (NSSize)minSize;
- (void)setRichText:(BOOL)flag;
- (void)setImportsGraphics:(BOOL)flag;
- (BOOL)importsGraphics;
- (void)setBackgroundColor:(NSColor *)color;
- (NSColor *)backgroundColor;
- (void)setMaxSize:(NSSize)newMaxSize;
- (NSSize)maxSize;
- (void)setUsesFontPanel:(BOOL)flag;
- (BOOL)usesFontPanel;
- (void)setFieldEditor:(BOOL)flag;
- (void)setAlignment:(NSTextAlignment)mode;
- (NSTextAlignment)alignment;
```

```
- (void)setVerticallyResizable:(BOOL)flag;
- (void)setFont:(NSFont *)obj;
- (NSFont *)font;
- (void)setTextColor:(NSColor *)color;
- (NSColor *)textColor;
- (void)setDrawsBackground:(BOOL)flag;
- (BOOL)drawsBackground;
- (void)setTextColor:(NSColor *)color range:(NSRange)range;
- (void)setEditable:(BOOL)flag;
- (void)setFont:(NSFont *)font range:(NSRange)range;
// Instance Methods
- (NSData *)RTFDFromRange:(NSRange)range;
- (NSData *)RTFFromRange:(NSRange)range;
- (void)alignLeft:(id)sender;
- (void)alignRight:(id)sender;
- (void)changeFont:(id)sender;
- (void)cut:(id)sender;
- (void)delete:(id)sender;
- (BOOL)isEditable;
- (void)alignCenter:(id)sender;
- (void)checkSpelling:(id)sender;
- (BOOL)isFieldEditor;
- (BOOL)isHorizontallyResizable;
- (BOOL)isRichText;
- (BOOL)isSelectable;
- (BOOL)isVerticallyResizable;
- (BOOL)readRTFDFromFile:(NSString *)path;
- (void)replaceCharactersInRange:(NSRange)range withRTF:(NSData *)rtfData;
- (void)replaceCharactersInRange:(NSRange)range withRTFD:(NSData *)rtfdData;
- (void)replaceCharactersInRange:(NSRange)range withString:(NSString *)aString;
- (void)scrollRangeToVisible:(NSRange)range;
- (void)selectAll:(id)sender;
- (void)sizeToFit;
- (void)subscript:(id)sender;
- (void)superscript:(id)sender;
- (void)toggleRuler:(id)sender;
- (void)underline:(id)sender;
- (void)unscript:(id)sender;
- (void)copy:(id)sender;
- (void)copyFont:(id)sender;
- (void)copyRuler:(id)sender;
- (BOOL)isRulerVisible;
- (void)paste:(id)sender;
- (void)pasteFont:(id)sender;
- (void)pasteRuler:(id)sender;
- (void)showGuessPanel:(id)sender;
- (BOOL)writeRTFDToFile:(NSString *)path atomically:(BOOL)flag;
// Methods Implementing NSChangeSpelling
- (void)changeSpelling:(id)sender;
// Methods Implementing NSIgnoreMisspelledWords
- (void)ignoreSpelling:(id)sender;
```

// Methods Implemented by the Delegate

- (void)**textDidBeginEditing**:(NSNotification *)*notification*;

- (void)**textDidChange**:(NSNotification *)*notification*;

- (void)**textDidEndEditing**:(NSNotification *)*notification*;

- (BOOL)**textShouldBeginEditing**:(NSText *)*textObject*;

- (BOOL)**textShouldEndEditing**:(NSText *)*textObject*;

// Notifications

NSTextDidBeginEditingNotification;

NSTextDidChangeNotification;

Subclasses

NSTextView

NSTextAttachment

Mac OS X 10.0

Instances of this class serve as values in an attributed string for the attribute NSAttachmentAttributeName. Text attachment cells are associated with an NSFileWrapper object that may represent either a file or a URL.

@interface **NSTextAttachment** : NSObject <NSCoding>

// Initializers

- (id)**initWithFileWrapper**:(NSFileWrapper *)*fileWrapper*;

// Accessor Methods

- (void)**setFileWrapper**:(NSFileWrapper *)*fileWrapper*;

- (NSFileWrapper *)**fileWrapper**;

- (void)**setAttachmentCell**:(id <NSTextAttachmentCell>)*cell*;

- (id <NSTextAttachmentCell>)**attachmentCell**;

// Methods Implementing NSCoding

- (void)**encodeWithCoder**:(NSCoder *)*aCoder*;

- (id)**initWithCoder**:(NSCoder *)*aDecoder*;

NSTextAttachmentCell

Mac OS X 10.0

This class implements the interface defined by the NSTextAttachmentCell protocol.

@interface **NSTextAttachmentCell** : NSCell <NSTextAttachmentCell>

// Methods Implementing NSTextAttachmentCell

- (void)**drawWithFrame**:(NSRect)*cellFrame* **inView**:(NSView *)*controlView*;

- (BOOL)**wantsToTrackMouse**;

- (void)**highlight**:(BOOL)*flag* **withFrame**:(NSRect)*cellFrame* **inView**:(NSView *)*controlView*;

- (BOOL)**trackMouse**:(NSEvent *)*theEvent* **inRect**:(NSRect)*cellFrame* **ofView**:(NSView *)*controlView*
    untilMouseUp:(BOOL)*flag*;
- (NSSize)**cellSize**;
- (NSPoint)**cellBaselineOffset**;
- (void)**setAttachment**:(NSTextAttachment *)*anObject*;
- (NSTextAttachment *)**attachment**;
- (void)**drawWithFrame**:(NSRect)*cellFrame* **inView**:(NSView *)*controlView* **characterIndex**:(unsigned)*charIndex*;
- (void)**drawWithFrame**:(NSRect)*cellFrame* **inView**:(NSView *)*controlView* **characterIndex**:(unsigned)*charIndex*
    layoutManager:(NSLayoutManager *)*layoutManager*;
- (BOOL)**wantsToTrackMouseForEvent**:(NSEvent *)*theEvent* **inRect**:(NSRect)*cellFrame* **ofView**:(NSView *)*controlView*
    atCharacterIndex:(unsigned)*charIndex*;
- (BOOL)**trackMouse**:(NSEvent *)*theEvent* **inRect**:(NSRect)*cellFrame* **ofView**:(NSView *)*controlView*
    atCharacterIndex:(unsigned)*charIndex* **untilMouseUp**:(BOOL)*flag*;
- (NSRect)**cellFrameForTextContainer**:(NSTextContainer *)*textContainer* **proposedLineFragment**:(NSRect)*lineFrag*
    glyphPosition:(NSPoint)*position* **characterIndex**:(unsigned)*charIndex*;

NSTextContainer

Mac OS X 10.0

This class is responsible for defining a region in which text will be laid out. The class NSLayoutManager manages a set of NSTextContainer objects and controls how text should fill these text containers. An NSTextContainer object, in turn, owns an instance of NSTextView that is responsible for putting the text up on screen. The default implementation of NSTextContainer defines a rectangular region of text; however, subclasses may be implemented to provide irregular shaped regions for text. In terms of the Model-View-Controller pattern, NSTextStorage is the model, NSTextView is the view, and NSLayoutManager and NSTextContainer serve as controllers between the data layer and the view layer. For more information on Cocoa's text layout engine, see Chapter 5.

@interface **NSTextContainer** : NSObject <NSCoding>
// Initializers
- (id)**initWithContainerSize**:(NSSize)*size*;
// Accessor Methods
- (void)**setLineFragmentPadding**:(float)*pad*;
- (float)**lineFragmentPadding**;
- (void)**setLayoutManager**:(NSLayoutManager *)*layoutManager*;
- (NSLayoutManager *)**layoutManager**;
- (void)**setHeightTracksTextView**:(BOOL)*flag*;
- (BOOL)**heightTracksTextView**;
- (void)**setWidthTracksTextView**:(BOOL)*flag*;
- (BOOL)**widthTracksTextView**;
- (void)**setTextView**:(NSTextView *)*textView*;
- (NSTextView *)**textView**;
- (void)**setContainerSize**:(NSSize)*size*;
- (NSSize)**containerSize**;
// Instance Methods
- (BOOL)**containsPoint**:(NSPoint)*point*;
- (BOOL)**isSimpleRectangularTextContainer**;

- (NSRect)**lineFragmentRectForProposedRect:**(NSRect)*proposedRect*
    sweepDirection:(NSLineSweepDirection)*sweepDirection*
    movementDirection:(NSLineMovementDirection)*movementDirection* **remainingRect:**(NSRectPointer)*remainingRect*;
- (void)**replaceLayoutManager:**(NSLayoutManager *)*newLayoutManager*;
// Methods Implementing NSCoding
- (void)**encodeWithCoder:**(NSCoder *)*aCoder*;
- (id)**initWithCoder:**(NSCoder *)*aDecoder*;

NSTextField

This control class implements an editable text entry and display field. NSTextField's companion cell class is NSTextFieldCell, a subclass of NSActionCell. Thus, NSTextField is capable of sending action messages to targets. By default, actions are sent to targets when the user completes editing by pressing the Return key.

Accessing the value of a text field is done using methods inherited from NSControl (indeed, these are the methods used to access the values of any control). To get the contents of the text field as a string, invoke stringValue. Alternatively, we may take the value as a number using intValue, floatValue, and doubleValue. Each of these methods has a corresponding set... method used to change the value displayed in the text field. See NSControl (earlier in this chapter) for more information.

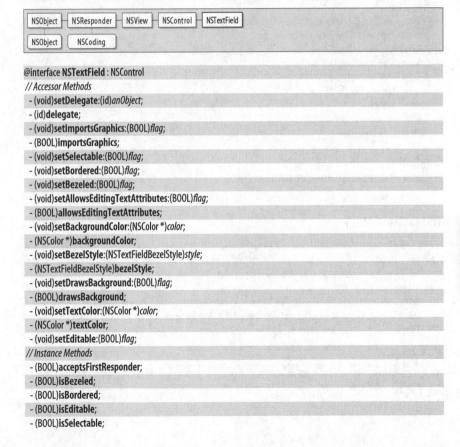

```
@interface NSTextField : NSControl
// Accessor Methods
- (void)setDelegate:(id)anObject;
- (id)delegate;
- (void)setImportsGraphics:(BOOL)flag;
- (BOOL)importsGraphics;
- (void)setSelectable:(BOOL)flag;
- (void)setBordered:(BOOL)flag;
- (void)setBezeled:(BOOL)flag;
- (void)setAllowsEditingTextAttributes:(BOOL)flag;
- (BOOL)allowsEditingTextAttributes;
- (void)setBackgroundColor:(NSColor *)color;
- (NSColor *)backgroundColor;
- (void)setBezelStyle:(NSTextFieldBezelStyle)style;
- (NSTextFieldBezelStyle)bezelStyle;
- (void)setDrawsBackground:(BOOL)flag;
- (BOOL)drawsBackground;
- (void)setTextColor:(NSColor *)color;
- (NSColor *)textColor;
- (void)setEditable:(BOOL)flag;
// Instance Methods
- (BOOL)acceptsFirstResponder;
- (BOOL)isBezeled;
- (BOOL)isBordered;
- (BOOL)isEditable;
- (BOOL)isSelectable;
```

AppKit
Classes

- (void)**selectText**:(id)*sender*;
- (void)**textDidBeginEditing**:(NSNotification *)*notification*;
- (void)**textDidChange**:(NSNotification *)*notification*;
- (void)**textDidEndEditing**:(NSNotification *)*notification*;
- (BOOL)**textShouldBeginEditing**:(NSText *)*textObject*;
- (BOOL)**textShouldEndEditing**:(NSText *)*textObject*;

Subclasses
NSComboBox, NSSecureTextField

NSTextFieldCell Mac OS X 10.0

This is the NSCell subclass that NSTextField objects use to draw the contents of the control.

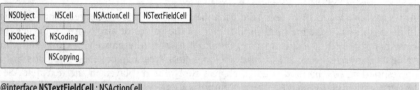

@interface **NSTextFieldCell** : NSActionCell
// Accessor Methods
- (NSText *)**setUpFieldEditorAttributes**:(NSText *)*textObj*;
- (void)**setBezelStyle**:(NSTextFieldBezelStyle)*style*;
- (NSTextFieldBezelStyle)**bezelStyle**;
- (void)**setBackgroundColor**:(NSColor *)*color*;
- (NSColor *)**backgroundColor**;
- (void)**setTextColor**:(NSColor *)*color*;
- (NSColor *)**textColor**;
- (void)**setDrawsBackground**:(BOOL)*flag*;
- (BOOL)**drawsBackground**;

Subclasses
NSComboBoxCell, NSSecureTextFieldCell, NSTableHeaderCell

NSTextStorage Mac OS X 10.0

This subclass of NSMutableAttributedString is the data model for Cocoa's text-handling system. NSTextStorage manages one or more NSLayoutManagers, which are responsible for determining how the text should be displayed. Two additional classes have an equally important role in the text-handling system, as does NSTextStorage: NSTextContainer and NSTextView. In terms of the Model-View-Controller pattern, NSTextStorage is the model, NSTextView is the view, and NSLayoutManager and NSTextContainer serve as controllers between the data layer and the view layer.

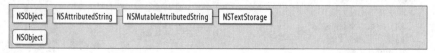

```
@interface NSTextStorage : NSMutableAttributedString
// Accessor Methods
    - (void)setParagraphs:(NSArray *)paragraphs;
    - (NSArray *)paragraphs;
    - (void)setForegroundColor:(NSColor *)color;
    - (NSColor *)foregroundColor;
    - (void)setCharacters:(NSArray *)characters;
    - (NSArray *)characters;
    - (void)setAttributeRuns:(NSArray *)attributeRuns;
    - (NSArray *)attributeRuns;
    - (void)setDelegate:(id)delegate;
    - (id)delegate;
    - (void)setWords:(NSArray *)words;
    - (NSArray *)words;
    - (void)setFont:(NSFont *)font;
    - (NSFont *)font;
// Instance Methods
    - (void)addLayoutManager:(NSLayoutManager *)obj;
    - (int)changeInLength;
    - (void)edited:(unsigned)editedMask range:(NSRange)range changeInLength:(int)delta;
    - (unsigned)editedMask;
    - (NSRange)editedRange;
    - (void)ensureAttributesAreFixedInRange:(NSRange)range;
    - (BOOL)fixesAttributesLazily;
    - (void)invalidateAttributesInRange:(NSRange)range;
    - (NSArray *)layoutManagers;
    - (void)processEditing;
    - (void)removeLayoutManager:(NSLayoutManager *)obj;
// Methods Implemented by the Delegate
    - (void)textStorageDidProcessEditing:(NSNotification *)notification;
    - (void)textStorageWillProcessEditing:(NSNotification *)notification;
// Notifications
    NSTextStorageDidProcessEditingNotification;
    NSTextStorageWillProcessEditingNotification;
```

NSTextTab

Mac OS X 10.0

This class is used by the class NSParagraphStyle to encapsulate information about a tab stop, such as alignment (left, right, center, etc.) and location of the stop relative to the alignment edge. To create a text tab object, use the method initWithType:location:. For more information on Cocoa's text handling infrastructure, see Chapter 5.

```
@interface NSTextTab : NSObject <NSCoding, NSCopying>
// Initializers
    - (id)initWithType:(NSTextTabType)type location:(float)loc;
```

```
// Instance Methods
- (float)location;
- (NSTextTabType)tabStopType;
// Methods Implementing NSCoding
- (void)encodeWithCoder:(NSCoder *)aCoder;
- (id)initWithCoder:(NSCoder *)aDecoder;
// Methods Implementing NSCopying
- (id)copyWithZone:(NSZone *)zone;
```

NSTextView

This class is the frontend class to Cocoa's text-manipulation architecture. For most purposes, programmers can use this class to interface with the text system; however, if more control is desired, than they may work with the individual component classes of the text system, which are NSTextStorage, NSTextContainer, NSLayoutManager, and this class. In terms of the Model-View-Controller pattern, NSTextStorage is the model, NSTextView is the view, and NSLayoutManager and NSTextContainer serve as controllers for the data layer and the view layer.

```
@interface NSTextView : NSText <NSTextInput>
// Initializers
- (id)initWithFrame:(NSRect)frameRect;
- (id)initWithFrame:(NSRect)frameRect textContainer:(NSTextContainer *)container;
// Accessor Methods
- (void)setImportsGraphics:(BOOL)flag;
- (BOOL)importsGraphics;
- (void)setBackgroundColor:(NSColor *)color;
- (NSColor *)backgroundColor;
- (void)setAcceptsGlyphInfo:(BOOL)flag;
- (BOOL)acceptsGlyphInfo;
- (void)setSelectable:(BOOL)flag;
- (void)setUsesRuler:(BOOL)flag;
- (BOOL)usesRuler;
- (void)setRulerVisible:(BOOL)flag;
- (void)setRichText:(BOOL)flag;
- (void)setTypingAttributes:(NSDictionary *)attrs;
- (NSDictionary *)typingAttributes;
- (void)setMarkedTextAttributes:(NSDictionary *)attributeDictionary;
- (NSDictionary *)markedTextAttributes;
- (void)setAlignment:(NSTextAlignment)alignment range:(NSRange)range;
- (void)setDelegate:(id)anObject;
- (id)delegate;
- (void)setSelectedRange:(NSRange)charRange;
- (void)setInsertionPointColor:(NSColor *)color;
- (NSColor *)insertionPointColor;
- (void)setAllowsUndo:(BOOL)flag;
- (BOOL)allowsUndo;
```

- (void)**setSelectedTextAttributes**:(NSDictionary *)*attributeDictionary*;
- (NSDictionary *)**selectedTextAttributes**;
- (void)**setSelectionGranularity**:(NSSelectionGranularity)*granularity*;
- (NSSelectionGranularity)**selectionGranularity**;
- (void)**setFieldEditor**:(BOOL)*flag*;
- (void)**setUsesFontPanel**:(BOOL)*flag*;
- (BOOL)**usesFontPanel**;
- (void)**setSelectedRange**:(NSRange)*charRange* **affinity**:(NSSelectionAffinity)*affinity*
    stillSelecting:(BOOL)*stillSelectingFlag*;
- (void)**setSmartInsertDeleteEnabled**:(BOOL)*flag*;
- (BOOL)**smartInsertDeleteEnabled**;
- (void)**setNeedsDisplayInRect**:(NSRect)*rect* **avoidAdditionalLayout**:(BOOL)*flag*;
- (void)**setTextContainerInset**:(NSSize)*inset*;
- (NSSize)**textContainerInset**;
- (void)**setTextContainer**:(NSTextContainer *)*container*;
- (NSTextContainer *)**textContainer**;
- (void)**setEditable**:(BOOL)*flag*;
- (void)**setDrawsBackground**:(BOOL)*flag*;
- (BOOL)**drawsBackground**;
- (void)**setContinuousSpellCheckingEnabled**:(BOOL)*flag*;
- (void)**setConstrainedFrameSize**:(NSSize)*desiredSize*;
// Class Methods
+ (void)**registerForServices**;
// Instance Methods
- (void)**cleanUpAfterDragOperation**;
- (NSArray *)**acceptableDragTypes**;
- (void)**clickedOnLink**:(id)*link v*
- (void)**alignJustified**:(id)*sender*;
- (void)**changeColor**:(id)*sender*;
- (void)**didChangeText**;
- (BOOL)**becomeFirstResponder**;
- (NSImage *)**dragImageForSelectionWithEvent**:(NSEvent *)*event* **origin**:(NSPointPointer)*origin*;
- (unsigned int)**dragOperationForDraggingInfo**:(id <NSDraggingInfo>)*dragInfo* **type**:(NSString *)*type*;
- (BOOL)**dragSelectionWithEvent**:(NSEvent *)*event* **offset**:(NSSize)*mouseOffset* **slideBack**:(BOOL)*slideBack*;
- (void)**insertText**:(id)*insertString*;
- (void)**invalidateTextContainerOrigin**;
- (BOOL)**isContinuousSpellCheckingEnabled**;
- (BOOL)**isEditable**;
- (BOOL)**isFieldEditor**;
- (BOOL)**isRichText**;
- (BOOL)**isSelectable**;
- (NSLayoutManager *)**layoutManager**;
- (void)**loosenKerning**:(id)*sender*;
- (void)**lowerBaseline**:(id)*sender*;
- (NSString *)**preferredPasteboardTypeFromArray**:(NSArray *)*availableTypes*
    restrictedToTypesFromArray:(NSArray *)*allowedTypes*;
- (void)**raiseBaseline**:(id)*sender*;
- (NSRange)**rangeForUserCharacterAttributeChange**;
- (NSRange)**rangeForUserParagraphAttributeChange**;
- (NSRange)**rangeForUserTextChange**;
- (BOOL)**readSelectionFromPasteboard**:(NSPasteboard *)*pboard*;
- (BOOL)**readSelectionFromPasteboard**:(NSPasteboard *)*pboard* **type**:(NSString *)*type*;

- (NSArray *)**readablePasteboardTypes**;

- (void)**replaceTextContainer**:(NSTextContainer *)*newContainer*;

- (BOOL)**resignFirstResponder**;

- (void)**drawInsertionPointInRect**:(NSRect)*rect* **color**:(NSColor *)*color* **turnedOn**:(BOOL)*flag*;

- (BOOL)**isRulerVisible**;

- (void)**pasteAsPlainText**:(id)*sender*;

- (void)**pasteAsRichText**:(id)*sender*;

- (void)**rulerView**:(NSRulerView *)*ruler* **didAddMarker**:(NSRulerMarker *)*marker*;

- (void)**rulerView**:(NSRulerView *)*ruler* **didMoveMarker**:(NSRulerMarker *)*marker*;

- (void)**rulerView**:(NSRulerView *)*ruler* **didRemoveMarker**:(NSRulerMarker *)*marker*;

- (void)**rulerView**:(NSRulerView *)*ruler* **handleMouseDown**:(NSEvent *)*event*;

- (BOOL)**rulerView**:(NSRulerView *)*ruler* **shouldAddMarker**:(NSRulerMarker *)*marker*;

- (BOOL)**rulerView**:(NSRulerView *)*ruler* **shouldMoveMarker**:(NSRulerMarker *)*marker*;

- (BOOL)**rulerView**:(NSRulerView *)*ruler* **shouldRemoveMarker**:(NSRulerMarker *)*marker*;

- (float)**rulerView**:(NSRulerView *)*ruler* **willAddMarker**:(NSRulerMarker *)*marker* **atLocation**:(float)*location*;

- (float)**rulerView**:(NSRulerView *)*ruler* **willMoveMarker**:(NSRulerMarker *)*marker* **toLocation**:(float)*location*;

- (NSSelectionAffinity)**selectionAffinity**;

- (NSRange)**selectionRangeForProposedRange**:(NSRange)*proposedCharRange*
    granularity:(NSSelectionGranularity)*granularity*;

- (BOOL)**shouldChangeTextInRange**:(NSRange)*affectedCharRange* **replacementString**:(NSString *)*replacementString*;

- (BOOL)**shouldDrawInsertionPoint**;

- (NSRange)**smartDeleteRangeForProposedRange**:(NSRange)*proposedCharRange*;

- (NSString *)**smartInsertAfterStringForString**:(NSString *)*pasteString*
    replacingRange:(NSRange)*charRangeToReplace*;

- (NSString *)**smartInsertBeforeStringForString**:(NSString *)*pasteString* **replacingRange**:(NSRange)*charRangeToReplace*;

- (void)**smartInsertForString**:(NSString *)*pasteString* **replacingRange**:(NSRange)*charRangeToReplace*
    beforeString:(NSString **)*beforeString* **afterString**:(NSString **)*afterString*;

- (int)**spellCheckerDocumentTag**;

- (void)**startSpeaking**:(id)*sender*;

- (void)**stopSpeaking**:(id)*sender*;

- (NSPoint)**textContainerOrigin**;

- (NSTextStorage *)**textStorage**;

- (void)**tightenKerning**:(id)*sender*;

- (void)**toggleContinuousSpellChecking**:(id)*sender*;

- (void)**toggleTraditionalCharacterShape**:(id)*sender*;

- (void)**turnOffKerning**:(id)*sender*;

- (void)**turnOffLigatures**:(id)*sender*;

- (void)**updateDragTypeRegistration**;

- (void)**updateFontPanel**;

- (void)**updateInsertionPointStateAndRestartTimer**:(BOOL)*restartFlag*;

- (void)**updateRuler**;

- (void)**useAllLigatures**:(id)*sender*;

- (void)**useStandardKerning**:(id)*sender*;

- (void)**useStandardLigatures**:(id)*sender*;

- (id)**validRequestorForSendType**:(NSString *)*sendType* **returnType**:(NSString *)*returnType*;

- (NSArray *)**writablePasteboardTypes**;

- (BOOL)**writeSelectionToPasteboard**:(NSPasteboard *)*pboard* **type**:(NSString *)*type*;

- (BOOL)**writeSelectionToPasteboard**:(NSPasteboard *)*pboard* **types**:(NSArray *)*types*;

// Methods Implementing NSTextInput

- (void)**insertText**:(id)*aString*;

- (void)**doCommandBySelector**:(SEL)*aSelector*;

- (void)**setMarkedText**:(id)*aString* **selectedRange**:(NSRange)*selRange*;

- (void)**unmarkText**;
- (BOOL)**hasMarkedText**;
- (long)**conversationIdentifier**;
- (NSAttributedString *)**attributedSubstringFromRange**:(NSRange)*theRange*;
- (NSRange)**markedRange**;
- (NSRange)**selectedRange**;
- (NSRect)**firstRectForCharacterRange**:(NSRange)*theRange*;
- (unsigned int)**characterIndexForPoint**:(NSPoint)*thePoint*;
- (NSArray*)**validAttributesForMarkedText**;
// Methods Implemented by the Delegate
- (void)**textView**:(NSTextView *)*textView* **clickedOnCell**:(id <NSTextAttachmentCell>)*cell*
    inRect:(NSRect)*cellFrame*;
- (void)**textView**:(NSTextView *)*textView* **clickedOnCell**:(id <NSTextAttachmentCell>)*cell*
    inRect:(NSRect)*cellFrame* **atIndex**:(unsigned)*charIndex*;
- (BOOL)**textView**:(NSTextView *)*textView* **clickedOnLink**:(id)*link*;
- (BOOL)**textView**:(NSTextView *)*textView* **clickedOnLink**:(id)*link* **atIndex**:(unsigned)*charIndex*;
- (BOOL)**textView**:(NSTextView *)*textView* **doCommandBySelector**:(SEL)*commandSelector*;
- (void)**textView**:(NSTextView *)*textView* **doubleClickedOnCell**:(id <NSTextAttachmentCell>)*cell*
    inRect:(NSRect)*cellFrame*;
- (void)**textView**:(NSTextView *)*textView* **doubleClickedOnCell**:(id <NSTextAttachmentCell>)*cell*
    inRect:(NSRect)*cellFrame* **atIndex**:(unsigned)*charIndex*;
- (BOOL)**textView**:(NSTextView *)*textView* **shouldChangeTextInRange**:(NSRange)*affectedCharRange*
    replacementString:(NSString *)*replacementString*;
- (NSRange)**textView**:(NSTextView *)*textView*
    willChangeSelectionFromCharacterRange:(NSRange)*oldSelectedCharRange*
    toCharacterRange:(NSRange)*newSelectedCharRange*;
- (void)**textView**:(NSTextView *)*view* **draggedCell**:(id <NSTextAttachmentCell>)*cell*
    inRect:(NSRect)*rect* **event**:(NSEvent *)*event*;
- (void)**textView**:(NSTextView *)*view* **draggedCell**:(id <NSTextAttachmentCell>)*cell* **inRect**:(NSRect)*rect*
    event:(NSEvent *)*event* **atIndex**:(unsigned)*charIndex*;
- (NSArray *)**textView**:(NSTextView *)*view* **writablePasteboardTypesForCell**:(id <NSTextAttachmentCell>)*cell*
    atIndex:(unsigned)*charIndex*;
- (BOOL)**textView**:(NSTextView *)*view* **writeCell**:(id <NSTextAttachmentCell>)*cell* **atIndex**:(unsigned)*charIndex*
    toPasteboard:(NSPasteboard *)*pboard* **type**:(NSString *)*type*;
- (void)**textViewDidChangeSelection**:(NSNotification *)*notification*;
- (NSUndoManager *)**undoManagerForTextView**:(NSTextView *)*view*;
// Notifications
NSTextViewDidChangeSelectionNotification;
NSTextViewWillChangeNotifyingTextViewNotification;

NSToolbar

Mac OS X 10.0

This class manages a toolbar in an application window. Every toolbar has an identifier, and multiple toolbars in an application with the same identifier (say, in multiple open document windows) will keep the same state. Toolbar objects take a delegate that provides the toolbar with NSToolbarItems to populate the toolbar and the toolbar customization sheet.

```
@interface NSToolbar : NSObject
// Initializers
- (id)initWithIdentifier:(NSString *)identifier;
// Accessor Methods
- (void)setConfigurationFromDictionary:(NSDictionary *)configDict;
- (void)setDelegate:(id)delegate;
- (id)delegate;
- (void)setVisible:(BOOL)shown;
- (void)setAllowsUserCustomization:(BOOL)allowCustomization;
- (BOOL)allowsUserCustomization;
- (void)setDisplayMode:(NSToolbarDisplayMode)displayMode;
- (NSToolbarDisplayMode)displayMode;
- (void)setSizeMode:(NSToolbarSizeMode)sizeMode;
- (NSToolbarSizeMode)sizeMode;
- (void)setAutosavesConfiguration:(BOOL)flag;
- (BOOL)autosavesConfiguration;
// Instance Methods
- (NSDictionary *)configurationDictionary;
- (NSString *)identifier;
- (BOOL)customizationPaletteIsRunning;
- (void)insertItemWithItemIdentifier:(NSString *)itemIdentifier atIndex:(int)index;
- (BOOL)isVisible;
- (NSArray *)items;
- (void)removeItemAtIndex:(int)index;
- (void)runCustomizationPalette:(id)sender;
- (void)validateVisibleItems;
- (NSArray *)visibleItems;
// Methods Implemented by the Delegate
- (NSToolbarItem *)toolbar:(NSToolbar *)toolbar itemForItemIdentifier:(NSString *)itemIdentifier
    willBeInsertedIntoToolbar:(BOOL)flag;
- (NSArray *)toolbarAllowedItemIdentifiers:(NSToolbar*)toolbar;
- (NSArray *)toolbarDefaultItemIdentifiers:(NSToolbar*)toolbar;
- (void)toolbarDidRemoveItem:(NSNotification *)notification;
- (void)toolbarWillAddItem:(NSNotification *)notification;
// Notifications
NSToolbarDidRemoveItemNotification;
NSToolbarWillAddItemNotification;
```

NSToolbarItem   Mac OS X 10.0

This class represents the controls that populate toolbars in the user interface. By
default, a toolbar item is an icon with a label attached. This icon functions as as simple
button. Like instances of NSButton, an NSToolbarItem object sends an action message to a
target when the user clicks the item. To initialize a toolbar item, we use the method
initWithItemIdentifier:. The identifier is simply a string used to uniquely identify the toolbar
item. AppKit has a number of prebuilt toolbar items that are used for common tasks,
such as opening the color panel or starting a print job. To take advantage of these standard toolbar items, initialize the toolbar item with one of the identifier strings listed in
the constants herein.

The second type of toolbar item is a custom **NSView** assigned to the toolbar item. The method **setView:** can be used to create a view in Interface Builder (or programatically) with a small set of controls suitable for a toolbar, and then create a toolbar item out of this view. This allows you to put standard AppKit controls (such as sliders or radio buttons) in the toolbar.

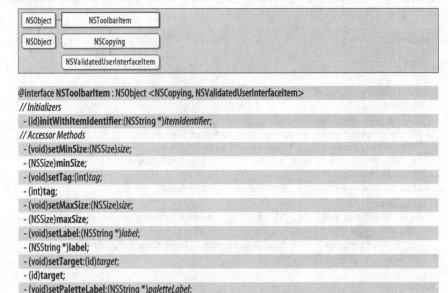

```
@interface NSToolbarItem : NSObject <NSCopying, NSValidatedUserInterfaceItem>
// Initializers
 - (id)initWithItemIdentifier:(NSString *)itemIdentifier;
// Accessor Methods
 - (void)setMinSize:(NSSize)size;
 - (NSSize)minSize;
 - (void)setTag:(int)tag;
 - (int)tag;
 - (void)setMaxSize:(NSSize)size;
 - (NSSize)maxSize;
 - (void)setLabel:(NSString *)label;
 - (NSString *)label;
 - (void)setTarget:(id)target;
 - (id)target;
 - (void)setPaletteLabel:(NSString *)paletteLabel;
 - (NSString *)paletteLabel;
 - (void)setEnabled:(BOOL)enabled;
 - (void)setAction:(SEL)action;
 - (SEL)action;
 - (void)setImage:(NSImage*)image;
 - (NSImage *)image;
 - (void)setToolTip:(NSString*)toolTip;
 - (NSString *)toolTip;
 - (void)setView:(NSView *)view;
 - (NSView *)view;
 - (void)setMenuFormRepresentation:(NSMenuItem *)menuItem;
 - (NSMenuItem *)menuFormRepresentation;
// Instance Methods
 - (BOOL)allowsDuplicatesInToolbar;
 - (BOOL)isEnabled;
 - (NSString *)itemIdentifier;
 - (NSToolbar *)toolbar;
 - (void)validate;
// Methods Implementing NSCopying
 - (id)copyWithZone:(NSZone *)zone;
// Methods Implementing NSValidatedUserInterfaceItem
 - (SEL)action;
 - (int)tag;
```

NSTypesetter

This abstract class provides an interface to objects that NSLayoutManager uses to layout lines in a text container. The Application Kit implements a single concrete subclass of NSTypesetter in NSSimpleHorizontalTypesetter. For more information about Cocoa's text layout system, see Chapter 5.

```
@interface NSTypesetter : NSObject
// Class Methods
+ (NSTypesetterBehavior)defaultTypesetterBehavior;
+ (NSSize)printingAdjustmentInLayoutManager:(NSLayoutManager *)layoutMgr
    forNominallySpacedGlyphRange:(NSRange)nominallySpacedGlyphsRange
    packedGlyphs:(const unsigned char *)packedGlyphs  count:(unsigned)packedGlyphsCount;
+ (id)sharedSystemTypesetter;
+ (id)sharedSystemTypesetterForBehavior:(NSTypesetterBehavior)theBehavior;
// Instance Methods
- (float)baselineOffsetInLayoutManager:(NSLayoutManager *)layoutMgr glyphIndex:(unsigned)glyphIndex;
- (void)layoutGlyphsInLayoutManager:(NSLayoutManager *)layoutManager
    startingAtGlyphIndex:(unsigned)startGlyphIndex maxNumberOfLineFragments:(unsigned)maxNumLines
    nextGlyphIndex:(unsigned *)nextGlyph;
```

Subclasses
NSSimpleHorizontalTypesetter

NSView

This is the Cocoa interface to Mac OS X's graphics APIs, including Quartz 2D, OpenGL (using NSOpenGLView), and QuickDraw (using NSQuickDrawView). Anything that is drawn to screen in Cocoa is done so within a view object. Developers can implement custom drawing behavior by subclassing NSView and overriding the drawRect: method. See Chapter 3 for more information on how views relate to other classes in the AppKit.

```
@interface NSView : NSResponder
// Initializers
- (id)initWithFrame:(NSRect)frameRect;
// Accessor Methods
- (void)setBoundsSize:(NSSize)newSize;
- (void)setFrameOrigin:(NSPoint)newOrigin;
- (void)setFrame:(NSRect)frameRect;
- (NSRect)frame;
- (void)setAutoresizingMask:(unsigned int)mask;
- (unsigned int)autoresizingMask;
- (void)setUpGState;
```

```
- (void)setBoundsRotation:(float)angle;
- (float)boundsRotation;
- (void)setAutoresizesSubviews:(BOOL)flag;
- (BOOL)autoresizesSubviews;
- (void)setNeedsDisplayInRect:(NSRect)invalidRect;
- (void)setBoundsOrigin:(NSPoint)newOrigin;
- (void)setFrameRotation:(float)angle;
- (float)frameRotation;
- (void)setNeedsDisplay:(BOOL)flag;
- (BOOL)needsDisplay;
- (void)setToolTip:(NSString *)string;
- (NSString *)toolTip;
- (void)setFrameSize:(NSSize)newSize;
- (void)setBounds:(NSRect)aRect;
- (NSRect)bounds;
- (void)setPostsFrameChangedNotifications:(BOOL)flag;
- (BOOL)postsFrameChangedNotifications;
- (void)setPostsBoundsChangedNotifications:(BOOL)flag;
- (BOOL)postsBoundsChangedNotifications;
// Class Methods
+ (NSMenu *)defaultMenu;
+ (NSView *)focusView;
// Instance Methods
- (BOOL)acceptsFirstMouse:(NSEvent *)theEvent;
- (NSView *)ancestorSharedWithView:(NSView *)aView;
- (void)addSubview:(NSView *)aView;
- (void)addSubview:(NSView *)aView positioned:(NSWindowOrderingMode)place relativeTo:(NSView *)otherView;
- (void)allocateGState;
- (NSToolTipTag)addToolTipRect:(NSRect)aRect owner:(id)anObject userData:(void *)data;
- (void)addCursorRect:(NSRect)aRect cursor:(NSCursor *)anObj;
- (NSTrackingRectTag)addTrackingRect:(NSRect)aRect owner:(id)anObject userData:(void *)data
    assumeInside:(BOOL)flag;
- (BOOL)autoscroll:(NSEvent *)theEvent;
- (void)beginDocument;
- (void)beginPageInRect:(NSRect)aRect atPlacement:(NSPoint)location;
- (BOOL)canDraw;
- (void)adjustPageHeightNew:(float *)newBottom top:(float)oldTop bottom:(float)oldBottom
    limit:(float)bottomLimit;
- (void)adjustPageWidthNew:(float *)newRight left:(float)oldLeft right:(float)oldRight limit:(float)rightLimit;
- (NSRect)adjustScroll:(NSRect)newVisible;
- (NSRect)centerScanRect:(NSRect)aRect;
- (NSPoint)convertPoint:(NSPoint)aPoint fromView:(NSView *)aView;
- (NSPoint)convertPoint:(NSPoint)aPoint toView:(NSView *)aView;
- (NSRect)convertRect:(NSRect)aRect fromView:(NSView *)aView;
- (NSRect)convertRect:(NSRect)aRect toView:(NSView *)aView;
- (NSSize)convertSize:(NSSize)aSize fromView:(NSView *)aView;
- (NSSize)convertSize:(NSSize)aSize toView:(NSView *)aView;
- (NSData *)dataWithEPSInsideRect:(NSRect)rect;
- (NSData *)dataWithPDFInsideRect:(NSRect)rect;
- (void)didAddSubview:(NSView *)subview;
- (void)discardCursorRects;
- (void)display;
```

- (void)**displayIfNeeded**;
- (void)**displayIfNeededIgnoringOpacity**;
- (void)**displayIfNeededInRect**:(NSRect)*rect*;
- (void)**displayIfNeededInRectIgnoringOpacity**:(NSRect)*rect*;
- (void)**displayRect**:(NSRect)*rect*;
- (void)**displayRectIgnoringOpacity**:(NSRect)*rect*;
- (void)**drawPageBorderWithSize**:(NSSize)*borderSize*;
- (void)**drawRect**:(NSRect)*rect*;
- (void)**drawSheetBorderWithSize**:(NSSize)*borderSize*;
- (NSScrollView *)**enclosingScrollView**;
- (void)**endDocument**;
- (void)**endPage**;
- (int)**gState**;
- (float)**heightAdjustLimit**;
- (NSView *)**hitTest**:(NSPoint)*aPoint*;
- (BOOL)**inLiveResize**;
- (BOOL)**isDescendantOf**:(NSView *)*aView*;
- (BOOL)**isFlipped**;
- (BOOL)**isOpaque**;
- (BOOL)**isRotatedFromBase**;
- (BOOL)**isRotatedOrScaledFromBase**;
- (BOOL)**knowsPageRange**:(NSRangePointer)*range*;
- (NSPoint)**locationOfPrintRect**:(NSRect)*aRect*;
- (void)**lockFocus**;
- (BOOL)**lockFocusIfCanDraw**;
- (NSMenu *)**menuForEvent**:(NSEvent *)*event*;
- (BOOL)**mouse**:(NSPoint)*aPoint* **inRect**:(NSRect)*aRect*;
- (BOOL)**mouseDownCanMoveWindow**;
- (BOOL)**needsPanelToBecomeKey**;
- (NSView *)**opaqueAncestor**;
- (BOOL)**performKeyEquivalent**:(NSEvent *)*theEvent*;
- (void)**print**:(id)*sender*;
- (NSString *)**printJobTitle**;
- (NSRect)**rectForPage**:(int)*page*;
- (void)**reflectScrolledClipView**:(NSClipView *)*aClipView*;
- (void)**releaseGState**;
- (void)**removeAllToolTips**;
- (void)**removeCursorRect**:(NSRect)*aRect* **cursor**:(NSCursor *)*anObj*;
- (void)**removeFromSuperview**;
- (void)**removeFromSuperviewWithoutNeedingDisplay**;
- (void)**removeToolTip**:(NSToolTipTag)*tag*;
- (void)**removeTrackingRect**:(NSTrackingRectTag)*tag*;
- (void)**renewGState**;
- (void)**replaceSubview**:(NSView *)*oldView* **with**:(NSView *)*newView*;
- (void)**resetCursorRects**;
- (void)**resizeSubviewsWithOldSize**:(NSSize)*oldSize*;
- (void)**resizeWithOldSuperviewSize**:(NSSize)*oldSize*;
- (void)**rotateByAngle**:(float)*angle*;
- (void)**scaleUnitSquareToSize**:(NSSize)*newUnitSize*;
- (void)**scrollClipView**:(NSClipView *)*aClipView* **toPoint**:(NSPoint)*aPoint*;
- (void)**scrollPoint**:(NSPoint)*aPoint*;
- (void)**scrollRect**:(NSRect)*aRect* **by**:(NSSize)*delta*;

- (BOOL)**scrollRectToVisible**:(NSRect)*aRect*;
- (BOOL)**shouldDelayWindowOrderingForEvent**:(NSEvent *)*theEvent*;
- (BOOL)**shouldDrawColor**;
- (void)**sortSubviewsUsingFunction**:(int (*)(id, id, void *))*compare* **context**:(void *)*context*;
- (NSArray *)**subviews**;
- (NSView *)**superview**;
- (int)**tag**;
- (void)**translateOriginToPoint**:(NSPoint)*translation*;
- (void)**unlockFocus**;
- (void)**viewDidEndLiveResize**;
- (void)**viewDidMoveToSuperview**;
- (void)**viewDidMoveToWindow**;
- (void)**viewWillMoveToSuperview**:(NSView *)*newSuperview*;
- (void)**viewWillMoveToWindow**:(NSWindow *)*newWindow*;
- (void)**viewWillStartLiveResize**;
- (id)**viewWithTag**:(int)*aTag*;
- (NSRect)**visibleRect**;
- (float)**widthAdjustLimit**;
- (void)**willRemoveSubview**:(NSView *)*subview*;
- (NSWindow *)**window**;
- (void)**writeEPSInsideRect**:(NSRect)*rect* **toPasteboard**:(NSPasteboard *)*pasteboard*;
- (void)**writePDFInsideRect**:(NSRect)*rect* **toPasteboard**:(NSPasteboard *)*pasteboard*;

// Notifications

NSViewBoundsDidChangeNotification;

NSViewFocusDidChangeNotification;

NSViewFrameDidChangeNotification;

NSViewGlobalFrameDidChangeNotification;

Subclasses

NSBox, NSClipView, NSControl, NSMenuView, NSMovieView, NSOpenGLView, NSProgressIndicator, NSQuickDrawView, NSRulerView, NSScrollView, NSSplitView, NSTabView, NSTableHeaderView, NSText

---

NSWindow
Mac OS X 10.0

This class declares an interface to application windows and is one of the key components of the Application Kit architecture. NSWindow objects are responsible for managing and displaying a hierarchy of views within the window, as well as handling mouse and keyboard events that occur in the window.

@interface **NSWindow** : NSResponder

// Initializers

- (id)**initWithContentRect**:(NSRect)*contentRect* **styleMask**:(unsigned int)*aStyle*
    backing:(NSBackingStoreType)*bufferingType* **defer**:(BOOL)*flag*;
- (id)**initWithContentRect**:(NSRect)*contentRect* **styleMask**:(unsigned int)*aStyle*
    backing:(NSBackingStoreType)*bufferingType* **defer**:(BOOL)*flag* **screen**:(NSScreen *)*screen*;
- (NSWindow *)**initWithWindowRef**:(void * /* WindowRef */)*windowRef*;
- (NSView *)**initialFirstResponder**;

```
// Accessor Methods
- (void)setAspectRatio:(NSSize)ratio;
- (NSSize)aspectRatio;
- (void)setOrderedIndex:(int)index;
- (int)orderedIndex;
- (void)setIsVisible:(BOOL)flag;
- (BOOL)isVisible;
- (void)setTitle:(NSString *)aString;
- (NSString *)title;
- (void)setIsMiniaturized:(BOOL)flag;
- (BOOL)isMiniaturized;
- (void)setRepresentedFilename:(NSString *)aString;
- (NSString *)representedFilename;
- (void)setTitleWithRepresentedFilename:(NSString *)filename;
- (void)setExcludedFromWindowsMenu:(BOOL)flag;
- (void)setIsZoomed:(BOOL)flag;
- (BOOL)isZoomed;
- (void)setMiniwindowTitle:(NSString *)title;
- (NSString *)miniwindowTitle;
- (void)setDelegate:(id)anObject;
- (id)delegate;
- (void)setToolbar:(NSToolbar*)toolbar;
- (NSToolbar *)toolbar;
- (void)setDefaultButtonCell:(NSButtonCell *)defButt;
- (NSButtonCell *)defaultButtonCell;
- (void)setParentWindow:(NSWindow *)window;
- (NSWindow *)parentWindow;
- (void)setFrame:(NSRect)frameRect display:(BOOL)flag;
- (NSRect)frame;
- (void)setFrameOrigin:(NSPoint)aPoint;
- (void)setFrameTopLeftPoint:(NSPoint)aPoint;
- (void)setFrame:(NSRect)frameRect display:(BOOL)displayFlag animate:(BOOL)animateFlag;
- (void)setResizeIncrements:(NSSize)increments;
- (NSSize)resizeIncrements;
- (void)setWindowController:(NSWindowController *)windowController;
- (id)windowController;
- (void)setMovableByWindowBackground:(BOOL)flag;
- (void)setIgnoresMouseEvents:(BOOL)flag;
- (BOOL)ignoresMouseEvents;
- (void)setAcceptsMouseMovedEvents:(BOOL)flag;
- (BOOL)acceptsMouseMovedEvents;
- (void)setMaxSize:(NSSize)size;
- (NSSize)maxSize;
- (void)setMiniwindowImage:(NSImage *)image;
- (NSImage *)miniwindowImage;
- (void)setCanHide:(BOOL)flag;
- (BOOL)canHide;
- (BOOL)setFrameAutosaveName:(NSString *)name;
- (NSString *)frameAutosaveName;
- (BOOL)setFrameUsingName:(NSString *)name;
- (void)setAutodisplay:(BOOL)flag;
- (BOOL)setFrameUsingName:(NSString *)name force:(BOOL)force;
```

- (void)**setFrameFromString**:(NSString *)*string*;
- (void)**setOpaque**:(BOOL)*isOpaque*;
- (void)**setAlphaValue**:(float)*windowAlpha*;
- (float)**alphaValue**;
- (void)**setHasShadow**:(BOOL)*hasShadow*;
- (BOOL)**hasShadow**;
- (void)**setReleasedWhenClosed**:(BOOL)*flag*;
- (void)**setDynamicDepthLimit**:(BOOL)*flag*;
- (void)**setHidesOnDeactivate**:(BOOL)*flag*;
- (BOOL)**hidesOnDeactivate**;
- (void)**setLevel**:(int)*newLevel*;
- (int)**level**;
- (void)**setBackingType**:(NSBackingStoreType)*bufferingType*;
- (NSBackingStoreType)**backingType**;
- (void)**setOneShot**:(BOOL)*flag*;
- (void)**setBackgroundColor**:(NSColor *)*color*;
- (NSColor *)**backgroundColor**;
- (void)**setMinSize**:(NSSize)*size*;
- (NSSize)**minSize**;
- (void)**setContentView**:(NSView *)*aView*;
- (id)**contentView**;
- (void)**setDocumentEdited**:(BOOL)*flag*;
- (void)**setInitialFirstResponder**:(NSView *)*view*;
- (void)**setShowsResizeIndicator**:(BOOL)*show*;
- (BOOL)**showsResizeIndicator**;
- (void)**setViewsNeedDisplay**:(BOOL)*flag*;
- (BOOL)**viewsNeedDisplay**;
- (void)**setDepthLimit**:(NSWindowDepth)*limit*;
- (NSWindowDepth)**depthLimit**;
- (void)**setContentSize**:(NSSize)*aSize*;

// Class Methods

+ (NSRect)**contentRectForFrameRect**:(NSRect)*fRect* **styleMask**:(unsigned int)*aStyle*;
+ (NSWindowDepth)**defaultDepthLimit**;
+ (NSRect)**frameRectForContentRect**:(NSRect)*cRect* **styleMask**:(unsigned int)*aStyle*;
+ (void)**menuChanged**:(NSMenu *)*menu*;
+ (float)**minFrameWidthWithTitle**:(NSString *)*aTitle* **styleMask**:(unsigned int)*aStyle*;
+ (void)**removeFrameUsingName**:(NSString *)*name*;
+ (NSButton *)**standardWindowButton**:(NSWindowButton)*b* **forStyleMask**:(unsigned int)*styleMask*;

// Instance Methods

- (BOOL)**canBecomeKeyWindow**;
- (BOOL)**canBecomeMainWindow**;
- (void)**becomeKeyWindow**;
- (NSArray *)**childWindows**;
- (void)**becomeMainWindow**;
- (void)**addChildWindow**:(NSWindow *)*childWin* **ordered**:(NSWindowOrderingMode)*place*;
- (NSTimeInterval)**animationResizeTime**:(NSRect)*newFrame*;
- (NSPoint)**cascadeTopLeftFromPoint**:(NSPoint)*topLeftPoint*;
- (NSWindow *)**attachedSheet**;
- (NSEvent *)**currentEvent**;
- (void)**cacheImageInRect**:(NSRect)*aRect*;
- (void)**close**;
- (BOOL)**canStoreColor**;

- (BOOL)**areCursorRectsEnabled**;
- (void)**center**;
- (NSRect)**constrainFrameRect**:(NSRect)*frameRect* **toScreen**:(NSScreen *)*screen*;
- (NSPoint)**convertBaseToScreen**:(NSPoint)*aPoint*;
- (NSPoint)**convertScreenToBase**:(NSPoint)*aPoint*;
- (NSData *)**dataWithEPSInsideRect**:(NSRect)*rect*;
- (NSData *)**dataWithPDFInsideRect**:(NSRect)*rect*;
- (NSScreen *)**deepestScreen**;
- (void)**deminiaturize**:(id)*sender*;
- (NSDictionary *)**deviceDescription**;
- (void)**disableCursorRects**;
- (void)**disableFlushWindow**;
- (void)**disableKeyEquivalentForDefaultButtonCell**;
- (void)**discardCachedImage**;
- (void)**discardCursorRects**;
- (void)**discardEventsMatchingMask**:(unsigned int)*mask* **beforeEvent**:(NSEvent *)*lastEvent*;
- (void)**display**;
- (void)**displayIfNeeded**;
- (void)**dragImage**:(NSImage *)*anImage* **at**:(NSPoint)*baseLocation* **offset**:(NSSize)*initialOffset*
    event:(NSEvent *)*event* **pasteboard**:(NSPasteboard *)*pboard* **source**:(id)*sourceObj* **slideBack**:(BOOL)*slideFlag*;
- (NSArray *)**drawers**;
- (void)**enableCursorRects**;
- (void)**enableFlushWindow**;
- (void)**enableKeyEquivalentForDefaultButtonCell**;
- (void)**endEditingFor**:(id)*anObject*;
- (NSText *)**fieldEditor**:(BOOL)*createFlag* **forObject**:(id)*anObject*;
- (NSResponder *)**firstResponder**;
- (void)**flushWindow**;
- (void)**flushWindowIfNeeded**;
- (int)**gState**;
- (id)**handleCloseScriptCommand**:(NSCloseCommand *)*command*;
- (id)**handlePrintScriptCommand**:(NSScriptCommand *)*command*;
- (id)**handleSaveScriptCommand**:(NSScriptCommand *)*command*;
- (BOOL)**hasCloseBox**;
- (BOOL)**hasDynamicDepthLimit**;
- (BOOL)**hasTitleBar**;
- (void)**invalidateCursorRectsForView**:(NSView *)*aView*;
- (void)**invalidateShadow**;
- (BOOL)**isAutodisplay**;
- (BOOL)**isDocumentEdited**;
- (BOOL)**isExcludedFromWindowsMenu**;
- (BOOL)**isFloatingPanel**;
- (BOOL)**isFlushWindowDisabled**;
- (BOOL)**isKeyWindow**;
- (BOOL)**isMainWindow**;
- (BOOL)**isMiniaturizable**;
- (BOOL)**isModalPanel**;
- (BOOL)**isMovableByWindowBackground**;
- (BOOL)**isOneShot**;
- (BOOL)**isOpaque**;
- (BOOL)**isReleasedWhenClosed**;
- (BOOL)**isResizable**;

- (BOOL)**isSheet**;
- (BOOL)**isZoomable**;
- (void)**keyDown**:(NSEvent *)*theEvent*;
- (NSSelectionDirection)**keyViewSelectionDirection**;
- (BOOL)**makeFirstResponder**:(NSResponder *)*aResponder*;
- (void)**makeKeyAndOrderFront**:(id)*sender*;
- (void)**makeKeyWindow**;
- (void)**makeMainWindow**;
- (void)**miniaturize**:(id)*sender*;
- (NSPoint)**mouseLocationOutsideOfEventStream**;
- (NSEvent *)**nextEventMatchingMask**:(unsigned int)*mask*;
- (NSEvent *)**nextEventMatchingMask**:(unsigned int)*mask* **untilDate**:(NSDate *)*expiration* **inMode**:(NSString *)*mode*
    dequeue:(BOOL)*deqFlag*;
- (void)**orderBack**:(id)*sender*;
- (void)**orderFront**:(id)*sender*;
- (void)**orderFrontRegardless**;
- (void)**orderOut**:(id)*sender*;
- (void)**orderWindow**:(NSWindowOrderingMode)*place* **relativeTo**:(int)*otherWin*;
- (void)**performClose**:(id)*sender*;
- (void)**performMiniaturize**:(id)*sender*;
- (void)**performZoom**:(id)*sender*;
- (void)**postEvent**:(NSEvent *)*event* **atStart**:(BOOL)*flag*;
- (void)**print**:(id)*sender*;
- (void)**registerForDraggedTypes**:(NSArray *)*newTypes*;
- (void)**removeChildWindow**:(NSWindow *)*childWin*;
- (void)**resetCursorRects**;
- (void)**resignKeyWindow**;
- (void)**resignMainWindow**;
- (int)**resizeFlags**;
- (void)**restoreCachedImage**;
- (void)**runToolbarCustomizationPalette**:(id)*sender*;
- (void)**saveFrameUsingName**:(NSString *)*name*;
- (NSScreen *)**screen**;
- (void)**selectKeyViewFollowingView**:(NSView *)*aView*;
- (void)**selectKeyViewPrecedingView**:(NSView *)*aView*;
- (void)**selectNextKeyView**:(id)*sender*;
- (void)**selectPreviousKeyView**:(id)*sender*;
- (void)**sendEvent**:(NSEvent *)*theEvent*;
- (NSButton *)**standardWindowButton**:(NSWindowButton)*b*;
- (NSString *)**stringWithSavedFrame**;
- (unsigned int)**styleMask**;
- (void)**toggleToolbarShown**:(id)*sender*;
- (BOOL)**tryToPerform**:(SEL)*anAction* **with**:(id)*anObject*;
- (void)**unregisterDraggedTypes**;
- (void)**update**;
- (void)**useOptimizedDrawing**:(BOOL)*flag*;
- (id)**validRequestorForSendType**:(NSString *)*sendType* **returnType**:(NSString *)*returnType*;
- (void * /*HWND*/)**windowHandle**;
- (int)**windowNumber**;
- (void * /* WindowRef */)**windowRef**;
- (BOOL)**worksWhenModal**;
- (void)**zoom**:(id)*sender*;

// Methods Implemented by the Delegate
- (void)**windowDidBecomeKey**:(NSNotification *)*notification*;
- (void)**windowDidBecomeMain**:(NSNotification *)*notification*;
- (void)**windowDidChangeScreen**:(NSNotification *)*notification*;
- (void)**windowDidDeminiaturize**:(NSNotification *)*notification*;
- (void)**windowDidEndSheet**:(NSNotification *)*notification*;
- (void)**windowDidExpose**:(NSNotification *)*notification*;
- (void)**windowDidMiniaturize**:(NSNotification *)*notification*;
- (void)**windowDidMove**:(NSNotification *)*notification*;
- (void)**windowDidResignKey**:(NSNotification *)*notification*;
- (void)**windowDidResignMain**:(NSNotification *)*notification*;
- (void)**windowDidResize**:(NSNotification *)*notification*;
- (void)**windowDidUpdate**:(NSNotification *)*notification*;
- (BOOL)**windowShouldClose**:(id)*sender*;
- (BOOL)**windowShouldZoom**:(NSWindow *)*window* **toFrame**:(NSRect)*newFrame*;
- (void)**windowWillBeginSheet**:(NSNotification *)*notification*;
- (void)**windowWillClose**:(NSNotification *)*notification*;
- (void)**windowWillMiniaturize**:(NSNotification *)*notification*;
- (void)**windowWillMove**:(NSNotification *)*notification*;
- (NSSize)**windowWillResize**:(NSWindow *)*sender* **toSize**:(NSSize)*frameSize*;
- (id)**windowWillReturnFieldEditor**:(NSWindow *)*sender* **toObject**:(id)*client*;
- (NSUndoManager *)**windowWillReturnUndoManager**:(NSWindow *)*window*;
- (NSRect)**windowWillUseStandardFrame**:(NSWindow *)*window* **defaultFrame**:(NSRect)*newFrame*;

// Notifications
NSWindowDidBecomeKeyNotification;
NSWindowDidBecomeMainNotification;
NSWindowDidChangeScreenNotification;
NSWindowDidDeminiaturizeNotification;
NSWindowDidEndSheetNotification;
NSWindowDidMiniaturizeNotification;
NSWindowDidMoveNotification;
NSWindowDidResignKeyNotification;
NSWindowDidResignMainNotification;
NSWindowDidResizeNotification;
NSWindowDidUpdateNotification;
NSWindowWillBeginSheetNotification;
NSWindowWillCloseNotification;
NSWindowWillMiniaturizeNotification;
NSWindowWillMoveNotification;

Subclasses
NSPanel

NSWindowController   Mac OS X 10.0

This is one of the three classes that makes up Cocoa's document-based application architecture; the other two classes are NSDocument and NSDocumentController. Instances of NSWindowController are responsible for managing a single window for a document. NSWindowController has a close relationship with windows contained in nib files, which is evident in the initializer initWithWindowNibName:. This initializer will load the window in the nib and take ownership over it. See Chapter 3 for more information on NSWindowController and its role in document-based applications.

@interface **NSWindowController** : NSResponder <NSCoding>

// Initializers
- (id)**initWithWindow**:(NSWindow *)*window*;
- (id)**initWithWindowNibName**:(NSString *)*windowNibName*;
- (id)**initWithWindowNibName**:(NSString *)*windowNibName* **owner**:(id)*owner*;
- (id)**initWithWindowNibPath**:(NSString *)*windowNibPath* **owner**:(id)*owner*;

// Accessor Methods
- (void)**setWindowFrameAutosaveName**:(NSString *)*name*;
- (NSString *)**windowFrameAutosaveName**;
- (void)**setWindow**:(NSWindow *)*window*;
- (NSWindow *)**window**;
- (void)**setDocumentEdited**:(BOOL)*dirtyFlag*;
- (void)**setShouldCloseDocument**:(BOOL)*flag*;
- (BOOL)**shouldCloseDocument**;
- (void)**setDocument**:(NSDocument *)*document*;
- (id)**document**;
- (void)**setShouldCascadeWindows**:(BOOL)*flag*;
- (BOOL)**shouldCascadeWindows**;

// Instance Methods
- (void)**close**;
- (BOOL)**isWindowLoaded**;
- (void)**loadWindow**;
- (id)**owner**;
- (IBAction)**showWindow**:(id)*sender*;
- (void)**synchronizeWindowTitleWithDocumentName**;
- (void)**windowDidLoad**;
- (NSString *)**windowNibName**;
- (NSString *)**windowNibPath**;
- (NSString *)**windowTitleForDocumentDisplayName**:(NSString *)*displayName*;
- (void)**windowWillLoad**;

// Methods Implementing NSCoding
- (void)**encodeWithCoder**:(NSCoder *)*aCoder*;
- (id)**initWithCoder**:(NSCoder *)*aDecoder*;

NSWorkspace

Mac OS X 10.0

This class makes available to Cocoa applications many of Mac OS X's "workspace" services, which are essentially those services provided by the Finder. NSWorkspace provides methods for discovering characteristics of the workspace, such as what GUI applications are running and what volumes are mounted. Additionally, applications can use NSWorkspace to open files and URLs as if they were opened in the Finder. Each

application has a single shared instance of **NSWorkspace** that is accessed with the method
sharedWorkspace.

```
@interface NSWorkspace : NSObject
// Class Methods
 + (NSWorkspace *)sharedWorkspace;
// Instance Methods
 - (NSDictionary *)activeApplication;
 - (void)checkForRemovableMedia;
 - (int)extendPowerOffBy:(int)requested;
 - (BOOL)fileSystemChanged;
 - (void)findApplications;
 - (NSString *)fullPathForApplication:(NSString *)appName;
 - (BOOL)getFileSystemInfoForPath:(NSString *)fullPath isRemovable:(BOOL *)removableFlag
     isWritable:(BOOL *)writableFlag isUnmountable:(BOOL *)unmountableFlag description:(NSString **)description
     type:(NSString **)fileSystemType;
 - (BOOL)getInfoForFile:(NSString *)fullPath application:(NSString **)appName type:(NSString **)type;
 - (void)hideOtherApplications;
 - (NSImage *)iconForFile:(NSString *)fullPath;
 - (NSImage *)iconForFileType:(NSString *)fileType;
 - (NSImage *)iconForFiles:(NSArray *)fullPaths;
 - (BOOL)isFilePackageAtPath:(NSString *)fullPath;
 - (BOOL)launchApplication:(NSString *)appName;
 - (BOOL)launchApplication:(NSString *)appName showIcon:(BOOL)showIcon autolaunch:(BOOL)autolaunch;
 - (NSArray *)launchedApplications;
 - (NSArray *)mountNewRemovableMedia;
 - (NSArray *)mountedLocalVolumePaths;
 - (NSArray *)mountedRemovableMedia;
 - (void)noteFileSystemChanged;
 - (void)noteFileSystemChanged:(NSString *)path;
 - (void)noteUserDefaultsChanged;
 - (NSNotificationCenter *)notificationCenter;
 - (BOOL)openFile:(NSString *)fullPath;
 - (BOOL)openFile:(NSString *)fullPath fromImage:(NSImage *)anImage at:(NSPoint)point inView:(NSView *)aView;
 - (BOOL)openFile:(NSString *)fullPath withApplication:(NSString *)appName;
 - (BOOL)openFile:(NSString *)fullPath withApplication:(NSString *)appName andDeactivate:(BOOL)flag;
 - (BOOL)openTempFile:(NSString *)fullPath;
 - (BOOL)openURL:(NSURL *)url;
 - (BOOL)performFileOperation:(NSString *)operation source:(NSString *)source destination:(NSString *)destination
     files:(NSArray *)files tag:(int *)tag;
 - (BOOL)selectFile:(NSString *)fullPath inFileViewerRootedAtPath:(NSString *)rootFullpath;
 - (void)slideImage:(NSImage *)image from:(NSPoint)fromPoint to:(NSPoint)toPoint;
 - (BOOL)unmountAndEjectDeviceAtPath:(NSString *)path;
 - (BOOL)userDefaultsChanged;
// Notifications
NSWorkspaceWillPowerOffNotification;
```

16

Application Kit Protocols

This chapter covers the protocols of the Application Kit. The Application Kit implements all of the graphical user interface components of Cocoa, including the complete standard Aqua widget set. Additionally, the Application Kit provides classes for interacting with the Quartz 2D drawing system, and for managing and accessing resources such as colors, fonts, and printers. The Application Kit is introduced in Chapter 3. Chapter 4 and Chapter 5 went into more detail about those aspects of the Application Kit.

NSAccessibility   Mac OS X 10.2

Cocoa provides support for accessibility, which gives Cocoa applications the ability to work with other assistive applications, such as screen readers. This informal protocol declares the methods that classes in an application must implement to interface with the accessibility system. The great majority of Application Kit classes implement this protocol, meaning that Cocoa applications are largely accessible to assistive technologies. However, if you do a great deal of customization to existing Cocoa classes, it may be necessary to implement portions of the protocol yourself.

```
@interface NSObject (NSAccessibility)
// Instance Methods
 - (NSArray *)accessibilityAttributeNames;
 - (id)accessibilityAttributeValue:(NSString *)attribute;
 - (BOOL)accessibilityIsAttributeSettable:(NSString *)attribute;
 - (void)accessibilitySetValue:(id)value forAttribute:(NSString *)attribute;
 - (NSArray *)accessibilityActionNames;
 - (NSString *)accessibilityActionDescription:(NSString *)action;
 - (void)accessibilityPerformAction:(NSString *)action;
 - (BOOL)accessibilityIsIgnored;
 - (id)accessibilityHitTest:(NSPoint)point;
 - (id)accessibilityFocusedUIElement;
@end
```

NSChangeSpelling

This protocol declares the single action method changeSpelling:, implemented to receive messages from the Spelling panel notifying them of text selections that need to be replaced. The sender of the changeSpelling: message is the Spelling panel. Classes should implement this method to query the sender for the word that the user has selected in the panel, and replace the current selection with that word.

```
@protocol NSChangeSpelling
// Instance Methods
 - (void)changeSpelling:(id)sender;
@end
```

NSColorPickingCustom

This protocol declares an interface for classes to conform to provide custom color pickers for the color-picker panel. This protocol is used closely with the NSColorPickingDefault protocol, which declares the basic interface for color pickers. The most straightforward way to create a custom color picker for your application is to subclass NSColorPicker, and implement the methods of this protocol in your subclass.

```
@protocol NSColorPickingCustom
// Instance Methods
 - (BOOL)supportsMode:(int)mode;
 - (int)currentMode;
 - (NSView *)provideNewView:(BOOL)initialRequest;
 - (void)setColor:(NSColor *)newColor;
@end
```

NSColorPickingDefault

This protocol declares an interface for classes to conform to in order to provide custom color pickers for the color-picker panel. This protocol is used closely with the NSColorPickingCustom protocol. The Application Kit implements the methods of this protocol in the NSColorPicker class. The most straightforward way to create a custom color picker for your application is to subclass NSColorPicker and implement the methods of NSColorPickingCustom in your subclass.

```
@protocol NSColorPickingDefault
// Instance Methods
 - (id)initWithPickerMask:(int)mask colorPanel:(NSColorPanel *)owningColorPanel;
 - (NSImage *)provideNewButtonImage;
 - (void)insertNewButtonImage:(NSImage *)newButtonImage in:(NSButtonCell *)buttonCell;
 - (void)viewSizeChanged:(id)sender;
 - (void)alphaControlAddedOrRemoved:(id)sender;
 - (void)attachColorList:(NSColorList *)colorList;
 - (void)detachColorList:(NSColorList *)colorList;
 - (void)setMode:(int)mode;
@end
```

NSComboBoxCellDataSource

NSComboBox controls rely on data source objects to provide the contents of the combo box. This informal protocol provides the interface for NSComboBoxCell data source objects to implement. It declares methods that not only provide the contents of the combo box list, but support autocompletion behavior (where a string is returned from the data source that matches a partially completed string typed into the combo box field). At a minimum, data source objects must implement the methods comboBoxCell:objectValueForItemAtIndex: and numberOfItemsInComboBoxCell:.

```
@interface NSObject (NSComboBoxCellDataSource)
// Instance Methods
  - (int)numberOfItemsInComboBoxCell:(NSComboBoxCell *)comboBoxCell;
  - (id)comboBoxCell:(NSComboBoxCell *)aComboBoxCell objectValueForItemAtIndex:(int)index;
  - (unsigned int)comboBoxCell:(NSComboBoxCell *)aComboBoxCell indexOfItemWithStringValue:(NSString *)string;
  - (NSString *)comboBoxCell:(NSComboBoxCell *)aComboBoxCell completedString:(NSString *)uncompletedString;
@end
```

NSComboBoxDataSource

This informal protocol provides methods for a class to implement to act as a data source for NSComboBox objects. This protocol declares methods that not only provide the contents of the combo box list, but support autocompletion behavior (where a string is returned from the data source that matches a partially completed string typed into the combo box field). At a minimum, data source objects must implement the methods comboBox:objectValueForItemAtIndex: and numberOfItemsInComboBox:.

```
@interface NSObject (NSComboBoxDataSource)
// Instance Methods
  - (int)numberOfItemsInComboBox:(NSComboBox *)aComboBox;
  - (id)comboBox:(NSComboBox *)aComboBox objectValueForItemAtIndex:(int)index;
  - (unsigned int)comboBox:(NSComboBox *)aComboBox indexOfItemWithStringValue:(NSString *)string;
  - (NSString *)comboBox:(NSComboBox *)aComboBox completedString:(NSString *)string;
@end
```

NSDraggingDestination

This informal protocol declares methods for objects to implement if they need to receive dragging operations. Several of the methods of NSDraggingDestination are implemented to respond to the movement of the drag operation of an destination object, while the remainder are implemented to execute and complete the dragging operation. Completing a drag operation involves retrieving and handling the data appropriately. To retrieve the data one must first obtain the NSPasteboard object in which the data is stored, for a dragging operation only knows about this pasteboard, not the data itself. The pasteboard may be obtained with the draggingPasteboard method. This is declared by the NSDraggingInfo protocol, and all dragging operation objects conform to this protocol. See the NSDraggingInfo protocol description and NSPasteboard class description for more information.

```
@interface NSObject (NSDraggingDestination)
// Instance Methods
 - (NSDragOperation)draggingEntered:(id <NSDraggingInfo>)sender;
 - (NSDragOperation)draggingUpdated:(id <NSDraggingInfo>)sender;
 - (void)draggingExited:(id <NSDraggingInfo>)sender;
 - (BOOL)prepareForDragOperation:(id <NSDraggingInfo>)sender;
 - (BOOL)performDragOperation:(id <NSDraggingInfo>)sender;
 - (void)concludeDragOperation:(id <NSDraggingInfo>)sender;
 - (void)draggingEnded:(id <NSDraggingInfo>)sender;
@end
```

NSDraggingInfo Mac OS X 10.0

This protocol declares methods that are used to provide an interface to objects that represent dragging sessions. When a dragging session begins, an object that conforms to this protocol is automatically created, and is the sender of all messages to the destination object, which implements the methods outlined in the NSDraggingDestination protocol. NSDraggingInfo exists to publish the interface for this object that represents the dragging operation, and as such developers never need to implement these methods.

```
@protocol NSDraggingInfo
// Instance Methods
 - (NSWindow *)draggingDestinationWindow;
 - (NSDragOperation)draggingSourceOperationMask;
 - (NSPoint)draggingLocation;
 - (NSPoint)draggedImageLocation;
 - (NSImage *)draggedImage;
 - (NSPasteboard *)draggingPasteboard;
 - (id)draggingSource;
 - (int)draggingSequenceNumber;
 - (void)slideDraggedImageTo:(NSPoint)screenPoint;
 - (NSArray *)namesOfPromisedFilesDroppedAtDestination:(NSURL *)dropDestination;
@end
```

NSDraggingSource Mac OS X 10.0

This informal protocol declares methods that a class must implement to serve as a source of data in dragging operations. This protocol declares a number of methods, but classes need only implement the method draggingSourceOperationMaskForLocal: to be a valid dragging operation source. Classes should implement this method to return a dragging source operation mask, which describes how data should be handled in a dragging operation. See NSDraggingInfo's listing (previously) for more information.

```
@interface NSObject (NSDraggingSource)
// Instance Methods
 - (NSDragOperation)draggingSourceOperationMaskForLocal:(BOOL)flag;
 - (NSArray *)namesOfPromisedFilesDroppedAtDestination:(NSURL *)dropDestination;
 - (void)draggedImage:(NSImage *)image beganAt:(NSPoint)screenPoint;
 - (void)draggedImage:(NSImage *)image endedAt:(NSPoint)screenPoint operation:(NSDragOperation)operation;
```

```
    - (void)draggedImage:(NSImage *)image movedTo:(NSPoint)screenPoint;
    - (BOOL)ignoreModifierKeysWhileDragging;
    - (void)draggedImage:(NSImage *)image endedAt:(NSPoint)screenPoint deposited:(BOOL)flag;
@end
```

NSIgnoreMisspelledWords

Mac OS X 10.0

This protocol declares the single action method ignoreSpelling:, which should be implemented by classes that need to work with Cocoa's Spelling panel. NSSpellChecker sends this message up the responder chain. Classes implement this method so that the *Ignore* button in the Spelling panel functions properly for the particular application or document implementation.

```
@protocol NSIgnoreMisspelledWords
// Instance Methods
    - (void)ignoreSpelling:(id)sender;
@end
```

NSInputServerMouseTracker

Mac OS X 10.0

This protocol declares an interface for mouse event handling that is tailored for use by text views. The methods of this protocol provide information about the character position of an event, in addition to the coordinates of the mouse location in the view.

```
@protocol NSInputServerMouseTracker
// Instance Methods
    - (BOOL)mouseDownOnCharacterIndex:(unsigned)theIndex atCoordinate:(NSPoint)thePoint
        withModifier:(unsigned int)theFlags client:(id)sender;
    - (BOOL)mouseDraggedOnCharacterIndex:(unsigned)theIndex atCoordinate:(NSPoint)thePoint
        withModifier:(unsigned int)theFlags client:(id)sender;
    - (void)mouseUpOnCharacterIndex:(unsigned)theIndex atCoordinate:(NSPoint)thePoint
        withModifier:(unsigned int)theFlags client:(id)sender;
@end
```

NSInputServiceProvider

Mac OS X 10.0

This protocol declares the interface for most of the functionality implemented by NSInputServer. Clients may use this class to implement their own input server classes, or to implement a delegate object that can be used with the standard NSInputServer.

```
@protocol NSInputServiceProvider
// Instance Methods
    - (void)insertText:(id)aString client:(id)sender;
    - (void)doCommandBySelector:(SEL)aSelector client:(id)sender;
    - (void)markedTextAbandoned:(id)sender;
    - (void)markedTextSelectionChanged:(NSRange)newSel client:(id)sender;
    - (void)terminate:(id)sender;
    - (BOOL)canBeDisabled;
    - (BOOL)wantsToInterpretAllKeystrokes;
```

```
- (BOOL)wantsToHandleMouseEvents;
- (BOOL)wantsToDelayTextChangeNotifications;
- (void)inputClientBecomeActive:(id)sender;
- (void)inputClientResignActive:(id)sender;
- (void)inputClientEnabled:(id)sender;
- (void)inputClientDisabled:(id)sender;
- (void)activeConversationWillChange:(id)sender fromOldConversation:(long)oldConversation;
- (void)activeConversationChanged:(id)sender toNewConversation:(long)newConversation;
@end
```

NSMenuItem

This protocol has been deprecated in favor of the class NSMenuItem, which takes over all of the functionality associated with this protocol. See the NSMenuItem class description for more information.

```
@protocol NSMenuItem
// Instance Methods
- (id)initWithTitle:(NSString *)aString action:(SEL)aSelector keyEquivalent:(NSString *)charCode;
- (void)setMenu:(NSMenu *)menu;
- (NSMenu *)menu;
- (BOOL)hasSubmenu;
- (void)setSubmenu:(NSMenu *)submenu;
- (NSMenu *)submenu;
- (void)setTitle:(NSString *)aString;
- (NSString *)title;
- (BOOL)isSeparatorItem;
- (void)setKeyEquivalent:(NSString *)aKeyEquivalent;
- (NSString *)keyEquivalent;
- (void)setKeyEquivalentModifierMask:(unsigned int)mask;
- (unsigned int)keyEquivalentModifierMask;
- (NSString *)userKeyEquivalent;
- (unsigned int)userKeyEquivalentModifierMask;
- (void)setMnemonicLocation:(unsigned)location;
- (unsigned)mnemonicLocation;
- (NSString *)mnemonic;
- (void)setTitleWithMnemonic:(NSString *)stringWithAmpersand;
- (void)setImage:(NSImage *)menuImage;
- (NSImage *)image;
- (void)setState:(int)state;
- (int)state;
- (void)setOnStateImage:(NSImage *)image;
- (NSImage *)onStateImage;
- (void)setOffStateImage:(NSImage *)image;
- (NSImage *)offStateImage;
- (void)setMixedStateImage:(NSImage *)image;
- (NSImage *)mixedStateImage;
- (void)setEnabled:(BOOL)flag;
- (BOOL)isEnabled;
- (void)setTarget:(id)anObject;
```

```
- (id)target;
- (void)setAction:(SEL)aSelector;
- (SEL)action;
- (void)setTag:(int)anInt;
- (int)tag;
- (void)setRepresentedObject:(id)anObject;
- (id)representedObject;
@end
```

NSMenuValidation

Mac OS X 10.0

This informal protocol declares the single method validateMenuItem:, which is implemented by classes of the a menu's target object. The class implements this method to return a BOOL specifying whether the menu item should be enabled or disabled. Whenever a menu is displayed, each menu item will send a validateMenuItem: message to its target (if the target responds), which then responds with YES or NO depending on whether or not the menu item should be enabled.

```
@interface NSObject (NSMenuValidation)
// Instance Methods
- (BOOL)validateMenuItem:(id <NSMenuItem>)menuItem;
@end
```

NSNibAwaking

Mac OS X 10.0

This informal protocol declares the single method awakeFromNib:, which is implemented by classes to perform any final initialization for objects that are being loaded from a nib. When this method is invoked, the outlets of an object are guaranteed to be connected to their respective objects.

```
@interface NSObject (NSNibAwaking)
// Instance Methods
- (void)awakeFromNib;
@end
```

NSOutlineViewDataSource

Mac OS X 10.0

Methods in this informal protocol are implemented by classes that provide the data contents for an NSOutlineView. An NSOutlineView data source delegate object must implement the following four required methods of the protocol: outlineView:child:ofItem:, outlineView:isItemExpandable:, outlineView:numberOfChildrenOfItem:, outlineView:objectValueForTableColumn:byItem:.

In each of these four methods, outlineView: is the NSOutlineView object invoking the method. Every outline view has a root item. In the invocation of the data source methods, an outline view indicates a root item as nil. Thus, if outlineView:numberOfChildrenOfItem: was invoked with nil at the item, the implementation of this method would return the number of children items for the root item.

```
@interface NSObject (NSOutlineViewDataSource)
// Instance Methods
- (id)outlineView:(NSOutlineView *)outlineView child:(int)index ofItem:(id)item;
- (BOOL)outlineView:(NSOutlineView *)outlineView isItemExpandable:(id)item;
- (int)outlineView:(NSOutlineView *)outlineView numberOfChildrenOfItem:(id)item;
- (id)outlineView:(NSOutlineView *)outlineView objectValueForTableColumn:(NSTableColumn *)tableColumn
      byItem:(id)item;
- (void)outlineView:(NSOutlineView *)outlineView v forTableColumn:(NSTableColumn *)tableColumn byItem:(id)item;
- (id)outlineView:(NSOutlineView *)outlineView itemForPersistentObject:(id)object;
- (id)outlineView:(NSOutlineView *)outlineView persistentObjectForItem:(id)item;
- (BOOL)outlineView:(NSOutlineView *)olv writeItems:(NSArray*)items toPasteboard:(NSPasteboard*)pboard;
- (NSDragOperation)outlineView:(NSOutlineView*)olv validateDrop:(id <NSDraggingInfo>)info
      proposedItem:(id)item proposedChildIndex:(int)index;
- (BOOL)outlineView:(NSOutlineView*)olv acceptDrop:(id <NSDraggingInfo>)info item:(id)item childIndex:(int)index;
@end
```

NSServicesRequests Mac OS X 10.0

This informal protocol declares the two methods writeSelectionToPasteboard:types: and read-SelectionFromPasteboard:, which classes may implement to interact with system services found in the Services menu. The first of these, writeSelectionToPasteboard:types:, is used to provide data to a service, while readSelectionFromPasteboard: is used to retrieve data from a service.

```
@interface NSObject (NSServicesRequests)
// Instance Methods
- (BOOL)writeSelectionToPasteboard:(NSPasteboard *)pboard types:(NSArray *)types;
- (BOOL)readSelectionFromPasteboard:(NSPasteboard *)pboard;
@end
```

NSTableDataSource Mac OS X 10.0

Methods in this informal protocol are implemented by classes that provide the data displayed in an NSTableView. At a minimum, data source classes must implement the methods numberOfRowsInTableView: and tableView:objectValueForTableColumn:row:. Both of these methods are called frequently, so they should be efficient.

```
@interface NSObject (NSTableDataSource)
// Instance Methods
- (int)numberOfRowsInTableView:(NSTableView *)tableView;
- (id)tableView:(NSTableView *)tableView objectValueForTableColumn:(NSTableColumn *)tableColumn row:(int)row;
- (void)tableView:(NSTableView *)tableView setObjectValue:(id)object forTableColumn:(NSTableColumn *)tableColumn
      row:(int)row;
- (BOOL)tableView:(NSTableView *)tv writeRows:(NSArray*)rows toPasteboard:(NSPasteboard*)pboard;
- (NSDragOperation)tableView:(NSTableView*)tv validateDrop:(id <NSDraggingInfo>)info proposedRow:(int)row
      proposedDropOperation:(NSTableViewDropOperation)op;
- (BOOL)tableView:(NSTableView*)tv acceptDrop:(id <NSDraggingInfo>)info row:(int)row
      dropOperation:(NSTableViewDropOperation)op;
@end
```

NSTextAttachmentCell

This protocol declares an interface for classes that draw text attachments and handle mouse events within a text attachment. NSCell implements all of the methods of this protocol, less three: cellBaselineOffset, setAttachment:, and attachment. NSTextAttachmentCell extends NSCell's interface by implementing these three methods.

```
@protocol NSTextAttachmentCell
// Instance Methods
- (void)drawWithFrame:(NSRect)cellFrame inView:(NSView *)controlView;
- (BOOL)wantsToTrackMouse;
- (void)highlight:(BOOL)flag withFrame:(NSRect)cellFrame inView:(NSView *)controlView;
- (BOOL)trackMouse:(NSEvent *)theEvent inRect:(NSRect)cellFrame ofView:(NSView *)controlView
     untilMouseUp:(BOOL)flag;
- (NSSize)cellSize;
- (NSPoint)cellBaselineOffset;
- (void)setAttachment:(NSTextAttachment *)anObject;
- (NSTextAttachment *)attachment;
- (void)drawWithFrame:(NSRect)cellFrame inView:(NSView *)controlView characterIndex:(unsigned)charIndex;
- (void)drawWithFrame:(NSRect)cellFrame inView:(NSView *)controlView characterIndex:(unsigned)charIndex
     layoutManager:(NSLayoutManager *)layoutManager;
- (BOOL)wantsToTrackMouseForEvent:(NSEvent *)theEvent inRect:(NSRect)cellFrame ofView:(NSView *)controlView
     atCharacterIndex:(unsigned)charIndex;
- (BOOL)trackMouse:(NSEvent *)theEvent inRect:(NSRect)cellFrame ofView:(NSView *)controlView
     atCharacterIndex:(unsigned)charIndex untilMouseUp:(BOOL)flag;
- (NSRect)cellFrameForTextContainer:(NSTextContainer *)textContainer proposedLineFragment:(NSRect)lineFrag
     glyphPosition:(NSPoint)position characterIndex:(unsigned)charIndex;
@end
```

NSTextInput

This protocol declares the methods that text view classes should implement to interface with Cocoa's input management system. In the Application Kit, NSText and NSTextView implement the methods of this protocol.

```
@protocol NSTextInput
// Instance Methods
- (void)insertText:(id)aString;
- (void)doCommandBySelector:(SEL)aSelector;
- (void)setMarkedText:(id)aString selectedRange:(NSRange)selRange;
- (void)unmarkText;
- (BOOL)hasMarkedText;
- (long)conversationIdentifier;
- (NSAttributedString *)attributedSubstringFromRange:(NSRange)theRange;
- (NSRange)markedRange;
- (NSRange)selectedRange;
- (NSRect)firstRectForCharacterRange:(NSRange)theRange;
- (unsigned int)characterIndexForPoint:(NSPoint)thePoint;
- (NSArray*)validAttributesForMarkedText;
@end
```

NSTextStorageScripting

This informal protocol declares methods for text storage classes to implement so that they may be scriptable. In the Application Kit, NSTextStorage implements all of the methods in this protocol as part of Cocoa's built-in support for scripting.

```
@interface NSObject (NSTextStorageScripting)
// Instance Methods
 - (NSArray *)attributeRuns;
 - (void)setAttributeRuns:(NSArray *)attributeRuns;
 - (NSArray *)paragraphs;
 - (void)setParagraphs:(NSArray *)paragraphs;
 - (NSArray *)words;
 - (void)setWords:(NSArray *)words;
 - (NSArray *)characters;
 - (void)setCharacters:(NSArray *)characters;
 - (NSFont *)font;
 - (void)setFont:(NSFont *)font;
 - (NSColor *)foregroundColor;
 - (void)setForegroundColor:(NSColor *)color;
@end
```

NSToolbarItemValidation

This informal protocol declares the method validateToolbarItem:, which allows targets of toolbar item actions to decide whether or not the toolbar item should be enabled. This method is similar in purpose and operation to the method validaeMenuItem:, which is found in the the NSMenuValidation protocol.

```
@interface NSObject (NSToolbarItemValidation)
// Instance Methods
 - (BOOL)validateToolbarItem:(NSToolbarItem *)theItem;
@end
```

NSToolTipOwner

This informal protocol declares a single method, view:stringForToolTip:point:userData:, which a class may implement to provide a tool-tip string to be displayed. For more information on tool tips, see the NSView and the NSView method addToolTip-Rect:owner:userData:.

```
@interface NSObject (NSToolTipOwner)
// Instance Methods
 - (NSString *)view:(NSView *)view stringForToolTip:(NSToolTipTag)tag point:(NSPoint)point userData:(void *)data;
@end
```

NSUserInterfaceValidations

Mac OS X 10.0

This protocol, in conjunction with NSValidatedUserInterfaceItem, declares methods that classes implement to provide user interface object validation. This protocol declares the single method validateUserInterfaceItem:, which enables or disables interface objects based on the return value.

```
@protocol NSUserInterfaceValidations
// Instance Methods
  - (BOOL)validateUserInterfaceItem:(id <NSValidatedUserInterfaceItem>)anItem;
@end
```

NSValidatedUserInterfaceItem

Mac OS X 10.0

Custom interface control objects may adopt this protocol to partake in the Application Kit's automated validation mechanism. User interface validation works by having user interface items, such as buttons or text fields, query the targets of their action about whether or not they should be enabled. This protocol is closely related to the NSUserInterfaceItemValidations protocol, which declares the method validateUserInterfaceItem: for target objects to implement.

```
@protocol NSValidatedUserInterfaceItem
// Instance Methods
  - (SEL)action;
  - (int)tag;
@end
```

NSWindowScripting

Mac OS X 10.0

This informal protocol declares the methods that must be implemented by window classes in order to be scriptable. The methods of this protocol define an interface to setting and retrieving properties of the window, as well as to control operations such as saving, printing, and closing the window. NSWindow implements all of the methods in this protocol as part of Cocoa's built-in support for scripting.

```
@interface NSObject (NSWindowScripting)
// Instance Methods
  - (BOOL)hasCloseBox;
  - (BOOL)hasTitleBar;
  - (BOOL)isFloatingPanel;
  - (BOOL)isModalPanel;
  - (BOOL)isResizable;
  - (BOOL)isZoomable;
  - (BOOL)isMiniaturizable;
  - (void)setIsZoomed:(BOOL)flag;
  - (void)setIsMiniaturized:(BOOL)flag;
  - (void)setIsVisible:(BOOL)flag;
  - (int)orderedIndex;
```

AppKit
Protocols

```
- (void)setOrderedIndex:(int)index;
- (id)handleSaveScriptCommand:(NSScriptCommand *)command;
- (id)handleCloseScriptCommand:(NSCloseCommand *)command;
- (id)handlePrintScriptCommand:(NSScriptCommand *)command;
@end
```

Method Index

The following index allows you to look up a method and find the Cocoa class in which it is defined. Use this index when you want to look up a method but don't know its class.

addEntriesFromDictionary: NSMutableDictionary

addEntry: NSForm

addFileWithPath: NSFileWrapper

addFileWrapper: NSFileWrapper

addFontTrait: NSFontManager

addItem: NSMenu

addItemWithObjectValue: NSComboBoxCell, NSComboBox

addItemWithTitle: NSPopUpButton, NSPopUpButtonCell

addItemWithTitle:action:keyEquivalent: NSMenu

addItemsWithObjectValues: NSComboBoxCell, NSComboBox

addItemsWithTitles: NSPopUpButton, NSPopUpButtonCell

addLayoutManager: NSTextStorage

addMarker: NSRulerView

addObject: NSAutoreleasePool, NSMutable-Array, NSMutableSet, NSCountedSet

addObjectsFromArray: NSMutableArray, NSMutableSet

addObserver:selector:name:object: NSDistributedNotificationCenter, NSNotificationCenter

addObserver:selector:name:object:suspension-Behavior: NSDistributedNotificationCenter

addPort:forMode: NSRunLoop

addRegularFileWithContents:preferred-Filename: NSFileWrapper

addRepresentation: NSImage

addRepresentations: NSImage

addRequestMode: NSConnection

addRow NSMatrix

addRowWithCells: NSMatrix

addRunLoop: NSConnection

addSubview: NSView

addSubview:positioned:relativeTo: NSView

addSuiteNamed: NSUserDefaults

addSymbolicLinkWithDestination:preferred-Filename: NSFileWrapper

addTabStop: NSMutableParagraphStyle

addTabViewItem: NSTabView

addTableColumn: NSTableView

addTemporaryAttributes:forCharacterRange: NSLayoutManager

addTextContainer: NSLayoutManager

addTimeInterval: NSDate

addTimer:forMode: NSRunLoop

addToolTipRect:owner:userData: NSView

addTrackingRect:owner:userData:assume-Inside: NSView

addTypes:owner: NSPasteboard

addWindowController: NSDocument

addWindowsItem:title:filename: NSApplication

address NSHost, NSSocketPort

addresses NSHost, NSNetService

adjustPageHeightNew:top:bottom:limit: NSView

adjustPageWidthNew:left:right:limit: NSView

adjustScroll: NSView

adjustSubviews NSSplitView

advancementForGlyph: NSFont

aeDesc NSAppleEventDescriptor

aeteResource NSScriptSuiteRegistry

afmDictionary NSFont

alignCenter: NSText

alignJustified: NSTextView

alignLeft: NSText

alignRight: NSText

alignment NSParagraphStyle, NSControl, NSCell, NSText

allBundles NSBundle

allConnections NSConnection

allFrameworks NSBundle

allKeys NSDictionary, NSColorList

allKeysForObject: NSDictionary

allObjects NSSet, NSEnumerator

allValues NSDictionary

alloc NSObject, NSProxy

allocWithZone: NSObject, NSPort, NSProxy

allocateGState NSView

allowsBranchSelection NSBrowser

allowsColumnReordering NSTableView

allowsColumnResizing NSTableView

allowsColumnSelection NSTableView

allowsDuplicatesInToolbar NSToolbarItem

allowsEditingTextAttributes NSCell,
   NSTextField

allowsEmptySelection NSTableView, NSMatrix,
   NSBrowser

allowsFloats NSNumberFormatter

allowsKeyedCoding NSCoder

allowsMixedState NSCell, NSButton

allowsMultipleSelection NSOpenPanel,
   NSTableView, NSBrowser

allowsNaturalLanguage NSDateFormatter

allowsTickMarkValuesOnly NSSliderCell

allowsTruncatedLabels NSTabView

allowsUndo NSTextView

allowsUserCustomization NSToolbar

alpha NSColorPanel

alphaComponent NSColor

alphaValue NSWindow

alphanumericCharacterSet NSCharacterSet

altIncrementValue NSSlider, NSSliderCell

alternateImage NSBrowserCell, NSButtonCell,
   NSButton

alternateSelectedControlColor NSColor

alternateSelectedControlTextColor NSColor

alternateTitle NSButtonCell, NSButton

altersStateOfSelectedItem NSPopUpButtonCell

ancestorSharedWithView: NSView

animate: NSProgressIndicator

animationDelay NSProgressIndicator

animationResizeTime: NSWindow

anyObject NSSet

appendAttributedString:
   NSMutableAttributedString

appendBezierPath: NSBezierPath

appendBezierPathWithArcFromPoint:
   NSBezierPath

appendBezierPathWithArcWithCenter:radius:
   NSBezierPath

appendBezierPathWithGlyph:inFont:
   NSBezierPath

appendBezierPathWithGlyphs:count:
   NSBezierPath

appendBezierPathWithOvalInRect:
   NSBezierPath

appendBezierPathWithPackedGlyphs:
   NSBezierPath

appendBezierPathWithPoints:count:
   NSBezierPath

appendBezierPathWithRect: NSBezierPath

appendBytes:length: NSMutableData

appendData: NSMutableData

appendFormat:... NSMutableString

appendString: NSMutableString

appendTransform: NSAffineTransform

appleEventClassCode
   NSScriptCommandDescription

appleEventCode NSScriptClassDescription,
   NSScriptCommandDescription

appleEventCodeForArgumentWithName:
   NSScriptCommandDescription

appleEventCodeForKey: NSScriptClassDescription

appleEventCodeForReturnType
   NSScriptCommandDescription

appleEventCodeForSuite: NSScriptSuiteRegistry

appleEventWithEventClass:eventID:target-
   Descriptor:returnID:transactionID:
   NSAppleEventDescriptor

application:delegateHandlesKey: NSApplication

application:openFile: NSApplication

application:openFileWithoutUI: NSApplication

application:openTempFile: NSApplication

application:printFile: NSApplication

applicationDidBecomeActive: NSApplication

applicationDidChangeScreenParameters:
   NSApplication

applicationDidFinishLaunching: NSApplication

applicationDidHide: NSApplication

applicationDidResignActive: NSApplication

applicationDidUnhide: NSApplication

applicationDidUpdate: NSApplication

applicationDockMenu: NSApplication

applicationIconImage NSApplication

applicationOpenUntitledFile: NSApplication

applicationShouldHandleReopen:hasVisible-
   Windows: NSApplication

applicationShouldOpenUntitledFile:
   NSApplication

applicationShouldTerminate: NSApplication

applicationShouldTerminateAfterLastWindow-
   Closed: NSApplication

applicationWillBecomeActive: NSApplication

autoresizesSubviews NSView

autoresizingMask NSView

autosaveExpandedItems NSOutlineView

autosaveName NSTableView

autosaveTableColumns NSTableView

autosavesConfiguration NSToolbar

autoscroll: NSClipView, NSView

autosizesCells NSMatrix

availableColorLists NSColorList

availableData NSFileHandle

availableFontFamilies NSFontManager

availableFontNamesWithTraits: NSFontManager

availableFonts NSFontManager

availableMembersOfFontFamily:
NSFontManager

availableResourceData NSURLHandle

availableStringEncodings NSString

availableTypeFromArray: NSPasteboard

awakeAfterUsingCoder: NSObject

B

backgroundColor NSImage, NSWindow,
NSTextFieldCell, NSTableView, NSTextView,
NSScrollView, NSClipView, NSMatrix,
NSTextField, NSText

backgroundLayoutEnabled NSLayoutManager

backgroundLoadDidFailWithReason:
NSURLHandle

backingType NSWindow

baseOfTypesetterGlyphInfo
NSSimpleHorizontalTypesetter

baseSpecifier NSRelativeSpecifier

baseURL NSURL

baseWritingDirection NSParagraphStyle

baselineLocation NSRulerView

baselineOffsetInLayoutManager:glyphIndex:
NSTypesetter

becomeFirstResponder NSResponder,
NSTextView

becomeKeyWindow NSWindow

becomeMainWindow NSWindow

becomesKeyOnlyIfNeeded NSPanel

beginDocument NSView

beginEditing NSMutableAttributedString

beginLoadInBackground NSURLHandle

beginModalSessionForWindow: NSApplication

beginModalSessionForWindow:relative-
ToWindow: NSApplication

beginPageInRect:atPlacement: NSView

beginSheet:modalForWindow:modal-
Delegate:didEndSelector:contextInfo:
NSApplication

beginSheetForDirectory:file:modalForWindow:
modalDelegate:didEndSelector:
contextInfo: NSSavePanel

beginSheetForDirectory:file:types:modalFor-
Window:modalDelegate:didEndSelector:con-
textInfo: NSOpenPanel

beginSheetWithPrintInfo:modalForWindow:
delegate:didEndSelector:contextInfo:
NSPrintPanel, NSPageLayout

beginUndoGrouping NSUndoManager

bestRepresentationForDevice: NSImage

bezelStyle NSTextFieldCell, NSButtonCell,
NSButton, NSTextField

bezierPath NSBezierPath

bezierPathByFlatteningPath NSBezierPath

bezierPathByReversingPath NSBezierPath

bezierPathWithOvalInRect: NSBezierPath

bezierPathWithRect: NSBezierPath

bitmapData NSBitmapImageRep

bitmapRepresentation NSCharacterSet

bitsPerPixel NSBitmapImageRep

bitsPerSample NSImageRep

blackColor NSColor

blackComponent NSColor

blendedColorWithFraction:ofColor: NSColor

blueColor NSColor

blueComponent NSColor

boldSystemFontOfSize: NSFont

boolForKey: NSUserDefaults

boolValue NSNumber

booleanForKey:inTable: NSPrinter

booleanValue NSAppleEventDescriptor

borderRect NSBox

borderType NSBox, NSScrollView

bottomMargin NSPrintInfo

boundingBox NSEPSImageRep,
NSPICTImageRep

boundingRectForFont NSFont
boundingRectForGlyph: NSFont
boundingRectForGlyphRange:inTextContainer:
    NSLayoutManager
bounds NSPDFImageRep, NSBezierPath, NSView
boundsRotation NSView
boxType NSBox
branchImage NSBrowserCell
breakLineAtIndex: NSSimpleHorizontalTypesetter
breakLock NSDistributedLock
brightnessComponent NSColor
brownColor NSColor
browser:createRowsForColumn:inMatrix:
    NSBrowser
browser:isColumnValid: NSBrowser
browser:numberOfRowsInColumn: NSBrowser
browser:selectCellWithString:inColumn:
    NSBrowser
browser:selectRow:inColumn: NSBrowser
browser:titleOfColumn: NSBrowser
browser:willDisplayCell:atRow:column:
    NSBrowser
browserDidScroll: NSBrowser
browserWillScroll: NSBrowser
builtInPlugInsPath NSBundle
bundleForClass: NSBundle
bundleForSuite: NSScriptSuiteRegistry
bundleIdentifier NSBundle
bundlePath NSBundle
bundleWithIdentifier: NSBundle
bundleWithPath: NSBundle
buttonNumber NSEvent
bytes NSData
bytesPerPlane NSBitmapImageRep
bytesPerRow NSBitmapImageRep

C

cString NSString
cStringLength NSString
cacheDepthMatchesImageDepth NSImage
cacheImageInRect: NSWindow
cacheMode NSImage
cachedHandleForURL: NSURLHandle
cachesBezierPath NSBezierPath

calcDrawInfo: NSCell
calcSize NSControl, NSMenuItemCell
calendarDate NSCalendarDate
calendarFormat NSCalendarDate
canBeCompressedUsing: NSBitmapImageRep
canBeConvertedToEncoding: NSString
canBecomeKeyWindow NSWindow
canBecomeMainWindow NSWindow
canChooseDirectories NSOpenPanel
canChooseFiles NSOpenPanel
canCloseDocument NSDocument
canCloseDocumentWithDelegate:should-
    CloseSelector:contextInfo: NSDocument
canDraw NSView
canHide NSWindow
canInitWithData: NSImageRep
canInitWithPasteboard: NSImage, NSSound,
    NSMovie, NSImageRep
canInitWithURL: NSURLHandle
canRedo NSUndoManager
canSpawnSeparateThread NSPrintOperation
canStoreColor NSWindow
canUndo NSUndoManager
cancel: NSSavePanel
cancelIncrementalLoad NSImage
cancelLoadInBackground NSURLHandle
cancelPerformSelector:target:argument:
    NSRunLoop
cancelPerformSelectorsWithTarget:
    NSRunLoop
cancelUserAttentionRequest: NSApplication
capHeight NSFont
capacityOfTypesetterGlyphInfo
    NSSimpleHorizontalTypesetter
capitalizeWord: NSResponder
capitalizedLetterCharacterSet NSCharacterSet
capitalizedString NSString
cascadeTopLeftFromPoint: NSWindow
caseInsensitiveCompare: NSString
caseSensitive NSScanner
catalogNameComponent NSColor
cell NSControl
cellAtIndex: NSForm
cellAtRow:column: NSMatrix

cellAttribute: NSCell

cellBackgroundColor NSMatrix

cellClass NSControl, NSMatrix, NSBrowser

cellFrameAtRow:column: NSMatrix

cellPrototype NSBrowser

cellSize NSCell, NSMatrix

cellSizeForBounds: NSCell

cellWithTag: NSMatrix

cells NSMatrix

center NSWindow

centerScanRect: NSView

centerSelectionInVisibleArea: NSResponder

changeCaseOfLetter: NSResponder

changeColor: NSTextView, NSApplication

changeCount NSPasteboard

changeCurrentDirectoryPath: NSFileManager

changeFileAttributes:atPath: NSFileManager

changeFont: NSFontManager, NSText

changeInLength NSTextStorage

changeWindowsItem:title:filename:
　　NSApplication

charValue NSNumber

characterAtIndex: NSString

characterCollection NSGlyphInfo

characterIdentifier NSGlyphInfo

characterIndexForGlyphAtIndex:
　　NSLayoutManager

characterIsMember: NSCharacterSet

characterRangeForGlyphRange:actual-
　　GlyphRange: NSLayoutManager

characterSetWithBitmapRepresentation:
　　NSCharacterSet

characterSetWithCharactersInString:
　　NSCharacterSet

characterSetWithContentsOfFile:
　　NSCharacterSet

characterSetWithRange: NSCharacterSet

characters NSTextStorage, NSEvent

charactersIgnoringModifiers NSEvent

charactersToBeSkipped NSScanner

checkForRemovableMedia NSWorkspace

checkSpaceForParts NSScroller

checkSpelling: NSText

checkSpellingOfString:startingAt:
　　NSSpellChecker

checkSpellingOfString:startingAt:lang-
　　uage:wrap:inSpellDocumentWithTag:word-
　　Count: NSSpellChecker

childSpecifier NSScriptObjectSpecifier

childWindows NSWindow

class NSObject, NSProxy

classCode NSObject

classDescription NSClassDescription

classDescriptionForClass: NSClassDescription

classDescriptionForKey: NSScriptClassDescription

classDescriptionWithAppleEventCode:
　　NSScriptSuiteRegistry

classDescriptionsInSuite: NSScriptSuiteRegistry

classForArchiver NSObject

classForClassName: NSKeyedUnarchiver

classForCoder NSObject

classForKeyedArchiver NSObject

classForPortCoder NSObject

className NSScriptClassDescription, NSObject

classNameDecodedForArchiveClassName:
　　NSUnarchiver

classNameEncodedForTrueClassName:
　　NSArchiver

classNameForClass: NSKeyedArchiver

classNamed: NSBundle

cleanUpAfterDragOperation NSTextView

cleanUpOperation NSPrintOperation

clear: NSMovieView

clearAttributesCache
　　NSSimpleHorizontalTypesetter

clearColor NSColor

clearCurrentContext NSOpenGLContext

clearDrawable NSOpenGLContext

clearGLContext NSOpenGLView

clearGlyphCache NSSimpleHorizontalTypesetter

clearRecentDocuments: NSDocumentController

clickCount NSEvent

clickedColumn NSTableView

clickedOnLink:atIndex: NSTextView

clickedRow NSTableView

clientView NSRulerView

clipRect: NSBezierPath

close NSWindow, NSDrawer, NSWindowController, NSDocument

close: NSDrawer

closeAllDocuments NSDocumentController

closeAllDocumentsWithDelegate: didCloseAllSelector:contextInfo: NSDocumentController

closeFile NSFileHandle

closePath NSBezierPath

closeSpellDocumentWithTag: NSSpellChecker

closestTickMarkValueToValue: NSSliderCell

coerceToDescriptorType: NSAppleEventDescriptor

coerceValue:toClass: NSScriptCoercionHandler

collapseItem: NSOutlineView

collapseItem:collapseChildren: NSOutlineView

color NSTabViewItem, NSColorWell, NSColorPanel

colorForControlTint: NSColor

colorFromPasteboard: NSColor

colorListNamed: NSColorList

colorNameComponent NSColor

colorPanel NSColorPicker

colorSpaceName NSColor, NSImageRep

colorUsingColorSpaceName: NSColor

colorUsingColorSpaceName:device: NSColor

colorWithAlphaComponent: NSColor

colorWithCalibratedHue:saturation: brightness:alpha: NSColor

colorWithCalibratedRed:green:blue:alpha: NSColor

colorWithCalibratedWhite:alpha: NSColor

colorWithCatalogName:colorName: NSColor

colorWithDeviceCyan:magenta:yellow: black:alpha: NSColor

colorWithDeviceHue:saturation:brightness: alpha: NSColor

colorWithDeviceRed:green:blue:alpha: NSColor

colorWithDeviceWhite:alpha: NSColor

colorWithKey: NSColorList

colorWithPatternImage: NSColor

colorizeByMappingGray:toColor: blackMapping:whiteMapping: NSBitmapImageRep

columnAtPoint: NSTableView, NSTableHeaderView

columnOfMatrix: NSBrowser

columnWithIdentifier: NSTableView

columnsInRect: NSTableView

comboBoxSelectionDidChange: NSComboBox

comboBoxSelectionIsChanging: NSComboBox

comboBoxWillDismiss: NSComboBox

comboBoxWillPopUp: NSComboBox

commandClassName NSScriptCommandDescription

commandDescription NSScriptCommand

commandDescriptionWithAppleEventClass: andAppleEventCode: NSScriptSuiteRegistry

commandDescriptionsInSuite: NSScriptSuiteRegistry

commandName NSScriptCommandDescription

commonPrefixWithString:options: NSString

compare: NSString, NSDecimalNumber, NSCell, NSNumber, NSDate

compare:options: NSString

compare:options:range: NSString

compare:options:range:locale: NSString

compileAndReturnError: NSAppleScript

complete: NSResponder

completePathIntoString:caseSensitive: matchesIntoArray:filterTypes: NSString

completedString: NSComboBoxCell

completes NSComboBoxCell, NSComboBox

components NSPortMessage

componentsJoinedByString: NSArray

componentsSeparatedByString: NSString

componentsToDisplayForPath: NSFileManager

compositeToPoint:fromRect:operation: NSImage

compositeToPoint:fromRect:operation:fraction: NSImage

compositeToPoint:operation: NSImage

compositeToPoint:operation:fraction: NSImage

concat NSAffineTransform

condition NSConditionLock

configurationDictionary NSToolbar

configureAsServer NSRunLoop

convertWeight:ofFont: NSFontManager
copiesOnScroll NSClipView
copy NSObject
copy: NSMovieView, NSText
copyAttributesFromContext:withMask:
    NSOpenGLContext
copyFont: NSText
copyPath:toPath:handler: NSFileManager
copyRuler: NSText
copyWithZone: NSObject
cornerView NSTableView
count NSDictionary, NSSet, NSArray
countForObject: NSCountedSet
countWordsInString:language: NSSpellChecker
coveredCharacterSet NSFont
createClassDescription NSCreateCommand
createCommandInstance
    NSScriptCommandDescription
createCommandInstanceWithZone:
    NSScriptCommandDescription
createContext NSPrintOperation
createConversationForConnection:
    NSConnection
createDirectoryAtPath:attributes:
    NSFileManager
createFileAtPath:contents:attributes:
    NSFileManager
createSymbolicLinkAtPath:pathContent:
    NSFileManager
createTexture:fromView:internalFormat:
    NSOpenGLContext
currentContainer
    NSSimpleHorizontalTypesetter
currentContext NSGraphicsContext,
    NSOpenGLContext
currentContextDrawingToScreen
    NSGraphicsContext
currentConversation NSConnection
currentCursor NSCursor
currentDirectory NSDocumentController
currentDirectoryPath NSTask, NSFileManager
currentDocument NSDocumentController
currentEditor NSControl
currentEvent NSWindow, NSApplication
currentHandler NSAssertionHandler

currentHost NSHost
currentInputManager NSInputManager
currentLayoutManager
    NSSimpleHorizontalTypesetter
currentMode NSRunLoop
currentOperation NSPrintOperation
currentPage NSPrintOperation, NSPDFImageRep
currentParagraphStyle
    NSSimpleHorizontalTypesetter
currentPoint NSBezierPath
currentRunLoop NSRunLoop
currentTextStorage
    NSSimpleHorizontalTypesetter
currentThread NSThread
currentVirtualScreen NSOpenGLContext
curveToPoint: NSBezierPath
customizationPaletteIsRunning NSToolbar
cut: NSMovieView, NSText
cyanColor NSColor
cyanComponent NSColor
cycleToNextInputLanguage: NSInputManager
cycleToNextInputServerInLanguage:
    NSInputManager

D

darkGrayColor NSColor
data NSData, NSTimeZone,
    NSAppleEventDescriptor
data1 NSEvent
data2 NSEvent
dataCell NSTableColumn
dataCellForRow: NSTableColumn
dataForKey: NSUserDefaults
dataForType: NSPasteboard
dataFromPropertyList:format:errorDescription:
    NSPropertyListSerialization
dataRepresentationOfType: NSDocument
dataSource NSTableView, NSComboBoxCell,
    NSComboBox
dataUsingEncoding: NSString
dataUsingEncoding:allowLossyConversion:
    NSString
dataWithBytes:length: NSData
dataWithBytesNoCopy:length: NSData

decodeInt64ForKey: NSKeyedUnarchiver, NSCoder

decodeIntForKey: NSKeyedUnarchiver, NSCoder

decodeNXColor NSCoder

decodeNXObject NSCoder

decodeObject NSCoder

decodeObjectForKey: NSKeyedUnarchiver, NSCoder

decodePoint NSCoder

decodePointForKey: NSCoder

decodePortObject NSPortCoder

decodePropertyList NSCoder

decodeRect NSCoder

decodeRectForKey: NSCoder

decodeSize NSCoder

decodeSizeForKey: NSCoder

decodeValueOfObjCType:at: NSCoder

decodeValuesOfObjCTypes:... NSCoder

decomposableCharacterSet NSCharacterSet

decomposedStringWithCanonicalMapping NSString

decomposedStringWithCompatibilityMapping NSString

deepestScreen NSScreen, NSWindow

defaultAttachmentScaling NSLayoutManager

defaultBehavior NSDecimalNumber

defaultButtonCell NSWindow

defaultCStringEncoding NSString

defaultCenter NSDistributedNotificationCenter, NSNotificationCenter

defaultConnection NSConnection

defaultDecimalNumberHandler NSDecimalNumberHandler

defaultDepthLimit NSWindow

defaultFlatness NSBezierPath

defaultLineCapStyle NSBezierPath

defaultLineHeightForFont NSFont

defaultLineHeightForFont: NSLayoutManager

defaultLineJoinStyle NSBezierPath

defaultLineWidth NSBezierPath

defaultManager NSFileManager

defaultMenu NSCell, NSView

defaultMiterLimit NSBezierPath

defaultNameServerPortNumber NSSocketPortNameServer

defaultParagraphStyle NSParagraphStyle

defaultPixelFormat NSOpenGLView

defaultPrinter NSPrintInfo

defaultQueue NSNotificationQueue

defaultSubcontainerAttributeKey NSScriptClassDescription

defaultTimeZone NSTimeZone

defaultTypesetterBehavior NSTypesetter

defaultWindingRule NSBezierPath

defaultWritingDirectionForLanguage: NSParagraphStyle

delegate NSImage, NSTextStorage, NSWindow, NSTableView, NSSound, NSKeyedUnarchiver, NSNetServiceBrowser, NSSplitView, NSText-View, NSNetService, NSLayoutManager, NSFontManager, NSDrawer, NSMatrix, NSApplication, NSCustomImageRep, NSPort, NSSpellServer, NSToolbar, NSKeyedArchiver, NSTabView, NSBrowser, NSConnection, NSTextField, NSText

delete: NSText

deleteBackward: NSResponder

deleteCharactersInRange: NSMutableString, NSMutableAttributedString

deleteForward: NSResponder

deleteGlyphsInRange: NSLayoutManager

deleteToBeginningOfLine: NSResponder

deleteToBeginningOfParagraph: NSResponder

deleteToEndOfLine: NSResponder

deleteToEndOfParagraph: NSResponder

deleteToMark: NSResponder

deleteWordBackward: NSResponder

deleteWordForward: NSResponder

deliverResult NSPrintOperation

deltaX NSEvent

deltaY NSEvent

deltaZ NSEvent

deminiaturize: NSWindow

depth NSScreen

depthLimit NSWindow

dequeueNotificationsMatching:coalesceMask: NSNotificationQueue

descender NSFont

description NSString, NSData, NSDictionary,
NSTimeZone, NSObject, NSSet, NSArray,
NSCalendarDate, NSDate, NSProxy

descriptionInStringsFileFormat NSDictionary

descriptionWithCalendarFormat:
NSCalendarDate

descriptionWithCalendarFormat:locale:
NSCalendarDate

descriptionWithCalendarFormat:time-
Zone:locale: NSDate

descriptionWithLocale: NSDictionary,
NSDecimalNumber, NSSet, NSArray,
NSNumber, NSCalendarDate, NSDate

descriptionWithLocale:indent: NSDictionary,
NSArray

descriptorAtIndex: NSAppleEventDescriptor

descriptorForKeyword: NSAppleEventDescriptor

descriptorType NSAppleEventDescriptor

descriptorWithBoolean:
NSAppleEventDescriptor

descriptorWithDescriptorType:bytes:length:
NSAppleEventDescriptor

descriptorWithDescriptorType:data:
NSAppleEventDescriptor

descriptorWithEnumCode:
NSAppleEventDescriptor

descriptorWithInt32: NSAppleEventDescriptor

descriptorWithString: NSAppleEventDescriptor

descriptorWithTypeCode:
NSAppleEventDescriptor

deselectAll: NSTableView

deselectAllCells NSMatrix

deselectColumn: NSTableView

deselectItemAtIndex: NSComboBoxCell,
NSComboBox

deselectRow: NSTableView

deselectSelectedCell NSMatrix

deserializeAlignedBytesLengthAtCursor:
NSData

deserializeBytes:length:atCursor: NSData

deserializeDataAt:ofObjCType:atCursor:
context: NSData

deserializeIntAtCursor: NSData

deserializeIntAtIndex: NSData

deserializeInts:count:atCursor: NSData

deserializeInts:count:atIndex: NSData

deserializePropertyListFromData:
atCursor:mutableContainers:
NSDeserializer

deserializePropertyListFromData:mutable-
Containers: NSDeserializer

deserializePropertyListLazilyFromData:
atCursor:length:mutableContainers:
NSDeserializer

destination NSNibConnector

destroyContext NSPrintOperation

detachColorList: NSColorPicker, NSColorPanel

detachDrawingThread:toTarget:withObject:
NSApplication

detachNewThreadSelector:toTarget:
withObject: NSThread

detachSubmenu NSMenuView

developmentLocalization NSBundle

deviceDescription NSScreen, NSWindow,
NSPrinter

dictionary NSDictionary, NSPrintInfo

dictionaryForKey: NSUserDefaults

dictionaryRepresentation NSUserDefaults

dictionaryWithCapacity: NSMutableDictionary

dictionaryWithContentsOfFile: NSDictionary

dictionaryWithContentsOfURL: NSDictionary

dictionaryWithDictionary: NSDictionary

dictionaryWithObject:forKey: NSDictionary

dictionaryWithObjects:forKeys: NSDictionary

dictionaryWithObjects:forKeys:count:
NSDictionary

dictionaryWithObjectsAndKeys:... NSDictionary

didAddSubview: NSView

didChangeText NSTextView

didLoadBytes:loadComplete: NSURLHandle

directParameter NSScriptCommand

directory NSSavePanel

directoryAttributes NSDirectoryEnumerator

directoryContentsAtPath: NSFileManager

disableCursorRects NSWindow

disableFlushWindow NSWindow

disableKeyEquivalentForDefaultButtonCell
NSWindow

disableUndoRegistration NSUndoManager

disabledControlTextColor NSColor

discardCachedImage NSWindow

discardCursorRects NSWindow, NSView

discardEventsMatchingMask:beforeEvent:
  NSWindow, NSApplication

dismissPopUp NSPopUpButtonCell

dispatch NSPortCoder

dispatchRawAppleEvent:withRawReply:
  handlerRefCon:
  NSAppleEventManager

display NSWindow, NSView

displayAllColumns NSBrowser

displayColumn: NSBrowser

displayIfNeeded NSWindow, NSView

displayIfNeededIgnoringOpacity NSView

displayIfNeededInRect: NSView

displayIfNeededInRectIgnoringOpacity:
  NSView

displayMode NSToolbar

displayName NSFont, NSDocument

displayNameAtPath: NSFileManager

displayNameForType: NSDocumentController

displayRect: NSView

displayRectIgnoringOpacity: NSView

dissolveToPoint:fraction: NSImage

dissolveToPoint:fromRect:fraction: NSImage

distantFuture NSDate

distantPast NSDate

dividerThickness NSSplitView

doClick: NSBrowser

doCommandBySelector: NSResponder

doDoubleClick: NSBrowser

document NSWindowController

documentClassForType: NSDocumentController

documentCursor NSScrollView, NSClipView

documentForFileName: NSDocumentController

documentForWindow: NSDocumentController

documentRect NSClipView

documentView NSScrollView, NSClipView

documentVisibleRect NSScrollView, NSClipView

documents NSDocumentController

doesNotRecognizeSelector: NSObject

domain NSPrinter, NSNetService

doubleAction NSTableView, NSMatrix,
  NSBrowser

doubleClickAtIndex: NSAttributedString

doubleValue NSString, NSProgressIndicator,
  NSControl, NSDecimalNumber, NSCell,
  NSNumber, NSActionCell

dragColor:withEvent:fromView: NSColorPanel

dragImage:at:offset:event:pasteboard:
  source:slideBack: NSWindow

dragImageForRows:event:dragImageOffset:
  NSTableView

dragImageForSelectionWithEvent:origin:
  NSTextView

dragOperationForDraggingInfo:type:
  NSTextView

dragSelectionWithEvent:offset:slideBack:
  NSTextView

draggedColumn NSTableHeaderView

draggedDistance NSTableHeaderView

draw NSImageRep

drawArrow:highlight: NSScroller

drawAtPoint: NSAttributedString, NSImageRep

drawAtPoint:fromRect:operation:fraction:
  NSImage

drawBackgroundForGlyphRange:atPoint:
  NSLayoutManager

drawBarInside:flipped: NSSliderCell

drawBorderAndBackgroundWithFrame:
  inView: NSMenuItemCell

drawCell: NSControl

drawCellAtIndex: NSForm

drawCellAtRow:column: NSMatrix

drawCellInside: NSControl

drawDividerInRect: NSSplitView

drawGlyphsForGlyphRange:atPoint:
  NSLayoutManager

drawGridInClipRect: NSTableView

drawHashMarksAndLabelsInRect:
  NSRulerView

drawImageWithFrame:inView: NSMenuItemCell

drawInRect: NSAttributedString, NSImageRep

drawInRect:fromRect:operation:fraction:
  NSImage

drawInsertionPointInRect:color:turnedOn:
  NSTextView

drawInteriorWithFrame:inView: NSCell

drawKeyEquivalentWithFrame:inView:
  NSMenuItemCell

drawKnob NSSliderCell, NSScroller

drawLabel:inRect: NSTabViewItem

drawMarkersInRect: NSRulerView

drawPackedGlyphs:atPoint: NSBezierPath

drawPageBorderWithSize: NSView

drawParts NSScroller drawRect:
    NSRulerMarker, NSView

drawRepresentation:inRect: NSImage

drawRow:clipRect: NSTableView

drawSelector NSCustomImageRep

drawSeparatorItemWithFrame:inView:
    NSMenuItemCell

drawSheetBorderWithSize: NSView

drawStateImageWithFrame:inView:
    NSMenuItemCell

drawSwatchInRect: NSColor

drawTitleOfColumn:inRect: NSBrowser

drawTitleWithFrame:inView: NSMenuItemCell

drawUnderlineForGlyphRange:underlineType:
    baselineOffset:lineFragmentRect:
    lineFragmentGlyphRange:containerOrigin:
    NSLayoutManager

drawWellInside: NSColorWell

drawWithFrame:inView: NSCell

drawerDidClose: NSDrawer

drawerDidOpen: NSDrawer

drawerShouldClose: NSDrawer

drawerShouldOpen: NSDrawer

drawerWillClose: NSDrawer

drawerWillOpen: NSDrawer

drawerWillResizeContents:toSize: NSDrawer

drawers NSWindow

drawingRectForBounds: NSCell

drawsBackground NSTextFieldCell,
    NSTextView, NSScrollView, NSClipView,
    NSMatrix, NSTabView, NSTextField, NSText

drawsCellBackground NSMatrix

drawsGrid NSTableView

drawsOutsideLineFragmentForGlyphAtIndex:
    NSLayoutManager

E

EPSOperationWithView:insideRect:toData:
    NSPrintOperation

EPSOperationWithView:insideRect:
    toData:printInfo: NSPrintOperation

EPSOperationWithView:insideRect:
    toPath:printInfo: NSPrintOperation

EPSRepresentation NSEPSImageRep

earlierDate: NSDate

echosBullets NSSecureTextFieldCell

edge NSDrawer

editColumn:row:withEvent:select:
    NSTableView

editWithFrame:inView:editor:delegate:event:
    NSCell

edited:range:changeInLength: NSTextStorage

editedColumn NSTableView

editedMask NSTextStorage

editedRange NSTextStorage

editedRow NSTableView

editingStringForObjectValue: NSFormatter

elementAtIndex: NSBezierPath

elementCount NSBezierPath

enableCursorRects NSWindow

enableFlushWindow NSWindow

enableFreedObjectCheck: NSAutoreleasePool

enableKeyEquivalentForDefaultButtonCell
    NSWindow

enableMultipleThreads NSConnection

enableRelease: NSAutoreleasePool

enableUndoRegistration NSUndoManager

enclosingScrollView NSView

encodeArrayOfObjCType:count:at: NSCoder

encodeBool:forKey: NSCoder, NSKeyedArchiver

encodeBycopyObject: NSCoder

encodeByrefObject: NSCoder

encodeBytes:length: NSCoder

encodeBytes:length:forKey: NSCoder,
    NSKeyedArchiver

encodeClassName:intoClassName: NSArchiver

encodeConditionalObject: NSCoder, NSArchiver

encodeConditionalObject:forKey: NSCoder,
    NSKeyedArchiver

encodeDataObject: NSCoder

encodeDouble:forKey: NSCoder,
    NSKeyedArchiver

encodeFloat:forKey: NSCoder, NSKeyedArchiver

encodeInt32:forKey: NSCoder, NSKeyedArchiver

encodeInt64:forKey: NSCoder, NSKeyedArchiver

encodeInt:forKey: NSCoder, NSKeyedArchiver

encodeNXObject: NSCoder

encodeObject: NSCoder

encodeObject:forKey: NSCoder,
NSKeyedArchiver

encodePoint: NSCoder

encodePoint:forKey: NSCoder

encodePortObject: NSPortCoder

encodePropertyList: NSCoder

encodeRect: NSCoder

encodeRect:forKey: NSCoder

encodeRootObject: NSCoder, NSArchiver

encodeSize: NSCoder

encodeSize:forKey: NSCoder

encodeValueOfObjCType:at: NSCoder

encodeValuesOfObjCTypes:... NSCoder

encodeWithCoder: NSComboBoxCell,
NSComboBox

encodingScheme NSFont

endDocument NSView

endEditing NSMutableAttributedString

endEditing: NSCell

endEditingFor: NSWindow

endLoadInBackground NSURLHandle

endModalSession: NSApplication

endPage NSView

endSheet: NSApplication

endSheet:returnCode: NSApplication

endSpecifier NSRangeSpecifier

endSubelementIdentifier NSWhoseSpecifier

endSubelementIndex NSWhoseSpecifier

endUndoGrouping NSUndoManager

enqueueNotification:postingStyle:
NSNotificationQueue

enqueueNotification:postingStyle:
coalesceMask:forModes:
NSNotificationQueue

ensureAttributesAreFixedInRange:
NSTextStorage

enterExitEventWithType:location:
modifierFlags:timetamp:
windowNumber:context:
eventNumber:trackingNumber:userData:
NSEvent

entryType NSCell

enumCodeValue NSAppleEventDescriptor

enumeratorAtPath: NSFileManager

environment NSProcessInfo, NSTask

establishConnection NSNibOutletConnector,
NSNibConnector, NSNibControlConnector

evaluate NSPositionalSpecifier

evaluatedArguments NSScriptCommand

evaluatedReceivers NSScriptCommand

evaluationErrorNumber NSScriptObjectSpecifier

evaluationErrorSpecifier NSScriptObjectSpecifier

eventClass NSAppleEventDescriptor

eventID NSAppleEventDescriptor

eventNumber NSEvent

exceptionWithName:reason:userInfo:
NSException

exchangeObjectAtIndex:withObjectAtIndex:
NSMutableArray

executablePath NSBundle

executeAndReturnError: NSAppleScript

executeAppleEvent:error: NSAppleScript

executeCommand NSScriptCommand

exit NSThread

expandItem: NSOutlineView

expandItem:expandChildren: NSOutlineView

extendPowerOffBy: NSWorkspace

extraLineFragmentRect NSLayoutManager

extraLineFragmentTextContainer
NSLayoutManager

extraLineFragmentUsedRect NSLayoutManager

F

failureReason NSURLHandle

familyName NSFont

fastestEncoding NSString

fieldEditor:forObject: NSWindow

fileAttributes NSFileWrapper,
NSDirectoryEnumerator

fileAttributesAtPath:traverseLink:
NSFileManager

fileAttributesToWriteToFile:ofType:
saveOperation: NSDocument

fileCreationDate NSDictionary

fileDescriptor NSFileHandle

fileExistsAtPath: NSFileManager

fileExistsAtPath:isDirectory: NSFileManager

fileExtensionHidden NSDictionary

fileExtensionsFromType:
  NSDocumentController

fileGroupOwnerAccountID NSDictionary

fileGroupOwnerAccountName NSDictionary

fileHFSCreatorCode NSDictionary

fileHFSTypeCode NSDictionary

fileHandleForReading NSPipe

fileHandleForReadingAtPath: NSFileHandle

fileHandleForUpdatingAtPath: NSFileHandle

fileHandleForWriting NSPipe

fileHandleForWritingAtPath: NSFileHandle

fileHandleWithNullDevice NSFileHandle

fileHandleWithStandardError NSFileHandle

fileHandleWithStandardInput NSFileHandle

fileHandleWithStandardOutput NSFileHandle

fileIsAppendOnly NSDictionary

fileIsImmutable NSDictionary

fileModificationDate NSDictionary

fileName NSDocument

fileNameExtensionWasHiddenInLastRunSave-
  Panel NSDocument

fileNameFromRunningSavePanelForSave-
  Operation: NSDocument

fileNamesFromRunningOpenPanel
  NSDocumentController

fileOwnerAccountID NSDictionary

fileOwnerAccountName NSDictionary

filePosixPermissions NSDictionary

fileSize NSDictionary

fileSystemAttributesAtPath: NSFileManager

fileSystemChanged NSWorkspace

fileSystemFileNumber NSDictionary

fileSystemNumber NSDictionary

fileSystemRepresentation NSString

fileSystemRepresentationWithPath:
  NSFileManager

fileType NSDictionary, NSDocument

fileTypeFromLastRunSavePanel NSDocument

fileURLWithPath: NSURL

fileWrapper NSTextAttachment

fileWrapperRepresentationOfType: NSDocument

fileWrappers NSFileWrapper

filename NSFileWrapper, NSSavePanel

filenames NSOpenPanel

fill NSBezierPath

fillAttributesCache
  NSSimpleHorizontalTypesetter

fillRect: NSBezierPath

finalWritePrintInfo NSPrintPanel

findApplications NSWorkspace

finishDecoding NSKeyedUnarchiver

finishEncoding NSKeyedArchiver

finishLaunching NSApplication

fire NSTimer

fireDate NSTimer

firstGlyphIndexOfCurrentLineFragment
  NSSimpleHorizontalTypesetter

firstLineHeadIndent NSParagraphStyle

firstObjectCommonWithArray: NSArray

firstResponder NSWindow

firstTextView NSLayoutManager

firstUnlaidCharacterIndex NSLayoutManager

firstUnlaidGlyphIndex NSLayoutManager

firstVisibleColumn NSBrowser

fixAttachmentAttributeInRange:
  NSMutableAttributedString

fixAttributesInRange: NSMutableAttributedString

fixFontAttributeInRange:
  NSMutableAttributedString

fixParagraphStyleAttributeInRange:
  NSMutableAttributedString

fixesAttributesLazily NSTextStorage

flagsChanged: NSResponder

flatness NSBezierPath

floatForKey: NSUserDefaults

floatForKey:inTable: NSPrinter

floatValue NSString, NSControl, NSCell,
  NSNumber, NSActionCell

flushBuffer NSOpenGLContext

flushBufferedKeyEvents NSResponder

flushCachedData NSURLHandle

flushGraphics NSGraphicsContext

flushHostCache NSHost

flushWindow NSWindow

flushWindowIfNeeded NSWindow

focusStack NSGraphicsContext

focusView NSView

font NSTextStorage, NSControl, NSCell,
    NSTabView, NSMenuView, NSText
fontAttributesInRange: NSAttributedString
fontManager:willIncludeFont: NSFontManager
fontMenu: NSFontManager
fontName NSFont
fontNamed:hasTraits: NSFontManager
fontPanel: NSFontManager
fontWithFamily:traits:weight:size:
    NSFontManager
fontWithName:matrix: NSFont
fontWithName:size: NSFont
foregroundColor NSTextStorage
formIntersectionWithCharacterSet:
    NSMutableCharacterSet
formUnionWithCharacterSet:
    NSMutableCharacterSet
format NSNumberFormatter
formatter NSControl, NSCell
forwardInvocation: NSUndoManager,
    NSObject, NSProxy
fractionOfDistanceThroughGlyphFor-
    Point:inTextContainer: NSLayoutManager
fragment NSURL
frame NSScreen, NSWindow, NSView
frameAutosaveName NSWindow
frameLength NSMethodSignature
frameOfCellAtColumn:row: NSTableView
frameOfColumn: NSBrowser
frameOfInsideOfColumn: NSBrowser
frameRectForContentRect:styleMask:
    NSWindow
frameRotation NSView
frameSizeForContentSize:
    hasHorizontaScroller:
    hasVerticalScroller:borderType:
    NSScrollView
fullJustifyLineAtGlyphIndex:
    NSSimpleHorizontalTypesetter
fullPathForApplication: NSWorkspace

G

gState NSWindow, NSView
generalPasteboard NSPasteboard
getArgument:atIndex: NSInvocation

getArgumentTypeAtIndex:
    NSMethodSignature
getBitmapDataPlanes: NSBitmapImageRep
getBytes: NSData
getBytes:length: NSData
getBytes:range: NSData
getCFRunLoop NSRunLoop
getCString: NSString
getCString:maxLength: NSString
getCString:maxLength:range:remainigRange:
    NSString
getCharacters: NSString
getCharacters:range: NSString
getCompression:factor: NSBitmapImageRep
getCyan:magenta:yellow:black:alpha: NSColor
getFileSystemInfoForPath:isRemovable:
    isWritable:isUnmountable:description:
    type: NSWorkspace
getFileSystemRepresentation:maxLength:
    NSString
getFirstUnlaidCharacterIndex:glyphIndex:
    NSLayoutManager
getGlyphs:range: NSLayoutManager
getGlyphsInRange:glyphs:characterIndexes:
    glyphInscriptions:elasticBits:
    NSLayoutManager
getGlyphsInRange:glyphs:characterIndexes:
    glyphInscriptions:elasticBits:bidiLevels:
    NSLayoutManager
getHue:saturation:brightness:alpha: NSColor
getInfoForFile:application:type: NSWorkspace
getLineDash:count:phase: NSBezierPath
getLineStart:end:contentsEnd:forRange:
    NSString
getNumberOfRows:columns: NSMatrix
getObjectValue:forString:errorDescription:
    NSFormatter
getObjects: NSArray
getObjects:range: NSArray
getPeriodicDelay:interval: NSButtonCell,
    NSCell, NSButton
getRed:green:blue:alpha: NSColor
getReturnValue: NSInvocation
getRow:column:forPoint: NSMatrix
getRow:column:ofCell: NSMatrix

Method Index

headerRectOfColumn: NSTableHeaderView

headerTextColor NSColor

headerView NSTableView

heightAdjustLimit NSView

heightTracksTextView NSTextContainer

helpRequested: NSMenu, NSResponder

hide NSCursor

hide: NSApplication

hideOtherApplications NSWorkspace

hideOtherApplications: NSApplication

hidesOnDeactivate NSWindow

highlight: NSButton, NSScroller

highlight:withFrame:inView: NSCell

highlightCell:atRow:column: NSMatrix

highlightColor NSColor

highlightColorInView: NSBrowserCell

highlightColorWithFrame:inView: NSCell

highlightMode NSStatusItem

highlightSelectionInClipRect: NSTableView

highlightWithLevel: NSColor

highlightedBranchImage NSBrowserCell

highlightedItemIndex NSMenuView

highlightedTableColumn NSTableView

highlightsBy NSButtonCell

hitPart NSScroller

hitTest: NSView

horizontalEdgePadding NSMenuView

horizontalLineScroll NSScrollView

horizontalPageScroll NSScrollView

horizontalPagination NSPrintInfo

horizontalRulerView NSScrollView

horizontalScroller NSScrollView

host NSPrinter, NSURL

hostName NSProcessInfo

hostWithAddress: NSHost

hostWithName: NSHost

hotSpot NSCursor

hourOfDay NSCalendarDate

hueComponent NSColor

hyphenationFactor NSLayoutManager

I

IBeamCursor NSCursor

icon NSFileWrapper

iconForFile: NSWorkspace

iconForFileType: NSWorkspace

iconForFiles: NSWorkspace

identifier NSTableColumn, NSTabViewItem, NSToolbar

ignoreWord:inSpellDocumentWithTag: NSSpellChecker

ignoredWordsInSpellDocumentWithTag: NSSpellChecker

ignoresAlpha NSColor

ignoresMouseEvents NSWindow

ignoresMultiClick NSControl

illegalCharacterSet NSCharacterSet

image NSSlider, NSBrowserCell, NSCursor, NSMenuItem, NSCell, NSToolbarItem, NSButton, NSImageView, NSRulerMarker, NSInputManager, NSStatusItem

image:didLoadPartOfRepresentation: withValidRows: NSImage

image:didLoadRepresentation:withStatus: NSImage

image:didLoadRepresentationHeader: NSImage

image:willLoadRepresentation: NSImage

imageAlignment NSImageCell, NSImageView

imageAndTitleOffset NSMenuView

imageAndTitleWidth NSMenuView

imageDidNotDraw:inRect: NSImage

imageDimsWhenDisabled NSButtonCell

imageFileTypes NSImage, NSImageRep

imageFrameStyle NSImageCell, NSImageView

imageInterpolation NSGraphicsContext

imageNamed: NSImage

imageOrigin NSRulerMarker

imagePasteboardTypes NSImage, NSImageRep

imagePosition NSButtonCell, NSButton

imageRectForBounds: NSCell, NSMenuItemCell

imageRectForPaper: NSPrinter

imageRectInRuler NSRulerMarker

imageRepClassForData: NSImageRep

imageRepClassForFileType: NSImageRep

imageRepClassForPasteboardType: NSImageRep

imageRepWithContentsOfFile: NSImageRep

imageRepWithContentsOfURL: NSImageRep

imageRepWithData: NSPDFImageRep, NSEPSImageRep, NSBitmapImageRep, NSPICTImageRep

imageRepWithPasteboard: NSImageRep

imageRepsWithContentsOfFile: NSImageRep

imageRepsWithContentsOfURL: NSImageRep

imageRepsWithData: NSBitmapImageRep

imageRepsWithPasteboard: NSImageRep

imageScaling NSImageCell, NSImageView

imageUnfilteredFileTypes NSImage, NSImageRep

imageUnfilteredPasteboardTypes NSImage, NSImageRep

imageWidth NSMenuItemCell

imageablePageBounds NSPrintInfo

importsGraphics NSTextView, NSCell, NSTextField, NSText

inLiveResize NSView

increaseLengthBy: NSMutableData

increment NSStepperCell, NSStepper

incrementBy: NSProgressIndicator

incrementalLoadFromData:complete: NSBitmapImageRep

indent: NSResponder

indentationMarkerFollowsCell NSOutlineView

indentationPerLevel NSOutlineView

independentConversationQueueing NSConnection

index NSIndexSpecifier

indexOfCellWithTag: NSForm

indexOfItem: NSPopUpButton, NSPopUpButtonCell, NSMenu

indexOfItemAtPoint: NSMenuView

indexOfItemWithObjectValue: NSComboBoxCell, NSComboBox

indexOfItemWithRepresentedObject: NSPopUpButton, NSPopUpButtonCell, NSMenu

indexOfItemWithSubmenu: NSMenu

indexOfItemWithTag: NSPopUpButton, NSPopUpButtonCell, NSMenu

indexOfItemWithTarget:andAction: NSPopUpButton, NSPopUpButtonCell, NSMenu

indexOfItemWithTitle: NSPopUpButton, NSPopUpButtonCell, NSMenu

indexOfObject: NSArray

indexOfObject:inRange: NSArray

indexOfObjectIdenticalTo: NSArray

indexOfObjectIdenticalTo:inRange: NSArray

indexOfSelectedItem NSPopUpButton, NSPopUpButtonCell, NSComboBoxCell, NSForm, NSComboBox

indexOfTabViewItem: NSTabView

indexOfTabViewItemWithIdentifier: NSTabView

indexOfTickMarkAtPoint: NSSliderCell

indicatorImageInTableColumn: NSTableView

indicesOfObjectsByEvaluatingWithContainer: count: NSScriptObjectSpecifier

infoDictionary NSBundle

init NSString, NSNetServiceBrowser, NSUserDefaults, NSDocumentController, NSLayoutManager, NSObject, NSSocketPort, NSDate, NSPipe, NSTask, NSDocument

initAndTestWithTests: NSLogicalTest

initAsTearOff NSMenuView

initByReferencingFile: NSImage

initByReferencingURL: NSImage

initDirectoryWithFileWrappers: NSFileWrapper

initFileURLWithPath: NSURL

initForIncrementalLoad NSBitmapImageRep

initForReadingWithData: NSKeyedUnarchiver, NSUnarchiver

initForWritingWithMutableData: NSKeyedArchiver, NSArchiver

initImageCell: NSCell

initListDescriptor NSAppleEventDescriptor

initNotTestWithTest: NSLogicalTest

initOrTestWithTests: NSLogicalTest

initRecordDescriptor NSAppleEventDescriptor

initRegularFileWithContents: NSFileWrapper

initRemoteWithProtocolFamily:socketType: protocol:address: NSSocketPort

initRemoteWithTCPPort:host: NSSocketPort

initSymbolicLinkWithDestination: NSFileWrapper

initTextCell: NSFormCell, NSCell

initTextCell:pullsDown: NSPopUpButtonCell

initWithAEDescNoCopy: NSAppleEventDescriptor

initWithArray: NSSet, NSArray, NSCountedSet

initWithArray:copyItems: NSArray

initWithAttributedString: NSAttributedString

initWithAttributes: NSOpenGLPixelFormat

initWithBitmapDataPlanes:pixelsWide:
pixelsHigh:bitsPerSample:
samplesPerPixel:hasAlpha:isPlanar:
colorSpaceName:bytesPerRow:
bitsPePixel:
NSBitmapImageRep

initWithBool: NSNumber

initWithBytes:length: NSData

initWithBytes:objCType: NSValue

initWithBytesNoCopy:length: NSData

initWithBytesNoCopy:length:freeWhenDone:
NSData

initWithCString: NSString

initWithCString:length: NSString

initWithCStringNoCopy:length:
freeWhenDone: NSString

initWithCapacity: NSMutableArray,
NSMutableData, NSMutableString,
NSMutableDictionary, NSMutableSet,
NSCountedSet

initWithChar: NSNumber

initWithCharacters:length: NSString

initWithCharactersNoCopy:length:freeWhen-
Done: NSString

initWithCoder: NSComboBoxCell, NSComboBox

initWithCommandDescription:
NSScriptCommand

initWithCondition: NSConditionLock

initWithContainerClassDescription:
containerSpecifier:key:
NSScriptObjectSpecifier

initWithContainerClassDescription:container-
Specifier:key:index: NSIndexSpecifier

initWithContainerClassDescription:
containerSpecifier:key:name:
NSNameSpecifier

initWithContainerClassDescription:
containerSpecifier:key:relativePosition:
baseSpecifier:
NSRelativeSpecifier

initWithContainerClassDescription:
containerSpecifier:key:startSpecifier:
endSpecifier: NSRangeSpecifier

initWithContainerClassDescription:
containerSpecifier:key:test:
NSWhoseSpecifier

initWithContainerClassDescription:
containerSpecifier:key:uniqueID:
NSUniqueIDSpecifier

initWithContainerSize: NSTextContainer

initWithContainerSpecifier:key:
NSScriptObjectSpecifier

initWithContentRect:style-
Mask:backing:defer: NSWindow

initWithContentRect:styleMask:backing:
defer:screen: NSWindow

initWithContentSize:preferredEdge: NSDrawer

initWithContentsOfFile: NSImage, NSString,
NSData, NSDictionary, NSArray

initWithContentsOfFile:byReference: NSSound

initWithContentsOfFile:ofType: NSDocument

initWithContentsOfMappedFile: NSData

initWithContentsOfURL: NSImage, NSString,
NSData, NSDictionary, NSArray

initWithContentsOfURL:byReference:
NSSound

initWithContentsOfURL:error: NSAppleScript

initWithContentsOfURL:ofType: NSDocument

initWithData: NSImage, NSSound, NSData,
NSPDFImageRep, NSEPSImageRep,
NSOpenGLPixelFormat, NSBitmapImageRep,
NSPICTImageRep

initWithData:encoding: NSString

initWithDateFormat:allowNaturalLanguage:
NSDateFormatter

initWithDecimal: NSDecimalNumber

initWithDelegate:name: NSInputServer

initWithDescriptorType:bytes:length:
NSAppleEventDescriptor

initWithDescriptorType:data:
NSAppleEventDescriptor

initWithDictionary: NSDictionary, NSPrintInfo

initWithDictionary:copyItems: NSDictionary

initWithDomain:type:name: NSNetService

initWithDomain:type:name:port:
NSNetService

initWithDouble: NSNumber

initWithDrawSelector:delegate:
NSCustomImageRep

---

initWithEventClass:eventID:
    targetDescriptor:returnID:transactionID:
    NSAppleEventDescriptor

initWithFileDescriptor: NSFileHandle

initWithFileDescriptor:closeOnDealloc:
    NSFileHandle

initWithFileWrapper: NSTextAttachment

initWithFireDate:interval:target:selector:
    userInfo:repeats: NSTimer

initWithFloat: NSNumber

initWithFocusedViewRect: NSBitmapImageRep

initWithFormat:... NSString

initWithFormat:arguments: NSString

initWithFormat:locale:... NSString

initWithFormat:locale:arguments: NSString

initWithFormat:shareContext:
    NSOpenGLContext

initWithFrame: NSTextView, NSControl,
    NSMatrix, NSView, NSMenuView

initWithFrame:mode:cellClass:numberOfRows:
    numberOfColumns: NSMatrix

initWithFrame:mode:prototype:numberOfRows:
    numberOfColumns: NSMatrix

initWithFrame:pixelFormat: NSOpenGLView

initWithFrame:pullsDown: NSPopUpButton

initWithFrame:textContainer: NSTextView

initWithHTML:baseURL:documentAttributes:
    NSAttributedString

initWithHTML:documentAttributes:
    NSAttributedString

initWithIdentifier: NSTableColumn,
    NSTabViewItem, NSToolbar

initWithImage:foregroundColorHint:
    backgroundColorHint:hotSpot: NSCursor

initWithImage:hotSpot: NSCursor

initWithInt: NSNumber

initWithItemIdentifier: NSToolbarItem

initWithLength: NSMutableData

initWithLocal:connection: NSDistantObject

initWithLong: NSNumber

initWithLongLong: NSNumber

initWithMachPort: NSMachPort

initWithMantissa:exponent:isNegative:
    NSDecimalNumber

initWithMovie: NSMovie

initWithName: NSTimeZone, NSColorList

initWithName:data: NSTimeZone

initWithName:fromFile: NSColorList

initWithName:host: NSInputManager

initWithName:reason:userInfo: NSException

initWithNativeHandle: NSFileHandle

initWithNativeHandle:closeOnDealloc:
    NSFileHandle

initWithNotificationCenter:
    NSNotificationQueue

initWithObjectSpecifier:comparisonOperator:
    testObject: NSSpecifierTest

initWithObjects:... NSSet, NSArray

initWithObjects:count: NSSet, NSArray

initWithObjects:forKeys: NSDictionary

initWithObjects:forKeys:count: NSDictionary

initWithObjectsAndKeys:... NSDictionary

initWithPasteboard: NSImage, NSSound,
    NSMovie

initWithPath: NSBundle, NSFileWrapper,
    NSDistributedLock

initWithPath:documentAttributes:
    NSAttributedString

initWithPickerMask:colorPanel: NSColorPicker

initWithPosition:objectSpecifier:
    NSPositionalSpecifier

initWithProtocolFamily:socketType:
    protocol:address: NSSocketPort

initWithProtocolFamily:socketType:
    protocol:socket: NSSocketPort

initWithRTF:documentAttributes:
    NSAttributedString

initWithRTFD:documentAttributes:
    NSAttributedString

initWithRTFDFileWrapper:
    documentAttributes: NSAttributedString

initWithReceivePort:sendPort: NSConnection

initWithReceivePort:sendPort:components:
    NSPortCoder

initWithRoundingMode:scale:
    raiseOnExactness:raiseOnOverflow:
    raiseOnUnderflow:raiseOnDivideByZero:
    NSDecimalNumberHandler

initWithRulerView:markerLocation:
    image:imageOrigin: NSRulerMarker

initWithScheme:host:path: NSURL

initWithScrollView:orientation: NSRulerView

initWithSendPort:receivePort:components:
NSPortMessage

initWithSerializedRepresentation:
NSFileWrapper

initWithSet: NSSet, NSCountedSet

initWithSet:copyItems: NSSet

initWithShort: NSNumber

initWithSize: NSImage

initWithSize:depth:separate:alpha:
NSCachedImageRep

initWithSource: NSAppleScript

initWithString: NSString, NSAttributedString,
NSURL, NSDecimalNumber,
NSCalendarDate, NSDate, NSScanner

initWithString:attributes: NSAttributedString

initWithString:calendarFormat:
NSCalendarDate

initWithString:calendarFormat:locale:
NSCalendarDate

initWithString:locale: NSDecimalNumber

initWithString:relativeToURL: NSURL

initWithSuiteName:className:dictionary:
NSScriptClassDescription

initWithSuiteName:commandName:dictionary:
NSScriptCommandDescription

initWithTCPPort: NSSocketPort

initWithTarget:connection: NSDistantObject

initWithTarget:protocol: NSProtocolChecker

• initWithTimeInterval:sinceDate: NSDate

initWithTimeIntervalSinceNow: NSDate

initWithTimeIntervalSinceReferenceDate:
NSDate

initWithTitle: NSMenu

initWithTitle:action:keyEquivalent:
NSMenuItem

initWithTransform: NSAffineTransform

initWithType:location: NSTextTab

initWithURL:byReference: NSMovie

initWithURL:cached: NSURLHandle

initWithURL:documentAttributes:
NSAttributedString

initWithUTF8String: NSString

initWithUnsignedChar: NSNumber

initWithUnsignedInt: NSNumber

initWithUnsignedLong: NSNumber

initWithUnsignedLongLong: NSNumber

initWithUnsignedShort: NSNumber

initWithUser: NSUserDefaults

initWithWindow: NSWindowController

initWithWindow:rect: NSCachedImageRep

initWithWindowNibName:
NSWindowController

initWithWindowNibName:owner:
NSWindowController

initWithWindowNibPath:owner:
NSWindowController

initWithWindowRef: NSWindow

initWithYear:month:day:hour:minute:
second:timeZone: NSCalendarDate

initialFirstResponder NSWindow,
NSTabViewItem

initialize NSObject

innerRect NSMenuView

insertAttributedString:atIndex:
NSMutableAttributedString

insertBacktab: NSResponder

insertColor:key:atIndex: NSColorList

insertColumn: NSMatrix

insertColumn:withCells: NSMatrix

insertDescriptor:atIndex:
NSAppleEventDescriptor

insertEntry:atIndex: NSForm

insertGlyph:atGlyphIndex:characterIndex:
NSSimpleHorizontalTypesetter,
NSLayoutManager

insertItem:atIndex: NSMenu

insertItemWithItemIdentifier:atIndex:
NSToolbar

insertItemWithObjectValue:atIndex:
NSComboBoxCell, NSComboBox

insertItemWithTitle:action:keyEquivalent:
atIndex: NSMenu

insertItemWithTitle:atIndex: NSPopUpButton,
NSPopUpButtonCell

insertNewButtonImage:in: NSColorPicker

insertNewline: NSResponder

insertNewlineIgnoringFieldEditor:
NSResponder

insertObject:atIndex: NSMutableArray

insertParagraphSeparator: NSResponder

insertRow: NSMatrix

insertRow:withCells: NSMatrix

insertString:atIndex: NSMutableString

insertTab: NSResponder

insertTabIgnoringFieldEditor: NSResponder

insertTabViewItem:atIndex: NSTabView

insertText: NSResponder, NSTextView

insertTextContainer:atIndex:
   NSLayoutManager

insertionContainer NSPositionalSpecifier

insertionIndex NSPositionalSpecifier

insertionKey NSPositionalSpecifier

insertionPointColor NSTextView

insertionReplaces NSPositionalSpecifier

instanceMethodForSelector: NSObject

instanceMethodSignatureForSelector: NSObject

instancesRespondToSelector: NSObject

int32Value NSAppleEventDescriptor

intAttribute:forGlyphAtIndex:
   NSLayoutManager

intForKey:inTable: NSPrinter

intValue NSString, NSControl, NSCell,
   NSNumber, NSActionCell

integerForKey: NSUserDefaults

intercellSpacing NSTableView,
   NSComboBoxCell, NSMatrix, NSComboBox

interfaceStyle NSResponder

interpretKeyEvents: NSResponder

interrupt NSTask

intersectSet: NSMutableSet

intersectsSet: NSSet

invalidate NSTimer, NSPort, NSConnection

invalidateAttributesInRange: NSTextStorage

invalidateClassDescriptionCache
   NSClassDescription

invalidateCursorRectsForView: NSWindow

invalidateDisplayForCharacterRange:
   NSLayoutManager

invalidateDisplayForGlyphRange:
   NSLayoutManager

invalidateGlyphsForCharacterRange:
   changeInLength:actualCharacterRange:
   NSLayoutManager

invalidateHashMarks NSRulerView

invalidateLayoutForCharacterRange:
   isSoft:actualCharacterRange:
   NSLayoutManager

invalidateShadow NSWindow

invalidateTextContainerOrigin NSTextView

inverseForRelationshipKey: NSClassDescription

invert NSMutableCharacterSet,
   NSAffineTransform

invertedSet NSCharacterSet

invocation NSDistantObjectRequest

invocationWithMethodSignature:
   NSInvocation

invoke NSInvocation

invokeWithTarget: NSInvocation

isARepeat NSEvent

isAbsolutePath NSString

isActive NSApplication, NSColorWell

isAtEnd NSScanner, NSUnarchiver

isAttached NSMenu, NSMenuView

isAutodisplay NSWindow

isAutoscroll NSMatrix

isBaseFont NSFont

isBezeled NSProgressIndicator, NSCell,
   NSTextField

isBordered NSCell, NSButton, NSColorWell,
   NSTextField

isBycopy NSPortCoder

isByref NSPortCoder

isCachedSeparately NSImage

isColor NSPrinter

isColumnSelected: NSTableView

isCompiled NSAppleScript

isContextHelpModeActive NSHelpManager

isContinuous NSControl, NSCell, NSColorPanel

isContinuousSpellCheckingEnabled
   NSTextView

isControllerVisible NSMovieView

isCopyingOperation NSPrintOperation

isDataRetained NSImage

isDaylightSavingTime NSTimeZone

isDaylightSavingTimeForDate: NSTimeZone

isDeletableFileAtPath: NSFileManager

isDescendantOf: NSView

isDirectory NSFileWrapper

isDisplayedWhenStopped NSProgressIndicator

isDocumentEdited NSWindow, NSDocument

isDragging NSRulerMarker

isDrawingToScreen NSGraphicsContext

isEditable NSTableColumn, NSTextView, NSCell, NSMovieView, NSImageView, NSColorList, NSTextField, NSText

isEmpty NSBezierPath

isEnabled NSControl, NSMenuItem, NSCell, NSFontManager, NSToolbarItem, NSFontPanel, NSStatusItem

isEntryAcceptable: NSCell

isEqualToArray: NSArray

isEqualToAttributedString: NSAttributedString

isEqualToData: NSData

isEqualToDate: NSDate

isEqualToDictionary: NSDictionary

isEqualToHost: NSHost

isEqualToNumber: NSNumber

isEqualToSet: NSSet

isEqualToString: NSString

isEqualToTimeZone: NSTimeZone

isEqualToValue: NSValue

isExcludedFromWindowsMenu NSWindow

isExecutableFileAtPath: NSFileManager

isExpandable: NSOutlineView

isExpanded NSSavePanel

isExtensionHidden NSSavePanel

isFieldEditor NSTextView, NSText

isFilePackageAtPath: NSWorkspace

isFileURL NSURL

isFixedPitch NSFont

isFlipped NSImage, NSView, NSRulerView

isFloatingPanel NSWindow, NSPanel

isFlushWindowDisabled NSWindow

isFontAvailable: NSPrinter

isHidden NSApplication

isHighlighted NSCell, NSMenuItemCell

isHorizontal NSMenuView

isHorizontallyCentered NSPrintInfo

isHorizontallyResizable NSText

isHostCacheEnabled NSHost

isIndeterminate NSProgressIndicator

isItemExpanded: NSOutlineView

isKey:inTable: NSPrinter

isKeyWindow NSWindow

isLeaf NSBrowserCell

isLoaded NSBundle, NSBrowserCell, NSBrowser

isLocationRequiredToCreateForKey: NSScriptClassDescription

isMainWindow NSWindow

isMiniaturizable NSWindow

isMiniaturized NSWindow

isModalPanel NSWindow

isMovable NSRulerMarker

isMovableByWindowBackground NSWindow

isMultiThreaded NSThread

isMultiple NSFontManager

isMuted NSMovieView

isNativeType: NSDocument

isOneShot NSWindow

isOneway NSMethodSignature

isOpaque NSWindow, NSButtonCell, NSFormCell, NSCell, NSImageRep, NSView

isOptionalArgumentWithName: NSScriptCommandDescription

isOutputStackInReverseOrder NSPrinter

isPaneSplitter NSSplitView

isPartialStringValid:newEditingString: errorDescription: NSFormatter

isPartialStringValid:proposedSelectedRange: originalString:originalSelectedRange: errorDescription: NSFormatter

isPlanar NSBitmapImageRep

isPlaying NSSound, NSMovieView

isReadOnlyKey: NSScriptClassDescription

isReadableFileAtPath: NSFileManager

isRedoing NSUndoManager

isRegularFile NSFileWrapper

isReleasedWhenClosed NSWindow

isRemovable NSRulerMarker

isResizable NSTableColumn, NSWindow

isRichText NSTextView, NSText

isRotatedFromBase NSView

isRotatedOrScaledFromBase NSView

isRowSelected: NSTableView

isRulerVisible NSTextView, NSText

isRunning NSApplication, NSTask

isScrollable NSCell

isSelectable NSTextView, NSCell, NSTextField, NSText

isSelectionByRect NSMatrix

isSeparatorItem NSMenuItem

isSetOnMouseEntered NSCursor

isSetOnMouseExited NSCursor

isSheet NSWindow

isSimpleRectangularTextContainer NSTextContainer

isSubclassOfClass: NSObject

isSubsetOfSet: NSSet

isSubviewCollapsed: NSSplitView

isSupersetOfSet: NSCharacterSet

isSymbolicLink NSFileWrapper

isTitled NSBrowser

isTornOff NSMenu, NSMenuView

isTransparent NSButtonCell, NSButton

isTrue NSScriptWhoseTest

isUndoRegistrationEnabled NSUndoManager

isUndoing NSUndoManager

isValid NSImage, NSTimer, NSPort, NSConnection

isValidGlyphIndex: NSLayoutManager

isVertical NSSlider, NSStatusBar, NSSplitView, NSSliderCell

isVerticallyCentered NSPrintInfo

isVerticallyResizable NSText

isVisible NSWindow, NSToolbar

isWellFormed NSScriptCommand

isWindowLoaded NSWindowController

isWordInUserDictionaries:caseSensitive: NSSpellServer

isWritableFileAtPath: NSFileManager

isZoomable NSWindow

isZoomed NSWindow

italicAngle NSFont

itemAdded: NSMenuView

itemArray NSPopUpButton, NSPopUpButtonCell, NSMenu

itemAtIndex: NSPopUpButton, NSPopUpButtonCell, NSMenu

itemAtRow: NSOutlineView

itemChanged: NSMenu, NSMenuView

itemHeight NSComboBoxCell, NSComboBox

itemIdentifier NSToolbarItem

itemObjectValueAtIndex: NSComboBoxCell, NSComboBox

itemRemoved: NSMenuView

itemTitleAtIndex: NSPopUpButton, NSPopUpButtonCell

itemTitles NSPopUpButton, NSPopUpButtonCell

itemWithTag: NSMenu

itemWithTitle: NSPopUpButton, NSPopUpButtonCell, NSMenu

items NSToolbar

J

jobDisposition NSPrintInfo

jobStyleHint NSPrintPanel, NSPrintOperation

K

keepBackupFile NSDocument

key NSScriptObjectSpecifier

keyClassDescription NSScriptObjectSpecifier

keyCode NSEvent

keyDown: NSWindow, NSResponder

keyEnumerator NSDictionary

keyEquivalent NSButtonCell, NSMenuItem, NSCell, NSButton

keyEquivalentFont NSButtonCell

keyEquivalentModifierMask NSButtonCell, NSMenuItem, NSButton

keyEquivalentOffset NSMenuView

keyEquivalentRectForBounds: NSMenuItemCell

keyEquivalentWidth NSMenuItemCell, NSMenuView

keyEventWithType:location:modifierFlags: timestamp:windowNumber:context: characters:charactersIgnoringModifiers: isARepeat:keyCode: NSEvent

keyForFileWrapper: NSFileWrapper

keySpecifier NSDeleteCommand, NSCloneCommand, NSMoveCommand, NSSetCommand

keyUp: NSResponder

keyViewSelectionDirection NSWindow

keyWindow NSApplication

keyWithAppleEventCode: NSScriptClassDescription

keyboardFocusIndicatorColor NSColor

keysSortedByValueUsingSelector:
 NSDictionary

keywordForDescriptorAtIndex:
 NSAppleEventDescriptor

knobColor NSColor

knobProportion NSScroller

knobRectFlipped: NSSliderCell

knobThickness NSSlider, NSSliderCell

knownTimeZoneNames NSTimeZone

knowsPageRange: NSView

L

label NSNibConnector, NSTabViewItem,
 NSToolbarItem

labelFontOfSize: NSFont

labelFontSize NSFont

language NSSpellChecker, NSInputManager

languageLevel NSPrinter

lastColumn NSBrowser

lastItem NSPopUpButton, NSPopUpButtonCell

lastObject NSArray

lastPathComponen NSString

lastVisibleColumn NSBrowser

laterDate: NSDate

launch NSTask

launchApplication: NSWorkspace

launchApplication:showIcon:autolaunch:
 NSWorkspace

launchPath NSTask

launchedApplications NSWorkspace

launchedTaskWithLaunchPath:arguments:
 NSTask

layoutControlGlyphForLineFragment:
 NSSimpleHorizontalTypesetter

layoutGlyphsInHorizontalLineFragment:base-
 line: NSSimpleHorizontalTypesetter

layoutGlyphsInLayoutManager:
 startingAtGlyphIndex:maxNumberOfLine-
 Fragments:nextGlyphIndex:
 NSSimpleHorizontalTypesetter, NSTypesetter

layoutManager NSTextView, NSTextContainer

layoutManager:didCompleteLayoutForText-
 Container:atEnd: NSLayoutManager

layoutManagerDidInvalidateLayout:
 NSLayoutManager

layoutManagerOwnsFirstResponderIn-
 Window: NSLayoutManager

layoutManagers NSTextStorage

layoutTab NSSimpleHorizontalTypesetter

leadingOffset NSDrawer

leftMargin NSPrintInfo

length NSString, NSAttributedString, NSData,
 NSStatusItem

letterCharacterSet NSCharacterSet

level NSWindow

levelForItem: NSOutlineView

levelForRow: NSOutlineView

levelsOfUndo NSUndoManager

lightGrayColor NSColor

limitDateForMode: NSRunLoop

lineBreakBeforeIndex:withinRange:
 NSAttributedString

lineBreakMode NSParagraphStyle

lineCapStyle NSBezierPath

lineFragmentPadding NSTextContainer

lineFragmentRectForGlyphAtIndex:
 effectiveRange: NSLayoutManager

lineFragmentRectForProposedRect:
 sweepDirection:movementDirection:
 remainingRect: NSTextContainer

lineFragmentUsedRectForGlyphAtIndex:
 effectiveRange: NSLayoutManager

lineJoinStyle NSBezierPath

lineRangeForRange: NSString

lineScroll NSScrollView

lineSpacing NSParagraphStyle

lineToPoint: NSBezierPath

lineWidth NSBezierPath

linkPath:toPath:handler: NSFileManager

listDescriptor NSAppleEventDescriptor

load NSBundle, NSObject

loadColumnZero NSBrowser

loadDataRepresentation:ofType: NSDocument

loadFileWrapperRepresentation:ofType:
 NSDocument

loadInBackground NSURLHandle

loadInForeground NSURLHandle

loadNibFile:externalNameTable:withZone:
 NSBundle

loadNibNamed:owner: NSBundle

matrixInColumn: NSBrowser

maxContentSize NSDrawer

maxSize NSWindow, NSToolbarItem, NSText

maxValue NSSlider, NSProgressIndicator, NSSliderCell, NSStepperCell, NSStepper

maxVisibleColumns NSBrowser

maxWidth NSTableColumn

maximum NSNumberFormatter

maximumAdvancement NSFont

maximumDecimalNumber NSDecimalNumber

maximumLineHeight NSParagraphStyle

measurementUnits NSRulerView

member: NSSet

menu NSPopUpButton, NSPopUpButtonCell, NSResponder, NSMenuItem, NSCell, NSStatusItem, NSMenuView

menuBarHeight NSMenuView

menuBarVisible NSMenu

menuChanged: NSWindow

menuChangedMessagesEnabled NSMenu

menuFontOfSize: NSFont

menuForEvent: NSView

menuForEvent:inRect:ofView: NSCell

menuFormRepresentation NSToolbarItem

menuItem NSMenuItemCell

menuItemCellForItemAtIndex: NSMenuView

menuRepresentation NSMenu

menuView NSMenuItemCell

menuZone NSMenu

messageFontOfSize: NSFont

methodForSelector: NSObject

methodReturnLength NSMethodSignature

methodReturnType NSMethodSignature

methodSignature NSInvocation

methodSignatureForSelector: NSObject, NSProxy

minColumnWidth NSBrowser

minContentSize NSDrawer

minFrameWidthWithTitle:styleMask: NSWindow

minSize NSWindow, NSToolbarItem, NSText

minValue NSSlider, NSProgressIndicator, NSSliderCell, NSStepperCell, NSStepper

minWidth NSTableColumn

miniaturize: NSWindow

miniaturizeAll: NSApplication

minimum NSNumberFormatter

minimumDecimalNumber NSDecimalNumber

minimumLineHeight NSParagraphStyle

minimumSize NSTabView

miniwindowImage NSWindow

miniwindowTitle NSWindow

minusSet: NSMutableSet

minuteOfHour NSCalendarDate

miterLimit NSBezierPath

mixedStateImage NSMenuItem

mnemonic NSMenuItem

mnemonicLocation NSMenuItem

modalWindow NSApplication

mode NSMatrix, NSColorPanel

modifierFlags NSEvent

modifyFont: NSFontManager

modifyFontViaPanel: NSFontManager

monthOfYear NSCalendarDate

mostCompatibleStringEncoding NSFont

mountNewRemovableMedia NSWorkspace

mountedLocalVolumePaths NSWorkspace

mountedRemovableMedia NSWorkspace

mouse:inRect: NSView

mouseDown: NSResponder, NSControl, NSMatrix

mouseDownCanMoveWindow NSView

mouseDownFlags NSCell, NSMatrix

mouseDragged: NSResponder

mouseEntered: NSCursor, NSResponder, NSButtonCell

mouseEventWithType:location:modifierFlags: timestamp:windowNumber:context: eventNumber:clickCount:pressure: NSEvent

mouseExited: NSCursor, NSResponder, NSButtonCell

mouseLocation NSEvent

mouseLocationOutsideOfEventStream NSWindow

mouseMoved: NSResponder

mouseUp: NSResponder

moveBackward: NSResponder

moveBackwardAndModifySelection: NSResponder

Method Index

openOnEdge: NSDrawer
openPanel NSOpenPanel
openTempFile: NSWorkspace
openURL: NSWorkspace
openUntitledDocumentOfType:display:
    NSDocumentController
operatingSystem NSProcessInfo
operatingSystemName NSProcessInfo
operatingSystemVersionString NSProcessInfo
orangeColor NSColor
orderBack: NSWindow
orderFront: NSWindow
orderFrontColorPanel: NSApplication
orderFrontFontPanel: NSFontManager
orderFrontRegardless NSWindow
orderFrontStandardAboutPanel: NSApplication
orderFrontStandardAboutPanelWithOptions:
    NSApplication
orderOut: NSWindow
orderWindow:relativeTo: NSWindow
orderedIndex NSWindow
orientation NSPrintInfo,
    NSRulerView
originOffset NSRulerView
otherEventWithType:location:modifierFlags:
    timestamp:windowNumber:context:
    subtype:data1:data2: NSEvent
otherMouseDown: NSResponder
otherMouseDragged: NSResponder
otherMouseUp: NSResponder
outlineTableColumn NSOutlineView
outlineView:shouldCollapseItem:
    NSOutlineView
outlineView:shouldEditTableColumn:item:
    NSOutlineView
outlineView:shouldExpandItem:
    NSOutlineView
outlineView:shouldSelectItem: NSOutlineView
outlineView:shouldSelectTableColumn:
    NSOutlineView
outlineView:willDisplayCell:forTableColumn:
    item: NSOutlineView
outlineView:willDisplayOutlineCell:
    forTableColumn:item: NSOutlineView
outlineViewColumnDidMove: NSOutlineView

outlineViewColumnDidResize: NSOutlineView
outlineViewItemDidCollapse: NSOutlineView
outlineViewItemDidExpand: NSOutlineView
outlineViewItemWillCollapse: NSOutlineView
outlineViewItemWillExpand: NSOutlineView
outlineViewSelectionDidChange:
    NSOutlineView
outlineViewSelectionIsChanging:
    NSOutlineView
outputFormat NSKeyedArchiver
owner NSWindowController

P

PDFOperationWithView:insideRect:toData:
    NSPrintOperation
PDFOperationWithView:insideRect:toData:
    printInfo: NSPrintOperation
PDFOperationWithView:insideRect:toPath:
    printInfo: NSPrintOperation
PDFRepresentation NSPDFImageRep
PICTRepresentation NSPICTImageRep
pageCount NSPDFImageRep
pageDown: NSResponder
pageLayout NSPageLayout
pageOrder NSPrintOperation
pageScroll NSScrollView
pageSizeForPaper: NSPrinter
pageUp: NSResponder
paletteFontOfSize: NSFont
paletteLabel NSToolbarItem
panel:compareFilename:with:caseSensitive:
    NSSavePanel
panel:isValidFilename: NSSavePanel
panel:shouldShowFilename: NSSavePanel
panel:userEnteredFilename:confirmed:
    NSSavePanel
panel:willExpand: NSSavePanel
panelConvertFont: NSFontPanel
paperName NSPrintInfo
paperSize NSPrintInfo
paragraphSpacing NSParagraphStyle
paragraphs NSTextStorage
paramDescriptorForKeyword:
    NSAppleEventDescriptor
parameterString NSURL

parentWindow NSWindow, NSDrawer

password NSURL

paste: NSMovieView, NSText

pasteAsPlainText: NSTextView

pasteAsRichText: NSTextView

pasteFont: NSText

pasteRuler: NSText

pasteboardByFilteringData:ofType:
NSPasteboard

pasteboardByFilteringFile: NSPasteboard

pasteboardByFilteringTypesInPasteboard:
NSPasteboard

pasteboardWithName: NSPasteboard

pasteboardWithUniqueName NSPasteboard

path NSURL, NSBrowser

pathComponents NSString

pathContentOfSymbolicLinkAtPath:
NSFileManager

pathExtension NSString

pathForAuxiliaryExecutable: NSBundle

pathForImageResource: NSBundle

pathForResource:ofType: NSBundle

pathForResource:ofType:inDirectory:
NSBundle

pathForResource:ofType:inDirectory:
forLocalization: NSBundle

pathForSoundResource: NSBundle

pathSeparator NSBrowser

pathToColumn: NSBrowser

pathWithComponents: NSString

pathsForResourcesOfType:inDirectory:
NSBundle

pathsForResourcesOfType:inDirectory:
forLocalization: NSBundle

pathsMatchingExtensions: NSArray

patternImage NSColor

patternPhase NSGraphicsContext

pause NSSound

performActionForItemAtIndex: NSMenu

performActionWithHighlightingForItem-
AtIndex: NSMenuView

performClick: NSButtonCell

performClickWithFrame:inView:
NSPopUpButtonCell

performClose: NSWindow

performDefaultImplementation
NSScriptCommand

performFileOperation:source:destination:
files:tag: NSWorkspace

performKeyEquivalent: NSMenu,
NSResponder, NSMatrix, NSButton, NSView

performMiniaturize: NSWindow

performSelector:target:argument:
order:modes: NSRunLoop

performSelector:withObject:afterDelay:
NSObject

performSelector:withObject:after-
Delay:inModes: NSObject

performSelectorOnMainThread:withObject:
waitUntilDone: NSObject

performSelectorOnMainThread:withObject:
waitUntilDone:modes: NSObject

performZoom: NSWindow

persistentDomainForName: NSUserDefaults

persistentDomainNames NSUserDefaults

pickedAllPages: NSPrintPanel

pickedButton: NSPrintPanel, NSPageLayout

pickedLayoutList: NSPrintPanel

pickedOrientation: NSPageLayout

pickedPaperSize: NSPageLayout

pickedUnits: NSPageLayout

pipe NSPipe

pixelFormat NSOpenGLView

pixelsHigh NSImageRep

pixelsWide NSImageRep

play NSSound

playsEveryFrame NSMovieView

playsSelectionOnly NSMovieView

pointSize NSFont

pointValue NSValue

pointerValue NSValue

poolCountHighWaterMark NSAutoreleasePool

poolCountHighWaterResolution
NSAutoreleasePool

pop NSCursor

popUpContextMenu:withEvent:forView:
NSMenu

port NSURL, NSPort

portCoderWithReceivePort:sendPort:
components: NSPortCoder

portForName: NSSocketPortNameServer, NSMessagePortNameServer, NSMachBootstrapServer, NSPortNameServer

portForName:host: NSSocketPortNameServer, NSMessagePortNameServer, NSMachBootstrapServer, NSPortNameServer

portForName:host:nameServerPortNumber: NSSocketPortNameServer

portWithMachPort: NSMachPort

poseAsClass: NSObject

positionOfGlyph:forCharacter:struckOverRect: NSFont

positionOfGlyph:precededByGlyph:isNominal: NSFont

positionOfGlyph:struckOverGlyph:metricsExist: NSFont

positionOfGlyph:struckOverRect:metricsExist: NSFont

positionOfGlyph:withRelation:toBaseGlyph: totalAdvancement:metricsExist: NSFont

positionsForCompositeSequence: numberOfGlyphs:pointArray: NSFont

positiveFormat NSNumberFormatter

postEvent:atStart: NSWindow, NSApplication

postNotification: NSNotificationCenter

postNotificationName:object: NSDistributedNotificationCenter, NSNotificationCenter

postNotificationName:object:userInfo: NSDistributedNotificationCenter, NSNotificationCenter

postNotificationName:object:userInfo: deliverImmediately: NSDistributedNotificationCenter

postsBoundsChangedNotifications NSView

postsFrameChangedNotifications NSView

precomposedStringWithCanonicalMapping NSString

precomposedStringWithCompatibilityMapping NSString

preferredEdge NSPopUpButton, NSPopUpButtonCell, NSDrawer

preferredFilename NSFileWrapper

preferredFontNames NSFont

preferredLocalizations NSBundle

preferredLocalizationsFromArray: NSBundle

preferredLocalizationsFromArray: forPreferences: NSBundle

preferredPasteboardTypeFromArray: restrictedToTypesFromArray: NSTextView

prefersColorMatch NSImage

prefersTrackingUntilMouseUp NSSliderCell, NSCell

prepareGState NSEPSImageRep

preparePageLayout: NSDocument

prepareSavePanel: NSDocument

prepareWithInvocationTarget: NSUndoManager

prependTransform: NSAffineTransform

pressure NSEvent

preventWindowOrdering NSApplication

principalClass NSBundle

print: NSWindow, NSView

printDocument: NSDocument

printInfo NSPrintOperation, NSPageLayout, NSDocument

printJobTitle NSView

printOperationWithView: NSPrintOperation

printOperationWithView:printInfo: NSPrintOperation

printPanel NSPrintPanel, NSPrintOperation

printShowingPrintPanel: NSDocument

printer NSPrintInfo

printerFont NSFont

printerNames NSPrinter

printerTypes NSPrinter

printerWithName: NSPrinter

printerWithName:domain:includeUnavailable: NSPrinter

printerWithType: NSPrinter

printingAdjustmentInLayoutManager: forNominallySpacedGlyphRange: packedGlyphs:count: NSTypesetter

privateFrameworksPath NSBundle

processEditing NSTextStorage

processIdentifier NSProcessInfo, NSTask

processInfo NSProcessInfo

processName NSProcessInfo

prompt NSSavePanel

propertyForKey: NSURL, NSURLHandle

propertyForKeyIfAvailable: NSURLHandle

propertyList NSString

rect NSCachedImageRep

rectArrayForCharacterRange:withinSelected-
    CharacterRange:inTextContainer:rectCount:
    NSLayoutManager

rectArrayForGlyphRange:
    withinSelectedGlyphRange:
    inTextContainer:rectCount:
    NSLayoutManager

rectForKey:inTable: NSPrinter

rectForPage: NSView

rectForPart: NSScroller

rectOfColumn: NSTableView

rectOfItemAtIndex: NSMenuView

rectOfRow: NSTableView

rectOfTickMarkAtIndex: NSSliderCell

rectValue NSValue

redColor NSColor

redComponent NSColor

redo NSUndoManager

redoActionName NSUndoManager

redoMenuItemTitle NSUndoManager

redoMenuTitleForUndoActionName:
    NSUndoManager

reflectScrolledClipView: NSScrollView, NSView

registerClassDescription: NSScriptSuiteRegistry

registerClassDescription:forClass:
    NSClassDescription

registerCoercer:selector:toConvertFromClass:
    toClass: NSScriptCoercionHandler

registerCommandDescription:
    NSScriptSuiteRegistry

registerDefaults: NSUserDefaults

registerForDraggedTypes: NSWindow

registerForServices NSTextView

registerImageRepClass: NSImageRep

registerLanguage:byVendor: NSSpellServer

registerName: NSConnection

registerName:withNameServer: NSConnection

registerPort:name: NSSocketPortNameServer,
    NSMachBootstrapServer, NSPortNameServer

registerPort:name:nameServerPortNumber:
    NSSocketPortNameServer

registerServicesMenuSendTypes:returnTypes:
    NSApplication

registerURLHandleClass: NSURLHandle

registerUndoWithTarget:selector:object:
    NSUndoManager

registerUnitWithName:abbreviation:
    unitToPointsConversionFactor:
    stepUpCycle:step-DownCycle: NSRulerView

registeredImageRepClasses NSImageRep

regularFileContents NSFileWrapper

relativeCurveToPoint: NSBezierPath

relativeLineToPoint: NSBezierPath

relativeMoveToPoint: NSBezierPath

relativePath NSURL

relativePosition NSRelativeSpecifier

relativeString NSURL

releaseGState NSView

releaseGlobally NSPasteboard

reloadColumn: NSBrowser

reloadData NSTableView, NSComboBoxCell,
    NSComboBox

reloadDefaultFontFamilies NSFontPanel

reloadItem: NSOutlineView

reloadItem:reloadChildren: NSOutlineView

remoteObjects NSConnection

removeAllActions NSUndoManager

removeAllActionsWithTarget: NSUndoManager

removeAllItems NSPopUpButton,
    NSPopUpButtonCell, NSComboBoxCell,
    NSComboBox

removeAllObjects NSMutableArray,
    NSMutableDictionary, NSMutableSet

removeAllPoints NSBezierPath

removeAllToolTips NSView

removeAttribute:range:
    NSMutableAttributedString

removeCharactersInRange:
    NSMutableCharacterSet

removeCharactersInString:
    NSMutableCharacterSet

removeChildWindow: NSWindow

removeClient: NSURLHandle

removeColorWithKey: NSColorList

removeColumn: NSMatrix

removeConnection:fromRunLoop:forMode:
    NSPort

removeContextHelpForObject: NSHelpManager

removeCursorRect:cursor: NSView

removeDecriptorAtIndex:
  NSAppleEventDescriptor
removeDescriptorAtIndex:
  NSAppleEventDescriptor
removeDescriptorWithKeyword:
  NSAppleEventDescriptor
removeDocument: NSDocumentController
removeEntryAtIndex: NSForm
removeEventHandlerForEventClass:
  andEventID: NSAppleEventManager
removeFile NSColorList
removeFileAtPath:handler: NSFileManager
removeFileWrapper: NSFileWrapper
removeFontTrait: NSFontManager
removeFrameUsingName: NSWindow
removeFromRunLoop:forMode:
  NSNetServiceBrowser, NSNetService, NSPort,
  NSMachPort
removeFromSuperview NSView
removeFromSuperviewWithoutNeedingDisplay
  NSView
removeItem: NSMenu
removeItemAtIndex: NSPopUpButton,
  NSPopUpButtonCell, NSMenu,
  NSComboBoxCell, NSComboBox, NSToolbar
removeItemWithObjectValue:
  NSComboBoxCell, NSComboBox
removeItemWithTitle: NSPopUpButton,
  NSPopUpButtonCell
removeLastObject NSMutableArray
removeLayoutManager: NSTextStorage
removeMarker: NSRulerView
removeObject: NSMutableArray, NSMutableSet,
  NSCountedSet
removeObject:inRange: NSMutableArray
removeObjectAtIndex: NSMutableArray
removeObjectForKey: NSUserDefaults,
  NSMutableDictionary
removeObjectIdenticalTo: NSMutableArray
removeObjectIdenticalTo:inRange:
  NSMutableArray
removeObjectsForKeys: NSMutableDictionary
removeObjectsFromIndices:numIndices:
  NSMutableArray
removeObjectsInArray: NSMutableArray

removeObjectsInRange: NSMutableArray
removeObserver: NSNotificationCenter
removeObserver:name:object: NSDistributed-
  NotificationCenter, NSNotificationCenter
removeParamDescriptorWithKeyword:
  NSAppleEventDescriptor
removePersistentDomainForName:
  NSUserDefaults
removePort:forMode: NSRunLoop
removePortForName:
  NSSocketPortNameServer, NSPortNameServer
removeRepresentation: NSImage
removeRequestMode: NSConnection
removeRow: NSMatrix
removeRunLoop: NSConnection
removeStatusItem: NSStatusBar
removeSuiteNamed: NSUserDefaults
removeTabStop: NSMutableParagraphStyle
removeTabViewItem: NSTabView
removeTableColumn: NSTableView
removeTemporaryAttribute:
  forCharacterRange: NSLayoutManager
removeTextContainerAtIndex:
  NSLayoutManager
removeToolTip: NSView
removeTrackingRect: NSView
removeVolatileDomainForName:
  NSUserDefaults
removeWindowController: NSDocument
removeWindowsItem: NSApplication
renewGState NSView
renewRows:columns: NSMatrix
replaceBytesInRange:withBytes:
  NSMutableData
replaceBytesInRange:withBytes:length:
  NSMutableData
replaceCharactersInRange:
  withAttributedString:
  NSMutableAttributedString
replaceCharactersInRange:withRTF: NSText
replaceCharactersInRange:withRTFD: NSText
replaceCharactersInRange:withString:
  NSMutableString,
  NSMutableAttributedString, NSText

Method Index

rightMouseUp: NSResponder

rootObject NSConnection

rootProxy NSConnection

rootProxyForConnectionWithRegisteredName:
host: NSConnection

rootProxyForConnectionWithRegisteredName:
host:usingNameServer:
NSConnection

rotateByAngle: NSView

rotateByDegrees: NSAffineTransform

rotateByRadians: NSAffineTransform

roundingBehavior NSNumberFormatter

rowAtPoint: NSTableView

rowForItem: NSOutlineView

rowHeight NSTableView

rowsInRect: NSTableView

ruleThickness NSRulerView

ruler NSRulerMarker

rulerAccessoryViewForTextView:paragraphStyle:
ruler:enabled: NSLayoutManager

rulerAttributesInRange: NSAttributedString

rulerMarkersForTextView:paragraphStyle:
ruler: NSLayoutManager

rulerView:didAddMarker: NSTextView,
NSRulerMarker

rulerView:didMoveMarker: NSTextView,
NSRulerMarker

rulerView:didRemoveMarker: NSTextView,
NSRulerMarker

rulerView:handleMouseDown: NSTextView,
NSRulerMarker

rulerView:shouldAddMarker: NSTextView,
NSRulerMarker

rulerView:shouldMoveMarker: NSTextView,
NSRulerMarker

rulerView:shouldRemoveMarker: NSTextView,
NSRulerMarker

rulerView:willAddMarker:atLocation:
NSTextView, NSRulerMarker

rulerView:willMoveMarker:toLocation:
NSTextView, NSRulerMarker

rulerView:willSetClientView: NSRulerMarker

rulerViewClass NSScrollView

rulersVisible NSScrollView

run NSApplication, NSSpellServer, NSRunLoop

runCustomizationPalette: NSToolbar

runInNewThread NSConnection

runLoopModes NSUndoManager

runModal NSSavePanel, NSPrintPanel,
NSPageLayout

runModalForDirectory:file: NSSavePanel

runModalForDirectory:file:
relativeToWindow: NSSavePanel

runModalForDirectory:file:types: NSOpenPanel

runModalForDirectory:file:types:
relativeToWindow: NSOpenPanel

runModalForTypes: NSOpenPanel

runModalForWindow: NSApplication

runModalForWindow:relativeToWindow:
NSApplication

runModalOpenPanel:forTypes:
NSDocumentController

runModalPageLayoutWithPrintInfo:
NSDocument

runModalPageLayoutWithPrintInfo:
delegate:didRunSelector:contextInfo:
NSDocument

runModalPrintOperation:delegate:
didRunSelector:contextInfo: NSDocument

runModalSavePanel:withAccessoryView:
NSDocument

runModalSavePanelForSaveOperation:
delegate:didSaveSelector:contextInfo:
NSDocument

runModalSession: NSApplication

runModalWithPrintInfo: NSPageLayout

runMode:beforeDate: NSRunLoop

runOperation NSPrintOperation

runOperationModalForWindow:delegate:
didRunSelector:contextInfo:
NSPrintOperation

runPageLayout: NSApplication, NSDocument

runToolbarCustomizationPalette: NSWindow

runUntilDate: NSRunLoop

S

samplesPerPixel NSBitmapImageRep

saturationComponent NSColor

saveAllDocuments: NSDocumentController

saveDocument: NSDocument

---

saveDocumentAs: NSDocument

saveDocumentTo: NSDocument

saveDocumentWithDelegate:
didSaveSelector:contextInfo: NSDocument

saveFrameUsingName: NSWindow

saveGraphicsState NSGraphicsContext

saveOptions NSQuitCommand,
NSCloseCommand

savePanel NSSavePanel

saveToFile:saveOperation:delegate:
didSaveSelector:contextInfo: NSDocument

scaleBy: NSAffineTransform

scaleUnitSquareToSize: NSView

scaleXBy:yBy: NSAffineTransform

scalesWhenResized NSImage

scanCharactersFromSet:intoString: NSScanner

scanDecimal: NSScanner

scanDouble: NSScanner

scanFloat: NSScanner

scanHexInt: NSScanner

scanInt: NSScanner

scanLocation NSScanner

scanLongLong: NSScanner

scanString:intoString: NSScanner

scanUpToCharactersFromSet:intoString:
NSScanner

scanUpToString:intoString: NSScanner

scannerWithString: NSScanner

scheduleInRunLoop:forMode: NSNetService-
Browser, NSNetService, NSPort, NSMachPort

scheduledTimerWithTimeInterval:invocation:
repeats: NSTimer

scheduledTimerWithTimeInterval:target:
selector:userInfo:repeats: NSTimer

scheme NSURL

screen NSWindow

screenFont NSFont

screens NSScreen

scriptErrorNumber NSScriptCommand

scriptErrorString NSScriptCommand

scrollBarColor NSColor

scrollCellToVisibleAtRow:column: NSMatrix

scrollClipView:toPoint: NSView

scrollColumnToVisible: NSTableView,
NSBrowser

scrollColumnsLeftBy: NSBrowser

scrollColumnsRightBy: NSBrowser

scrollItemAtIndexToTop: NSComboBoxCell,
NSComboBox

scrollItemAtIndexToVisible: NSComboBoxCell,
NSComboBox

scrollLineDown: NSResponder

scrollLineUp: NSResponder

scrollPageDown: NSResponder

scrollPageUp: NSResponder

scrollPoint: NSView

scrollRangeToVisible: NSText

scrollRect:by: NSView

scrollRectToVisible: NSView

scrollRowToVisible: NSTableView

scrollToPoint: NSClipView

scrollViaScroller: NSBrowser

scrollView NSRulerView

scrollWheel: NSResponder, NSScrollView

scrollerWidth NSScroller

scrollerWidthForControlSize: NSScroller

scrollsDynamically NSScrollView

searchForAllDomains NSNetServiceBrowser

searchForRegistrationDomains
NSNetServiceBrowser

searchForServicesOfType:inDomain:
NSNetServiceBrowser

secondOfMinute NSCalendarDate

secondarySelectedControlColor NSColor

secondsFromGMT NSTimeZone

secondsFromGMTForDate: NSTimeZone

seekToEndOfFile NSFileHandle

seekToFileOffset: NSFileHandle

selectAll: NSTableView, NSResponder,
NSMovieView, NSMatrix, NSBrowser, NSText

selectCell: NSControl

selectCellAtRow:column: NSMatrix

selectCellWithTag: NSMatrix

selectColumn:byExtendingSelection:
NSTableView

selectFile:inFileViewerRootedAtPath:
NSWorkspace

selectFirstTabViewItem: NSTabView

selectItem: NSPopUpButton, NSPopUpButtonCell

selectItemAtIndex: NSPopUpButton, NSPopUpButtonCell, NSComboBoxCell, NSComboBox

selectItemWithObjectValue: NSComboBoxCell, NSComboBox

selectItemWithTitle: NSPopUpButton, NSPopUpButtonCell

selectKeyViewFollowingView: NSWindow

selectKeyViewPrecedingView: NSWindow

selectLastTabViewItem: NSTabView

selectLine: NSResponder

selectNextKeyView: NSWindow

selectNextTabViewItem: NSTabView

selectParagraph: NSResponder

selectPreviousKeyView: NSWindow

selectPreviousTabViewItem: NSTabView

selectRow:byExtendingSelection: NSTableView

selectRow:inColumn: NSBrowser

selectTabViewItem: NSTabView

selectTabViewItemAtIndex: NSTabView

selectTabViewItemWithIdentifier: NSTabView

selectText: NSSavePanel, NSMatrix, NSTextField

selectTextAtIndex: NSForm

selectTextAtRow:column: NSMatrix

selectToMark: NSResponder

selectWithFrame:inView:editor:delegate: start:length: NSCell

selectWord: NSResponder

selectedCell NSControl, NSMatrix, NSBrowser

selectedCellInColumn: NSBrowser

selectedCells NSMatrix, NSBrowser

selectedColumn NSTableView, NSMatrix, NSBrowser

selectedColumnEnumerator NSTableView

selectedControlColor NSColor

selectedControlTextColor NSColor

selectedFont NSFontManager

selectedItem NSPopUpButton, NSPopUpButtonCell

selectedKnobColor NSColor

selectedMenuItemColor NSColor

selectedMenuItemTextColor NSColor

selectedRange NSText

selectedRow NSTableView, NSMatrix

selectedRowEnumerator NSTableView

selectedRowInColumn: NSBrowser

selectedTabViewItem NSTabView

selectedTag NSControl

selectedTextAttributes NSTextView

selectedTextBackgroundColor NSColor

selectedTextColor NSColor

selectionAffinity NSTextView

selectionGranularity NSTextView

selectionRangeForProposedRange: granularity: NSTextView

selectionShouldChangeInOutlineView: NSOutlineView

selectionShouldChangeInTableView: NSTableView

selector NSInvocation

selectorForCommand: NSScriptClassDescription

sendAction NSFontManager, NSMatrix, NSBrowser

sendAction:to: NSControl

sendAction:to:forAllCells: NSMatrix

sendAction:to:from: NSApplication

sendActionOn: NSControl, NSCell, NSStatusItem

sendBeforeDate: NSPortMessage

sendBeforeDate:components:from:reserved: NSPort

sendBeforeDate:msgid:components: from:reserved: NSPort

sendDoubleAction NSMatrix

sendEvent: NSWindow, NSApplication

sendPort NSPortMessage, NSConnection

sendsActionOnArrowKeys NSBrowser

sendsActionOnEndEditing NSCell

separatesColumns NSBrowser

separatorItem NSMenuItem

serializeAlignedBytesLength: NSMutableData

serializeDataAt:ofObjCType:context: NSMutableData

serializeInt: NSMutableData

serializeInt:atIndex: NSMutableData

serializeInts:count: NSMutableData
serializeInts:count:atIndex: NSMutableData
serializePropertyList: NSSerializer
serializePropertyList:intoData: NSSerializer
serializedRepresentation NSFileWrapper
server NSInputManager
servicesMenu NSApplication
servicesProvider NSApplication
set NSBrowserCell, NSCursor, NSColor, NSSet,
NSAffineTransform, NSFont
setAcceptsArrowKeys: NSBrowser
setAcceptsGlyphInfo: NSTextView
setAcceptsMouseMovedEvents: NSWindow
setAccessoryView: NSSavePanel, NSPrintPanel,
NSPrintOperation, NSFontPanel,
NSSpellChecker, NSColorPanel,
NSPageLayout, NSRulerView
setAction: NSControl, NSMenuItem, NSCell,
NSFontManager, NSToolbarItem,
NSActionCell, NSColorPanel, NSStatusItem
setActionName: NSUndoManager
setAlignment: NSMutableParagraphStyle,
NSControl, NSCell, NSActionCell, NSText
setAlignment:range: NSTextView,
NSMutableAttributedString
setAllowsBranchSelection: NSBrowser
setAllowsColumnReordering: NSTableView
setAllowsColumnResizing: NSTableView
setAllowsColumnSelection: NSTableView
setAllowsEditingTextAttributes: NSCell,
NSTextField
setAllowsEmptySelection: NSTableView,
NSMatrix, NSBrowser
setAllowsFloats: NSNumberFormatter
setAllowsMixedState: NSCell, NSButton
setAllowsMultipleSelection: NSOpenPanel,
NSTableView, NSBrowser
setAllowsTickMarkValuesOnly: NSSliderCell
setAllowsTruncatedLabels: NSTabView
setAllowsUndo: NSTextView
setAllowsUserCustomization: NSToolbar
setAlpha: NSImageRep
setAlphaValue: NSWindow
setAltIncrementValue: NSSlider, NSSliderCell

setAlternateImage: NSBrowserCell,
NSButtonCell, NSButton
setAlternateTitle: NSButtonCell, NSButton
setAltersStateOfSelectedItem:
NSPopUpButtonCell
setAnimationDelay: NSProgressIndicator
setAppleMenu: NSApplication
setApplicationIconImage: NSApplication
setArgument:atIndex: NSInvocation
setArguments: NSTask, NSScriptCommand
setArray: NSMutableArray
setArrowPosition: NSPopUpButtonCell
setArrowsPosition: NSScroller
setAspectRatio: NSWindow
setAssociatedPoints:atIndex: NSBezierPath
setAttachmentCell: NSTextAttachment
setAttachmentSize:forGlyphRange:
NSLayoutManager
setAttributeDescriptor:forKeyword:
NSAppleEventDescriptor
setAttributeRuns: NSTextStorage
setAttributedAlternateTitle: NSButtonCell,
NSButton
setAttributedString:
NSMutableAttributedString
setAttributedStringForNil:
NSNumberFormatter
setAttributedStringForNotANumber:
NSNumberFormatter
setAttributedStringForZero:
NSNumberFormatter
setAttributedStringValue: NSControl, NSCell
setAttributedTitle: NSButtonCell, NSFormCell,
NSButton, NSStatusItem
setAttributes: NSOpenGLPixelFormat
setAttributes:range:
NSMutableAttributedString
setAutodisplay: NSWindow
setAutoenablesItems: NSPopUpButton,
NSPopUpButtonCell, NSMenu
setAutorepeat: NSStepperCell, NSStepper
setAutoresizesAllColumnsToFit: NSTableView
setAutoresizesOutlineColumn: NSOutlineView
setAutoresizesSubviews: NSView
setAutoresizingMask: NSView

setAutosaveExpandedItems: NSOutlineView

setAutosaveName: NSTableView

setAutosaveTableColumns: NSTableView

setAutosavesConfiguration: NSToolbar

setAutoscroll: NSMatrix

setAutosizesCells: NSMatrix

setBackgroundColor: NSImage, NSWindow, NSTextFieldCell, NSTableView, NSTextView, NSScrollView, NSClipView, NSMatrix, NSTextField, NSText

setBackgroundLayoutEnabled: NSLayoutManager

setBackingType: NSWindow

setBaseSpecifier: NSRelativeSpecifier

setBaseWritingDirection: NSMutableParagraphStyle

setBecomesKeyOnlyIfNeeded: NSPanel

setBezelStyle: NSTextFieldCell, NSButtonCell, NSButton, NSTextField

setBezeled: NSProgressIndicator, NSCell, NSForm, NSActionCell, NSTextField

setBitsPerSample: NSImageRep

setBool:forKey: NSUserDefaults

setBorderType: NSBox, NSScrollView

setBordered: NSCell, NSForm, NSButton, NSColorWell, NSActionCell, NSTextField

setBottomMargin: NSPrintInfo

setBounds: NSView

setBoundsOrigin: NSView

setBoundsRotation: NSView

setBoundsSize: NSView

setBoxType: NSBox

setButtonType: NSButtonCell, NSButton

setCacheDepthMatchesImageDepth: NSImage

setCacheMode: NSImage

setCachedSeparately: NSImage

setCachesBezierPath: NSBezierPath

setCalendarFormat: NSCalendarDate

setCanChooseDirectories: NSOpenPanel

setCanChooseFiles: NSOpenPanel

setCanHide: NSWindow

setCanSelectHiddenExtension: NSSavePanel

setCanSpawnSeparateThread: NSPrintOperation

setCaseSensitive: NSScanner

setCell: NSControl

setCellAttribute:to: NSCell

setCellBackgroundColor: NSMatrix

setCellClass: NSControl, NSMatrix, NSBrowser

setCellPrototype: NSBrowser

setCellSize: NSMatrix

setCharacterIndex:forGlyphAtIndex: NSLayoutManager

setCharacters: NSTextStorage

setCharactersToBeSkipped: NSScanner

setChildSpecifier: NSScriptObjectSpecifier

setClass:forClassName: NSKeyed Unarchiver

setClassName:forClass: NSKeyedArchiver

setClientView: NSRulerView

setClip NSBezierPath

setColor: NSTabViewItem, NSColorWell, NSColorPanel

setColor:forKey: NSColorList

setColorSpaceName: NSImageRep

setCompletes: NSComboBoxCell, NSComboBox

setCompression:factor: NSBitmapImageRep

setConfigurationFromDictionary: NSToolbar

setConstrainedFrameSize: NSTextView

setContainerClassDescription: NSScriptObjectSpecifier

setContainerIsObjectBeingTested: NSScriptObjectSpecifier

setContainerIsRangeContainerObject: NSScriptObjectSpecifier

setContainerSize: NSTextContainer

setContainerSpecifier: NSScriptObjectSpecifier

setContentSize: NSWindow, NSDrawer

setContentView: NSWindow, NSBox, NSScrollView, NSDrawer

setContentViewMargins: NSBox

setContextHelp:forObject: NSHelpManager

setContextHelpModeActive: NSHelpManager

setContextMenuRepresentation: NSMenu

setContinuous: NSControl, NSCell, NSColorPanel

setContinuousSpellCheckingEnabled: NSTextView

setControlSize: NSProgressIndicator, NSCell, NSTabView, NSScroller

setControlTint: NSProgressIndicator, NSCell, NSTabView, NSScroller

setCopiesOnScroll: NSClipView

setCornerView: NSTableView

setCurrentContext: NSGraphicsContext

setCurrentDirectoryPath: NSTask

setCurrentOperation: NSPrintOperation

setCurrentPage: NSPDFImageRep

setCurrentVirtualScreen: NSOpenGLContext

setData: NSMutableData

setData:forType: NSPasteboard

setDataCell: NSTableColumn

setDataRetained: NSImage

setDataSource: NSTableView, NSComboBoxCell, NSComboBox

setDecimalSeparator: NSNumberFormatter

setDefaultAttachmentScaling: NSLayoutManager

setDefaultBehavior: NSDecimalNumber

setDefaultButtonCell: NSWindow

setDefaultFlatness: NSBezierPath

setDefaultLineCapStyle: NSBezierPath

setDefaultLineJoinStyle: NSBezierPath

setDefaultLineWidth: NSBezierPath

setDefaultMiterLimit: NSBezierPath

setDefaultNameServerPortNumber: NSSocketPortNameServer

setDefaultPrinter: NSPrintInfo

setDefaultTimeZone: NSTimeZone

setDefaultWindingRule: NSBezierPath

setDelegate: NSImage, NSTextStorage, NSWindow, NSSavePanel, NSTableView, NSSound, NSKeyedUnarchiver, NSNetServiceBrowser, NSSplitView, NSTextView, NSNetService, NSLayoutManager, NSFontManager, NSDrawer, NSMatrix, NSApplication, NSPort, NSSpellServer, NSToolbar, NSKeyedArchiver, NSTabView, NSBrowser, NSConnection, NSTextField, NSText

setDepthLimit: NSWindow

setDescriptor:forKeyword: NSAppleEventDescriptor

setDestination: NSNibConnector

setDictionary: NSMutableDictionary

setDirectParameter: NSScriptCommand

setDirectory: NSSavePanel

setDisplayMode: NSToolbar

setDisplayedWhenStopped: NSProgressIndicator

setDocument: NSWindowController

setDocumentCursor: NSScrollView, NSClipView

setDocumentEdited: NSWindow, NSWindowController

setDocumentView: NSScrollView, NSClipView

setDoubleAction: NSTableView, NSMatrix, NSBrowser

setDoubleValue: NSProgressIndicator, NSControl, NSCell

setDrawsBackground: NSTextFieldCell, NSTextView, NSScrollView, NSClipView, NSMatrix, NSTabView, NSTextField, NSText

setDrawsCellBackground: NSMatrix

setDrawsGrid: NSTableView

setDrawsOutsideLineFragment:forGlyphAtIndex: NSLayoutManager

setDropItem:dropChildIndex: NSOutlineView

setDropRow:dropOperation: NSTableView

setDynamicDepthLimit: NSWindow

setEchosBullets: NSSecureTextFieldCell

setEditable: NSTableColumn, NSTextView, NSCell, NSMovieView, NSImageView, NSTextField, NSText

setEnabled: NSControl, NSMenuItem, NSCell, NSFontManager, NSToolbarItem, NSFontPanel, NSActionCell, NSStatusItem

setEndSpecifier: NSRangeSpecifier

setEndSubelementIdentifier: NSWhoseSpecifier

setEndSubelementIndex: NSWhoseSpecifier

setEntryType: NSCell

setEntryWidth: NSForm

setEnvironment: NSTask

setEvaluationErrorNumber: NSScriptObjectSpecifier

setEventHandler:andSelector:forEventClass:andEventID: NSAppleEventManager

setExcludedFromWindowsMenu: NSWindow

setExtensionHidden: NSSavePanel

setExtraLineFragmentRect:usedRect:textContainer: NSLayoutManager setFieldEditor: NSTextView, NSText

setFileAttributes: NSFileWrapper

setFileName: NSDocument

setFileType: NSDocument

setFileWrapper: NSTextAttachment

setFilename: NSFileWrapper

setFireDate: NSTimer

setFirstLineHeadIndent:
NSMutableParagraphStyle

setFlatness: NSBezierPath

setFlipped: NSImage

setFloat:forKey: NSUserDefaults

setFloatValue: NSControl, NSCell

setFloatValue:knobProportion: NSScroller

setFloatingPanel: NSPanel

setFloatingPointFormat:left:right: NSControl,
NSCell, NSActionCell

setFocusStack: NSGraphicsContext

setFont: NSTextStorage, NSControl,
NSButtonCell, NSCell, NSTabView,
NSActionCell, NSMenuView, NSText

setFont:range: NSText

setFontManagerFactory: NSFontManager

setFontMenu: NSFontManager

setFontPanelFactory: NSFontManager

setForegroundColor: NSTextStorage

setFormat: NSNumberFormatter

setFormatter: NSControl, NSCell

setFrame: NSView

setFrame:display: NSWindow

setFrame:display:animate: NSWindow

setFrameAutosaveName: NSWindow

setFrameFromContentFrame: NSBox

setFrameFromString: NSWindow

setFrameOrigin: NSWindow, NSView

setFrameRotation: NSView

setFrameSize: NSView

setFrameTopLeftPoint: NSWindow

setFrameUsingName: NSWindow

setFrameUsingName:force: NSWindow

setFullScreen NSOpenGLContext

setGradientType: NSButtonCell

setGraphicsState: NSGraphicsContext

setGridColor: NSTableView

setGroupsByEvent: NSUndoManager

setHasHorizontalRuler: NSScrollView

setHasHorizontalScroller: NSScrollView,
NSBrowser

setHasShadow: NSWindow

setHasThousandSeparators:
NSNumberFormatter

setHasUndoManager: NSDocument

setHasVerticalRuler: NSScrollView

setHasVerticalScroller: NSComboBoxCell,
NSScrollView, NSComboBox

setHeadIndent: NSMutableParagraphStyle

setHeaderCell: NSTableColumn

setHeaderView: NSTableView

setHeightTracksTextView: NSTextContainer

setHiddenUntilMouseMoves: NSCursor

setHidesOnDeactivate: NSWindow

setHighlightMode: NSStatusItem

setHighlighted: NSCell, NSMenuItemCell

setHighlightedItemIndex: NSMenuView

setHighlightedTableColumn: NSTableView

setHighlightsBy: NSButtonCell

setHorizontal: NSMenuView

setHorizontalEdgePadding: NSMenuView

setHorizontalLineScroll: NSScrollView

setHorizontalPageScroll: NSScrollView

setHorizontalPagination: NSPrintInfo

setHorizontalRulerView: NSScrollView

setHorizontalScroller: NSScrollView

setHorizontallyCentered: NSPrintInfo

setHorizontallyResizable: NSText

setHostCacheEnabled: NSHost

setHyphenationFactor: NSLayoutManager

setIcon: NSFileWrapper

setIdentifier: NSTableColumn, NSTabViewItem

setIgnoredWords:inSpellDocumentWithTag:
NSSpellChecker

setIgnoresAlpha: NSColor

setIgnoresMouseEvents: NSWindow

setIgnoresMultiClick: NSControl

setImage: NSSlider, NSBrowserCell,
NSMenuItem, NSCell, NSToolbarItem,
NSButton, NSImageView, NSRulerMarker,
NSActionCell, NSStatusItem

setImageAlignment: NSImageCell, NSImageView

setImageDimsWhenDisabled: NSButtonCell

setImageFrameStyle: NSImageCell, NSImageView

setImageInterpolation: NSGraphicsContext

setImageOrigin: NSRulerMarker

setImagePosition: NSButtonCell, NSButton

setImageScaling: NSImageCell, NSImageView

setImportsGraphics: NSTextView, NSCell, NSTextField, NSText

setIncrement: NSStepperCell, NSStepper

setIndentationMarkerFollowsCell: NSOutlineView

setIndentationPerLevel: NSOutlineView

setIndependentConversationQueueing: NSConnection

setIndeterminate: NSProgressIndicator

setIndex: NSIndexSpecifier

setIndicatorImage:inTableColumn: NSTableView

setInitialFirstResponder: NSWindow, NSTabViewItem

setInsertionClassDescription: NSPositionalSpecifier

setInsertionPointColor: NSTextView

setIntAttribute:value:forGlyphAtIndex: NSLayoutManager

setIntValue: NSControl, NSCell

setInteger:forKey: NSUserDefaults

setIntercellSpacing: NSTableView, NSComboBoxCell, NSMatrix, NSComboBox

setInterfaceStyle: NSResponder

setInterlineSpacing: NSForm

setIsMiniaturized: NSWindow

setIsPaneSplitter: NSSplitView

setIsVisible: NSWindow

setIsZoomed: NSWindow

setItemHeight: NSComboBoxCell, NSComboBox

setJobDisposition: NSPrintInfo

setJobStyleHint: NSPrintPanel, NSPrintOperation

setKey: NSScriptObjectSpecifier

setKeyEquivalent: NSButtonCell, NSMenuItem, NSButton

setKeyEquivalentFont: NSButtonCell

setKeyEquivalentFont:size: NSButtonCell

setKeyEquivalentModifierMask: NSButtonCell, NSMenuItem, NSButton

setKnobThickness: NSSlider, NSSliderCell

setLabel: NSNibConnector, NSTabViewItem, NSToolbarItem

setLanguage: NSSpellChecker

setLastColumn: NSBrowser

setLaunchPath: NSTask

setLayoutManager: NSTextContainer

setLeadingOffset: NSDrawer

setLeaf: NSBrowserCell

setLeftMargin: NSPrintInfo

setLength: NSMutableData, NSStatusItem

setLevel: NSWindow

setLevelsOfUndo: NSUndoManager

setLineBreakMode: NSMutableParagraphStyle

setLineCapStyle: NSBezierPath

setLineDash:count:phase: NSBezierPath

setLineFragmentPadding: NSTextContainer

setLineFragmentRect:forGlyphRange:usedRect: NSLayoutManager

setLineJoinStyle: NSBezierPath

setLineScroll: NSScrollView

setLineSpacing: NSMutableParagraphStyle

setLineWidth: NSBezierPath

setLoaded: NSBrowserCell

setLocale: NSScanner

setLocalizesFormat: NSNumberFormatter

setLocation:forStartOfGlyphRange: NSLayoutManager

setLoopMode: NSMovieView

setMainMenu: NSApplication

setMark: NSResponder

setMarkedTextAttributes: NSTextView

setMarkerLocation: NSRulerMarker

setMarkers: NSRulerView

setMatchesOnMultipleResolution: NSImage

setMatrixClass: NSBrowser

setMaxContentSize: NSDrawer

setMaxSize: NSWindow, NSToolbarItem, NSText

setMaxValue: NSSlider, NSProgressIndicator, NSSliderCell, NSStepperCell, NSStepper

setMaxVisibleColumns: NSBrowser
setMaxWidth: NSTableColumn
setMaximum: NSNumberFormatter
setMaximumLineHeight:
  NSMutableParagraphStyle
setMeasurementUnits: NSRulerView
setMenu: NSPopUpButton, NSPopUpButtonCell,
  NSResponder, NSMenuItem, NSCell,
  NSStatusItem, NSMenuView
setMenuBarVisible: NSMenu
setMenuChangedMessagesEnabled: NSMenu
setMenuFormRepresentation: NSToolbarItem
setMenuItem: NSMenuItemCell
setMenuItemCell:forItemAtIndex:
  NSMenuView
setMenuRepresentation: NSMenu
setMenuView: NSMenuItemCell
setMenuZone: NSMenu
setMinColumnWidth: NSBrowser
setMinContentSize: NSDrawer
setMinSize: NSWindow, NSToolbarItem, NSText
setMinValue: NSSlider, NSProgressIndicator,
  NSSliderCell, NSStepperCell, NSStepper
setMinWidth: NSTableColumn
setMinimum: NSNumberFormatter
setMinimumLineHeight:
  NSMutableParagraphStyle
setMiniwindowImage: NSWindow
setMiniwindowTitle: NSWindow
setMiterLimit: NSBezierPath
setMixedStateImage: NSMenuItem
setMnemonicLocation: NSMenuItem
setMode: NSColorPicker, NSMatrix, NSColorPanel
setMovable: NSRulerMarker
setMovableByWindowBackground: NSWindow
setMovie: NSMovieView
setMsgid: NSPortMessage
setMuted: NSMovieView
setName: NSImage, NSSound, NSNameSpecifier
setNeedsDisplay NSControl
setNeedsDisplay: NSMenuItemCell, NSView
setNeedsDisplayForItemAtIndex: NSMenuView
setNeedsDisplayInRect: NSView

setNeedsDisplayInRect:
  avoidAdditionalLayout: NSTextView
setNeedsSizing: NSMenuItemCell, NSMenuView
setNegativeFormat: NSNumberFormatter
setNextResponder: NSResponder
setNextState NSCell, NSButton
setNotShownAttribute:forGlyphAtIndex:
  NSLayoutManager
setNumberOfTickMarks: NSSliderCell
setNumberOfVisibleItems: NSComboBoxCell,
  NSComboBox
setObject:forKey: NSUserDefaults,
  NSMutableDictionary
setObjectBeingTested:
  NSScriptExecutionContext
setObjectValue: NSControl, NSCell, NSActionCell
setObjectZone: NSCoder, NSUnarchiver
setOffScreen:width:height:rowbytes:
  NSOpenGLContext
setOffStateImage: NSMenuItem
setOnMouseEntered: NSCursor
setOnMouseExited: NSCursor
setOnStateImage: NSMenuItem
setOneShot: NSWindow
setOpaque: NSWindow, NSImageRep
setOpenGLContext: NSOpenGLView
setOrderedIndex: NSWindow
setOrientation: NSPrintInfo, NSRulerView
setOriginOffset: NSRulerView
setOutlineTableColumn: NSOutlineView
setOutputFormat: NSKeyedArchiver
setPageOrder: NSPrintOperation
setPageScroll: NSScrollView
setPaletteLabel: NSToolbarItem
setPanelFont:isMultiple: NSFontPanel
setPaperName: NSPrintInfo
setPaperSize: NSPrintInfo
setParagraphSpacing:
  NSMutableParagraphStyle
setParagraphStyle: NSMutableParagraphStyle
setParagraphs: NSTextStorage
setParamDescriptor:forKeyword:
  NSAppleEventDescriptor
setParentWindow: NSWindow, NSDrawer

Method Index

setSelectionFrom:to:anchor:highlight:
 NSMatrix
setSelectionGranularity: NSTextView
setSelector: NSInvocation
setSendsActionOnArrowKeys: NSBrowser
setSendsActionOnEndEditing: NSCell
setSeparatesColumns: NSBrowser
setServicesMenu: NSApplication
setServicesProvider: NSApplication
setSet: NSMutableSet
setSharedPrintInfo: NSPrintInfo
setSharedScriptSuiteRegistry:
 NSScriptSuiteRegistry
setShouldAntialias: NSGraphicsContext
setShouldCascadeWindows:
 NSWindowController
setShouldCloseDocument:
 NSWindowController
setShouldCreateUI: NSDocumentController
setShowPanels: NSPrintOperation
setShowsAlpha: NSColorPanel
setShowsBorderOnlyWhileMouseInside:
 NSButtonCell, NSButton
setShowsControlCharacters: NSLayoutManager
setShowsInvisibleCharacters:
 NSLayoutManager
setShowsResizeIndicator: NSWindow
setShowsStateBy: NSButtonCell
setSize: NSImage, NSImageRep
setSizeMode: NSToolbar
setSmartInsertDeleteEnabled: NSTextView
setSound: NSButtonCell, NSButton
setSource: NSNibConnector
setStandardError: NSTask
setStandardInput: NSTask
setStandardOutput: NSTask
setStartSpecifier: NSRangeSpecifier
setStartSubelementIdentifier:
 NSWhoseSpecifier
setStartSubelementIndex: NSWhoseSpecifier
setState: NSMenuItem, NSCell, NSButton
setState:atRow:column: NSMatrix
setString: NSMutableString, NSText
setString:forType: NSPasteboard

setStringValue: NSControl, NSCell
setStyle: NSProgressIndicator
setSubmenu: NSMenuItem
setSubmenu:forItem: NSMenu
setSupermenu: NSMenu
setSuspended: NSDistributedNotificationCenter
setTabStops: NSMutableParagraphStyle
setTabViewType: NSTabView
setTableView: NSTableColumn,
 NSTableHeaderView
setTag: NSControl, NSMenuItem, NSCell,
 NSToolbarItem, NSActionCell
setTailIndent: NSMutableParagraphStyle
setTakesTitleFromPreviousColumn: NSBrowser
setTarget: NSControl, NSMenuItem, NSCell,
 NSToolbarItem, NSActionCell, NSColorPanel,
 NSStatusItem, NSInvocation
setTearOffMenuRepresentation: NSMenu
setTemporaryAttributes:forCharacterRange:
 NSLayoutManager
setTest: NSWhoseSpecifier
setTextAlignment: NSForm
setTextAttributesForNegativeValues:
 NSNumberFormatter
setTextAttributesForPositiveValues:
 NSNumberFormatter
setTextColor: NSTextFieldCell, NSTextField,
 NSText
setTextColor:range: NSText
setTextContainer: NSTextView
setTextContainer:forGlyphRange:
 NSLayoutManager
setTextContainerInset: NSTextView
setTextFont: NSForm
setTextStorage: NSLayoutManager
setTextView: NSTextContainer
setThousandSeparator: NSNumberFormatter
setThreadPriority: NSThread
setTickMarkPosition: NSSliderCell
setTimeZone: NSCalendarDate
setTitle: NSSlider, NSPopUpButton, NSWindow,
 NSSavePanel, NSPopUpButtonCell, NSMenu,
 NSSliderCell, NSButtonCell, NSBox,
 NSFormCell, NSMenuItem, NSCell, NSButton,
 NSStatusItem

setTitle:ofColumn: NSBrowser

setTitleAlignment: NSFormCell, NSForm

setTitleCell: NSSlider, NSSliderCell

setTitleColor: NSSlider, NSSliderCell

setTitleFont: NSSlider, NSSliderCell, NSBox,
NSFormCell, NSForm

setTitlePosition: NSBox

setTitleWidth: NSFormCell

setTitleWithMnemonic: NSMenuItem

setTitleWithRepresentedFilename: NSWindow

setTitled: NSBrowser

setToolTip: NSToolbarItem, NSStatusItem,
NSView

setToolTip:forCell: NSMatrix

setToolbar: NSWindow

setTopLevelObject: NSScriptExecutionContext

setTopMargin: NSPrintInfo

setTrailingOffset: NSDrawer

setTransformStruct: NSAffineTransform

setTransparent: NSButtonCell, NSButton

setTreatsFilePackagesAsDirectories:
NSSavePanel

setType: NSCell

setTypesetter: NSLayoutManager

setTypesetterBehavior: NSLayoutManager

setTypingAttributes: NSTextView

setUndoManager: NSDocument

setUniqueID: NSUniqueIDSpecifier

setUpFieldEditorAttributes: NSTextFieldCell,
NSCell

setUpGState NSView

setUpPrintOperationDefaultValues NSPrintInfo

setUserFixedPitchFont: NSFont

setUserFont: NSFont

setUsesDataSource: NSComboBoxCell,
NSComboBox

setUsesEPSOnResolutionMismatch: NSImage

setUsesFontPanel: NSTextView, NSText

setUsesItemFromMenu: NSPopUpButtonCell

setUsesRuler: NSTextView

setUsesScreenFonts: NSLayoutManager

setUsesThreadedAnimation:
NSProgressIndicator

setUsesUserKeyEquivalents: NSMenuItem

setValidateSize: NSMatrix

setValueWraps: NSStepperCell, NSStepper

setValues:forParameter: NSOpenGLContext

setVersion: NSObject

setVertical: NSSplitView

setVerticalLineScroll: NSScrollView

setVerticalMotionCanBeginDrag: NSTableView

setVerticalPageScroll: NSScrollView

setVerticalPagination: NSPrintInfo

setVerticalRulerView: NSScrollView

setVerticalScroller: NSScrollView

setVerticallyCentered: NSPrintInfo

setVerticallyResizable: NSText

setView: NSOpenGLContext, NSTabViewItem,
NSToolbarItem, NSStatusItem

setViewsNeedDisplay: NSWindow

setVisible: NSToolbar

setVolatileDomain:forName: NSUserDefaults

setVolume: NSMovieView

setWidth: NSTableColumn

setWidthTracksTextView: NSTextContainer

setWindingRule: NSBezierPath

setWindow: NSWindowController, NSDocument

setWindowController: NSWindow

setWindowFrameAutosaveName:
NSWindowController

**setWindowFrameForAttachingToRect:
onScreen:preferredEdge:
popUpSelectedItem:** NSMenuView

setWindowsMenu: NSApplication

setWindowsNeedUpdate: NSApplication

setWithArray: NSSet

setWithCapacity: NSMutableSet

setWithObject: NSSet

setWithObjects:... NSSet

setWithObjects:count: NSSet

setWithSet: NSSet

setWordFieldStringValue: NSSpellChecker

setWords: NSTextStorage

setWorksWhenModal: NSPanel

setWraps: NSCell

shadowColor NSColor

shadowWithLevel: NSColor

Method Index

sharedAppleEventManager
NSAppleEventManager

sharedApplication NSApplication

sharedCoercionHandler
NSScriptCoercionHandler

sharedColorPanel NSColorPanel

sharedColorPanelExists NSColorPanel

sharedDocumentController
NSDocumentController

sharedFontManager NSFontManager

sharedFontPanel NSFontPanel

sharedFontPanelExists NSFontPanel

sharedFrameworksPath NSBundle

sharedHelpManager NSHelpManager

sharedInstance NSSocketPortNameServer,
NSSimpleHorizontalTypesetter,
NSMessagePortNameServer,
NSMachBootstrapServer

sharedPrintInfo NSPrintInfo

sharedScriptExecutionContext
NSScriptExecutionContext

sharedScriptSuiteRegistry
NSScriptSuiteRegistry

sharedSpellChecker NSSpellChecker

sharedSpellCheckerExists NSSpellChecker

sharedSupportPath NSBundle

sharedSystemTypesetter NSTypesetter

sharedSystemTypesetterForBehavior:
NSTypesetter

sharedWorkspace NSWorkspace

shortValue NSNumber

shouldAntialias NSGraphicsContext

shouldBeTreatedAsInkEvent: NSResponder

shouldCascadeWindows NSWindowController

shouldChangePrintInfo: NSDocument

shouldChangeTextInRange:
replacementString: NSTextView

shouldCloseDocument NSWindowController

shouldCloseWindowController: NSDocument

shouldCloseWindowController:delegate:
shouldCloseSelector:contextInfo:
NSDocument

shouldCollapseAutoExpandedItemsFor-
Deposited: NSOutlineView

shouldCreateUI NSDocumentController

shouldDelayWindowOrderingForEvent:
NSView

shouldDrawColor NSView

shouldDrawInsertionPoint NSTextView

shouldRunSavePanelWithAccessoryView
NSDocument

showAttachmentCell:inRect:characterIndex:
NSLayoutManager

showContextHelp: NSResponder

showContextHelpForObject:locationHint:
NSHelpManager

showController:adjustingSize: NSMovieView

showGuessPanel: NSText

showHelp: NSApplication

showPackedGlyphs:length:glyphRange:
atPoint:font:color:printingAdjustment:
NSLayoutManager

showPanels NSPrintOperation

showPools NSAutoreleasePool

showWindow: NSWindowController

showWindows NSDocument

showsAlpha NSColorPanel

showsBorderOnlyWhileMouseInside
NSButtonCell, NSButton

showsControlCharacters NSLayoutManager

showsInvisibleCharacters NSLayoutManager

showsResizeIndicator NSWindow

showsStateBy NSButtonCell

size NSImage, NSAttributedString, NSImageRep

sizeForKey:inTable: NSPrinter

sizeForMagnification: NSMovieView

sizeForPaperName: NSPrintInfo

sizeLastColumnToFit NSTableView

sizeMode NSToolbar

sizeOfLabel: NSTabViewItem

sizeOfTypesetterGlyphInfo
NSSimpleHorizontalTypesetter

sizeToCells NSMatrix

sizeToFit NSTableColumn, NSMenu,
NSProgressIndicator, NSControl, NSBox,
NSMenuView, NSText

sizeValue NSValue

skipDescendents NSDirectoryEnumerator

sleepUntilDate: NSThread

slideImage:from:to: NSWorkspace

smallSystemFontSize NSFont

smallestEncoding NSString

smartDeleteRangeForProposedRange:
    NSTextView

smartInsertAfterStringForString:
    replacingRange: NSTextView

smartInsertBeforeStringForString:
    replacingRange: NSTextView

smartInsertDeleteEnabled NSTextView

smartInsertForString:replacingRange:
    beforeString:afterString: NSTextView

socket NSSocketPort

socketType NSSocketPort

sortSubviewsUsingFunction:context: NSView

sortUsingFunction:context: NSMutableArray,
    NSMatrix

sortUsingSelector: NSMutableArray, NSMatrix

sortedArrayHint NSArray

sortedArrayUsingFunction:context: NSArray

sortedArrayUsingFunction:context:hint:
    NSArray

sortedArrayUsingSelector: NSArray

sound NSButtonCell, NSButton

sound:didFinishPlaying: NSSound

soundNamed: NSSound

soundUnfilteredFileTypes NSSound

soundUnfilteredPasteboardTypes NSSound

source NSAppleScript, NSNibConnector

spellCheckerDocumentTag NSTextView

spellServer:didForgetWord:inLanguage:
    NSSpellServer

spellServer:didLearnWord:inLanguage:
    NSSpellServer

spellServer:findMisspelledWordInString:
    language:wordCount:countOnly:
    NSSpellServer

spellServer:suggestGuessesForWord:
    inLanguage: NSSpellServer

spellingPanel NSSpellChecker

splitView:canCollapseSubview: NSSplitView

splitView:constrainMaxCoordinate:
    ofSubviewAt: NSSplitView

splitView:constrainMinCoordinate:
    ofSubviewAt: NSSplitView

splitView:constrainSplitPosition:
    ofSubviewAt: NSSplitView

splitView:resizeSubviewsWithOldSize:
    NSSplitView

splitViewDidResizeSubviews: NSSplitView

splitViewWillResizeSubviews: NSSplitView

standardError NSTask

standardInput NSTask

standardOutput NSTask

standardUserDefaults NSUserDefaults

standardWindowButton: NSWindow

standardWindowButton:forStyleMask:
    NSWindow

standardizedURL NSURL

start: NSMovieView

startAnimation: NSProgressIndicator

startPeriodicEventsAfterDelay:withPeriod:
    NSEvent

startSpeaking: NSTextView

startSpecifier NSRangeSpecifier

startSubelementIdentifier NSWhoseSpecifier

startSubelementIndex NSWhoseSpecifier

startTrackingAt:inView: NSCell

state NSMenuItem, NSCell, NSDrawer, NSButton

stateImageOffset NSMenuView

stateImageRectForBounds: NSMenuItemCell

stateImageWidth NSMenuItemCell,
    NSMenuView

statistics NSConnection

status NSURLHandle

statusBar NSStatusItem

statusForTable: NSPrinter

statusItemWithLength: NSStatusBar

stepBack: NSMovieView

stepForward: NSMovieView

stop NSSound, NSNetServiceBrowser,
    NSNetService

stop: NSMovieView, NSApplication

stopAnimation: NSProgressIndicator

stopModal NSApplication

stopModalWithCode: NSApplication

stopPeriodicEvents NSEvent

stopSpeaking: NSTextView

stopTracking:at:inView:mouseIsUp: NSCell

string NSString, NSAttributedString, NSScanner, NSText

stringArrayForKey: NSUserDefaults

stringByAbbreviatingWithTildeInPath NSString

stringByAppendingFormat:... NSString

stringByAppendingPathComponent: NSString

stringByAppendingPathExtension: NSString

stringByAppendingString: NSString

stringByDeletingLastPathComponent NSString

stringByDeletingPathExtension NSString

stringByExpandingTildeInPath NSString

stringByPaddingToLength:withString:startingAtIndex: NSString

stringByResolvingSymlinksInPath NSString

stringByStandardizingPath NSString

stringByTrimmingCharactersInSet: NSString

stringForKey: NSUserDefaults

stringForKey:inTable: NSPrinter

stringForObjectValue: NSFormatter

stringForType: NSPasteboard

stringListForKey:inTable: NSPrinter

stringValue NSControl, NSCell, NSAppleEventDescriptor, NSNumber, NSActionCell

stringWithCString: NSString

stringWithCString:length: NSString

stringWithCapacity: NSMutableString

stringWithCharacters:length: NSString

stringWithContentsOfFile: NSString

stringWithContentsOfURL: NSString

stringWithFileSystemRepresentation:length: NSFileManager

stringWithFormat:... NSString

stringWithSavedFrame NSWindow

stringWithString: NSString

stringWithUTF8String: NSString

stringsByAppendingPaths: NSString

stroke NSBezierPath

strokeLineFromPoint:toPoint: NSBezierPath

strokeRect: NSBezierPath

style NSProgressIndicator

styleMask NSWindow

subarrayWithRange: NSArray

subdataWithRange: NSData

submenu NSMenuItem

submenuAction: NSMenu

subpathsAtPath: NSFileManager

subscript: NSText

subscriptRange: NSMutableAttributedString

substituteFontForFont: NSLayoutManager

substringFromIndex: NSString

substringToIndex: NSString

substringWithRange: NSString

subtype NSEvent

subviews NSView

suiteForAppleEventCode: NSScriptSuiteRegistry

suiteName NSScriptClassDescription, NSScriptCommandDescription

suiteNames NSScriptSuiteRegistry

superclass NSObject

superclassDescription NSScriptClassDescription

supermenu NSMenu

superscript: NSText

superscriptRange: NSMutableAttributedString

superview NSView

supportedWindowDepths NSScreen

supportsCommand: NSScriptClassDescription

suspend NSTask

suspended NSDistributedNotificationCenter

swapWithMark: NSResponder

symbolicLinkDestination NSFileWrapper

synchronize NSUserDefaults

synchronizeFile NSFileHandle

synchronizeTitleAndSelectedItem NSPopUpButton, NSPopUpButtonCell

synchronizeWindowTitleWithDocument-Name NSWindowController

systemDefaultPortNameServer NSPortNameServer

systemFontOfSize: NSFont

systemFontSize NSFont

systemStatusBar NSStatusBar

systemTimeZone NSTimeZone

systemVersion NSCoder, NSUnarchiver

T

textFileTypes NSAttributedString

textPasteboardTypes NSAttributedString

textShouldBeginEditing: NSTableView, NSMatrix, NSTextField, NSText

textShouldEndEditing: NSTableView, NSMatrix, NSTextField, NSText

textStorage NSTextView, NSLayoutManager

textStorage:edited:range:changeInLength: invalidatedRange: NSLayoutManager

textStorageDidProcessEditing: NSTextStorage

textStorageWillProcessEditing: NSTextStorage

textUnfilteredFileTypes NSAttributedString

textUnfilteredPasteboardTypes NSAttributedString

textView NSTextContainer

textView:clickedOnCell:inRect: NSTextView

textView:clickedOnCell:inRect:atIndex: NSTextView

textView:clickedOnLink: NSTextView

textView:clickedOnLink:atIndex: NSTextView

textView:doCommandBySelector: NSTextView

textView:doubleClickedOnCell:inRect: NSTextView

textView:doubleClickedOnCell:inRect: atIndex: NSTextView

textView:draggedCell:inRect:event: NSTextView

textView:draggedCell:inRect:event:atIndex: NSTextView

textView:shouldChangeTextInRange: replacementString: NSTextView

textView:willChangeSelectionFromCharacter-Range:toCharacterRange: NSTextView

textView:writablePasteboardTypesForCell: atIndex: NSTextView

textView:writeCell:atIndex:toPasteboard: type: NSTextView

textViewDidChangeSelection: NSTextView

textViewForBeginningOfSelection NSLayoutManager

thickness NSStatusBar

thicknessRequiredInRuler NSRulerMarker

thousandSeparator NSNumberFormatter

threadDictionary NSThread

threadPriority NSThread

tickMarkPosition NSSliderCell

tickMarkValueAtIndex: NSSliderCell

tightenKerning: NSTextView

tile NSTableView, NSScrollView, NSBrowser

timeInterval NSTimer

timeIntervalSince1970 NSDate

timeIntervalSinceDate: NSDate

timeIntervalSinceNow NSDate

timeIntervalSinceReferenceDate NSDate

timeZone NSCalendarDate

timeZoneForSecondsFromGMT: NSTimeZone

timeZoneWithAbbreviation: NSTimeZone

timeZoneWithName: NSTimeZone

timeZoneWithName:data: NSTimeZone

timerWithTimeInterval:invocation:repeats: NSTimer

timerWithTimeInterval:target:selector: userInfo:repeats: NSTimer

timestamp NSEvent

title NSSlider, NSWindow, NSSavePanel, NSMenu, NSSliderCell, NSButtonCell, NSBox, NSFormCell, NSMenuItem, NSCell, NSButton, NSStatusItem

titleAlignment NSFormCell

titleBarFontOfSize: NSFont

titleCell NSSlider, NSSliderCell, NSBox

titleColor NSSlider, NSSliderCell

titleFont NSSlider, NSSliderCell, NSBox, NSFormCell

titleFrameOfColumn: NSBrowser

titleHeight NSBrowser

titleOfColumn: NSBrowser

titleOfSelectedItem NSPopUpButton, NSPopUpButtonCell

titlePosition NSBox

titleRect NSBox

titleRectForBounds: NSCell, NSMenuItemCell

titleWidth NSFormCell, NSMenuItemCell

titleWidth: NSFormCell

toManyRelationshipKeys NSClassDescription

toOneRelationshipKeys NSClassDescription

toggle: NSDrawer

toggleContinuousSpellChecking: NSTextView

toggleRuler: NSText

toggleToolbarShown: NSWindow

toggleTraditionalCharacterShape: NSTextView

toolTip NSToolbarItem, NSStatusItem, NSView

toolTipForCell: NSMatrix

toolTipsFontOfSize: NSFont

toolbar NSWindow, NSToolbarItem

toolbar:itemForItemIdentifier:willBeInserted-
IntoToolbar: NSToolbar

toolbarAllowedItemIdentifiers: NSToolbar

toolbarDefaultItemIdentifiers: NSToolbar

toolbarDidRemoveItem: NSToolbar

toolbarWillAddItem: NSToolbar

topAutoreleasePoolCount NSAutoreleasePool

topLevelObject NSScriptExecutionContext

topMargin NSPrintInfo

totalAutoreleasedObjects NSAutoreleasePool

trackKnob: NSScroller

trackMarker:withMouseEvent: NSRulerView

trackMouse:adding: NSRulerMarker

trackMouse:inRect:ofView:untilMouseUp:
NSCell

trackRect NSSliderCell

trackScrollButtons: NSScroller

trackWithEvent: NSMenuView

trackingNumber NSEvent

trailingOffset NSDrawer

traitsOfFont: NSFontManager

transactionID NSAppleEventDescriptor

transform NSAffineTransform

transformBezierPath: NSAffineTransform

transformPoint: NSAffineTransform

transformSize: NSAffineTransform

transformStruct NSAffineTransform

transformUsingAffineTransform: NSBezierPath

translateOriginToPoint: NSView

translateXBy:yBy: NSAffineTransform

transpose: NSResponder

transposeWords: NSResponder

treatsFilePackagesAsDirectories NSSavePanel

truncateFileAtOffset: NSFileHandle

tryLock NSDistributedLock, NSConditionLock,
NSLock, NSRecursiveLock

tryLockWhenCondition: NSConditionLock

tryToPerform:with: NSWindow, NSResponder,
NSApplication

turnOffKerning: NSTextView

turnOffLigatures: NSTextView

type NSPrinter, NSNetService, NSCell, NSEvent

typeCodeValue NSAppleEventDescriptor

typeForArgumentWithName:
NSScriptCommandDescription

typeForKey: NSScriptClassDescription

typeFromFileExtension: NSDocumentController

types NSPasteboard

typesFilterableTo: NSPasteboard

typesetter NSLayoutManager

typesetterBehavior NSLayoutManager

typesetterLaidOneGlyph:
NSSimpleHorizontalTypesetter

typingAttributes NSTextView

U

URL NSSavePanel, NSMovie

URL:resourceDataDidBecomeAvailable:
NSObject

URL:resourceDidFailLoadingWithReason:
NSObject

URLFromPasteboard: NSURL

URLHandleClassForURL: NSURLHandle

URLHandleUsingCache: NSURL

URLResourceDidCancelLoading: NSObject

URLResourceDidFinishLoading: NSObject

URLWithString: NSURL

URLWithString:relativeToURL: NSURL

URLs NSOpenPanel

URLsFromRunningOpenPanel
NSDocumentController

UTF8String NSString

unarchiveObjectWithData: NSKeyedUnarchiver,
NSUnarchiver

unarchiveObjectWithFile: NSKeyedUnarchiver,
NSUnarchiver

unarchiver:cannotDecodeObjectOfClassName:
originalClasses: NSKeyedUnarchiver

unarchiver:didDecodeObject: NSKeyedUnarchiver

unarchiver:willReplaceObject:withObject:
NSKeyedUnarchiver

unarchiverDidFinish: NSKeyedUnarchiver

unarchiverWillFinish: NSKeyedUnarchiver

underline: NSText

underlineGlyphRange:underlineType:
   lineFragmentRect:
   lineFragmentGlyphRange:
   containerOrigin: NSLayoutManager

underlinePosition NSFont

underlineThickness NSFont

undo NSUndoManager

undoActionName NSUndoManager

undoManager NSResponder, NSDocument

undoManagerForTextView: NSTextView

undoMenuItemTitle NSUndoManager

undoMenuTitleForUndoActionName:
   NSUndoManager

undoNestedGroup NSUndoManager

unhide NSCursor

unhide: NSApplication

unhideAllApplications: NSApplication

unhideWithoutActivation NSApplication

unionSet: NSMutableSet

uniqueID NSUniqueIDSpecifier

uniqueSpellDocumentTag NSSpellChecker

unlock NSDistributedLock

unlockFocus NSImage, NSView

unlockWithCondition: NSConditionLock

unmountAndEjectDeviceAtPath: NSWorkspace

unregisterDraggedTypes NSWindow

unregisterImageRepClass: NSImageRep

unscript: NSText

unscriptRange: NSMutableAttributedString

unsignedCharValue NSNumber

unsignedIntValue NSNumber

unsignedLongLongValue NSNumber

unsignedLongValue NSNumber

unsignedShortValue NSNumber

update NSWindow, NSOpenGLView, NSMenu,
   NSOpenGLContext, NSMenuView

updateAttachmentsFromPath:
   NSMutableAttributedString

updateCell: NSControl

updateCellInside: NSControl

updateChangeCount: NSDocument

updateCurGlyphOffset
   NSSimpleHorizontalTypesetter

updateDragTypeRegistration NSTextView

updateFontPanel NSTextView

updateFromPath: NSFileWrapper

updateFromPrintInfo NSPrintPanel

updateInsertionPointStateAndRestartTimer:
   NSTextView

updateRuler NSTextView

updateScroller NSBrowser

updateSpellingPanelWithMisspelledWord:
   NSSpellChecker

updateWindows NSApplication

updateWindowsItem: NSApplication

uppercaseLetterCharacterSet NSCharacterSet

uppercaseString NSString

uppercaseWord: NSResponder

usableParts NSScroller

useAllLigatures: NSTextView

useFont: NSFont

useOptimizedDrawing: NSWindow

useStandardKerning: NSTextView

useStandardLigatures: NSTextView

usedRectForTextContainer: NSLayoutManager

user NSURL

userData NSEvent

userDefaultsChanged NSWorkspace

userFixedPitchFontOfSize: NSFont

userFontOfSize: NSFont

userInfo NSException, NSTimer, NSNotification

userKeyEquivalent NSMenuItem

usesDataSource NSComboBoxCell, NSComboBox

usesEPSOnResolutionMismatch NSImage

usesFontPanel NSTextView, NSText

usesItemFromMenu NSPopUpButtonCell

usesRuler NSTextView

usesScreenFonts NSLayoutManager

usesThreadedAnimation NSProgressIndicator

usesUserKeyEquivalents NSMenuItem

V

validRequestorForSendType:returnType:
   NSWindow, NSResponder, NSTextView,
   NSApplication

validate NSToolbarItem

validateEditing NSControl

validateMenuItem: NSDocumentController,
   NSDocument

Appendix

Unlike the rest of the book's sections, there is only one short appendix in Part III of *Cocoa in a Nutshell*. Regardless of your experience level as a Mac developer, the *Appendix* contains valuable resources for Cocoa programmers, including details on how you can partner with Apple to market your application.

Appendix: Resources for Cocoa Developers

Appendix:
Resources for Cocoa Developers

If your mission is to produce commercial-quality software for Mac OS X, your journey can be made easier by knowing where to look for more information. This appendix lists information about the documents referred to in this book, and points you to other resources that can further help your Cocoa application development. These resources include:

- Developer documentation from Apple
- Cocoa and Mac OS X books aimed at the general programmer audience
- Articles and postings about particular Cocoa programming topics
- Cocoa developer mailing lists and newsgroups
- Partnership programs with Apple Computer

Apple Documentation

Many of the best resources on Cocoa development are installed on your hard drive when you install Apple's Developer Tools. These documents, mirrored online (*http://developer.apple.com/techpubs*), include but aren't limited to the following:

Mac OS X Release Notes
> Updated with every release of Mac OS X, these notes are typically one step ahead of the rest of Apple's documentation. You should read through these every time you update your system so that you can stay on top of the latest changes to the system.
>
> */Developer/Documentation/ReleaseNotes*

The Objective-C Programming Language
> This is the definitive reference for the Objective-C programming language, and is a must-read for all Cocoa developers. HTML and PDF versions of this document can be found on the Cocoa Documentation web site and on your system.
>
> */Developer/Documentation/Cocoa/ObjectiveC/ObjC.pdf*

Foundation Reference for Objective-C

This is a two-volume set, published by Apple through Vervanté, contains the complete reference documentation for the Foundation framework. This is the same material found online at Apple's Cocoa documentation web site, and on your hard drive as part of the developer tools installation.

/Developer/Documentation/Cocoa/Reference/Foundation/ObjC_classic/ Foundation.pdf

Application Kit Reference for Objective-C

Like the Foundation Reference for Objective-C, this book is a three-volume set that contains the complete reference documentation for the Application Kit framework.

/Developer/Documentation/Cocoa/Reference/ApplicationKit/ObjC_classic/ AppKit.pdf

Inside Mac OS X: System Overview

This overview of Mac OS X is valuable for anyone doing software development with Cocoa. You should read Inside Mac OS X: System Overview to familiarize yourself with the architecture of Mac OS X so you can take advantage of its design. This guide not only describes the features and capabilities of the operating system, it also describes concepts, facilities, and conventions common to the system's Carbon, Cocoa, Java, and BSD application environments.

/Developer/Documentation/Essentials/SystemOverview/SystemOverview.pdf

Inside Mac OS X: Aqua Human Interface Guidelines

This book, commonly referred to as "The HIG," describes how to design your application for Mac OS X's user interface (known as Aqua). The HIG provides examples of how to use such Aqua interface elements as windows, controls, dialogs, and icons so that the users of your Cocoa application will be familiar and comfortable with your product the moment they double-click its icon.

/Developer/Documentation/Essentials/AquaHIGuidelines/AquaHIGuidelines.pdf

Inside Mac OS X: Performance

This book tells you how to enhance your program to achieve maximum performance and how to use the development tools to analyze and tune your code. Topics include: managing virtual memory; accessing files efficiently; optimizing Carbon applications; building efficient C, C++, and Java code; using the Mac OS X performance measurement and analysis tools; and optimizing the in-memory layout of your program.

/Developer/Documentation/Essentials/Performance/performance.pdf

Core Foundation Developer Documentation

Cocoa is built upon the Core Foundation framework. Occasionally, you will need to use functionality at the Core Foundation level that isn't exposed in the Cocoa APIs.

/Developer/Documentation/CoreFoundation/corefoundation_carbon.html

If you prefer print over PDF, you can order printed, bound copies of many selected Apple documents, including the full Cocoa API reference, from Apple's print-on-demand service from Vervanté. For more information, or to order an Apple document, see:

> *http://www.vervante.com/apple*

In total, the complete bound Objective-C references for Foundation and Application Kit span 5 volumes and nearly 3,000 pages of material.

Related Books

Fast on the heels of the release of Mac OS X 10.0, O'Reilly began publishing a series of books as part of its ADC series, a joint-publishing agreement between Apple and O'Reilly. The books published in the ADC series are aimed at Mac OS X developers. Included in this series are several excellent Cocoa books:

Cocoa Design Patterns
> As more users "Switch" from Unix and Windows to the Mac, programmers need to stay ahead of the curve and develop their applications using Apple's Cocoa frameworks. This book illustrates the core design patterns of Cocoa programming, and transfers knowledge about the structure and rationale of Cocoa—something that isn't covered in any other book in print. The book explains the essential patterns of objects that are used in Cocoa, and describes problems solved by Cocoa and the consequences of each solution. At the time of this writing, this book is still in development, but should be released by O'Reilly & Associates in the summer of 2003.

Learning Cocoa with Objective-C
> Now in its second edition, *Learning Cocoa with Objective-C*, by James Duncan Davidson, is a great first book for Cocoa beginners. It eases you into the experience of Cocoa development not merely by reading, but by doing. After introductions to Project Builder and Interface Builder, you'll quickly come up to speed on the concepts of object-oriented programming with Objective-C.

Objective-C Pocket Reference
> This small book by Andrew M. Duncan provides a quick and concise introduction to Objective-C for programmers already familiar with either C or C++. In addition to covering the essentials of Objective-C syntax, it also covers important facets of the language such as memory management, the Objective-C runtime, dynamic loading, distributed objects, and exception handling.

Building Cocoa Applications: A Step-by-Step Guide
> This book by Simson Garfinkle and Michael Mahoney walks the reader through four full-fledged Cocoa applications from start to finish. In the course of each application the reader is immersed in Cocoa techniques and Mac OS X as a development platform.

In addition to *Cocoa*, there are several more books published by O'Reilly that are worth mentioning:

Cocoa Programming for Mac OS X
> This book by Aaron Hillegass is an example driven approach to learning Cocoa that is an excellent resource for the beginning Cocoa developer.

Cocoa Programming
> If you've tapped out all of your current Cocoa resources, consider this book to take you to the next level. This 1,200-page tome by Scott Anguish, Erik M. Buck, and Don Yacktman covers many of the less-talked-about aspects of Cocoa, including such subjects as advanced optimization and debugging techniques.

Cocoa Recipes for Mac OS X: The Vermont Recipes
> This book by Bill Cheeseman builds a Cocoa application from start to finish with a practical step-by-step approach. Each stage of the application development is explained in clear detail.

To become an effective Cocoa programmer a thorough understanding of the C language is a must. Additionally, knowledge of object-oriented programming principles is essential. To expand the minds of all developers, Cocoa and others alike, we heartily recommend having the following books nearby:

The C Programming Language
> To be an effective Objective-C programmer, you need to know C. This book, written by the creators of the C programming language, Kernighan and Ritchie—commonly referred to as "K&R"—is the definitive reference on the C language. Don't let the 1988 publication date deter you; this book is an essential.

Practical C Programming
> Whenever anyone asks about books for learning C, Mike always recommends this book, which is the book he learned C from. This book covers everything that is in K&R, but from a different angle. Mike keeps both *Practical C Programming* and K&R close at hand.

Design Patterns
> This is the book that codified what developers had known about object-oriented programming for many years prior to its publication. *Design Patterns* is hailed as a landmark book in the OOP community, and rightly so, as it defined a language for communicating ideas about OOP at a level more abstracts than level. Cocoa developers can take pride in the fact that NeXT-STEP (If you don't know the story yet, Cocoa is a direct descendent of NeXTSTEP) is cited repeatedly throughout the text for its use of design patterns.

Web Sites

The Web provides a cornucopia of information about Cocoa (as it does about everything else). We've found it useful to use Google (*http://www.google.com*, or directly from the Safari web browser's interface) to provide help for the most arcane of issues, including odd compiler error messages. Just type it into the search field and go.

These are the sites that we browse most often for Cocoa information:

Apple Developer Connection (ADC)
> Apple uses the Developer Documentation area of this web site to post new documents, and update existing ones, on a frequent basis. In addition, being

an ADC member (the basic, online membership is free) gives you access to the latest Developer Tools releases.

http://developer.apple.com

O'Reilly's Macintosh DevCenter
Affiliated with O'Reilly & Associates, Inc., the O'Reilly Network is home to the Mac DevCenter, a hub site that offers news, FAQs, original articles, and other technical information for Mac developers and users alike.

http://www.macdevcenter.com

MacTech magazine
MacTech's web site contains a lot of downloadable source code and a monthly column from the print magazine that provides online technologies and resources. These resources include links to web pages, shareware archives, newsgroups, mailing lists, and castanet channels aimed at Macintosh programmers.

http://www.mactech.com

Stepwise
One of the original Cocoa sites, Stepwise was created as a resource for NeXT-STEP developers; it serves as an excellent resource for Cocoa and WebObjects programming.

http://www.stepwise.com

The Vermont Recipes
Published on Stepwise, this group of articles written by Bill Cheeseman, serves as a cookbook for developing Mac OS X applications with Cocoa using a no-nonsense, hands-on, step-by-step approach.

http://www.stepwise.com/Articles/VermontRecipes

Cocoa Dev Central
This site is updated fairly frequently with tips, tricks, and tutorials for novice Cocoa developers.

http://www.cocoadevcentral.com

CocoaDev Wiki
This user-editable web site is by and for the Mac OS X developer community. If you've never used the WikiWeb before, this style of site gives literally anyone the capability to view and add information on the site.

http://www.cocoadev.com

Mailing Lists

Many programmers find online mailing lists to be the best way to stay on top of what's fresh and new in the Cocoa community. In addition, they are an excellent place to get help on a problem; just be sure to search the archives first before asking!

cocoa-dev
Apple's moderated email list focused exclusively on Cocoa development issues.

http://lists.apple.com/mailman/listinfo/cocoa-dev

projectbuilder-users
>Apple's moderated email list focused on Project Builder issues.

>>*http://lists.apple.com/mailman/listinfo/projectbuilder-users*

macosx-dev
>This mailing list is hosted by one of the premiere Cocoa development houses, The Omni Group. This list is open to a wide variety of topics for Mac OS X developers.

>>*http://www.omnigroup.com/developer/mailinglists/macosx-dev*

MacDev-1
>A source of news, information, updates, and special offers for Macintosh developers.

>>*http://www.mactech.com/macdev-1*

Mamasam's Cocoa List Archive
>A browsable, searchable archive of Apple's *cocoa-dev* and The Omni Group's *macosx-dev* mailing lists.

>>*http://cocoa.mamasam.com*

Partnering with Apple

Apple knows that your success is Apple's success. Apple wants developers like you to create successful applications that make customers clamor for Apple computers.

You should tap into some of the programs, products, and services offered by the Apple Developer Connection (ADC). Aimed at both large and small developers, the stated purpose of the ADC is "to help you successfully develop, test, market, and distribute software and hardware products for Apple platforms and technologies."

In addition to publishing the Developer web site at *developer.apple.com* (which includes the Cocoa Developer Documentation suite), hosting an annual Apple Worldwide Developer's Conference (WWDC), and championing developer needs to Apple's own development engineers, the ADC offers several program packages useful to you and other developers.

You should become a member of one of these programs. At the minimum, sign up for the Online program... it's free! The Online program allows you to download up-to-date development tools, gain access to certain early software releases, and receive weekly technical updates via email.

If you'd rather have this type of information mailed to you, you can pay to become an ADC Mailing customer. You'll then receive the latest in development tools, system software, development kits, and reference materials via a CD or DVD series delivered to you monthly via snail mail.

A low-cost ADC Student Program is targeted at university students around the world. ADC Student developers receive special introductory tools, access to a student community of Mac developers, and other educational opportunities, including the chance to win scholarships to the WWDC.

The priciest ADC programs are called Select and Premier. These programs offer a multitude of plush products and services, including fat discounts on Apple hardware and third-party products and services, as well as access to Apple's technical support engineers.

For information on signing up for any of these programs, go to the following URL:

http://developer.apple.com/membership

ADC members also receive discounts on O'Reilly's books and conferences. For more information about the discounts available to ADC members, go to the following URL:

http://developer.apple.com/mkt/programs/oreilly.html

Index

We'd like to hear your suggestions for improving our indexes. Send email to *index@oreilly.com*.

N

naming conventions, 17
network classes hierarchy, 114
network domains, 274
network services, 118, 273
  creating and publishing, 119
networking, 114–127
nib files, 58
notifications, 49, 275, 276
  center, 275
    defined, 49
  changing delivery behavior, 50
  defined, xi
  distributed, 130
  observers, 49
  removing, 50
  suspended, 131
NSAccessibility class
  global variables, 213, 214, 215
  protocol, 441
NSAccessibilityPostNotification
      function, 221
NSAccessibilityUnignoredAncestor
      function, 221
NSAccessibilityUnignoredChildren
      function, 221
NSAccessibilityUnignoredChildren-
      ForOnlyChild function, 222
NSAccessibilityUnignoredDescendant
      function, 222
NSActionCell class (Application
      Kit), 319–320
NSAffineTransform class, 101
  Application Kit, 320–321
NSAffineTransformStruct data
      type, 188
NSAllHashTableObjects function, 180
NSAllMapTableKeys function, 181
NSAllMapTableValues function, 181
NSAllocateMemoryPages function, 187
NSAllocateObject function, 182
NSAppleEvent Timeouts global
      variable, 170
NSAppleEventDescriptor class, 228
NSAppleEventManager class, 230
NSAppleScript class, 230
NSApplication class, 57, 60
  Application Kit, 321–324
  delegate object, 62
  enumeration, 205
  global variables, 216

NSApplicationLoad function, 222
NSApplicationMain function, 61, 222
NSApplicationTerminateReply data
      type, 188
NSArchiver class, 44, 231
NSArgumentDomain class, 46
NSArray class, 27, 231
NSAssert function, 176
NSAssert1 through NSAssert5
      functions, 176
NSAssertionHandler class, 233
NSAttributedString class, 23, 234
  attributes, 92
  enumeration, 205
  global variables, 216
NSAutoreleasePool class, 236
NSAvailableWindowDepths
      function, 225
NSBackingStoreType data type, 188
NSBeep function, 227
NSBeginAlertSheet function, 226
NSBeginCriticalAlertSheet
      function, 226
NSBeginInformationalAlertSheet
      function, 226
NSBestDepth function, 225
NSBezelStyle data type, 189
NSBezierPath class, 84, 88
  Application Kit, 324–326
  constructing complex shape, 85
NSBezierPathElement data type, 189
NSBitmapImageFileType data type, 189
NSBitmapImageRep class, 99
  Application Kit, 326–327
  global variables, 216
  subclass, 98
NSBitsPerPixelFromDepth
      function, 225
NSBitsPerSampleFromDepth
      function, 225
NSBorderType data type, 189
NSBox class (Application Kit), 327
NSBoxType data type, 189
NSBrowser class (Application
      Kit), 327–329
NSBrowserCell class (Application
      Kit), 330
NSBundle class, 41, 236
  loading code, 43
  loading resources, 42

observers (notification center), 49
Omni Frameworks, 152
 OmniAppKit, 152
 OmniBase, 152
 OmniFoundation, 152
 OmniHTML, 152
 OmniNetworking, 152
 OWF, 152
Omni Group, The web site, 152
Open panel, 382
OpenGL API, 380
OpenGL functions (Application
 Kit), 225
outlets
 actions and, 59
 defined, x, 59
outline view, 383
overriding a superclass method, 11

P

Page Layout panel, 384
page-view, 110
paginating text, 110
panel functions (Application Kit), 226
paragraph style, 379
parent window, defined, 72
pasteboard functions (Application
 Kit), 226
pasteboard server, 386
path flatness, 88
path utilities functions, 183
PDF image rendering, 387
persistent domains, 46
point functions, 184
pop-up button interface, 388
port name servers, 266, 298
port registration services, 283
PPD file, 390
presentation layer, 104
primary identifier, 139
print job information, 391
Print panel, 393
Print Preview window, 111
printf-style formatting web site, 19
@private, 8
process discovery, 50
Project Builder, defined, x
property keys (AddressBook
 framework), 138

property list objects, 251, 285, 295
proposed rectangle, 107
@protected, 8
protocols, 16
 Application Kit, 441–452
 defining, 16
 Foundation, 313–318
proxies, 285
@public, 8

Q

Quartz, 60
 2D API, 82
 composite images and, 95
 Compositor, 82
 defined, 82
 path-based drawing API, 84
querying the contents of the array, 231
quick reference, how it was
 generated, xv
QuickDraw drawing commands, 395
QuickTime movie data, 377

R

range functions, 184
rect functions, 185
reference counting mechanism, 13
Rendezvous network services, 118
 web site, 118
resources, application, 41
 loading resources, 42
resources for Cocoa
 developers, 515–521
 Apple documentation, 515
 Apple partnering programs, 520
 mailing lists, 519
 related books, 517
 web sites, 518
responder chain, 76, 78
 pattern, defined, xi
retrieve objects from an archive, 231
root class, 7, 279
rotating, 101
ruler view, 398
run loops, 62, 288, 304
 defined, 61

About the Authors

Michael Beam lives in Houston, Texas, and is a Unix applications developer for a seismic data processing firm. (X11 and Motif are a far cry from Cocoa!) Mike graduated from the University of Texas at Austin (Hook 'Em!) in 2001, where he studied physics and astronomy. When he's not at his day job, or writing about Cocoa in his night job, Mike spends his time with his friends and his soon-to-be-wife, Heather. To unwind from the stresses of life, Mike enjoys a good book, practices Chayon-Ryu martial arts, and indulges in his favorite sin, watching *South Park*.

James Duncan Davidson is a freelance author, software developer, and consultant focusing on Mac OS X, Java, XML, and open source technologies. He is the author of *Learning Cocoa with Objective-C* (O'Reilly) and is a frequent contributor to the O'Reilly Network web site, as well as publisher of his own web site, x180 (*http://www.x180.net*), where he keeps his popular weblog.

Duncan was the creator of Apache Tomcat and Apache Ant, and was instrumental in their donation to the Apache Software Foundation by Sun Microsystems. While working at Sun, he authored two versions of the Java Servlet API specification, as well as the Java API for XML processing.

Duncan regularly presents at conferences all over the world on topics ranging from open source and collaborative development to programming Java effectively. He didn't graduate with a computer science degree, but sees that as a benefit in helping explain how software works. His educational background is in architecture (the bricks and mortar kind), the essence of which he applies to every software problem that finds him. He currently resides in San Francisco, CA.

Colophon

Our look is the result of reader comments, our own experimentation, and feedback from distribution channels. Distinctive covers complement our distinctive approach to technical topics, breathing personality and life into potentially dry subjects.

The animal on the cover of *Cocoa in a Nutshell* is an Irish setter. Bred as a sporting dog in the 19th century, the Irish setter's agility and energy made it a prime companion for pheasant and quail hunters. By the 1890s, the dog's attractive, silky red coat and elegant build boosted its popularity as a show dog. For the past century, breeders have created a larger dog with a longer coat, with deep chestnut red or patches of red and white hair. The dog is also popular as a family pet. Described as loyal, gentle, energetic, and happy, the Irish setter gets along well with children. Some hospitals, nursing homes, and rehabilitation centers also adopt the Irish setter as a therapy dog.

Colleen Gorman was the production editor, and Colleen Gorman and Ann Schirmer were the copyeditors for *Cocoa in a Nutshell*. Mary Brady, Jane Ellin, Claire Cloutier, and Linley Dolby provided quality control. Reg Aubry wrote the index.

Emma Colby designed the cover of this book, based on a series design by Edie Freedman. The cover image is a 19th-century engraving from the Dover Pictorial Archive. Emma Colby produced the cover layout with QuarkXPress 4.1 using Adobe's ITC Garamond font.

David Futato and Bret Kerr designed the interior layout. This book was converted by Andrew Savikas to FrameMaker 5.5.6 with a format conversion tool created by Erik Ray, Jason McIntosh, Neil Walls, and Mike Sierra that uses Perl and XML technologies. The text font is Linotype Birka; the heading font is Adobe Myriad Condensed; and the code font is LucasFont's TheSans Mono Condensed. The illustrations that appear in the book were produced by Robert Romano and Jessamyn Read using Macromedia FreeHand 9 and Adobe Photoshop 6. The tip and warning icons were drawn by Christopher Bing. This colophon was written by Ann Schirmer.

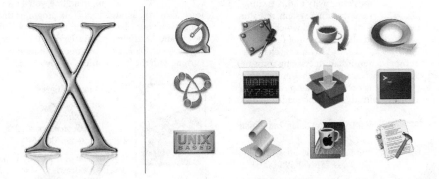
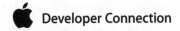

Other Titles Available from O'Reilly

Macintosh Power Users

Mac OS X: The Missing Manual, 2nd Edition

By David Pogue
2nd Edition October 2002
728 pages, ISBN 0-596-00450-8

David Pogue applies his scrupulous objectivity to this exciting new operating system, revealing which new features work well and which do not. This second edition offers a wealth of detail on the myriad changes in OS X 10.2. With new chapters on iChat (Apple's new instant-messaging software), Sherlock 3 (the Web search tool that pulls Web information directly onto the desktop), and the new Finder (which reintroduces spring-loaded folders).

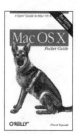

Mac OS X Pocket Guide, 2nd Edition

By Chuck Toporek
2nd Edition November 2002
150 pages, ISBN 0-596-00458-3

Updated to cover Mac OS X 10.2 (nicknamed "Jaguar"), Mac OS X Pocket Guide, 2nd Edition is the perfect guide for unleashing the power of this amazing operating system. Easy to take and use anywhere for quick problem solving, the second edition features an overview of the System Preferences, the Terminal application, and the Developer Tools, along with new tips and tricks for working with Mac OS X. This handy book also includes quick references for creating special characters, and a listing of basic keyboard commands.

Mac OS X in a Nutshell

By Jason McIntosh, Chuck Toporek & ChrisStone
1sr Edition January 2003
826 pages, ISBN 0-596-00370-6

Mac OS X in a Nutshell offers a thorough treatment of Mac OS X version 10.2, from its BSD Unix foundation to Aqua, the new user interface. The book's "Unix Command Reference" is the most complete and thorough coverage of Mac OS X Unix commands you can find anywhere. Each command and option in this section has been painstakingly tested and checked against Jaguar.

Learning Unix for Mac OS X, 2nd Edition

By Dave Taylor & Brian Jepson
2nd Edition December 2002
158 pages, ISBN 0-596-00470-2

This compact book provides a user-friendly tour of your Mac's Unix base. As you explore Terminal and familiarize yourself with the command line, you'll also learn about the hundreds of Unix programs that come with your Mac and begin to understand the power and flexibility of Unix. Updated to cover Jaguar (Mac OS X, 10.2), this book will keep you current with the latest features of your Mac.

Mac OS X for Unix Geeks

By Brian Jepson & Ernest E. Rothman
1st Edition September 2002
216 pages, 0-596-00356-0

If you're one of the many Unix developers drawn to Mac OS X for its BSD core, you'll find yourself in surprisingly unfamiliar territory. Even if you're an experienced Mac user, Mac OS X is unlike earlier Macs, and it's radically different from the Unix you've used before, too. Their new book is your guide to figuring out the BSD Unix system and Mac-specific components that are making your life difficult and to help ease you into the Unix inside Mac OS X.

Office X for Macintosh: The Missing Manual

By Nan Barber, Tonya Engst & David Reynolds
1st Edition July 2002
728 pages, ISBN 0-596-00332-3

This book applies the urbane and readable Missing Manuals touch to a winning topic: Microsoft Office X for Apple's stunning new operating system, Mac OS X. In typical Missing Manual style, targeted sidebars ensure that the book's three sections impart business-level details on Word, Excel, and the Palm-syncable Entourage, without leaving beginners behind. Indispensable reference for a growing user base.

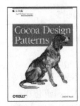

Macintosh Developers

AppleScript in a Nutshell

By Bruce W. Perry
1st Edition June 2001
528 pages, ISBN 1-56592-841-5

AppleScript in a Nutshell is the first complete reference to Apple-Script, the popular programming language that gives both power users and sophisticated enterprise customers the important ability to automate repetitive tasks and customize applications. *AppleScript in a Nutshell* is a high-end handbook at a low-end price—an essential desktop reference that puts the full power of this user-friendly programming language in every AppleScript user's hands.

Building Cocoa Applications: A Step-by-Step Guide

By Simson Garfinkel & Mike Mahoney
1st Edition May 2002
648 pages, ISBN 0-596-00235-1

Building Cocoa Applications is a step-by-step guide to developing applications for Apple's Mac OS X. It describes, in an engaging tutorial fashion, how to build substantial, object-oriented applications using Cocoa. The primary audience for this book is C programmers who want to learn quickly how to use Cocoa to build significant Mac OS X applications. The book takes the reader from basic Cocoa functions through the most advanced and powerful facilities.

REALbasic: The Definitive Guide, 2nd Edition

By Matt Neuburg
2nd Edition September 2001
752 pages, ISBN 0-596-00177-0

Design astonishingly fast, full-fledged Mac applications with REALbasic! Even if you're a beginning programmer, this book will teach you the essential concepts for programming every aspect of REALbasic. It's a vital reference for the expanding legion of developers who are discovering the power and flexibility of REALbasic. Now covers REALbasic 3, so you can generate your project for Mac OS 8/9, Mac OS X, and Windows.